Guide to Rural England

THE HEART OF ENGLAND

Derbyshire, Herefordshire, Leicestershire, Lincolnshire, Northamptonshire, Nottinghamshire, Rutland, Shropshire, Staffordshire, Warwickshire, West Midlands, Worcestershire

By Peter Long

© Travel Publishing Ltd

Published by:
Travel Publishing Ltd
7a Apollo House, Calleva Park
Aldermaston, Berkshire RG7 8TN
ISBN 1-904-43464-9
EAN 9781904434641
© Travel Publishing Ltd
Country Living is a registered trademark of The National
Magazine Company Limited.

First Published: 2001
Second Edition: 2004
Third Edition: 2007

COUNTRY LIVING GUIDES:

East Anglia	Scotland
Heart of England	The South of England
Ireland	The South East of England
The North East of England	The West Country
The North West of England	Wales

PLEASE NOTE:

All advertisements in this publication have been accepted in good faith by Travel Publishing and they have not necessarily been endorsed by *Country Living* Magazine.

All information is included by the publishers in good faith and is believed to be correct at the time of going to press. No responsibility can be accepted for errors.

Editor:	Peter Long
Printing by:	Scotprint, Haddington
Location Maps:	© Maps in Minutes ™ (2007) © Crown Copyright, Ordnance Survey 2007
Walks:	Walks have been reproduced with kind permission of the internet walking site www.walkingworld.com
Walk Maps:	Reproduced from Ordnance Survey mapping on behalf of the Controller of Her Majesty's Stationery Office, © Crown Copyright. Licence Number MC 100035812
Cover Design:	Lines & Words, Aldermaston
Cover Photo:	Bridge over River Arrow, Eardisland, Herefordshire © www.loopimages.com
Text Photos:	Text photo: © www.picturesofbritain.co.uk and © Bob Brooks, Weston-super-Mare

Foreword

From a bracing walk across the hills and tarns of The Lake District to a relaxing weekend spent discovering the unspoilt hamlets of East Anglia, nothing quite matches getting off the beaten track and exploring Britain's areas of outstanding beauty.

Each month, *Country Living Magazine* celebrates the richness and diversity of our countryside with features on rural Britain and the traditions that have their roots there. So it is with great pleasure that I introduce you to the *Country Living Magazine Guide to Rural England* series. Packed with information about unusual and unique aspects of our countryside, the guides will point both fair-weather and intrepid travellers in the right direction.

Each chapter provides a fascinating tour of the Heart of England area, with insights into local heritage and history and easy-to-read facts on a wealth of places to visit, stay, eat, drink and shop.

I hope that this guide will help make your visit a rewarding and stimulating experience and that you will return inspired, refreshed and ready to head off on your next countryside adventure.

Susy Smith

Susy Smith
Editor, Country Living magazine

PS To subscribe to *Country Living Magazine* each month, call 01858 438844

Introduction

This is the 3rd edition of the *Country Living Guide to Rural England - The Heart of England* and we are sure that it will be as popular as its predecessors. Regular readers will note that the page layouts have been attractively redesigned and that we have provided more information on the places, people, and activities covered. Also, in the introduction to each village or town we have summarized and categorized the main attractions to be found there which makes it easier for readers to plan their visit. Peter Long, a very experienced travel writer has, of course, completely updated the contents of the guide and ensured that it is packed with vivid descriptions, historical stories, amusing anecdotes and interesting facts on hundreds of places in Derbyshire, Herefordshire, Leicestershire, Lincolnshire, Northamptonshire, Nottinghamshire, Rutland, Shropshire, Staffordshire, Warwickshire, the West Midlands and Worcestershire.

The coloured advertising panels within each chapter provide further information on places to see, stay, eat, drink, shop and even exercise! We have also selected a number of walks from walkingworld.com (full details of this website may be found to the rear of the guide) which we highly recommend if you wish to appreciate fully the beauty and charm of the varied rural landscapes of the Heart of England.

The guide however is not simply an "armchair tour". Its prime aim is to encourage the reader to visit the places described and discover much more about the wonderful towns, villages and countryside of the Heart of England. In this respect we would like to thank all the Tourist Information Centres who helped us to provide you with up-to-date information. Whether you decide to explore this region by wheeled transport or on foot we are sure you will find it a very uplifting experience.

We are always interested in receiving comments on places covered (or not covered) in our guides so please do not hesitate to use the reader reaction forms provided at the rear of this guide to give us your considered comments. This will help us refine and improve the content of the next edition. We also welcome any general comments which will help improve the overall presentation of the guides themselves.

For more information on the full range of travel guides published by Travel Publishing please refer to the order form at the rear of this guide or log on to our website (see below).

Travel Publishing

Did you know that you can also search our website for details of thousands of places to see, stay, eat or drink throughout Britain and Ireland? Our site has become increasingly popular and now receives monthly hundreds of thousands of visits. Try it!

website: www.travelpublishing.co.uk

Contents

LOCATOR MAP

LOCATOR MAP

ADVERTISERS AND PLACES OF INTEREST

🏛 historic building   🏛 museum   🏛 historic site   ⚘ scenic attraction   🌿 flora and fauna

1| Herefordshire

"Wherever one goes, there will not be a mile that is visually unrewarding." Sir Nikolaus Pevsner was clearly impressed, and today's visitors will also find delights at every turn in the rolling landscape, the pretty villages and the charming market towns. Herefordshire had few natural resources, so the industrial scars that spoil many counties are mercifully absent; the beauty and peace remain relatively intact, and motorists will generally find traffic-free roads. Apples and hops are the traditional crops of Herefordshire, and the cider industry is still a thriving one. The days when almost every farm produced its own cider are long gone, but many of the old mills are preserved on the farms or in museums. Large areas (over 9,500 acres) of the county are given over to cider orchards, and 63 million gallons of cider are produced here each year - well over half the UK total. The Cider Museum in Hereford is a good starting point for taking the Cider Route, which tours the Herefordshire countryside and includes more than a dozen cider-makers.

In western Herefordshire perry is something of a speciality, the drink being made on similar lines to cider but with pears instead of apples. Hops have been cultivated in the county since the 16th century and once provided late summer work for thousands of pickers, mainly from the Black Country and south Wales. The industry is considerably smaller than before, and mechanisation has greatly reduced the need for human effort. The poles and wires are a less common sight than previously, but they can still be seen, along with the occasional kiln for drying the hops - the Herefordshire equivalent of Kent's oast houses. Among the animals, sheep and cattle are a familiar sight; Hereford cattle still abound, and their stock are now to be found in many parts of the world, particularly in the Americas.

Industry was never developed to any great extent, partly through the remoteness of the location and the poverty of communications, and the visible traces of the county's heritage are confined largely to castles (this is Border territory) and churches. The castles were mainly of the straightforward motte and bailey variety, the motte being a tower-topped earthen mound surrounded by a small court, the bailey a larger yard with the stables and workshops and accommodation. Skirmishes with the Welsh were a common occurrence for many centuries, and one of the county's best-known landmarks, Offa's Dyke, was built in the 8th century as a defence against the Welsh marauders.

The Golden Valley, near Peterchurch

THE OLD COURT HOTEL & DINING ROOM

Symonds Yat West,
Herefordshire HR9 6DA
Tel: 01600 890367
Fax: 01600 890964
e-mail: Victoria@oldcourthotel.co.uk
website: www.oldcourthotel.co.uk

The Old Court Hotel is an ideal base for exploring the Wye Valley, a part of the world that's particularly rich in history, heritage and scenic beauty. Victoria and Jono welcome guests into their 16th century home, whether it's for a drink, a snack, a meal or an overnight stay or longer break. The 18 named and themed bedrooms, all with en suite facilities or adjacent private bathrooms, are divided between the original house and the modern wing; all are beautifully decorated and furnished and equipped with TV, radio-alarm clock, direct-dial phone, broadband connection for laptops and hot drinks tray.

The Cotswold Bar is equally popular with locals and visitors, and when the sun shines the patio and garden come into their own. Hot and cold food is served in the bar, while the main menu is available every day in the restaurant that occupies the former Great Hall. Dishes on a typical menu range from oak-roast salmon and a cheese and leek filo tart to steaks, chicken with tarragon, and pork normande with apple, cream and calvados. The Elizabethan Function Room is an atmospheric setting for a birthday, reunion or wedding celebration (the hotel holds a civil wedding licence).

The main building retains many handsome original features, and boasts a distinguished list of former occupants. These include Thomas Gwillim, aide-de-camp to General Wolfe at the Battle of Quebec, and John Graves Simcoe, the first Governor-General of Upper Canada and the founder of the city of Toronto. Local attractions include walking and climbing in this lovely setting and boat trips on the River Wye, and with easy access to the main road network, all the major sights are within easy reach, including Monmouth, Ross-on-Wye, Tintern Abbey and the Forest of Dean.

🏛 historic building   🏛 museum   🏛 historic site   ♨ scenic attraction   🌿 flora and fauna

South Herefordshire

The River Wye rises in the Plynlimon mountains east of Aberystwyth, near the spot where the Severn also has its source. The Wye enters England by Hay-on-Wye and winds its way through some of the most delightful scenery in the whole land, changing mood and direction from time to time and finally joining its original neighbour at the Severn Estuary. The whole of its length offers great touring and walking country, and the Wye Valley Walk, waymarked with the logo of the leaping salmon, follows the river closely for 112 miles, almost half of which are in Herefordshire. The valley was designated an Area of Outstanding Natural Beauty (AONB) in 1971, and the river itself was the first to be recognised as a Site of Special Scientific Interest (SSSI). The salmon logo is, of course, wholly appropriate, as the Wye is a Mecca for anglers. In the 18th century artists, poets and the leisured classes enjoyed the Wye Tour, a highly agreeable alternative to the European Grand Tour, and two centuries later the car, train and bicycle have brought the charm of the valley within the reach of all.

SYMONDS YAT
5 miles NE of Monmouth off the A40 and B4164

🏛 Seven Sisters Rock   🏛 Merlin's Cave

🐦 Jubilee Park   🍃 Amazing Hedge puzzle

Travelling upstream, a journey through the southern part of the county starts at the beauty spot of Symonds Yat, an inland resort to which visitors flock to enjoy the views, the walks, the river cruises, the wildlife (peregrine falcons nest at Coldwell Rocks), the history and the adventure. Into the last category fall canoeing - rushing down the Wye gorge south of the village - and rock climbing. Symonds Yat (yat means gap) is divided into east and west by the Wye, with no vehicular bridge at that point. Pedestrians can make use of the punt ferry, pulled across the river by chain, but the journey by car is 4.5 miles. Walking in the area is an endless delight and, at The Biblins, a swaying suspension bridge provides vertiginous thrills across the river. Notable landmarks include the **Seven Sisters Rocks**, a collection of oolitic limestone crags; **Merlin's Cave**; King Arthur's Cave, where the bones of mammoths and other prehistoric creatures have been found; Coldwell Rocks and Yat Rock itself, rising to 500 feet above sea level at a point where the river performs a long and majestic loop.

Symonds Yat

🎭 stories and anecdotes   🍴 famous people   🎨 art and craft   🍃 entertainment and sport   🚶 walks

Also on the Symonds Yat walkabout is a massive boulder measuring 60 feet by 40 feet, one of the largest in the country.

Other entertainment in the area is provided by the **Amazing Hedge Puzzle** devised by brothers Lindsay and Edward Heyes to celebrate Queen Elizabeth's 1977 Jubilee. On the same site is a museum of mazes and a puzzle shop with the largest collection of puzzle games in the UK. In the **Jubilee Park**, the attractions include a garden centre with an extensive range of plants plus garden furniture and a gift shop. The church in Symonds Yat, built in the 14th century, is dedicated to St Dubricius, a local who converted the area to Christianity and who, according to legend, crowned King Arthur.

In 1993 Symonds Yat provided the backdrop for the film *Shadowlands*.

WHITCHURCH
4½ miles NE of Monmouth off the A40

🏛 Goodrich Castle   🐾 Zoo

At **Symonds Yat West**, close to the village of Whitchurch, the **Butterfly Zoo** gives visitors the chance to experience the warmth of a tropical hothouse with butterflies flitting freely

about their heads. A little further up, just off the A40, is Kerne Bridge, a settlement which grew around a bridge built in 1828, where coracles are still made, and from where the energetic walker can hike into history at the majestic **Goodrich Castle** in a commanding position above the Wye. Built of red sandstone in the 11th century by Godric Mapplestone, the castle is now ruined but still magnificent. It was the last bastion to fall in the Civil War, attacked by 'Roaring Meg', a siege gun cast in Whitchurch which could hurl a 200lb ball and which can now be seen in Hereford. The siege lasted four-and-a-half months and marked the end of the castle's 'working life'. English Heritage maintains the ruins in excellent condition, and the 12th century keep and elements from the next two centuries are well worth a visit, to walk the ramparts or just to imagine the glorious sight it once presented.

Torwood, near Whitchurch, is an interesting cottage garden by the village school, specialising in shrubs, conifers and herbaceous plants. Private visits welcome.

GOODRICH
6 miles NE of Monmouth off the A40

Goodrich village is notable for the landmark

Goodrich Castle

14th century broach spire of its parish church. The vicar at a critical point in the Civil War was one Thomas Swift, grandfather of Jonathan Swift, author of *Gulliver's Travels*. This staunch royalist hid some of the church's treasures, including a superb silver chalice, from the marauders and, it is said, sewed 300 pieces of gold into his waistcoat to take to the king.

🏛 historic building   🖼 museum   🏚 historic site   🌿 scenic attraction   🐾 flora and fauna

WELSH NEWTON
4 miles N of Monmouth on the A466

The village lies right on the A466, and just off it stands Pembridge Castle, now in use as a private house. In the village churchyard of St Mary the Virgin lies the body of John Kemble, a Roman Catholic who was executed in 1679 for daring to hold a mass in the castle. A plain slab commemorates this martyr, who was 80 years of age when he met his violent end. Several more castles along the River Monmow are further reminders that this pretty part of the world was once very turbulent.

ST WEONARDS
9 miles N of Monmouth on the A466

🏛 Violette Szabo   🏛 Museum

This little hilltop village is named after an obscure Welsh saint who is portrayed in the church named after him in early-16th century stained glass. Most of the church is of that period but a 13th century doorway in the porch has survived.

About three miles north of St Weonards, at **Wormelow Tump**, the **Violette Szabo GC Museum** celebrates the bravery of the young woman who was parachuted into Nazi-occupied France to work with the Maquis. While trying to save a key agent, using a sten gun single-handed, she was captured, imprisoned, tortured and shot in January 1945. The 1950s film *Carve Her Name With Pride*, with Virginia McKenna in the title role, tells her dramatic story. The museum, opened in June 2000, contains memorabilia of this remarkable woman and is open on Wednesdays from April to October.

LLANROTHAL
6 miles NW of Monmouth off the A466

Standing in isolation at the end of a lane by the river is the Church of St John the Baptist, built in the 12th and 13th centuries and restored from almost total ruin in the 1920s.

SKENFRITH
7 miles NW of Monmouth on the B4521

🏰 Skenfrith Castle

A drive or an energetic walk takes in the remains of **Skenfrith Castle** (the round tower is an impressive sight), an ancient mill and the Church of St Bridget, dating, like the castle, from the 12th and 13th centuries. All in Skenfrith!

GARWAY
9 miles NW of Monmouth on a minor road

🏰 Dovecote   ⛰ Garway Hill

Marvellous views from the wild and remote **Garway Hill** take in the river valley, the Forest of Dean beyond Symonds Yat to the east, and the Black Mountains. The church at Garway was built by the Knights Templar and the influences from the Holy Sepulchre in Jerusalem can clearly be seen. During the purges of Henry VIII's reign, the Abbot of Monmouth was one of many who sought refuge in the church tower. The most unusual building in Garway is undoubtedly the famous **Dovecote**, the first of several to be mentioned in this book. Built in the 1300s (probably the work of the same good knights) it stands in a farmyard next to the church and has precisely 666 pigeon-holes.

GROSMONT
12 miles NW of Monmouth on the B4347

In the village of Grosmont lies another castle with impressive remains, and another interesting church, this one dedicated to St Nicolas of Myra.

A little way beyond Grosmont is Kentchurch Court, a one-time border castle rebuilt by John Nash around 1800 and featuring some splendid wood carvings by Grinling Gibbons. The Court has for many centuries been the home of the Scudamore family, one of whose number married Owen Glendower.

Ross-on-Wye

🏛 Market House   🌿 Festival

The lovely old market town of Ross-on-Wye is signalled from some way out by the towering spire of St Mary's Church, surrounded up on its sandstone cliffs by a cluster of attractive houses. Opposite the church is a row of Tudor almshouses which have an ancient yet ageless look and which show off the beauty of the rosy-red sandstone to great effect. The town was visited by the Black Death in 1637, and over 300 victims are buried in the churchyard. A simple stone cross commemorates these hapless souls, who were interred in the dead of night in an effort to avoid panicking the populace. Notable features in the church include 15th century stained glass figures and a tomb chest with effigies of William Rudhall, Attorney General to Henry Vlll and founder of the almshouses, and his wife. Pride of place in the market square goes to the 17th century **Market House**, with an open ground floor and pillars supporting the upper floor, which is a Heritage Centre. Spot the relief of Charles ll on the east wall.

Ross is full of interesting buildings, and besides those already noted is Thrushes Nest, once the home of Sir Frederick Burrows, a railway porter who rose above his station to become the last Governor of Bengal. Opposite Market House stands the half-timbered house (now shops) of the town's greatest benefactor, John Kyrle. A wealthy barrister who had studied law at the Middle Temple, Kyrle settled in Ross around 1660 and dedicated the rest of his life to philanthropic works: he donated the town's main public garden, The Prospect; he repaired St Mary's spire; he provided a constant supply of fresh water; and he paid for food and education for the poor. Alexander Pope was as impressed as anyone by this benefactor, penning these lines some time after the great man died in 1724 at the age of 87:

Market House, Ross-on-Wye

Rise, honest Muse, and sing the Man of Ross,
Health to the sick and solace to the swain,
Whose causeway parts the vale in shady rows,
Whose seats the weary traveller repose,
Who taught that heav'n directed spire to rise?
'The Man of Ross', each lisping babe replies.

The Ross International Festival of music, opera, theatre, comedy and film takes place each August and grows in stature year by year. In and around Ross are several examples of modern public art, including leaping salmon metal sculptures (Edde Cross Street) and a mural celebrating the life of locally-born playwright Dennis Potter. At Ross-on-Wye Candlemakers in Gloucester Road are a shop and workshop showing the manufacture of all types of candles, with evening demonstrations and group visits by appointment.

Around Ross-on-Wye

WESTON-UNDER-PENYARD
2 miles E of Ross on the A40

🌿 Hope Mansell Valley 🌿 Forest of Dean

Leave the A40 at Weston Cross to Bollitree Castle (a folly), then turn left to Rudhall and you'll come upon Kingstone Cottages, whose delightful informal gardens contain the National Collection of old pinks and carnations. Private visits welcome.

South of Weston lies **Hope Mansell Valley**, tucked away between the River Wye and the Forest of Dean, and certainly one of the loveliest and most fertile valleys in the region. It is an area of wooded hills and spectacular views, of farms and small settlements, with the tiny village of Hope Mansell itself at the far end. The **Forest of Dean**, over the border in Gloucestershire, is a vast and ancient woodland full of beauty and

mystery, with signs of an Iron Age settlement. Later a royal hunting ground, and the home of charcoal-burners and shepherds, it became the first National Forest Park.

YATTON
5 miles NE of Ross on the A449

In a remote farmyard setting off the B4224, Yatton Chapel, disused for many years, is a simple little church with a 12th century doorway, a wooden belfry, agricultural floor and largely unplastered walls.

MUCH MARCLE
7 miles NE of Ross on the A449

🏛 Church 🏛 Hellens 🍎 Cider Mill

🏛 Cider Museums 🌳 Great Marcle Yew

🌳 Newbridge Farm Park

This is Big Apple Country, with major cider connections in the shape of **Westons Cider Mill** and Lyne Down Farm, where traditional methods of making cider and perry are still employed. Among the many attractions are free cider tasting, the **Bottle Museum**, a wetland nature reserve, the award-winning Henry Weston Garden, a traditional and rare breeds farm, shire horse dray rides and a tea room. Tours start every day at 2.30pm. The **Church of St Bartholomew** is notable for some superb tombs and monuments, amongst them an effigy of Much Marcle's 'Sleeping Beauty'. The well-preserved effigy portrays Blanche Mortimer, daughter of the 1st Earl of March, who died in 1347. As was customary at that time, the effigy depicts her as aged around 30 – the supposed age at which Christ was crucified – suggesting the possibility of marriage to Him in heaven.

The church contains another striking effigy, a rare painted wooden effigy, carved from solid oak, which is thought to be the likeness

🎭 stories and anecdotes 🦜 famous people ✍ art and craft 🖉 entertainment and sport 🚶 walks of a 14th century landowner called Walter de Helyon. Up until the 1970s he was painted a rather sombre stone colour, but was then loaned for an exhibition of Chaucer's London and was repainted in his original colours. The **Great Marcle Yew** is a talking point among all visitors to the village, its massive trunk hollowed out allowing up to eight people to enjoy cosy comfort on the bench inside.

A short distance north of Much Marcle, **Hellens** is an untouched Tudor/Stuart house set in 15 acres of grounds with coppices, lawns and fishponds. The house contains a wealth of period furnishings and decorations, fine paintings, miniatures and artefacts.

Closer to Ledbury, on the A4172 at Little Marcle, is **Newbridge Farm Park**, where families can enjoy a day out on the farm in the company of a large assortment of friendly farm animals.

LEDBURY
10 miles NE of Ross on the A449

🏛 Barrett Browning Institute   🏛 Market House

🏛 Church   🏛 Eastnor Castle

🏛 Butchers Row Museum   🏛 Heritage Centre

A classic market town filled with timber-framed black-and-white buildings, mentioned in the Domesday Book as Ledeberge and accorded its market status in the 12th century. The centre of the town is dominated by the **Barrett Browning Institute** of 1892, erected in memory of the author Elizabeth Barrett Browning, whose family lived at nearby Colwall. Alongside it are the almshouses of St

---

TINSMITHS

8a High Street, Ledbury, Herefordshire HR8 1DS
Tel: 01531 632083   Fax: 01531 635822
website: www.tinsmiths.co.uk

Tinsmiths owner, Phoebe Clive, is passionate about people and textiles, so visitors receive a friendly welcome and are offered an informed, personal service. Tinsmiths' two courtyard showrooms couldn't be more different. Old Tinsmiths, a timber framed building has a traditional draper-shop feel with a large selection of high-quality cottons and linens sold off the roll for curtains, blinds and upholstery and Phoebe offers a full making-up service from her workroom on the premises. Adjacent is the new showroom, an unexpectedly modern steel and glass building designed by Phoebe's husband Alex Clive and worth visiting in its own right. It houses a range of contemporary furniture, lighting and homeware.

Tinsmiths is the only provincial stockist of Ian Mankin's natural woven cottons and linens: work by other talented textile designers include Kate Foreman, Angela Lewin and Orla Kiely with her superb oilcloths and ceramic designers include Sophie Conran, Stuart Houghton and Arwyn Jones' hand-thrown stoneware.

Shop hours are 10 to 5 Tuesday to Saturday, or customer's can request fabric samples and make orders via a comprehensive website.

🏛 historic building   🏛 museum   🏛 historic site   🌳 scenic attraction   🌱 flora and fauna

Market House, Ledbury

Katherine's Hospital, founded in 1232 for wayfarers and the poor. Church Lane, much in demand for calendars and film location scenes, is a cobbled medieval street where some of the buildings seem almost to meet across the street. In the **Heritage Centre,** in a timber-framed former grammar school, visitors can learn about Ledbury's past, John Masefield and Elizabeth Barrett Browning, and try their hand at timber framing. Opposite the Heritage Museum is the **Butchers Row Museum**, a tiny museum depicting Victorian life. The house used to stand in the middle of the High Street but was demolished in about 1830. It was re-erected in 1979 by the Ledbury & District Society.

The town's symbol is the **Market House**, dating from about 1650 and attributed to John

SEZ

5 High Street, Ledbury, Herefordshire HR8 1DS
Tel: 01531 631136
website: www.sez.uk.com

Classic ladies' clothes with a contemporary feel fill the shelves and racks of the three branches of **Sez**. Founder and owner Sarah Handley has been sourcing ranges of clothes from British and European designers and manufacturers since 1986, and is as well informed as anyone in the business. She believes that shopping should be fun, so she is happy to let customers browse at leisure among the wide range of garments. Customers are encouraged to put together their own 'look' by selecting from among the carefully chosen co-ordinates, and Sarah and her friendly, on-the-ball staff are always ready if advice or help is needed.

All occasions, from fun to formal, are catered for, and the shops carry a wide range of bags, scarves and other complementary accessories from Dents, and jewellery by Danté. Among the labels featured are Karelia, Libra, Gelco, Poppy, Emreco, Oscar B and Intown . Opening hours are 9.30 to 5 Monday to Saturday. Also at:

17 High Street, Bromyard Tel: 01885 482399

17 Drapers Lane, Leominster Tel: 01568 613850

📺 stories and anecdotes 🦜 famous people 🎨 art and craft 🎭 entertainment and sport 🚶 walks

MRS MUFFINS

1 Church Lane, Ledbury, Herefordshire HR8 1DL
Tel: 01531 633579
website: www.mrsmuffins.co.uk e-mail: leanne@mrsmuffins.co.uk

Mrs Muffins offers scrumptious, award-winning food set in a
beautiful 16th Century oak beamed building with a secluded
courtyard garden. The menu offers tempting and tasty meals
using local cheeses and rare breed meats, homemade soup, salads, local Ledbury ice cream and
homemade cakes and scones. Favourite dishes include Gloucester Old Spot bacon and brie
jacket potato, little Hereford sage cheese and apricot chutney toastie and hungry Hereford
ploughmans. Mrs Muffins' cream teas, with homemade scones and Herefordshire clotted cream
are a real treat. Mrs Muffins is licensed for a tempting range of local beers and wines, and sells
a selection of local produce including jams, chutneys, ice cream and chocolates. Open from
10am Mon - Sat and from 11am on summer Sundays.

Abel, the royal carpenter, and another notable
landmark is the Norman parish **Church of St
Michael and All Angels**, with a soaring 18th
century spire set on a separate 13th century
tower, a golden weather vane, some
magnificent medieval brasses, fine monuments
by Westmacott, Flaxman and Thornycroft, and
bullet holes in the door - the scars of the
Battle of Ledbury. The town's history has in
general been fairly placid, but its peace was

THE SEVEN STARS

11 The Homend, Ledbury, Herefordshire HR8 1BN
Tel: 01531 631317 Fax: 01531 630168
website: www.sevenstarsledbury.com

On one of the best-known and most interesting streets in
Ledbury, the **Seven Stars** is a marvellous Grade II listed
coaching inn dating back to the 16th century. It was
largely destroyed by fire in 2001, and hard work and
dedication have allowed it to rise from the ashes in all its
glory. The distinctive cream-painted frontage features
beams, a red-tiled roof and a tall brick chimney, and the
promise of the exterior is fully realised inside, carefully
updated while retaining its traditional charm and appeal.
The bar, which is open throughout the day, is well stocked
with beers, lagers, wines, spirits and soft drinks, providing
a convivial, welcoming spot to enjoy a drink and a chat.

Hospitable tenants Paul and Nikki Baker are passionate
about food, and they have created excellent all-day
menus based as far as possible on prime local produce,
including rare-breed meats. The guest accommodation
comprises three oak-beamed bedrooms – a double and
two family rooms – with en suite facilities, TV, telephone,
free WI/FI access and hot drinks tray. The Seven Stars is
admirably placed for exploring the town: the Tourist Information Centre is almost next door, and
the Heritage Centre, the Butchers Row Museum, the 17th century Market House and the Church
of St Michael & All Angels are all an easy walk away.

🏛 historic building   🏛 museum   🏛 historic site   ⚘ scenic attraction   🌱 flora and fauna broken with a vengeance in April 1645, when Royalist troops under Prince Rupert surprised a Roundhead advance from Gloucester. In the fierce fighting that followed there were many deaths, and 400 men were taken prisoner.

Annual events at Ledbury include a poetry festival in July, a street carnival in August and a hop fair in the autumn. Among the famous sons of the town is one of our most distinguished Poets Laureate, John Masefield, born in 1878 in a house called The Knapps. William Langland, who wrote *Piers Plowman*, was born in 1332 in nearby Colwall. The town is a great place for walking and, on the fringes, nature-lovers will find plenty to delight in Dog Hill Wood, Frith Wood and Conigree Wood, as well as on Wellington Heath and along the Old Railway Line.

Two-and-a-half miles outside Ledbury on the A438 towards Tewkesbury stands **Eastnor Castle**, overlooking the Malvern Hills. This fairytale castle, surrounded by a deer park, arboretum and lake, has the look of a medieval fortress but was actually built between 1812 and 1824 and is a major example of the great Norman and Gothic architectural revival of the time. The first Earl Somers wanted a magnificent baronial castle, and, with the young and inspired architect Robert Smirke in charge, that's exactly what he got; the combination of inherited wealth and a judicious marriage enabled the Earl to build a family home to impress all his contemporaries. The interior is excitingly beautiful on a massive scale: a vast 60ft hall leads into a series of state rooms including a

---

WOODSIDE LODGES COUNTRY PARK

Falcon Lane, Ledbury, Herefordshire HR8 2JN
Tel: 01531 670269   Fax: 0560 1153922
e-mail: info@woodsidelodges.co.uk
website: www.woodsidelodges.co.uk

Owned and run since 1991 by the Davies family, **Woodside Lodges Country Park** enjoys a lovely rural setting off the A438 2 miles west of Ledbury, with woodland, grassland, fishing pools and waterfalls. Luxury Scandinavian self-catering lodges make an ideal base for walking, cycling, discovering the many attractions in the region, or just relaxing and enjoying the surroundings. Sleeping from 2 to 6 in three variations, they are all centrally heated and double-glazed, with open-plan lounge/kitchen/dining areas, TV, CD player, Hi-fi, bathrooms with bath and shower and verandas; the smallest (Kites Nest) and largest (Falcon Wood and Tanglewood) also boast saunas. Laundrette facilities are available.

The site includes an award-winning conservation area with trees, shrubs, 300 native water plants and 100 varieties of wild flowers. One part is grassland stocked with a flock of 100 Wiltshire Horn breeding ewes. The owners are always striving to add to the many attractions of the Park: plans include turning redundant farm buildings into a visitor centre, which will also create a stop for walkers on the long-distance Herefordshire Trail that passes through the site.

📖 stories and anecdotes   🐦 famous people   🎨 art and craft   ✎ entertainment and sport   🚶 walks

BLUE RIDGE & TICKLED PINK

5 The Homend, Ledbury, Herefordshire HR8 1BN
Tel: 01531 636492
e-mail: enquiries@tickledpinkledbury.co.uk
website: www.tickledpinkledbury.co.uk

Behind the cheerful frontage of **Blue Ridge & Tickled Pink**, run by sisters Emma O'Boyle and Helen Davies, you'll find a wide range of clothes, accessories, gifts and toys. The shop is packed with its very varied stock, but there's plenty of room to browse the ever-changing selection. They sell clothes for men, women and children, and ranges for kids include Lucy Lockett and Toby Tiger; among other brands featured are Crew, Chilli Pepper and Weird Fish casual and everyday wear.

Kids are particularly well catered for, with a wealth of creative things to keep them happy and busy – jewellery, fairy wings, wands, shoes, toys and trinkets. There are gifts for adults too, including watches, pens, Leathermans, binoculars.....The shop is full of surprises: one of them is a classic blue beach hut used as a changing room!

Winner of a Good Citizens of Ledbury Award 2006, the shop stands next to the Tourist Information Centre and close to the Market House, the focal point of the town. Opening hours are 9.30 to 5.30 Monday to Saturday.

library in Italian Renaissance style containing a treasure house of paintings and tapestries, and a spectacular Gothic drawing room designed by Pugin. The grounds, part of which are a Site of Special Scientific Interest, are home to a wonderful variety of flora and fauna, and throughout the year the castle is the scene of special events.

The Edwardian gardens at **How Caple Court**, set high above the Wye in park and woodland, are magnificent indeed, with formal terraces, yew hedges, statues, pools, a sunken Florentine water garden and woodland walks. How Caple's medieval **Church of St Andrew and St Mary** contains a priceless 16th century German diptych depicting, among other subjects, the martyrdom of St Clare and St Francis, and Mary Magdalene washing the feet of Christ.

BROCKHAMPTON
5 miles N of Ross off the B4224

🏛 Church   ⚖ Marcle Ridge

The **Church of All Saints** is one of only two thatched churches in the country and dates from 1902, designed by William Lethaby, who

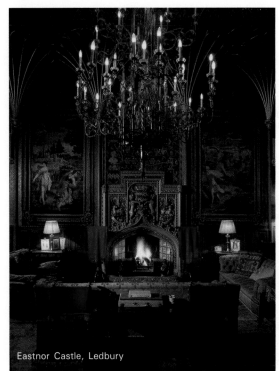

Eastnor Castle, Ledbury

Wuliva, the sister of Lady Godiva who owned the manor in the 11th century. In the 13th century sandstone **Church of St George** is a modern stained-glass window depicting the siblings. Godiva rides through the streets on her white horse (all in the best possible taste), is seen petting a cat and a dog, while her sister has a dog and some rabbits at her feet.

WILTON
1 mile W of Ross on the A40

🏰 Castle

Wilton, just a short walk from Ross, stands at a crossing point of the River Wye. The bridge was built in 1599, some years after a river disaster which claimed 40 lives. Over the bridge are the ruins of **Wilton Castle**, of which some walls and towers still stand. An 18th century sundial on the bridge bears this numinous inscription:

> *"Esteem thy precious time,*
> *which pass so swiftly away:*
> *Prepare them for eternity*
> *and do not make delay."*

had close ties with Westminster Abbey, and built by Alice Foster, a wealthy American, as a memorial to her parents. The Norfolk thatch is not the only unusual aspect here, as the church also boasts stained glass made in the Christopher Whall studios and tapestries from the William Morris workshop from Burne-Jones designs.

This is, like so much of the county, great walking country, with the **Marcle Ridge** and the 500ft Woolhope Dome.

WOOLHOPE
7 miles N of Ross off the B4224

⛪ Church

A small village enjoying lovely views of the Black Mountains, Woolhope is named after

PETERSTOW
2 miles W of Ross on A49

🌿 Broome Farm   🌿 Kyrle House

At **Broome Farm**, half a mile off the A49, traditional farmhouse cider has been brewed since the early 1980s, winning many prizes throughout the 1990s and featuring apples with evocative names like Fox Whelp or Yarlington Mill. Also at Peterstow is **Kyrle House**, whose country garden contains herbaceous borders, a small grotto, sunken

 stories and anecdotes   🐿 famous people   🎨 art and craft   🎭 entertainment and sport   🚶 walks garden and secret garden. Private visits are welcome.

FOWNHOPE
7 miles NW of Ross on the B4224

A pleasant village set beside the River Wye. Every year on Oak Apple Day, in May or June, the Green Man Inn celebrates the restoration of Charles II with the Heart of Oak Club Walk. The inn's most famous landlord was Tom Spring, a champion bare-knuckle prizefighter who died in 1851. Fownhope's church, known as the 'Little Cathedral', has a special treasure in the form of a Norman tympanum depicting the Virgin and Child with a winged lion and eagle amongst foliage.

HOLME LACY
8 miles NW of Ross on the B4399

🏛 Hole Lace	🏛 St Cuthbert's Church
🏛 Dinedor Court	🏛 Rotherwas Chapel

Holme Lacy was originally the estate of the de Lacy family in the 14th century, but later passed into the hands of the illustrious Scudamore family. The 1st Viscount Scudamore was the first person to classify the varieties of cider apple, and actually introduced the well-known Red Streak Pippin strain. The fine Palladian mansion dates from 1672 and once sported woodwork by Grinling Gibbons. **St Cuthbert's Church**, standing away from the village on a bend of the Wye, has a remarkable collection of 16th and 17th century monuments of the Scudamores, and also some fine furnishings and medieval stalls with misericords.

Near the village of Holme Lacy is **Dinedor Court**, a splendid 16th century listed farmhouse with an impressive oak-panelled dining hall. English Heritage is responsible for **Rotherwas Chapel** in **Dinedor**. This is a Roman Catholic chapel dating from the 14th and 16th centuries and featuring an interesting mid-Victorian side chapel and high altar.

SELLACK
3 miles NW of Ross on minor roads or off the A49

A popular waymarked walk takes in three marvellous churches in three delightful

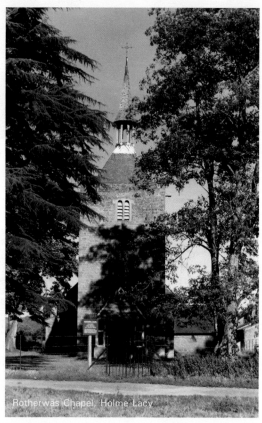

Rotherwas Chapel, Holme Lacy

villages. The church in Sellack is uniquely dedicated to St Tysilio, son of a king of Powys, and is Norman in origin.

A short drive north of Sellack, in the churchyard at King's Caple, is a plague cross remembering victims of the Black Death of 1348. The church dates mainly from the 13th century and a fascinating little detail is to be found on the benefactors' board on the west wall. The local charities listed include Cake Money, a gift in perpetuity from a former vicar of King's Caple and Sellack. Pax cakes, signifying peace, are still distributed to the congregations on Palm Sunday.

HOARWITHY
6 miles NW of Ross off the A49

🏛 Church   🐑 Glenda Spooner Farm

By far the most extraordinary of the three walk-linked churches lies in the unspoilt village of Hoarwithy on the willow-lined banks of the Wye. **St Catherine's Church** is a splendid piece of architecture which owes its origin to the Reverend William Poole, who arrived in 1854, didn't like what he saw – the chapel was, he said, "as bare as the palm of the hand". Poole spent the next 30 years supervising the building of a new church round the chapel. The result is an Italianate building complete with a campanile, arcades, beautiful tiled floors and a white marble altar with lapis lazuli inlay. The **International League for the Protection of Horses Glenda Spooner Farm** is a recovery and rehabilitation centre for horses and ponies set in glorious countryside. In a quiet lane easily reached from

the A49, it's a peaceful haven for around 50 animals at any one time. Open for visits Wednesday and Saturday. Worth a look in Little Birch, just to the north west, is Higgin's Well, named after a local farmer and restored at the time of Queen Victoria's Diamond Jubilee in 1897.

Hereford

🏛 Cathedral   🏛 Chained Library   🏛 Mappa Mundi
🏛 Museums   🍺 Cider Mills   🖼 Hatton Gallery
🎵 Three Choirs Festival

The county town-to-be was founded as a settlement near the unstable Welsh Marches

Hereford Cathedral

after the Saxons had crossed the Severn in the 7th century. A royal demesne in the 11th century, it had a provincial mint, and was an important centre of the wool trade in the Middle Ages. Fragments of Saxon and medieval walls can still be seen, but the city's crowning glory is the magnificent '**Cathedral of the Marches**'. Largely Norman, it also has examples of Gothic, Early English, Decorated, Perpendicular and Modern architecture. The Cathedral demands an extended visit, as it contains, in the impressive New Library building, two of the country's most important historical treasures. **Mappa Mundi** is the renowned medieval world map, the work of Richard of Haldingham. Drawn on vellum, it has Jerusalem as its centre and East at the top, indicating that direction as the source of all things good and religiously significant. Richard was Treasurer of Lincoln Cathedral, which might explain why Lincoln appears rather more prominently on the map than Hereford. The Cathedral has many other treasures, including the shrine of St Thomas of Hereford in stone and marble, the Norman font, the Bishop's Throne and the John Piper tapestries. There's also a brass-rubbing centre. For details of the Cathedral's opening hours and guided tours call 01432 374202.

The **Chained Library** at All Saints Church, houses more than 1,400 rare books, including over 200 medieval manuscripts, all chained to their original 17th century book presses. The actor/theatre manager David Garrick was born in Hereford in 1717 and was christened at All Saints. Another notable child of Hereford was

🏛 historic building   🏛 museum   🏛 historic site   🐿 scenic attraction   🌼 flora and fauna

Nell Gwyn(ne), favourite of Charles II. Born in 1650, she is remembered by a plaque on the wall of the Bishop's Garden.

Hereford is full of fascinating buildings and museums which visitors should try to include in their tour. **Hereford Museum and Art Gallery** has a changing art gallery programme and hands-on exhibitions. The **Old Hall Museum**, right in the centre of High Town, brings alive the 17th century in a three-storey black-and-white house filled with fascinating exhibits. **Churchill House Museum**, whose grounds

Waterworks Museum, Hereford

include a fragrant garden, displays furniture, costumes and paintings from the 18th and 19th centuries; among its rooms are a costume exhibition gallery and Victorian nursery, parlour, kitchen and butler's pantry. The

---

C V OSBORNE GOLDSMITH AND JEWELLER

20 Union Street, Hereford, Herefordshire HR1 2BT
Tel/Fax: 01432 263226

Owner Colin Osborne and his two assistants bring a wealth of experience and expertise to everything they do at **C V Osborne**, which stands behind Chads in Union Street. Colin himself has been a goldsmith for 25 years, Tina has designed and made jewellery for 20 years and Ron has been in the jewellery trade for over 40 years. Between them they produce a variety of superb pieces that include rings, bracelets, cufflinks and tiaras, to bespoke designs or to customers' individual specifications. Tina also attends regular courses in gemmology.

Pieces range from traditional to contemporary, classic to bizarre; opals, pearls and amber are specialities, along with unusual gems such as morganite or kunzite. A workshop at the back of the shop has a traditional work bench for making pieces and for repairs and alterations. Friendly, personal service and consistent high quality of workmanship attracts business from as far away as London to this outstanding establishment.

📖 stories and anecdotes   🕊 famous people   🎨 art and craft   🎭 entertainment and sport   🚶 walks

Hatton Gallery shows the work of local artist Brian Hatton. **The Coningsby Museum & St John Medieval's Museum** at Coningsby is a 13th century building in an ancient quadrangle of almshouses. Displays include costume models of Nell Gwynne, a famous daughter of Hereford, and the history of the Ancient Order of St John and its wars during the Crusades. Open by appointment only Tel: 01432 358134. Hereford's restored pumping station is home to the **Waterworks Museum**, where Victorian technology is alive and well in the shape of a collection of pumps (some of which can be operated by visitors), a Lancashire Boiler and Britain's largest triple expansion engine. The **Herefordshire Light Infantry Museum** houses an important collection of uniforms, colours, medals, equipment, documents and photographs connected with the regiment set up in 1960. Visits by appointment only, Tel: 01432 50328.

Hereford and cider are old friends, and the **Cider Museum** tells the interesting story of cider production down the years. One of the galleries houses the King Offa Distillery, the first cider brandy distillery to be granted a licence for more than 200 years. Among the many attractions are the reconstructed farm ciderhouse, the champagne cider cellars, the vat house, the coopers' workshop and beautiful old books illustrating the varieties of cider apples and perry pears grown from earliest times. The Strongbow Vat, which holds 7.4 million litres and is more than 20 metres high, is the largest in the world. Visitors can sample cider brandy, liqueur and aperitif, all produced at the distillery, which is open for visits throughout the year. Tel: 01432 354207. On the outskirts

---

BERRY RED

29 Church Street, Hereford HR1 2LR
Tel: 01432 274805 Fax: 01432 263858
e-mail: enquiries@berryred.co.uk website: www.berryred.co.uk

Located down a small cobbled lane adjacent to Hereford's historic Cathedral is the Country Lifestyle Boutique **Berry Red** and its sister shop **Berry Red Children**. Opened by London émigrés Karon and Simon Hamilton, both shops specialise in individually designed products a world away from the standard High Street fare.

On display are textiles, fabrics, embroidered wares, quilts, cushions, and unusual painted decorative furniture, glassware, enamelware and ceramics, mirrors, clocks and lighting, all selected to fit into a relaxed country theme. As well as products for the home, the Lifestyle Shop also affords the opportunity to indulge in some personal retail therapy. No 29 Church Street offers a fabulous selection of mainly French toiletries together with personal accessories such as scarves, hats, slippers, nightwear and vintage-style jewellery. In the old panelled Garden Room at the side of the building is an equally alluring selection of items for the garden. From ornaments and planters to hammocks and Raj style parasols. It's all very eclectic and colourful and a paradise for browsers.

No 9 Church Street is the Children's Store, and like its elder sister is full of wonderful surprises. Its unashamedly old fashioned and stocks the kind of toys you remember from your own childhood; no batteries or plastic in this shop! Treasures like rag dolls, wicker prams, traditional teddy bears, spinning tops and bows & arrows are typical of the stock carried together with a lovely selection of Mother and Baby. The shop also stocks children's clothes from D'Arcy Brown, London, as well as smaller collections from individual designers such as the intricately hand crocheted fair trade dresses and pram coats made from organic cotton and sourced in Peru.

🏛 historic building   🏛 museum   🏛 historic site   ⚘ scenic attraction   🌿 flora and fauna

CASTLE CLIFFE EAST

14 Quay Street, Hereford HR1 2NH
Tel: 01432 272096
e-mail: mail@castlecliffe.net website: www.castlecliffe.net

Castle Cliffe is a medieval watergate that has been beautifully restored to provide luxury holiday accommodation for six people on the banks of the River Wye. Surrounded by historic parkland, with riverside gardens and views of Bishop's Meadow beyond, the house is wonderfully tranquil yet only a few minutes walk from shops, restaurants, the cathedral and Mappa Mundi Exhibition. Period furniture and open fires throughout, make Castle Cliffe the ideal place to relax with friends and family.

of the city are the Cider Mills of HP Bulmer, the world's leading cider producer.

The original Saxon part of the city includes historic Church Street, full of 17th century listed buildings (most of them modernised in the 19th century). Church Street and Capuchin Yard - the name derives from the hood worn by the Franciscan friars who built a chapel nearby - are renowned for their small specialist shops and craft workshops.

Hereford stages important musical events throughout the year, and every third year hosts the **Three Choirs Festival**, Europe's oldest music festival.

The Golden Valley

KILPECK
8 miles SW of Hereford off the A465

🏛 Church

The parish **Church of St Mary and St David** is one of the most fascinating in the whole county and generally regarded as the most perfect Norman church in England. Built by Hugh de Kilpeck (son of William Fitznorman, who built Kilpeck Castle) round an earlier Saxon church, it has changed little since the 12th century. Much of the church is unique in

its rich decoration, but the gem is the portal over the south doorway, with all manner of elaborate carvings. Most of the carvings throughout the church have no apparent religious significance, with some bordering on the bizarre, if not downright bawdy! Very little remains of the castle, it having been largely demolished by Cromwell's men, but on a clear day the castle mound affords very fine views.

EWYAS HAROLD
12 miles SW of Hereford on the B4347

A village at the foot of the lovely Golden Valley, in an area of fine walks. West of the village lay the ancient Welsh kingdom of Ewias; the motte and bailey castle that was part of the border defences has disappeared, leaving only the distinctive mound. A Cistercian Abbey was founded here in the 12th century and the building, which was substantially restored by John Abel in the 17th century, is still in use as a parish church.

ABBEY DORE
12 miles SW of Hereford on the B4347

🏛 Abbey   🌿 Abbey Dore Court

🌿 Pentwyn Cottage Garden

Occupying a sublimely beautiful setting beside the river are the impressive remains of a 12th

Llangua and the Monnow Valley Walk

Distance: *4.5 miles (7.2 kilometres)*

Typical time: *120 mins*

Height gain: *180 metres*

Map: *Explorer OL 13*

Walk: *www.walkingworld.com ID:2701*

Contributor: *Pat Roberts*

Parking is in a layby on the minor road to Llangua, just off the A465 from Abergavenny to Hereford, just south of the traffic lights and bridge over the River Monnow south of Pontrilas.

The Monnow Valley Walk has been produced in book form by Ira and Harry Steggles and traces the River Monnow from Monmouth to Hay-on-Wye, On this walk we follow part of it on the outward route before returning across Cupid's Hill and re-joining the River Monnow and following the river bank back to Llangua.

Hills or Fells, River, Wildlife, Birds, Flowers, Great Views, Butterflies

1 | Walk on the verge of the A465 towards the traffic lights. Cross the bridge on the painted footpath and then cross the road to the west side. We are now following the Monnow Valley Walk.

2 | Immediately after the traffic lights go through the gate on the left. Ignore the finger post on the side of the road as it is misleading. Through the gate bear diagonally left to reach a post bearing the Monnow Valley Logo and walk under the railway bridge. Through a gate and left to walk with the River Monnow on your left. Over a stile and continue, reaching a wood and a footbridge. Half way across the next field bear slightly right to reach a stile in the hedge.

3 | Over the stile onto a lane and right and up. The lane becomes tarmaced and bends left. At the top the lane bends right but we continue on a track ahead, signed "Vroe". The track drops down to pass between the two houses and reaches a ford.

4 | Just before the ford take the footbridge over the stream. Through a gate/stile and, keeping about 40 metres from the left hedge, up to another stile. Over the stile and diagonally left up quite a steep field to reach another gate/stile.

5 | Over the stile and immediately left over another stile. We have now left the Monnow Valley Walk. Keep to the left of the next 3 fields, climbing stiles as nessessary. The fourth field starts to lose height half way across. Start to bear slightly right to a kissing gate.

6 | Through the kissing gate and head across the field to a metal gate onto the railway. CROSS WITH CAUTION and up to another field. Continue across to a metal bridge over the monnow and on to the A465. Cross with care.

7 | Up the steps, over the stile and up diagonally left to reach a fence. Turn left with the fence on your right. Reach a stile in the corner, over and down to another stile and onto a farm drive.

8 | Cross the drive diagonally and over the stile. Follow the arrow left to another hedge where turn right to walk up with the hedge on your left. Take time to look back and enjoy the views back over the walk and over to the Black Mountains. Through a gate and up the next field to another gate. Through this gate and slightly left to a stile onto the road where turn right and up for 200 metres.

9 | Just before Little Kingsfield Cottage left and onto the farm drive. From here the path has been moved and does not match some maps. PLEASE FOLLOW SIGNS.

10 | Before reaching the bend in the drive look out for the gate and footpath sign on the right. Through the gate and down the field, hedge on your right to a stile. Over and immediately left to the gates before the house. Follow arrows right over stile and small footbridge and immediately left to walk with hedge on your left. Through gate and follow hedge in next field to another stile. Down the next field to reach the river bank where we re-join the Monnow Valley Walk.

11 | Left with the River Monnow on your right, over stiles and across fields as nessessary to reach a stile onto the road next to the car park.

Abbey Dore Court Gardens

century **Cistercian Abbey**, part of which is still in use as the parish church. Most of the building dates from around 1180 but the battlemented tower was added in the 1660s by the Scudamore family, lords of the manor. They also commissioned the noted carpenter John Abel to create the impressive wooden chancel roof and the superb, heavily carved screen.

On the other side of the river, the garden at **Abbey Dore Court** is home to many unusual shrubs and perennials along with specialist collections of euphorbias, hellebores and peonies. There's also a small nursery, a gift shop and a restaurant.

In Bacton itself, a mile along the same B4347, is **Pentwyn Cottage Garden**, where visitors can walk round the peaceful garden before enjoying a cream tea. From the remote, lonely roads that lead west towards Offa's Dyke and the boundary with Wales, motorists should leave their cars, stretch their legs and drink in the wonderful scenery.

The villages of Longtown and Clodock lie at the foot of the Olchon Valley, while further north are the Olchon Waterfall, Black Hill, the rocky ridge of the Cat's Back and the ruins of Craswall Priory, which was founded in the 13th century by the rare Grandmontine order and abandoned 200 years later.

PETERCHURCH
10 miles W of Hereford on the B4348

The chief village of the Golden Valley, with a very fine parish church. In 786, King Offa brought monks to the village to found the original church. It was a sign of Offa's great power and influence that a bishop from Rome was included in the missionary party established here.

DORSTONE
12 miles W of Hereford off the B4348

🏛 Snodhill Castle   🏛 Arthur's Stone

A very attractive village with neat sandstone cottages set around the green. St Faith's Church has a connection with Canterbury, as Richard de Brito, one of the knights who murdered Thomas à Becket, established a church here after serving 15 years' penance in the Holy Land for his crime. He returned to build the church and is buried in the churchyard.

South of Dorstone lie the ruins of **Snodhill Castle**, from which the views are spectacular even for this part of the world. To the north, on wild, exposed Merbach Hill, is the much-visited landmark of **Arthur's Stone**, a megalithic tomb of great antiquity which was used for the burial of tribal chieftains. Some say (but few believe) that the body of King Arthur himself was buried here.

Along the Wye Valley

The A465 out of Hereford soon reaches **Belmont Abbey**, whose architect, the renowned Pugin, was responsible for part of the House of Commons. One of the stained-glass windows in the church at Clehonger is probably also his work.

SWAINSHILL
3 miles W of Hereford on the A438

🌿 The Weir

The Weir (National Trust) in Swainshill is a charming riverside garden, spectacular in early spring, with 'drifts of flowering bulbs'. The garden enjoys grand views of the Wye and the Welsh Hills.

MADLEY
6 miles W of Hereford on the B4352

🏛 Lulham Pew

There's more fine stained glass from the early 1300s in the Church of the Nativity of the Virgin at Madley, which also claims to have one of the largest stone fonts in the country. A curiosity here is the **Lulham Pew** in the north aisle. Constructed mostly from a medieval screen it has high sides and curtains, thus allowing the Lulham family to pursue their devotions in privacy. They didn't even emerge to take Communion but received it through a small door in the pew. According to legend, St Dyfrig, the man who some say crowned King Arthur, was born at Madley.

MOCCAS
10 miles W of Hereford off the B4352

🏛 Moccas Court

Moccas Court, designed by Robert Adam and built by local architect Anthony Keck, stands in seven acres of Capability Brown parkland on the south bank of the Wye. In the grounds stands the beautiful Church of St Michael, built in Norman times using the local stone known as tufa limestone. Dominating the chancel is the impressive effigy of a 14th century knight with a dog lying at his feet – contemporaries would understand this signified that the knight had not died on the battlefield but in his own bed.

🏛 historic building   📷 museum   🏛 historic site   🌿 scenic attraction   🌿 flora and fauna

HAY-ON-WYE

18 miles W of Hereford on the B4348

⚑ Book Festival

And so to the border town of Hay-on-Wye, where bookworms will wriggle with delight as they browse through its dozens of secondhand bookshops. Richard Booth, known as the King of Wye, opened the first bookshop here 40 years ago, and is a leading player in the annual **Hay Book Festival**. The famous diarist Francis Kilvert was a local man, and his *Diary* is just one of millions of books on sale. But books are not the only attraction:

THE GRANARY

Broad Street, Hay-on-Wye, Herefordshire HR3 5DB
Tel: 01497 820790 e-mail: info@granaryhay.co.uk

Opposite the Clock Tower in the border book town of Hay-on-Wye, **The Granary** has been providing wholesome home-cooked food for 26 years. Owned by sisters Jeannette Barker and Caroline Pryce Mason, this atmospheric former agricultural warehouse extends over two floors, with seating for 160 and also pavement tables. The menus offer an all day choice that runs from meat, fish and game main courses, to usually three different soups which are self serve with locally baked granary bread and unusual salads. Home-baked apple strudel, meringues, pies and cheesecake and local fruit summer puddings are also available. There's always a good and imaginative choice of vegetarian and vegan food. The Granary is open seven days a week from 10am to 5.30pm, also in the evening during the Easter Holidays, Hay Festival of Literature and the summer holidays.

F W GOLESWORTHY & SONS

17 Broad Street, Hay-on-Wye,
Powys HR3 5DB
Tel: 01497 820491
website: www.golesworthys.com

F W Golesworthy & Sons is a venerable business established in 1877, making it one of the oldest menswear shop in Britain still run by the founding family.

Robert Golesworthy has been at the helm for 35 years, carrying on the family tradition as a complete men's outfitter (with also a smaller range for women).

Behind the handsome Victorian shopfront, 2,500 square feet of display space provides top-quality country and outdoor wear – everything that the well-dressed male could need: clothes from Barbour and Joules, Bladen sports jackets, Brasher traditional footwear for comfort and performance, Viyella shirts and Stetson and Tilley hats.

Maps, tools, knives and other accessories complete the list of must-haves for the serious, well-dressed outdoor man.

📽 stories and anecdotes 🐦 famous people ✍ art and craft 🎭 entertainment and sport 🚶 walks

Hay also has a large number of antiques, crafts and clothes shops, and is home to a major conkers championship. The River Wye is never far away, with its shifting moods and ever-changing scenery. Just north of Hay stand the ruins of Clifford Castle, where in 1140 Jane Clifford, 'Fair Rosamund', mistress of King Henry II, was born.

North of Hereford

MORDIFORD
4 miles E of Hereford on the B4224

🖼 Mordiford Dragon   🌲 Haugh Wood

Mordiford was once a centre of the mining industry and now free from the baleful man-eating **Mordiford Dragon**. The story goes that the dragon was found by a local girl while it was still small. She nurtured it lovingly, and although it was at first content to feed on milk, and later chickens and the odd duck, it eventually developed a taste for cows and finally people. The beast terrorised the locals, and indeed one of the paths leading from the woods is still known as Serpents Lane. It was here that he would slink along the river to drink, and it is said that no grass ever grows there. No one was brave enough to face the beast until a man called Garson, who happened to be awaiting execution, decided that he had nothing to lose. He hid in a barrel by the river, and when the creature appeared he shot it through the heart. That was the end of the dragon, and also of poor Garson, who was killed in the fiery breath of the dragon's death throes. Mordiford stands on the River Lugg, just above the point where it joins the Wye, and the River Frome joins the Lugg a little way above the village. Mordiford Bridge, with its elegant span of nine arches, was once the source of regular revenue for the kings of

this land: apparently every time the king crossed the bridge the local lords had to provide him with a pair of silver spurs as a levy on the manor.

The Forestry Commission's **Haugh Wood** is best approached from Mordiford.

SUTTON ST NICHOLAS
4 miles NE of Hereford off the A465

🏛 Wergin Stone   🏛 Sutton Walls

Just outside the village is a group of stones known collectively as the **Wergin Stone**. In the hollow base of one of the stones, rents or tithes were laid, to be collected later by the local squire. There is a story that in 1652 the Devil picked up the stone and removed it to a spot a little distance away. It took a team of nine oxen to return the stone to its original place, though why the villagers bothered is not related. South of the village is the Iron Age hill fort of **Sutton Walls**, where King Offa once had a palace. One day in 794, Offa, the King of Mercia, promised the hand of his daughter Alfreda to Ethelbert, King of East Anglia. Ethelbert journeyed to Sutton Walls, but the trip was full of bad omens: the earth shook, there was an eclipse of the sun, and he had a vision that his mother was weeping bloody tears. In spite of all this he pressed on, but after he had reached the palace, and before the wedding ceremony, Offa had him beheaded. There is little now to see at the camp, as a lot of the land has been worked on. Many skeletons have been unearthed, some showing signs of very violent ends.

Just outside Sutton, Overcourt Garden Nursery is situated in the grounds of a Grade II listed 16th century house with connections to the Crusader Knights of St John. A wide range of unusual plants is for sale. Private visits are welcome.

BROMYARD

13 miles NE of Hereford on the A44

🏠 Teddy Bear Museum   🏠 Heritage centre

🍃 Great Hereford Show   🍃 Folk Festival

Bromyard is an attractive market town on the River Frome with hills and good walking all around. In the town itself the **Teddy Bear Museum** (see panel below), housed in a former bakery, is a magical little world of bears, dolls and Disney-related toys. It also has a bear hospital.

Bromyard Heritage Centre tells the stories of the local hop-growing industry, the

Teddy Bears of Bromyard Museum

*The Old Bakery, 12 The Square, Bromyard,
Herefordshire HR7 4BP
Tel: 01885 488329*

A visit to Teddy Bears of Bromyard really is a trip down memory lane, an experience to treasure for ever. The museum is one of the most informative you will visit, with hundreds of rare and exciting exhibits – all well displayed behind glass. You will see antique bears, dolls, Disney toys, prams, pedal cars, a huge steiff bear and the smallest golly.

Opening Times Museum and Shop: 10.30am to 4.30pm Tues – Sat
April 1st to October 31st

LITTLEBRIDGE HOUSE B&B

*Tedstone Wafer, Bromyard, Herefordshire HR7 4PN
Tel: 01885 482471
e-mail: littlebridge-1@tiscali.co.uk
website: www.littlebridgehouse.com*

Littlebridge House has been the family home of Gill Williams for 50 years, and since 1989 she has been offering good-value Bed & Breakfast accommodation in a lovely rural setting on the B4203 north of Bromyard.

The early-Victorian house has three comfortable guest bedrooms with en suite shower room, co-ordinated fabrics, TV, radio-alarm, shaver point, hairdryer and hospitality tray. Cots are available on request, and babysitting can be arranged.

The house has a lounge with a woodburning stove and a sunny dining room where a full English breakfast and an optional evening meal are served, both making excellent use of local or home-grown produce.

Three acres of gardens are perfect for a leisurely stroll, and well-known nearby walks offer stunning views over National Trust land to the Black Mountains and Malvern Hills.

🎬 stories and anecdotes   🐦 famous people   ✏️ art and craft   🎭 entertainment and sport   🚶 walks

LEGGES OF BROMYARD

Tenbury Road, Bromyard, Herefordshire HR7 4LW
Tel: 01885 482417 Fax: 01885 485968

Owner Anthony Legge opened a butchers shop in
Bromyard in 1999 and in November 2006 moved 300
yards to these premises on the site of the old livestock
market. He takes great pride in the traditional quality that
is evident in everything on display.

The beef sold at **Legges of Bromyard** comes from the
family farm and is hung for four weeks to produce outstanding
flavour, and the other meat comes from more than 40 of the very
best local suppliers.

Seasonal game includes venison, partridge, pheasant and mallard,
and fresh fish is delivered daily. Legges makes its own excellent
sausages, burgers and pies, and the shop also sells homemade
pickles and preserves, bread and cakes, organic fruit, vegetables,
dairy products and ice cream, local beer, cider and wine and fresh
flowers cut each day. The family also owns Shortwood Family Farm
at nearby Pencombe, a working organic dairy farm where children can
help with feeding the animals.

railway age and life in Bromyard through the
centuries. Well worth a look is the 12th
century St Peter's Church with its historic
Walker organ. Late June and early July see
Bromyard's **Great Hereford Show and
Steam Rally**, an event which has built up to
major proportions over the years. Later on, in
early September, Bromyard's **Folk Festival**
brings in the crowds.

EDVIN LOACH

3 miles N of Bromyard off the B4203

Here are the remains of one of Britain's rare
Saxon churches. The church at nearby Edwyn
Ralph is noted for its unusual monument and
medieval effigies under the tower.

LOWER BROCKHAMPTON

2 miles E of Bromyard off the A44

🏛 Lower Brockhampton Estate

The 1,900 acres of wood and farmland that
comprise **Lower Brockhampton Estate**

(National Trust) are the essence of
Herefordshire. Springtime sees the park at its
best when daffodils provide a mass of colour
but there are delightful woodland and
lakeside nature walks to be enjoyed
throughout the year. Within the grounds
stands a late-14th century half-timbered
moated manor house with a very unusual
detached gatehouse and the ruins of a 12th
century chapel.

STANFORD BISHOP

3 miles SE of Bromyard off the B4220

The Church at Stanford Bishop once
possessed an old oak chair in which it is
believed St Augustine sat when he presided
over a synod of bishops here in 603. The
chair was retrieved by an antiquarian visiting
the church during a 19th century restoration,
minutes before workmen were about to chop
it up for firewood. The chair is now in
Canterbury Cathedral.

🏛 historic building   🏛 museum   🏛 historic site   🞀 scenic attraction   🌱 flora and fauna

BISHOP'S FROME
3 miles S of Bromyard on the B4214

🏛 Church   ✿ Hop Pocket Craft Centre

St Mary's Church is notable for its massive font more than 700 years old. Entry to the church is by way of a handsome lychgate, a 19th century porch and a beautiful Norman doorway. Inside, a battered figure of a knight in armour lies sword in hand and with a lion at his feet. Lying close to the Worcestershire border, in hop country, is the **Hop Pocket Craft Centre**, which has working kilns and machinery, a craft shop and a restaurant. It lies just off the A4103 Hereford-Worcester road.

HOPE UNDER DINMORE
8 miles N of Hereford on the A49

🌳 Queen's Wood Country Park   🌱 Hampton Court

To the south of the village, at Dinmore Hill, stretch the green spaces of **Queenswood Country Park**, a popular place for walking and enjoying the panoramic views. The Park includes 67 acres of arboretum with 500+ rare and exotic trees from all over the world and 103 acres of SSSI-designated woodland rich in wildlife. It offers waymarked trails, panoramic views, picnic areas, barbecue facilities, a children's adventure play area and a Tourist Information Centre. Open all year

GREEN ACRES ORGANIC FARM SHOP

Dinmore, Herefordshire HR4 8ED
Tel: 01568 797045
website: www.greenacresorganics.co.uk

Green Acres Organic Farm Shop stands on prime farming land at Dinmore, off the A49 halfway between Leominster and Hereford. Sheila and David Jenkins started selling their produce from a roadside wheelbarrow, and when they opened their shop in 1982 it was the first organic farm shop in the county. It won the Soil Association seal of approval in that year and has retained it every year since. The list of produce on sale in the shop is long and impressive: free-range pork and beef; organically reared lamb, chickens and Christmas turkeys; home-grown and local vegetables and salads; French, runner and broad beans; 15 varieties of squash and four of pumpkins; cabbage, potatoes, leeks and kale; soups, jams, chutneys, tea, coffee, dairy, chocolate; and local crafts including handmade jewellery.

The 17 acres on the south side of Dinmore Hill are fed by a natural spring, and the riverbank is a designated Site of Special Scientific Interest. An apple and pear orchard produces crops for their own and local ciders and perrys, and also supplies major firms like Westons and Dunkertons.

The Farm Shop is open from 9 to 5.30 Tuesday to Saturday.

🎞 stories and anecdotes   🐦 famous people   ✿ art and craft   🖌 entertainment and sport   🐾 walks

THE LION GALLERY

15b Broad Street, Leominster, Herefordshire HR6 8DT
Tel: 01568 611898
e-mail: info@liongallery.com
website: www.liongallery.com

Leominster is an attractive town with many unusual independent businesses in handsome period buildings. One of the most interesting is **The Lion Gallery** in the historic Lion House in front of the splendid restored 19th century ballroom.

Owner Andrea Jackson established her gallery in 2005 to show high-quality contemporary British art and craft, reflecting a wide range of talented artists and makers in the area. The well laid-out exhibits include original paintings in watercolours, oils and acrylic, limited edition prints, screenprints and etchings, sculpture, ceramics, jewellery, textiles, glass and woodwork.

Fresh work is regularly introduced, featured artists change monthly, and commissions can be arranged. Regular exhibitors include ceramicists Jon & Julie Harbottle, Bridget Drakeford and Jennifer Hall; sculpture by Rachel Ricketts; jewellery by Blake & Janette Mackinnon, Helen Brice, Georgina Franklin and Lynn Antley; glass by Stuart Ackroyd; glass engraving by Julia Linstead; prints by Christopher Noble and textiles by Poppy Treffry and Sarah Roberts.

The Gallery is open Monday to Saturday from 10am to 5pm.

DRAPERS LANE BUTCHERS

16 Drapers lane, Leominster, Herefordshire HR6 8ND
Tel: 01568 613981

Stuart Fletcher has been in the business for 20 years and took over **Drapers Lane Butchers** in 2002. Behind a traditional shopfront the interior has a cosy, old-world look, and everything on display is of the highest quality.

Welsh Black beef is hug for 21 days, and all the meat is traceable to the farms of origin, all local and therefore keeping the 'food miles' to a minimum. The shop is licensed to deal in game, and pheasant, partridge, wild duck, snipe, woodcock, pigeon, hare, rabbit and venison all make their seasonal appearances as available. Customers come for miles around for the meat, the pork pies, the dry-cured bacon and particularly for the award-winning sausages, which come in many tempting varieties, including pork with apple & cider, with spring onions & ginger, and with leeks & chilli (Welsh Dragon); beef with Guinness; smoked bacon with tomato and lamb with lemon & honey.

Hampton Court Estate

the title. In the 7th century, Merewald, King of Mercia, was renowned for his bravery and ferocity and earned the nickname of 'the Lion'. He is said to have had a dream concerning a message from a Christian missionary, while at the same time a religious hermit had a vision of a lion coming to him and eating from his hand. They later met up at what was to be Leominster almost by accident, and when the King heard of the hermit's strangely coincidental dream, he was persuaded to convert to Christianity. Later, the King requested that a convent and church be built in the town; a stone lintel on the west door of the church depicts the chance meeting of King and hermit. Other, more likely explanations of the name revolve around Welsh and medieval Latin words for 'stream' and 'marsh'.

dawn to dusk; free entry.

A more recent addition to the county's notable gardens is **Hampton Court**, magnificent organic gardens in historic castle grounds. Within the 1,000-acre estate surrounding a fortified medieval manor house are walled vegetable and flower gardens, canals, island pavilions, a maze with a secret tunnel and a waterfall in a sunken garden. There are river and woodland walks, a restaurant and shop. Tel 01568 797777

The magnificent ruins of the **Priory Church of St Peter and St Paul**, originally King Merewald's convent, was founded in

Leominster

🏛 Priory Church 🏛 Grange Court 🏛 Museum

The hub of the farming community and the largest town in this part of the county, Leominster was made wealthy in the Middle Ages through the wool trade of its local Ryeland sheep; the fleeces came to be known as 'Leminster Ore' meaning Leominster Gold. The town still prospers today and is well known as one of the most important antiques centres in the region. Some have linked the unusual name with Richard the Lionheart, but there was in fact an earlier king who earned

Priory Church, Leominster

DOCKLOW MANOR

Docklow, nr Leominster,
Herefordshire HR6 0RX
Tel: 01568 760668
e-mail: enquiries@docklow-manor.co.uk
website: www.docklow-manor.co.uk

At the end of a long private drive two miles east of Leominster, **Docklow Manor** is a wonderful secluded spot for a break or a holiday. Set in a rambling Victorian garden and five acres of grounds, two superb properties provide self-catering accommodation of a very high standard. Manor Cottage is a romantic hideaway sleeping two or three; the ground floor, originally the kitchen for the manor, is now an open-plan kitchen/sitting room, with French windows opening on to a courtyard with a splendid old stone cider mill.

The upstairs bedroom has a magnificent four-poster bed, with an extra bed, suitable for a child, tucked away under the stairs. Yew Tree Cottage, with two bedrooms and a combined sitting room and kitchen, has its own secluded garden leading to a shady orchard. Both are provided with TV and video, books and games. Amenities include croquet, table tennis and table football, and the grounds of the manor are home to an abundance of trees and wildlife. A welcome hamper filled with local produce greets guests on arrival, and the owners offer the option of an evening meal – an option well worth taking up, as the Manor has won Flavours of Hereford awards for the quality of its food.

GROVE FARM SHOP WITH TEA ROOM AND B&B

Kimbolton, Nr Leominster, Herefordshire HR6 0HE
e-mail: Bookings@Grovefarmdirect.f9.co.uk
website: www.grovefarmdirect.co.uk

Small family-run livestock and fruit farm on the outskirts of Kimbolton Village is where Tim and Fiona Bunting have converted the Cider Mill Barn and Grain Loft into a beautiful annexe housing two en-suite double bedrooms upstairs (for B&B) together with farm shop and tea room downstairs. The old Cider mill is now situated in the Tea Garden. The shop sells the farm's own Aberdeen Angus beef, Suffolk lamb, free range eggs, garden fruit and vegetables. Also for sale is a wide range of delicious breads, cakes, and preserves together with homemade ready meals cooked in the Aga. Also stocked is a variety of local organic dairy products and Fair Trade produce. Bacon, pork and chicken are bought in off other local producers.

The Tea Room prides itself on its homemade farmhouse dishes which can be enjoyed sitting in front of the fire throughout the winter or in the Tea Garden on a warm summer's day. Beautiful views to be had in every direction of farming and rural life in general. Great walking and cycling country. Children, dogs and horse/ponies are all very welcome! For those staying overnight there is an excellent pub within walking distance and a host of other local attractions.

Opening Hours: 10am til late Monday-Saturday, 11.30am – 5pm Sunday

🏛 historic building   🏛 museum   🏛 historic site   ✇ scenic attraction   ❦ flora and fauna

1123, and the three naves, built in the 12th, 13th and 14th centuries, attest to its importance. A curio here, standing in the north aisle, is the last ducking stool to be used in England. It's recorded that the miscreant was one Jennie Pipes, the year was 1809, but it's not known which of the two crimes that were punished in this way she had committed – being a 'scold' or selling adulterated goods.

A short walk away, in Priory Park, is **Grange Court**, a fine timbered building which for many years stood in the market place. Built in 1633, it is the work of the royal carpenter John Abel, and shows typical Abel flamboyance in its elaborate carvings.

Other buildings to be visited in Leominster are the Leominster **Folk Museum**, the Lion Gallery, featuring the best of local arts and crafts, and The Forbury, a 13th century chapel dedicated to Thomas à Becket.

Around Leominster

KIMBOLTON
3 miles NE of Leominster off the A49

There are two delightful gardens to visit near Kimbolton. At Stockton Bury (turn right off the A49 on to the A4112) the sheltered four-acre garden has an extensive variety of plants set among medieval buildings, a kitchen garden, pigeon house, tithe barn, cider press and ruined chapel.

ASHTON
4 miles N of Leominster on the A49

🏛 Berrington Hall

Four miles north of Leominster on the road to Ludlow stands the National Trust's **Berrington Hall**, an elegant late-18th century mansion designed by Henry Holland (later architect to the Prince Regent) in parkland laid out by his father-in-law Capability Brown. Features of the interior include a spectacular staircase hall, gilt tracery, fine furniture and paintings, a nursery, Victorian laundry and tiled Georgian dairy. Most notable of all are perhaps the beautifully decorated ceilings: in the drawing room, the central medallion of Jupiter, Cupid and Venus is a composite scene taken from The Council and The Banquet of the Gods by Penni and del Colle in the Villa Farnesina in Rome. In the grounds are a walled garden with a collection of pre-1900 local apple trees, a woodland walk and a living willow tunnel in the children's play area.

YARPOLE
4 miles N of Leominster off the B4361

🏛 Churches   🏛 Croft Castle

In this delightful village with its jumble of cottages and their colourful gardens stands the **Church of St Leonard**, which has a detached bell tower, a wooden structure with a stone outer wall. At neighbouring **Eye** are Eye Manor and the **Church of St Peter and St Paul**, where Thomas Harley, a Lord Mayor of London, is buried. An unusual feature of this church is the pulpit with carvings of Native Americans.

Near Yarpole, reached from the B4362 between Bircher and Mortimer's Cross, stands **Croft Castle**, an atmospheric property in the care of the National Trust. Behind a defensive exterior that tells of the troubled times of Marcher territory, the state rooms are elegant and comfortable, with rare furniture, fine plasterwork and portraits of the Croft family, who have been associated with the house since 1086. In the park are ancient oaks and an avenue of 350-year-old Spanish chestnut trees. Also looked after by the National Trust, and just a short walk away, is Croft Ambrey, an Iron Age fort which affords stunning views.

ORLETON
6 miles N of Leominster off the B4361

🏛 Richard's Castle

The churchyard at Orleton is thought by some to be the likely setting for the Resurrection at the Day of Judgment, and for that reason people from all over the country used to ask to be buried here in the hope that they would be among the first in the queue when life began again. The road north from Orleton leads to **Richard's Castle** on the Shropshire border. This Norman castle, which lies in ruins on the hillside above the church, was, like so many others, built as a defence against the marauding Welsh. The church played a similar role, and in the 14th century it was refurbished for use as a chapel by the Knights Hospitallers.

MORTIMER'S CROSS
7 miles NW of Leominster on the A4110/B4362

🏛 Battle Site

The site of one of England's greatest and bloodiest battles. Here, on the 3rd February 1461, was enacted a decisive episode in the War of the Roses, with the Yorkists defeating the Lancastrians. Hundreds died that day, but 19-year-old Edward Mortimer, the Duke of York's eldest son, survived and was crowned King Edward IV in the following month. Visit the **Battle Centre** at Watermill.

WIGMORE
11 miles NW of Leominster on the A4110

🏛 Castle and Abbey

A few miles on from Mortimer's Cross, Wigmore is noted for its ruined **Castle and Abbey**. With its impressive vantage point, the

---

LOWER HOUSE COUNTRY GUEST HOUSE

Adforton, nr Leintwardine, Shropshire SY7 0NF
Tel: 01568 770223
e-mail: reservations@sy7.com   website: www.sy7.com

Lower House is a family-run guest house in a quiet lane amongst the Welsh Border hills. Resident owners Anne and Bill Brandrick offer a choice of accommodation in these very pleasant surroundings. In the main house, a farmhouse dating in part from the early-17th century, are four rooms, three with en suite facilities, the other with its own private bathroom, all with television, radio and tea/coffee tray. Rooms can be booked individually, and the house is also an ideal choice for family get-togethers, reunions or parties. A few steps away from the main house, Stable Cottage has two twin-bedded rooms; the room on the ground floor is suitable for less mobile guests and is wheelchair-accessible. The Cottage is a good choice for a family

of four or two couples. Anne is an excellent cook, and her Aga-cooked breakfasts are definitely not to be missed. A three-course evening meal is available by prior arrangement, served at 7 o'clock in the oak-beamed dining room (the house is not licensed, but guests can bring their own wine). The guest lounge, with an open log fire, is an ideal spot for planning the day's activities, and guests can enjoy a stroll in the beautiful gardens. Lower House is a perfect base for relaxing, for walking (the Mortimer Trail and Offa's Dyke are nearby) and for discovering the numerous scenic and historic delights of the region.

🏛 historic building   🏛 museum   🏛 historic site   🍂 scenic attraction   �０ flora and fauna hillside at Wigmore was a natural site for building a castle, which is what William FitzOsbern did in the 11th century. This was one of a chain of fortifications built along the Welsh border. By the time of his death in 1071, FitzOsbern had also built Chepstow, Berkeley, Monmouth, Guenta (perhaps Winchester?) and Clifford, and had rebuilt Ewyas Harold. Wigmore passed into the hands of the Clifford family, then the ambitious Mortimers, and it was no doubt here that the future Edward IV prepared himself for the battle at Mortimer's Cross. Enough of the ruins remain to show that Wigmore was once a very serious castle, and one which protected the village and its environs for many centuries until the Civil War.

BRAMPTON BRYAN
16 miles NW of Leominster on the A4113

Many of the thatched cottages in the village as well as its castle, had to be rebuilt after a siege during the Civil War in 1643. The chief relic of the castle is the gatehouse, which now stands in the gardens of a charming 18th century house near the Church of St Barnabus. Sir Robert Harley, a relation of Thomas Harley of Berrington Hall, owned the castle and it was due to his allegiance to Cromwell that it was besieged not once but twice by the Royalist army. Following the eventual destruction of the castle by the Royalists, Harley fell out with Cromwell. They remained at loggerheads until the day that Cromwell died, and on that day in September 1658 it is said that a violent storm swept through Brampton Bryan Park, destroying a great number of trees. Harley was

convinced that the storm was caused by the Devil dragging Cromwell down to Hell.

SHOBDON
8 miles W of Leominster on the B4362

🏛 Church 🏛 Shobdon Arches 🌿 Lingen Nursery
🌿 Bryan's Ground

The **Church of St John the Evangelist**, which stands on the site of a 12th century priory, is the most amazing in the county. In the 1750s, Lord Bateman demolished the medieval priory (relocating selected fragments as a hilltop folly a quarter of a mile away), and built a new church which has been described as "a pastiche of the Countess' boudoir in Mozart's opera *The Marriage of Figaro*". The overall effect is of being inside a giant wedding cake, with white and pale blue icing everywhere, and lovely stained glass adding to the dazzling scene. Such is its flamboyance, the *Shell Guide* declared that this church was "an inconceivable place to hold a funeral". It has to be seen to be believed.

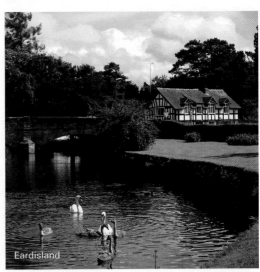
Eardisland

Just north of the village are the '**Shobdon Arches**', a collection of Norman sculptures which have sadly been greatly damaged by centuries of exposure to the elements, but which still demonstrate the high skills of the sculptors of the 12th century.

Country roads signposted from the B4362 lead west from Shobdon to Lingen, where the **Nursery and Garden** are a horticultural haven for visitors to this remote area of the Marches. The gardens are home to National Collections of Iris Sibirica and Herbaceous Campanula.

Even nearer the Welsh border, between Kinsham and Stapleton (signs from the B4362 at Combe) is **Bryan's Ground**, a three-acre Edwardian garden with towers and topiary, follies and fragrant flowers, a specialist collection of old roses, formal pools and potager, and paths to a five-acre arboretum beside the river.

EARDISLAND
8 miles W of Leominster on the B4529

🏛 Church   🏛 Dovecote   🏛 Burton Court

"An uncommonly pretty village", said Pevsner of this renowned spot on the banks of the River Arrow. Certainly glorious, Eardisland is one of the most beautiful villages in the county (and the competition is very strong), and with its inns, bowling green, river and charming buildings spanning the centuries, this is essential England. Dominating the scene is the 12th century **Church of St Mary the Virgin** where, each year, from Easter until late autumn, an exhibition of village and parish life is staged. At Holmlea stands the **Eardisland Dovecote**, a unique Georgian dovecote in a beautiful riverside setting in the centre of a conservation village. A mile outside Eardisland is **Burton Court**, whose

centrepiece is the sumptuous 14th century Great Hall. Many additions have been made to the building down the years, and the present entrance, dating from 1912, is the work of Sir Clough Williams-Ellis of Portmeirion fame. Highlight of the various attractions is a collection of European and Oriental costumes, but of interest, too, are a model ship collection, a wide range of natural history specimens and a working model fairground. The Court is open only for pre-arranged group visits.

PEMBRIDGE
10 miles W of Leominster on the A44

🏛 Church and Belfry   🎨 Old Chapel Gallery

The influential Mortimer family were responsible for the medieval prosperity of historic Pembridge, and many handsome buildings bear witness to their patronage and its legacy. The most famous building is the 14th century **Church**, a three-storey structure in stone and timber with a marvellous timber **Belfry**. The bell and the clock mechanism can be viewed from inside the church. Two other buildings which the visitor should not miss are the delightful 16th century Market Hall standing on its eight oak pillars and the **Old Chapel Gallery** in a converted Victorian chapel. This gallery contains an exciting range of contemporary arts and crafts and hosts regular exhibitions. A little way south of Pembridge is Dunkerton's Cider Mill, where cider and perry are produced from organically grown local fruit. Open Monday to Saturday.

LYONSHALL
14 miles W of Leominster on the A480

🏛 Church and Castle

The remains of the **Church and Castle** are at some distance from the main body of the village, a fact which is often attributed to the plague causing older settlements to be abandoned. The Church of St Michael and All Angels dates mainly from the 13th century and was restored in 1870 when close to collapse. The ruins of the castle include some walls and part of the moat, making this the most 'complete' of all the castle ruins in the area. Among the fine old buildings in the village itself are the Royal George Inn, Ivy House, The Wharf and The Woodlands. There are two 12th century water corn mills in the parish, one of them, Bullock's Mill, being documented continuously from 1580 to 1928.

KINGTON

15 miles W of Leominster on the A44

🏛 Cwmmau Farmhouse   🏛 Museum

🏛 Wapley Hill   🏛 Offa's Dyke

🌿 Farm Park Small Breeds & Owl Centre

🌿 Hergest Croft Gardens   🏛 Hergest Court

The road up to Kington passes many places of interest, and for two in particular a short pause will be well worth while. The National Trust's **Cwmmau Farmhouse**, which lies four miles south of Kington between the A4111 and A438 at Brilley, is an imposing

timber-framed and stone-tiled farmhouse dating from the early-17th century. Viewing is by guided tour only. Call 01497 831251. **Kington Museum** tells the story of Kington from Roman times to the present day.

A splendid place for a family visit is the **Small Breeds Farm Park and Owl Centre**. The Owl Centre houses one of the finest displays of owls in the UK, and in the Per Animal House can be seen guinea pigs, mice, chinchillas, rabbits and chipmunks. Other creatures on the site include ducks, geese and swans in the landscaped waterfowl enclosure, colourful pheasants, doves, bantams and red squirrels. Tel 01544 231109

Half a mile off the A44 on the Welsh side of Kington are **Hergest Croft Gardens** (see panel below), four distinct gardens for all seasons from spring bulbs to autumn colour that include a valley of giant rhododendrons, spectacular azaleas, an old-fashioned kitchen garden and a marvellous collection of trees and shrubs. Hergest holds National Collections of maples, birches and zelkovas.

Nearby is the impressive Hergest Ridge, rising to around 1,400 feet, and, on its southern edge, **Hergest Court**, once owned by the Vaughan family. Two members of the

Hergest Croft Gardens

Kington, Herefordshire HR5 3EG
Tel: 01544 230160
Fax: 01544 232031
e-mail: gardens@hergest.co.uk
website: www.hergest.co.uk

Four gardens for all seasons from spring bulbs to autumn colour include an old-fashioned kitchen garden growing unusual vegetables, with spring and summer borders and roses. Brilliantly coloured rhododendrons and azaleas up to 30ft grow in Park Wood with over 60 champion trees in one of the finest collections in the British Isles.

🎬 stories and anecdotes   🐦 famous people   🎨 art and craft   🎭 entertainment and sport   🚶 walks family who gained particular notoriety were Thomas 'Black' Vaughan and his wife, who was known as Gethen the Terrible. She is said to have taken revenge on a man who killed her brother by taking part in an archery competition disguised as a man. When her turn came to compete, she shot him dead at point blank range and escaped in the ensuing melee. Thomas died at the Battle of Banbury in 1469, but, being a true Vaughan, that was not the last of him. He is said to have haunted the church in the guise of a bull, and even managed to turn himself into a horsefly to annoy the local horses. He was back in taurine form when he was finally overcome by a band of clerics. One of the band managed to shrink him and cram him into a snuff box, which was quickly consigned to the waters of Hergest Pool. Later owners of the estate found and unwittingly opened the box, letting Black Vaughan loose once more. The next band of intrepid clerics confined the spirit under an oak tree, but he is currently at large again - though not sighted for many years. These feisty Vaughans are buried in the Vaughan Chapel in Kington parish church.

Kington itself lies on the England/Wales border and, like other towns in the area known as the Marches, had for many years to

look closely to the west, whence the wild Welsh would attack. Kington's castle was destroyed many centuries ago, but outside the town, on **Wapley Hill**, are earthworks of an ancient hill fort which could be the site of King Caractacus' last stand.

Most notable by far of all the defences in the region is **Offa's Dyke**, the imposing ditch that extends for almost 180 miles along the border, from the Severn Estuary at Sedbury Cliffs near Chepstow, across the Black Mountain ridge, through the Wye Valley and north to Prestatyn on the North Wales coast. Offa was a Mercian king of great influence, with strong diplomatic links with the Popes and Charlemagne, who ruled the land south of the Humber from 757 to 796. Remnants of wooden stakes unearthed down the years suggest that the Dyke had a definite defensive role, rather than acting merely as a psychological barrier. It was a truly massive construction, in places almost 60 feet wide, and although nowadays it disappears in places, much of it can still be walked, particularly in the Wye Valley. A stretch north of Kington is especially well preserved and provides excellent, invigorating walking for the energetic. The walk crosses, at Bradnor Hill, the highest golf course, over 1,200 feet above sea level. Other major traces of the Dyke remain, notably between Chepstow and Monmouth and by Oswestry, and at many points Offa's Dyke Path, opened by the Countryside Commission in 1971, diverts from the actual Dyke into magnificent scenery. At Kington, Offa's Dyke links to the Mortimer Trail, a 30-mile route to Ludlow, following the ridges of the hills and woods in the northwest corner of Herefordshire.

Weobley

🏢 historic building   🏛 museum   🏚 historic site   🌺 scenic attraction   🌱 flora and fauna

DILWYN

7 miles SW of Leominster on the A4112

The village lies in a hollow, so its Old English name of 'Secret Place' is an appropriate one. The main body of the parish church was built around 1200, with additions in the following century and a spire put up in the 1700s. The workmen who built the church were also associated with nearby Wormsley Priory, and one of the figures in Dilwyn's church is thought to be a member of the Talbot family, founders of the priory. The church registers go back over 400 years, providing a valuable trail of local history.

WEOBLEY

9 miles SW of Leominster on the B4230

🏛 Museum

The steeple of the parish church of St Peter and St Paul is the second highest in the county, a reminder that this prettiest of places (pronounced Webbly) was once a thriving market town. One of its more unusual sources of wealth was a successful glove-making industry which flourished in the early-19th century when the Napoleonic Wars cut off the traditional French source of gloves. At certain times in its history Weobley returned two Members of Parliament, but there have been none since 1832. One of the effigies in the church is of Colonel John Birch, who was rewarded for his successes with Cromwell's army with the Governorship of Hereford and who later became a keen Royalist and Weobley's MP. Little but the earthworks remain of Weobley Castle, which was built before the Norman Conquest and was captured by King Stephen in 1138. One of Weobley's many interesting buildings is called The Throne, but it was called The Unicorn

when King Charles I took refuge after the Battle of Naseby in 1645. One of the most interesting exhibitions in **Weobley Museum** focuses on the history of timber-framed buildings, with interactives showing how various types of timber joints are put together.

KINNERSLEY

5 miles SW of Weobley on the A4112

🏰 Castle

On the main road lie the village and **Kinnersley Castle**, which has the look of a fortified manor house. Famous occupants down the years include the Morgans (the 17th century buccaneer Sir Henry Morgan was one of them) and the Vaughans. Black Vaughan's huge dog is believed to have been the inspiration for Conan Doyle's Hound of the Baskervilles.

EARDISLEY

8 miles W of Weobley on the A4111

🏰 Church   🌳 Great Oak

The greatest treasure of Eardisley's **Church of St Mary Magdalene** is its font, dating from the early-12th century. The figures depicted round the font represent not only familiar religious themes but also two men in armed struggle. It is thought that these are a 12th century lord of the manor, Ralph de Baskerville, and his father-in-law, Lord Drogo, whom he killed in a dispute over land. As a penance, Ralph was ordered by the church authorities to commission this extraordinary font.

Outside this pretty village, the most notable feature, standing majestically by an old chapel, is the **Great Oak**, which is believed to be some 800 years old.

🎭 stories and anecdotes   🦜 famous people   🎨 art and craft   ✏ entertainment and sport   🚶 walks

LOCATOR MAP

ADVERTISERS AND PLACES OF INTEREST

🏢 historic building   🏛 museum   🏛 historic site   🍃 scenic attraction   🌱 flora and fauna

2 | Worcestershire

In the southern part of the county lies the spectacular ridge of the Malvern Hills, with marvellous walking and breathtaking views. Moving eastwards we reach the towns of Upton-upon-Severn, Pershore and Evesham, along with many charming villages and ancient sites. The Vale of Evesham is one of the country's most important and prolific horticultural regions, and in springtime the Vale is alive with colour from the blossom of the fruit trees. High-quality fruit and vegetables are distributed from here throughout the land, and motorists will come across numerous roadside stalls selling a wonderful array of produce. At the eastern edge of this part of the county lies Broadway, a quintessential Cotswold village of outstanding beauty, beloved of tourists and not to be missed on any visit to this most delightful county.

Set on either side of the curving River Severn, Worcester is a bustling county capital and cathedral city. Its architecture spans many centuries and there are some marvellous examples from all of them. In the heart of England, this is an area characterised by red earth, apple orchards, hop yards, quiet inns, stone farmhouses and black-and-white timbered dwellings. As a visible legacy of the ancient forest that once surrounded Worcester, the half-timbered buildings lend colour and variety to the villages around this historic city.

Most of Worcestershire's industry was centred in the northern part of the county, and there are numerous examples of industrial archaeology to interest the historian. Salt and scythes, carpets, porcelain and needles all contributed to the local economy, along with ironworks and corn mills, and many fine old buildings survive as monuments to industries which have dwindled or disappeared.

Canals here were once as important as roads, and in this part of the county the Worcester & Birmingham Canal, the Staffordshire & Worcester Canal and the Droitwich Canal were a quicker means of transport than the Severn and more reliable than the roads. They lost a good deal of their practical advantages when the railways arrived. The railway network has shrunk considerably over the last 40 years, so it's back to the roads for most local communications. The Severn Valley Railway, from Kidderminster to Bridgnorth, has survived and flourished, and today people come from far and wide for the chance to ride behind a steam engine through some incredibly beautiful scenery. Enthusiasts have also ensured that much of the canal system has survived, finding a new role as a major leisure and tourist attraction.

The route north from Droitwich towards Bromsgrove takes in much that is of interest to the industrial historian, including the Worcester & Birmingham Canal. Opened in 1815 and 30 miles in length, the canal passes Stoke Works and Stoke Prior, where John Corbett set up his salt works after leaving Droitwich.

Great Malvern

🏛 Church of St Mary & St Michael   🏛 Museum

🏛 St Anne's Well   🌿 Theatres   🌲 Malvern Hills

🌲 The Worcestershire Way

Beneath the northeastern slopes of the **Malvern Hills**, Great Malvern is known for its porcelain, its annual music and drama festivals, Malvern water and Morgan cars. Though invaded by tourists for much of the year, Great Malvern has retained its dignity and elegance, with open spaces, leafy avenues and handsome houses. Close to the start of the Malvern walking trail, on a path leading up from the town, is a Regency cottage housing one source of the water – **St Anne's Well** – where one can sample the water and drink in the views. Great Malvern was for many centuries a quiet, little-known place with a priory at its heart, and even when the curative properties of its spring waters were discovered, it took a long time for it to become a fashionable spa resort. Hotels, baths and a pump room were built in the early-19th century, and the arrival of the railway provided easy access from the middle of the century. The station is one of many charming Victorian buildings, and with its cast-iron pillars, stone ornaments and beautifully painted floral designs, is a tourist attraction in its own right.

The **Priory Church of St Mary and St Michael** is a dominant feature in the centre of the town. Its windows, the west a gift from

---

GREENLINK ORGANIC FOODS

11 Graham Road, Great Malvern, Worcestershire WR14 2HR
Tel: 01684 576266
e-mail: greenlinkorganics@tiscali.co.uk
website: www.greenlinkorganics.co.uk

Just off Church Street in the centre of Great Malvern, **Greenlink Organic Foods** is stocked with an excellent selection of the very best organic produce. Hands-on owner Mike Gattis, here since 1990, keeps his many customers happy with a full range that includes seasonal fruit and vegetables, pulses and grains, nuts, seeds and cereals, dried fruits, fruit juices, oils, pasta, cakes, biscuits and vitamins. A small café, with seats inside and outside, serves Fair Trade teas and coffees, light lunches and seasonal salads.

SIDNEY HOUSE

40 Worcester Road, Great Malvern,
Worcestershire WR14 4AA
Tel: 01684 574994

Built in 1823 and now Grade II listed, **Sidney House** is a warm and welcoming Bed & Breakfast establishment run by friendly resident owners Len and Jan McLeod. All the bedrooms have alarm clock/radio, hot drinks tray, TV and hairdryer, and rooms with private facilities and family rooms are available. Sidney House, a non-smoking hotel, has a comfortable lounge, ample car parking space and a garden, and from its elevated position it commands superb views over the Severn Valley towards the Vale of Evesham and the Cotswolds. The shops, the Festival Theatre, the Winter Garden and Priory Park are within a few minutes' walk of the house.

🏛 historic building   🏛 museum   🏛 historic site   🌿 scenic attraction   🌲 flora and fauna

Richard III, the east from Henry VII, contain a wonderful collection of 15th century stained glass, and another unique feature is a collection of more than 1,200 wall tiles on the chancel screens. These also date from the 15th century. Among many interesting graves in the cemetery is that of Jenny Lind, The Swedish Nightingale, who was born in Stockholm in 1820 and died at Wynd's Point, Malvern, which she used as a summer retreat, in 1887. In the churchyard at West Malvern Peter Mark Roget (the Thesaurus man) is buried (interred, entombed, coffined, laid to rest, consigned to earth). The

St Anne's Well

14th century Abbey Gateway, whose huge wooden gateposts can be seen in the archway, houses the **Malvern Museum**. Open Easter to October, its displays include the geology of

FOLEY HOUSE ANTIQUES CENTRE

28 Worcester Road, Great Malvern,
Worcestershire WR14 4QW
Tel: 01684 575750
e-mail: foleyhouseantiquescentre@yahoo.co.uk
website: www.foleyhouseantiques.com

Sixteen dealers under one roof regale visitors to **Foley House** with a fine range of affordable quality antiques, furnishings, books and collectables. The handsome Georgian house on the A449 in the centre of Great Malvern was home in the years around the Second World War to a famous marionette company; it acquired its current role in 2003, when dealers moved mainly from the former Malvern Links Antiques Centre. In eight rooms on three floors, the stock includes 18th to 20th century furniture, decorative antiques, jewellery, silver, tea sets, clocks, mirrors, porcelain, china, books and toys.

Foley House will carry out restoration work including French polishing and upholstery work, and will deliver nationwide; it also undertakes valuations for insurance and probate. Opening hours are 10 to 5.30 Monday to Saturday, 11 to 5 Sunday. The excellent website is regularly updated with examples of the constantly changing stock.

the Malvern Hills, the history of Malvern spring water and the development of Morgan cars. In Tanhouse Lane stands the factory of Boehm of Malvern, where the remarkable American, Edward Marshall Boehm (call it 'Beam'), founded the centre which has become known worldwide for the quality of its porcelain. Great Malvern has a distinguished tradition of arts and culture, much of it the legacy of Sir Edward Elgar and George Bernard Shaw, and The **Malvern Theatres** are an exciting setting for performances of music and drama including pre-West End runs. Malvern is the home of the excellent English Symphony Orchestra, formed in 1980 by William Boughton. In addition, The Malvern Theatres host many superb performances by notable singers, actors and speakers.

Great Malvern is the largest of six settlements that make up the Malverns: to the south are Malvern Wells and Little Malvern, to the north North Malvern and to the northeast Malvern Link. The **Worcestershire Way** is a 31-mile walking trail that links Great Malvern with Bewdley, through Abberley, Knightley and Markwick and the valleys of the Teme and Severn.

Around Great Malvern

LITTLE MALVERN
4 miles S of Great Malvern on the A449

🏛 Court and Priory   🏛 St Peter's Church

🏛 British Camp

At Little Malvern stands the Church of St Wulstan, where a simple headstone marks the

---

BLUE-GINGER

Home End Farm, Stiffords Bridge, Cradley, nr Malvern, Worcestershire WR13 5NW
Tel/Fax: 01886 880240
e-mail: sue@blue-ginger.com website: www.blue-ginger.com

The motto of **Blue-Ginger** is 'arts, crafts and inspirational ideas', and a visit promises a real treat for the senses. A converted barn in the grounds of a 16th century farmhouse houses an eclectic array of the work of British and international artists, with a special emphasis on local talent.

The collections include ceramics and pottery, paintings and prints, textiles, glass, wood and jewellery. Within the gallery is a friendly, relaxed coffee shop where visitors can enjoy Fairtrade tea and coffee, homemade cakes and light savouries.

Hands-on owner Sue Lim organises an ongoing programme of craft workshops and courses. Home End Farm has two delightful B&B rooms for holiday visitors to the area, and these are also available for workshop participants. Blue-Ginger enjoys a pleasant rural setting on the A4103 at Cradley, four miles from Malvern and 10 from Worcester. Opening hours are 10am to 5.30pm Wednesday to Sunday (late night opening Friday to 8pm). Close Jan and Feb.

🏛 historic building   🏛 museum   🏛 historic site   🐾 scenic attraction   🌿 flora and fauna grave of Sir Edward Elgar and his wife Caroline. Their daughter is buried next to them.

Little Malvern Court, off the A4104, enjoys a glorious setting on the lower slopes of the Malvern Hills. It stands next to Little Malvern Priory, whose hall, the only part that survived the Dissolution, is now incorporated into the Court. Of the priory church, only the chancel tower and south transept remain. The Court was once a Catholic safe house, with a chapel reached by a secret staircase. The Court and gardens are open Wednesday and Thursday afternoons from mid-April to mid-July.

Just to the north at Malvern Wells, where the first medicinal wells were discovered, stands **St Peter's Church**, dating from 1836 and notable for some original stained glass and a William Morris window of 1885.

The showground at Malvern Wells hosts major Spring and Autumn garden shows as well as antiques and crafts shows.

Around the Malverns

The whole area is glorious walking country, with endless places to discover and explore. **British Camp**, on Herefordshire Beacon, two miles west of Little Malvern, is one of the most important Roman settlements in Britain, and a little way south is Midsummer Hill, site of another ancient settlement.

COLWALL
2 miles SW of Great Malvern off the B4218

🌱 Picton Garden

On the west side of the Malverns, Colwall lies just across the border in Herefordshire. Its chief claim to fame is the enormous lump of limestone which stands at its centre. How it got there no one knows, but the Devil and a local giant are among the suspects. Less mysterious are the attractions of the **Picton Garden**, which contains a National Collection of Michaelmas Daisies which flower in September/October. The 14th century poet William Langland, author of *Piers Plowman*, lived at Colwall.

Birtsmorton
7 miles S of Great Malvern off the B4208

In the Church of St Peter and St Paul are monuments to the Nanfan family, owners of the nearby **Birtsmorton Court**. Other notable residents of this magnificent building (not open to the public) include William Huskisson, a

Little Malvern

Birtsmorton Court

UPTON-ON-SEVERN
7 miles SE of Great Malvern on the A4104

🏛 The Pepperpot   🏛 The Tudor House

An unspoilt town which gained prominence as one of the few bridging points on the Severn. The first records indicate that it was a Roman station, and it is mentioned in the Domesday Book. It became an important medieval port, and its strategic position led to its playing a role in the Civil War. In 1651, Charles sent a force to Upton to destroy the bridge, but after a long and bloody struggle the King's troops were routed and Cromwell regained the town. A Dutch gabled building used for stabling during the War still stands. The medieval church, one of the most distinctive buildings in the whole county, is affectionately known as **The Pepperpot**, because of its handsome tower with its copper-covered cupola. This former place of worship is now a heritage centre, telling of the Civil War battles and the town's history. The Church of St Peter and St Paul, built in 1879, has an interesting talking point in a large metal

former colonial secretary, who in 1830 became the first person to be killed in a railway accident.

HANLEY CASTLE
6 miles SE of Great Malvern on the B4209

The village takes its name from the castle, which was originally a hunting lodge for King John, and which disappeared, except for its moat, many centuries ago. There's still plenty to see in this attractive little spot, including picturesque cottages, a 15th century inn (The Three Kings), a 16th century grammar school and the Church of St Mary in stone and brick.

abstract hanging above the altar. The **Tudor House**, which contains a museum of Upton past and present, is open daily on summer afternoons. The White Lion Hotel, in the High Street, has a history going back to 1510 and was the setting for some scenes in Henry Fielding's Tom Jones. The commercial trade has largely left the Severn, replaced by a steady stream of summertime pleasure craft.

RIPPLE
10 miles SE of Great Malvern off the A38

🐦 Giant's Grave

The village square with its stocks and whipping post is tiny, making the Church of St Mary seem even larger than it is. Note the series of 12 misericords each depicting the seasonal activities of country life. They are full of detail and wondrously carved. In the churchyard is the **Giant's Grave**, the final resting place of Robert Reeve who was said to be 7ft 4in tall when he died in 1626, aged 56. On his well-preserved gravestone the epitaph reads:

> *Ye who pass by behold my length*
> *But never glory in your strength*

EARLS CROOME
6 miles SE of Great Malvern on the A4104

🏛 Croome Park

There are several attractions in the area of Earls Croome. **Croome Park** was Capability Brown's first complete landscape. Commissioned by the 6th Earl of Coventry in 1751, the Park made Brown's reputation and set a pattern for parkland design that lasted half a century. At Croome he established the English Landscape Style, a vision of Ideal Nature that was admired and copied throughout the Western world. The restoration of the park, one of the largest

landscape restoration projects undertaken, has included the replanting of many unusual trees and shrubs, the establishment of a wild flower meadow and pasture, and the creation of new pathways to the ice house through the Wild Walk shrubbery. The buildings have equally distinguished pedigrees, with Robert Adam and James Wyatt as architects. The Hill Croome Dovecote is a very rare square building next to the church in Hill Croome. Dunstall Castle folly at Dunstall Common is a folly in the style of a Norman castle, put up in the 18th century and comprising two round towers and one square, connected by arches.

At Croome d'Abitot, a little way north of Earls Croome, the 18th century Church of St Mary Magdalene is filled with memorials to the Coventry family – it stood on their estate.

ECKINGTON
10 miles SE of Great Malvern on the B4080

🌳 Bredon Hill

The small village of Eckington can be traced back to 172AD; it was originally a Roman settlement on land belonging to the British tribe of Dobuni. The bridge over the Avon, which dates from the 15th century, has an adjacent car park which is a popular picnic site.

The area south of Pershore towards the boundary with Gloucestershire is dominated by **Bredon Hill**, which is surrounded by charming villages such as Great and Little Comberton and Elmley Castle on the north side, and Bredon, Overbury and Kemerton to the south. Bredon Hill is almost circular, a limestone outcrop of the Cotswolds covering 12 square miles, accessible from many of the villages that ring it, and rising to over 900 feet. On the crest of its northern slope, best accessed from Great Comberton, are the remains – part of the earthworks – of the pre-

BLUE GECKO PLANTS

Tewkesbury Road, Eckington, nr Pershore,
Worcestershire WR10 3DE
Tel: 01386 751802 e-mail: cath@bluegeckoplants.com
website: www.bluegeckoplants.com

Catherine Thorpe revived an old nursery on the Tewkesbury road
out of the village of Eckington to establish the delightfully named
Blue Gecko Plants. The specialities, mostly grown on the premises, include shrubs, herbaceous
perennials, small trees and conifers, camellias, herbs and vegetable plants. Visitors will also find
a variety of garden ornaments, ceramic pots and gift ideas. Information and advice on planting is
always available at this friendly, family-run nursery. Garden gift vouchers are sold and accepted
at the nursery. Opening hours are 10am to 5pm Tuesday to Sunday.

Roman settlement. Much more visible on the
top is a curious brick tower called Parsons
Folly, built by a Mr Parsons in the 18th
century.

ELMLEY CASTLE

13 miles SE of Great Malvern on a minor road

Just one of the many enchanting villages
around Bredon Hill, no longer boasting a
castle but with this memorandum of 1540:
"The late Castle of Elmley standing on high
and adjoining the Park, compassed in with
wall and ditch is uncovered and in decay."

The village's main street is very wide and
lined with trees, with a little brook flowing to
one side. Picturesque
cottages with thatched roofs
lead up to a well-preserved
15th century cross, then to
St Mary's Church with its
handsome tower and
battlements. Inside are some
of the finest monuments to
be found anywhere in
England, most notably the
17th century alabaster tomb
of William Savage, his son
Giles and Giles' wife and
children.

BREDON

14 miles SE of Great Malvern off the B4080

🏛 Bredon Barn

Plenty to see in this sizeable village, notably
the Church of St Giles with its 14th century
stained glass and some very elaborate stone
monuments; an Elizabethan rectory with
stone figures on horseback on the roof; and
some fine 18th century stables. **Bredon Barn**,
owned by the National Trust, is a huge 14th
century barn built of local Cotswold stone.
132 feet in length, it has a dramatic aisled
interior, marvellous beams and two porches at
the wagon entrances. Open April-November.

Bredon Barn

PERSHORE

9 miles E of Great Malvern on the A4104

🏛 Abbey 🌱 Pershore College

A gem of a market town, with fine Georgian architecture and an attractive setting on the banks of the Avon. Its crowning glory is the **Abbey**, which combines outstanding examples of Norman and Early English architecture. The Abbey was founded by King Oswald in 689, and in 972 King Edgar granted a charter to the Benedictine monks. Only the choir remains of the original church, but it is still a considerable architectural treasure. The south transept is the oldest part, while among the most impressive features is some superb vaulting in the chancel roof.

Pershore Bridge, a favourite picnic spot, still bears the marks of damage done during the Civil War. A mile east of town on the B4084 is **Pershore College**. Originally part of the Wyke Estate, the college has been developed round an early 19th century mansion and is the Royal Horticultural Society's Centre for the Midlands and the Regional Centre of Excellence for the food and drink industry. The grounds contain many unusual trees and shrubs, and in the glasshouses are tropical, temperate and cool decorative plants. The College houses the National Collections of Penstemons and Philadelphus.

Pershore's main horticultural claim to fame are its plums, and a new variety called Pershore Emblem joins the long-established Pershore Purple and Pershore Yellow Egg.

REVILLS FARM SHOP & TEA ROOMS

Bourne Road, Defford, nr Pershore,
Worcestershire WR8 9BS
Tel: 01386 750466
e-mail: darren@revillsfarmshop.co.uk
website: www.revillsfarmshop.co.uk

The Revills are a prominent local farming family and it is son in law Darren Hedges who runs **Revills Farm Shop**, which is located in the village of Defford, off the A4104 two miles southwest of Pershore. Darren and his staff take justifiable pride in the quality of the produce sourced direct from the growers or locally through farmers' markets. The shop sells a fine variety of food, from meat (frozen or fresh to order), free-range poultry, seasonal game and fish from St Ives to eggs and cheese, preserves and pickles, homemade cakes, speciality breads, ice creams, and popular vegetable boxes and fruit baskets that reflect what's best throughout the seasons – these include superb soft fruits in summer and the first crop of asparagus in the county.

Shoppers will also find wines, beers, cider and perry, a small deli selection and some splendid pottery from Boleslawiec in Poland. The Old Stables Tea Room, with seats inside and outside, is open for morning coffee, light lunches and cream teas; a gallery showcases the work of local artists. Revills is open from 9am to 6pm (5.30pm in winter), Sunday 10am to 4pm.

🎬 stories and anecdotes 🦜 famous people 🎨 art and craft 🎭 entertainment and sport 🥾 walks

Great Comberton and Little Comberton

Distance: *3.5 miles (5.6 kilometres)*

Typical time: *120 mins*

Height gain: *25 metres*

Map: *Explorer 190*

Walk: *www.walkingworld.com ID:2627*

Contributor: *Ron and Jenny Glynn*

ACCESS INFORMATION:

On unclassified road off the A44 south of Pershore. Considerate parking on the village streets please.

DESCRIPTION:

A gentle little walk in Worcestershire farmland from Great Comberton to Little Comberton, and to the edge of Bricklehampton with the splendid backdrop of Bredon Hill for most of the way. The old and lovely thatched and timbered Tudor cottages of Little Comberton are quite breathtaking, and the church with its large tower is another pleasure to behold.

FEATURES:

Pub, Church, Wildlife, Birds, Flowers, Great Views, Butterflies, Mostly Flat

WALK DIRECTIONS:

1 | From the junction, a few yards from the War Memorial, walk along the road signed to Little Comberton and Elmley Castle, and take the public footpath on the right. Head diagonally left over field where there is a footbridge by a telegraph pole. Go on over it and continue in same direction to a gate, then over a field following a line of telegraph poles. Take footbridge to walk on in meadow to far corner, then a stile to walk between houses in Little Comberton.

2 | Turn right past pretty cottages and houses. Turn right into Manor Lane and pass beautiful Tudor half

timbered houses, following lane round to pass the lovely church. Turn left for few yards along road.

3 | Turn right into a large lawned area and head for the right of a large lime at far end. Take the gate 'neath its branches and turn left, then right, to walk round edge of field with the tree clad Bredon Hill opposite. Continue over a stile, turning left, then right, beside hedge. Pass two stiles on the right and continue round edge of field and into another, with Nash's Farm over on the left. Eventually reach an obscured stile in corner, and climb over it to walk on an overgrown path by Old House Farm, taking another stile into an orchard. Take stile on left and walk over to a gate beside a bungalow on a narrow, overgrown path.

4 | Come out into Little Comberton and turn left to walk along to telephone kiosk, then turn right along main road through village, leaving it to walk on past pretty cottages.

5 | Turn left through a large gate and walk along to field corner, through a gate, then over a footbridge into pastures. Go on to climb a stile out onto road.

6 | Turn left along it, the magnificent Bredon Hill ahead, and follow road round, and along to Great Comberton.

Tewkesbury

🏫 Abbey 🏛 Museums ⛪ Battle of Tewkesbury

Actually just across the border into Gloucestershire, Tewkesbury is a town of historic and strategic importance close to the confluence of the Severn and Avon rivers. At the centre of the town is **Tewkesbury Abbey**, the cathedral-sized parish church of St Mary. Founded in the 8th century and completely rebuilt in the 11th, it was one of the last to be dissolved by Henry VIII, and in 1540 it was saved from destruction by the townspeople, who raised £453 to buy it from the Crown. Many of its features are on a truly grand scale, and the vast main tower is the tallest surviving Norman main tower in the world. Three museums tell the story of the town and its environs: the **Little Museum**, laid out in a typical old merchant's house; **Tewkesbury Museum**, with displays on the social history and archaeology of the area; and the John Moore Countryside Museum, a natural history collection displayed in a 15th century timber-framed house. The **Battle of Tewkesbury**, one of the fiercest in the Wars of the Roses, took place in 1471 in a field south of the town which ever since has been known as Bloody Meadow. The 17-year-old son of Henry VI was killed in the conflict, and a plaque marking his final resting place can be seen in the Abbey.

THE BECKFORD

Cheltenham Road, Beckford, nr Tewkesbury, Worcestershire GL20 7AN
Tel: 01386 881532 Fax: 01386 882021
e-mail: Norman@thebeckford.com website: www.thebeckford.com

The Beckford is a traditional family-run country inn – lively, welcoming, with good wholesome food, a fine range of drinks and comfortable guest accommodation. Dating from the 18th century, the Cotswold stone building has the look of a country mansion, and when owners Sue and Norman Hughes arrived in August 2005 they oversaw a complete refurbishment that has kept it in immaculate order. They guarantee the warmest of welcomes to all their visitors, whether it's for a drink, a lunch, an evening meal or a short break. The bar is well stocked with real ales (always including a local brew) and other beers, lagers and ciders, and wines by bottle or

glass to enjoy on their own or to complement a meal. The excellent choice of freshly prepared food ranges from bar snacks to a full à la carte, daily specials and traditional Sunday lunch.

The restaurant seats 85 in comfort and, in the summer, picnic tables are set out on the lawned gardens at the front and side of the inn. Typical choices on the main menu might include garlic king prawns with a provençal sauce, oven-baked salmon with a chilli honey glaze, Herefordshire fillet steak, lamb's liver with bubble & squeak, and four-cheese cannelloni. The Beckford holds a civil wedding license and a marquee can be made available or there is a separate function room which can accommodate up to 60 people. The Beckford's eight spotless bedrooms in the modern wing are equipped with en suite shower and WC, central heating, TV, radio-alarm clock, hairdryer, trouser press, kettle, teas and coffee and mineral water. One room of great character in the old part has a sloping floor and splendid brass bed. The Beckford is open from 11am to 11pm (Sunday 12 noon to 10.30pm) and food is served in the restaurant and bar from 12 noon to 2.30pm and 6.30pm to 9.30pm, also morning coffee and afternoon tea.

📺 stories and anecdotes 🦃 famous people 🎨 art and craft 🎭 entertainment and sport 🚶 walks

Evesham

Almonry Heritage Centre	Spring Blossom Trail
Country Park	

A bustling market town at the centre of the Vale of Evesham, an area long known as the Garden of England, with a prolific harvest of soft fruits, apples, plums and salad vegetables. The **Spring Blossom Trail** is a circular driving trail around the Vale of Evesham, taking the sights and smells of springtime blossom. The River Avon performs a loop round the town, and the Abbey park is a good place for a riverside stroll; it is also the start point for boat trips. The magnificent 110ft bell tower is the only major building remaining of the Abbey, which was founded around 700 by Egwin, Bishop of Worcester, and was one of the largest and grandest in the whole country. It was knocked down by Henry VIII's men at the time of the Dissolution of the Monasteries. The story of the town is told in vivid detail at the **Almonry Heritage Centre**, which was formerly the home of the Abbey Almoner and was built around 1400. The almoner was responsible for the distribution of alms to poor pilgrims and townspeople during the 850-year lifetime of the Abbey. It now houses a unique collection of artefacts as well as exhibitions showing the history of the Abbey, the defeat of Simon de Montfort at the Battle of Evesham (the Leicester Tower stands on the site of the Battle), the involvement of the town in the Civil War, and stories from more recent campaigns. The Almonry gardens have more exhibits, including agricultural equipment and a cannon from the Crimea campaign of 1854.

There are many other interesting buildings in Evesham, including the neighbouring churches of All Saints and St Lawrence. The former is entered through a porch built by Abbot Lichfield in the 16th century, and the Lichfield Chapel, with a lovely fan-vaulted ceiling, contains his tomb. Much of the building, as well as the stone pulpit, dates from Victorian times, when major restoration work was carried out. The latter, declared redundant in 1978, was also the subject of extensive restoration, in the 1830s and again in the 1990s. In the market place is a free-standing grand old timbered building called the Round House – a curious name, because it is actually square. One theory claims that it was so called because "you can walk all round it".

A little way north of Evesham is **Evesham Country Park**, where the attractions include a

Bell Tower, Evesham

🏠 historic building	🏛 museum 🏛 historic site 🍃 scenic attraction 🌿 flora and fauna

stretch of the River Avon, a wildlife visitor centre, shops, a garden centre and the charming Evesham Vale Light Railway. Nearby, in the village of Offenham, is a rare sight – a terrace of seven half-timbered medieval cottages from the 1460s which share one long continuous thatched roof. They stand on Main Street at the end of which is another rarity – a permanent Maypole of red, white and blue crowned by a golden cockerel.

Around Evesham

ASHTON UNDER HILL
5 miles SW of Evesham off the A46

Ashton under Hill sits at the foot of Bredon Hill, its main street flanked by stone half-timbered, black and white buildings. At the crossroads stands an unusual survival, an 18th century cross with a sundial.

BROADWAY
6 miles SE of Evesham on the A44

🏠 Broadway Tower   🏃 Broadway Beacon

🌱 Snowshill Lavender

One of the most beautiful villages in England and a magnet for tourists throughout the year. The quintessential Cotswold village, its eponymous broad main street is lined with houses and cottages built of golden Cotswold stone. Broadway was settled as far back as 1900BC, and later the Romans came and occupied the hill above the village. Broadway was probably re-established after the Battle of Dyrham in AD557 by conquering Saxons advancing towards Worcester. The parish records tell of hospitality being offered at a Broadway hostelry as early as 1532. This was the time of the advent of the horse-drawn carriage, when Broadway became an important staging post. A journey from London to Worcester took about 17 hours including stops and a change of horse, and at one time Broadway boasted an incredible 33 public houses.

In the centre of Broadway is a wide village green from where the main street continues gently upwards for nearly a mile, with the surrounding hills always in view. The gradient increases at Fish Hill then rises to more than 1,000 feet above sea level at **Broadway Beacon**. At the top of the Beacon is **Broadway Tower**, standing in a delightful country park with something to interest all ages, from animal enclosures and adventure playground to nature walks and barbecue sites. The tower was built as a folly by the 6th Earl

---

COWLEY HOUSE

Church Street, Broadway, Worcestershire
WR12 7AE
Tel: 01386 858148

Broadway is one of the most beautiful villages in England and a magnet for tourists. Visitors in search of a quiet, comfortable base need look no further than **Cowley House**, a lovely property recently totally renovated by owner Joan Reading. The six bedrooms, all re-decorated to a very high standard, have new en suite shower rooms with quality toiletries, and TVs with CD players. Joan is a charming, welcoming host, greeting arrivals with tea and biscuits, and the day starts with a super breakfast served in the stylish modern dining room.

🎬 stories and anecdotes   🕊 famous people   🎨 art and craft   🎭 entertainment and sport   🏃 walks of Coventry in 1799 as part of the great movement of the time towards picturesque and romantic landscapes. James Wyatt designed the tower, which now contains various displays and exhibitions including the William Morris Room – Morris used the Tower as a country retreat.

Broadway's St Michael's Church (1839) boasts an intricate Elizabethan pulpit which came from the nearby St Eadburga's Church and was installed in a thanksgiving service marking the end of World War I.

In the late 19th century Broadway was a haunt of artists, musicians and writers, including JM Barrie, Ralph Vaughan Willams, Henry James, Edward Elgar and John Singer Sargent. It was later a centre of the Arts & Crafts Movement.

Broadway Tower

SHEEPSCOMBE HOUSE

Snowshill, nr Broadway, Worcestershire WR12 7JU
Tel: 01386 853769
e-mail: reservations@snowshill-broadway.co.uk
website: www.broadway-cotswolds.co.uk/sheepscombe.html
www.cotswoldsbreakfast.com/accommodation/sheepscombe-house.html

There's an almost endless list of things to do and see in this lovely part of the world, and **Sheepscombe House** provides an ideal base for discovering them. Tim and Jacki Harrison's Bed & Breakfast accommodation comprises three beautifully equipped, spacious en suite bedrooms that fully deserve their 4- Star Gold rating. Amenities include new TV/DVD players. The house stands on a hillside, with a lovely secluded garden and glorious views down the Snowshill Valley to Broadway and beyond.

The Cotswold Way runs nearby, and local amenities include two golf courses and a riding school. Guests start the day with a truly splendid breakfast that features the pick of local produce, including bacon and sausages from Gloucester Old Spot pigs, home-laid eggs, Netherend Farm butter, homemade marmalade, Costwold honey and Benson's Cox's apple juice.

🏛 historic building   🏛 museum   🏛 historic site   🌳 scenic attraction   🌿 flora and fauna

South of Broadway, at Snowshill, **Snowshill Lavender** comprises 53 acres of rolling lavender fields, with more than 30 varieties.

CHILDSWICKHAM
4 miles SE of Evesham off the A44

🏛 Cider Mill Museum

The Church of St Mary the Virgin, its tall, slender spire a prominent landmark, is a good place to start a walk round the old part of the village. Close by, on the Broadway road, is the Barnfield **Cider Mill Museum**, where visitors can see a display of cider-making down the years before sampling cider, perry or one of the wines produced from local plums and berries.

BRETFORTON
4 miles E of Evesham on the B4035

🏛 Fleece Inn

A pub in the care of the National Trust is a rarity indeed, and it's well worth a trip to Bretforton to visit the **Fleece Inn**, a medieval half-timbered building that was originally a farmhouse. It has changed very little since being first licensed in 1848, and an interesting feature is the Witches' Marks carved in the hearth to prevent witches coming down the chimney. The Church of St Leonard boasts a number of interesting and intricate carvings, notably a scene depicting St Margaret emerging (through a hole she made with her cross) from the side of the dragon which has just swallowed her.

HONEYBOURNE
4 miles E of Evesham on minor roads off the B4035

🕊 Domestic Fowl Trust and Honeybourne Rare Breeds

The **Domestic Fowl Trust and Honeybourne Rare Breeds** is a conservation centre for rare breeds of poultry and livestock. Over 100 breeds are on view on the 29-acre farm. Visitors can wander along the grass pathways to see breeding flocks of chickens (including British and American bantams), ducks, geese and turkeys. The farm animals include the rare Irish Moiled cows and some of the rarest breeds of sheep and goats. Books, gifts and animal equipment and feedstuffs are available from the shop, and the centre also has an activity room for children, a poultry museum and an information centre.

MIDDLE LITTLETON
3 miles NE of Evesham off the B4085

🏛 Tithe Barn 🕊 Windmill Hill Nature Reserve

The Littletons – North, Middle and South – lie close to each other and close to the River Avon. In Middle Littleton is a huge and wonderful **Tithe Barn**, built in the 13th century and once the property of the Abbots of Evesham. Now owned by the National Trust, it is still in use as a farm building, but can be visited.

Nearby, a bridleway leads off the B4510 to **Windmill Hill Nature Reserve**, an area of fertile limestone which continues up to Cleeve Prior, where the Church of St Andrew is well worth a visit.

Worcester

🏛 Cathedral   🏛 Greyfriars   🏛 City Museum
🏛 Royal Worcester Porcelain
🏛 Commandery Civil War Centre
🏛 Museum of Local Life   🌿 Three Choirs Festival
🏃 Worcester Woods Country Park

The **Cathedral**, with its 200ft tower, stands majestically beside the Severn. The 11th century crypt is a classic example of Norman

GRAYS AT THE NORTHWICK INTERIORS & LIFESTYLE

142 Ombersley Road, Worcester WR3 7HA
Tel: 01905 754040   Fax: 01905 757676
e-mail: graysatthenorthwick@yahoo.co.uk   website: www.graysatthenorthwick.co.uk

David and Helen Gray deserve an Oscar for creating a new starring role for what was until recently a sad, derelict cinema. The classic 1938 Art Deco cinema had lain neglected for 12 years before they turned it into a vibrant, glamorous setting for displaying a wide variety of furniture, fabrics, accessories, gifts and collectables. Much of the furniture is in keeping with the spirit of the cinema, including mirrored cabinets and dressers, monochromatic dining sets, pieces in pale wood and glass and striking crystal chandeliers.

Supporting the furniture, but definitely not B features, are fabrics by the best-known makers, plants and decorative cast-iron garden seats and tables, gifts and lifestyle items to suit all pockets and a splendid café selling all-day breakfasts, sandwiches, panini, terrific pies (steak & ale, chicken & mushroom, fisherman's) and excellent coffee. Grays is open from 9 to 5.30 (Sunday 10 to 4.30).

🏛 historic building 🏛 museum 🏛 historic site ♧ scenic attraction 🌿 flora and fauna architecture and was built by St Wulstan, who is remembered in a stone carving. He was the only English bishop not to be replaced by a Norman after the Conquest. To many of the local people the task of building the Cathedral must have seemed endless; the central tower collapsed in 1175 and a fire destroyed much of the building in 1203. The Cathedral had only just been re-dedicated after these disasters when Bishop Blois began pulling it down again, only to rebuild it in the fashionable Gothic style. The nave was rebuilt in the 14th century under the auspices of Bishop Cobham, but the south side was not completed until much later, and in a far less elaborate style. King John requested that he be buried in the choir, and his tomb stands near the high altar. It is a masterpiece of medieval sculpture, showing the King flanked by the Bishops Oswald and Wulstan. Prince Arthur, elder brother of Henry VIII, is also entombed near the high altar. One of the many stories about the Cathedral concerns the 'Grumpy Monk', so grumpy that his brothers decided to get their own back when he died. They buried him under a step in the cloisters so they could have the satisfaction of treading on him whenever they passed by. He lies there to this day, still being trodden on by visitors.

There's a great deal more to see than the Cathedral, of course, and in the **City Museum and Art Gallery** are contemporary art and archaeological displays, a 19th century chemist's shop and the military collections of the Worcestershire Regiment and the Worcestershire Yeomanry Cavalry. Friar Street has many lovely old timber houses. **Greyfriars**, in the care of the National Trust, is a medieval house that has managed to survive right in the heart of the city, and passing through its archway visitors will come across a pretty walled garden. The imposing Guildhall in the High Street is a marvellous example of Queen Anne architecture, designed by a local man, Thomas White. The **Commandery Civil War Centre** is a stunning complex of buildings behind a small timber-framed entrance. At the Battle of Worcester in 1651 the Commandery was used as the Royalist headquarters, and today period rooms offer a fascinating glimpse of the architecture and style of Tudor and Stuart times while acting as the country's only museum devoted to the story of the Civil War. The story takes in the trial of Charles I, visits a Royalist encampment on the eve of the

Greyfriars, Worcester

battle and enacts the last battle of the war narrated by Charles II and Oliver Cromwell.

The **Royal Worcester Porcelain Visitor Centre** is an absolute must on any sightseer's list. Royal Worcester is Britain's oldest continuous producer of porcelain and is world famous for its exquisite bone china. The factory was founded in 1751 by Dr John Wall with the intention of creating "a ware of a form so precise as to be easily distinguished from other English porcelain". The collection in the museum contains some of the finest treasures of the factory, and visitors can take a guided tour of the factory to observe the many stages of production. The premises include a shop and a restaurant where the food is, naturally, served on Royal Worcester china. In the 1930s the company was acquired by (Charles William) Dyson Perrins, the grandson of William Perrins, founder of the Worcester Sauce company.

The **Museum of Local Life** reflects the history of Worcester and its people, with displays covering the past 700 years. There's a Victorian kitchen scene, a turn-of-the-century schoolroom and a variety of changing exhibitions throughout the year. The site is a 16th century timber-framed building in wonderful Friar Street. Famous sons of Worcester, where the **Three Choirs Festival** was first held in 1717, include Sir Edward Elgar, born at nearby Broadheath; his statue is a notable landmark opposite the Cathedral.

To the east of the city and signposted from the M5 (J6) and from the city centre via the A44, **Worcester Woods Country Park**, open daily, has 50 hectares of ancient oak woodland, 10 hectares of traditional wildflower meadow, waymarked trails, a picnic area, children's play area, visitor centre, café and shop.

Around Worcester

POWICK
2 miles S of Worcester on the A449

Powick Bridge was the scene of the first and last battles in the Civil War; the last, in 1651, ending with Charles hiding in the Boscobel Oak before journeying south to nine year's exile in France. Cromwell's power had been overwhelming, and the long years of strife were at an end. Powick Bridge's skyline is today dominated by Worcester's first power station, built in 1894.

SPETCHLEY
3 miles E of Worcester on the A422

🏛 Church

All Saints Church, 14th century with a 16th century chapel, is home to a fine collection of monuments to the Berkeley family, who owned adjoining Spetchley Park. The park, which extends over 12 hectares, has lovely formal gardens, wooded areas, lawns and a lake with an ornamental bridge.

HUDDINGTON
6 miles E of Worcester on minor roads

🏛 Huddington Court

Two buildings of particular note: the simple little Church of St James, with a timber-framed bell turret; and **Huddington Court**. The Court has been described as the most picturesque house in Worcestershire. An excellent example of a 16th century timber-framed building, it was once the home of the Wintours, a staunchly Catholic family who were involved in the Gunpowder Plot. When the plot was exposed and the conspirators finally arrested, both Thomas and Robert Wintour, cousins of Robert Catesby,

MANOR HOUSE FARM

Ab Lench, nr Evesham, Worcestershire WR11 4UP
Tel: 01386 462226 Fax: 01386 462563

Set serenely in a lovely garden, **Manor House Farm** is the perfect antidote to the bustle of urban life. The 250-year-old house has two guest bedrooms – a double with en suite bathroom with the morning sun and views of the garden and a twin with original beams and a private bathroom a few steps away. Owner Sheila Virr is the most welcoming of hosts, and her three delightful little Maltese terriers can be guaranteed to provide their own waggy greeting. Tea is served to arriving guests in the drawing room, and guests also have the use of two reception rooms and a study with TV. A splendid traditional English breakfast starts the day, and an evening meal can be served by arrangement.

confessed their guilt and were executed. The Court is a private residence, but you can get a good view of it from the churchyard.

A mile or so north of Huddington lies the village of Himbleton, where the Church of St Mary Magdalene has a picturesque bell turret with a memorial clock.

ROUS LENCH

7 miles E of Worcester on a minor road

🏠 Rous Lench Court

The Lenches are attractive little villages in an area known for its particularly rich soil. Rous Lench church has a chapel with monuments to the Rous family and an oil painting of Jesus in the house of Simon the Pharisee. The road to the hilltop village of Church Lench (a mile south), with the church at the very top of the hill, passes by **Rous Lench Court**, the seat of the Rous family for many centuries from 1382. The Court is a splendid half-timbered mansion with a tall Italianate tower in the beautiful gardens.

INKBERROW

8 miles E of Worcester off the A42

🏠 Old Bull Inn

A very pleasant and pretty spot to pause awhile, with the Church of St Peter (note the

alabaster of John Savage, a High Sheriff of Worcester who died in 1631), the inn and other buildings round the village green, some in red brick, others black and white half-timbered. The **Old Bull Inn** has two claims to fame, one that William Shakespeare stayed there in 1582, the other that it is the original of The Bull at Ambridge, home of The Archers. Photographs of the cast adorn the walls, and the inn has become a place of pilgrimage for fans of the programme.

The Old Vicarage, a handsome 18th century building in the Tudor style, was host in an earlier guise to King Charles I, who stayed there on his way to Naseby; some maps he left behind are kept in the church.

At nearby Dormston, a timber-framed Dovecote stands in front of the Moat farmhouse.

One mile south of Inkberrow is the village of Abbots Morton, whose dwellings are mainly 17th century yeomen's houses. The village was once the site of the Abbot of Evesham's summer residence, but only some mounds and fishponds now remain.

ODDINGLEY

5 miles NE of Worcester on minor roads

The parish church of Oddingley stands on a

STAR YARD INTERIORS

17 High Street, Droitwich, Worcestershire WR9 8EJ
Tel/Fax: 01905 772276

Owner Andrew Brooker-Carey has made a superb job of converting a 16th century salt merchant's house into a furniture and interiors business of the highest quality. **Star Yard Interiors** is set on three floors and comprises 12 beautifully

appointed rooms with individual, old-world settings. Andrew is an accomplished furniture designer and finisher, and the pieces on display are either antiques, or made-to-order on traditional lines using traditional skills.

He sources primarily Georgian or country furniture, and among his specialities are furniture for libraries and kitchens.

Mirrors and lighting are also featured strongly, and Andrew and his staff are on hand with assistance for clients wishing to furnish anything from a small flat to a large house or a barn conversion. Opening times are Tuesday to Friday 10am to 3pm, Saturday 10am to 5pm, or by prior arrangement. Plans for 2007 include a tea shop on the ground floor by the entrance.

hill overlooking the Worcester & Birmingham Canal. Its principal treasure is the mostly 15th century stained glass in the east window which is regarded as some of the finest of that period. Behind the communion rail is a memorial to a rector, George Parker, who was murdered in 1806 because of a dispute over tithes.

DROITWICH
6 miles NE of Worcester on the A38

🏰 Chateau Immpney   🏰 Church of the Scared Heart

🏛 Heritage & Information Centre

🌿 Salwarpe Valley Nature Reserve

This was Salinae, the place of salt, in Roman times. Salt deposits, a legacy from the time when this area was on the seabed, were extracted for 2,000 years until the end of the

19th century. The natural Droitwich brine contains about 2.5 pounds of salt per gallon - ten times as much as sea water - and is often likened to the waters of the Dead Sea. The brine is pumped up from an underground lake which lies 200 feet below the town. Visitors do not drink the waters at Droitwich as they do at most other spas, but enjoy the therapeutic properties floating in the warm brine. The first brine baths were built in the 1830s and were soon renowned for bringing relief to many and effecting seemingly miraculous cures. By 1876, Droitwich had developed as a fashionable spa, mainly through the efforts of John Corbett, known as the Salt King.

This typical Victorian businessman and philanthropist introduced new methods of

BEAUBELLES

44 St Andrews Square, Droitwich Spa, Worcestershire WR9 8HE
Tel: 01905 772229 Fax: 01905 798546
e-mail: beaubelles_06@yahoo.co.uk

An eye-catching window display makes it difficult to walk past **Beaubelles**, and once inside customers will find literally thousands of interesting gifts for all ages, all occasions and all pockets, something for the home or a well-deserved personal treat.

Items filling the shelves, tables and floors in the two rooms range from silver and costume jewellery and jewel boxes, jewel trees, scarves, hand bags, hand-made and 3D pop up greeting cards, penguin books, bouncy balls, solar key rings, souvenirs and marble coasters.

There are china figures small and large, glassware, candles, mirrors, soft toys, Sheaffer pens, perfume bottles, picture frames, trinkets, cuff-links, handkerchiefs, hobby clocks and leather wallets. Coffee Shop opening very soon.

This is definitely not a place to visit just once: the stock changes constantly, so every time you go you'll find an array of new and different goods for browsing and buying.

THE HADLEY BOWLING GREEN INN

Hadley Heath, nr Droitwich, Worcestershire WR9 0AR
Tel: 01905 620294 Fax: 01905 620771
e-mail: enquiries@hadleybowlinggreen.com   website: www.hadleybowlinggreen.com

The **Hadley Bowling Green Inn** has a history of hospitality that dates back more then 400 years. Darkwood furniture, hop-hung beams and log fires paint a delightfully traditional scene in the bars, creating an inviting, relaxing setting for enjoying a glass or two of real ale. In fine weather it's very pleasant sit outside overlooking the green.

Food is an important side of the business and patrons can have a full meal, or just a snack such as Upton rarebit or black pudding and bacon stack with a Dijon sauce. Typical main courses include cod cooked in a guest ale batter, salmon with sesame and chilli dressing on a broccoli stir-fry, steaks or homemade burgers. Risotto and pasta options are available as starter or main courses and a fine meal might end with a scrumptious apple pie served with apple and cinnamon ice cream. Complementing the food is a wide-ranging 100-strong wine list with a dozen or more champagnes. The inn offers special menus for celebration events such as Valentine's Day and Mother's Day.

Twelve well-appointed bedrooms provide excellent accommodation for an overnight stay or a base for touring the region. The bowling green, after which the inn is named, is the oldest in the British Isles. Existing records date back only as far as 1775, but the green was in existence long before that. Visitors are more than welcome to try their hand at bowling, and the inn keeps several sets of bowls. This famous old inn, which opens long hours every day, is a short drive from the M5 (J5 or 6).

extracting the brine and moved the main plant to Stoke Prior. The enterprise was beset with various problems in the 1870s and Corbett turned his attention to developing the town as a spa resort. He was clearly a man of some energy as he also served as an MP after the 1874 General Election. Many of the buildings in present-day Droitwich were owned by Corbett, including the Raven Hotel (a raven was part of his coat of arms) in the centre. His most remarkable legacy is undoubtedly **Chateau Impney**, on the eastern side of town at Dodderhill. It was designed by a Frenchman, Auguste Tronquois, in the style of an ornate French chateau, with soaring turrets, mansard roof and classical French gardens. It was intended as a home for Corbett and his wife Anna, but she apparently didn't like the place; their increasingly stormy marriage ended in 1884, nine years after the completion of the flamboyant chateau, which is now a high-class hotel and conference centre.

The **Heritage and Information Centre** includes a local history exhibition (Salt Town to Spa) and a historic BBC radio room.

In the centre of the town is St Andrew's Church, part of whose tower was removed because of subsidence, a condition which affected many buildings and which can be seen in some fairly alarming angles. One of the chapels, dating from the 13th century, is dedicated to St Richard de Wyche, the town's patron saint, who became Bishop of Chichester. On the southern outskirts of Droitwich is the **Church of the Sacred Heart**, built in Italianate style in the 1930s and remarkable for its profusion of beautiful mosaics made from Venetian glass. Many of these mosaics also commemorate the life of St Richard.

One of Droitwich's most famous sons is

Edward Winslow, born the eldest of eight children in 1595. He was one of the pilgrims who set sail for the New World to seek religious freedom and he later became Governor of the colony. A bronze memorial to Edward Winslow can be seen in St Peter's Church.

Salwarpe on the southwest fringes of Droitwich, is truly a hidden hamlet, approached by a stone bridge over James Brindley's Droitwich Canal. Opened in 1771, the canal linked the town to the River Severn at Hawford. The Church of St Michael, by the edge of the canal, has several monuments to the Talbot family, who owned nearby Salwarpe Court. **Salwarpe Valley Nature Reserve** is one of very few inland sites with salt water, making it ideal for a variety of saltmarsh plants and very well worth a visit.

HAWFORD
4 miles N of Worcester off the A449

The site of another amazing dovecote, this one half-timbered, dating from the 16th century and owned by the National Trust.

OMBERSLEY
6 miles N of Worcester off the A449

St Andrew's Church

A truly delightful and very English village with some superb black-and-white timbered dwellings with steeply-sloping roofs. **St Andrew's Church**, rebuilt in 1825, contains memorials to the Sandys family and also their family pew. Large and square, it stands beside the pulpit and is comfortably furnished with cushioned seats, matching blue embroidered kneelers and an ornate open fireplace. For their heating, the congregation had to rely on the impressive Howden Heating Stove, set against the north wall. Installed in 1829, it

GWILLAMS FARM SHOP

Ombersley Road, Claines, Worcester WR3 7RH
Tel: 01905 756490
e-mail: gwillams@btconnect.com

Mary and Neville are the third generation of
Gwillams to farm here, becoming owners in 1982
and opening the farm shop in 1996. The speciality
for which **Gwillams Farm Shop** has become
particularly well known is the superb beef, bred in
Exmoor and reared on the farm's corn and silage,
slaughtered in Herefordshire and vacuum-packed for
sale in the shop. Traditional free-range pork is
another speciality, and the cold cabinets contain a
wide range of beef and pork in joints and cuts of all
sizes, steaks, mince and sausages.

The shop also sells a fine variety of top-quality
seasonal fruit and vegetables (many grown on the
farm, with pick-your-own available); the best eggs,
milk, cream and English cheeses; dressings, sauces,
pickles and chutneys from Kit's Kitchen at Egdon;
fruit juices; wines; local Hobson beer and Knights &
Westons cider, locally baked cakes and hand-baked
biscuits from Cheshire. Gwillams Farm Shop has
built up a loyal following in the locality, as well as further afield. Their customers know that they
will always find the very best and have no need to go anywhere near a supermarket for their
meat, dairy produce, fruit and vegetables.

rises some 12 feet and is in the shape of a
miniature church tower complete with
buttresses, arcaded top and a fuel opening just
like a church doorway.

The Sandys family lived at nearby
Ombersley Court (private), a splendid
Georgian mansion which can be seen from
the churchyard.

WICHENFORD
5 miles NW of Worcester on the B4204

🏛 Dovecote

A famous landmark here is the National
Trust's **Wichenford Dovecote**, a 17th century
timber-framed construction with a lantern on
top. With its 557 nesting holes, it is the largest
surviving dovecote in England. When it was
constructed, only the Lord of the Manor had

the right to build one and to kill the birds for
winter meat – a source of resentment to the
villagers whose crops were pillaged by these
voracious birds.

CLIFTON
10 miles NW of Worcester on the B4204

🏛 Church of St Kenelm

In lovely countryside near the River Teme, the
village boasts a number of charming dwellings
around the green and the **Church of St
Kenelm**. Parts of the church go back to the
12th and 14th centuries. Collectors of unusual
tombstones will find two here. Just inside the
porch is the grave of "Elizabeth Taylor,
Gent." who "Lived and dyed A Virgin"; on
the north wall a marble tablet includes an
inscription recording that "William" achieved

🏛 historic building   🏛 museum   🏛 historic site   🗸 scenic attraction   🌿 flora and fauna the intriguing feat of being born on August 22nd 1714 and dying on November 23rd 1713.

There are other interesting churches at nearby Shelsey Beauchamp, in red sandstone, and Shelsey Walsh, with many treasures including the tomb of Sir Francis Walsh. The name of Shelsey Walsh will be familiar to fans of motor sport as the location of a very famous hill climb.

LOWER BROADHEATH
3 miles W of Worcester off the A44

☞ Elgar Birthplace Museum

The **Elgar Birthplace Museum** is a redbrick cottage that is crammed with items from the great composer's life. He was born here in 1857 and, despite long periods spent elsewhere, Broadheath remained his spiritual home. The violin was his first instrument, though he

Elgar Birthplace Museum

The Elgar Birthplace Museum

Crown East Lane, Lower Broadheath, Worcester
Tel: 01905 333224
e-mail: birthplace@elgarmuseum.org
website: www.elgarmuseum.org

Visit the historic Birthplace Cottage and modern Elgar Centre for a fascinating insight into the life and music, family and friends, development and inspirations of Sir Edward Elgar, one of England's greatest composers. Explore the unique displays of manuscripts and memorabilia illustrating the man and his music, and enjoy the free introductory video and audio tour. Browse in the Museum Shop with its unrivalled range of appealing gifts including CDs, sheet music, souvenirs, greeting cards and much more. Enjoy the annual programme of concerts, talks, special weekends and holiday activities.

Open daily 11.00 am – 5.00 pm (last admission 4.15 pm).
Closed Christmas to end January

🎭 stories and anecdotes 🎏 famous people 🖼 art and craft 🎭 entertainment and sport 🎿 walks called Edmund Colles is said to have robbed one of his colleagues who was returning from Worcester and known to be carrying a full purse. It was a dark, gloomy night, and as Colles reached out to grab the man's horse, holding on to the bridle, the other struck at him with a sword. When he visited Edmund the next day, the appalling wound testified to the man's guilt; although forgiven by his intended victim, Colles died shortly after and his ghost once haunted the area. A phantom coach pulled by four fire-breathing steeds would appear and race down the hill to the church by Leigh Court, where they would leap over the tithe barn and disappear beneath the waters of the River Teme. A midnight service attended by 12 clergymen eventually laid the ghost to rest. Leaping over the tithe barn was no mean feat (though easier of course if you're a ghost), as the 14th century barn is truly massive, with great cruck beams and porched wagon doors. Standing in the grounds of Leigh Court, a long gabled mansion, the barn is open for visits on summer weekends.

Leigh Brook is a tributary of the Teme and wends its way through a spectacular valley cared for by Worcestershire Nature Conservation Trust. The countryside here is lovely, and footpaths make the going easier. Up on Old Storridge Common, birch, ash, oak and bracken have taken a firm hold, and there is a weird, rather unearthly feel about the place. Nearby, the hamlet of Birch Wood is where Elgar composed his *Dream of Gerontius*.

ALFRICK
7 miles W of Worcester off the A44

🌿 Nature Reserves

Charles Dodgson (Lewis Carroll) once preached at the village Church of St Mary

Magdalene, which enjoys a delightful setting above the village green. In the vicinity are two major attractions for nature-lovers. A little way to the northwest is **Ravenshill Woodland Nature Reserve** with waymarked trails through woodland that is home to many breeding birds, while a mile south of Alfrick is the **Knapp and Papermill Nature Reserve**, with 25 hectares of woodland and meadows rich in flora and fauna.

Bromsgrove

🏛 Avoncraft Museum of Historic Buildings

🏛 Museum

🏛 BT National Telephone Kiosk Collection

🏛 Church of St John the Baptist   🌿 AE Housman

A visit to the **Avoncraft Museum of Historic Buildings**, just south of Bromsgrove, is a walk through seven centuries of English history, with each building providing a snapshot of life in its particular period. The first building, a timber-framed merchant's house from Bromsgrove, was brought to the site in 1967, since when over 20 more have been installed. In addition to the buildings themselves, the Museum has regular demonstrations of such crafts as wood-turning, windmilling, racksawing, brick-making, chain-making and nail-making. There's also a shop, refreshment area, picnic site, a children's area, horse-drawn wagon rides and farm animals wandering around freely. One of the most treasured exhibits is the original 14th century beamed roof of Guesten Hall from Worcester Cathedral, now covering a modern brick building. In an area behind the shop is another unique collection, the **BT National Telephone Kiosk Collection**.

Bromsgrove Museum, near the town centre, has displays of local crafts and industries, including glass, salt and nail, and the Bromsgrove Guild, an organisation of craftsmen founded in 1894. The Guild of highly skilled craftsmen had its finest hour when commissioned to design and make the gates and railings of Buckingham Palace. Another popular exhibit is a street scene of Victorian shops.

Besides the museums, there is plenty to see, including some very handsome timber-framed buildings in the High Street, where stands a statue of **AE Housman**, the town's most famous son. Alfred Edward Housman was born one of seven children at Fockbury, Bromsgrove, in 1859, and spent his schooldays in the town. After a spell at Oxford University and some time teaching at his old school, he entered the Civil Service in London, where he found time to resume his academic studies. He was appointed Professor of Latin at University College, London, in 1892 and soon afterwards he published his first and best-known collection of poems – *A Shropshire Lad*. His total output was not large, but it includes some of the best-loved poems in the English language. He died in 1936 and is buried in the churchyard of St Lawrence in Ludlow. The forming, in 1972, of a Housman Society brought his name to the forefront of public attention and in the region of Bromsgrove walking and motoring trails take in the properties and places associated with him.

Bromsgrove has a prestigious annual music festival held during the month of May, when the town plays host to a wide range of musical entertainment from orchestral concerts to jazz, and featuring many well-known artists. Another annual event is the revival of the

Bromsgrove Museum

Court Leet, an ancient form of local administration. A colourful procession moves through the town and there's a lively Elizabethan street market.

The **Church of St John the Baptist** – see his statue over the south porch entrance – contains some superb 19th century stained glass and an impressive collection of monuments, notably to members of the Talbot family. Side by side in the churchyard are the tombs of two railwaymen who were killed in 1840 when the boiler of their engine exploded while climbing the notorious Lickey Incline (see Burcot below).

BURCOT
3 miles NE of Bromsgrove on the B4184

🏠 Locks at Tardebigge

Burcot was long associated with the Floyd family of blacksmiths, who had been blacksmiths in Ireland for 500 years before coming here to work at the long-established forge. During World War I three members of the Floyd family and one employee made 25,000 shoes for cavalry horses.

The stretch of railway that includes the Lickey Incline is, at 1 in 37.7, the steepest gradient on the whole of the British rail network. One specially powerful locomotive, 58100 (better known as Big Bertha), spent its days, up until the late 1950s, helping trains up the bank, a task which was later performed by massive double-boilered locomotives that were the most powerful in the then British Railways fleet. The steepness of the climb is due to the same geographical feature that necessitated the construction of the unique flight of **Locks at Tardebigge**, between Bromsgrove and Redditch. In the space of 2.5 miles the canal is lifted by no fewer than 30 locks. In the actual village of Tardebigge, on the A448, the Church of St Bartholomew enjoys a lovely setting with views across the Severn lowlands. Built in 1777 to the design of Francis Horn of Warwick, it has a slender tower capped by a delicate needle spire.

Around Bromsgrove – South

HANBURY
3 miles S of Bromsgrove off the B4090

🏤 Hanbury Hall   🪷 Jinney Ring Craft Centre

Hanbury Hall is a fine redbrick mansion in William & Mary style, completed by Thomas Vernon in 1701. Internal features include murals by Sir James Thornhill, known particularly for his Painted Hall in the Royal Naval Hospital, Greenwich, and frescoes in the dome of St Paul's. See also a splendid collection of porcelain, the Long Gallery, the Moorish gazebos at each corner of the

forecourt and the formal gardens with orangery and 18th century ice house.

In beautiful rural surroundings a mile north of the village of Hanbury stands the award-winning **Jinney Ring Craft Centre**. Richard and Jenny Greatwood created this marvellous place by restoring and converting a collection of old timbered barns next to their 17th century farmhouse home. Craftspeople with many diverse skills can be seen at work in their own craft studios, including two potters, a violin-maker, a jeweller, a picture-framer, a leatherworker, a sign-maker and an antiques restorer. Also on the premises is a craft gallery with changing exhibitions by British craftsmen and artists, and a clothes and knitwear department.

Woodland near Hanbury

🏤 historic building   📷 museum   🏛 historic site   🌣 scenic attraction   🌱 flora and fauna

FECKENHAM

7 miles SE of Bromsgrove on the B4090

A pretty village with half-timbered, redbrick and Georgian houses and the fine Church of St John the Baptist. Inside the church a board displays the benefaction which Charles I bestowed upon the village in 1665 - £6. 13 shillings and fourpence, payable out of forest land to the school. The forest in question once surrounded the village, but the trees were all felled for fuelling the saltpans and no trace of the forest now remains.

REDDITCH

6 miles E of Bromsgrove on the A448

🏠 Forge Mill Needle Museum

🏃 Arrow Valley Country Park

A New Town from the `60s, but there is plenty of history here, as well as some great walking. The **Arrow Valley Country Park**, comprises a vast expanse of parkland with nature trails, picnic areas and lovely walks. Sailing, canoeing, windsurfing and fishing are popular pastimes on the lake. There is a café, shop and countryside centre. One walk follows the river upstream to the ruins of Bordesley Abbey, a medieval Cistercian Abbey. Nearby is the **Forge Mill Needle Museum** telling the fascinating story of the Redditch needle-making industry.

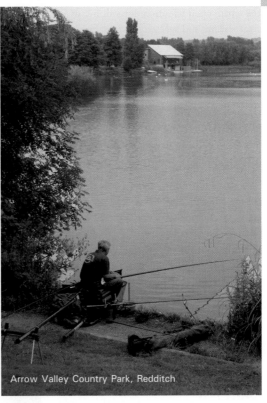

Arrow Valley Country Park, Redditch

WYTHALL

10 miles NE of Bromsgrove on the A435

🏠 Museum of Transport

Right on the other side of Redditch, and well on the way to Birmingham, is the **Birmingham and Midland Museum of Transport**. Founded in 1977, the museum's two large halls house a marvellous collection of some 100 buses and coaches, battery vehicles and fire engines, many having seen service in Birmingham and the West Midlands. It includes the largest collection of buses from the Midland Red fleet. Open Saturday and Sunday in summer.

WASELEY HILL

5 miles N of Bromsgrove of the B4551

🏃 Lickey Hills

Five miles north of Bromsgrove lies Wasely

Hill where open hillside and woodland offers great walking and spectacular views from the top of Windmill Hill. There is also a visitor centre. Just to the east there is more great walking and views in a varied landscape around the **Lickey Hills** which also has a visitor centre.

BELBROUGHTON
6 miles N of Bromsgrove on the B4188

🎄 Clent Hills

This village was once a centre of the scythe-making industry. Holy Trinity Church occupies a hillside site along with some pleasing Georgian buildings.

A little to the north are the village of Clent and the **Clent Hills**, an immensely popular place for walking and drinking in the views. On the top are four large upright stones which could be statement-making modern art but for the fact that they were put there over 200 years ago by Lord Lyttleton of Hagley Hall. Walton Hill is over 1,000 feet above sea level.

HAGLEY
8 miles N of Bromsgrove off the A491

🏛 Hagley Hall

George, 1st Lord Lyttleton, commissioned in 1756 the creation of what was to be the last great Palladian mansion in Britain, **Hagley Hall**. Imposing without, exotic and rococo within; notable are the Barrell Room with panelling from Holbeach Hall, where two of the Gunpowder Plotters – the Wintour brothers – were caught and later put to death in the favourite way of hanging, drawing and quartering. Temples, cascading pools and a ruined castle are some of the reasons for lingering in the park, which has a large herd of deer.

Another attraction at Hagley is the Falconry Centre on the A4565, where owls, hawks, falcons and eagles live and fly.

DODFORD
3 miles W of Bromsgrove off the A448

Not far out of Bromsgrove, north of the A448, lies the village of Dodford, whose Church of the Holy Trinity and St Mary is an outstanding example of an Arts and Crafts church, designed in 1908 by the Bromsgrove Guild in their interpretation of the neo-Gothic style.

CHADDESLEY CORBETT
4 miles W of Bromsgrove on the A448

A fairly sizeable village, dominated at its southern end by the 14th century Church of St Cassian. It is the only church in England to be dedicated to this saint, who was born in

Harvington Hall

Alexandria in the 5th century and became a bishop in Africa. He was also a schoolmaster and was apparently killed by his pupils.

HARVINGTON
5 miles W of Bromsgrove near junction of A448/A450

🏰 Harvington Hall

Harvington Hall is a moated medieval and Elizabethan manor house with a veritable maze of rooms. Mass was celebrated here during times when it was a very dangerous thing to do, and that is perhaps why the Hall has more priest holes than any other house in the land.

Kidderminster

🏰 St Mary's Church   🏛 Railway Museum

🌱 Stone House Cottage Garden

Known chiefly as a centre of the carpet-making industry, which began here early in the 18th century as a cottage industry. The introduction of the power loom brought wealth to the area and instigated the building of carpet mills. Standing on the River Stour, the town has a variety of mills, whose enormous chimneys dominate the skyline and serve as architectural monuments to Kidderminster's heritage. **St Mary's Church**, on a hill overlooking the town, is the largest parish church in the county and contains some superb tomb monuments. The Whittall Chapel, designed in 1922 by Sir Charles Gilbert Scott, was paid for by Matthew Whittall, a native of Kidderminster who went to America and made a fortune in carpets. Three beautiful windows depicting the Virgin Mary, Joan of Arc and Florence Nightingale, were given by his widow in his memory.

Kidderminster's best-known son is Rowland Hill, who founded the modern postal system and introduced the penny post; he was also a teacher, educationalist and inventor. His statue stands outside the Town Hall. By the station on the Severn Valley Railway is the **Kidderminster Railway Museum** with a splendid collection of railway memorabilia. Run by volunteers, it is housed in an old GWR grain store.

Just outside town, at Stone, on the A448, is **Stone House Cottage Garden**, a lovely walled garden with towers. Unusual wall shrubs, climbers and herbaceous plants are featured, most of them for sale in the nursery.

In the Stour Valley just north of Kidderminster is the village of Wolverley, with charming cottages and pretty gardens, the massive Church of St John the Baptist, and the remains – not easy to see – of prehistoric cave dwellings in the red sandstone cliffs.

Around Kidderminster

HARTLEBURY
7 miles W of Bromsgrove off the A449

🏰 Castle   🏛 Museum   🌱 Leapgate Country Park

Hartlebury Castle (see panel on page 72), a historic sandstone castle of the Bishops of Worcester and a prison for captured Royalist troops in the Civil War, now houses the **Worcester County Museum**. In the former servants' quarters in the north wing numerous permanent exhibitions show the past lives of the county's inhabitants from Roman times to the 20th century. Visitors can also admire the grandeur of the three Castle State Rooms.

🎭 stories and anecdotes   🎭 famous people   🎨 art and craft   🎭 entertainment and sport   🚶 walks

Hartlebury Castle

Hartlebury, Nr Kidderminster DY11 7XZ
Tel: 01299 250416
e-mail: museum@worcestershire.gov.uk
www.worcestershire.gov.uk/museum

Worcestershire County Museum is housed in
the servants quarters of Hartlebury Castle,
home to the Bishop of Worcester for over
600 years. The museum collection ranges
from fascinating toys and domestic items to
beautiful costume and ancient archaeological finds. The building also contains room
sets such as the Schoolroom as well as original rooms within the Castle including the
Scullery, Housekeeper's Room and Nursery. On most days visitors can also view the
Bishop's State rooms.

Within the grounds of the Castle you can also visit the Cider Mill and the Transport
Gallery housing a fascinating array of horse-drawn vehicles including a fire engine,
hansom cab and a large collection of Gypsy caravans.

A café area in the historic Castle Kitchen serves a range of freshly made lunches,
afternoon teas and refreshments using both local and fair trade products. The café is
also available for private hire and functions. There are also two outdoor picnic areas in
Old Moat Coppice and the Orchard. An external glass lift gives all visitors access to
the first and second floors of the Museum.

Opening Times: The County Museum and the
Castle Kitchen Café are open: 10am-5pm Tuesday

On Hartlebury Common, **Leapgate
Country Park** is a nature reserve in heath and
woodland, with the county's only acid bog.

SHATTERFORD

3 miles NW of Kidderminster on the A442

🌵 Wildlife Sanctuary   🌵 Kingsford Country Park

Shatterford **Wildlife Sanctuary** is home to
Sika deer, red deer, goats, sheep, wild boar,
pot-bellied pigs and koi carp.

Two miles further north, off the A442,
Kingsford Country Park covers 200 acres of
heath and woodland that is home to a wide
variety of birdlife. It extends into Kinver
Edge, across the border into Staffordshire,
and many waymarked walks start at this point.

BEWDLEY

3 miles W of Kidderminster on the A456

🏛 Museum   🏛 Severn Valley Railway

On the western bank of the Severn, linked to
its suburb Wribbenhall by a fine Thomas
Telford Bridge, Bewdley was once a
flourishing port, but lost some of its
importance when the Staffordshire &
Worcestershire Canal was built. It's a quiet,
civilised but much visited little town with
some good examples of Georgian
architecture, and has won fame with another
form of transport, the **Severn Valley
Railway**. Guaranteed to excite young and old
alike, the Severn Valley Railway operates a
full service of timetabled trains hauled by a

🏛 historic building   🏛 museum   🏛 historic site   🏞 scenic attraction   🌵 flora and fauna variety of steam locomotives. These include two Collett-designed ex-GWR 0-6-0 Pannier Tanks, 5764 and 7714; Ivatt 2-6-0 46443; and Stanier 2-6-0 42968. A distinguished summer visitor is Stanier Pacific 46223 *Duchess of Sutherland*. The service runs from Kidderminster to Bridgnorth, home of the railway since 1965, and the route takes in such scenic attractions as the Wyre Forest and the Severn Valley Country Park and Nature Reserve. Each of the stations – Bridgnorth, Hampton Loade, Country Park Halt, Highley, Arley, Bewdley and Kidderminster – is an architectural delight, and there are buffets at Bridgnorth and Kidderminster, and a tea room at Bewdley. New for 2007 is the Engine House at Highley (in Shropshire), with a large display of steam locomotives and a Visitor and Education centre. Visitors can realise a childhood dream by driving and firing a steam locomotive - call 01299 403816 for all information concerning the railway, the timetables and the special events that take place throughout the year.

Bewdley Museum, which also incorporates the Tourist Information Centre, is a great place for all the family, with exhibitions themed around the growth and trades of the town, including basket and besom makers, charcoal burners, pewterers, brass founders and wheelwrights. There are daily demonstrations of rope-making and clay pipe-making, and a fascinating programme of events throughout the year. Bewdley was the birthplace of Stanley Baldwin, three times Prime Minister between the World Wars. On the A456 between Bewdley and Kidderminster, the West Midland Safari & Leisure Park at Spring Grove provides a fantastic day out for the whole family.

CALLOW HILL
5 miles W of Kidderminster on the A456

🚶 Wyre Forest

The **Wyre Forest** Visitor Centre is set among mature oak woodland with forest walks, picnic area, gift shop and restaurant. Wyre Forest covers a vast area starting northwest of Bewdley and extending into Shropshire. The woodland, home to abundant flora and fauna, is quite dense in places. It was once inhabited by nomadic people who made their living from what was around them, weaving baskets and brooms, burning charcoal and making the little wooden whisks which were used in the carpet-making process. Just south of Callow Hill, the village of Rock has an imposing Norman church in a prominent hillside position with some lovely windows and carving.

STOURPORT-ON-SEVERN
3 miles S of Kidderminster on the A451

At the centre of the Worcestershire waterways is the unique Georgian 'canal town' of

Stourport-on-Severn

Stourport, famous for its intricate network of canal basins. There was not much trade, nor even much of a town, before the canals came, but prosperity came quickly once the Staffordshire & Worcestershire Canal had been dug. The commercial trade has gone, but the town still prospers, the barges laden with coal, timber, iron and grain having given way to pleasure craft. Many of the old barges have been renovated and adapted to this new role.

ASTLEY
5 miles S of Kidderminster on the A451

Stanley Baldwin (1867-1947), born in Bewdley, died at Astley Hall, opposite which stands a memorial stone inscribed "Thrice Prime Minister". (His ashes are buried in the nave of Worcester Cathedral.) Astley is also home to Astley Vineyards, a working vineyard producing award-winning white wines, with a vineyard trail and a shop. Visitors can arrive by car, by bus – or by boat, as they have mooring facilities.

ABBERLEY
7 miles SW of Kidderminster off the A451

🏛 Church

A truly delightful little place, surrounded by hills. The Norman **Church of St Michael** was saved from complete dilapidation in the 1960s, and the part that survives, the chancel, is certainly well worth a visit, not only for its charming ambience but also for the treasures it holds. On the other side of the hill is Abberley Hall, now a school, with a Big Ben-like bell tower that can be seen for miles around. Old Boys include former Foreign Secretary Geoffrey Howe and the late actor Sir Anthony Quayle.

GREAT WITLEY
8 miles SW of Kidderminster on the A443

🏛 Church   🏛 Witley Court

🖋 Jerwood Sculpture Path

There are two great reasons not to miss this place. **Great Witley Church**, almost ordinary from the outside, has an unbelievable interior of Baroque flamboyance that glows with light in a stunning ambience of gold and white. Masters of their crafts contributed to the interior, which was actually removed from the Chapel of Canons in Edgware: Joshua Price stained glass, 23 ceiling paintings by Antonio Bellucci, plasterwork by Bagutti.

Next to the church are the spectacular and hauntingly beautiful remains of **Witley Court**, a palatial mansion funded by the riches of the Dudley family. Destroyed by fire in 1937, it stood a neglected shell for years, until English Heritage took over these most splendid of ruins and started the enormous task of making them safe and accessible. If you only see one ruin in the whole county, this should be it. Restoration work on the West Wing has made several rooms accessible to the public for the first time. Across from the ruins is a magnificent fountain, said to be the largest in Britain. Inspired by Bernini's fountains in Rome, it rises 26ft feet and is crowned by an opulent sculpture that depicts Perseus rescuing Andromeda from a sea-monster. Also within the grounds is the **Jerwood Sculpture Park** which has a permanent collection including work by Elizabeth Frink and Anthony Gormley and also stages temporary exhibitions during the summer months.

THE FOOD HALL

Cromer House, Teme Street, Tenbury Wells,
Worcestershire WR15 8AA
Tel: 01584 810071

Owners Philip Saxon and Brian Howells have put their long experience to excellent use at **The Food Hall**, where they have built up a fine reputation for quality, consistency and prompt, friendly service.

The meat choice is absolutely outstanding, from prime beef from Herefordshire and Scotland to Gloucester Old Spot pork, local lamb, free-range chickens, game in season, cooked hams, bacon, homemade sausages and locally-made pies.

They also sell fresh fish, of which hot smoked salmon is their speciality, fine English cheeses, delicatessen items such as salami, salads and olives, Dairy House yoghurt from Weobley and Just Rachel ice cream from Ledbury with wonderful flavours such as honeycomb or treacle toffee. The Food Hall occupies a modern building next to the Library in the centre of town.

TENBURY WELLS

12 miles SW of Kidderminster on the A456

🏛 Museum 🌳 Burford House

The A443 leads from Great Witley towards Shropshire and the border town of Tenbury Wells in a delightfully rural setting on the River Teme. The 'Wells' was added when a source of mineral water was discovered, but its heyday as a spa resort was very brief. **Tenbury Museum** tells the spa story and depicts other aspects of local life, including hop-growing and the railway days. In the market place is a curious oval-shaped building with rather ecclesiastical-looking windows. This is the Market House, which was built in 1811 and used as a corn and butter market.

Set in sweeping lawns on the banks of the River Teme, in the village of Burford a mile west of Tenbury (and just in Shropshire) stands **Burford House**, whose four-acre gardens are filled with well over 2,000 varieties of plants. This is the home of the National Collection of Clematis, and in the nursery attached to the garden almost 400 varieties of clematis are for sale, along with many other plants and gifts. The ground floor of the house is open as a gallery of contemporary art. Teas and light meals are served in the Burford Buttery.

LOCATOR MAP

ADVERTISERS AND PLACES OF INTEREST

🏚 historic building   🏛 museum   🏛 historic site   🏞 scenic attraction   🌿 flora and fauna

3| Shropshire

The tranquil, romantic face of Shropshire belies an often turbulent past that is revealed at scores of sites by the remains of dykes, ramparts and hill forts, and by the castles of the Marcher Lords, who seem to have divided their time between fighting the Welsh and fighting each other. The county boasts some of Britain's most important Roman sites, notably at Wroxeter, which at one time was the fourth largest Roman town in the land. Shropshire beckons with a landscape of great variety: the little hills and valleys, the lakes and canals of the northwest, the amazing parallel hill ranges towards the south, the rich farming plains around Oswestry, the forests of Clun and Wyre, Ironbridge Gorge, called the birthplace of the Industrial Revolution. This stretch of the Severn Valley is now a World Heritage Centre, which ranks it alongside the Pyramids, the Grand Canyon and the Taj Mahal, and several interesting museums can be found here. Add to this the historic towns of Shrewsbury, Ludlow and Oswestry, the churches and the stately homes and the glorious gardens and you have a part of the world just waiting to be explored, whether by car, on a bike or on foot. South Shropshire affords a trip through history, including the wonderful town of Ludlow and the spectacular scenery of Wenlock Ridge, Long Mynd and Clun.

The Mere, Ellesmere

Ludlow

🏛 Castle   🏛 Church of St Lawrence   🏛 Museum

🍃 Festival

Often called 'the perfect historic town', Ludlow is an enchanting place with more than 500 listed buildings and a medieval street pattern that has been kept virtually intact. There are some lovely walks along the banks of the River Teme with its plentiful wildlife, markets on Mondays, Wednesdays, Fridays and Saturdays, a livestock market on Mondays, and regular flea markets on Sundays.

Ludlow Castle was built by the Normans in the 11th century, one of a line of castles along the Marches to keep out the Welsh. Under its protection a large town was planned and built - and prospered, due to the collection and sale of wool and the manufacture of cloth. The Castle has been home to many distinguished families and to Royalty: Edward V, Prince Arthur and other Royal children were brought up in Ludlow, and the Castle became the headquarters of the Council of the Marches, which governed Wales and the border counties until 1689. The parish **Church of St Laurence** is one of the largest in the county, reflecting the town's affluence at the time of its rebuilding in the 15th century. There are fine misericords and stained glass, and the poet AE Housman, author of *A Shropshire Lad*, is commemorated on the outer wall of the church; his ashes lie outside the north door. Other places which should be seen include Castle Lodge, once a

ANDREW FRANCIS

1 Market Street, Ludlow,
Shropshire SY8 1BD
Tel: 01584 872008 Fax: 01584 711785

Andrew Francis has been a butcher for 25 years, 15 of them in Ludlow and the last two here in the centre of town a short walk from the Castle.

Quality is the keynote throughout the range on sale: Hereford and Welsh black beef, Berkshire and Gloucester Old Spot pork, prime local lamb, wild venison from Mortimer Forest in steaks, joints, casserole meat and sausages, wild duck, rabbit, pigeon, home-cured bacon and ham, free-range poultry and eggs. Andrew's award-winning sausages, pork pies and steak pies are all cooked on the premises.

Outside catering includes hog roasts and barbecues, and the shop supplies many of the top local pubs, restaurants and hotels, including the renowned Feathers Hotel a few streets away. In spring and summer, hanging baskets make a colourful sight outside the shop, which is open from 7am to 5pm (6am to 5pm Friday and Saturday; closed Sunday)

Ludlow Castle

archaeology. At one time in the last century glove-making was one of the chief occupations in the town. Nine master glovers employed some 700 women and children, each required to produce ten pairs of gloves a week, mainly for the American market.

The Ludlow Festival, held annually since 1960 and lasting a fortnight in June/July, has become one of the major arts festivals in the country. The centrepiece of the festival, an open-air performance of a Shakespeare play in the Castle's inner bailey, is supported by a number of events that have included orchestral concerts, musical recitals, literary and historical lectures, exhibitions, readings and workshops.

prison and later home of the officials of the Council of the Marches, and the fascinating houses that line Broad Street.

Ludlow Museum, in Castle Street has exhibitions of local history centred on, among other things, the Castle, the town's trade and special features on local geology and

BROMLEY COURT

Lower Broad Street, Ludlow, Shropshire SY8 1PQ
Tel: 01584 876996   Fax: 01584 873666
e-mail: phil@ludlowhotels.com   website: www.ludlowhotels.com

Three handsome Tudor cottages in a conservation area of Ludlow have been converted to provide outstanding Bed & Breakfast accommodation for visitors to this historic town. Each of the three cottages at **Bromley Court** forms a private suite, individually decorated and furnished,

bedroom with en suite bathroom (bath and shower) and a comfortable sitting room. The properties have a wealth of oak beams, and two of the suites boast inglenook fireplaces.

Each suite has a breakfast bar provided with everything needed for a Continental breakfast, or for a more substantial start to the day guests can wander along to the Bull Hotel at the Bull Ring, where they can enjoy a full traditional English breakfast. Ludlow is a

delightful place with a wealth of history and more than 500 listed buildings.

Visitors should put plenty of time aside to discover everything the town has to offer, and there's no more comfortable a base than Bromley Court.

BROAD BEAN WHOLEFOOD

60 Broad Street, Ludlow, Shropshire SY8 1NH
Tel: 01584 874239
e-mail: ianbox2004-bean@yahoo.co.uk
website: www.broad-bean.co.uk

In the heart of Ludlow, **Broad Bean Wholefood** provides a relaxed environment for shopping for an exciting range of wholefood, drink and health products. Opened in 1977 by the Jones family from London, the shop originally just sold wholefoods from sacks. The range expanded over the years, particularly after 2001, when the business was acquired by Ian Maxwell Muller. Best sellers naturally keep their place on the shelves, and new items are continually being added.

The stock includes organic meat and fish, more than 20 cheeses, chilled dairy and deli products, nuts, grains, seeds and dried fruits, cakes, speciality flour, teas, infusions, coffees, juices and alcoholic drinks (organic and non-organic wines, own label and other beers, organic cider, meads and speciality liqueurs). Also for sale are dietary supplements, gluten- and wheat-free foods, homeopathic remedies and beauty products.

Personal service is a watchword, and though browsing is encouraged (and very enjoyable!) Ian and his staff are always on hand with help and advice.

Around Ludlow

CLEOBURY MORTIMER
8 miles E of Ludlow on the A4117

🏛 Church

A famous landmark in this pleasing small town just west of the Forest of Wyre is the crooked spire of **St Mary's Church**, whose east window commemorates the 14th century poet, William Langland. His best known work is *Piers Plowman*, an indignant tract against rural poverty in a landscape still recognisable as south Shropshire.

It was in Cleobury Mortimer that Maisie Bloomer, a witch, gained notoriety in the 18th century. Curses and love potions were her speciality, and the villagers were in no doubt

that she was in league with the Devil.

Two miles east of Cleobury stands Mawley Hall, an 18th century stone house with some very fine internal features.

CLEE HILL
4 miles E of Ludlow on the A4117

🦌 Brown Clee

The Clee Hills to the north of the village include the highest peaks in the county. The summit of **Brown Clee** is 1,750 feet above sea level.

STANTON LACY
2 miles NW of Ludlow off the B4365

This charming little village with its black and white cottages sits on the bank of the River Corve and is notable for its Church of St

SEIFTON COURT

Seifton, nr Ludlow, Shropshire SY8 2DG
Tel: 01584 861214
e-mail: seiftoncourt@fsmail.net
website: www.seiftoncourt.co.uk

Five miles from Ludlow in the heart of the
tranquil Corvedale Valley, **Seifton Court** is the
perfect place for a relaxing break away from
the hustle and bustle of city life. The Tudor
farmhouse, which has a 4 Diamond rating, is
the family home of Jane Tomkinson. The
house has retained much of its old-world

charm, with sturdy beams and inglenook fireplaces, and the two en
suite bedrooms combine period character with modern comfort and
amenities. The cosy guest lounge has television and open fires, and
the garden is a pleasant place for a stroll.

Jane uses local produce, including vegetables and herbs from her
garden, in the excellent breakfasts and optional evening meals that
start and end the day. The house is an ideal base for walking and
sightseeing, with Stokesay Castle and the Shropshire Hills Discovery
centre nearby, and Ludlow, described by John Betjeman as 'England's
finest town', a few minutes' drive away. A unique offering at Seifton
Court is Mind & Body Detox Weekends, which include group and one-
to-one yoga sessions, meditation and delicious Ayurvedic meals. Jane
is also part of the Marches Horse Trails which provides B&B for riders
and their horses (www.marcheshorsetrails.co.uk).

Peter, which has some Saxon features and
Victorian stained glass.

BROMFIELD
3 miles NW of Ludlow on the A49

🏠 Church   🐎 Racecourse

Although the busy A49 runs through the centre
of the village, **St Mary's Church** is beautifully
sited close to where the River Teme joins up
with the River Onny. Originally a priory, it
became a private residence for one George
Foxe following the dissolution of the
monasteries. What is now the chancel was once
the dining room but the extraordinary painted
ceiling was created after the building once again
became a church in the mid-1600s. The swirling
figures with their ribbons bearing biblical texts
have been described as "the best example of

the worst style of ecclesiastical art". Another
striking feature here is the huge mural coat of
arms of Charles II on the south wall.

About a mile northeast of Bromfield is
Ludlow Racecourse (National Hunt) where
Bronze Age barrows have been brought to
light.

ONIBURY
5 miles NW of Ludlow off the A49

🐓 The Wernlas Collection

"I didn't know chickens could be so
beautiful," was the comment of one visitor to
The Wernlas Collection, a living museum of
rare poultry. The setting of this 20-acre
smallholding is a joy in itself, and the
collection is an internationally acclaimed
conservation centre and vital gene pool where

🎭 stories and anecdotes   🕊 famous people   🎨 art and craft   🎪 entertainment and sport   🚶 walks over 15,000 chicks are hatched each year, all year round. Besides the 220 breeds of chickens there are rare breeds of goats, sheep and pigs, and some donkeys. The gift shop is themed on chickens - a chickaholic's paradise, in fact - and eggs and vaccinated and salmonella tested chicks are also on sale.

STOKESAY
7 miles NW of Ludlow off the A49

🏚 Castle 🏚 Church

The de Say family of nearby Clun started **Stokesay Castle** in about 1240, and a Ludlow wool merchant, Lawrence de Ludlow, made considerable additions, including the Great Hall and fortified south tower. It is the oldest fortified manor house in England and is substantially complete, making it easy to see how a rich medieval merchant would have lived. Entrance to this magnificent building is through a splendid timber-framed gatehouse and the cottage-style gardens are an extra delight. An audio tour guides visitors round the site.

The adjacent parish **Church of St John the Baptist** is unusual in having been restored during Cromwell's rule after sustaining severe damage in the Civil War. A remarkable feature in the nave is a series of biblical texts written in giant script on the walls. The 17th century box pews and pulpit are still in use and, outside, the churchyard is managed as semi-wild, allowing some 88 species of wild flowers to flourish.

Craven Arms

🏛 Secret Hills

The village takes its name from the hotel and pub built by the Earl of Craven. The coming of the railways caused the community to be developed, and it was also at the centre of

several roads that were once used by sheep-drovers moving their flocks from Wales to the English markets. In its heyday Craven Arms held one of the largest sheep auctions in Britain, with as many as 20,000 sheep being sold in a single day.

Shropshire's landscape has inspired the music of Vaughan Williams, the poems of AE Housman and the novels of Mary Webb. At the **Secret Hills,** Shropshire Hills Discovery Centre, visitors can discover the heritage, wildlife and traditions of the area in a striking all-weather building with a grass roof made from 1,000 square metres of turf weighing more than 70 tons. Rocks that have travelled 7,000 miles from the equator over the last 560 million years; a mammoth skeleton from Shropshire's last Ice Age 13,000 years ago, and a simulated balloon flight over the hills are just some of the attractions. Outside, visitors can wander through 25 acres of attractive meadows sloping down to the River Onny. The centre has a gift shop, café and information point, and there's a programme of regular events and craft exhibitions throughout the year.

Around Craven Arms

CLUN
8 miles W of Craven Arms on the A488/ B4368

🏚 Castle 🏚 Church 🏛 Museum 🏛 Bury Ditches

A quiet, picturesque little town in the valley of the River Clun, overlooked by the ruins of its **Castle**, which was once the stronghold of the Fitzalan family. The shell of the keep and the earthworks are the main surviving features. The **Church of St George** has a fortress-like tower with small windows and a lovely 17th century tiered pyramidal top. There are also some splendid Norman arcades with circular pillars and scalloped capitals. The 14th century north aisle roof and restored nave roof are an impressive sight that will keep necks craning for some time. Some wonderful Jacobean woodwork and a marvellous medieval studded canopy are

Clun Castle

other sights worth lingering over at this beautiful church, which is a great tribute to GE Street, who was responsible for its restoration in 1876. Geological finds are the main attractions in the little **Local History** **Museum** in the Town Hall. The real things are to be found on site at **Bury Ditches**, north of Clun on the way to Bishop's Castle. The Ditches are an Iron Age fort on a seven-acre tree-covered site.

THE ORGANIC SMOKEHOUSE

Clunbury Hall, Clunbury,
Shropshire SY7 0HG
Tel/Fax: 01588 661206
e-mail: info@organicsmokehouse.com
website: www.organicsmokehouse.com

Near Craven Arms in the beautiful Shropshire countryside, **The Organic Smokehouse** provides the very finest award-winning organic smoked food. 'Exceptional ingredients – perfectly smoked' sums up the reputation gained by this outstanding enterprise, which is run by Deborah and Michael Leviseur. Michael learned his smoking expertise in the Outer Hebrides, where, incidentally, he also became a qualified weaver of Harris Tweed. Salmon, obtained where possible from smaller suppliers, is slowly cold-smoked over Shropshire oak for the finest possible flavour.

Other equally superb products of the smokehouse include smoked salmon mousse, salmon fillets, smoked sea salt, smoked butter, smoked cheeses – cheddar, parmesan, soft sheep's cheese – and smoked extra virgin olive oil from Crete. Goods can be ordered by phone, by e-mail, by fax or by post.

stories and anecdotes   famous people   art and craft   entertainment and sport   walks

Nipstone Rock

Distance: *2.5 miles (4.0 kilometres)*

Typical time: *90 mins*

Height gain: *80 metres*

Map: *Explorer 216*

Walk: *www.walkingworld.com ID:2541*

Contributor: *Jim Grindle*

Stiperstones village and the Bog are signposted from the A488 near Minsterly; the A488 joins the A5 Shrewsbury by-pass. There is ample free parking by the Bog crossroads. For travel information call 0870 608 2608.

At the crossroads is an outdoor activity centre in an old school. At summer weekends, and mid-week at times, a volunteer group offers refreshments here; there are also toilets. For details e-mail info@thresholdscentre.co.uk or look at www.shropshire-cc.gov.uk/discover.nsf

Mary Webb, the Shropshire author, set one of her novels, 'The Golden Arrow', in the Stiperstones area and there are many legends concerning the rocks - don't spend the night in the Devil's Chair for instance, or else...... A film of her novel, 'Gone to Earth', was made here. The district has been known since Roman times though, as an intensively industrialised mining area, mainly lead and barytes, and many chimneys and spoil heaps can be seen the western slopes. The main geological feature is the quartz capping of the ridge, some 480 million years old and shattered by frost in the last Ice Age resulting in the huge outcrops we see today.

The walk starts from The Bog an area which even 50 years ago had some fading signs of the intense industrial activity of Victorian days. The start is relatively high and gives good views for very little climbing. Some mapped areas of woodland have been removed to restore the heather habitat, part of the Stiperstones Purple Project by English Nature.

Hills or Fells, Pub, Toilets, Birds, Flowers, Great Views, Butterflies, Good for Kids, Industrial Archaeology, Tea Shop, Woodland

1 | At the higher end of the Bog car park is a signpost for two waymarked walks. Turn right, following The Mucklewick Walk. This takes you past a small pond where you are directed to the left through trees. You reach a flight of steps going up to the right. At the top is a stile next to the telegraph pole. Cross the stile and follow the line of poles uphill to a stile in a fence. After this the footpath goes diagonally left away from the line of poles and ends at a stile on a lane.

2 | Don't cross this stile but turn round and look across the large field. Go first just to the left of the telegraph pole in front and then follow the line of trees making for the extreme left end of the wood in front.

3 | At the end of the wood and to the right of the more obvious gate is a stile with signposts for the Shropshire Way (a buzzard) and the Mucklewick Walk. Cross this and follow a path along the edge of the wood to a stile at its far end. At the moment you can go around the stile. Just in sight is a crossing track with signposts.

4 | Cross the track and go through the gate. The route is now well signposted both for the Mucklewick Walk and the Shropshire Way (the buzzard symbol). It leads past the Nipstone Rock, the last of the Stiperstones, over to your right across the fence. After this it goes into another plantation where you must watch for a signpost at the bottom of a drop in the ground.

5 | At this point the two waymarked routes divide - our route goes to the right, following the Mucklewick Walk. 100m away it comes to a stile and a lane. Cross the lane to the far stile and then go to the hedge and fence beyond. At the fence the Mucklewick Walk is signposted to the left but our route goes to the right, following a farm track for a very short distance almost as far as a gateway with cattlegrid.

6 | Leave the track and follow the hedge to a stile. Continue by the hedge (really a line of trees with some laburnum) until you see the way into the next field. There is no gate, just a gap. When you have gone through it you will have a fence on your right with a farm behind it. Follow the fence, which bends a few times, to its corner where there is a stile leading into a wood.

7 | The path goes along the edge of the wood but soon ends at a newish forest road. Cross this onto a grassy firebreak and continue when the surfaced is stony. The route is well signposted at all junctions. There is no change in direction and several gates. After passing a reedy lake which you can just about make out on your left, the forest paths end at a metal gate. Keep straight ahead over the crossing track and you will come to a lane.

8 | Turn left and after about 20m you will see the wide open area which is the car park. Turn right and cross to the far side where the walk started.

Down the valley are other Cluns: **Clunton**, **Clunbury** and **Clungunford**. The quartet were idyllically described by AE Housman in *A Shropshire Lad*:

> *In valleys of springs and rivers,*
> *By Onny and Teme and Clun,*
> *The country for easy livers,*
> *The quietest under the sun.*

ASTON ON CLUN
3 miles W of Craven Arms off the B4368

🌳 Arbor Tree Dressing

Not one of Housman's Cluns, but well worth a mention and a visit. The village's **Arbor Tree Dressing** ceremony has been held every year since 1786. Following the Battle of Worcester in 1651, King Charles spent some time up a tree (see under Boscobel) and to commemorate his escape he proclaimed Arbor Day, a day in May, as a national holiday when tree-dressing took place. The custom generally died out but was revived here in 1786 when a local landowner married. As Aston was part of his estate he revived the tradition of dressing the Black Poplar in the middle of the village, a custom that still survives.

BISHOP'S CASTLE
9 miles NW of Craven Arms off the A488

🏛 Museum   🏛 Mitchell's Fold   ⚔ Stiperstones

This small and ancient town lies in an area of great natural beauty in solitary border country. Little remains of the castle, built in the 12th century for the Bishops of Hereford, which gave the place its name, but there is no shortage of fine old buildings for the visitor to see. The **House on Crutches Museum**, sited in one of the oldest and most picturesque of these buildings, recounts the town's history. Its gable end is supported on wooden posts – hence the name. North of Bishop's Castle lie the **Stiperstones**, a rock-strewn quartzite outcrop rising to a height of 1,700ft at the Devil's Chair. A bleak place of brooding solitude, the ridge is part of a 1,000-acre National Nature Reserve and on the lower slopes gaunt chimneys, derelict buildings and neglected roads and paths are silent reminders of the lead-mining industry that flourished here from Roman times until the 19th century. To the west, on the other

---

GET AHEAD HATS

Middle Aston, near Bishop's Castle, Powys SY15 6TA
Tel: 01588 638246
website: www.getaheadhats.co.uk and
www.getaheadhats/montgomery.php

Special hats for special occasions - that's the proud boast of **Get Ahead Hats**! Nowela Swanson opened her boutique five years ago, selling and hiring out hats exclusively designed by herself and some of the top UK milliners. Elegance and style are the watchwords here, and there are flexible opening hours with evenings by appointment. There is also a wide range of beautiful accessories, such as jewellery, handbags and shoes.

COUNTRY WORKS

Broad Street, Montgomery, Powys SY15 6PH
Tel: 01686 668866
e-mail: countryworks@btconnect.com
website: www.countryworksgallery.co.uk

For over 19 years, **Country Works,** a small, exclusive gallery, has been exhibiting and selling original works of art, including paintings etchings, jewellery, ceramics, glass clothes and cards. It is owned and managed by Barbara Geddes, who brings a wealth of experience to showcasing the work of local artists and craftspeople. She is determined to stock and sell only the best artistic works, and everything is keenly priced so that you, the customer, can own a work of art that you will treasure and admire for many years. The shop was opened in 1987, and Barbara has been here now for four years, offering friendly, helpful advice to people who call in. Country Works has been an award winner in the *Country Living* Small Business Award schemes!

There are two floors, with the upstairs floor being given over to exhibitions of paintings and such like. These exhibitions change every six weeks, and they have featured such local artists as Jenny Jones and Anna Ravenscroft. There have also been exhibitions of pottery, glass and even books.

Country Works is open 10am to 5.30pm from Monday to Saturday and from 1pm to 5pm on Sundays. It closes over Christmas and New Year, but stays open on bank holidays.

---

side of the A49 near **Chirbury**, is **Mitchell's Fold** stone circle, a Bronze Age circle of 15 stones. This is Shropshire's oldest monument, its origins and purpose unknown.

ACTON SCOTT
5 miles NE of Craven Arms off the A49

🐑 Working Farm

Signposted off the A49 just south of Church Stretton, **Acton Scott Historic Working Farm** offers a fascinating insight into farming and rural life as practised in the South Shropshire hills at the close of the 19th century. Owned by Shropshire County Council, it is a living museum with a commitment to preserving both traditional farming techniques and rural craft skills. Every day visitors can see milking by hand

and butter-making in the dairy. There are weekly visits from the wheelwright, farrier and blacksmith, while in the fields the farming year unfolds with ploughing, sowing and harvesting. Special attractions include lambing, shearing, cider-making and threshing with steam and flail. The waggoner and his team of heavy horses provide the power to work the land, while the stockman looks after the farm's livestock, among which are many rare breeds of cattle, sheep and pigs.

Church Stretton

🏛 Church 🚶 Long Mynd 🚶 Carding Mill Valley

🚶 Rectory Wood

The town has a long history - King John granted a charter in 1214 - and traces of the

CHADSTONE

Aston Munslow, nr Craven Arms, Shropshire SY7 9ER
Tel: 01584 841675 Fax: 01584 841620
e-mail: chadstone.lee@btinternet.com
website: chadstonebandb.co.uk

Chadstone is a spacious modern dormer bungalow standing in two acres of grounds in the Corvedale, with lovely countryside all around and splendid views of the Clee Hills. Owner Judith Lee keeps out the welcome mat for her guests, offering friendly personal service and every comfort in three luxuriously appointed bedrooms. These comprise two twin-bedded rooms and a double, all tastefully decorated and furnished, with shower and bath en suite, TV, hot beverage tray and hairdryer. Rooms are booked on a B&B basis, but an evening meal is available by arrangement.

Winner of a Visit Britain Silver Award, Chadstone lies on the B4368 a short drive from the A49 at Craven Arms. It is an ideal base for exploring the tranquil Shropshire countryside and guests will find plenty of books and local information in the roomy lounge. Aston Munslow is the start point of a number of interesting local walks, and Ludlow, Church Stretton, Wenlock Edge, the historic working farm at Acton Scott and several National Trust properties are within easy reach.

CHOCOLATE HAVEN

Shop 2, Sandford Court, Sandford Avenue,
Church Stretton, Shropshire SY6 6BH
Tel: 01694 722630
e-mail: enquiries@chocolatehaven.co.uk
website: www.chocolatehaven.co.uk

Many people dream of owning and running a chocolate shop, but very few realise those dreams. One of those lucky few is Lavinia Ratcliffe, who opened her **Chocolate Haven** in 1999. The great majority of the goodies on display are top-quality Belgian chocolates, all either totally handmade or hand-finished. All the leading brands are featured, along with some local Shropshire chocolates and some that are sugar-free. But the shop sells much more than chocolates.

Other temptations include handmade fudge and nougat, Turkish Delight, marzipan, praline, truffles, and the sort of sweets we'd almost forgotten: six flavours of toffee bonbons, mint imperials, sweet tobacco, jellies, sugar mice. Bennett's Farmhouse ice creams come in vanilla, vanilla with seeds and 20 other flavours, and among other local goods are flavour-packed preserves. This is a perfect place to find a gift, and customers can have their own gift boxes made up. Chocolate haven is open from 10am to 5pm Monday to Saturday, and on Sundays from 12 noon to 5pm.

MALT HOUSE FARM B&B

Lower Wood, Church Stretton, Shropshire SY6 6LF
Tel/Fax: 01694 751379

Malt House Farm B&B is located on a beef and sheep farm in a secluded position on the lower slopes of the Long Mynd. Lyn and Don Bloor are delightful hosts, and the atmosphere in their house is warm and welcoming. The en suite bedrooms are both charming and very comfortable, and the day rooms include a sitting room with books and magazines and a dining room with a huge inglenook fireplace, all decorated and furnished in keeping with the age of the house – it was first modernised in 1772!

The owners provide a hearty breakfast to start the day, setting up their guests for a day exploring the region, and evening meals are available with a little notice. The area round the house is a paradise for walkers and lovers of the great outdoors, and riding, golf and tennis are available nearby. Church Stretton is just three miles away, and Shrewsbury, Ludlow and Iron Bridge and a number of castles and country houses are within an easy drive. The Malt House is a no-smoking establishment, with no children or pets to disturb the peace.

🏠 historic building 🏛 museum 🏚 historic site 🌱 scenic attraction 🌿 flora and fauna medieval town are to be seen among the 18th and 19th century buildings in the High Street.

Elsewhere in the town, many of the black-and-white timbered buildings are not so old as they look, having been built when the town had ideas of becoming a health resort. Just behind the High Street stands the **Church of St Laurence**, with Saxon foundations, a Norman nave and a tower dating from about 1200. Over the aisle is a memorial to a tragic event that happened in 1968 when three boys were killed in a fire. The memorial is in the form of a gridiron, with flakes of copper simulating flames. The gridiron is the symbol of St Laurence, who was burnt to death on one in AD258. The Victorian novelist Sarah Smith, who wrote under the name of Hesba Stretton, was a frequent visitor to nearby All Stretton, and there is a small memorial window to her in the south transept.

A mile from the town centre are **Carding Mill Valley** and the extensive ridge known as **Long Mynd**. The valley and the moorland into which it runs are National Trust property and very popular for walking and picnicking. This wild area of heath affords marvellous views across Shropshire to the Cheshire Plains and the Black Mountains. Just below Long Mynd is Rectory Wood, which once formed part of the rectory church at Church Stretton. Three marked walks in the vicinity of the woods include a sculpture trail, and the woodland itself provides a valuable habitat for birds, bats and other wildlife.

Long Mynd

Around Church Stretton

LITTLE STRETTON
2 miles S of Church Stretton on the B4370

🏛 Church

The village of Little Stretton nestles in the Stretton Gap, with the wooded slopes of Ragleth to the east and Long Mynd to the west. It is a peaceful spot, bypassed by the A49, and is a delightful place for a stroll. The most photographed building is **All Saints Church**, with a black and white timbered frame, a thatched roof and the general look of a cottage rather than a church. When built in 1903 it had an iron roof, but this was soon found to be too noisy and was replaced with thatch (heather initially, then the straw that tops it today). Among many other interesting buildings are Manor House, a cruck hall dating

JOHN ALLEN UPHOLSTERY

Unit 3, Home Farm, Leebotwood, Shropshire SY6 6LX
Tel/Fax: 01694 751780
website: www.antique-upholstery.co.uk

Based in a rural village workshop, master upholsterer John Allen has been specialising in the creation and restoration of fine upholstery for well over 30 years. Working with a wide variety of materials and fabrics, in styles

ranging from classic to the modern, John employs the meticulous, time-honoured methods of the traditional craftsman, serving everyone from private clients to such prestigious customers as English Heritage and the National Trust.

His reputation now firmly established, commissions are available to order, and John has recently launched his own range of inexpensive antique-style French painted furniture, which can be upholstered by hand in the fabric of your choice.

HEATHER BRAE

Leebotwood, nr Church Stretton, Shropshire SY6 6LU
Tel: 01694 751757
website: www.heatherbraeshropshire.co.uk

Jane Taylor and Mary Mullock renovated an old garage and turned it into a delightful lifestyle shop that has quickly won many loyal friends. **Heather Brae** is filled with a carefully chosen, eclectic selection of items large and small for the house and garden, and a wide variety of gift ideas. On display are chinaware and pottery, tins and jars and other kitchenalaia, brooches, vintage and contemporary jewellery, semi-precious stones, home-made soaps, candles and

lanterns, leather goods, embroidery, dolls and toys and mobiles, leather goods, watercolours and cards for all occasions.

For the outside and garden there are sculptures and ornaments, benches, and superb locally made wrought-iron arches. It's a great place for browsing and the stock is constantly changing, so every visit is guaranteed to reveal new and delightful surprises. Hard to beat when looking for a personal treat or an unusual present, Heather Brae is open from 10 to 5.30 every day except Tuesday.

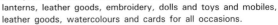

MYND HOUSE GUEST HOUSE

Little Stretton, nr Church Stretton,
Shropshire SY6 6RB
Tel: 01694 722212
e-mail: info@myndhouse.co.uk
website: www.myndhouse.co.uk

Mynd House is a Bed & Breakfast guest house located in an unspoilt village at the foot of the extensive heathland ridge known as Long Mynd. Seven spacious letting rooms cater for singles, couples, families and small groups of friends.

Top of the range are the romantic four-poster suite with a spa bath and an intimate sitting area for two, and the family room with a Queen-size bed in one room and two single beds in a connecting room, with space for a third bed if needed. Owners Sue and Dave Pember provide an excellent breakfast to start the day, and packed lunches and afternoon teas can be arranged.

This is a wonderful part of the world for walking, cycling and riding, Sue and Dave have a good selection of books and maps detailing local walks and places of interest. The house has a drying area for wet clothes and storage space for bikes.

from 1500, and Bircher Cottage, of a similar vintage.

'Switzerland without the wolves and avalanches' is a description sometimes applied to this beautiful, serene part of the world.

ACTON BURNELL
7m NE of Church Stretton off the A49

This charming small village takes its name from Robert Burnell who was Bishop of Bath and Wells and Lord Chancellor to Edward I. In his latter role he entertained the king here in 1283 and one of the first true Parliaments took place in the castle (more of a fortified residence, really) whose ruins of bright red sandstone stand behind the church. Burnell had built the church of St Mary only a decade before the king's visit. It's an elegantly

proportioned Early Gothic building with a simple interior that shows off to advantage the impressive late-16th century alabaster tomb of a later Lord of the Manor, Sir Richard Lee.

Bridgnorth

🏛 Castle 🏛 Bishop Percy's House 🏚 Museums
🚋 Cliff Railway 🚂 Severn Valley Railway

The ancient market town of Bridgnorth, straddling the River Severn, comprises Low Town and, 100 feet up sandstone cliffs, High Town. The year 1101 is a key date in its history – the year in which the Norman **Castle** was built by Robert de Belesme from Quatt. All that remains of the castle is part of the keep tower, which leans at an angle of about 17 degrees (more than that of the Leaning Tower of Pisa) as a result of an attempt to demolish it after the Civil War. The castle grounds offer splendid views of the river, and when King Charles 1 stayed here in 1642 he declared the view from the **Castle Walk** to be the finest in his dominion. The **Northgate Museum** is a good place to start a tour of this interesting town. It occupies rooms over the arches of the North Gate, which is the only one of the town's original fortifications to survive - though most of it was rebuilt in the 18th century. The **Costume and Childhood Museum** incorporates a costume gallery, a complete Victorian nursery and a collection of rare minerals. It's a really charming place that appeals to all ages. The Civil War caused great damage in Bridgnorth and the lovely Town Hall is one of many timber-framed buildings put up just after the war. The sandstone arched base was completed in 1652 and later covered in brick; Charles II took a great interest in it and, when improvements were needed, he made funds available from his own purse and from a collection he ordered be made in every parish in England.

St Mary's Street is one of the three streets off High Street which formed the planned new town of the 12th century. Many of the houses, brick faced over timber frames, have side passages leading to gardens which contained workshops and cottages. **Bishop Percy's House** is the oldest house standing in the town, a handsome building dating from 1580 and one of the very few timber-framed houses to survive the fire of 1646. It is named after the Reverend Dr Percy, who was born in

Bishop Percy's House, Bridgnorth

the house in 1729 and became Bishop of Dromore.

For many visitors the most irresistible attraction in Bridgnorth is the **Castle Hill Cliff Railway**, funicular railway built in 1892 to link the two parts of the town. The track is 200 feet long and rises over 100 feet up the cliff. Originally it operated on a water balance system but it was converted in 1943 to electrically driven colliery-type winding gear. John Betjeman likened a ride on this lovely little railway to a journey up to heaven. For all but the very energetic it might feel like heaven compared to the alternative ways of getting from Low to High Town - seven sets of steps or Cartway, a meandering street that's steeped in history.

🏛 historic building 🏛 museum 🏛 historic site 🌣 scenic attraction 🌿 flora and fauna

The bridge across the Severn, rebuilt in 1823 to a Thomas Telford design, has a clock tower with an inscription commemorating the building, in 1808, of the first steam locomotive at John Hazeldine's foundry a short distance upstream.

Talking of steam locomotives, Bridgnorth is the northern terminus of the wonderful **Severn Valley Railway** (see under Bewdley in Worcestershire).

One of the stations on this marvellous railway is at Highley, where a new attraction is the Visitor and Education centre in the Engine Shed, with an exhibition and a large display of steam locomotives.

Around Bridgnorth

QUATT
4 miles SE of Bridgnorth on the A442

🏛 Dudmaston Hall

Quatt is the location of the National Trust's **Dudmaston Hall** (see panel below), a late-

17th century house with fine furniture, Dutch flower paintings, modern pictures and sculptures (Hepworth, Moore), botanical art, watercolours, family and natural history and colourful gardens with lakeside walks, a rockery and a wooded valley. The church at Quatt contains some splendid monuments and memorials to the Wolryche family.

BILLINGSLEY
5 miles S of Bridgnorth on the B4363

🐦 Rays Farm Country Matters   🏇 Jack Mytton Way

In a beautiful wooded valley near the village, **Rays Farm Country Matters** is home to many farm animals including Highland cattle, deer, donkeys, goats and pigs, plus more than 50 owls. The longest bridleway in Shropshire, and one of the longest in the country, passes close by. This is the **Jack Mytton Way**, named after a 19th century hard-living squire and sometime MP for Shrewsbury. It runs all the way to Llanfair Waterdine in the Teme Valley, a distance of some 70 miles. At nearby Highley, on the Severn Valley Railway, several

Dudmaston (National Trust)

Quatt, nr Bridgnorth, Shropshire WV15 6QN
Tel: 01746 780866
e-mail: dudmaston@nationaltrust.org.uk
website: www.nationaltrust.org.uk

Late 17th-century mansion with art collection, lakeside garden and estate

The house with its intimate family rooms contains fine furniture and Dutch flower paintings, as well as one of Britain's most important public collections of contemporary art in a country house setting. The delightful gardens are a mass of colour in spring and visitors can enjoy walks in the Dingle, a wooded valley, or the popular 'Big Pool' walk. There are also estate walks to and from Hampton Loade. Dudmaston is the home of Colonel and Mrs Hamilton-Russell. *(Photo by Michael Caldwell).*

📖 stories and anecdotes   🐦 famous people   🎨 art and craft   🎭 entertainment and sport   🏇 walks steam locomotives are on display at the Engine House (see under Bewdley in Worcestershire).

MUCH WENLOCK
8 miles NW of Bridgnorth on the A458

🏛 Guildhall   🏛 Museum   🏛 Priory of St Milburga

The narrow streets of Much Wenlock are a delight to explore, and among the mellow buildings are some absolute gems. The **Guildhall** is one of them, dating from 1540 and added to in 1577 with a chamber over the stone medieval prison. The Guildhall was until recently used as a courtroom, and the Town Council still meets here once a month. The **Museum** is housed in the former market hall, which was built in 1878. There are interesting displays on the geology, flora and fauna of Wenlock Edge (see below), as well as local history items including Dr William Penny Brookes' Olympian Games. A forerunner of, and inspiration for the modern Olympic Games, they are an annual event in the town every year, having started in 1850. The good doctor lived in Wilmore Street.

Holy Trinity Church, 'mother' to ten churches in villages around Much Wenlock, is a dominant presence in the town, though less conspicuous than it was until 1931 when its spire was removed. Its nave and chancel are Norman, the porch 13th century. The Parish Registers date from 1558.

The sight that simply must not be missed on a visit here is the ruined **Priory of St Milburga**, maintained by English Heritage. The Priory was originally a nunnery, founded in the 7th century by a Mercian princess and destroyed some 200 years later. Leofric, Earl of Mercia and husband of Lady Godiva, re-established it as a priory in 1050 and the current spectacular ruins belong to the Cluniac Priory rebuilt in the 12th and 13th centuries. The best remaining features are the wall carvings in the cloisters and the Norman interlacing of arches and doorways in the Chapter House. **The Prior's Lodge**, dating from about 1500, is particularly impressive with its steeply pitched roof of sandstone tiles above the rows of mullioned windows. Away from the main site is St Milburga's Well, whose waters are reputed to cure eye diseases.

WENLOCK EDGE
7 miles W of Bridgnorth on the B4371

Wenlock Edge is one of the most spectacular and impressive landmarks in the whole county, a limestone escarpment dating back 400 million years and a paradise for naturalists and lovers of the outdoors. It runs for 15 miles all the way down to Craven Arms. For centuries its quarries have produced the stone used in many of the local buildings; it was also a source of lime for agricultural fertiliser and much went into the blast furnaces that fired the Industrial Revolution.

EARDINGTON
2 miles SW of Bridgnorth on the B4555

🏛 Daniel's Mill

Eardington is a southern suburb of Bridgnorth where, a mile out of town on the B4555, stands **Daniel's Mill**, a picturesque working watermill powered by an enormous (38ft) wheel. Family-owned for 200 years, the mill still produces flour.

MORVILLE
2 miles W of Bridgnorth on the A458

🏛 Morville Hall   🌱 Dower House Garden

Morville Hall, 16th century with 18th century additions, stands at the junction of the A458 and B4368. Within its grounds, the

HURST FARM HOLIDAY COTTAGES

Morville, nr Bridgnorth, Shropshire WV16 4TF
Tel: 01746 714375 Fax: 01746 714133
e-mail: info@cottagefishingholidays.co.uk
web: www.hurstfarmcottages.co.uk

Situated in an Area of Outstanding Natural Beauty in the heart of Shropshire, **Hurst Farm Holiday Cottages** are ideally suited to exploring the county's many scenic and historic attractions. They are set within landscaped gardens, with easy parking and a patio and barbecue area. The smallest of the five self-catering cottages, called Stables, sleeps two, the others up to five or six, and all are finished to the highest modern standards.

The single-storeyed Stables is designed for full wheelchair access and use, and some of the other cottages have ground-floor bedrooms suitable for older or less mobile guests. The main farmhouse offers Bed & Breakfast accommodation in beautifully appointed en suite twin-bedded rooms, and a bonus for all guests at Hurst Farm is free fishing on the pools and lakes in the grounds. This is very much a working farm, and guests are welcome to meet Lucy the cow, Sage and Onion the Kune Kune pigs, Ken and Mike the pygmy goats, and the horses and ponies, the hens and the dogs.

Bridgnorth, with its historic cliff railway and many other attractions, is just five minutes' drive from the cottages, and Ironbridge 10 minutes.

Dower House Garden is a 1.5 acre site designed by Dr Katherine Swift and begun in 1989. Its aim is to tell the history of English gardens in a sequence of separate gardens designed in the style of different historical periods. Particular attention is given to the use of authentic plants and construction techniques. Old roses are a speciality of the garden. Parking is available in the churchyard of the fine Norman Church of St Gregory, which is also well worth a visit.

Telford

🏛 Steam Railway Trust   🌱 Hoo Farm

🌿 Wonderland

Telford is a sprawling modern development that absorbed several existing towns in the region of the Shropshire coalfield. Wellington, Hadley, Ketley, Oakengates, Madeley and Dawley were among the towns to be incorporated, and the name chosen in the 1960s commemorates Thomas Telford, whose influence can be seen all over the county. Thomas Telford was a Scot, born in Eskdale in 1757, who came to Shrewsbury in 1786. Appointed County Surveyor, he quickly got to work on such enterprises as Shrewsbury jail, Bridgnorth, a host of bridges, an aqueduct, canals and the Holyhead Road. He designed distinctive milestones for the road, one of which is now at the Blists Hill Museum. Telford's many ambitious developments include the huge (450-acre) Town Park, with nature trails, sports fields, lakes, gardens and play areas. **Wonderland** is an enchanting and enchanted woodland whose fairytale attractions

🎭 stories and anecdotes 🦜 famous people 🎨 art and craft 🎪 entertainment and sport 🚶 walks

THE HUNDRED HOUSE HOTEL

Bridgnorth Road (A442), Norton, nr Telford,
Shropshire, TF11 9EE
Tel: 01952 730353 Fax: 01952 730355
e-mail: reservations@hundredhouse.co.uk
website: www.hundredhouse.co.uk

The Hundred House Hotel takes its name from the ancient divisions of shires into 'hundreds'. The oldest part of the building is a 14th century thatched courthouse. Opposite the hotel are the remains of the old stocks and whipping post used for dispensing quick justice. The main hotel is Georgian, and the interior boasts old quarry-tiled floors, exposed brickwork, beamed ceilings and oak panelling. Celebrating 21 years under family ownership, the Phillips' have made some new improvements to ensure your experience remains up to date, whilst retaining the friendly welcoming atmosphere, which marries hospitality, eccentricity, warmth and wit in an irresistible combination.

The ten guest bedrooms are furnished with antique or period furniture and adorned with herbs and plants. Some have half-tester or four-poster beds, the sheets are lavender-scented and the superior rooms have the unique attraction of velvet-covered swings.

The herb/plant theme continues into the restaurant and bars, with drying herbs, flowers and gourds. Chef/Patron Stuart, the younger son produces great meals on brasserie and restaurant menus that combine classic skills with many innovative touches, as well as making use of over 100 sorts of herbs that grow in the garden. Typical choices on both their Bar/Brasserie menu and the Restaurant menu run from griddled scallops with a red pepper coulis for starters, to their "soon to be famous" steak and kidney pie with home made pastry, home-made sausages, traditional ploughmans with local cheeses, fresh fish of the day and vegetarians can enjoy selections including roast mushrooms with lentil Dahl served with chick pea salad and courgettes. Traditional roasts are served between 12 and 7pm on Sundays.

A door opposite the bar leads to a path marked Lovers Walk and grounds laid out to show the changing colours of the seasons. The gardens are the creation of Sylvia, who travelled the land with her husband Henry to find the stones, artefacts and plants that grace this extraordinary garden. The hotel has a lovely old tithe barn that's an ideal venue for meetings, conferences or special occasions. The Hundred House is also fully licensed for Civil Ceremonies.

🏛 historic building   🏛 museum   🏛 historic site   🍃 scenic attraction   🌿 flora and fauna include Snow White's Cottage, the Three Little Pigs and the Wrekin Giant. On the northern outskirts, at Preston-on-the-Weald Moor, is **Hoo Farm Animal Kingdom**, which numbers among its inhabitants ostriches, chipmunks, deer and llamas. Events include lamb feeding, milking and the famous sheep steeplechase.

Telford Steam Railway Trust keeps a number of old locomotives, some of them ex-Great Western Railway, in working condition at the old shed and yard at Horsehay.

Around Telford

OAKENGATES
1 mile NE of Telford on the A5

Oakengates, on the eastern edge of the metropolis of Telford, is the birthplace of Sir Gordon Richards, perhaps the greatest jockey this country has ever produced. His father was a miner and the young Gordon first learned to ride on pit ponies. When he retired from the saddle, he had ridden 4,872 winners and was champion jockey for 20 years. Frankie Dettori and Kieren Fallon have a long way to go!

SHIFNAL
3 miles E of Telford on the A464

🏛 RAF Museum

Once a staging post on the Holyhead Road, Shifnal has an unexpectedly large church with a Norman chancel arch, a 14th century east window, carved Italian pulpit and an Italian reredos.

On the A41, at **Cosford** near Shifnal, the **RAF Museum** is home to an important

---

THE SANDSTONE BARN B&B

Cosford Grange Farm, Shifnal,
Shropshire TF11 9JB
Tel: 01902 373062
website: www.thebandbdirectory.co.uk

In 2001, Ralph Young converted a barn on the family farm to provide comfortable, characterful Bed & Breakfast accommodation. The **Sandstone Barn**, which dates from the 17th century, has two centrally heated letting bedrooms, a double with en suite bathroom and a twin with a private bathroom; both have television and hot drinks tray. A quality English or Continental breakfast is served in the Oak Gallery, which contains Ralph's fascinating collection of prints and artefacts.

Guests can relax with a good book or plan the next day's activities in the spacious beamed sitting room, and they have unlimited access to the Woodland Walk, a private 25-acre nature reserve alongside the garden. The Walk snakes through woodland with sandstone cliffs, a stream and wildlife pond and the evocative ivy-clad ruins of a watermill. The Sandstone Barn is a very pleasant

and civilised base for touring the area – RAF Cosford and Air Museum is just 2 miles away, David Austin Roses 1 mile and Boscobel, Weston Park and Ironbridge are all within easy reach.

🎦 stories and anecdotes 🕊 famous people 🎨 art and craft 🎵 entertainment and sport 🚶 walks

CORNER FARM ANTIQUES

Corner Farm, Weston Heath, nr Newport,
Shropshire TF11 8RX
Tel: 01952 691543
e-mail: cornerfarmantiques@btopenworld.com
website: www.cornerfarmantiques.com

Corner Farm Antiques is a well-established family antiques business which operates from delightful converted farm buildings 4 miles south of the market town of Newport. In a prominent position, situated on the main A41, they are leading antiques retailers and offer by far the largest choice of furniture and clocks in Shropshire. Moreover everything is available at realistic, affordable prices.

Owner Tim Dams together with his manager Tim Gittins, who heads a team of highly qualified craftsmen, provide the perfect combination of experience and expertise which is unequalled. Their proud boast is that no-one can match their extensive range of clean quality stock nor offer better service or value for money. With over 500 items of specially chosen furniture and clocks the complex opens up like a tardis to reveal an Aladdins cave for you to browse and enjoy in a relaxed and friendly atmosphere.

The main specialities are dining furniture, period oak, longcase (grandfather) clocks, other clocks and barometers. Within the 12 carpeted showrooms are individual room settings showing off the vast selection of dining tables, sets of chairs, sideboards, chiffoniers, bookcases, bureaux, cabinets, desks, chests of drawers, dressers, mirrors, all complemented by a multitude of accessories. Over 1,000 individual smaller items include lovely china and glass, boxes and caddies, copper and brass and other desirable collectables.

The choice of clocks and barometers has to be seen to be believed. Over 200, yes 200, all thoroughly overhauled and ready for you to use and enjoy. Over 60 longcase clocks from £1,800 to £18,000! Each is fully guaranteed and ready to be delivered and set up in your home by their professionals.

Visitors can take a break from browsing by relaxing in the attractive tea room, or sitting outside in the gardens. Take the family along, there's a children's play area with swings and slide and a menagerie with birds, rabbits and guinea pigs.

There's a big turnover of stock in all categories, so customers can be sure that they will find many pieces that were not there on their last visit. Corner Farm Antiques is open seven days a week, (including Bank Holidays) and their excellent website shows a comprehensive selection of what is currently available at this outstanding place.

Please note; their website is updated weekly so add them to your favourites to see what's new.

🏚 historic building   🏛 museum   🏛 historic site   🍃 scenic attraction   🌿 flora and fauna collection of aircraft, from the little Red Arrows Gnat to the mighty Belfast, Britain's largest operational transport aircraft, along with aero engines and missiles from all over the world. The latest attraction is the National Cold War Exhibition, reflecting the social, cultural and political history of the Cold War era, c1947 to 1991. It features Britain's three famous V Bombers, the Vulcan, Victor and Valiant, and others suspended as if in flight, including a Dakota, Canberra, Meteor and Lightning. Admission to the Museum is free.

NEWPORT
6 miles NE of Telford off the A41

A handsome town which lost many of its buildings in a fire in 1665. Most of the buildings on the broad main street are Georgian or early Victorian. There's plenty to keep the visitor active in the area, including the Lilleshall National Sports Centre and the ruins of Lilleshall Abbey, the extensive and evocative remains of an Augustinian abbey.

TONG
5 miles E of Telford on the A41

🏛 Church

Tong is an attractive village which once had a castle, founded, according to legend, by the wizard Merlin. Where was he when the castle was blown up in 1954? The Vernons and the Durants were the Lords of the Manor in Tong for many years and they are commemorated in the 15th century **Church of St Bartholomew**. The Vernons were a particularly distinguished lot: one was a Speaker of the House of Commons and another was Lord High Constable to Henry V.

THE FIRE PLACE
19 Chetwynd End, Newport, Shropshire TF10 7JJ
Tel: 01952 811443
website: www.thedoorknockercompany.co.uk

The **Fire Place** is a specialist supplier of solid-fuel fireplaces, grates, ranges, stoves and fireside accessories. It also stocks a wide range of British-made brass and ironware, and period fixtures and fittings for the home and garden in a variety of materials, including marble, stone, cast iron, slate and granite. Smaller items include doorknobs and door knockers, hooks and brackets,

finger plates, hinges and bolts. Owner Rachel Webb, here since 1999, has built up a worldwide list of customers, including collectors and interior designers as well as home improvers. The business is proud to support local foundries, thus helping the community and ensuring better quality and competitive prices.

📖 stories and anecdotes 🐦 famous people 🎨 art and craft 🎭 entertainment and sport 🚶 walks

Old Church Ruins, Tong

years later was restored to the throne. The house has changed considerably since Charles's time, but it's still full of atmosphere and interest, with an exhibition giving a vivid account of the King's adventures. Every visitor naturally wants to see the famous oak in which he hid, but it is no longer standing, destroyed by souvenir-hunting loyalists. Today there stands a descendant of the original, itself now more than 300 years old.

In the Golden Chapel, which has a superb gilded, fan-vaulted ceiling, there is a bust of Arthur Vernon, who was a don at Cambridge University. Venetia Stanley, descended from the Vernons and the Earls of Derby, was a famed beauty who was lauded by poets and artists. She counted Ben Jonson, Van Dyck and the Earl of Dorset among her lovers, but in 1625 she made the unfortunate move of marrying Sir Kenelm Digby, whose father had been executed for his part in the Gunpowder Plot. She died tragically young, some say at the hands of her jealous husband.

Boscobel

7 miles E of Telford off the A41

🏛 Boscobel House

After Charles II was defeated by the Roundheads at the Battle of Worcester in 1651, he fled for his life and was advised to seek refuge in a remote hunting lodge called **Boscobel House**, already known as a safe house for royals on the run. By day the King hid in the branches of an old oak tree, while at night he would creep into the house and hide in secret rooms with one of his trusty officers. He eventually escaped, of course, and nine

BROSELEY

5 miles S of Telford on the B4373

🏛 Benthall Hall   🏛 Pipe Museum

Broseley, which stands on the south side of the River Severn opposite Ironbridge, was the headquarters of John Wilkinson, the great ironmaster and head of a giant empire. It was while he was living at The Lawns in Broseley that he commissioned the Shrewsbury architect Thomas Pritchard to design the world's first iron bridge. He also launched the first iron boat, *The Trial*, on the Severn in 1787 and even designed his own iron coffin. Broseley was the centre of an ancient local industry in clay products and tobacco pipes, and the **Broseley Pipeworks Clay Tobacco Pipe Museum** untouched for more than 40 years, is a time-capsule factory where the famous Broseley Churchwarden pipes were made for 350 years until 1957. Tools lie on benches where they were left, clay is stacked in the yard ready for use, and saggars lean against each other waiting to be filled. Just north of Broseley, off the B4375, on a plateau above a gorge, stands **Benthall Hall**, a 16th century building in the care of the National Trust, with mullioned windows and a magnificent interior with a carved oak staircase, elaborate plaster ceilings and the Benthall family's collection of furniture, ceramics and paintings. There's a carefully restored plantsman's garden and, in the grounds, an interesting Restoration church.

IRONBRIDGE AND IRONBRIDGE GORGE

4 miles SW of Telford on the B4373

🏛 Museums	Buildwas Abbey	🏛 Bridge
🏛 Tar Tunnel		

This is it, the town at the centre of Ironbridge Gorge, an area which has been designated a World Heritage Centre by UNESCO, ranking it alongside the likes of the Pyramids, the Grand Canyon and the Taj Mahal. It was the first British site on the list. The **Bridge** itself is a pedestrian right of way with a museum in the tollgate at one end, and the series of museums that spread along the banks of the Severn in **Ironbridge**, **Coalbrookdale**, **Coalport** and **Jackfield** pay tribute to the momentous events that took place here 250 years ago. The first iron wheels were made here, and also the first iron rails and the first steam railway locomotive.

The **Museum of the Gorge** offers the ideal introduction to the attractions, filled with stories of how industry changed the Gorge. The **Museum of Iron** in **Coalbrookdale** in the most historic part of the valley shows the whole story of how the Darby family

THE WHITE HART

The Wharfarge, Ironbridge, Shropshire TF8 7AW
Tel: 01952 433547
e-mail: info@ironfowhitehartironbridge.com
website: www.whitchurchironbridge.com

The **White Hart** stands on the main road through Ironbridge, 300 yards from the famous bridge. The pub dates from the mid-18th century and is thus older than the bridge, and it is likely that it provided shelter and hospitality for workers who built the bridge. It has now been developed by Malthouse Pubs into a light, modern pub that combines a contemporary, almost Continental style with a traditional welcome and warm, friendly ambience. It's a great place to meet for a drink or a meal, and a comfortable, convenient base for discovering the many historic attractions within walking distance.

A regularly changing menu of worldwide inspiration caters for all tastes and appetites, with typical dishes ranging from lunchtime baguettes, salads, pasta and old favourites like ham, egg & chips or spaghetti Bolognese to a tapas selection, baked salmon, fish pie, lamb tagine, steak & ale pie, Cajun chicken breast and Mediterranean vegetable stack. To finish in style, perhaps chocolate pudding or redcurrant crème brûlée. Children can choose from their own menu or have a half-portion of most dishes on the main menu; high chairs and colouring pads are available. The guest accommodation comprises eight rooms, the two largest rooms overlooking the river. All have en suite high-pressure showers and big fluffy towels, TV and DVD player.

📖 stories and anecdotes　🦢 famous people　🎨 art and craft　🎭 entertainment and sport　🚶 walks

The Bridge, Ironbridge

revolutionised early iron making. The Great Warehouse is full of surprises, including classical statues, garden ornaments, magnificent furniture and curious objects, all made of iron. Next to it is the original furnace used by Abraham Darby when he first smelted iron with coke; a little way north are **Rosehill House**, one of the homes of the Darby family, and **Dale House**, where Abraham Darby's grandson made his plans for the iron bridge.

Also in Coalbrookdale is **Enginuity,** the latest of Ironbridge's ten museums to open. Here, visitors can become apprentice engineers for the day, free to experiment with all the gadgets and acquire the know-how involved in producing everyday items. You can find out whether you can pull a real

locomotive; test your speed and accuracy against a robot; control water to generate electricity or work as a team to make the Crazy Boiler blow its top!

The Old Police Station, owned by John and Lynn Youngman, is one of Ironbridge's less well-known museums, but one that is well worth a visit, and for a variety of reasons. The Victorian station and its cells have been painstakingly restored to provide a fascinating insight into the judicial and prison systems at the turn of the century. After it closed for duty in 1964 it was used for various purposes before becoming home to police memorabilia from handcuffs and truncheons to uniforms and documents. The cells are particularly arresting – Cell 4 was the birching centre for Shropshire, and a birching stool still stands in the middle of the room. In the upper-floor theatre, using the unique backdrop of the former station and courthouse, Courthouse Productions puts on a wide variety of corporate and personal events, from plays with a buffet supper to Courtroom trial re-enactments; from Victorian Music Halls to jazz and other musical events. Also on the premises is a tearoom where home baking, traditional afternoon teas and a Victorian buffet are among the offerings. Weddings are catered for at the station, and for an eve-of-wedding night with a difference the groom and best man can spend a night in the cells after the evening's celebrations, then wake up to a healthy breakfast before being delivered in style to the church! Also to be found in the Police Station is the **Left Centre**, which holds a vast stock of knives, scissors, kitchen tools and writing aids for left-handers, plus anti-clockwise clocks and "the best of ambidextrous".

Also at Coalbrookdale is the **Ironbridge**

Open Air Museum of Steel Sculpture, a collection of 60 modern steel sculptures of all shapes and sizes set in ten acres of beautiful countryside.

The **Jackfield Tile Museum** (see panel below), on the south bank, stands on the site of a world centre of the tile-making industry. The museum houses a fine collection of wall and floor tiles from Victorian times to the 1950s. Demonstrations of traditional tile-making take place regularly, and visitors can have a go in one of the hands-on workshops. Back across a footbridge to the **Coalport China Museum**, with its marvellous displays of two centuries of porcelain. The National Collections of Coalport and Coughley China are displayed in the original riverside buildings in which many of the pieces were made. Coalport was once one of the country's largest manufacturers of porcelain, starting

The Jackfield Tile Museum

Ironbridge Gorge, Shropshire
Tel: 01952 435900 Ironbridge TIC Tel: 01952 884 391
website: www.ironbridge.org.uk

The Jackfield Tile Museum in Shropshire's Ironbridge Gorge has re-opened its doors after major restoration with a spectacular new suite of tiled period room settings which capture the extravagance and beauty of Victorian 'tile mania' – a great source of inspiration for room designers today.

Also on offer are galleries filled with thousands of sumptuous tiles, hands-on workshops where families can decorate their own tiles and visits to the Craven Dunnill tile factory alongside. Here skilled crafts people can be seen making intricately designed tiles by hand for private homes, historic houses and public spaces.

For anyone who has broken or damaged a special tile, the Craven Dunnill team offer a custom service to restore or replicate the design to bring the display back to its original splendour – a great bonus for today's interior designers as well as those restoring historic buildings. Alternatively visitors can create their own designs, or order from the extensive selection of British hand-made tiles displayed in the museum shop.

Jackfield Tile Museum is housed in the original Craven Dunnill factory built in the 1870s. Visitors can view five themed galleries starting with the history of tile making in the Severn Valley followed by the restored 19th century, gas-lit Tile Trade Showroom. This large vaulted room would have been used by commercial buyers and architects to select ranges of tiles for retailing and decoration prior to the production of trade catalogues. Other galleries display examples of different decorative styles and art pottery as well as explain the various tile making processes, such as encaustic production, tube lining, embossed and hand painted designs.

The museums are open seven days a week from 10am until 5pm; activities and workshops vary day-to-day.

🎞 stories and anecdotes   🐦 famous people   ✏ art and craft   ✒ entertainment and sport   🚶 walks life here but moving its factory to Stoke in the 1920s. Nearby is the extraordinary **Tar Tunnel** with its pools of natural bitumen. It was a popular attraction for tourists in the 18th century, and it remains one of the most interesting geological phenomena in Britain. The tunnel was started in 1786, under the direction of ironmaster William Reynolds, who intended that it should be used for a canal to reach the shafts to the coal seams three quarters of a mile away on Blists Hill. After they had driven the tunnel about 300 yards the miners struck a spring of natural bitumen. Reynolds immediately recognised the scientific interest of the discovery and sent samples of the bitumen to eminent scientists, who declared that the properties of the bitumen were superior to those of tar made of coal. The tunnel was almost forgotten over the years, but in 1965 the Shropshire Mining Club persuaded the owner of the village shop in **Coalport** to let them explore the darkness which lay beyond a door opening from his cellar. They rediscovered the Tar Tunnel, but it was another 18 years before visitors were allowed access to a short stretch.

At **Blists Hill Victorian Town** visitors can experience the atmosphere and way of life of a working Victorian community; there's a shop, domestic animals, a squatter's cottage, a schoolhouse and a bank which distributes its own tender.

Passport tickets are available to admit holders to all the Ironbridge Gorge Museums – call 01952 884391 for all details.

Two miles west of Ironbridge, on a minor road off the B4378, stands **Buildwas Abbey**, one of the finest ruined abbeys in England. After 850 years the church is virtually complete except for the roof, and the setting, in a meadow by the Severn against a backdrop

of wooded grounds, is both peaceful and evocative. The place is full of things of interest, like the lead-glazed tiles depicting animals and birds in the Chapter House.

WELLINGTON
2 miles NW of Telford on the A442

🏛 Sunnycroft   🏛 Aqueduct   🌄 The Wrekin

Wellington is part of the new town of Telford but still retains much of its Victorian look. The Church of All Saints is the work of George Steuart, better known for St Chad's in Shrewsbury. A recent addition to the town's attractions is the National Trust's **Sunnycroft**, a late-Victorian gentleman's suburban villa typical of the kind that were built for wealthy business and professional men. The house and its contents are largely unaltered, and in the grounds are pig sties, a kitchen garden, orchards, a conservatory and a Wellingtonia avenue.

A couple of miles north of Wellington, at **Longdon-on-Tern**, stands the **Aqueduct** built by Thomas Telford as a pilot for other, better-known constructions.

South of here, on the other side of the M54/A5, is one of the best-known landmarks in the whole country. **The Wrekin**, which reaches up over 1,300 feet, is the site of a prehistoric hill fort, visible for many miles around and accessible by a network of public footpaths. The reward for reaching the top is a beautiful panoramic view stretching to the neighbouring counties. In Roman times it was used as a base by the Cornovii tribe before they were moved to Viroconium. Shropshire folklore tells us that it was 'put' there by a malicious giant who was carrying a huge load of earth to dam the Severn and flood Shrewsbury, simply because he didn't like the people. The giant met a cobbler, who persuaded him against this evil act, whereupon the giant dropped the load he was carrying – and that's The Wrekin.

WROXETER
7 miles W of Telford on the B4380

🏛 Viroconium

In the village of Wroxeter, beside the B4380, is one of the most important Roman sites ever brought to light. **Viroconium** was the first town to be established by the Romans in this part of the country and developed into the 4th largest city in Roman Britain with more than 5,000 soldiers and civilians living here. It's an absolutely fascinating place, where the highlights include extensive remains of a 2nd century bathhouse complex. Some of the major excavated items are on display here, many more at Rowley's House Museum in Shrewsbury. Also in the village is Wroxeter

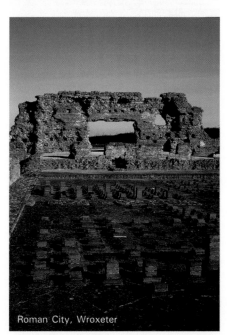
Roman City, Wroxeter

Roman Vineyard where there is not only a vineyard producing both red and white wines but additional attractions in the shape of rare-breed animals and a lavender field.

ATCHAM
7 miles W of Telford on the B4380

🏛 Attingham Park   🌱 Attingham Home Farm

The village stands at the point where the Severn is crossed by the Roman road. The splendid old seven-arched bridge is now redundant, having been replaced by a new neighbour some time ago, but is still in situ. The old bridge was designed by John Gwynne, who was a founder member of the Royal Academy and the designer of Magdalen Bridge in Oxford.

Attingham Park, run by the National Trust, is perhaps the finest house in Shropshire, a splendid neo-classical mansion set in 250 delightful acres. Designed by George Steuart for the 1st Lord Berwick, it has the grandest of Regency interiors, ambassadorial silver, Italian furniture and Grand Tour paintings hanging in the John Nash gallery. The tea room is lined with paintings of the 5th Lord Berwick's Herefordshire cattle. Humphrey Repton landscaped the park where visitors can enjoy woodland and riverside walks and see the deer.

From the park visitors can take a trailer ride to **Attingham Home Farm**, the original home farm of the grand house. It comprises buildings dating mainly from about 1800 and the yard retains the atmosphere of a traditional Shropshire farm. Many breeds of farm animals are represented: pigs - Oxford, Sandy, Iron Age, Vietnamese pot-bellied; sheep - Jacob, Shetland and Ryeland; cattle - Jerseys, Longhair, Dexter, Red Poll, British

White. The rabbit house is particularly popular with youngsters, and there are usually some orphaned lambs for children to bottle-feed.

Shrewsbury

🏛 Castle   🏛 Abbey   🏛 Lord's Hill Column

🏛 St Chad's   🏛 St Mary's Church

🏛 Bear Steps   🌲 Quarry Park

🌲 Brother Cadfael Walk   🏚 Coleham Pumping Station

🏛 Battlefield   🏚 Shropshire Regimental Museum

High the vanes of Shrewsbury gleam,
Islanded in Severn stream

So wrote AE Housman in *A Shropshire Lad* and the town is indeed almost an island, caught in a wandering loop of the River Severn. It was on two hills within this protected site that the Saxon town developed. The Normans under Roger de Montgomery took over after the conquest, building the castle and the great Benedictine abbey. In the 15th and 16th centuries Shrewsbury prospered through the wool trade, and evidence of its affluence shows in the many "Magpie" black-and-white timbered buildings that still line the streets. In Victorian times steam made Shrewsbury an important railway centre whilst at the same time Charles Darwin, born and educated in the town, was rocking the world with his theories. Everywhere there is a sense of history, and the Museums do a particularly fine job of bringing the past to life, in terms of both human and natural history. Rowley's House is a glorious timber-framed building of the late-16th century, with an adjoining brick and stone mansion of 1618, the home of William Rowley, 17th century draper, brewer and leading citizen. The collection of pieces from Viroconium and spectacular displays of costumes, natural

Rowley's House, Shrewsbury

history and geology that were until the end of 2006 housed here will be shown in the Music Hall, which already has the TIC and is being developed as a museum. Rowley's house remains a building of some significance. A short walk away is Clive House, where Clive of India lived in 1762 while he was Mayor. It is now a private house.

Noted for its commanding position and wonderful views, **Shrewsbury Castle** was founded in 1083. That was when Roger de Montgomery, a kinsman of William the Conqueror, was granted Shrewsbury and much of Shropshire as a reward for loyalty, and the Castle was part of the Norman attempt to control the lawless Welsh border. By the time of Elizabeth I it had become a virtual ruin, and of the original structure only the gateway survives, along with one side and two towers

🏛 historic building   🏚 museum   🏛 historic site   🌿 scenic attraction   🌱 flora and fauna

River Severn, Shrewsbury

dating from the 13th century. It last saw action in the Civil War and was converted by Thomas Telford into a private residence. It now houses the **Shropshire Regimental Museum**, which tells the story of the four Shropshire regiments – the King's Shropshire Light Infantry, the Shropshire Yeomanry Cavalry, the Shropshire Royal Horse Artillery and the 4th Battalion King's Shropshire Light Infantry TA. Among the many treasures on display are colours bearing battle honours, regimental silver and china, weapons and medals, including three Victoria Crosses.

ZEBRA (SHREWSBURY) LTD

11 Fish Street, Shrewsbury, Shropshire SY1 1UR
Tel/Fax: 01743 247770
e-mail: hannah@zebrashrewsbury.co.uk
website: www.zebrashrewsbury.co.uk

Hannah Taylor brought years of retailing experience when she opened **Zebra** in the historic heart of Shrewsbury.

The shop sells a wide and constantly changing stock of ladies clothes and accessories sourced from the UK and from Ireland, France, Italy, Germany and Denmark. Up-to-the-minute styles covering casual, formal, day wear and occasion wear are designed to flatter and to make the wearer feel confident, and many of the styles are available in sizes up to 24.

The setting, in a medieval timber-framed building with wattle & daub walls and many other original features, adds to the pleasure of a visit to Zebra, where customers looking for something a little bit different from the run-of-the-mill High Street stores can browse and buy between 10am and 5pm Monday to Saturday.

stories and anecdotes　famous people　art and craft　entertainment and sport　walks

Begun in the same year as the castle, **Shrewsbury Abbey** survived the dissolution of the monasteries in 1540 and still serves as the parish church. The Abbey, like the Castle, was founded by Roger de Montgomery on the site of a Saxon wooden church. In 1283 a parliament met in the Chapter House, the first national assembly in which the Commons were involved. The Abbey Church remains a place of worship, and in 1997 a stained glass window depicting St Benedict was dedicated to the memory of Edith Pargeter. This lady, writing under the name of Ellis Peters, created the character of Brother Cadfael, who lived at the Abbey and became one of the country's best-loved fictional characters when portrayed by Derek Jacobi in the television series.

To the east of the abbey, in front of the Shire Hall, rises the lofty **Lord Hill's Column**. Four magnificent sculpted lions guard the base of this, the largest Grecian Doric column in the world, which reaches a total height of 133 feet 6 inches. Inside, there's a spiral staircase which unfortunately is not open to the public because of safety reasons. Completed in 1816, the column celebrates Rowland Hill who was born in Shropshire and achieved distinction as a soldier in the Napoleonic wars, notably at Waterloo. He was created a viscount and later succeeded the Duke of Wellington as commander-in-chief.

Shrewsbury has more than 30 churches and among the finest are St Mary's and St Chad's. **St Mary's**, the town's only complete medieval

---

HUNTERS

1 Wyle Cop, Shrewsbury, Shropshire SY1 1UT
Tel/Fax: 01743 232823
e-mail: shop@hunters-shrewsbury.co.uk
website: www.huntersofshrewsbury.co.uk

In a conservation area of Shrewsbury at the top of historic Wyle Cop, **Hunters** is Shropshire's largest independent china shop.

Behind the alluring window display David and Glenis Young have filled their shop with china, tableware, crystal, art glass, studio pottery, cutlery, jewellery and collectable ornaments. Among the leading brands always in stock are Wedgwood, Vera Wang, Royal Doulton, Royal Worcester, Spode, Portmeirion, Denby and Villeroy & Boch; Border Fine Arts, Willow Tree, Lilliput Lane, Moorcroft and Anita Harris; crystal by Dartington, Stuart and Waterford; and cutlery by Arthur Price and Villeroy & Boch.

The well-informed and always helpful staff are much more than sales assistants and are specialists in wedding lists. They can put customers in touch with repairers and restorers of china and can point you to suppliers of discontinued ranges.

🏛 historic building   🏛 museum   🏛 historic site   ☘ scenic attraction   🌿 flora and fauna church, originated in the late Saxon period, but the earliest features of the present building are of the 12th century. The stained glass, monuments and fittings are quite out of the ordinary, and the spire has claims to being the third highest in the land. One of the memorials is to Admiral Benbow, a national hero who died in 1702 who is also remembered in innumerable pub signs. **St Chad's** is the work of Attingham Hall's designer George Steuart, who was commissioned to design a replacement for the original, which fell down in 1788. His church is very unusual in having a circular nave.

The best examples of Shrewsbury's Tudor buildings are to be found in **Bear Steps**, close to the main square. This charming group of Tudor cottages and a timbered hall now houses two floors of paintings and craft exhibits, usually featuring local artists and images.

Guided tours and suggested walks cover all aspects of this marvellous town, including a **Brother Cadfael Trail** and walks in the beautiful countryside that is all around. One walk takes in the spot to the north of town now known as **Battlefield**, where in 1403 the armies of Henry IV and the insurgent Harry Percy (Harry Hotspur) met. Fifty thousand men were deployed in all, and in the brief but bloody battle Hotspur was among the many casualties. A church was built near the mass grave, where 1,600 bodies are buried, a monument to the fallen and also an oasis of wildlife in the town environment. Battlefield Church is open at weekends during the summer.

Complementing the town's Museum and Archaeological Services, a records and research service was opened in a new building in 1995. Shropshire Archives has 5.5 miles of material relating to Shropshire past and present, including many original records and extensive microfilm records.

A museum with a difference is **Coleham Pumping Station** at **Longden Coleham**, which houses the splendid Renshaw pumping engines that powered Shrewsbury's sewerage system until 1970.

Shrewsbury Flower Show is Britain's best two-day summer show. Each August for more than a century the show has been held in the picturesque grounds of **Quarry Park**, which slopes down to the Severn. At the centre of the 29-acre site is The Dingle, a colourful sunken flower garden.

Around Shrewsbury

WOLLASTON
8 miles W of Shrewsbury on the A458

The church here has a memorial to Thomas Parr, widely claimed to be the longest-lived Englishman, dying at the ripe old age of 152. He lived through ten reigns, married for the first time at 88, raised a family and married again at 122. He is buried in Westminster Abbey, so someone must have believed his story.

MONTFORD
4 miles W of Shrewsbury off the A5

It's worth pausing at Montford to look at the church where Charles Darwin was buried for a time. His body was subsequently moved to Westminster Abbey, showing that the furore caused by his theories had largely died down soon after his death – but not entirely, as *The Origin of Species* and *The Descent of Man* can still arouse fierce debate. Just beyond Montford are the ruins of Shrawardine Castle.

CHURNCOTE FARM SHOP

Welshpool Road. Bicton Heath, Shrewsbury,
Shropshire SY3 5EB
Tel: 01743 850273
e-mail: info@churncote.co.uk
website: www.churncote.co.uk

Sue and David Clarke own and run **Churncote Farm Shop** on a 400-acre mixed livestock and arable farm three miles from Shrewsbury, on the A458, the main road into Wales. They have turned an 18th century cow shed into a roomy, well-laid out, state-of-the-art farm shop selling a wide variety of top-quality produce. Home-produced or local beef, lamb and pork head the list, which also includes their own sausages, burgers, dry-cured bacon and black pudding. Eggs are free-range, vegetables local and seasonal, and fruit includes plums, apples, gooseberries, raspberries, blackcurrants and redcurrants.

Among the dairy produce are farm butter, cut cheeses (up to 25 varieties) and ice creams from Top House and Foxberry. Also not to be missed are the jams and preserves, homemade lemon curd, honey, pickles and tracklements.

The shop is open from 10am to 5.30pm Monday, Tuesday and Wednesday; 9am to 5.30pm Thursday, Friday and Saturday; and 10am to 4pm Sunday.

MELVERLEY

10 miles W of Shrewsbury off the B4393

🏛 Church of St Peter

Country lanes lead to the remarkable **Church of St Peter**, which stands serenely, if somewhat precariously, on the banks of the River Vyrnwy. From the outside, flanked by two massive yew trees, the church looks rather like a black-and-white manor house; the interior reveals one of England's few timber-framed churches. It was built in 1406 after its predecessor was destroyed by Owen Glendower. Great open screens of oak divide the interior into three areas and most of the furnishings - pulpit, altar table and chairs - are Jacobean.

NESSCLIFFE

9 miles NW of Shrewsbury on the A5

🌳 Country Park

Near the village of Nesscliffe, which lies halfway between Shrewsbury and Oswestry, is **Nesscliffe Hill Country Park**, where paths lead up through woodland to the summit and fine views over Shropshire. The hill is a sandstone escarpment, popular for walking and rock climbing; cut into the face of an abandoned quarry are caves, one of them reputedly the lair of the 16th century worthy-turned-highwayman Humphrey Kynaston.

A short distance north of Nesscliffe, on the B4397, is the village of **Ruyton-XI-Towns**, which acquired its unusual name in medieval

🏛 historic building   🏛 museum   🏛 historic site   🌳 scenic attraction   🌱 flora and fauna times when 11 communities were united into the borough of Ruyton.

HADNALL

5 miles NE of Shrewsbury on the A49

Hadnall is the burial place of Rowland Hill – not the man who conceived the idea of the Penny Post in Victorian times but the distinguished soldier who was Wellington's right hand man during the Peninsula War and covered himself with glory by routing Napoleon's Imperial Guard at the Battle of Waterloo. Hill was created a viscount and after succeeding Wellington as Commander in Chief retired to Hardwicke Grange near Hadnall. That house no longer stands and the viscount himself is buried beneath the church tower.

Oswestry

🏛 Church of St Oswald   🏛 Croeswylan Stone

🏛 Heritage Centre   🏚 Wat's Dyke

🏛 Cumbrian Museum of Transport

🏚 Old Oswestry   🏚 St Oswald's Well

Close to the Welsh border, Oswestry is an important market town whose look is mainly Georgian and Victorian, due in part to the fires which regularly ravaged timber-framed buildings. The town grew up around **St Oswald's Well**. Oswald was a Saxon king who was killed in a battle in 642 against a rival Saxon king, Penda of Mercia. Oswald's body was dismembered and hung on the branches of a tree. An eagle swooped and carried off one of his arms and where the limb fell to the

MAB & CO

26-28 Church Street, Oswestry,
Shropshire SY11 2SP
Tel/Fax: 01691 661328
website: www.mabandco.net

Julie Bennion spent many years in the jewellery and silverware retail trade, including spells in the USA and Australia, before opening **Mab & Co** in Oswestry in 1998.

Her first shop was in English Walls, and she relocated to larger premises here in Church Street in November 2006. She still specialises in contemporary jewellery and silver, but also on display are gold items, precious and semi-precious stones, beautiful glassware, chandeliers, mirrors, tableware, clocks, bags, leatherware, soft toys and many other ideas to enhance the home or to give as a special present for any occasion.

Among the many leading brands represented are Alessi, Dr Hauschka, Nigella Lawson, Storm, Leonardo, Bath House, Muddy Dog, Liz Cox, Bombay Duck, Radley Hidesign handbags and Newgate Clocks of Oswestry.

Mab & Co is a real gem of a shop, and, with the stock changing all the time, every visit will reveal something new and exciting.

THE WALLS RESTAURANT & BAR OSWESTRY

Welsh Walls, Oswestry, Shropshire SY11 1AW
Tel: 01691 670970 Fax: 01691 653820
e-mail: info@the-walls.co.uk

The expertise and enthusiasm of Geoff Hughes and Kate Bottoms and their team have established the high reputation of The Walls as the top place in Oswestry for food and entertainment. Geoff & Kate re-purchased the business they founded in 1993, a little over 18 months ago. The place has never looked better!

Geoff along with Simon Newbery, The Walls head chef, run a very dynamic kitchen with constantly changing seasonally driven menus compiled from local meats, vegetables, cheeses and expertly sourced fish. This wide ranging food is served in two main dining areas, both immensely impressive- roomy and comfortable, with lofty raftered ceilings, wooden floorboards and feature brick hearth & walls. The grander wing has a raised seating area, sofas galore and a frequently used grand piano.

An amazing wine list featuring over 20 wines available by the glass, runs to almost 200 wines and range in price from £12.00 a bottle up to £800.00. This is complemented by one of the widest range of spirits and liqueurs we've ever seen. The Walls offers a choice of a la carte, excellent value fixed price menu and a "Market Forces" menu and dishes on offer range from traditional conservative fare to the more exotic and adventurous. The latest a la carte features a double baked goats cheese soufflé and a impressive looking seafood vol au vent in the shape of a fish filled with scallops, salmon, prawns and herbs. Sunday sees the famous carvery with an unrivalled range of high quality roast joints, Yorkshire puddings and all manner of indulgent puddings and cheeses: its always very popular.

But The Walls is much more than a very good restaurant: it can cater for special events for up to 200 guests and is highly regarded as a most suitable wedding venue. Two areas are licensed for civil ceremonies. Regular and diverse art exhibition are a year round feature and add to the general interest of this quirky business. Geoff is a great host and communicator and customers are kept up to date with a regular news letter- The Walls Street Journal! - which can be down-loaded from the website.

Open Every day from 10 a.m. for lunch, teas, coffees and dinner, including Sundays. Last orders for lunch, 2.30p.m., last orders for Dinner 9.30.p.m.

Closed Boxing Day and 27th & 28th of December and 1,2,3, of January.

ground a spring bubbled up to mark the spot. Thus St Oswald's Well came into being, soon to become a place of pilgrimage renowned for its healing powers.

There are many fine old buildings in Oswestry, none finer than the **Church of St Oswald**. It played an important part in the Civil War, when it was used as an observation point during the siege of the town by the Parliamentarians. The oldest section is the tower, which dates back to around 1200. The interior is beautiful, and among the treasures are a font presented by Colonel Lloyd of Llanforda as a thanksgiving for the restoration of the monarchy, a Gilbert Scott war memorial and a memorial to Hugh Yale, a member of the family that founded Yale University.

Standing in the grounds of the church is the 15th century Holbache House. Once a grammar school, this handsome building now houses the Tourist Information Centre and the **Heritage Centre** with displays of local interest and exhibitions of arts and crafts. Ferrequinologists (railway buffs) will make tracks for the **Cambrian Museum of Transport** on Oswald Road. Oswestry was the headquarters of the Cambrian Railway Company until it amalgamated with the Great Western Railway in 1922, and as late as the 1960s there were over 1,000 railwaymen in the area. Locomotives, carriages and wagons have been built and repaired in Oswestry for over 100 years, and the maintenance of 300 miles of track was directed from offices in the station building. One of the old engine sheds now houses a small museum with a collection of railway memorabilia and also some old

DAVID J KEEGAN

Market Square, Llanrhaeadr Y.M., Oswestry, Powys SY10 0JL
Tel: 01691 780251
e-mail: davidkeegan@onetel.com

Many visitors to the quiet rural village of Llanraeadr Ym Mochnant are on their way to Pistyll Rhaeadr, the highest waterfall south of the Scottish Highlands and one of the Seven Wonders of Wales. For its many loyal customers **David J Keegan** is *the* local wonder, serving a wide variety of consistently high-quality meats at very competitive prices.

The meat, including lamb, pork and beef (rare-breed Welsh) comes from Ross of Wrexham and local meat markets; other highlights include traditional dry-cured bacon, sausages made on the premises, cooked meats and pies, and pastries from the local bakery.

David also provides meat for the deep freeze and supplies many local pubs and restaurants as well as his loyal band of private customers. Llanrhaeadr lies on the B4580 west of Oswestry, just over the Welsh border in Powys.

Old Oswestry

bicycles and motorbikes. One of the locomotives is regularly steamed up by the volunteers of the Cambrian Railway Society.

In 1559 a plague killed almost a third of the town's population and the **Croeswylan Stone** commemorates this disaster, marking the spot to which the market was moved during the plague. It is sometimes referred to as the Cross of Weeping.

On the northern edge of town, **Old Oswestry** is an impressive example of an Iron Age fortress, first occupied in about 300BC. It was on the border of the territory held by the Cornovii and is one of several in the region. At the southwest corner of the fort can be seen **Wat's Dyke**, built at the same time and for the same purpose – delineating the border between Saxon Mercia and the Welsh – as the better-known Offa's Dyke. Who was Wat? We know not, but he could have been one of Offa's officers.

Around Oswestry

MAESBURY
2 miles S of Oswestry off the A5 or A483

The village was one of the main transit points on the Montgomery Canal, and many of the canal buildings at Maesbury Marsh are still standing, along with some boatmen's cottages.

Immediately south of Maesbury Marsh is the village of Woolston, where St Winifred's Well is said to have been a resting place for saints' bones being carried to their final destinations.

LLANYMYNECH
7 miles S of Oswestry on the A483

🌲 Llanymynech Hills   🌲 Offa's Dyke

🌲 Montgomery Canal

A small diversion is well worthwhile to visit Llanymynech, once a town of some standing,

---

🏛 historic building   🏛 museum   🏛 historic site   🌀 scenic attraction   🌱 flora and fauna with a major canal and a thriving industry based on limestone. It was also a railway junction. The **Llanymynech Hills**, which include a section of **Offa's Dyke**, make for good walking, with the old limestone workings to add interest – you can still see the old bottle lime kilns and an unusual Hoffman rotary kiln. The quarried limestone was taken to the kilns on a tramway and, after processing, to the nearby canalside wharf. Part of the quarry is now a designated nature reserve and supports abundant bird life. On top of the hill are traces of an ancient hill fort. **The Montgomery Canal** was built at the end of the 18th century mainly for the transportation of limestone from the Llanymynech quarries. Large sections of it are now unnavigable, indeed dry, but a restoration

project aims to open 35 miles of waterway from Oswestry through Welshpool to Newtown. Until the boats return there are some delightful walks along the towpath, as well as fishing where it is possible.

ELLESMERE
8 miles NE of Oswestry on the A495

🏛 Old Town Hall	🏛 Old Railway Station
🏛 Welshampton Church	🏚 Llangollen Canal
🜍 The Mere	

The centre of Shropshire's Lakeland, Ellesmere is a pretty market town where the market is held every Tuesday, just as it has been since 1221. The town has been regional winner of the Britain in Bloom competition in both 2000 and 2001 and along its medieval

---

MERESIDE FARM B&B

Ellesmere, Shropshire SY12 0PA
Tel/Fax: 01691 622404
e-mail: nicky@meresidefarm.co.uk
website: www.meresidefarm.co.uk

Mereside Farm B&B stands in 14 acres of farmland near the Llangollen and Shropshire Union Canals and only half a mile from the centre of Ellesmere. In their 18th century farmhouse, friendly hosts Rodney and Nicky Stokes and their family guarantee a pleasant, relaxed stay in comfortable, well-appointed accommodation. A full farmhouse breakfast includes sausages made by Rodney in converted farm buildings where he also makes his renowned Ellesmere Pork Pies. Picnic lunches can be arranged for guests spending a day exploring the area. The two bedrooms in the main house have recently been joined by three apartments in an adjacent building. Ideal for families and with disabled access, the new apartments have under floor heating throughout, super king size beds,

en suite bathrooms, digital flat screen TV, free wireless broadband, mini-kitchens which include a fridge and microwave, and direct access to a walled garden. Country walks start from the doorstep. Cyclists, walkers and dogs are all welcome.

Opposite Mereside Farm is The Mere - the largest of seven meres which are all within three miles of each other, they offer excellent walking, boating, fishing and birdwatching; there are other country walks in the vicinity, and buses run from outside the farm. Mereside Farm has an alarmed lock-up for bicycles, laundry facilities and a drying room for outdoor clothing.

🎬 stories and anecdotes   🐦 famous people   🎨 art and craft   🎭 entertainment and sport   🜍 walks

FANCY THAT!

3 Scotland Street, Ellesmere,
Shropshire SY12 0DE
Tel: 01691 624058

Fancy That! The perfect name for a lovely little shop that's full of surprises. Isabel Scott started the shop from scratch in 2003 and it's now on many local lists as *the* place to look for a gift with a difference or something nice for the home. Behind the cheerful frontage with its attractive window display, the bright, well-presented interior is filled with unusual gift ideas. Affordable designer jewellery in sterling silver set with semi-precious stones or art glass are examples of the high-class goods that fill the display space.

streets rise Georgian and half-timbered buildings. The **Old Town Hall** and the **Old Railway Station** are two of the most striking buildings, but nothing except the mound remains of the castle. The most impressive of all is the parish church of St Mary the Virgin, built by the Knights of St John. It is particularly beautiful inside, with an exceptional 15th century carved roof in the chapel.

The church overlooks **The Mere**, largest of several lakes that are an equal delight to boating enthusiasts, anglers and birdwatchers. Herons, Canada geese and swans are among the inhabitants of The Mere. For an insight into the creation some 15,000 years ago of the Shropshire meres, a browse around the Meres Visitor Centre is recommended. From the centre, there's a pleasant half-mile promenade along the lakeside and through Cremorne Gardens.

Ellesmere forms the hub of a regional canal network with the **Llangollen Canal** linking the Shropshire Union Canal to the Mersey. It was from his offices in Ellesmere that Thomas Telford designed and supervised the building of the entire canal

whose most spectacular feature is the aqueduct, 125 feet high and 1,000 feet long, which spans the Vale of Llangollen. The project was initiated by the Duke of Bridgewater who in just one day raised over a million (18th century) pounds at a hotel in the town to fund the scheme.

A mile or so east of Ellesmere, on the A495, is **Welshampton**, whose **Church** was built by Sir George Gilbert Scott in 1863. One of its memorial windows is dedicated to a Basuto chieftain; he had been a student of theology at Canterbury and part of his studies brought him to Welshampton, where he lodged with the vicar. Unfortunately he fell ill and died in the same year that saw the completion of the church.

Market Drayton

🏠 Buttercross   🌶 Shropshire Union Canal

🌶 Newcastle Way   🌶 Discovery Trail

Market Drayton was mentioned in the Domesday Book as Magna Draitune. It changed its name when Abbot Simon Combermere obtained a Royal Market Charter

FORDHALL FARM

Tern Hill Road, Market Drayton, Shropshire TF9 3PS
Tel: 01630 638255
e-mail: info@fordhallfarm.com website: www.fordhallfarm.com

When Arthur Hollins started **Fordhall Farm** more than 60 years ago, it was one of the very first organic farms in the country and the first to make its own yoghurt. The farm is now in the ownership of the Community Land Initiative, who lease it back to Arthur's youngest children Ben and Charlotte to farm. This they do according to their father's organic principles, and in the farm shop they sell beef and lamb raised on the farm, pork from Gloucester Old Spot pigs, locally grown organic vegetables – even organic drinks and ice cream. The farm attracts many family visits with its nature trails, farm animals, picnic areas, wildlife habitats and a programme of summer events. Open: Wednesday, Saturday and Sunday 11am-4pm, Friday 11am-6pm.

in 1245:

Know that we have granted and by this our present charter confirmed to Brother Simon Abbot of Combermere and the monks serving God there that they and their successors forever shall have a weekly market in their manor of Drayton on Wednesday.

And so they have, every Wednesday since.

The fire of 1651 razed most of the town, so there is now quite a diversity of styles among the buildings, including black and white half-timbered residences and former coaching inns. One of the most interesting structures is the **Buttercross**, built in 1842 to enable farmers' wives to display their wares protected from the weather. The crest it carries is of the Corbet family, Lords of the Manor since 1650.

Market Drayton is often referred to as 'The Home of the Gingerbread'. Gingerbread was baked here for more than 200 years. The bakery is no longer here but traditional Billington's Gingerbread can still be bought in local shops in the town. Traditionally it was dunked in port. Also available is a selection of Gingerbread figures made in all shapes and sizes by a local business called Image on Food. Gingerbread is very good to nibble on the **Discovery Trail** that takes in the sights of the

town. Gingerbread dates back far more than 200 years, of course, and Shakespeare had a good word for it:

An' I had but one penny in the world thou shouldst have it to buy gingerbread.

Just a few hundred yards from the town centre, the **Shropshire Union Canal** gives boaters the chance to moor up and explore the town, while the towpath walk takes in flights of locks, wharfside cottages and the breathtaking 40-steps Aqueduct.

Market Drayton's most famous son (actually born just outside) was Clive of India, whose childhood escapades in the town included climbing the church tower and sitting on one of the gargoyles, and building a dam to flood a shop whose owner was unwilling to pay protection money. Baron Clive of India, Governor of Bengal, was MP for Shrewsbury from 1760 until his death. He is buried in St Margaret's Church, Moreton Say, 12 miles northwest of Shrewsbury. The **Newcastle Way** is a long-distance walking route that runs for 25 miles between Market Drayton and Mow Cop in Staffordshire. It links the Staffordshire Way at Mow Cop with the Shropshire Union Canal towpath at Market Drayton.

Around Market Drayton

HODNET
4 miles SW of Market Drayton on the A53

🏛 Hodnet Hall

The sizeable village of Hodnet is overlooked by the church of St Luke from its hilltop position. The church is Norman, with some unusual features including a christening gate and wedding steps, and it has a very distinctive octagonal tower. There are some ornate carvings around the 17th century font, and a chapel is dedicated to the Heber-Percy family, owners of **Hodnet Hall**. The most illustrious member of the family was Bishop Heber, who wrote, among many other hymns, *From Greenland's Icy Mountains.* Hodnet Hall is an Elizabethan-style mansion built in the 1870s, but the real reason for a visit here is the wonderful gardens, which extend over 60 acres and were carefully planted (Brigadier Heber-Percy masterminded the transformation) to provide a show of colour throughout the seasons. The gardens are only open to the public on certain weekends during the summer. Call 01630 685786 for dates.

MARCHAMLEY
4 miles SW of Market Drayton on the A442

🏛 Hawkestone Hall

The beautiful Georgian mansion **Hawkestone Hall** was the ancestral home of the Hill family from 1556 until 1906. The Hall is now the seat of a religious order, but the principal rooms, including the splendid Venetian Saloon, are open for a

THE FOUR ALLS

Newport Road, Woodseaves, Market Drayton, Shropshire TF9 2AG
Tel: 01630 652995 Fax: 01630 653930
e-mail: inn@thefouralls.com
website: www.thefouralls.com

Sharon Thorpe is the hard-working owner and host at the **Four Alls**, a popular inn and hotel on the A529 a mile south of Market Drayton. It enjoys a quiet rural setting, but is also well placed for discovering many of Shropshire's major visitor attractions. The centrally heated guest accommodation – en suite rooms with hot drinks trays and radio alarm clocks – are located in a motel-style building unit, with access from the large car park; each has its own entrance.

Food is also big business, and diners have a choice between bar and restaurant menus; the main menu is supplemented by daily specials and a lunchtime carvery. The restaurant has seats for 100, with 50 more outside, and the inn has a self-contained function room. And the unique name? It's based on a medieval concept regarding the division of Society:

The King: I rule All
The Priest: I pray for All
The Knight: I fight All
The Peasant: I pay for All

POTFORD HOUSE

Little Bolas, Telford TF6 6PS
Tel: 01952 541362
e-mail: dsadler@potford.fsnet.co.uk
website: www.shropshirebedandbreakfast.com

Potford House is a comfortable family home set in picturesque open countryside a few miles north of Telford and Wellington and just half a mile off the main A442. The guest accommodation consists of three double rooms, one with en suite facilities, the other two sharing an immaculate bathroom. The tariff includes a full English breakfast, and an evening meal is available with prior notice.

Owners Janet and Derek Sadler know everything about the local countryside and tourist attractions, and guests can plan their day's outings in the sitting room. This is good walking country, and among the places of interest within easy reach are Hawkstone Park, the splendid ruins of Moreton Corbet Castle, the Shropshire Union Canal and the towns of Telford, Wellington and Market Drayton.

short time in the summer Tel: 01630 685242. The Pleasure Gardens comprise terraces, lily pond, herbaceous borders and extensive woodland.

MORETON CORBET

6 miles N of Shrewsbury on the B5063

🏰 Castle

Take the A53 to Shawbury and turn left on to the B5063 and you'll soon come across the splendid ruins of **Moreton Corbet Castle**, seat of the local bigwig family. Its stark greystone walls are an entrancing and moving sight, and not at all like a castle. In fact, what remains is the shell of a grand Italian-influenced mansion which was never completed (Corbet funds ran out) and was severely damaged in the Civil War.

WEM

11 miles N of Shrewsbury on the B5476

🏰 Astley House

A peaceful enough place now, but Wem has seen its share of strife, being virtually destroyed in the Wars of the Roses and attacked in the Civil War. On the latter occasion, in 1643, Lord Capel at the head of 5,000 Royalist troops got a pretty hostile reception, and his defeat by a much smaller band, including some townswomen, gave rise to this mocking couplet:

The women of Wem and a few volunteers
Beat the Lord Capel and all his Cavaliers.

It was another woman – actually a 14-year-old girl called Jane Churm – who nearly did what Capel proved incapable of doing. In

SOULTON HALL

nr Wem, Shrewsbury,
Shropshire SY4 5RS
Tel: 01939 232786 Fax: 01939 234097
e-mail: enquiries@soultonhall.co.uk
website: www.soultonhall.co.uk

Soulton Hall is a superb country manor house
lying two miles east of Wem on the B5065.
The family who have owned and run the Hall
for more than six centuries offer luxurious
guest accommodation in the main house and
in the coach house across the lawn; they also
have the option of self-catering
accommodation in three cottages on the
estate. In the main house the four double
bedrooms (three en suite) are individual in
style and character, with many architectural
features from the 16th century. The two
spacious doubles in the coach house have en
suite bathrooms and fine views across to
Soulton Wood.

The cottages are perfect for a quiet,
relaxed, come-as-you-please stay, and, again,
each has its own individual appeal. Keeper's
Cottage in white Grinshill sandstone has three
bedrooms and a sitting room with picture
windows commanding views of the lawns and
woodland. Central heating, hot water and
kitchen appliances are all electric. Shooter's
Lodge is a 1970s bungalow with four
bedrooms with oak-finished fitted units,
farmhouse tables and chairs in the dining
room, oil-fired central heating, lawns at the
front and back and a garage. Ploughman's
Cottage has three bedrooms, a sitting room,
kitchen-dining room, electric power and a
large garden with fruit trees, lawns and flower
beds. The fields, woodland and river banks on

the estate are a haven for wildlife, with foxes,
rabbits, birds and insects to be spotted. Soulton Hall is built of Tudor brick and incorporates
parts of an older property. Roland Hill, the first Protestant Lord Mayor of London, was an early
owner and his descendants have kept the mansion much as it was then.

The present owner is Ann Ashton, who invites guests to share the marvellous atmosphere
generated by the age of the Hall and the care with which it has been maintained. The mullion-
windowed bar is a convivial spot to meet for a drink, and in the elegant dining room a leisurely
five-course dinner uses fresh home-grown or locally sourced produce in a choice of dishes that
combine traditional and contemporary elements. Soulton is a working farm, and guests are
welcome to take an interest in the farming activities. There are ponies for riding, and pony &
trap rides, clay target shooting, musket shooting, archery and coarse fishing can all be arranged;
the Hall is also a wonderful traditional setting for family or Christmas parties.

setting alight the thatch on the roof of her home she started a fire that destroyed 140 properties in one hour. Some notable buildings survived, including **Astley House**, home of the painter John Astley. This and many of the town's most impressive houses are in Noble Street. Famous people associated with Wem include Judge Jeffreys of Bloody Assize fame, who became Baron Wem in 1685, with his official residence at Lowe Hall. Wem is the home of the modern sweet pea, developed by the 19th century nurseryman Henry Eckford. The Sweet Pea Show and the carnival are great occasions in the Wem calendar.

WHITCHURCH
17 miles N of Shrewsbury on the A49

🏛 Church

First developed by the Romans as

Mediolanum, Whitchurch is the most important town in the northern part of the county. Its main street is dominated by the tall sandstone tower of **St Alkmund's Church**, in whose chapel lies the body of Sir John Talbot, 1st Earl of Shrewsbury, who was killed at the Battle of Castillon, near Bordeaux, in 1453.

The Shropshire Way passes nearby, so too the Llangollen Canal, and nature-lovers can explore the local wetland habitats – Brown Moss is two miles to the south off the A41. Whitchurch is the home of Joyce Clocks, the oldest tower clockmakers in the world, and is also, somewhat oddly, where Cheshire cheese was created.

Hidden away in the heart of the town are the Old Town Hall Vaults, where the composer Edward German (*Merrie England, Tom Jones*) was born in 1862.

🎞 stories and anecdotes 🦅 famous people 🖌 art and craft 🎭 entertainment and sport 🚶 walks

ADVERTISERS AND PLACES OF INTEREST

LOCATOR MAP

🏠 historic building   🏛 museum   🏚 historic site   🐦 scenic attraction   🌿 flora and fauna

4 | Staffordshire

The southwest of Staffordshire encompasses many changing landscapes, from the busy industrial towns of Stafford and Burton-on-Trent to the peace and quiet of Cannock Chase. Along with the Hednesford Hills, the Chase provides a wonderful open area of woodland and moorland that is one of the county's great recreational centres. Well-supported by an interesting and informative visitors' centre, the Chase is a must for anyone visiting this part of Staffordshire. The southeast of Staffordshire, although lying close to the Black Country – the depressing product of the heavy industrialisation of the 18th and 19th centuries – has managed to escape in the main. One legacy of the era and a feature throughout the whole of Staffordshire, however, is the canal network. Built to link Birmingham with the Trent & Mersey Canal, the less well known Coventry Canal and the Birmingham & Fazeley Canal pass through tiny villages and hamlets and the towpaths provide the opportunity to walk in some unexpectedly scenic countryside.

Extending along the southern edge of the Peak District, the Staffordshire moorlands certainly rival their neighbour in terms of scenic attraction. The undulating pastures of the moorlands, along with the fresh air and ancient weather-worn crags, make this the ideal place to walk, cycle or trek. It is also an area full of character, with charming scattered villages, historic market towns and a wealth of history. The Industrial Revolution also left its mark on the landscape, though the two great reservoirs of Rudyard and Tittesworth, built to provide a water supply to the growing industry and population of the Midlands, now offer peaceful havens for a wide variety of plants, animals and birds as well as recreational facilities such as fishing and boating.

The area around Stoke-on-Trent is famous the world over for its pottery industry. Originally centred on the five towns of Stoke, Tunstall,

Burslem, Hanley and Longton, the Potteries were at the heart of the Industrial Revolution. Both coal and clay were found locally which gave rise to the start of the industry, though imported clay from Cornwall was later used - but it was the foresight and ingenuity of men such as Wedgwood and Minton that really turned the cottage industry into production on a much larger scale. To support the industry in and around the centre, a network of canals and, later, railways was begun. The Trent & Mersey Canal, built by James Brindley with the support of Wedgwood and his friend the Duke of Bridgewater, was finally completed in 1777 and made possible navigation from coast to coast, between the busy ports of Liverpool and Hull. Together, the Trent & Mersey Canal, the Staffordshire & Worcester Canal, begun in the same year, the Shropshire Union Canal to the west and the Middlewich branch of the Llangollen Canal, form a wonderful four counties ring that can be undertaken wholly or partly by boat. These canals, with their accessible towpaths, run through the very heart of the towns as well as through the often delightful countryside.

Mow Cop Castle, Harriseahead

Stafford

The county town of Staffordshire has its origins in Saxon times, but the most impressive site is Norman. At **Stafford Castle** visitors can follow the castle trail, wander around the medieval herb garden and explore the visitor centre built in the style of a Norman Guardhouse. The Castle grounds are often used for historical re-enactments by such groups as the Napoleonic Society and are the site for Sealed Knot battles as well as other outdoor entertainment. Stafford originally had a medieval town wall and evidence of it can still be seen today in the names of the town's main streets. However, only the East Gate remains

Ancient High House, Stafford

of the structure. Stafford lies on the banks of the River Sow, and Green Bridge marks the site of the ancient ford across the river. There has been a bridge on this spot since the late 1200s but the gate in the town's medieval walls that was also at this point was demolished in 1777. Just to the east of the Bridge is **Victoria Park**, opened in 1908 and later extended to incorporate land reclaimed from the River Sow. There are many pleasant walks through the Park, which includes a mill pond and a weir, in particular to the Windmill at Broad Eye. Built in 1796 by John Wright, the mill moved over to steam power in 1847 and continue to be used until 1880. Like many towns today, Stafford has its busy shopping streets and also an impressive shopping centre. However, many picturesque cobbled lanes still remain and provide the visitor with a quiet and relaxing contrast to the hurly burly of the 21st century. Of particular note are Church Lane, with its timbered buildings, and Mill Street with a varied array of shops, restaurants and pubs.

A place well worth visiting during any stay in Stafford is **The Ancient High House**, a beautiful Elizabethan house built in 1595 and now the largest surviving timber-framed town house in England. Through painstaking efforts over several years, Stafford Borough Council has restored this breathtaking piece of architecture to its former glory. Today the building houses the Museum of the Staffordshire Yeomanry. The Ancient High House's varied history can be followed through the permanent displays in the period room settings taking the visitor through the 17th, 18th and 19th centuries and telling the stories of people who came to know this House so intimately. Not surprisingly, the house has royal connections: both King Charles I and Prince Rupert having stayed here in 1642. The House also has a small heritage shop selling a variety of interesting and locally crafted gifts. The Shire Hall Gallery (1798) on the market square was the assize court and still retains the original panelled courtrooms. It is now a venue for contemporary exhibitions and children's workshops, and has a teashop and a workshop.

Close to the High House is the **Collegiate Church of St Mary**, an unusual building

Stafford Castle

which dates in part from the late 1100s, but has received additions in the early English, Gothic and Victorian styles. The huge tower arches in the nave seem to divide the building into two, which is, in fact, exactly what they were intended to do, as St Mary's is two churches under one roof. The nave was the parish church of Stafford with its own altar while the chancel beyond was used by the Deans of the College of St Mary whose duty it was to pray for deceased members of the Royal family. Although the College was abolished in 1548, the screens which divided the Church remained until 1841 and today the Church is still referred to as the Collegiate. Izaak Walton was baptised here on 21st September, 1593 and his bust can be seen on the north wall of the nave. Each year, at a civic service, a wreath is placed around the bust to commemorate his probable birthday (9th August). Those interested in ecclesiastical architecture should also find time to visit the little Norman and medieval Church of St Chad.

Best known today for his work *The Compleat Angler*, **Izaak Walton** was famous throughout his lifetime as a writer of biographies. However, the story of his own life is somewhat

obscure, though it is certain that he was born in Stafford in 1593. From humble origins, Walton became accepted in the intellectual and ecclesiastical circles of the day and, during the Civil War, he remained a staunch Royalist and stayed in the Stafford area.

St Mary's Mews dates back to the mid-19th century and is a Grade II listed building. The architect was the renowned Gilbert Scott, the famous church restorer of the 1850s. Other notable buildings include The Infirmary, designed by Benjamin Wyatt and completed in 1772; the Noell Almshouses dating back to 1680 and Chetwynd House, the 17th century town house of the Chetwynd family and now used as the town's main Post Office.

Around Stafford

GNOSALL
6 miles W of Stafford on A518

🛶 Canal

Some beautiful ash and sycamore trees form a delightful shaded arch over the road through this village (the name is pronounced 'No Sull') and it also has its very own ghost! On the night of January 21st, 1879 a man was attacked at Gnosall canal bridge by an alarming black monster with enormous white eyes. The police were quite sure it was the ghost of a man–monkey who had haunted the bridge for years after a man was drowned in the canal. It is worth staying a while in the village, ghost permitting, to have a look around the fine collegiate Church of St Lawrence. As well as containing some of the best Norman work to be seen in the county, the church, most of which dates from the 13th and 15th centuries, has a particularly ornate west crossing arch.

Despite its name, a large portion of the **Shropshire Union Canal**, some 23 miles, lies within the county of Staffordshire. Indeed, much of this southern section passes through wonderful countryside. Extending from Ellesmere Port, Cheshire, on the Manchester Ship Canal to Autherley junction near Wolverhampton, the Shroppie, as it is affectionately known, has a long history.

Built by three separate companies, at three different times, the canal was begun as early as 1772 but not finished until 1835, a few months after the death of Thomas Telford, who had worked on its construction. In order to compete with the new railways, the canal had to be built as simply and economically as possible and so, unlike many canals before it, the Shropshire Union's route was short and straight, cutting deeply through hills and crossing lower ground on embankments rather than talking the longer route on level ground.

The canal's Cowley Tunnel, near the village, was originally intended to be longer than its actual 81 yards but, as it was being constructed, the rock towards the southern end, being softer, gave way. The dramatic fault, where the more solid sandstone of the

northern end meets the soft marlstones, can still be seen by taking the towpath through the tunnel and cutting.

WESTON-UNDER-LIZARD
11 miles SW of Stafford on the A5

🏛 Weston Park

Situated on the site of a medieval manor house, **Weston Park** has been the home of the Earls of Bradford for 300 years. Disraeli was a frequent visitor here and, on one visit, presented the house with a grotesque stuffed parrot. The parrot became famous when the present Earl, after leaving Cambridge, published a book entitled *My Private Parts and the Stuffed Parrot*. The stuffed parrot still enjoys the hospitality of Weston Park. The parkland at Weston has matured over several hundred years into a masterpiece of unspoilt landscape. Many have left their mark, yet each successive generation has taken note of its predecessors. Disraeli loved the Park. In one of his letters to Selina, 3rd Countess of Bradford, he refers to the 'stately woods of Weston'. There are some wonderful architectural features in the Park, including the Roman Bridge and the Temple of Diana, both designed and built by James Paine for Sir Henry Bridgeman in about 1760. Fallow deer and rare breeds of sheep roam the vast parklands and there are plenty of other interesting attractions for visitors of all ages including nature trails, a miniature railway and a Museum of Country Bygones.

FEATHERSTONE
12 miles S of Stafford off the A449

🏛 Moseley Old Hall

Just to the south of the village is **Moseley Old Hall**, which visitors can be forgiven for thinking belongs to the 19th century. In fact, it dates from the first Elizabethan Age and, inside, much of the original panelling and timber framing is still visible. The Hall once sheltered King Charles II for a short time following his defeat at the Battle of Worcester in 1651, and it is for this that the house is best remembered. Under cover of darkness the defeated King, disguised as a woodcutter, was escorted into the house by Thomas Whitgreave, the owner, and his chaplain, John Huddlestone. He rested here for two days and even evaded capture when Parliamentarians visited the house in search of the monarch before leaving, again in disguise, and fleeing to France. In 1940, the house was acquired by the Wiggin family and in 1962 it became the property of the National Trust. At that time it had no garden to speak of, but fairly soon two experts recreated the garden in the style of the century. The outstanding feature is the knot garden with its box hedges and gravel beds. There is interest everywhere in this wonderful garden, which is full of rare 17th century plants and herbs. In the barn is an exhibition showing the escape of King Charles.

GREAT HAYWOOD
5 miles E of Stafford on the A51

🏛 Shugborough Hall

This ancient village is famous for having the longest packhorse bridge in England. Built in the 16th century, the Essex Bridge (named after the Elizabethan Earl who lived nearby at Shugborough Hall when hunting in the area) still has 14 of its original 40 arches spanning the River Trent. Here, too, is the interesting Roman Catholic Church of St John the

WESTON HALL

Weston, Staffordshire ST18 0BA
Tel: 01889 271700 Fax: 01889 271400
e-mail: info@westonhall.co.uk
website: www.westonhall.co.uk

Weston Hall is a magnificent Grade II listed building dating back to the 16th century set in beautifully landscaped gardens and grounds on the A518 five miles from Stafford. It's a perfect place to relax and rest, an ideal base for touring the local attractions and a perfect venue for wedding and other celebrations. It was long ago the home of wealthy ironmongers but eventually fell into neglect before being sympathetically restored in the 1990s. Many handsome original features survive, including oak beams and open stone fireplaces. The accommodation comprises eight superbly appointed en suite rooms, including two for families, with a four-poster and twin beds.

The star of the show is the Western Suite with a superb stone fireplace, a four-poster bed and a 14ft beamed ceiling. This room and several others enjoy glorious views over the picturesque Trent Valley. The Alexander Restaurant is an elegant, intimate room with exposed stone walls, beams, an open fireplace and cosy candlelit nooks – a lovely setting for a memorable meal using the finest seasonal ingredients and complemented by a fine wine list. The Hall has versatile conference and meeting rooms and is licensed for civil wedding ceremonies, with two suites and the restaurant for celebrations after the knot is tied.

Baptist. Built in 1828, in 1845 the whole church was moved from its original site at Tixall to Great Haywood by the local Roman Catholic community. With an ornate west front and Perpendicular windows, it is the richness of the west gallery that is the highlight of the building.

Most visitors to the village however, pass swiftly through it on their way to one of the most impressive attractions in the county, **Shugborough Hall**, the 17th century seat of the Earls of Lichfield. This magnificent 900-acre estate includes Shugborough Park Farm, a Georgian farmstead built in 1805 for Thomas, Viscount Anson, and now home to rare breed animals and to demonstrations of traditional farming methods such as hand milking, butter and cheese making and shire horses at work. The former servants' quarters have been restored to the days of the 19th century and offer an insight into life below stairs. The mansion itself is a splendid piece of architecture, altered several times over its 300 years, but always retaining its distinct grandeur. Outside, in the beautiful parkland, can be found an outstanding collection of neoclassical monuments dotted around and the Lady Walk leads along the banks of the River Sow to the delightful terraced lawns and rose garden.

INGESTRE
4 miles E of Stafford off the A51

🏛 Church

The beautiful **Church of St Mary the Virgin**, in this small estate village, is something of a surprise. Standing close to the Jacobean Ingestre Hall, the sophisticated church was built in 1676 and has been attributed to Sir Christopher Wren. One of the few churches that Wren designed outside London, it has an elegant interior with a rich stucco nave ceiling

and some of the earliest electrical installations in any church. The chancel, which is barrel vaulted, is home to a delightful garlanded reredos and there are many monuments to the Chetwynds and Talbots, who were Earls of Shrewsbury from 1856 and had their seat in the village.

STOWE-BY-CHARTLEY
5 miles E of Stafford on the A518

On the A518 Stafford-Uttoxeter road, a mile east of Weston, Amerton Farm and Craft Centre has something for everyone.

RUGELEY
7 miles SE of Stafford on the A51

🏛 The Old Chancel   ⚜ Ridware Arts Centre

🌿 Wolseley Centre

On first arriving in the town, visitors can be mistaken for thinking that Rugeley is all modern but, at its heart, there are some fine 17th and 18th century buildings that have survived the years of industrialisation. Between 1860 and 1967, the cattle market was held behind the inn and a market bell was rung from the steps of the hostelry to summon the farmers back from their lunch.

Rugeley's original parish church, the **Old Chancel**, was founded in the 1100s though it is only the tower, chancel and north chapel that remain from those early days; the rest of the building dates back to the 13th and 14th centuries. The nave was demolished in 1823 to help pay for the building of the imposing new church which, too, is well worth a visit.

Next to the Old Chancel is Church Croft, a fine Georgian house and the birthplace of William Palmer. Later in life, as Dr William Palmer, he brought unhappy notoriety to the town in Victorian times as he poisoned his hapless victims after insuring them.

🏛 historic building   🏛 museum   🏛 historic site   ⚜ scenic attraction   🌿 flora and fauna

Eventually he was caught, put on trial, found guilty of murder and publicly hanged in Stafford in 1856. The Tudor house rented by the evil Dr Palmer still stands.

Ridware Arts Centre, just outside the town, is within the Tudor walls of the ancient manorial site of Hamstall Hall and is home to a fascinating group of shops, studios and a restaurant. Also nearby is the **Wolseley Centre**, a haven of wildlife and plant life and the headquarters of the Staffordshire Wildlife Trust.

CANNOCK CHASE
5 miles SE of Stafford on the A34

🏛 Museum   🏰 Castle Ring   🏰 Broadhurst Green

🍃 Coppice Hill   🍃 Brereton Spurs

Though close to areas of dense population, Cannock Chase is a surprisingly wild place of heath and woodland that has been designated an Area of Outstanding Natural Beauty. Covering some 20,000 acres, the Chase was once the hunting ground of Norman kings and, later, the Bishops of Lichfield. Deer are still plentiful. Conifers now dominate but it is still possible to find the remains of the ancient oak forest and, in the less well-walked marshy grounds, many rare species survive. A popular place for leisurely strolls, the Chase is also ideal for more strenuous walking and other outdoor recreational activities. Excellent view points can be found at **Coppice Hill** and **Brereton Spurs**, while **Castle Ring**, an impressive Iron Age hill fort, is well worth the effort to find.

Amid all this natural beauty, there are also reminders of the 20th century and, in

CANNOCK CHASE TREKKING CENTRE

Chase Side Stables, Teddesley Coppice,
Staffordshire ST19 5RP
Tel: 01785 711177
website: www.cannockchasetrekking.co.uk

Cannock Chase Trekking Centre offers the opportunity to enjoy 'an ultimate riding experience through the tranquil forests of Cannock Chase'. The surroundings are peaceful and serene, the scenery superb, and the woods are home to 800 fallow deer. Part of the forest is a designated Area of Outstanding Natural Beauty and the open heathland is a Site of Special Scientific Interest.

Owner Lisa Hyde has a lifetime's experience with horses and when she established the trekking centre in 1995 she was following in the footsteps of her father Joe Gregory, who owned and ran a riding stables when she was very young. She and her team have an excellent selection of horses and ponies, and riders will find a combination of professionalism and fun.

Accompanied rides for both novice and experienced riders take place throughout the day. The options are: 1 hour for novices; 2 hours for mixed ability; 2 hours for experienced riders; all-day rides; and evening rides in the summer. The minimum age for these rides is 7, and there are paddock rides for youngsters aged between 4 and 7.

🎭 stories and anecdotes   🐦 famous people   🎨 art and craft   ✒ entertainment and sport   🚶 walks

SIR AMICS PAINTA

Coppice House, Teddesley Coppice, Penkridge,
Staffordshire ST19 5RP
Tel: 01785 711483
e-mail: info@siramicspainta.co.uk

At **Sir Amics Painta**, pottery painting is a real pleasure, providing fun for all the family in making a unique piece to keep or to give as a special, personal present. The studio fee of £5 covers paints, glazing and firing for up to three pieces of pottery per person, and the choice of items to paint – some functional, some decorative, many both – ranges from under £5 to £30. The steps are to choose a piece; work out a design and paint the piece; leave it to be glazed and fired; collect it five days later; enjoy it and win admiration all round!

Designs could be tailored to a special occasion, perhaps a new baby, moving house or a retirement, and customers can paint their own or commission them; takeaway packs can be bought to paint a pot at home. The studio, which lies on the A34 between Stafford and Cannock, holds special pottery evenings and ladies only evenings, and parties and groups of all ages can arrange a session outside normal hours, which are 10am to 6pm Wednesday to Sunday.

particular, the unique military cemeteries near **Broadhurst Green**, where some 5,000 German soldiers from the First World War lie buried. Cannock Chase was used as a training ground during that war and was the last billet for many thousands of soldiers before they left for France. The remnants of the training area can still be seen, as can the prisoner of war camp. The use of the Chase as a training ground was not a new idea: in 1873, there were extensive manoeuvres here with one army base at Etching Hill and the other at Hednesford Hills.

The **Museum of Cannock Chase** illustrates the rich social and industrial heritage of the area, from medieval hunting forest to coal field community, reflecting the social and domestic life of times past. The Toys and Games gallery has a collection of toys from the Victorian era right up to the present day, including loads of things to do for kids of all ages. Temporary exhibitions and a full events diary ensure that there is always something new to see or do at the Museum. Visitors can take a self-guided walk round the Museum – admission is free – and then enjoy a walk over the adjacent Hednesford Nature Reserve following the Colliery Trail or using one of the many other walk leaflets available in the Museum.

HEDNESFORD
8 miles S of Stafford on the A460

🌱 Hazel Slade Reserve   🏛 Cockpit Hill

🏛 Hednesford Hills

This former mining town lies on the edge of Cannock Chase and its oldest building, The

🏛 historic building   🏛 museum   🏛 historic site   🏛 scenic attraction   🌱 flora and fauna

Cross Keys Inn, dates from about 1746. The Anglesey Hotel, built in 1831 by Edmund Peel of Fazeley, was originally designed as a form of summerhouse in a Tudor style with stepped gables and this, too, lies at the heart of Hednesford.

Nearby, the **Hazel Slade Reserve** shows the adaptability of nature with an old-fashioned countryside of small fields, hedges, streams, marshes and woodland. In the 1960s the old broadleaf wood was felled for timber; hedges were planted and cattle grazed the cleared fields. However, a small area of the wood managed to recover and grew from the stumps and seeds that remained in the ground. Then, five years later, a pool and marsh started to form as the land began to subside as a result of the local mining activity. The Reserve is a popular place for fishermen as well as those interested in natural history.

Rising over 700 feet above sea level, the **Hednesford Hills** are a prominent local landmark, which bring the countryside of Cannock Chase into the heart of Hednesford. Originally covered in oak and birch, these 300 acres of heathland have been the scene of varied activities over the years. They have been quarried for sand and gravel, mined for coal and used for military training. The land is now a registered common and the hills are a tract of wild landscape with a plethora of heathland plants, abundant wildlife and the opportunity for recreation for the people who live nearby.

The hills have other sporting connections, too. Cockfighting once took place at **Cockpit Hill** though the exact location of the old

ROSEDALE TREES & SHRUBS

Pillaton Hall Farm, Penkridge, Staffordshire ST19 5RZ
Tel: 01785 713444 Fax: 01785 713666
e-mail: rosedaletrees@aol.com

Rosedale Trees & Shrubs is the enterprise of David Morris and David Moore, where they raise and sell a huge variety of plants, trees, shrubs, grasses and herbs. The nursery is always filled with an excellent selection of all kinds of plants, all gown from seed, and the vegetables are grown from seed, some in polytunnels, for flavour and not, as too often is the case elsewhere, for shelf life.

Vegetables grown on the raised beds in the nursery are a demonstration of what is grown in the nearby kitchen garden. The two Davids and their hardworking staff have an extensive knowledge of all aspects of plants and gardening and are always on the spot with advice and help. The staff

are also responsible for the eyecatching flower displays that every season adorn the centre of Penkridge, and the owners also run a successful landscaping business.

cockpit is unknown. In the 1900s, prize fighters prepared themselves at the nearby Cross Keys Inn for boxing bouts on the hills, and racehorses were trained on the land. Race meetings were held here regularly until 1840 when the racetrack at Etchinghill, near Rugeley, became more popular. In particular, three Grand National winners were stabled and trained on the Hednesford Hills: Jealousy won the race in 1861, Eremon in 1907 and Jenkinstown in 1910.

CANNOCK
9 miles S of Stafford on the A34

Lying on the southern edge of Cannock Chase, this colliery town goes back to the time of the Norman Conquest and appears as 'Chenet' in the Domesday Book. It was an important market town for centuries (Henry III granted the charter in 1259), and the attractive market place still holds busy market days on Tuesdays, Fridays and Saturdays.

On the far side of the market place is the Parish Church of St Luke which, according to the records, had a chantry and a grammar school linked to it as early as 1143. The battlemented church tower dates from the 1300s and, together with the west end of the nave, is the oldest surviving part of the building. The arms of Humphrey de Stafford, who was killed at the Battle of Northampton in 1460, are on display.

The ancient bowling green has been there since time immemorial and, overlooking the green, is an imposing Georgian house that was once home to the Council. Nearby is the former conduit head building of Cannock Conduit Trust. Founded in 1736 to bring a water supply to the town, the Trust building, known as the Tank House, supplied water to the area until 1942.

Burton-on-Trent

🏛 Coors Visitor Centre   🌱 Washlands

The 'capital' of East Staffordshire, Burton-on-Trent is famous for its brewing industry. It began many centuries ago, and even the monks of the Benedictine Abbey, founded here in 1100, were not the first to realise that the Burton well water was specially suited to brewing. William Bass began brewing in Burton in 1777, and by 1863 the brewery had grown to produce half a million barrels of beer each year on a 150-acre site. In 1998 Bass acquired the Burton premises of Carlsberg-Tetley, creating the biggest brewery site in the UK – 115 acres, brewing 5.5 million barrels yearly. The **Coors Visitor Centre** in Horninglow Street is the present name of the Bass Museum, the UK's premier museum dedicated to brewing. Occupying a t10-acre site, the centre offers a unique insight into the history of brewing in Burton. The original joiners' shop, a Grade II listed building dating from 1866, has three floors of historic galleries, and among the many other attractions are the brewing process exhibition, a vintage vehicle collection (including the famous Daimler Worthington White Shield Bottle Car), the famous Shire horses and a working stationary steam engine. England's oldest micro-brewery also operates from the Visitor Centre with working vessels dating back as far as 1830. The Centre is open seven days a week, and tours of the brewery and latest technology packaging plant take place from Tuesday to Thursday.

A Benedictine Abbey, founded by a Saxon earl called Wulfric Spot, was established on the banks of the River Trent, where the Market Place now stands. The focus of Burton, it was from here that the town grew.

In the 12th century, the monks constructed a large stone bridge of some 36 arches across the River Trent – today's bridge replaced the medieval structure in 1864. The area along the banks of the Trent, between Burton Bridge and the later structure of Ferry Bridge, which opened in 1889, is known as the **Washlands**. Rich in native wildlife, the Washlands is a haven for all manner of birds, small mammals, trees and plants. This ancient area, now a wonderful, traditionally managed recreational centre for the town, has a history dating back beyond that of Burton itself. It was at Washlands, in the 7th century, that St Modwen is said to have built her chapel and settlement on Andresey Island. No evidence of the constructions remain and they are thought to have been destroyed in a Danish raid in 874. The site of the chapel is marked by a cherry orchard and some yew trees.

Around Burton-on-Trent

TUTBURY
4 miles N of Burton on the A50

🏰 Castle

The historic village of Tutbury is dominated by the imposing remains of the Castle, which has stood on a naturally defensive outcrop of rock for many centuries. From 1086 to 1265, **Tutbury Castle** belonged to the Ferrers family, who had connections here and in Derbyshire, and for a time it belonged to the Duchy of Lancaster. Today, the Castle is in ruins but it remains an attraction particularly for those interested in Mary, Queen of Scots, who was imprisoned here for a while. During the Civil War, Tutbury Castle remained loyal to the Crown while the town was under the control of Parliament. After a three-week

THE BAY TREE DELICATESSEN

*8 High Street, Tutbury, nr Burton-upon-Trent,
Derbyshire DE13 9LP
Tel: 01283 810055*

The Newberry family opened the **Bay Tree Delicatessen** in 2006 in the historic village of Tutbury, on the A50 four miles north of Burton. A mouthwatering array of top-quality produce includes deli items with a Mediterranean flavour, among them salamis and other charcuterie, olives and olive oil, vinegars, sun-dried tomatoes, pasta and sauce mixes, along with free-range eggs, local cheese and dairy produce.

Sandwiches and rolls are made up to order in bread baked daily on the premises, and other goodies include preserves from Cottage Delight, Forest chutneys and preserves, hand-made chocolates and Turkish Delight. Baskets and picnic hampers can be made to order. Shop hours are 9 to 5 Monday to Friday, 9 to 4.30 Saturday.

Tutbury Castle

churches. The town itself is both charming and full of character with many Georgian-fronted shops and a wide variety of antiques showrooms in the Tutbury Mill Mews, which was originally an ironmongery and wheelwright.

HOAR CROSS
7 miles W of Burton off the B5234

🏠 Church

The magnificent Roman Catholic **Church of the Holy Angels** is by the Victorian architect GF Bodley and it so impressed Sir John Betjeman that he called it Bodley's masterpiece. It was commissioned by the widow of Hugo Francis Meynell Ingram, in

siege, the Castle surrendered and in the following year, 1647, Parliament ordered its destruction. In the shadow of the castle stands the Priory Church of St Mary the Virgin, one of the finest of all Norman

🏠 historic building   🏛 museum   🏚 historic site   🌥 scenic attraction   🌿 flora and fauna his memory, and much of its beauty it due to this remarkable lady.

ABBOTS BROMLEY
10 miles W of Burton on the B5234

🏛 Hurst Chapel

This delightful 13th century village in the Vale of Trent has some notable timber-framed buildings, among which are the Goat's Head Inn and the village school. The butter cross in the centre of the village is where the local farmers used to sell their produce. Abbots Bromley is known chiefly for its annual Horn Dance, and the ancient reindeer horns used in the ceremony are kept in the **Hurst Chapel** of the Church of St Nicholas. The origins of this dance are lost in the mists of time, but it is thought that it was first performed at the three-day Bartelmy Fair, granted to the Abbots of Burton by Henry III in 1226 to celebrate St Bartholomew's Day. In early September each year, six male dancers carry

the horns around the village with six others and a fool, a hobby horse, a bowman and Maid Marian, the last being a man dressed up as a woman. There's dancing and even mock battles with deer heads and reindeer antlers. The procession starts at about 8am and passes by some local farms before arriving at Blithfield Hall around midday. After lunch, the procession wends its way back to the village, where the horns are returned to the church.

Lichfield

🏛 St John's Hospital & Chapel   🏛 Cathedral

🚶 Stone and Minster Pools   🏛 Heritage Centre

🏛 Wall Roman Site   🎨 The Curborough Collection

🐦 Samuel Johnson Birthplace Museum

🐦 Erasmus Darwin Centre

Despite its 18th century prominence, Lichfield lagged behind other towns in extensive rebuilding programmes and consequently it still retains its medieval grid pattern streets with elegant Georgian houses and, mixed in among them, black and white Tudor cottages. First settled by the Celts and also close to the crossroads of the two great Roman roadways, Rykneld Street (now the A38) and Watling Street (now the A5), Lichfield was one of the most important towns of ancient days; the King of Mercia offered St Chad the seat of Lichfield and, on his death, the town became a place of pilgrimage and an important ecclesiastical centre.

The first cathedral was built here in 669 but no traces of this building, or the later Norman structure, remain. The **Lichfield Cathedral** seen today dates from the 12th century and is particularly famous for the three magnificent spires which dominate the City skyline. Inside

Lichfield Cathedral

 stories and anecdotes   famous people   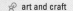 art and craft   🖊 entertainment and sport   🚶 walks there are many treasures, including the beautiful 8th century illuminated manuscript *The Lichfield Gospels* and Sir Francis Chantrey's famous sculpture *The Sleeping Children*.

The surrounding Cathedral Close is regarded by many as the most original and unspoilt in the country. Since it is separated from the rest of the city by **Stowe and Minster Pools**, it is also a peaceful haven of calm. These two wonderful pools, Stowe and Minster, are used for fishing, while Beacon Park is the venue for the Festival fireworks display each July. The Minster Pool is particularly beautiful – it was landscaped in the late 1700s by Anna Seward and is now a haven for wildfowl.

At the very heart of Lichfield is the **Lichfield Heritage Centre**, part of St Mary's Centre in the Market Place. The Staffordshire Millennium Embroideries are on display here. A church has stood on this site since the 12th century and the present building, the third, dates from 1868. As with many ecclesiastical buildings, the decline in the church-going population made St Mary's redundant and, to save it from being demolished altogether, the Centre was formed. A stroll round here is a fascinating experience and, for the energetic, there are spectacular views across the city from the viewing platform on the spire. There are exhibitions on the history and everyday life of the city as seen through the eyes of its inhabitants over the centuries and it also includes the story of the siege of Lichfield Cathedral during the Civil War and displays of the city's silver, ancient charter and archives.

The City has been a place of pilgrims and travellers for centuries and, in 1135, **St John's Hospital** was founded to offer shelter to those passing through Lichfield. One of the finest Tudor brick buildings in the country, the

Hospital is now a home for the elderly. The **Hospital Chapel**, with its magnificent stained glass window by the designer of the celebrated east window at Coventry Cathedral, John Piper, is open daily. A statue of *Noah and the Dove* by Simon Manby was installed here in 2006.

The Guildhall, the meeting place of the city governors for over 600 years, has, at various times been a courthouse, police station and prison. Behind its Victorian façade, lie the remains of the city jail, complete with stocks and cells and the City Dungeons can be visited on Saturdays throughout the summer.

Lichfield's most famous son is Dr Samuel Johnson, the poet, novelist and author of the first comprehensive English dictionary. The son of a bookseller, Johnson was born in 1709 in Breadmarket Street, and the house is now home to the **Samuel Johnson Birthplace Museum**. Open every day, with free entry, the Museum, as well as exhibiting artefacts relating to his life and works, also has a series of tableaux showing how the house looked in the early 1700s. Dr Johnson was justly proud of his city:

'I lately took my friend Boswell (a Londoner) and showed him genuine civilised life in an English provincial town. I turned him loose in Lichfield, that he might see for once real civility.'

Here are a few more Johnson gems:

'A tavern chair is the throne of human felicity.'

'Depend on it sir, when a man knows he is to be hanged in a fortnight, it concentrates the mind wonderfully.'

'When two Englishman meet their first talk is of the weather.'

Memorials to Dr Johnson's stepdaughter, Lucy Porter, can be seen in the medieval St Chad's Church, which has a Norman tower. In

DAME OLIVER'S

19 Dam Street, Lichfield, Staffordshire WS13 6AE
Tel: 01543 256600
e-mail: alf.hall@virgin.net

Set in historic Dam Street, just off the Market Square, **Dame Oliver's** is an Aladdin's Cave crammed full of all sorts of wonderful things. Womenswear (created using natural fibres such as silk, cotton, linen and wool), accessories, a huge range of costume jewellery, silver jewellery and body jewellery, scarves and stoles, bags, hats and fascinators (these can be made to order for that special occasion). The owner, Louise, is constantly on the lookout for something different and new stock arrives weekly throughout the year. Dress sizes 8 to 24, prices from 10p to £250. Affordable individuality!

the churchyard is a well in the place where St Chad used to baptise people in the 7th century. The ancient practice of well-dressing was revived at St Chad's in 1995 to celebrate the 50th anniversary of Christian Aid and is now an annual event.

Apart from the historic pleasure that Lichfield gives, there is also plenty of parkland to enjoy and, in particular, the Beacon Park and Museum Gardens. The 75-acre Park encloses playing fields and a small boating lake and, in the Museum Gardens, can be found a statue of Commander John Smith,

captain of the ill-fated *Titanic*, sculpted by Lady Katherine Scott, widow of Scott of the Antarctic.

Anna Seward, the landscaper of Minster Pool, is another of Lichfield's famous sons and daughters. She lived in the Bishop's Palace and was a poet and letter writer as well as being at the centre of a Lichfield-based literary circle in the late 1700s. Erasmus Darwin, the doctor, philosopher, inventor, botanist and poet, and the closest friend of Josiah Wedgwood, lived in a house in Beacon Street on the corner of The Close. The

Erasmus Darwin Centre

Beacon Street, Lichfield, Staffordshire WS13 7AD
Tel: 01543 306260
e-mail: Erasmus.d@virgin.net
website: www.erasmus-darwin.org

Visitors to Lichfield can find a covered alley way in-between the houses and bookshop opposite the majestic, three spired Cathedral.

Walking up the alley, they are led to the right, discovering a secluded courtyard of ancient houses, surrounding the herb garden of Erasmus Darwin's House. Through an iron gateway, the visitor then reaches the entrance door to the Doctor's former home. Indoors, an introductory video gives a short biography and audio-guides take the visitor back in time as they journey through the rooms. Touch screen computers, working models, and a silhouette booth are some of the interactives that compliment the historical artefacts on display.

🎞 stories and anecdotes 🐟 famous people 🎨 art and craft 🎭 entertainment and sport 🚶 walks

Erasmus Darwin Centre, just three minutes from the Cathedral, is a fascinating place to visit, with touch-screen computers to access Darwin's writings and inventions, and a garden where herbs and shrubs that would have been familiar to the doctor are grown. Erasmus was the grandfather of Charles Darwin, and had his own theories about evolution. David Garrick, probably the greatest actor-manager of the 18th century theatre, had a home which stands opposite the west gate of the Cathedral. The new Lichfield Garrick Theatre opened in 2003. Lichfield is a festival city, the premier event being the Lichfield International Arts Festival held in July.

Wall Roman Site, Lichfield

Just north of the Lichfield, **The Curborough Collection** is a traditional craft centre with an amazing array of crafts and antiques, found in 24 separate units. To the south can be found the impressive **Wall Roman Site**. Known to the Romans as Letocetum, is has the remains of a bath house and mansion, the most substantial to be found in the country.

Around Lichfield

BURNTWOOD
4 miles W of Lichfield on the A5190

🌱 Chasewater Heaths   🏛 Chasewater Railway

The 700 acres of land and water known as **Chasewater Heaths** are an unexpected find in this otherwise urban setting. On the fringes of the village, Chasewater offers a true wilderness experience with a combination of heath and woodland environments. Criss-crossed by paths and bridleways, the collection of plants and

animals found here is so rare that a large area has been designated a Site of Special Scientific Interest. The volunteer-run **Chasewater Railway**, a former colliery railway in what is now Chasewater Country Park, operates passenger services behind tank engines between Brownhills West and Norton Lakeside stations. The two-mile trip takes about 25 minutes and trains run every 45 minutes on Sundays and Bank Holiday Mondays from March to October. Old buildings from the industrial days of coal mining can still be seen, as can reminders of the time when this was an inland waterside resort.

ARMITAGE
5 miles NW of Lichfield on the A513

Situated on the banks of the Trent and Mersey Canal, the village is synonymous with sanitary ware – the manufacturer Armitage Shanks is still located on the canalside. Less well known is the splendid Norman font in the church. Close to the village is the only tunnel along the Trent and Mersey Canal with a towpath. Cut through red sandstone rock, it withstood the test of time and the vibrations of the traffic crossing over it, until, finally the heavy lorries of the late-20th century took their toll. The tunnel was opened out completely but the tunnel effect remains as the widened road still crosses the cutting.

ALREWAS
5 miles NE of Lichfield on the A38

🌱 National Memorial Arboretum

The main street of this enchanting village is lined with delightful black and white thatched cottages, some of which date back to the 1400s. The village Church of All Saints is equally beautiful. Its doorways are all that remain of the original Norman church; the chancel was built in the 13th century.

The National Memorial Arboretum, on the A513 Alrewas-Tamworth road, is the first large arboretum and wildlife reserve to be created in Britain for 200 years. A substantial grant from the Millennium Commission has transformed a 150-acre former gravel quarry into a sylvan temple whose theme is remembrance, essentially for those who have lost their lives or suffered in the service of their country. The central feature of the Arboretum, which is run by the British Legion, is the Millennium Avenue, created from cuttings from a 2,000-year-old lime tree. In the unique Millennium Chapel, the Last Post, two minutes' silence and Reveille are observed at 11am daily. October 2007 will see the opening of the Armed Forces Memorial – a national monument that commemorates members of the UK armed forces killed on duty or as a result of terrorist action since the Second World War. The Memorial will be built and maintained by The Armed Forces Memorial Trust, a separate charitable trust whose patron is HRH The Prince of Wales.

CURBOROUGH HALL FARM SHOP

Watery Lane, Curborough, nr Lichfield,
Staffordshire WS13 8ES
Tel: 01543 418599
website: www.curboroughcrafts.co.uk

Since 2003, John and Faye Evans have run the **Curborough Hall Farm Shop**, part of a traditional arts and crafts centre a short distance north east of the centre of Lichfield. Customers really matter to the owners, and it's always a pleasure to visit the shop. Meat comes from the very best local sources, including beef and lamb reared on the farm and Packington free range pork, all neatly and hygienically packaged for your convenience by award winning local butchers Peter Coates of Alrewas.

Fresh bread daily from a local baker, locally produced milk and cheeses, top quality fresh seasonal fruit and vegetables. Other quality produce includes seasonal game, free-range chickens, local free range chicken, duck and goose eggs, pickles and preserves, dressings, oils and herbs, luxurious Red Lion Farm ice cream available in 20 different flavours, teas, health foods and vitamins, even soft-eating natural licorice. The farm shop, which supplies many local hotels, restaurants and gastro-pubs, is open from 9.30 to 5, seven days a week.

THE HEART OF THE COUNTRY VILLAGE

*London Road, Lichfield,
Staffordshire WS14 9RQ*
Tel: 01543 481612
website: www.heartofthecountryvillage.com
Open: 10am - 5pm Tues- Sun, Bank Holiday Monday

Most people (albeit some secretly) enjoy shopping and most people would agree that variety is the spice of life. Those who believe both are in for a real treat at the **Heart of the Country Village**. For a relaxed, convenient shopping experience, where an amazing range of exclusive products is backed up by old-fashioned standards of service, shoppers form many miles around look no further than this shopping village at Swinfen, 2 miles south of Lichfield and just off the A38.

The village, next to the top-class Swinfen Hall Hotel, comprises a range of shops and two eating places in a group of converted farm building set around attractive courtyards. Each has its own unique style and appeal, with reputations built firmly on high quality and friendly personal service, and a source of unique gifts and design-led ideas to enhance the house and garden.

The variety is truly impressive: bespoke kitchens and bedrooms; solid, durable classic furniture in oak, pine, beech and cedar; French-style furniture; designer landscaping for gardens and driveways; lighting and other home accessories; bed linen and table linen; country lifestyle clothing; stunning ceramics; limited edition prints; contemporary jewellery; a made-to-measure service for curtains and blinds; and a range of inspirational gift ideas and lifestyle items sourced from around the world. Visitors can take a break from retail therapy with a drink and a snack in the Barn Café or Pear Tree Crêperie.

FRADLEY
4 miles NE of Lichfield off the A38

🌿 Fradley Pool Nature Reserve

Another dimension in the history of the canal age is revealed in the opening of **Fradley Pool Nature Reserve** at Fradley Junction, where the Coventry Canal joins the Trent & Mersey Canal. The reservoir site includes a variety of habitats, a bird hide, tree sculptures, pools, and gateways and a willow tunnel designed and made by local school groups. On the other side of the canal are a café and a British Waterways Information Centre and shop.

EDINGALE
5 miles E of Lichfield off the A513

🌳 National Forest

A regional forest, **National Forest**, is

reshaping the landscape between this village and Alrewas to the west. The project, which stretches over the three counties, blends the new plantations with ancient woodland and includes farmland, villages and open country.

WHITTINGTON
3 miles SE of Lichfield off the A51

🏛 Museum of the Staffordshire Regiment

Whittington is home to the **Museum of the Staffordshire Regiment** (The Prince of Wales'), housed in the Victorian Whittington Barracks. The regiment incorporates the former South and North Staffordshire Regiments which were amalgamated in 1959. The Regiment's origins go back to 1705 when the 38th Foot (later the 1st Battalion of the South Staffordshire Regiment) was raised at

THE OLD STABLES FARM SHOP

Packington Moor Farm, Lichfield,
Staffordshire WS14 9QB
Tel: 01543 481223   Fax: 01543 481259
e-mail: rosemary@packingtonmoor-events.co.uk
website: www.packingtonmoor/events.com

The Old Stables Farm Shop is located on Packington Moor, a working arable and livestock farm just off the A51 midway between Tamworth and Lichfield. The farm has been run by the Barnes family since 1921, and the third generation, John and Rosemary, live and work here. They run farm shop, bakery and café and produce the best Pick Your Own summer fruits. The farm shop is stocked with a wide range of prime produce, including the famous free-range Packington pork, which is specially butchered and packaged for the Old Stables; game and poultry; farm eggs, fruit and vegetables; British cheeses, local preserves and delicatessen products. Snacks, lunches and suppers are served in the Courtyard Café, and the spacious Country Garden and the 18th century Oat Barn are popular venues for weddings, functions and other special occasions. The Old Stables also offers a full outside catering service.

The farm shop is open from 8am to 6pm Tuesday to Friday and from 8am to 5pm on Saturday.

Lichfield. The Museum exhibits a good range of uniforms, shako and helmet plates, belt plates and clasps, badges and buttons, and weapons from pistols to machine guns. There's a full-scale WW1 trench system, Anderson shelters and relics from the Sikh Wars, the Crimean, Indian Mutiny, Zulu War, Egypt, Sudan, South Africa and both World Wars. Among the medals on display there are no fewer than 13 Victoria Crosses. Regimental archives are available for research by prior appointment.

TAMWORTH
8 miles SE of Lichfield off the A5

🏛 Castle   🏛 Town Hall

A modern, busy town, Tamworth is actually much older than it first appears. Straddling the famous Roman Watling Street (now the A5), it has a fascinating and turbulent past. The first reference to the town dates back to the 8th century when it was the capital of the Kingdom of Mercia. King Offa built a palace here. Raiding Danes managed to destroy the town twice and it was later invaded by other Scandinavians who left evidence of their visit in some of the street names such as Gungate.

Alfred's daughter, Ethelfleda, was busy here, too, and excavations in the town centre have revealed Saxon fortifications. Dominating Tamworth today is the fine Norman motte and bailey **Castle** set in the Pleasure Grounds, which have truly magnificent floral terraces. The sandstone castle, with its superb herringbone wall, dates originally from the 1180s, having replaced a wooden tower on the present

artificial mound constructed shortly after the Norman Conquest. Behind the ancient fortress walls, Tudor and Jacobean buildings tower over the medieval timer-framed Great Hall. Restored period rooms give a fascinating glimpse into life above and below stairs down the centuries. A Saxon nun, Editha, is said to haunt Tamworth Castle, her ghost appearing first in 1139. The story goes that when de Marmion took possession of his lands he expelled the nuns from a nearby convent. The order had been founded by Editha in the 9th century so the expelled nuns summoned her from her grave. Editha attacked de Marmion in his bedroom and, as a result of her severe beating, he restored the nuns to their home. The Parish Church of St Editha, founded in 963, is vast and was rebuilt after the Norman Conquest; then, again, after the Great Fire of Tamworth in 1345. The splendid 15th century tower at the west end contains a most remarkable double staircase. The mixture of Victorian and modern stained glass found inside is surprisingly harmonious.

The **Town Hall**, built in 1701, is charming with open arches and Tuscan columns below. The building was paid for by Thomas Guy, the local Member of Parliament, who is probably more famous as the founder of the London

Dining Room, Tamworth Castle

hospital that bears his name. Thomas Guy also gave the town its 14 almshouses in Lower Gungate, which were rebuilt in 1913.

FAZELEY
9 miles SE of Lichfield on the A4091

🏛 Canal

Drayton Manor Family Theme Park has over a million visitors a year. Besides the scary rides and a G-Force rollercoaster, it has a zoo, farm and garden centre and two museums, one of which is particularly interesting as it charts the history of the Peel family, former owners of Drayton Manor.

The **Birmingham & Fazeley Canal**, which joins up with the Trent & Mersey Canal to the west of Alrewas, made this small town one of the key centres of the English canal system for over 200 years and in the 18th century it had one of the most complete cotton mill complexes in the country. Not only did the Peel family set up their cotton factory here to take full advantage of the canal network but other cotton manufacturers also saw the potential for business at Fazeley. The old factory buildings and mills are being restored to their former glory and a wander along the towpath provides interesting glimpses into the industrial history of the area.

SWINFEN
3 miles S of Lichfield on the A38

🌱 Heart of the Country Village

On the A38 between Swinfen Island and Weeford Island stands the **Heart of the**

BLACKBROOK ANTIQUES VILLAGE

London Road, Weeford, nr Lichfield,
Staffordshire WS14 0PS
Tel: 01543 481450   Fax: 01543 480275
e-mail: info@blackbrook.co.uk
website: www.blackbrook.co.uk

For anyone looking to renovate, improve or enhance a property, a visit to **Blackbrook Antiques Village** will provide a wealth of ideas and an eclectic, ever-changing stock of everything from reclaimed bricks to fine furnishings and everything for the garden. The stock is sourced from throughout the UK, with a few choice pieces brought from Europe. Every piece is chosen for quality, interest and individuality and is displayed for sale in impeccable condition after restoration by in-house specialist craftsmen.

There are gates and doors, chimneypieces, fireplaces and fire surrounds, antiques in cast iron, marble, timber and stone, dining room furniture, hall stands, sideboards, cabinets, candelabra and classic lighting, kitchen ranges and kitchenalia, garden statuary, water features......and always unique, eyecatching one-offs such as an antique butter churn or a French rustic dog kennel. Staff are always ready with expert advice and support services, and for those who can't get to Blackbrook on the London Road (A38) south of Lichfield the excellent website is well worth a visit.

RUSSELLS THE BUTCHER

25 Main Street, Shenstone, nr Lichfield,
Staffordshire WS14 0LZ
Tel: 01543 480269

Russell Edwards has lived in the area since his schooldays and bought this business in the late 1980s. He sources the finest farm-assured meats for **Russell the Butcher**, including Bretby lamb from the South Derbyshire hills, Packington pork from Staffordshire and prime beef from Givendale in the Yorkshire Wolds. His poultry, cooked meats, cheeses and preserves are equally carefully sourced, and he is well-known in the region for his superb homemade sausages, which come in up to 20 varieties.

Country Village, a country centre set around attractive courtyards in converted farm buildings with a range of shopping outlets and two restaurants.

Leek

🏠 Butter Cross   🏠 Nicholson Institute

🏛 Brindley Water Museum   🚶 River Churnet

🚶 Tittesworth Reservoir   🏠 War Memorial

Known as the 'Capital of the Moorlands', Leek is an attractive textile centre on the banks of the River Churnet, noted for its range and variety of antiques shops. It was here that French Huguenots settled, after fleeing from religious oppression, and established the silk industry that thrived due to the abundance of soft water coming off the nearby moorland. Until the 19th century, this was a domestic industry with the workshops on the top storeys of the houses; many examples of these 'top shops' have survived to this day. Leek also became an important dyeing town, particularly after the death of Prince Albert, when 'Raven Black' was popularised by Queen Victoria, who remained in mourning for her beloved husband for many years.

William Morris, founder of the Arts and Crafts movement, lived and worked in Leek for long periods between 1875 and 1878. Much of his time here was spent investigating new techniques of dyeing with Thomas Wardle but he also revived the use of traditional dyes. Thomas Wardle's wife, Elizabeth, founded the Leek School of Embroidery, with much encouragement from William Morris.

Leek is by no means a recent town that grew up in the shadow of the Industrial Revolution. An ancient borough, granted its charter in 1214, Leek was a thriving market centre rivalling Macclesfield and Congleton. The **Butter Cross**, which now stands in the Market Place, was originally erected near the junction of Sheep Market and Stanley Street by the Joliffe family in 1671.

Every road coming into the town seems to converge on the old cobbled Market Place and the road to the west leads down to the Parish Church. Dedicated to Edward the Confessor (the full name is St Edward's and All Saints' Church), the original Church was burnt down in 1297 and rebuilt some 20 years later though the building is now largely 17th century. The timber roof of the nave is well worth a second look and is the church's pride and joy – it is said that each of the cross beams was hewn from a separate oak tree. In the west part of the nave, an enormous 18th century gallery rises up, tier on tier, giving the impression of a theatre's dress circle!

PERIOD FEATURES

17 Broad Street, Leek, Staffordshire ST13 5NR
Tel: 01538 372202 e-mail: enquiries@periodfeatures.net
website: www.periodfeatures.net

Leek is well known for its many antique shops and Period Features complements them perfectly. This very special shop is an excellent source of products for period homes.It has been under the new ownership of Suzy Dymock since September 2006 and stocks a vast range of fittings and accessories for the home, both antique and high quality reproduction. You will find an excellent selection of door knobs, letter plates, bell pushes, servant's bells, old fashioned light switches, shelf brackets, toilet roll holders, light pulls, door knockers, cupboard knobs, lighting, curtain poles and much more. Suzy and her staff also supply old fashioned homewares including carbolic soap, candles, wax furniture polishes, jute rugs, kitchen accessories and many more different products for period gardens.

   Period Features is proud to stock a wide range of traditional paints by Farrow & Ball, including sample pots in all 150 colours. The Farrow & Ball wallpaper books are also available for browsing. Period Features is open from 10am to 5pm, Monday to Saturday. Although the actual shop looks and smells like a Victorian hardware store, it also has an e-commerce site which is open for business 24 hours a day. Visit the website to view and purchase many of the products.

BAMBOO ELEGANT FASHIONS

12 Market Place, Leek, Staffordshire ST13 5HH
Tel: 01538 382838

Leek has a long connection with the silk and textiles industries, so it's an entirely appropriate setting for **Bamboo Elegant Fashions**. In spacious premises on the market place, owner Gaynor Fullbrook has filled her shop with a wide range of clothes and accessories for the well-dressed lady. The huge shop-wide window display gives a generous glimpse of what shoppers will find inside. Gaynor personally chooses her stock from some of the leading houses in the UK and Europe including Denmark, Holland and Germany, names like Sandwich, Steilman, Fransa, Olsen and award winning Oui Set; bags by Oriano; costume jewellery by Dante; scarves by Passigitti; hosiery and lingerie by Charnos, Legaby, Triumph and Elle Macpherson.

   Staff are always ready with help and advice, and the regular turnover means that every visit offers something new and exciting to wear. Regular clients come from many miles around to shop at Bamboo, which is open from 10 to 5 Monday to Saturday.

🏛 historic building   🏚 museum   🏛 historic site   ◔ scenic attraction   🌱 flora and fauna

Although much has been altered inside the church, most notably in 1865 when GE Street rebuilt the chancel, reredos, sanctuary, pulpit and stalls, there still remains a rather unusual wooden chair. Traditionally this is believed to have been a ducking stool for scolds, that was used in the nearby River Churnet. William Morris designed one of the rose windows, and the church also contains work by the Leek School of Embroidery. Outside, in the churchyard, can be found a rather curious inscription on a gravestone: "James Robinson interred February the 28th 1788 Aged 438"! To the north side of the Church is an area still known locally as 'Petty France'; it holds the graves of many Napoleonic prisoners of war who lived nearby. An oft-told local story relates that one day Bonnie Prince Charlie was passing through the town and knocked on the door of the vicarage asking for accommodation. The vicar's wife was so surprised that she expired from shock on the spot.

Another building worthy of a second glance is the imposing **Nicholson Institute**, with its copper dome. Completed in 1884 and funded by the local industrialist Joshua Nicholson, the Institute offered the people of Leek an opportunity to learn and also expand their cultural horizons. Many of the great Victorian literary giants, including George Bernard Shaw and Mark Twain, came here to admire the building. The town's **War Memorial**, built in Portland stone and with a clock tower, has a dedication to the youngest Nicholson son, who was killed in the First World War. Leek was the home of James Brindley, the 18th century engineer who built much of the early canal network. A water-powered corn mill built by him in 1752 in Mill Street has been restored and now houses the **Brindley Water Museum**, which is devoted to his life and work. Visitors can see corn being ground and see displays of

EDWARDIAN CHARM MEMORABILIA

8 Stanley Street, Leek, Staffordshire ST13 5HG
Tel: 01538 384384
website: www.edwardiancharm.co.uk

'Remember a bygone age and feel the nostalgia'. That's the message on a sign inside **Edwardian Charm**, whose ample display space is filled to bursting with memorabilia and gifts for all occasions and all pockets. Recently opened by Glenn and Maureen Evans in a pedestrianised area of town, this really is a paradise for anyone with a longing for the good old days.

Just a few of the items in the constantly changing stock: Robert Opie classic scrapbooks; postcards from the '50s and '60s; tin boats and cars and trams and soldiers, tin boxes; tins of sweets; retro radio sets; canvas prints and mirrors with vintage advertisements for the likes of Colman's Mustard and Oxo; gollies and teddy bears; dolls and soft toys; jewellery holders; money boxes in the shape of post boxes and handbags; fairies and figurines; picture frames; silk flowers; lavender pots, soaps and toiletries. There is no better place for browsing for a personal treat or a special gift, and if you can't get to the shop, the excellent website illustrates many of the wonderful things in store.

FOX COUNTRY FURNITURE

The Old Cheese Factory, Reapsmoor,
Longnor, nr Buxton,
Derbyshire SK17 0LG
Tel/Fax: 01298 84467
e-mail: peter@foxfurniture.co.uk
website: www.foxfurniture.co.uk

The Fox family are closely involved in three outstanding enterprises in Longnor. Peter started his working life as a mechanic and later joined his father in **Fox Country Furniture**. He is now the driving force behind the business that his father George had started in 1983 in the Old Cheese Factory with a few small machines and lots of (at the time) surplus space. Peter, who loves living and working in the beautiful Peak District countryside, has greatly expanded the business since the early days, creating a wide range of hand-made hardwood furniture of a clean, simple and practical design that emphasises the natural beauty of the (mainly native) wood.

The output is divided about equally between the standard range and custom-made pieces, and new designs are exhibited in the showroom at the **Longnor Craft Centre** (Tel: 01298 83587 web: longnorcrafts.co.uk). The Centre, located in the Victorian Market Hall at the top of the market square, was created in 1991 as a showroom for the Fox furniture. It is run by Peter's wife Alison and her father Abbie (Albert), a master baker and tenor singer of note. They added a coffee shop in 1993, completely transforming a rather bare, uninviting space and heralding the rise of the Craft Centre, which is now home to up to 60 talented local craft makers and artists.

The coffee shop sells Taylor's beverages, Abbie's superb home-baked cakes and light lunches, and regularly added new items keep the menu fresh and appealing. **Forest Flame** is the brainchild of Nick Egan, an expert in steel fabrication, in collaboration with Peter. The main product is wood-fired hot tubs, the standard-bearer being the Western Red Cedar Tub, a much-refined version of a Swedish original. It's made in a similar way to a barrel, with a stainless steel woodburning stove built in. You fill it with water, light the fire, keep it stocked for 2 to 4 hours, step in and relax. The tub is ecologically sympathetic: no plumbing or wiring; few or no chemicals, and the water can be drained off for use in the garden. Website: www.forestflame.co.uk

J W ASH & SONS QUALITY BUTCHERS

19-21 Ball Haye Street, Leek, Staffordshire
Tel: 01538 383094

Peter Lymer has more than 30 years' experience in the business, and when he acquired **J W Ash & Sons** in 2005 he was taking over one of the very best butchers in the region. Almost all his beef, lamb and pork comes from within a 10-mile radius of the shop, thus ensuring full traceability of the supply chain and minimising food miles. Game is also popular in season, some of it shot at the weekend by members of Peter's staff.

Pies are another speciality – ten varieties in all, including pork, steak, chicken and bacon & egg – and the pâtés, quiches, fruit pies and tarts, scones and mince pies are also top-notch. The shop can provide outside catering for anything from dinner parties to barbecues, hog roasts and wedding receptions. The week's special offers are chalked up outside the shop, which is open from 7 to 5 Monday to Saturday (half day Thursday).

millwrighting skills. Leek has a traditional outdoor market every Wednesday, a craft and antiques market on Saturday and an indoor 'butter market' on Wednesday, Friday and Saturday.

The **River Churnet**, though little known outside Staffordshire, has a wealth of scenery and industrial archaeology and, being easily accessible to the walker, its valley deserves better recognition. The river rises to the west of Leek in rugged gritstone country but for most of its length it flows through softer red sandstone countryside in a valley that was carved out during the Ice Age. Though there are few footpaths directly adjacent to the riverbank, most of the valley can be walked close to the river using a combination of canal towpaths and former railway tracks.

Four miles to the north of Leek on the A53 rise the dark, jagged gritstone outcrops of The Roaches, Ramshaw Rocks and Hen Cloud.

Roaches is a corruption of the French word 'roches' or rocks and was reputedly given by Napoleonic prisoners: 'cloud' is a local word used for high hills. Just below The Roaches there is another delightful stretch of water, **Tittesworth Reservoir**, which is extremely popular with trout fishermen. It has some super trails, a visitor centre with an interactive exhibition, a restaurant and a gift shop.

Around Leek

LONGNOR
8 miles NE of Leek off the B5053

🏛 Market Hall   ✂ Craft centre

🏛 Church of St Bartholomew

Over the county line into Staffordshire yet in the heart of the Peak District, on a gentle slope between the River Manifold and the River Dove, Longnor was once the meeting-

🏛 stories and anecdotes   🐦 famous people   ✎ art and craft   ● entertainment and sport   🚶 walks point of several packhorse routes. Its **Market Hall** was built in 1873 – outside the hall there is a posting of the market charges of the time. The town's prosperity declined with the onset of the agricultural depression, and there was an accompanying fall in the population. However, this decline has in recent years been reversed. Longnor is now a conservation area and has attracted a good many craftspeople.

Main showroom for the work of local craftspeople and artisans, **Longnor Craft Centre** occupies the beautifully restored Market Hall in the centre of Longnor village. The village also has some fascinating narrow flagged passages which seem to go nowhere but suddenly emerge into the most beautiful scenery.

Though the late 18th century **Church of St Bartholomew** is rather plain, the churchyard has a most interesting gravestone. The epitaph tells the tale of the life of William Billinge, born in 1679, died in 1791 – which made him 112 years old at the time of his death! As a soldier Billinge served under Rooke at Gibraltar and Marlborough at Ramillies; after being sent home wounded, he recovered to take part in defending the King in the Jacobite rebellions of 1715 and 1745.

RUDYARD
2 miles NW of Leek off the A523

🦌 Kinver Edge

In fond memory of the place where they first met in 1863, Mr and Mrs Kipling named their famous son, born in 1865, after this village. The nearby two-mile long Rudyard Lake was built in 1831 by John Rennie to feed the Caldon Canal. With steeply wooded banks the lake is now a leisure centre where there are facilities for picnicking, walking, fishing and sailing. On summer weekends and Bank Holidays, visitors can enjoy a magical three-mile return trip alongside the lake behind the vintage locomotives of the Rudyard Lake Steam Railway. The west shore of the Reservoir is also a section of the Staffordshire Way, the long distance footpath which runs from Mow Cop to **Kinver Edge**, near Stourbridge. This is a sandstone ridge covered in woodland and heath, and with several famous rock houses which were inhabited until the 1950s.

Back in Victorian days, Rudyard was a popular lakeside resort – in 1877 more than 20,000 people came here to see Captain Webb, the first man to swim the English Channel, swim in the Reservoir.

RUSHTON SPENCER
5 miles NW of Leek on the A523

🏛 Chapel in the Wilderness

Well known for its lonely church, the '**Chapel in the Wilderness**', this is a pleasant, moorland village nestling under the Cloud. Originally built of wood in the 14th century, the church, which served both Rushton Spencer and neighbouring Rushton James, has been almost rebuilt in stone. One of the graves is that of Thomas Meakin, who died in 1781 but whose grave faces the wrong way. He was originally buried in Stone, but there was a suspicion that he was buried alive. When the grave was opened scratches were found in the coffin and the body was lying face down. When he was laid to rest in Rushton Spencer the grave was positioned the wrong way round in order to keep the ghost in.

BIDDULPH
6 miles W of Leek on the A527

🏛 Biddulph Grange

John Wesley was a frequent visitor to this isolated moorland town but the history of

Biddulph goes back to long before the days of Methodism. After the Norman Conquest, the manor of Biddulph was granted by William the Conqueror to Robert the Forester, an overlord of what was then the extensively forested area of Lyme. The Biddulphs, a staunchly Catholic family, took control of the area. John Biddulph fought under the Royal flag during the Civil War and was killed at the Battle of Hopton Heath. His son entrusted the defence of Biddulph Hall to Lord Brereton who withstood a determined siege until 1644 when he was finally subjected to heavy artillery. The Hall was then demolished to prevent its being re-garrisoned.

Biddulph Grange belonged to the Cistercian monks of the Abbey at Hulton until the Dissolution and its garden is one of the most unusual and remarkable in the whole country. It was created by James Bateman in the mid-1800s as a series of connected parts to show specimens from his extensive collection which he had harvested from all parts of the globe. Highlights include an Egyptian garden with a pyramid and yew obelisks, a Chinese garden with a joss house, temple and watch tower, a splendid Scottish glen, a dahlia walk and a Wellingtonia avenue.

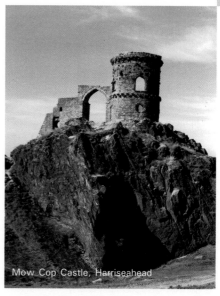
Mow Cop Castle, Harriseahead

HARRISEAHEAD
6 miles W of Leek off the A527

🏰 Mow Cop Castle   🏛 Englesea Brook Chapel

Close to the village and perched on top of a hill is **Mow Cop Castle**, which lies exactly on the boundary of Staffordshire and Cheshire. However, the Castle is not all that it appears. The ruined medieval fortress and remains of the round tower are, in fact, what is left of an elaborate summerhouse built by Randle Wilbraham, of nearby Rode Hall, in 1754. The history of the site goes back much further and

the remains of a prehistoric camp have been found here. In 1807, this ancient site gave birth to Primitive Methodism when Hugh Bourne, a Stoke-on-Trent man, and William Clowes, a champion dancer from Burslem, called a meeting on the hill which lasted almost 14 hours. When Mow Cop Castle was given to the National Trust in 1937, 10,000 Methodists marked the occasion with a meeting at the summit.

A small museum of Primitive Methodism can be visited in the school room of **Englesea Brook Chapel** just north of **Balterley**. The chapel is one of the oldest Primitive Methodist chapels to survive. Mow Cop is at one end of the Newcastle Way that runs to Market Drayton.

ENDON
4 miles SW of Leek on the A53

This small village is unusual in that it is the only place in Staffordshire which continues the ancient custom of well-dressing that is so common in neighbouring Derbyshire. Probably based on an ancient pagan ritual, the present ceremony, which was revived in 1845, takes place during the Spring Bank Holiday and includes the coronation of a Well-Dressing Queen.

On the Bank Holiday Monday a village fete and fair is held, where there are traditional Morris dancers and the rural competition of 'Tossing the Sheaf' also takes place. In the days before combine harvesters, a heavy sheaf of corn was heaved by pitchfork over a bar which was gradually raised. Today, the game is similar except that a 15lb sack of straw is used.

CHEDDLETON
3 miles S of Leek on the A520

🏛 Flint Mill   🏛 Churnet Valley Railway

🌾 Deep Hayes Country Park

The restored **Cheddleton Flint Mill**, in the rural surroundings of the Churnet Valley, makes an interesting visit. The water-powered machinery was used to crush flint that had been brought in by canal and then transported, again by water to Stoke where it was used in the hardening of pottery. The small museum includes a rare 18th century 'haystack' boiler and a Robey steam engine. There are also collections of exhibits relating to the preparation of raw materials for the pottery industry. Trips by narrow boats along the Caldon Canal can be taken from the mill.

The village station is home to the **Churnet Valley Railway**, which will give great delight to all railway enthusiasts. The Railway has a nostalgic collection of beautifully preserved steam locomotives, diesel multiple units and other railway memorabilia, and delights visitors with a 10½-mile return journey through the valley. Leekbrook Junction (no boarding or

alighting) is at the northern end, which runs through Cheddleton and Consall to the impressive North Staffordshire Railway-style station at Kingsley & Froghall. The railway is accessible from Cheddleton or Kingsley & Froghall.

To the west of Cheddleton is **Deep Hayes Country Park**, which lies in a secluded valley by the Caldon Canal and Staffordshire Way. From the ridge there are breathtaking views but, for the less energetic, there is a very pleasant walk around two pools which has many offshoots into lovely countryside.

CONSALL
4 miles S of Leek off the A520

🌾 Nature Park

This is a beautiful spot hidden in a particularly deep section of the Churnet Valley downstream from Cheddleton. The little cottages keep close company with the small bridges over the Caldon Canal. Originally known as Consall Forge, the hamlet took its name from an old iron forge that existed here in the first Elizabethan Age. As iron making became uneconomic here, the forge altered its operation and became one of the major lime making centres after the completion of the Caldon Canal.

Reached through Consall village is **Consall Nature Park**, an RSPB reserve that is a quiet and peaceful haven with much to delight the avid birdwatcher. It is accessible only on foot or by canal. The village itself is very popular with walkers and boaters and has a pub to provide the necessary refreshment. Consall Forge Pottery produces hand-thrown stoneware ceramics – teapots are a speciality.

The splendid **Consall Hall Landscape Gardens** (see panel opposite) cover 70 acres

CONSALL HALL LANDSCAPE GARDENS

Consall, nr Stoke-on-Trent, Staffordshire ST9 0AG
Tel: 01782 551947
website: www.consallgardens.co.uk

Consall Hall Landscape Garden covers an exceptional 70 acre site where four small valleys have been combined into an enchanting natural landscape. The beauty has been enhanced by the creation of six lakes, grottoes, follies, bridges and a charming cottage style summer house all surrounded by shelter belts planted with swathes of different trees to accentuate the valleys and create beautiful backgrounds.

The manor of Consall is first mentioned in the Domesday Book and the present hall was started in 1807. 150 years ago the area was ravaged by mining when 2,000 miners formed large pit banks which destroyed the views over the valleys. These scars were removed 48 years ago by William Podmore OBE when he began the restoration of the landscape and produced the beauty that can be seen today; a series of astonishing vistas which have been made easily accessible by linking with four miles of paths.

The vistas were composed in the same way as a painting starting with an interesting foreground, drawing the eye over grass or water to an eye catcher set against a stunning background. Each viewpoint is provided with a seat and some are covered to provide shelter whatever the weather, as well as framing the vista to form a carefully composed living picture, which continually changes throughout the day as well as with the seasons and the weather.

and are a true delight to visit. An assortment of lakes, follies, packhorse bridges and summer houses amidst the spectacular planting, provide a surprise at every turn. Light lunches and afternoon teas are also available in the Halcyon Room.

FROGHALL

7 miles S of Leek on the A52

🏛 Froghall Wharf   🏠 Caldon Canal

🏠 Manifold Valley Light Railway

Froghall Wharf was built along the banks of the **Caldon Canal** to act as a trans-shipment area for limestone as it came down a railway incline from the quarries to the south of Waterhouses. Here the limestone was tipped into narrow boats and, from the mid-1800s, into railway wagons, to be carried to Stoke-on-Trent. The once-busy Wharf declined after 1920 following the construction of the **Manifold Valley Light Railway**, which directly linked the quarries

Caldon Canal

🎭 stories and anecdotes   🐦 famous people   🎨 art and craft   ✒ entertainment and sport   🏃 walks

NEWFIELDS GALLERY

Foxt, nr Froghall, Staffordshire Moorlands ST10 2HS
Tel: 01538 266334
website: www.peakdistrictproducts.co.uk/newfieldsgallery

In a lovely rural setting on a south-facing hill farm, **Newfields Gallery** displays and sells only the work of owners Roger Sutton and Gail Keep, artists in ceramics and wood. They started working together in the 1970s, and in 1977 they established their own business Ceramico Designs. In

this setting of hedgerow, woodland, meadow and streams in the Staffordshire Moorlands their keen observation of wildlife has informed their work and inspired many of their detailed relief designs for jewellery, boxes and miniature wall plaques.

Roger carves English oak, specialising in plant forms and foliage, and he also makes the array of chisels he uses for the fine detailed carving. The Gallery is open most days between 9 and 5, but it's best to phone to check that they're open before setting out. Everything sold in the gallery is unique; ceramics range from £10 to about £120, woodcarvings start at £300.

with Leek and the national railway network. From then on the Canal and Wharf fell into a state of disrepair and it was only due to the efforts of the Caldon Canal Society that the navigation has survived. The Canal, once again open to traffic, is now the sole preserve of pleasure craft and, at the leisurely pace of literally one horse power, narrowboats take visitors along to Consall Forge and back.

CAULDON
8 miles SE of Leek off the A52

This was the site of the quarry from which wagons travelled, down a railway track, to Froghall Wharf.

OAKAMOOR
9 miles S of Leek on the B5417

🍃 Hawksmoor Nature Reserve

This village was once the home of the

Thomas Bolton & Sons copper works that produced some 20,000 miles of copper wire for the first transatlantic cable in 1856. Little now remains of the works, which were demolished in the 1960s, but the site of the mill has been turned into an attractive picnic site complete with the very large mill pond. Nearby **Hawksmoor Nature Reserve** and bird sanctuary covers some 300 acres of the Churnet Valley and is managed by a local committee. The trail through the Reserve includes glorious landscapes, abundant natural history and industrial architecture.

ALTON
11 miles SE of Leek off the B5032

🖋 Alton Towers   🏰 Castle   🐿 Toot Hill Rock

The world-famous **Alton Towers** leisure park is the main attraction here, but even this spot has its quieter, lesser known corners.

🏛 historic building   🖼 museum   🏛 historic site   🐿 scenic attraction   🍃 flora and fauna

Originally the home of the Earls of Shrewsbury, who also owned much of the surrounding area, the 19th century mansion by Pugin is now just a gutted shell. The surrounding gardens and parkland (which contain most of the attractions) are older and were laid out by Capability Brown. Hundreds of workmen were employed to convert a whole valley into what is still a magnificent mix of formal gardens and parkland. As well as many fountains and pools there are also numerous paths which lead to charming features such as a cast-iron Chinese pagoda, a Dutch garden, an Italian garden, a Swiss Chalet, a Gothic temple and a vast rock garden. The village of Alton has plenty to offer the visitor. The view up from the valley bottom to the **Castle**, perched on a sandstone rock above the River Churnet, has given this area of Staffordshire the nickname of 'Rhineland', and the steep climb up to **Toot Hill Rock** is rewarded by magnificent views. The Castle, in its present form, was built mainly by Pugin, who also built the now restored Italianate railway station. Note, too, the old lock-up and water mill.

UTTOXETER
16 miles SE of Leek on the A518

🏛 Church ⚓ Racecourse

Today, the town is perhaps best known for its **Racecourse**, a popular National Hunt track which lies to the southeast of town. Highlight of the course's calendar is the stamina-sapping **Midlands Grand National** run in the spring. Uttoxeter is a traditional, rural market town, with a busy livestock and street market on Wednesdays. There are several pleasant, old, timbered buildings in Uttoxeter but fires in

MANOR HOUSE FARM & KEEPER'S COTTAGE

Prestwood, Denstone, nr Uttoxeter, Staffordshire ST14 5DD
Tel: 01889 590415 Fax: 01889 342198
e-mail: cm-ball@yahoo.co.uk website: www.4posteraccom.com

Chris and Margaret Ball offer guests a choice of accommodation at **Manor House Farm**, which stands at the confluence of the Dove and Churnet Valleys. The rambling country farmhouse, which dates mainly from the 17th century, takes visitors back to another age with its antique furniture and oak-panelled dining room, and the four en suite bedrooms, all with four-poster beds, provide abundant comfort and character; they look out over the beautiful garden with its birdlife, the farm and the dramatic Weaver Hills. Thirty of the farm's 170 acres are a grazing area for the very rare breed of Irish Moiled cattle.

An alternative to the farmhouse rooms is a beautiful 18th century cottage with two bedrooms (one with a four-poster) and everything needed for a self-catering holiday. Next to the Victorian summer house are facilities for tennis, croquet and barbecues. Chris was born on the farm, and he and Margaret always have time for their guests, from a warm and genuine welcome to providing information on local walks and sights. Alton Towers is just two miles away, and other attractions within easy reach include stately homes and the potteries and museums of Stoke-on-Trent.

**PANACHE INSPIRED INTERIORS
& JEWELLERY**

*Lion Building, 8 Market Place, Uttoxeter,
Staffordshire ST14 8HP
Tel: 01889 560955　e-mail: jill_panache@hotmail.com*

Owner Jill Arme's passion for high-quality homewares
developed from a hobby to a business when she opened
Panache Inspired Interiors and Jewellery tucked away off the
market place at Uttoxeter. This passion is reflected in the stock that fills her shop, including
Hultquist Danish jewellery, Lampe Berger scented lamps, Danon jewellery from Israel, fashion
handbags, French furniture and top-quality glassware and lighting. Shop hours are 10am to 5pm
Monday to Saturday, and some parking spaces are available outside the shop for customers.

1596 and 1672 destroyed most of the town's
architectural heritage. As well as a visit to the
Heritage Centre, housed in some old timber-
framed cottages in Carter Street, **St Mary's
Church** should also appear on a sightseer's
itinerary; it has a typical 'preaching box' dating
from 1828.

Stoke-on-Trent

🏛 Museums in Stoke, Burslem and Etruria

The city was established as late as 1910 when
Fenton joined the five towns (Tunstall,
Burslem, Hanley, Longton and Stoke)
immortalised by the novels of Arnold Bennett.
Once fiercely independent, the towns became
progressively involved with each other as
improvements in roads, water supplies and
other amenities forced them towards
amalgamation. The new city's crest, of an
ancient Egyptian potter at his wheel in one
quarter, sums up the fortune on which the
wealth of the area was created. Each of the old
towns is also represented in the crest, and the
joint motto translates as "Strength is stronger
for unity".

It was the presence of the essential raw
materials for the manufacture and decoration
of ceramics, in particular marl clay, coal and
water, that led to the concentration of pottery
manufacture in this area. Though production
started in the 1600s it was the entrepreneurial
skills of Josiah Wedgwood and Thomas
Minton, who brought the individual potters
together in factory-style workplaces, that
caused the massive leap forward in production
that took place in the 18th century. Their
factories were large but there were also
hundreds of small establishments producing a
whole range of more utilitarian chinaware;
production in the Potteries reached its height
towards the end of the 19th century. For those
interested in pottery and industrial architecture,
Stoke-on-Trent is a wonderful place to visit,
with many museums and factories open to the
public to tell the story of the city. The **Spode
Museum & Visitor Centre** in Church Street is
one of several famous establishments open to
visitors.

Hanley, one of the five towns of The
Potteries, and part of the Stoke-on-Trent
conurbation, was the birthplace of Arnold
Bennett, Sir Stanley Matthews and John Smith
(the captain of the ill-fated *Titanic*). **The
Potteries Museum & Art Gallery** houses the
world's finest collection of Staffordshire
ceramics and offers many more attractions,
including a natural history gallery and a lively
programme of exhibitions, talks, tours and

workshops. The Potteries shopping centre, situated in the heart of Hanley, is every shopper's dream with a fantastic range of famous shops all brought together in a beautiful environment. Natural daylight cascades through the centre's many glazed roofs and plants, trees and water features create an outdoor feel.

Burslem, in the northern suburbs, is the home of **Burleigh Earthenware Pottery**, founded in 1851 by William Leigh and famous for its elegant blue and white patterns; the pottery's products are still made by hand using traditional methods such as underglaze transfer printing. Also in Burslem is the **Royal Doulton Visitor Centre**, which contains the world's largest display of Royal Doulton figures and many other treasures from the company's rich heritage. there are factory tours, demonstrations, a video-theatre, gallery, restaurant and shop. Another Burslem

attraction is Ceramica, located in the Old Town Hall, with a huge kiln and an Arnold Bennett study area. Bennett was educated in Burslem and his first novel, *Anna of the Five Towns*, is set in the Potteries. His ashes are buried at Burslem cemetery.

Etruria, to the west of the city centre, was created by Josiah Wedgwood in 1769 as a village for the workers at the pottery factory he built in this once rural valley. Though the factory has gone (it moved to Barlaston in the 1940s), Etruria Hall, Wedgwood's home, is still standing in what is now the National Garden Festival site. The pottery industry dominated the village and the **Etruria Industrial Museum**, next to the Trent & Mersey and Caldon Canals, displays a steam-powered potters' mill as well as other exhibits connected with the industry. Wedgwood died at Etruria Hall and is buried in the churchyard of St Peter and Vincula, Stoke-on-Trent.

Around Stoke-on-Trent

CHEADLE
5 miles E of Stoke-on-Trent on the A521

The glory of this busy market town is the Roman Catholic Church of St Giles, commissioned in 1841 and designed by AWN Pugin. The church has a 200ft spire, and the interior is an exuberant display of bright painting, brass, carving, gilding and Wedgwood and Minton tiles.

KIDSGROVE
5 miles N of Stoke-on-Trent on the A50

🏠 Harecastle Tunnels

Now chiefly a residential town, Kidsgrove is well worth a visit for anyone interested in canals. The two **Harecastle Tunnels** were major engineering feats of their time and they carry the Trent and Mersey Canal from Cheshire into The Potteries. It was Josiah Wedgwood who first dreamt of building a canal to link the area with the major Trent and Mersey navigation and thus create a waterway link right across the country from Liverpool to Hull. He fought long and hard to get the necessary Bill passed through Parliament, undaunted by the fact that a 3,000 yard long tunnel would be needed to go through Harecastle Hill. The Bill was passed and, though many scoffed at his plans, Wedgwood's canal and required tunnel, both built by James Brindley, were constructed over an 11-year period.

Those who had their doubts about Wedgwood's grand plan nearly had the last laugh when, some years later, there was almost a catastrophe as Harecastle started to subside. Fortunately, Thomas Telford was on hand to come to the rescue and another tunnel was built alongside the first thus averting disaster.

FINE FEATHERS FARM SHOP, TEA ROOMS & RARE BREEDS

Postbridge Cottage Farm, Post Lane, Endon, nr Stoke-on-Trent, Staffordshire ST9 9DT
Tel: 01782 504460
website: www.finefeathersofendon.co.uk

Surie and Andrew Goldstraw have turned an early-18th century farmhouse and gardens by the Caldon Canal into one of the most interesting places to visit in the region. The most unusual attraction at **Fine Feathers** is the unique collection of home-bred animals, from goats, pigs, sheep, racoons, cats and dogs (Rottweilers and Alaskan Snow Dogs) to exotic birds, ostriches, emus, waterfowl, poultry and Koi carp. The owners are specialist breeders of rare animals and also provide a unique animal rescue service, and they organise regular tours of the farm.

The farm shop on the site sells high-quality meat, exotic meat and game, home-made pies and cakes, dairy produce, vegetables, pickles and preserves, arts and crafts and boating supplies. Visitors can enjoy many of the shop's superb produce in home-cooked dishes, including an all-day breakfast, served in the little restaurant. Canal cruises on the Caldon Canal can be booked from here in high season, and narrow-boat moorings are available. Fine Feathers is open from 8 to 6 seven days a week.

🏠 historic building   🏛 museum   🏛 historic site   🌀 scenic attraction   🌿 flora and fauna

The two tunnels can still be seen today and make a very impressive sight: although Josiah's original tunnel is not in use, the Telford tunnel has been restored.

LONGTON
2 miles SE of Stoke-on-Trent on the A50

🏛 Gladstone Working Pottery Museum

The **Gladstone Working Pottery Museum** (see panel below) on Uttoxeter Road is a fascinating museum of the British pottery industry housed in a Victorian building. It tells visitors the story of how 19th century potters worked, with the display of traditional skills, the original workshops, the cobbled yard and the huge bottle kilns creating a unique atmospheric time-warp. As the brochure proclaims: 'throwing, jiggering, fettling, saggar making, glazing, dipping, firing, painting, sponging, moulding, casting – it's all at Gladstone'. Aynsley China, John Tams and Staffordshire Enamels have their factory shops in Longton.

BARLASTON
5 miles S of Stoke-on-Trent off the A34

🏛 Wedgwood Visitor Centre & Museum

A visit to The Potteries would not be complete without a visit to the **Wedgwood Visitor Centre and Museum** (see panel on page 160), set in a beautiful 500-acre country estate just outside Barlaston. The Museum traces the history of Wedgwood from the founding of the factory in 1759 to the present day through the displays of Queen's Ware, Jasper, Black Basalt and fine bone china. In rooms designed to recapture the style of specific periods there are hundreds of Wedgwood pieces from those eras. George Stubbs and Joshua Reynolds both painted portraits of the Wedgwood family, these hang in the centre's art gallery. In the craft centre, potters and decorators can be watched as they use traditional skills to create today's Wedgwood products. The centre is open every day.

HANCHURCH
5 miles S of Stoke-on-Trent on the A5182

🌱 Trentham Gardens

This tiny hamlet itself is unlikely to ring any bells with visitors as they pass by, but the nearby gardens are world famous. **Trentham Gardens** were landscaped by Capability Brown and given a more formal style by Sir Charles Barry, whose work can be observed in the lovely Italian gardens. Although the Hall was demolished in 1911, this style can still be recognised in such buildings as the orangery

---

Gladstone Pottery Museum

Uttoxeter Road, Longton, Stoke-on-Trent ST3 1PQ
Tel: 01782 237777
e-mail: gladstone@stoke.gov.uk website: www.stoke.gov.uk/museums

Gladstone is the only complete Victorian pottery factory from the days when coal burning ovens made the world's finest bone china. Traditional skills, original workshops, the cobbled yard and huge bottle kilns create an atmospheric time-warp that has no equal. Also visit the gift shop and Gladstone Parlour Tea Room serving morning coffee, delicious hot and cold lunches and afternoon tea. Please allow 2-3 hours for your visit.

📖 stories and anecdotes   🐦 famous people   🎨 art and craft   🎭 entertainment and sport   🚶 walks

THE WEDGWOOD VISITOR CENTRE

Barlaston, nr Stoke-on-Trent, Staffordshire ST12 9ES
Tel: 01782 282986   Fax: 01782 223063
e-mail: bookings@wedgwood.com
website: www.thewedgwoodvisitorcentre.com

WEDGWOOD
Visitor Centre

Wedgwood is probably the best known name in pottery, and the **Wedgwood Visitor Centre**, set in a beautiful 200-acre estate in the Heart of England, celebrates the life and achievements of the company's founder, Josiah Wedgwood, known as the 'Father of English Potters'. Visits include a tour of the real working factory that provides an insight into the making and decorating of Wedgwood ceramics. The full story of Wedgwood's history in an audio-guided exhibition featuring many rare and valuable items from the world famous company. A demonstration area offers the chance to create a unique souvenir of the visit and to chat to the skilled craftspeople at work. In the film theatre, a 20-minute film allows a leisurely assimilation of the Wedgwood story.

The Wedgwood Visitor Centre

The Centre has award winning catering facilities, the Ivy House Restaurant is a perfect place for morning coffee, lunch or afternoon tea - all served on Wedgwood Fine Bone China, of course. In the Wedgwood Shop is a wonderful selection of gift and tableware designs. Additionally, the seconds area within the shop tempts anyone with an eye for a bargain. In April 2008 a new £10 million Museum will open on the site, complementing the facilities of the Visitor Centre and anticipating the 250th anniversary of the Company's founding in 2009.

Hand on opportunities

Craft Skills

The New Wedgwood Museum

 historic building   museum   historic site   scenic attraction   flora and fauna

and sculpture gallery which remain today and form a framework for the outstanding conference, exhibition and banqueting centre that is Trentham.

NEWCASTLE-UNDER-LYME

2 miles W of Stoke-on-Trent on the A53

🏛 Guildhall 🏛 Museum

This ancient borough, which received its first charter from Henry II in 1173, was, for several centuries, the largest town in north Staffordshire. Today, the town maintains its individuality from its close neighbour, Stoke-on-Trent, and its centre is designated a conservation area. One of the best ways of exploring the delights of Newcastle-under-Lyme is to follow either, or both, of the town trails which take in many of the town's most notable buildings. Both begin in Nelson Place and the first takes in not only the early 19th century Church of St George and Mayer House, the former home of a famous

veterinary family, but also some fine Georgian houses and, in Marsh Parade, the vast 19th century building which once housed the town's first silk mill.

The second of the two trails takes in the particularly eye-catching Merrial Street before moving on to St Giles's Church, where the base of the tower dates from the 13th century. The original medieval Church was replaced by a brick building in 1720, and in 1870 it was again rebuilt, this time by George Gilbert Scott, who managed to capture much of the beauty of medieval times.

One of Newcastle-under-Lyme's oldest buildings also features on the route; **The Guildhall**, built in 1713 to replace an earlier timber building, stands beside the base of a medieval cross. The **Borough Museum & Art Gallery**, set in eight acres of parkland, houses a wonderful collection of assorted items from clocks to teapots, paintings to clay

---

BROOKFIELDS FARM SHOP

Stone Road, Blackbrook, nr Newcastle-under-Lyme, Staffordshire ST5 5EG
Tel: 01782 680833

For a pleasant, relaxed way to shop for food, a visit to **Brookfields Farm Shop** is takes a lot of beating. Beryl Lockett, Alan, Adam and Gill make this very much a family affair, and lots of the produce on sale is home-grown on the farm. Potatoes, beans, carrots, onions, leeks, courgettes and pumpkins are gathered for sale in their seasonal prime, and other lines include locally produced bacon, sausages and gammon, eggs, cheese, jams and honey, chutneys and pickles, fresh bread, cakes and pastries, ice cream and cut flowers.

The choice is impressive, and success has seen the shop expanding in size and range for 2007. It stands near the junction of the A51 and A53, 200 yards from the well-known Swan with Two Necks pub and 5 miles west of Newcastle-under-Lyme. Opening hours are 10 to 5 on Monday, 9 to 6 Tuesday to Saturday and 10 to 4 on Sunday.

📖 stories and anecdotes   🐦 famous people   🎨 art and craft   🎭 entertainment and sport   🚶 walks

SLATER'S EXCLUSIVE SHOPPING VILLAGE

Stone Road, Baldwin's Gate, nr Newcastle-under-Lyme,
Staffordshire ST5 5ED
Tel: 01782 680052 Fax: 01782 680136
e-mail: enquiries@slaterscountryinn.co.uk
website: www.slaterscountryinn.co.uk

'Something for Everyone.....Whatever the Weather.

Farm buildings dating from the 18th century have
been stylishly converted into **Slater's Exclusive
Shopping Village**, which lies on the A51, close to the
junction with the A53 and a ten-minute drive from
J15 of the M6.

The independently run business units in the Village
offer an impressive variety of top-quality products:
hand-made designer gifts, craft supplies and local deli
produce at Sunflower; beautiful Italian ceramics and
gifts at Artigiano; Oriental furniture, porcelain, lamps
and gifts at Oriental Experience; indoor and outdoor
furniture and accessories at Hiltons Outdoor living;
bedroom and dining room furniture at Modern Living;
antiques at Ottovinelli's; Authentic Canadian and
American products at Western Reflections; children's
clothing at Mommy Motz; traditional wooden toys,
jigsaws, teddy bears and books at Paddingtons;
stylish jewellery, furniture, lamps and gifts at La
Maison; ladies fashions, toiletries and giftware at the
Little White Cottage; collectable gifts at Inspired by
Nature; Masquerade hair & beauty salon; handmade
confectionery and Snugbury's Jersey ice cream at
Daniel's Delights.

The outlets, all under cover, are open from 10 to 5, seven days a week, and shoppers can
take a break in the award-winning Slater's Café Bar serving home-cooked food including
breakfasts, light lunches and home-made cakes. There's also a traditional country inn on the
site. The easy access (including disabled facilities), the ample free parking, the agreeable rural
setting, the seven-day opening, the wide range of top-quality goods and services, and friendly,
motivated staff all add up to make this one of the most pleasant and civilised shopping
experiences, and one that attracts customers from an ever wider area.

KNIT 2 TOGETHER SPECIALIST WOOLS

63 High Street, Wolstanton, Newcastle-under-Lyme, Staffordshire
Tel: 01782 862332
e-mail: sales@cucumberpatch.co.uk   website: www.cucumberpatch.co.uk

An amazing range of specialist wools keep the customers flocking to **Knit 2 Together**, which since opening in 2001 has established itself as *the* place for people who love to knit. The two shops, 100 yards apart at 63 and 97 High Street, stock all the famous names in the knitting business, and several less well known: Rowan, Jaeger, Hanne Falkenberg, Addi, Debbie Bliss, Colinette, Noro, Patons, RY Classic, Sirdar, Wendy, Katia, Louisa Harding, Robin, Weardowney, Stylecraft, Angora, Adriafil, Gedifra, Elle, Bergère de France, Lantern Moon, Laines du Nord, Artesano, Alpaca, Filati FF and Denise. And they naturally stock all the accessories, including a wide range of needles (Lantern Moon Ebony needles and silk cases, Brittany, Addi Turbo and Clover wooden needles) and hundreds of patterns.

Owners Jane and Martin Eccles and their staff are always ready to share their knowledge and experience with their customers at the Knit 2 Together shops, which are open from 10 to 4 Monday to Saturday. Online shopping is available by e-mail or at www.cucumberpatch.co.uk

---

pipes, a reconstruction of a Victorian street and exhibitions of local and national artists. A mile from the town centre, the New Victoria Theatre was Europe's first purpose-built 'theatre-in-the-round'.

MADELEY
7 miles W of Stoke-on-Trent on the A525

🏰 Castle   🌿 The Pool

Situated on an ancient packhorse route from Newcastle-under-Lyme, this village's name comes from the Anglo-Saxon 'maden lieg', which means 'clearing in the woods'. The focal point of this enchanting place, which has been designated a conservation area, is **The Pool**, formed by damming the River Lea to provide water power for the corn mill that still stands at its northern end. The pool is a haven for a variety of bird life. Madeley's grandest building is the Old Hall, an excellent example of a 15th

Madeley Old Hall

🎬 stories and anecdotes   🐦 famous people   🎨 art and craft   🖌 entertainment and sport   🚶 walks century squire's timber-framed residence. The village's large sandstone church can be seen through the trees from the mill pond. Standing in a raised churchyard, with ancient yew trees, All Saints Parish Church was originally Norman but was extensively enlarged in the 1400s; the chapel was rebuilt in 1872.

Stone

Augustinian monks founded a priory here in the 12th century, of which only one arch and some cloisters now remain, and in 1251 Henry II granted the monks a charter to hold a market. In its heyday as a trading town, some 38 coaches pulled up daily at the bow-windowed Crown Hotel, still one of the most attractive buildings along the High Street. Built during this period of prosperity, the early Gothic Revival Parish Church of St Michael contains several interesting monuments including a bust of Admiral John Jervis, Earl St Vincent, the hero of the great naval victory off Cape St Vincent in 1797. The Trent & Mersey Canal played a large part in Stone's early economic development and today it still brings work to the town through the building of holiday canal cruisers and a growing tourist trade. The Canal was begun in 1766 and, by 1771, it had reached Stone. The celebrations

which accompanied its opening here were so boisterous that one of the four locks in the town and a bridge collapsed under the weight of people! Stone is a true canal town, the dry docks and workshops are still busy today, as they have been for well over 200 years.

Around Stone

ECCLESHALL
5 miles SW of Stone on the A519

🏰 Castle   🏛 Pumping Station

For over a 1,000 years **Eccleshall Castle** was the palace of the bishops of Lichfield but, at the beginning of the 19th century, it became a family home when the Carter family moved here from Yorkshire. The present simple sandstone house is typical of the best architecture of the William and Mary period and incorporates part of the earlier 14th century Castle. The interior of the house has been augmented by successive members of the family, one of whom added a magnificent Victorian staircase and dome. Perhaps to remind them of the county from which they came, the Carters have collected a very interesting number of 19th century paintings by Yorkshire artists. The gardens have been created around the ruins of the old castle and

---

WILLIAM PERRY THE BUTCHERS

19 Stafford Street, Eccleshall, Staffordshire ST21 6BL
Tel: 01785 850288

2007 sees the 80th anniversary of **William Perry the Butchers**, where the owner and excellent staff take justifiable pride in the quality and consistency of what they sell. The meat comes almost exclusively from local farms, ensuring traceability and minimising 'food miles'. The shop has its own abattoir, and the beef is hung for 3 weeks to allow the full flavours to develop.
They make their own sausages, with at least six varieties available at any one time, and their own steak & kidney and chicken & mushroom pies are also among the best-sellers. Bread is delivered fresh daily, and there's always a good choice of cheese, much of it local.

🏰 historic building   🏛 museum   🏛 historic site   🌿 scenic attraction   🌱 flora and fauna

THE OLD SMITHY

Castle Street, Eccleshall, Staffordshire ST21 6DF
Tel: 01785 851567 Fax: 01785 859973
e-mail: enquiries@theoldsmithyeccleshall.co.uk
website: www.thebestofstaffordshire.co.uk

Eccleshall attracts visitors with an interest in history with its Castle, but for those with an interest in good food the town has a major new attraction. Punch Taverns have stylishly refurbished the **Old Smithy**, which they have relaunched as a gastropub serving a wide range of authentic Italian favourites interspersed with a few British pub classics. Food is served from 12 to 9.30 Monday to Saturday and from 12 to 5 on Sunday, when traditional roasts are added to the choice. Lunchtimes bring a selection of familiar favourites, from filled ciabattas and omelettes to jacket potatoes and spaghetti bolognese, cottage pie and chilli con carne. The main menu, served in the evening, shows the full repertoire of the Italian chef, from classic pasta dishes to well-loved

favourites such as pollo cacciatore, saltimbocca, fegato alla veneziana and steak valdostana.

   The chef also has a few of his own special creations, including fish soup with salmon, swordfish, cod, prawns, cockles and more, and medallions of pork tenderloin cooked with shallots, wild mushrooms, apricots and honey in a port and brandy cream sauce. Excellent wines complement the fine food, including well-priced house wines, Barolo and Montepulciano reds and Pinot Grigio white. The inn has a pleasant bar area where diners can peruse the menu over an aperitif or a glass of real ale.

have a great deal of romantic appeal.

   A little way north of Eccleshall, on the A519 at Cotes Heath, is **Mill Meece Pumping Station**, where two magnificent steam engines that once pumped more than three million gallons of water each day, are kept in pristine condition.

SHALLOWFORD
4 miles SW of Stone off the B5026

🐟 Izaaak Walton's Cottage

Set in beautiful grounds in this tiny hamlet in the heart of the Sow Valley, **Izaak Walton's Cottage** is a pretty 17th century half-timbered cottage once owned by the renowned biographer and author of *The Compleat Angler*. Fishing collections are on show, and there's a small souvenir shop. Within the grounds are an authentic 17th century herb garden, a lovely picnic area and orchard. The Cottage is

open daily Tuesday to Sunday and Bank Holidays from April to October.

SANDON
4 miles SE of Stone on the B5066

🏛 Sandon Hall

Near the village stands the ancestral home of the Earl of Harrowby, **Sandon Hall**. Rebuilt in 1850 after the earlier house had been damaged by fire, the Hall is surrounded by 400 acres of parkland, which include a notable arboretum. The Hall is steeped in history and, along with the impressive interior, makes an interesting and informative visit. The family, too, has led a fascinating life with no less than seven generations in parliament and three successive members of the family holding office in the Cabinet. The museum tells of their lives and also includes costumes, toys and the duelling pistols of William Pitt the Younger.

🎬 stories and anecdotes　🐟 famous people　🎨 art and craft　🎭 entertainment and sport　🚶 walks

ADVERTISERS AND PLACES OF INTEREST

LOCATOR MAP

🏢 historic building 🏛 museum 🏛 historic site 🌾 scenic attraction 🌱 flora and fauna

5| Derbyshire

Traditionally, Derbyshire marks the start of the north of England, and the county was also at the forefront of modern thinking at the beginning of the Industrial Revolution. The chief inheritor of this legacy is Derby, the home of Rolls-Royce and Royal Crown Derby porcelain, and it remains a busy industrial centre today. An early landmark of this new age is Richard Arkwright's mill and associated village at Cromford. In the south of the county are Calke Abbey and the charming ancient town of Repton.

However, the county is dominated by the Peak District National Park that covers much of its area. The first of the ten National Parks, it is often divided into White and Dark peak as the landscape changes from deep limestone valleys to bleak, isolated moorland.

Along with numerous attractive villages and small towns, ancient monuments and caves and caverns, the park is home to two of the finest stately homes not just in Derbyshire but in the whole country – Haddon Hall and Chatsworth.

The southern section of the Peak District is probably best known for beautiful Dovedale. The large car park near Thorpe that gives general access to the Dale is often crowded, but there is plenty of room for everyone and the wonderful valley, just a few hundred yards from the car park, is well worth experiencing. It is also the place to have a go at crossing a river on stepping stones, something that has delighted children for many, many years. The River Dove

is also a Mecca for keen fishermen. It was a favourite spot for Izaak Walton, who wrote his book *The Compleat Angler* in the area.

The ancient custom of well-dressing is almost exclusively confined to the limestone areas of the county. The porous rock, through which rainfall seeped leaving the surface completely dry just a few hours after heavy rainfall, meant that, for the people of these close-knit communities, the well or spring was of the utmost importance. If this dried up, the lives of the whole community were at risk.

The area of northeast Derbyshire with the District of Bolsover centres around Chesterfield. This was the heart of the county's coal-mining area and many of the towns and villages reflect the prosperity the mines brought in Victorian times. Sadly, the vast majority of the collieries are now closed; there was for a while a period of decline, but visitors today will be surprised at the wealth of history and fine architecture to be seen throughout the region.

Haddon Hall

The Peak District

The Peak District National Park was the first of Britain's National Parks to be established, in 1951, and ever since then its 555 square miles of glorious scenery have been protected from 'inappropriate development'. Of all the world's national parks, it is the second most popular – only Mount Fuji in Japan attracts more visitors each year.

Referred to as the Dark Peak as well as the High Peak, the northern area of the Peak District National Park is not as foreboding as its name might suggest. These high moors are ripe for exploring on foot, and a walk from the Kinder Reservoir will lead to the western edge of Kinder Scout. This whole area is really a series of plateaux, rather than

mountains and valleys, with the highest point on Kinder Scout some 2,088 feet above sea level. In this remote and wild area the walker can feel a real sense of freedom - however, it is worth remembering that the moors, with their treacherous peat bogs and unpredictable mists which can rise quickly even in summer, should not be dismissed as places for a casual ramble.

To the eastern side of this region are the three reservoirs created by flooding of the upper valley of the River Derwent. Howden, Derwent, and Ladybower provide water for Sheffield and the East Midlands but their remote location, along with the many recreational activities found there, make them popular places to visit. The Derwent dam is particularly famous as the site of practice

---

🏯 historic building   🏛 museum   🏚 historic site   🏞 scenic attraction   🌿 flora and fauna

exercises for the Dambusters of the Second World War.

Buxton

🏛 The Crescent 🏛 Opera House

🏛 St Anne's Church 🏛 Devonshire Royal Hospital

🏛 Museum 🌳 Pavilion Gardens

🏛 Church of St John the Baptist

With a population of barely 20,000, the elegant Georgian town of Buxton is nevertheless the largest settlement within the boundaries of the Peak District National Park. (The second largest town, Bakewell, has fewer than 5,000 inhabitants). Buxton's gracious architecture can be attributed mainly to the efforts of the 5th Duke of Devonshire who

hoped to establish a northern spa town that would rival, possibly surpass, the attractions of Bath in the southwest. In both locations it was the Romans who first exploited the healing waters of apparently inexhaustible hot springs as a commercial enterprise. The Romans name for Buxton was *Aquae Arnemetiae* – the Spa of the Goddess of the Grove. The waters still bubble up at Buxton, always maintaining an incredibly constant temperature of 82 degrees fahrenheit (28 degrees centigrade). Buxton water is reputed to be particularly pure and especially effective in mitigating the symptoms of rheumatism. Countless sufferers from rheumatism are on record attesting that the balmy Buxton water helped to soothe their painful symptoms: Mary, Queen of Scots, a political prisoner

📰 stories and anecdotes 🐦 famous people ✂ art and craft 🎵 entertainment and sport 🚶 walks

detained at nearby Chatsworth but allowed out on day release to Buxton, was one of them.

In the 18th century, the 5th Duke of Devonshire commissioned the building of **The Crescent** to ensure that visitors would flock here. Designed by John Carr of York, the building is similar to the architecture found in Bath and, after suffering from neglect, is about to undergo a huge restoration programme. As with many places, the coming of the railway to Buxton in 1863 marked the height of popularity of the town. Nothing, however, could be done to alter the harsh climate, and the incessant rainfall meant that the Duke's dream of making Buxton the 'Bath of the North', was never truly realised.

Among the other notable architectural features of the town is the **Devonshire Royal Hospital**. This was originally built as stables for hotel patrons of The Crescent and, after their conversion by the 6th Duke in 1858, the largest unsupported dome in the world (50 metres in diameter) was built to enclose the courtyard in 1880.

Originally built in 1905, the attractive **Opera House** was restored in 1979 to its grand Edwardian style. After being used as a cinema for many years, it is once again the host of live performances and, as well as offering a comprehensive and popular programme throughout the year, also has one of the largest stages in England.

The **Pavilion Gardens** have a conservatory and octagon within the grounds – antique markets and arts shows are often held here, and it is a very pleasant

---

THE COACH HOUSE FISH & CHIP SHOP & RU CRAFTY2

3 Scarsdale Place, Buxton, Derbyshire SK17 6EF
Tel: 01298 23345 Fax: 01298 71393
e-mail: info@rucrafty2.co.uk

The **Coach House Fish & Chip Shop** is a popular 44-seat café and takeaway on a corner site on the busy market place. It has a traditional look and feel, and the décor includes paintings and vintage photographs of local places of interest. It's owned by Sue and Wesley Darbyshire, a cheerful, hardworking couple with three children and a multitude of interests (the business was started in 1976 by Wesley's mum). The fish all comes from sustainable stock, and other favourites on a menu that caters for all appetites include home made steak pies and cheese & onion pies. Uniformed waitresses provide friendly, professional service, and the shop holds regular charity evenings in support of the RNLI and Rotary Club.

Sue's interests include card crafting and scrapbooking, and with her mother-in-law Barbara she runs **RU Crafty2** in a two room shop next to the chippy. This super little shop is filled with cardmaking and scrapbooking materials, paints and punches and rubber stamps, beads and jewellery, kids' kits and crafts, and they hold regular demos and weekly workshops. Sue got the idea for the shop after making a scrapbook of her daughter Danielle's first 18 years.

🏠 historic building   🏛 museum   🏚 historic site   🍃 scenic attraction   🌿 flora and fauna

place to walk around any time of year. Laid out in 1871 by Edward Milner, with money donated by the Dukes of Devonshire, the 23 acres include formal gardens, serpentine walks and decorative iron bridges across the River Wye. The conservatory was reopened in 1982 following extensive renovation; there is also a swimming pool filled with warm spa water.

St John the Baptist church was built in Italian style in 1811 by Sir Jeffrey Wyatville. That same year Wyatville laid out The Slopes, the area below the Market Place in Upper Buxton. The grand Town Hall was built between 1887 and 1889 and dominates the Market Place. Further down Terrace Road is the **Buxton Museum**, which explores the Wonders of the Peak through seven time zones. As well as housing an important local archaeology collection, the Museum also has a fine collection of Ashford Marble, Blue John ornaments, paintings, prints, pottery and glassware.

St Anne's Church, built in 1625, reflects the building work performed here before Buxton's 18th century heyday when limestone was the most common construction material rather than the mellow sandstone that dominates today.

Buxton, which rivals Ambleside for the title of the highest town in England, is surrounded by some of the most glorious of the Peak District countryside. These moorlands also provide one of the town's specialities – heather honey. Several varieties of heather grow on the moors: there is *ling*, or common heather which turns the land purple in late summer; there is bell-heather which grows on dry rocky slopes; and there is cross-leaved heather which can be found on wet, boggy ground.

Around Buxton

🏚 Poole's Cavern   🖈 Axe Edge

To the west of the town lies **Axe Edge**, the highest point of which rises to 1,807 feet above sea level. From this spot on a clear day (and the weather here is notoriously changeable) the panoramic views of Derbyshire are overwhelming. Just beyond, at 1,690 feet above sea level, the Cat and Fiddle Inn is the second highest pub in England. **Axe Edge Moor**, which receives an average annual rainfall of over four feet, is strictly for hardened walkers. It should come as no surprise that this Moor is the source of several rivers which play important roles in the life of the Peak District. The River Dove and the River Manifold, which join at Ilam, rise not far from one another; the River Wye rises above Buxton to join the Derwent further south; the River Goyt, a major source of the Mersey, rises to the west of Axe Edge. The entire length of the River Goyt can be walked, from its source to its confluence with the River Etherow to the north and just outside the boundaries of the National Park.

Those who venture to Errwood Reservoir will be surprised to see rhododendrons growing near the banks of a man-made lake. They once stood in the grounds of Errwood Hall, which was built in the 1830s for the Grimshawe family. The house was demolished before the Reservoir was flooded, but the gardens were left to grow wild. Not far away can be seen the strange-looking Spanish Shrine. Built by the Grimshawes in memory of their Spanish governess, it is a small stone building with an unusual beehive roof.

Also to the west of town, **Poole's Cavern** on Green Lane is a natural limestone cave which was used by tribes from the Neolithic period onwards. It was visited by Mary, Queen of Scots and the 'chair' she used is pointed out during the regular tours of the cave on offer. Above the cavern and about 20 minutes' walk away is Grin Low Country Park and the prominent folly and scenic viewpoint, built in 1896, known as Solomon's Temple.

COMBS
3 miles N of Buxton off the A6

🌱 Chestnut Centre

Combs Reservoir southwest of Chapel-en-le-Frith is crossed at one end by Dickie's Bridge. 'Dickie' is said to have resided at a farm in Tunstead where he was known as Ned Dixon. Apparently murdered by his cousin, he nevertheless continued his 'working life' as a sort of guard-skull, alerting the household whenever strangers drew near. Various strange occurrences are said to have ensued when

attempts were made to move the skull.

On Castleton Road just a few miles northeast of the town, the **Chestnut Centre** is a fascinating wildlife conservation centre, popular with children and adults alike. It is famed for its otters, with award-winning otter and owl enclosures set along an extensive circular nature trail which meanders through some historic wooded parkland.

CHAPEL-EN-LE-FRITH
4 miles N of Buxton off the A6

🏛 Chapel of St Thomas

This charming town is often overlooked by travellers on the bypass between Buxton and Stockport, but it repays a closer look. In 1225 the guardians of the High Peak's Royal Forest purchased land from the Crown and built a **Chapel** here, dedicating it to **St Thomas à Becket** of Canterbury. A century later the chapel was replaced with a more substantial building; further modernisation took place in the early 1700s. The building of the original chapel led to the foundation of the town and also its name, which is Norman French for 'chapel in the forest'. A curious legacy has been passed down allowing owners of freehold land in the district the right to choose their vicar. The interior of the church boasts 19th century box pews and a monument to 'the Apostle of the Peak', William Bagshawe of nearby Ford Hall, a

Chapel-en-le-Frith

Nonconformist minister of the late 17th century. In 1648 the church was used as a gaol for 1,500 Scottish prisoners and the dreadful conditions arising from such close confinement caused unimaginable suffering. Their ordeal lasted for 16 days; a total of 44 men died.

WHALEY BRIDGE
6 miles N of Buxton off the A5004

This small industrial town at the gateway to the Goyt Valley grew up around the coal-mining and textile industries. Both have now gone, but the Peak Forest Canal flowing through the town remains very much the centre of activity. The 'bridge' of the village's name crosses the River Goyt, on the site of what may once have been a Roman crossing.

Many of the old warehouses in Whaley Bridge have been restored and converted to meet the needs of the 21st century and, where once narrow boats transported goods and raw materials to and from the town, boats can now be hired. The Toddbrook Reservoir was built in 1831 to be a feeder for the Peak Forest Canal. The wharf here is dotted with picturesque narrowboats.

LYME PARK
8 miles NW of Buxton off the A6

Lyme Park (National Trust) is an ancient estate originally granted to Sir Thomas Danyers in 1346 by a grateful King Edward III after a battle at Caen. Danyers then passed the estate to his son-in-law, Sir Piers Legh, in 1388. It remained in the family until 1946, when it was given to the Trust. Not much remains of the original Elizabethan manor house; today's visitors are instead treated to the sight of a fantastic Palladian mansion, the work of Venetian architect Giacomo Leoni.

Not daunted by the bleak landscape and climate of the surrounding Peak District, Leoni built a corner of Italy here in this much harsher countryside. Inside the mansion there is a mixture of styles: the elegant Leoni-designed rooms with rich Roccoco ceilings, the panelled Tudor drawing room, and two surviving Elizabethan rooms. Much of the three-dimensional internal carving is attributed to Grinling Gibbons, though a lot of the work was also undertaken by local craftsmen. As well as the fantastic splendour of the mansion, the estate includes a late 19th century formal garden and a medieval deer park.

HAYFIELD
9 miles N of Buxton off the A624

Kinder Downfall Kinder Scout

This small town below the exposed moorland of **Kinder Scout** is a popular centre for exploring the area and offers many amenities for hillwalkers. Like its neighbour New Mills, Hayfield grew up around the textile industry, in this case wool weaving and calico printing. Many of the houses seen today were originally weavers' cottages. One of Hayfield's best-known sons was the much-loved actor Arthur Lowe (1914-1982).

Three miles northeast of the town is **Kinder Downfall**, the highest waterfall in the county, found where the River Kinder flows off the edge of Kinder Scout. In low temperatures the fall freezes solid – a sight to be seen. It is also renowned for its blow-back effect: when the wind blows, the fall's water is forced back against the rock and the water appears to run uphill! There are not many natural waterfalls in Derbyshire, so Kinder Downfall appears on most visitors' itineraries.

Hayfield and Lantern Pike

Distance: *5.6 miles (9.0 kilometres)*

Typical time: *180 mins*

Height gain: *300 metres*

Map: *Explorer Outdoor Leisure 1*

Walk: *www.walkingworld.com ID:2905*

Contributor: *Jim Grindle*

ACCESS INFORMATION:

The start of the walk is at the junction of the A624 and the A6015 and is not far from New Mills on the A6. There is a bus connection with Manchester and a well signposted car park at the start.

ADDITIONAL INFORMATION:

The Sett Valley Trail is traffic-free and was bought from British Rail in 1973 to provide a walking, cycling and horse riding route. Previously it was a popular holiday line for Manchester as well as an essential part of the industrial scene of the valley with its many cotton mills, calico printing works and paper mills. The route has been developed for wildlife too, with numbers of reed-beds and copses. Lantern Pike is owned by the National Trust to whom it was presented by the Ramblers Association as a memorial to a past president, Edwin Royce. There is a viewfinder/memorial on the summit. The Pennine Bridleway now runs as far north as Burnley and is suitable for mountain bikes and walkers as well as for horse riders.

DESCRIPTION:

This short circular walk has a reasonable height gain, but the summit of Lantern Pike is easily attained by a very gradual climb. Much of the walk follows the Sett Valley Way and the Pennine Bridleway which means fewer stiles than usual. There are outstanding views, of the Kinder Scout plateau in particular.

FEATURES:

Pub, Toilets, Church, National Trust/NTS, Wildlife, Birds, Flowers, Great Views, Butterflies, Cafe, Gift Shop, Food Shop, Good for Kids, Industrial Archaeology, Moor, Public Transport, Restaurant, Tea Shop, Woodland

WALK DIRECTIONS:

1 | The building is the Information Centre/Toilet block. If you walk past it you will be on the Sett Valley Trail. Follow this until it is interrupted by a road. Leave the Trail and turn right following the road. Drop to a bridge over the Sett and then look for a Pennine Bridleway sign by a cobbled track going uphill on the right.

2 | The Trail climbs to another road by a group of houses.

3 | Cross the road, turn right and almost at once left to continue on the Trail. This climbs slowly again and brings you to a gate with a National Trust sign behind it. Here you go through the gate and up to the left to reach the summit of Lantern Pike.

4 | The well-worn path leads over the hill and down to the exit from the National Trust land.

5 | Follow the direction of the signpost across the open moorland to a wall on the far side. There you will find a signpost with five arms.

6 | Just to the right of the signpost (and out of shot) is a bridleway gate with a Pennine Bridleway sign. Go through onto an enclosed track and follow it until it divides at Matleymoor Farm.

7 | Turn right and pass the farm. After 100m there is another division in the track. Ignore the turning on the left. Carry on downhill for 1km on the tarred track and look for another tarred track coming from the right.

8 | Here you turn right, doubling back on your route and climbing steeply. Just before a green metal footpath sign about 200m away is a turning on the left leading to a farm. Follow this to a stile and gate at its end. Go through and ahead at first before turning left and following a path across the slope. Cross a stream and avoid taking paths leading downhill on the left. The path leads through a wood and to a high stone wall with a ladder stile by two Scots pines. If you don't find the stile it will be because you have not kept high enough - just go uphill almost to the corner of the field.

9 | Once over this stile keep by the wall on your right to another stile. Cross and maintain direction with the wall now on your left. The path ends at a stile by a tarred drive with some houses. Cross this stile but not the one immediately opposite across the track. Continue on the drive until it bends sharply to the left. On the right you will find an enclosed track.

10 | Turn down this track until you see a stile on the left just before a bend to the right.

11 | Cross this stile and go down a steepish enclosed path. This leads you down to the outskirts of Hayfield. Turn left on joining a road and watch for a footpath sign by a gate on the right just before you reach a flyover.

12 | The sign directs you across a playing field to the riverbank. Follow the river on your right to a footbridge. Cross the bridge and follow the path to a road. Just over a wall is the car park.

GLOSSOP
13 miles N of Buxton off the A624

🚗 Snake Pass

Glossop is an interesting mix of styles: the industrial town of the 19th century with its towering Victorian mills and the 17th century village with its charming old cottages and cobbled streets.

From Glossop, the A57 east is an exhilarating stretch of road with hair-pin bends, known as the **Snake Pass**. The road is frequently made impassable by landslides, heavy mist and massive snowfalls in winter but, weather permitting, it is an experience not to be missed. For much of the length of the turnpike road that Thomas Telford built across Snake Pass in 1821, the route follows the line of an ancient Roman road, known as Doctor's Gate, which ran between Glossop and a fort at Brough. The route was so named after it was rediscovered, in the 16th century, by Dr Talbot, a vicar from Glossop.

HADFIELD
14 miles N of Buxton off the A624

🏛 Woodhead Chapel   🚶 Longendale Trail

The small village of Hadfield is the terminus of the **Longdendale Trail**, a route following the line of a former railway line and part of the Trans-Pennine Trail. Old Hall in The Square is the oldest building in the village, built in 1646. The Roman Catholic Church of St Charles was built in 1868 by Baron Howard of Glossop; members of the Howard family are buried here.

The Longdendale Trail continues eastward from here. Longdendale itself is the valley of the River Etherow, and is a favourite place for day-trippers. Along the footpath through this wild and desolate valley there are many reminders of the past, including **Woodhead**

Chapel, the graveyard of which has numerous memorials to the navvies, and their families, who died in an outbreak of cholera in 1849 while working on the Sheffield to Manchester railway line. Hadfield is Royston Vasey in *The League of Gentlemen*.

EDALE

8 miles NE of Buxton off the A625

⋏ Pennine Way

In the valley of the River Noe, Edale marks the start of the **Pennine Way**. Opened in 1965, this long-distance footpath follows the line of the backbone of Britain for some 270 miles from here to Kirk Yetholm, just over the Scottish border. Though the footpath begins in the lush meadows of this secluded valley, it is not long before walkers find themselves crossing wild and bleak moorland before heading further north to Bleaklow. Many travellers have spoken of Derbyshire as a

Peveril Castle, Castleton

county of contrasts, and nowhere is this more apparent than at Edale. Not only does the landscape change dramatically within a short distance from the heart of the village, but the weather can alter from brilliant sunshine to snowstorms in the space of a couple of hours.

Tourism first came to Edale with the completion of the Manchester to Sheffield railway in 1894, though at that time there was little in the way of hospitality for visitors. Today there are several hotels, camping sites, a large Youth Hostel and adventure and walking centres.

CASTLETON

8 miles NE of Buxton off the A625

🏰 Peveril Castle   ⛰ Winnats Pass

⛏ Blue John Mine & Caverns   ⛰ Mam Tor

Situated at the head of the Hope Valley, Castleton is sheltered by the Norman ruin of **Peveril Castle** with its spectacular views over Castleton and the surrounding countryside. The Castle, originally called Castle of the Peak, was built as a wooden stockade in 1080 by William Peveril, illegitimate son of William the Conqueror. Later rebuilt in stone, the keep was added by Henry II. It remains the only surviving example of a Norman castle in Derbyshire, and is among the best preserved and most complete ruins in Britain. Approaching Castleton from the west along the A625, the road runs through the **Winnats Pass**, a narrow limestone gorge. Thought to have been formed under the sea, from currents eroding the seabed, the gorge has been used as a road for centuries and is still the only direct route to the village from the west.

Originally laid out as a planned town below its castle, the shape of the village has changed little over the years and it has become a popular tourist centre. The mainly 17th century Church

🏰 historic building   📷 museum   ⛩ historic site   ⛰ scenic attraction   🌱 flora and fauna of St Edmund was heavily restored in 1837, but retains its box pews and a fine Norman arch, as well as a Breeches Bible dated 1611.

The hills to the west of Castleton are famous for their caves. The **Blue John Mine and Caverns**, which have been in the hands of the Ollerenshaw family for many years, are probably one of Derbyshire's most popular attractions. Amazing trips down into the caves themselves can be made. Above ground, in the gift shops various items can be bought made with the distinctive Blue fluorspar with its attractive purplish veining. It was once prized by the Romans, and it is said that Petronius paid the equivalent of around £40,000 for a wonderfully ornate vase carved from the stone. It is said that in a fit of petty-mindedness he preferred to smash the vase

rather than relinquish it to the Emperor Nero.

At the bottom of Winnats Pass lies Speedwell Cavern, a former lead mine which used boats on an underground canal to ferry the miners and lead ore to and from the rock face. Visitors can follow the same boat journey underground in the company of a guide. The mine had a short life: it started up in 1771 and, despite an investment of £14,000, closed in 1790 after only £3,000 worth of lead ore had been extracted.

Peak Cavern, reached by a delightful riverside walk, has the widest opening of any cave in Europe. Up until the 17th century, little cottages used to stand within the entrance. The rope-makers who lived in these tiny dwellings used the cave entrance, dry in all weathers, for making rope: the ropewalk,

VALLEY GIFTS

How Lane, Castleton, Hope Valley S33 8WF
Tel: 01433 623401

Pamela Richardson has owned and run **Valley Gifts** since 1999. It stands in a small row of businesses on the Hope side of Castleton, in the heart of the Peak District National Park. The open-plan display area is filled with lovely things, from ladies' ethnic clothing to candles and lamps, teddy bears, clocks, mirrors, cards and other personally chosen craft goods, gift ideas and things for the home.

Pamela's knitting skills are legendary, and she will accept commissions to knit something wonderful in wool. The famous Blue John and other caves, the Castle, the 17th village church and some superb walks and climbs are among the attractions in the vicinity, but visitors looking for a special treat or gift should definitely find time to visit Valley Gifts, which is open from 10 to 5.30 every day except Monday.

which dates back some 400 years, can still be seen. Guides re-enact the process of making rope, and one rope-maker's cottage is still extant. The cave was used by the BBC to film an episode of *The Chronicles of Narnia* series. Over the years successive Kings and Queens would entertain deep within the belly of the cave, which would be festooned with candles and other open flames – visitors can see the ledge on which the Royal musicians would perch. Peak Cavern was originally known as The Devil's Arse, but the fastidious Victorians felt this was 'inappropriate' and changed it to the name it carries today.

No description of Castleton would be complete without a mention of **Mam Tor**. The name means 'Mother Hill', and locally the tor is referred to as Shivering Mountain, because the immense cliff face near the summit is constantly on the move owing to water seepage. A climb to the top of the ridge is well worth while, as the views are splendid – in particular of the two diverse rock formations which separate the White (limestone) Peak from the northern Dark (gritstone) Peak.

HOPE
9 miles NE of Buxton off the A625

🏛 **Church of St Peter**

Hope gets its first mention in 926 as the site of a battle won by King Athelstan. By the time of the Domesday survey of 1086, the parish of Hope had extended to embrace much of the High Peak area and included places such as Buxton, Chapel-en-le-Frith and Tideswell. It remained one of the largest parishes in the country until the 19th century, though a

---

THE HOPE CHEST & COURTYARD CAFÉ/ RESTAURANT

The Courtyard, Castleton Road, Hope, Derbyshire S33 6RD
Tel: 01433 620072

Owner Cath Klapsia is passionate about food, and she runs the **Hope Chest & Courtyard Café/Restaurant** with help from her family and a small group of local staff. The setting is a Victorian gritstone building with a conservatory extension and a pleasant garden. The Hope Chest is a delicatessen selling a mouthwatering selection of good things to eat, including cooked meats, cheeses, cakes and pastries, sandwiches made to order in a variety of breads, and the range of excellent products in jars from the French company La Belle Chouvienne. Cath will make up picnic baskets with a little notice, and the deli offers an outside catering service.

The Café is open from 8 to 5 serving everything from an all-day breakfast to sandwiches, pasties, Derbyshire oatcakes with a choice of fillings and hot main dishes such as tuna pasta bake, chicken jalfrezi, liver & bacon, sausage casserole swerved in a giant Yorkshire pudding and always plenty for vegetarians, along with super home-made cakes and pastries. The Restaurant is open for bookings for atmospheric candlelit dining from 7 o'clock Monday to Saturday (and Sunday by special arrangement). Temptations on the à la carte and fixed-price menus tempt with classics such as rack of lamb, and tournedos Rossini. The dining room can be hired for private parties, and home catering is available.

🏛 historic building   🏛 museum   🏛 historic site   ⬥ scenic attraction   🌱 flora and fauna market charter was not granted until 1715. Hope lies at the point where the River Noe meets Peakshole Water; the stream rises in Peak's Hole (better known as Peak Cavern), hence its name.

The parish **Church of St Peter** was built at the beginning of the 1200s; the only part remaining from the original church is the Norman font. The Latin inscription on a chair in the north aisle reads (in translation) 'You cannot make a scholar out of a block of wood' and is said to have been carved for Thomas Bocking, the vicar and schoolmaster here during the 17th century. His name also appears on the fine pulpit; his Breeches Bible is displayed nearby. The Hope Agricultural Show is held every year on August Bank Holiday Monday.

BAMFORD
11 miles NE of Buxton off the A6013

🏛 Church   🏚 Bamford Mill   ⚑ Ladybower

This charming village situated between the Hope Valley and Ladybower Reservoir, stands at the heart of the Dark Peak below Bamford Edge and close to the Upper Derwent Valley Dams. When the Derwent and Howden Dams were built in the early years of the 20th century, the valley of the Upper Derwent was flooded, submerging many farms under the rising waters. The 1,000 or so labourers and their families were housed at Birchinlee, a temporary village which came to be known locally as 'Tin Town' because of its plethora of corrugated iron shacks. During the Second World War the third and largest reservoir, the **Ladybower**, was built. This involved the inundating of two more villages – Derwent and Ashopton. The dead from Derwent's church were re-interred in the churchyard of St John the Baptist in Bamford. The living

were rehoused in Yorkshire Bridge, a purpose-built hamlet located below the embankment of the Ladybower Dam. There is a Visitor Centre at Fairholmes (in the Upper Derwent Valley) which tells the story of these 'drowned villages'.

The topography hereabouts was similar to that of the Ruhr Valley and the Lancaster bombers of 617 Squadron, the Dambusters, used the reservoir to practise dropping Barnes Wallis' Bouncing bombs prior to their attack on the Ruhr Dam in 1943. Parts of the film *The Dambusters* were filmed here in 1954.

Bamford's **Church of St John the Baptist** is unlike any other in Derbyshire. Designed in 1861 by the famous church architect William Butterfield, it has a slender tower and an extra-sharp spire. Also worthy of note, particularly to lovers of industrial architecture, is **Bamford Mill**, just across the road by the river. This cotton mill was built in 1820; it retains its huge waterwheel and also has a 1907 tandem-compound steam engine.

The village lies in the heart of hill-farming country, and each Spring Bank Holiday Bamford plays host to one of the most famous of the Peak District Sheepdog Trials.

Along the A57 towards Sheffield, the road dips and crosses the gory-sounding Cutthroat Bridge. The present bridge dates back to 1830, but its name comes from the late 1500s, when the body of a man with his throat cut was discovered under the bridge which then stood here.

HATHERSAGE
12 miles NE of Buxton off the A625

🏛 Moorseats   🏚 Museum   🎬 Churchyard

Once a centre for needle-making, it is difficult to know whether to classify Hathersage as a large village or a small town. In either event, it

Grave of Little John, Hathersage

the 1780s, a 32-inch thighbone was discovered. This would certainly indicate that the owner was well over seven feet tall.

Bakewell and the White Peak

This region of the Derbyshire Dales, sometimes also known as the Central Peaks and occupying the central area of the Peak District National Park, is less wild and isolated than the remote High Peak area. The two main rivers, the Wye and the Derwent, which both have their source further north, are, in this region, at a more gentle stage of their course. Over the centuries, the fast-flowing waters were harnessed to provide power to drive the mills situated on the riverbanks; any walk taken along these riverbanks will not only give the opportunity to discover a wide range of plant and animal life, but also provide the opportunity to see the remains of buildings that once played an important part in the economy of north Derbyshire.

is a pleasant place with interesting literary connections. Charlotte Brontë stayed at Hathersage vicarage, and the village itself appears as 'Morton' in her novel *Jane Eyre*. The name Eyre was probably gleaned from the monuments to the prominent local landowners with this surname, as can be seen in the village Church of St Michael and its churchyard. The 15th century head of the family, Robert Eyre, lived at Highlow Hall. Within sight of this Hall he built seven houses, one for each of his seven sons. North Lees was one, and another was **Moorseats**, where Charlotte Brontë stayed on holiday and used as the inspiration for Moor House in *Jane Eyre*.

In **Hathersage Churchyard** lie the reputed remains of Little John, Robin Hood's renowned companion. Whether or not the legend is to be believed, it is worth mentioning that when the grave was opened in

Bakewell

🏛 Haddon Hall   🏛 Church

🏠 Museum

The only true town in the Peak District National Park, Bakewell attracts many day-trippers, walkers and campers as well as locals who come to take advantage of its many amenities. The beautiful medieval five-arched bridge spanning the River Wye is still in use today as the main crossing point for traffic. A stone-built town set along the banks of the River Wye, Bakewell enjoys a picturesque setting among well-wooded hills. With only 4,000 inhabitants it is nevertheless generally

🏛 historic building   🏠 museum   🏛 historic site   🔆 scenic attraction   🌿 flora and fauna acknowledged as the capital of the Peak District National Park.

However, for most people it is a dessert that has made the name of Bakewell so famous, but please remember it is referred to locally as a pudding and most definitely not as a tart! Its invention is said to have been an accident when what was supposed to have been a strawberry tart turned into something altogether different. The cooking mishap took place in the kitchens of the Rutland Arms Hotel, which was built in 1804 on the site of a coaching inn.

Medieval Bridge, Bakewell

Bakewell is the market town for this whole central area of the Peak District – markets were held here well before the granting of a charter in 1330. Monday is now Bakewell's

---

ID INTERIOR DESIGN

Matlock Street, Bakewell, Derbyshire DE45 1EE
Tel: 01629 813263   Fax: 01629 814361
e-mail: interior.design@btconnect.com

On one of the main shopping streets in the centre of Bakewell, **ID Interior Design** has gained a reputation starting in Sheffield over 60 years for providing a high-quality, personal design service. The studio provides a bespoke interior design consultancy service, and the team of professionally trained designers led by Sarah Cooper are able to undertake a wide range of projects, from individual rooms to complete houses, offices or hotels. The specialists include craftsmen for paint effect, carpet fitting and upholstery, and the workrooms are undoubted leaders in making up of curtains, pelmets, bedspreads and loose covers. Quality and attention to detail are to the fore in everything they do, and no job is too big or too small.

The showrooms on two floors are home to an exciting and inspirational mix of fabrics and upholstery, carpets and rugs, wallpapers and paints, furniture and mirrors, curtain poles, lighting and unusual gifts to suit all budgets. Every item is chosen for good design, quality and individuality.

Owner Sarah Cooper came here in 1982 with a Degree in Interior Design and her customers will testify that she is as keen as ever: her reward is the satisfaction of successfully transforming a room or a whole house for her clients.

🎬 stories and anecdotes   🦜 famous people   ✿ art and craft   ✏ entertainment and sport   🎋 walks

THE STYLE HOUSE

Anchor Square, Bakewell, Derbyshire DE45 1DR
Tel: 01629 813030   Fax: 01629 814432
e-mail: ceri.rocca@thestylehouse.co.uk
website: www.thestylehouse.co.uk

Ceri Rocca began her career at the age of 17, and after qualifying with a degree and a diploma she spent several years designing the interiors of 5-star hotels, palaces and offices in Dubai and elsewhere. She established the **Style House** in 1999 to provide a professional interior design service as well as offering beautiful interior accessories for the discerning buyer at affordable prices. The consultancy undertakes any level of project, from a refurbishment to a complete rebuild, right through from the initial concept to the complete design, full working drawings, and project management and supervision to handover.

The Style House sells a full range of products to turn a house into a home, from large items of traditional and contemporary furniture to fabrics and wallpapers, paints, china and glassware, cutlery, candles, cushions, handmade cards and exquisite wrapping paper and ribbons. The building is one of the oldest in Bakewell, and behind a deceptively small exterior the ground floor is given over to smaller items while the first floor is set out as room settings to display the furniture and other larger pieces.

CRITCHLOWS FARM SHOP & ASHFORD FARM HOLIDAY COTTAGES

2 Bridge Street, Bakewell, Derbyshire DE45 1DS
Tel: 01629 812010
Website: www.ashfordfarmcottages.co.uk

Critchlows Farm Shop: Visit this farm shop in Bakewell, where the beef and lamb is reared and sourced locally. Try their selection of award winning sausages and home cured bacon or buy a pork pie baked daily in their bakery. They also sell ready made meals, bread and savoury pies and a fine selection of English cheeses. So, if you want tasty and natural food to accompany your holiday do call in to Critchlows Farm Shop, 2 Bridge Street, Bakewell.

Ashford Farm Holiday Cottages: Four star rated barn conversions set in the picturesque village of Ashford, 3 miles from the market town of Bakewell. All furnished to the highest standards and set in glorious countryside. Ideal base for walking.

Further information: Tel: 01629 812376 or go to www.ashfordfarmcottages.co.uk.

 historic building   museum   historic site   scenic attraction   flora and fauna

market day and the cattle market, one of the largest in Derbyshire, is an important part of the area's farming life. The annual Bakewell Show started in 1819 and has gone on to become one of the foremost agricultural shows in the country. Across the River Wye stands the enormous, new Agricultural and Business Centre, where the livestock market takes place.

The large parish **Church of All Saints** was founded in Saxon times, as revealed by the ancient preaching crosses and stonework. Its graceful spire, with an octagonal tower, can be seen for miles around. Bakewell is one of the few places in Derbyshire in the Domesday Book to record two priests and a church, and the churchyard and church itself contain a wonderful variety of headstones and coffin

slabs and, near the porch, a most unusual cross. Over 1,200 years old, it stands an impressive eight feet high. On one side it depicts the Crucifixion, on the other are the Norse gods Odin and Loki. The Vernon Chapel in the south aisle contains impressive monuments to 'The King of the Peak', Sir George Vernon of Haddon Hall, who died in 1567, and also to Sir John Manners, who died in 1584, and his wife Dorothy Vernon – these latter two feature in one of the great romantic legends of the Peak District.

Behind the church is the lovely **Old House Museum**, housed in a building on Cunningham Place which dates back to 1534. It is thought to be the oldest house in Bakewell. This beautiful building narrowly escaped demolition but has been lovingly

LACE

Orme Court, Granby Road, Bakewell, Derbyshire DE45 1ES
Tel: 01629 814933
e-mail: lace.bakewell@virgin.net

Lace was once an important industry in Bakewell, and Sue Haywood's shop **Lace** is a worthy inheritor of the name and the heritage. Sue has been in the lingerie business for 25 years, and has run her own shop for the past 15.

Behind an inviting window display the shop is stocked with exclusive lingerie, seductive nightwear and exquisite swimwear. Sue is unfailingly friendly and helpful and she and her staff are always ready with advice. Lace offers an excellent fitting service, and when asked will keep a record of customers' fittings. This means that husbands and boyfriends looking for a surprise present will be sure of at least getting the size right! And if the local speciality Bakewell puddings (don't call them tarts, please!) have taken their toll, the ladies can go back to be refitted.

Among the top names regularly held at Lace are Prima Donna, Marie Jo and Aubade, and for swimwear, Nicole Olivia, Gideon Oberson and Charmline. Bakewell has plenty to attract the visitor, including the beautiful medieval five-arched bridge and the Church of All Saints with its graceful spire, but for the graceful, style-conscious lady all roads point to Lace, which is open from 9.30 to 5 Monday to Saturday.

CE GIFTS & BEARS

5 Hebden Court, Matlock Street, Bakewell, Derbyshire DE45 1EE
Tel: 01629 814811 Fax: 01629 814820
e-mail: info@cegifts.co.uk website: www.cegifts.co.uk

Ce Gifts & Bears is a charming shop located in the corner of a Victorian courtyard reached through an archway off the main street of Bakewell. Tracey Baker and her mother Angela have filled their welcoming shop with a beautiful selection of gifts that offer good value for money and you won't find in the High Street shops. Among the items on display on the ground floor are hand-painted glassware, ceramics, picture frames, magnetic/therapy bracelets, hand-finished cards and unusual bird houses and feeders. And upstairs are the Teddy Bears – hundreds of them, for the serious collector or just to be hugged – and dolls' house furniture and accessories. Open seven days a week.

restored by the Bakewell Historical Society and now displays its original wattle and daub interior walls. Now established as a folk museum, it houses a fascinating collection of rural bygones.

The town is full of delightful, mellow stone buildings, many of which date from the early 1600s and are still in use today. The Old Town Hall is now the Peak District National Park Visitor Centre. Few buildings remain from the days when Bakewell was a minor spa town, but the Bath House, on Bath Street, is one such building. Built in 1697 for the Duke of Rutland, it contained a large bath which was filled with the spa water and kept at a constant temperature of 59 degrees Fahrenheit.

South of Bakewell down the Matlock Road, on a bluff overlooking the Wye, the romantic **Haddon Hall** stands hidden from the road by a beech hedge. The home of the Dukes of Rutland for over 800 years, the

Hall has enjoyed a fairly peaceful existence, in part no doubt because it stood empty and neglected for nearly 300 years after 1640, when the family chose Belvoir Castle in Leicestershire as their main home. Examples of work from every century from the 12th to the 17th are evident in this architectural treasure trove.

Little construction work has been carried out on the Hall since the days of Henry VIII and it remains one of the best examples of a medieval and Tudor manor house. The 16th

Haddon Hall

🏛 historic building   🏛 museum   🏛 historic site   ♧ scenic attraction   ♣ flora and fauna century terraced gardens are one of the chief delights of the Hall and are thought by many to be the most romantic in England. The Hall's splendour and charm have led it to be used as a backdrop to television and film productions including *Jane Eyre*, *Moll Flanders* and *The Prince and the Pauper*. Nikolaus Pevsner described the Hall as, "the English castle par excellence, not the forbidding fortress on an unassailable crag, but the large, rambling, safe, grey, loveable house of knights and their ladies, the unreasonable dream-castle of those who think of the Middle Ages as a time of chivalry and valour and noble feelings. None other in England is so complete and convincing".

The Hall's chapel is adorned with medieval wall paintings; the kitchens are the oldest extant part of the house, and feature time-worn oak tables and dole cupboards. The oak-panelled Long Gallery features boars' heads and peacocks in the panelling.

Around Bakewell

EDENSOR
2 miles NE of Bakewell off the B6012

🏛 Chatsworth House

This model village (the name is pronounced Ensor) was built by the 6th Duke of Devonshire between 1838 and 1842 after the original village had been demolished because it spoilt the view from Chatsworth House. The village church was built by Sir George Gilbert Scott; in the churchyard is buried the late President Kennedy's sister Kathleen, who had married into the Cavendish family. Both she and her husband, the eldest son of the 10th Duke, were killed during the Second World War.

The home of the Dukes of Devonshire, **Chatsworth House**, known as the Palace of the Peak, is without doubt one of the finest of the great houses in Britain. The origins of the House as a great showpiece must be attributable to the redoubtable Bess of Hardwick, whose marriage into the Cavendish family helped to secure the future of the palace.

Bess' husband, Sir William Cavendish, bought the estate for £600 in 1549. It was Bess who completed the new House after his death. Over the years, the Cavendish fortune continued to pour into Chatsworth, making it an almost unparalleled showcase for art treasures. Every aspect of the fine arts is here, ranging from old masterpieces, furniture, tapestries, porcelain and some magnificent alabaster carvings.

The gardens of this stately home also have some marvellous features, including the Emperor Fountain, which dominates the Canal Pond and reaches a height of 290 feet. It was built by Sir Joseph Paxton to celebrate a visit by the Tsar of Russia in 1844. Paxton also built the world's largest greenhouse here as a prototype for the Crystal Palace built for the Great Exhibition of 1851. The glasshouse was demolished in 1920. There is a maze and a Laburnum Tunnel and, behind the house, the famous Cascades. The overall appearance of the park as it is seen today is chiefly due to the talents of Capability Brown, who was first consulted in 1761.

GRINDLEFORD
6 miles N of Bakewell off the B6521/B6001

🏛 Padley Chapel   🌲 Longshaw Country Park

This is one of the smallest Peak District villages and from here, each year in July, there is a pilgrimage to **Padley Chapel** to

🎬 stories and anecdotes   🐦 famous people   🎨 art and craft   🎭 entertainment and sport   🚶 walks

Calton Lees and Edensor

Distance: *4.2 miles (6.7 kilometres)*

Typical time: *120 mins*

Height gain: *140 metres*

Map: *Explorer Outdoor Leisure 24*

Walk: *www.walkingworld.com ID:2434*

Contributor: *Phil and Sue Eptlett*

ACCESS INFORMATION:

The start point is from the Calton Lees free car park adjacent to the Chatsworth Garden Centre just off the B6012. From whichever direction you approach just follow the signs for Chatsworth House

ADDITIONAL INFORMATION:

There is an abundance of wildlife to be seen including fish and birds of all types and deer which are free to roam on the estate.

In about 1760 the 4th Duke of Devonshire asked Capability Brown a noted landscape designer to improve the park the results of which can be seen today. Most notably the creation of Stand Wood which creates an impressive backdrop to the House and the wide open pastures to the front. He also altered the course of the river. One of the features of the gardens is the Emperor Fountain opened in 1844, which is fed by a 15" pipe from the Emperor Lake at the top of

the woods and reaches a height of approx. 270 ft. Fine views of the surrounding area can be seen from Waypoint 7 which include Froggatt Edge, Curber Edge and the house surrounded by Stand Wood.

DESCRIPTION:

Starting from the car park at Calton Lees the walk soon follows the bank of the River Derwent across rolling meadow towards Chatsworth House which is open to the public from Easter to Christmas. Upon reaching the river bridge leading to the house cross the road and take the path to the village of Edensor which up until the 1830's was sited across the river from the house but was moved to improve the view for His

Lordship. After passing through the village you take a path rising up a large landscaped meadow towards woodland with panoramic views all across the estate and surrounding countryside. Proceeding through the wood and a field a farm track is soon reached which leads back to the car park. Here refreshments can be had at the Garden Centre.

FEATURES:

Toilets, Church, Stately Home, Wildlife, Birds, Flowers, Great Views, Butterflies, Food Shop

WALK DIRECTIONS:

1 | Leave the car park by a path adjacent to the access road and go through the white gate. Immediately cross the road and go directly across the grassland to a weir on the River Derwent.

2 | From the weir walk upstream keeping the river on your right. As you proceed the house comes into view with its impressive west face and the Emperor Fountain can be seen in the gardens if it is working. Follow the river until you reach the bridge carrying the access road to the house. If you wish this is the point to visit the house and gardens

3 | Cross the road and take the path opposite going diagonally across the open parkland to the B6012 road and the village of Edensor.

4 | Cross the road, go through the white gates at the village entrance and proceed taking the road to the right of the church. As you pass through the village which has not changed since it was moved in the 1830's note the mix of architectural styles particularly Hollybush Cottage with its unusual spiral chimneys.

5 | Shortly after Hollybush Cottage take the footpath on the left signed to Rowsley. Go up the steps and turn left up further steps immediately before a cottage then go through a small gate onto open countryside. Here the path is non existent so starting with your back to the church spire walk across the rising open ground following the very infrequent footpath markers. Upon reaching the first crest head to the right side of a fenced off copse of trees.

6 | From the copse keep going upward in a straight line towards woodland on the horizon. As the woodland is approached head for the gate in the wall adjacent to some benches. This is the perfect spot to sit and rest and take in the fine view of the house, parkland and surrounding countryside.

7 | When suitably rested go through the gate and follow the track through woodland to a further gate. Go through this gate and proceed across the meadow to a wall and follow this keeping it on your left until another gate is reached.

8 | Again go through the gate and follow the stone track between two cottages and yet another gate.

9 | Keep on the track as it winds down a meadow to the bottom where it turns sharp left. Now follow this track keeping the wall and a stream on your right.

10 | Eventually you come to the final gate, go through and proceed straight ahead where the track becomes a tarmaced estate road. Follow this back to the car park.

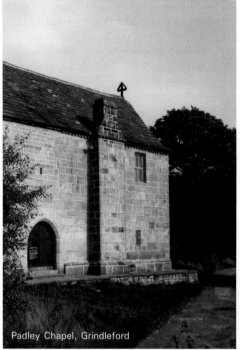

Padley Chapel, Grindleford

commemorate two Catholic martyrs of 1588. The ruins of ancient Padley Manor House, found alongside the track bed of the old railway line, are all that remain of the home of two devout Roman Catholic families. It was from the manor house that two priests, Robert Ludlam and Nicholas Garlick, were taken to Derby and sentenced to death by hanging, drawing and quartering. The then owner of the house, Thomas Fitzherbert, died in the Tower of London three years later, while his brother died at Fleet Prison in 1598. In 1933, the charming chapel seen today was converted from the still standing farm buildings.

To the northwest of the village is the **Longshaw Country Park**, some 1,500 acres of open moorland, woodland, and the impressive Padley Gorge. Originally the Longshaw estate of the Dukes of Rutland, the land was acquired by the National Trust in the 1970s.

STONEY MIDDLETON
4 miles N of Bakewell off the A623

🜨 Lover's Leap   ⚔ Middleton Dale

This village, known simply as Stoney locally, is certainly well named as, particularly in this part of **Middleton Dale**, great walls of limestone rise up from the valley floor. Further up the Dale there are also many disused limestone quarries as well as the remains of some lead mines. Not all industry has vanished from the area, as this is the home of nearly three-quarters of the country's fluorspar industry. Another relic from the past also survives, a shoe- and boot-making company operates from the village and is housed in a former corn mill.

The unusual octagonal village church was built by Joan Padley in thanksgiving for the safe return of her husband from the Battle of Agincourt in the 15th century. The lantern storey was added to the Perpendicular tower in 1759.

Higher up the dale from the village is the dramatically named **Lover's Leap**. In 1762, a jilted girl, Hannah Badderley, tried to jump to her death by leaping from a high rock. Her voluminous skirts, however, were caught on some brambles and she hung from the ledge before gently rolling down into a pit and escaping serious injury.

EYAM
5 miles N of Bakewell off the B6521

🏠 Eyam Hall   📺 Plague Village

Pronounced 'Eem', this village will forever be known as the **Plague Village**. In 1666, a local

🏠 historic building   🖼 museum   🏛 historic site   🜨 scenic attraction   🌱 flora and fauna tailor received a bundle of plague-infected clothing from London. Within a short time the infection had spread and the terrified inhabitants prepared to flee the village. However, the local rector, William Mompesson, persuaded the villagers to stay put and, thanks to his intervention, most neighbouring villages escaped the disease. Eyam was quarantined for over a year, relying on outside help for supplies of food which were left on the village boundary. Out of a total of 350 inhabitants, only 83 survived.

The home of the Wright family for over 300 years, **Eyam Hall** is a wonderful, unspoilt 17th century manor house that is now open to the public. As well as touring the house and seeing the impressive stone-flagged hall, tapestry room and the magnificent tester bed, visitors can pause in the café and gift shop. The Eyam Hall Crafts Centre, housed in the farm building, contains several individual units, which specialise in a variety of unusual and skilfully-fashioned crafts.

BRADWELL
9 miles N of Buxton off the B6049

🏛 Bagshawe Cavern

Usually abbreviated in the unique Peak District way to 'Bradder', Bradwell is a charming little limestone village sheltered by Bradwell Edge. At one time this former lead-mining community was famous as the place where miners' hardhats – hard, black, brimmed hats in which candles were stuck to light the way underground – were made; thus these hardhats came to be known as Bradder Beavers.

A key attraction here is the massive **Bagshawe Cavern**, a cave reached by a descending flight of 98 steps through an old lead mine. Along the half-mile walk to the main show cave there are wonderful rock formations and other interesting sights. For the more adventurous caving trips are available.

ASHFORD IN THE WATER
1 mile NW of Bakewell off the A6

🏛 Church   🏛 Sheepwash Bridge

Not exactly in the water, but certainly on the River Wye, Ashford is another candidate for Derbyshire's prettiest village. It developed around a ford across the river and was once an important crossing place on the ancient Portway. The medieval **Sheepwash Bridge** crosses the Wye, with overhanging willows framing its low arches. It is one of three bridges in the village, and a favourite with artists. There is a small enclosure to one side that provides a clue to its name, as this is still occasionally used for its original purpose – crowds gather to witness sheep being washed in the river to clean their fleece before they are shorn. Mill Bridge dates back to 1664.

The great limestone parish **Church of the Holy Trinity**, largely rebuilt in 1871 but retaining the base of a 13th century tower, has a fine Ashford marble table on show as well as a tablet to the memory of Henry Watson, the founder of the marble works who was also an authority on the geology of the area. Several of the pillars within the church are made of the rare Duke's Red marble, which is only found in the mine at Lathkill Dale owned by the Duke of Devonshire. Hanging from the roof of Ashford's church are the remains of four 'virgin's crants' – paper garlands carried at the funerals of unmarried village girls.

Ashford is perhaps most famous for its six beautifully executed well-dressings, which are held annually in early June. The village also

IBBOTSON'S OF ASHFORD

Ashford-in-the-Water, Derbyshire DE45 1QB
Tel: 01629 812528
Fax: 01629 815023

In a handsome old greystone building on a corner site in a pretty village on the River Wye, **Ibbotson's of Ashford** is one of the most delightful and individual food shops in the whole region.

It is owned and run by Ken and Kathryn Ibbotson, who have built up a loyal clientele since opening in 2000.

Ken's pickled onions have become a business in themselves, selling to retail outlets and to the trade, and the shop also sells a good range of made-to-order sandwiches, cooked meats, Italian and other delicatessen products, chutneys, preserves, coffees, ice creams and fresh fruit and vegetables.

River Wye, Monsal Dale

has a pleasant range of mainly 18th century cottages, and a former tithe barn which now serves as an art gallery.

MONSAL HEAD
3 miles NW of Bakewell off the B6465

🜨 Monsal Dale

Monsal Head is a deservedly renowned beauty spot from which there are tremendous views, particularly over **Monsal Dale** through which the River Wye flows.

WARDLOW
6 miles NW of Bakewell off the B6465

At a crossroads near Wardlow the highwayman Anthony Lingard was hanged in 1812 for the murder of a local widow. He was the last felon to hang in the county, and his

🏛 historic building   🏛 museum   🏛 historic site   🜨 scenic attraction   🌵 flora and fauna execution drew an enormous crowd – so much so that the local lay preacher at Tideswell found himself preaching to virtually empty pews. Determined not to waste this opportunity to speak to so large a congregation, he relocated to the gallows in order to deliver his sermon.

TIDESWELL
8 miles NW of Bakewell off the B6049

🏠 Church

One of the largest villages in the area, Tideswell takes its name from a nearby ebbing and flowing well. Over 900 feet above sea level, the surrounding countryside offers many opportunities to wander, stroll, or take a leisurely (or energetic) hike through some varied and impressive scenery.

Known as the 'Cathedral of the Peak', the magnificent 14th century **Church of St John the Baptist** has a wealth of splendid features. The tower is impressive, the windows are beautiful, there is a fine collection of brasses inside and the 'Minstrel of the Peak', William Newton, is buried in the churchyard.

Today the village is home to a number of craftspeople working in buildings converted from other uses. The excellence of their work is apparent not only in the items they display but also in the splendid well-dressing they help to enact annually on the Saturday nearest St John the Baptist's Day (24th June).

PEAK FOREST
11 miles NW of Bakewell off the A623

🏠 Church 🗽 Eldon Hole

High on the White Peak plateau, Peak Forest takes its name from the fact that it once stood at the centre of the Royal Forest of the Peak. The parish **Church of King Charles the Martyr** speaks of the fierce independence of the village inhabitants. It was built in 1657 by the wife of the 2nd Earl of Devonshire, during a time when there was a ban on building churches. The church that stands today on the site of the former chapel was built in 1878.

A quirk of ecclesiastical law ensured – up until early in the 19th century – that the village was outside the jurisdiction of the bishop. Thus it was not subject to the laws regarding posting the banns before marriage; hence it became known as 'the Gretna Green of the Peak'. If one or other of the couple has lived in the village for 15 days prior to the ceremony, to this day they can still be married in the church without banns being read.

Within walking distance of Peak Forest is the 'bottomless' pit of **Eldon Hole**. Once thought to be the Devil's own entrance to Hell, stories abound in which various people were lowered down on increasingly longer pieces of rope. They all returned, in differing states of mental anguish, but none ever reached the bottom! However, seasoned potholers, who view the hole as no more than a practice run, maintain that it is, in fact, 'only' 180 feet deep.

SHELDON
3 miles W of Bakewell off the A6

🏠 Magpie Mine

Magpie Mine, to the south of the village, produced lead for over 300 years. This important site of industrial archaeology has been preserved, from the Cornish-style chimney stack, engine house and dynamite cabin right down to the more recent corrugated-iron-roofed buildings. It is now owned by the Peak District Mines Historical Society which conducts guided tours of the site.

🗽 stories and anecdotes   🕊 famous people   🎨 art and craft   ✐ entertainment and sport   🚶 walks

MONYASH

5 miles W of Bakewell off the B5055

🜊 Lathkill Dale

Monyash was once at the centre of the Peak District's lead mining industry and had its own weekly market (the charter being granted in 1340); the old market cross still stands on the village green.

Today, Monyash, which is situated at the head of **Lathkill Dale**, is busy during the season with walkers keen to explore the valley of the River Lathkill, a road-free beauty spot with ash and elm woods that was designated a National Nature Reserve in 1972. The River Lathkill, like others in the limestone area of the Peak District, disappears underground for parts of its course. In this case the river rises in winter from a large cave above Monyash, known as Lathkill Head Cave. In summer, the river emerges further downstream at Over Haddon

ROWSLEY

4 miles SE of Bakewell off the A6

🏛 Caudwell's Mill

This small village, at the confluence of the Rivers Wye and Derwent, is home to the impressive Peacock Hotel. Built originally as a private house, it is aptly named since the carved peacock over the porch is actually part of the family crest of the Manners family, whose descendants still live at nearby Haddon Hall.

On the banks of the River Wye lies **Caudwell's Mill**, a unique Grade II listed historic flour mill. A mill has stood on this site for at least 400 years; the present mill was built in 1874, powered by water from the River Wye, and was run as a family business for over a century up until 1978. Since then the mill has undergone extensive restoration

by a group of dedicated volunteers and, using machinery that was installed at the beginning of this century, the mill is once again producing wholemeal flour. Other mill buildings on the site have been converted to house a variety of craft workshops, shops and a restaurant.

On Chatsworth Road near the terminus of the Peak Rail line, Peak Village is an extensive factory outlet shopping centre offering a range of ladies' and men's fashion, sports and outdoor wear, home furnishings, jewellery, toys and books, and eateries. Also on-site is the charming Wind in the Willows attraction, created by an award-winning team of craftsmen and designers to bring the adventures of Ratty, Mole, Badger and Mr Toad to life.

Matlock

🏛 Church of St Giles   🏛 Riber Castle   🏛 Peak Rail

As the northern, gritstone landscape of the Peak District is often referred to as the Dark Peak, the southern, limestone plateaux have gained the equally obvious name of White Peak. Though the hilltops are often windswept and bleak, the numerous dales, cut deep into the limestone, provide a lush and green haven for all manner of wild and plant life. Several of the rivers are famous for their trout, particularly the Lathkill, which was greatly favoured by the keen angler and writer Izaak Walton.

Matlock is a bustling town nestling in the lower valley of the River Derwent, and is the administrative centre of Derbyshire as well as being a busy tourist centre bordering the Peak District National Park. There are actually eight Matlocks making up the town, along with several other hamlets. Most have simply been engulfed and have lost their identity as the town grew, but **Matlock Bath**, the site of the spa, still maintains its individuality.

Matlock itself, at one time, had the steepest-gradient (a 1-in-5½) tramway in the world; it was also the only tram system in the Peak District. Opened in 1893, the tramcars ran until 1927 and the Depot can still be seen at the top of Bank Street. The old Ticket Office and Waiting Room at Matlock station have been taken over by the Peak Rail Society and here can be found not only their shop, but also exhibitions explaining the history and aims of the society. **Peak Rail** has its southernmost terminus just a few minutes' walk from the mainline station; from here the railway runs through the charming rural station of Darley Dale to the terminus at Rowsley South. In future it is hoped that the line can be extended to Bakewell. Run entirely by volunteers, this

lovely old steam train operates on different days throughout the year. A restaurant car is fitted for every journey. The full journey (one way) takes just 20 minutes, and passengers can alight to enjoy the picnic area at the entrance to Rowsley South Station, or the exhibition coach at Darley Dale platform to learn about the history of the re-opening of the line. Special events are held throughout the year, and engine-driving courses can be taken – the perfect gift for the steam enthusiast!

Inside Matlock's **Church of St Giles** can be seen the faded and preserved funeral garlands or 'virgin crants' that were once common all over Derbyshire. Bell-shaped, decorated with rosettes and ribbons and usually containing a personal item, the garlands were made in memory of a deceased young girl of the parish. At her funeral the garlands were carried by the dead girl's friends and, after the service, would be suspended from the church rafters above the pew she had normally occupied.

High up on the hill behind the town is the brooding ruin of **Riber Castle**. The castle was built between 1862 and 1868 by John Smedley, a local hosiery manufacturer who became interested in the hydropathic qualities of Matlock. He drew up the designs for the building himself and spent lavishly on its interior décor. Smedley constructed his own gas-producing plant to provide lighting for the Castle and it even had its own well.

Following the death of first Smedley and then his wife, the castle was sold and for a number of years it was boys' school. During the Second World War the castle was used as a food store before it was left to become a ruined shell.

Peak Rail, Matlock

🎞 stories and anecdotes 🕊 famous people ✿ art and craft ✐ entertainment and sport 🚶 walks

Around Matlock

DARLEY DALE
2 miles NW of Matlock off the A6

🏠 Red House Stables   🌱 The Darley Yew

The charming name for this straggling village along the main road north from Matlock dates only from the 19th century, and was either devised by the commercially-minded railway company at work in the area or by the romantically-inclined vicar of the parish. Darley Dale makes up one of three stops on the Matlock-to-Rowsley South Peak Rail line.

One of the most unassuming heroines of this part of Derbyshire must be Lady Mary Louisa Whitworth, the second wife of Sir Joseph Whitworth, the famous Victorian engineer. Following his death in 1887, Lady

Church and Yew, Darley Dale

Mary undertook sweeping changes to the lifestyle of the local poor and needy. The Whitworth Institute was opened in 1890, bringing to the community a wide range of facilities including a swimming pool, an assembly hall, a natural history museum and a library. Lady Whitworth died in France in 1896, and is buried next to her husband at the parish Church of St Helen, in the hamlet of Churchtown. The churchyard is also home to the **Darley Yew**, one of the oldest living trees in Britain which has a girth of some 33 feet. The yew pre-dates the Norman origins of the Church and may even be older than the Saxon fragments found here in the mid-1900s.

Darley Dale has an extensive park which is very pretty in all seasons. Another of this small village's attractions is **Red House Stables**, a working carriage museum featuring some fine examples of traditional horse-drawn vehicles and equipment. One of the finest collections in the country, it consists of nearly 40 carriages, including one of the very few surviving Hansom cabs, a stage coach, Royal Mail coach, Park Drag and many other private and commercial vehicles. Carriage rides are available, making regular trips through the countryside to places such as Chatsworth and Haddon Hall, and the carriages and horses can be hired for special occasions.

STANTON IN PEAK
5 miles NW of Matlock off the B5056

🏛 Nine Ladies   🏛 Rowtor Rocks   ⚔ Stanton Moor

The gritstone landscape of **Stanton Moor**, which rises to some 1,096 feet and overlooks the village, is encircled by footpaths and is a popular walking area. There are also several interesting features on the moorland. The folly, Earl Grey's Tower, was built in 1832 to

🏛 historic building   🏠 museum   🏛 historic site   ⚔ scenic attraction   🌱 flora and fauna

Nine Ladies Stone Circle, Stanton

upturned and used as a sundial. Inside, the working font is Norman and still retains its stoop for holding the Holy Water. It is well worth taking the time to have a look at, since it is the only such font in England. The Church also contains a small tomb with an equally small alabaster effigy; dated 1488, it is a memorial to Thomas Cockayne, who was killed in a brawl when only in his teens.

commemorate the reform of Parliament. There is also an ancient stone circle, dating from the Bronze Age, with over 70 burial mounds. Known as the **Nine Ladies**, the stone circle has a solitary boulder nearby called the King's Stone. Legend has it that one Sunday nine women and a fiddler came up onto the moor to dance and, for their act of sacrilege, they were turned to stone.

The nearby **Rowtor Rocks** contain caves which were carved out at some stage in the 1600s. Not only was the living space made from the rock but tables, chairs and alcoves were also made to create a cosy retreat for the local vicar, Rev Thomas Eyre. Prior to these home improvements, the caves were reputedly used by the Druids, who did not believe in such creature comforts.

Further up the village's main street is Thimble Hall, the smallest market hall in the Peak District and still used for selling goods today. Typical of the White Peak area of Derbyshire, the Hall dates from 1656 and there are also some rather grand Georgian houses to be found in the village.

Lathkill Dale, which can really only be experienced by walking along the path by the banks of the quiet river, is noted for its solitude and, consequently, there is an

YOULGREAVE
6 miles NW of Matlock off the B5056

🏛 Church   🏃 Lathkill Dale

This straggling village, known locally as Pommey, lies in Bradford Dale. The village **Church of All Saints** contains some parts of the original Saxon building though its ancient font is, unfortunately,

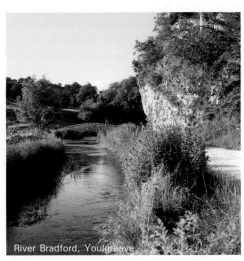

River Bradford, Youlgreave

abundance of wildlife in and around the riverbank meadows. The upper valley is a National Nature Reserve; those who are lucky enough may even spot a kingfisher or two. One of the country's purest rivers, the Lathkill is famed for the range of aquatic life that it supports as well as being a popular trout river. Renowned for many centuries, it was Izaak Walton who said of the Lathkill, back in 1676;

"the purest and most transparent stream
that I ever yet saw, either at home or abroad;
and breeds, 'tis said, the reddest
and best Trouts in England."

MIDDLETON BY YOULGREAVE
7 miles NW of Matlock off the A5012

🏛 Lomberdale Hall

Just outside this leafy village is **Lomberdale Hall**, once the home of Thomas Bateman, the 19th century archeologist who was responsible for the excavation of some 500 barrows in the Peak District over a 20 year period - it is said that he managed to reveal four in one single day! Many of the artefacts he unearthed can be seen in Sheffield Museum. The village lies in the valley of the River Bradford, at the point where it becomes Middleton Dale, and is unusual among villages in this area of the Peak District in that it has a large number of trees.

BIRCHOVER
4 miles W of Matlock off the B5056

🏛 Rocks of Rowtor

The strange **Rocks of Rowtor**, behind The Druid Inn, are said to have been used for Druidical rites. The Revd Thomas Eyre, who died in 1717, was fascinated by these rocks and built the strange collection of steps, rooms and seats which have been carved out of the gritstone rocks on the summit of the

outcrop. It is said that the Reverend would take his friends there to admire the view across the valley below – a view which nowadays is obscured by trees.

The equally strange outcrops of Robin Hood's Stride and Cratcliff Tor can be found nearby. A medieval hermit's cave, complete with crucifix, can be seen at the foot of Cratcliff Tor hidden behind an ancient yew tree.

WINSTER
4 miles W of Matlock off the B5056

🏛 Market House

This attractive gritstone village was once a lead-mining centre and market town. Today, it is a pleasant place with antique shops in the high street and some fine late-18th century houses. Less splendid than the surrounding houses, but no less interesting, are the ginnels – little alleyways – that run off the main street. The most impressive building here, however, must be the **Market House**, owned by the National Trust and found at the top of the main street. The Trust's first purchase in Derbyshire, the rugged, two-storey Market House dates from the late-17th and early-18th centuries and is a reminder of Winster's past importance as a market town. Built from an attractive combination of brickwork and stone, the House is open to the public and acts as an information centre and shop for the Trust.

The annual Shrove Tuesday Pancake Race, from the Crown Inn to the Market House is a much-anticipated event that is taken seriously in the village. Small frying pans are issued to the men, women and children, it is an open event, and the pancakes are specially made with an emphasis on durability rather than taste.

Although Morris dancing is traditionally associated with the Cotswold area, two of the best known and most often played tunes, *The Winster Gallop* and *Blue-eyed Stranger*, originate from the village. Collected many years ago by Cecil Sharpe, a legend in the world of Morris dancing, they were rediscovered in the 1960s. The Winster Morris men traditionally dance through the village at the beginning of Wakes Week in June, finishing, as all good Morris dances do, at one of the local pubs.

MATLOCK BATH
1 mile S of Matlock off the A6

🏠 Peak District Mining Museum   ⛏ Caverns

🏛 Aquarium   🌿 Countryside Centre

⛰ Heights of Abraham   🌿 Gullivers Kingdom

🏔 High Tor Grounds

As with many other spa towns up and down the country, it was not until the Regency period that Matlock Bath reached its peak. As

The Peak District Mining Museum

The Pavilion, Matlock Bath, Derbyshire DE4 3NR
Tel:01629 583 834
e-mail: mail@peakmines.co.uk
website: www.peakmines.co.uk

Visit a hands-on museum where you can experience and wonder at the almost forgotten world of a Derbyshire lead miner. For centuries men have toiled underground in cramped and hazardous conditions to earn a meagre living by extracting the mineral *galena*, lead ore.

See the tools they used and the clothes they wore and encounter the problems that the miner overcame - flooding, explosions and roof falls. Experience the maze of twisting tunnels and shafts and observe the advances in technology and the great importance of lead in our modern day lives. Refresh yourself in the cafe and browse in the well-stocked shop. See the magnificent water pressure engine that was rescued from deep down in a local lead mine.

You can find out what "nicking" means and discover for yourself the amazing network of tunnels that exist under your feet and wonder at the crystals glistening in the walls. This two-man, working lead and fluorspar mine will give you an authentic insight into life underground and the tools and equipment involved. Gold! Gold! The magic word in mining. Stand in a real gold strike, then try your hand at panning for "gold" - but you won't get rich quick with the sort of gold that you recover! Don't think that the museum is a dry-as-dust, wet weather activity. The average family will be enthralled by the many hands-on, interactive and novel opportunities.

🎭 stories and anecdotes   🐦 famous people   🎨 art and craft   🎢 entertainment and sport   🚶 walks well as offering cures for many of the ills of the day, Matlock Bath and the surrounding area had much to offer the visitor. The spa town was compared to Switzerland by Byron and it has also been much admired by Ruskin, who stayed at the New Bath Hotel in 1829. Many famous people have visited the town, including the young Victoria before she succeeded to the throne.

One of the great attractions of the town is **The Aquarium**, which occupies what was once the old Matlock Bath Hydro that was established in 1833. The original splendour of the Bath Hydro can still be seen in the fine stone staircase and also in the thermal large pool which is now without its roof. The pool, maintained at a constant temperature of 68 degrees fahrenheit, was where the rheumatic patients came to immerse themselves in the waters and relieve their symptoms. Today, the pool is home to a large collection of Large Mirror, Common and Koi Carp while the upstairs consulting rooms now house tanks full of native, tropical and marine fish. Down by the riverbank and housed in the old Pavilion can be found the **Peak District Mining Museum and Temple Mine** (see panel on page 197), the only one of its kind in the world. Opened in 1978 and run by the Peak District Mines Historical Society, the Museum tells the story of lead mining in the surrounding area from as far back as Roman times to the 20th century. The Museum also houses a huge engine, dating from 1819, which was recovered from a mine near Winster.

Located in the Victorian Railway Station buildings is the **Whistlestop Countryside Centre**, which aims to

inform and educate the public on the wildlife of the county as well as manage wildlife conservation. Set up by the Derbyshire Wildlife Trust and run by volunteers, the Centre has an interesting and informative exhibition and a gift shop and the staff are qualified to lead a range of environmental activities.

For spectacular views of Matlock Bath, nothing beats a walk on **High Tor Grounds**. There are 60 acres of nature trails to wander around, while some 400 feet below the River Derwent appears like a silver thread through the gorge. A popular viewing point for Victorian visitors to the town, today rock climbers practise their skills climbing the precipitous crags of the Tor.

On the opposite side of the valley are the beautiful wooded slopes of Masson Hill, the southern face of which has become known as the **Heights of Abraham**. The name was chosen after General Wolfe's victory in Quebec – this part of the Derwent valley being seen to resemble the gorge of the St Lawrence River and the original Heights of Abraham lying a

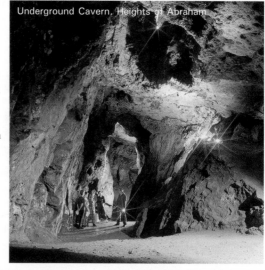
Underground Cavern, Heights of Abraham

mile north of Quebec. It features steep rocky gorges, vast caverns, fast-running rivers, panoramic views and a cable car. The cable car ticket includes access to all the site's attractions, which include two spectacular undergrounds caverns. The 60-acre country park also features woodland walks, the Owl Maze, the Explorers Challenge, a rocks and fossil shop, coffee shop, restaurant and play and picnic areas.

In 1812, the **Great Rutland Show Cavern**, on the slope, was opened to the public, a new experience for tourists of the time, and it was visited by many including the Grand Duke Michael of Russia and Princess Victoria. Following this success, in 1844, the **Great Masson Cavern** was opened and construction of the Victoria Prospect Tower was begun. Built by redundant lead miners, the Tower became a new landmark for the area and today still provides a bird's eye view over Derbyshire.

To the south of the town centre is a model village with a difference; **Gulliver's Kingdom** theme park makes a great day out for all the family. Set on the side of a wooded hill, each terrace is individually themed with styles including Fantasy Land, the Old Wild West and the Royal Mine ride. There are plenty of fun rides, a monorail, water slides and other diversions, as well as a cafe and restaurant.

CROMFORD
2 miles S of Matlock off the A5012

🏚 Mill 🏚 Steam Museum 🏚 Pumping Station

🏃 Cromford Canal 🏃 High Peak Trail

Cromford is a model village known the world over. It was developed by Richard Arkwright

ROBIN MAYCOCK

Leashaw Road, Holloway, nr Matlock, Derbyshire DE4 5AT
Tel/Fax: 01629 534333

Robin and Glynis Maycock came to the picturesque village of Holloway 30 years ago and took over a modest butchers shop. Through hard work and ambition they built up the business, and 22 years ago they knocked down the old building and replaced it with the present slate-roofed stone building that has allowed them to expand. The aim at **Robin Maycock – award-winning butchers and bakers** has always been to sell their own produce, and almost all the meat is reared on their own farm and killed in the slaughterhouse at the back of the shop. This means that all the meat is fully traceable from farm to shop counter, and quality has always been a watchword, along with friendly personal service.

Son Jonathan runs the butchery side, while daughter Emily is in charge of the bakery and the preparation of the ready meals that are an increasingly important part of the business. Lasagne, curries, chicken à la King, liver & onions, steak & kidney pie and blackberry & apple pie are just a few of the ready-to-go meals prepared on the premises, and customers are encouraged to bring their own dishes to be filled: more and more of the regular customers are surprising their dinner guests with their new-found cooking skills!

Cromford Bridge

Derbyshire. **Cromford Mill** and the associated buildings are now an International World Heritage site. Tours of the mill and Cromford village are available throughout the year.

Cromford has a rather odd 15th century bridge, which has rounded arches on one side and pointed arches on the other. It was from this bridge, in 1697, so local folklore has it, that a horse and rider took a flying leap from the parapet, plunged into the river 20 feet below and lived to tell the tale.

into one of the first industrial towns. In addition to housing, he also provided his workers with a market place and a village lock-up. Born in Lancashire in 1732, Arkwright was the inventor of the waterframe, a machine for spinning cotton that was powered by water. He built his first mill at Cromford in 1771, the project taking a further 20 years to complete. It was the world's first successful water-powered cotton spinning mill. The area he had chosen proved to be perfect: the River Derwent, described by Daniel Defoe as "a fury of a river", provided an ample power supply; there was an unorganised but very willing workforce, as the lead-mining industry was experiencing a decline and, probably most importantly, Cromford was away from the prying eyes of Arkwright's competitors. In 1792, Arkwright commissioned the building of the village church, where he now lies. The Mill proved to be a great success and became the model for others both in Britain and abroad, earning Arkwright the accolade 'Father of the Factory System'. His pioneering work and contributions to the great Industrial Age resulted in a knighthood in 1786, and one year later he became High Sheriff of

For lovers of waterways, there is an opportunity at **Cromford Canal** to potter along the five-mile stretch of towpath to Ambergate. The old **Leawood Pumping Station**, which transferred water from the River Derwent to the Cromford Canal, has been fully restored. Inside the engine house is a preserved Cornish-type beam engine which is occasionally steamed up. Close by the Pump House is the Wigwell Aqueduct, which carries the Canal high over the River Derwent.

The **High Peak Trail**, which stretches some 17 miles up to Dowlow near Buxton, starts at Cromford and follows the trackbed of the Cromford and High Peak Railway. First opened in 1880, the railway was built to connect the Cromford Canal with the Peak Forest Canal and is somewhat reminiscent of a canal as it has long level sections interspersed with sharp inclines (instead of locks) and many of the stations are known as wharfs. After walking the trail it is not surprising to learn that its chief engineer was really a canal builder! The railway was finally closed in 1967; the old stations are now car parks and picnic areas; there is an information office in the former Hartington station signal box. Surfaced with clinker rather than limestone, the trail is suitable for walkers, cyclists and horses.

WIRKSWORTH
4 miles S of Matlock off the B5023

🏛 Church   🏛 Heritage Centre

🏛 National Stone Centre   🏛 North End Mills

🏛 Steeple Grange Light Railway Society

Nestling in the lush green foothills of the Peak District where north meets south, Wirksworth is home to a distinctive **Heritage Centre** housed in a former silk mill. Visitors can travel through time from the Romans in Wirksworth to the present day. Quarrying, lead-mining and local customs such as clypping the church (a ceremony in which the parish church is encircled by the congregation holding hands around it) and well-dressing are explored with interactive and fascinating exhibits. One of the town's most interesting sights is the jumble of cottages linked by a maze of jitties on the hillside between The Dale and Greenhill, in particular the area known locally as 'The Puzzle Gardens'. Babington House dates back to Jacobean Wirksworth. Another former lead-merchant's house, Hopkinsons House, was restored in 1980 as part of a number of restoration schemes initiated by the Civic Trust's Wirksworth Project. The ancient parish **Church of St Mary** is a fine building standing in a tranquil close and bounded by Elizabethan 'Gell Almshouses' and the former (Georgian) grammar school. The church holds one of the oldest stone carvings in the country: known as the Wirksworth Stone, it is

a coffin lid dating from the 8th century.

The **National Stone Centre** tells "the story of stone", with a wealth of exhibits, activities such as gem-panning and fossil-casting, and outdoor trails tailored to introduce topics such as the geology, ecology and history of the dramatic Peak District landscape. Nearby, the **Steeple Grange Light Railway Society** runs along a short line over the High Peak Trail between Steeplehouse Station and Dark Lane Quarry. Power is provided by a battery-electric locomotive; passengers are carried in a manrider salvaged from Bevercotes Colliery in Nottinghamshire. Visitors to **North End Mills** are able to witness hosiery being made as it has been for over half a century; a special viewing area offers an insight into some of the items on sale in the Factory Shop.

Ashbourne

🏛 Market Square   🏛 The Mansion   🏛 Church

🏛 Green Man & Black's Head Royal Hotel

Ashbourne is one of Derbyshire's finest old towns, with a wealth of wonderful Georgian architecture as well as some older buildings, notably the Gingerbread Shop which is timber framed and probably dates from the 1400s. The triangular cobbled **Market Square** was part of the new development begun in the 1200s that shifted the town to the east, away from the church. Weekly markets have been held in the square since 1296, and still take place every Thursday and Saturday. It was in this market place, once lined with ale houses, that Bonnie Prince Charlie proclaimed his father as King James III, and so started the Jacobite Rebellion. Traditional Ashbourne gingerbread is said to be made from a recipe that was acquired from French prisoners of war who were kept in the town during the Napoleonic Wars.

Also worthy of a second glance is the **Green Man and Black's Head Royal Hotel**. The inn sign stretches over St John's Street and was put up when the Blackamoor Inn joined with the Green Man in 1825. Though the Blackamoor is no more, the sign remains and it claims to be the longest hotel name in the country. Of Georgian origin, the amalgamated hotel has played host to James Boswell, Dr Johnson and the young Princess Victoria. Ashbourne was, in fact, one of Dr Johnson's favourite places; he came to the town on several occasions between 1737 and

1784. He also visited the hotel so often that he had his own chair with his name on it! The chair can still be seen at the Green Man.

A stroll down Church Street, described by Pevsner as one of the finest streets in Derbyshire, takes the walker past many interesting Georgian houses – including the Grey House which stands next to the Grammar School. Founded by Sir Thomas Cockayne on behalf of Elizabeth I in 1585, the school was visited on its 400th anniversary by the present Queen. Almost opposite the Grey House is **The Mansion**, the late-17th century home of the Reverend Dr John Taylor, oldest friend of Dr Johnson. In 1764, a domed, octagonal drawing room was added

---

WIGLEYS SHOES

18-20 St John Street, Ashbourne, Derbyshire DE6 1GH
Tel: 01335 342884

Established as long ago as 1830, **Wigleys Shoes** has an excellent reputation built on variety, value for money and friendly, helpful service. It keeps a wide-ranging stock of shoes for toddlers and children by Startrite. Brands for men include Grenson, Loake, Ecco, Rockport, Padders and Joseph Seibel; for ladies, Van Dal, Laceys, Ecco, Gabor, Pikolinos, Joseph Seibel and Nordika slippers. They also sell clothes by In Town, Steilmann, Fransa and others, and accessories including stylish bags and costume jewellery.

NATURAL CHOICE

24 St John Street, Ashbourne, Derbyshire DE6 1GH
Tel: 01335 346096
e-mail: naturalchoice@tiscali.co.uk
website: www.naturalhealthchoice.co.uk

'Natural Foods, Natural Living, **Natural Choice**.' 2007 sees the 20th anniversary of this excellent place, which has evolved from humble beginnings into a busy, popular store selling a wide range of natural products. These include natural wholefoods, some locally produced; organic and fairtrade goods, natural remedies, nutritional supplements, cruelty-free cosmetics and bodycare ranges and environmentally friendly cleaning products. There is also an holistic therapy centre with several specialist practitioners.

🏛 historic building   🏛 museum   🏛 historic site   🍀 scenic attraction   🌱 flora and fauna to the house, and a new brick façade built facing the street. Next to The Mansion are two of the many almshouses established in Ashbourne during the 17th and 18th centuries. Ashbourne also retains many of its narrow alleyways, in particular Lovatt's Yard, where the town lock-up can be seen.

In **St Oswald's Parish Church**, Ashbourne has one of the most impressive and elegant churches in the country, described by George Eliot as "the finest mere parish church in England". James Boswell said that the church was "one of the largest and most luminous that I have seen in any town of the same size". St Oswald's stands on the site of a minster church mentioned in the Domesday Book, though most of what stands today dates from rebuilding work in the 13th century.

The alabaster tombs and monuments to the Bradbourne and Cockane families in the north transept chapel are justly famous. Perhaps the best-known monument is that to Penelope Boothby, who died in 1791 at the tender age of five. Thomas Banks' white Carrara marble figure of the sleeping child is so lifelike that she still appears to be only sleeping. The moving epitaph reads: "She was in form and intellect most exquisite; the unfortunate parents ventured their all on this frail bark, and the wreck was total". It is said that Penelope's parents separated at the child's grave and never spoke to each other again.

Ashbourne is home to the famous Shrovetide football game played on Shrove Tuesday and Ash Wednesday. The two teams, the 'Up'ards' (those born north of the Henmore Brook) and the 'Down'ards' (those born south of it) begin their match at 2pm behind the Green Man Hotel. The game continues until well into the evening. The two goals are situated three miles apart, along the Brook, on the site of the old mills at Clifton and Sturston. It is rare for more than one goal to be scored in this slow-moving game.

Around Ashbourne

HOGNASTON
4 miles NE of Ashbourne off the B5035

🐾 Carsington Water

This hillside village, with its extraordinary Norman carvings over the church doorway, lies close to **Carsington Water**, Britain's newest reservoir, owned by Severn Trent Water. There is plenty to do here besides the more usual water sports such as canoeing, sailing and fishing. Opened by the Queen in 1992, the reservoir has already blended well with the local countryside. Unlike many of the Peak District reservoirs, which draw their water from the acid moorland, Carsington is able to support a whole host of wildlife. One controversial resident is the American ruddy duck. Once unknown outside wildlife reserves, the duck escaped and in little over 50 years the breed has become widespread throughout Europe.

HOPTON
8 miles NE of Ashbourne off the B5035

This village, now by-passed by the main road, is dominated by the Carsington Water Reservoi. The land rises to the north of Hopton and here can be found the **Hopton Incline**, once the steepest railway incline in the British Isles. Lying on the **High Peak Railway** line, carriages on their journey from Cromford to Whaley Bridge were hauled up using fixed engines. It is now part of the High Peak Trail.

BRASSINGTON

7 miles NE of Ashbourne off the B5056

🏛 Rainster Rocks 🏛 Harborough Rocks

Protected from the wind by the limestone plateau that soars some 1,000 feet above sea level, the village sits by strange shaped rocks, the result of weather erosion, with names like **Rainster Rocks** and **Harborough Rocks**. Stone Age man found snugs among these formations and there is evidence that animals like the sabre-toothed tiger, brown bear, wolf and hyena also found comfort here in the caves. As late as the 18th century families were still living in the caves.

FENNY BENTLEY

2 miles N of Ashbourne off the A515

🏛 Church

Inside **St Edmund's Church** can be found the tomb of Thomas Beresford, the local lord of the manor who fought alongside eight of his 16 sons at Agincourt. The effigies of Beresford and his wife are surrounded by those of their 21 children – each covered by a shroud because by the time the tombs were built nobody could remember what they had looked like! During the Civil War, much of the Church and its rectory were destroyed. On returning to his parish after the restoration of Charles II in 1661, the rector resolved to rebuild the rectory, which was all but rubble, and restore the Church to its former glory. Both of these he managed. The 15th century square tower of the fortified manor house, now incorporated into Cherry Orchard Farm which belonged to the Beresford family and was once the home of Charles Cotton, is a local landmark that can be seen from the main road.

TISSINGTON

4 miles N of Ashbourne off the A515

🏛 Tissington Hall ⚔ Tissington Trail

Sitting at the foothills of the Pennines, Tissington is, perhaps, most famous for its

Fortified Manor, Fenny Bentley

🏛 historic building 🏛 museum 🏛 historic site 🔱 scenic attraction 🌿 flora and fauna ancient festival of well-dressing, a ceremony which dates back to at least 1350. Today this starts on Ascension Day and draws many crowds who come to see the spectacular folk art created by the local people.

There are plenty of theories as to why well-dressing began or was revived at Tissington. One centres on the purity of the Tissington wells during the Black Death which swept through the country in the mid-1300s. During this time some 77 of the 100 clergy in Derbyshire died and the surviving villagers simply returned to the pagan custom of well-dressing. Another plausible theory dates back only as far as the great drought of 1615, when the Tissington wells kept flowing though water everywhere was in very short supply. Whichever theory is true, one thing is certain, that in the last 50 years or so many villages who had not dressed a well for centuries, if ever, are now joining in the colourful tradition.

A total of six wells are dressed at Tissington: the Hall, the Town, the Yew Tree, the Hands, the Coffin and the Children's Wells. Each depicts a separate scene, usually one from the Bible. Visitors should follow the signs in the village or ask at the Old Coach House.

Home of the FitzHerbert family for 500 years, **Tissington Hall** is a distinguished and impressive stately home which was built by Francis FitzHerbert in 1609. The estate consists of 2,400 acres comprising 13 farms, 40 cottages and assorted lettings. The Hall boasts a wealth of original pieces, artwork, furnishings and architectural features tracing the times and tastes of the FitzHerbert family (now headed by Sir Richard FitzHerbert) over the centuries. Tissington Hall and Gardens are open to the public on 28 afternoons throughout the summer.

Following the old Ashbourne to Parsley Hay railway line, the **Tissington Trail** is a popular walk which can be combined with other old railway trails in the area or country lanes to make an enjoyable circular country walk. The Tissington Trail passes through some lovely countryside and, with a reasonable surface, is also popular with cyclists. Along the route can also be found many of the old railway line buildings and junction boxes and, in particular, the old Hartington station, which is now a picnic site with an information centre in the old signal box.

ALSOP-EN-LE-DALE
5 miles N of Ashbourne off the A515

🏛 Viator's Bridge

The old station on the Ashbourne-Buxton line which once served this tiny hamlet is today a car park on the Tissington Trail. The tranquil hamlet itself is on a narrow lane east of the main road towards Parwich, just a mile from Dovedale. Alsop-en-le-Dale's parish church of St Michael is Norman, though it was rebuilt substantially during Victorian times. The nave retains Norman features, with impressive double zigzag mouldings in the arches, but the west tower is only imitation Norman, and dates from 1883. One unusual feature which dominates this small church is its extraordinary 19th century, square mock-Gothic pulpit.

The renowned **Viator's Bridge** at Milldale is only a mile away to the west. It was immortalised in Izaak Walton's *The Compleat Angler* by a character who complains to another about the size of the tiny, two-arched packhorse bridge, deeming it "not two fingers broad".

🎬 stories and anecdotes   🦅 famous people   🎨 art and craft   🎭 entertainment and sport   🚶 walks

HART IN THE COUNTRY

Market Place, Hartington, Buxton, Derbyshire SK17 0AL
Tel: 01298 84459

On the B5054, in the heart of the Peak District National Park, **Hart in the Country** is one of the largest gift shops in the countryside, with a wide range of lifestyle items and presents for the whole family and all budgets. The list of goods in stock is long and varied: Regatta, Jack Murphy and Gelert outdoor wear; Farfield fleeces from Cumbria; Poppy ladies T-shirts and cardigans; Kakadu Aussie leather hats; leather handbags, purses and wallets; sheepskin hats,

slippers and rugs; hats, gloves and socks; bed throws and cushions; walking sticks and umbrellas; books, maps and greetings cards; soft and wooden toys; photo frames; jewellery; ladies fashion separates; garden ornaments and accessories; local artists' prints; fancy goods and kitchenware; preserves and biscuits.

Owner Christine Coxon likes the personal touch and makes sure that every visitor gets a genuinely friendly welcome. Hart in the Country is open every day from 10 to 5.30, or use the mail order facility.

ARBOR LOW

13 miles N of Ashbourne off the A515

🏛 Stone Circle

This remote **Stone Circle** is often referred to as the "Stonehenge of the Peaks", and although many of the stones now lie on the ground it is still an impressive sight. There are several stone circles in the Peak District but none offer the same atmosphere as Arbor Low, nor the same splendid views. Built around 4,000 years ago by the early Bronze

Arbor Low Stone Circle

🏠 historic building 🏛 museum 🏛 historic site 🌣 scenic attraction 🌱 flora and fauna

Age people, there are a total of 40 stones each weighing no less than eight tonnes. Probably used as an observatory and also a festival site, it is likely that the stones, which have been placed in pairs, never actually stood up.

MAPPLETON
2 miles NW of Ashbourne off the A515

Mappleton is a secluded and charming village of the Dove Valley, with attractive views and a wealth of exciting natural beauty. The 18th century Church of St Mary's is unusual in that it has a dome rather than a tower or steeple.

The village's main claim to fame is its annual New Year's Day charity bridge jump when ten teams of three people each paddle down half a mile of the River Dove and then jump off a bridge. The Dove is not easily navigable, the bridge is 30 feet high and after the jump there is a 500-yard sprint to the pub. It is a grand spectator sport and hundreds of people come to watch.

THORPE
3 miles NW of Ashbourne off the A515

Thorpe Cloud   Dovedale and River Dove

Thorpe lies at the confluence of the Rivers Manifold and Dove, and is dominated by the conical hill of **Thorpe Cloud** which guards the entrance to **Dovedale**. Although the Dale becomes over-crowded at times, there is always plenty of open space to explore on the hill as well as excellent walking. For much of its 45-mile course from Axe Edge to its confluence with the River Trent, the **River Dove** is a walker's river as it is mostly

HILLCREST HOUSE

Thorpe, Dovedale, Ashbourne,
Derbyshire DE6 2AW
Tel: 01335 350436
e-mail: info@hillcresthousedovedale.co.uk
website: www.hillcresthousedovedale.co.uk

Hillcrest House started life in the 19th century as a coaching inn called the Dovedale Hotel, providing lodging and refreshment for travellers and a change of horses. The tradition of hospitality continues in its present role as a comfortable private guest house owned and run by Dan and Margaret Sutton. The seven letting rooms run from a single and a twin to doubles (some with four-posters) and a family room.

A full English breakfast starts the day, featuring homemade bread and jams and locally produced yoghurts, and packed lunches can be arranged with a little notice. When the weather is fine, guests can relax in the large garden, complete with summer house, or even cook supper on the barbecue. Hillcrest is an excellent base for a walking holiday, and the owners have

lots of information on the best local walks, including the 1,000ft Thorpe Cloud; cyclists can follow the trackbed of the old Ashbourne- Buxton railway line.

Ilam, Dove Dale and Thorpe

Distance: *4.0 miles (6.4 kilometres)*

Typical time: *90 mins*

Height gain: *100 metres*

Map: *Explorer Outdoor Leisure 24*

Walk: *www.walkingworld.com ID:2183*

Contributor: *Phil and Sue Eptlett*

ACCESS INFORMATION:

By car from Ashbourne, take the A515 Buxton road north and after about a mile turn left at the sign for Ilam and Dove Dale. Follow this road through Thorpe to Ilam village. There is limited roadside parking in the village, or use the National Trust car park at Ilam Hall (charge). There is a bus service from Ashbourne three times per day each way, excluding Sunday. Ring 0870-608-2608 for details.

ADDITIONAL INFORMATION:

The National Trust property at Ilam Hall, part of which is a youth hostel, is surrounded by gardens and woodland and is worth a visit. Dove Dale, which stretches for about three miles to Milldale, is a steep-sided gorge created by the River Dove and was the favourite haunt of Izaak Walton, author of 'The Complete Angler'.

DESCRIPTION:

This walk starts in the quaint village of Ilam with its curious tile-clad houses and no intrusion by late 20th Century architecture.

A stroll alongside the River Manifold brings you to the grand stone Coldwell Bridge which was part of the old pack-horse route to Cheadle. A track then ascends to the second of our unspoilt villages at Thorpe. Here the village green and old church take you back to a more tranquil age.

After crossing a meadow and the short walk down Lin Dale you will arrive at Dove Dale and the well-known stepping-stones which cross the River Dove.

From this point the more energetic can take a short diversion up the conically shaped Thorpe Cloud for fine views of the surroundings.

Continuing down the lower part of Dove Dale brings you to a car park where refreshments can be purchased. It is then a short walk back to the start point at Ilam.

FEATURES:

Hills or Fells, River, Toilets, Stately Home, National Trust/NTS, Wildlife, Birds, Flowers, Great Views, Butterflies, Cafe

WALK DIRECTIONS:

1 | From the village, take the road to the right of the memorial cross and proceed over the river-bridge.

2 | Take the stile and steps on the left immediately after crossing the bridge, which lead down into a meadow. Follow a well-defined, curving path adjacent to the River Manifold, crossing three stiles.

3 | Where the path bends away from the river cross the stile, turn half-left and take the rising path away from the river and through some trees, following the footpath markers. On emerging from the trees to a crest, follow the green path across open meadow in the direction of a wooded hillside.

4|When a stony track is reached, go through the gate and bear slightly left, heading towards a large stone bridge over the river.

5|This is Coldwell Bridge, which is accessed via a stile adjacent to the gate at the end. After pausing to admire the view of the river from the bridge, continue along the rising old pack-horse route to the village of Thorpe.

6|Enter Thorpe via a gate and take the tarmac road through the village, passing the ancient church and the community centre and pausing at the village green where there is a convenient seat to rest. Continue past the postbox, following the road as it bears right to join the road to Ilam.

7|Go across the road and carry on through the car park, passing the toilets and exiting onto a stone track going up the meadow beyond.

8|On reaching a rocky outcrop, turn left on an indistinct path and head for a cluster of trees.

9|At the trees, follow the path down Lin Dale, keeping the wall to your left. Lin Dale is a short grassy dale under the shadow of conically-shaped Thorpe Cloud.

10|This brings us to Dove Dale with its popular stepping-stones. Here the more energetic can take a diversion up to the summit of Thorpe Cloud for fine views of the surrounding area. From here take the left path along the bank of the River Dove, or alternatively cross stepping-stones and take the tarmac road on the opposite bank.

11|Upon reaching a footbridge across the river, cross it and turn left, walking along the opposite bank to a car park where there are toilets and refreshments. Opposite the car park entrance, cross the stile signed to Ilam.

12|After approximately 100 metres, mount the steps on the right, pass through some trees and go over a stile into a meadow. It is now a straight path across several fields, passing the rear of the Izaak Walton Hotel and a farmyard, heading towards Ilam.

13|As you reach the outskirts of the village, the path descends to the road via a small gate, from which it is a short walk along the road back to the start point.

inaccessible by car. The steep sides to its valley, the fast-flowing water and the magnificent white rock formations all give Dovedale a special charm. Dovedale, however, is only a short section of the valley. Above Viator's Bridge it becomes Mill Dale and further upstream again are Wolfscote Dale and Beresford Dale.

ILAM
4 miles NW of Ashbourne off the A52

🏛 Ilam Hall

Now a model village of great charm, Ilam was originally an important settlement belonging to Burton Abbey. Following the Reformation in the 16th century, the estate was broken up and Ilam came into the hands of the Port family. In the early 1800s the family sold the property to Jesse Watts Russell, a wealthy industrialist. As well as building a fine mansion, **Ilam Hall**, for himself, Russell also spent a great deal of money refurbishing the attractive cottages. Obviously devoted to his wife, he had the Hall built in a romantic Gothic style and, in the centre of the village, he had the Eleanor Cross erected in her memory. Ilam Hall is now a Youth Hostel.

Many places in the Peak District have provided the inspiration for writers over the years and Ilam is no exception. The peace and quiet found here helped William Congreve create his bawdy play *The Old Bachelor*, while Dr Johnson wrote *Rasselas* while staying at the Hall. Ilam lies in the valley of the River Manifold and is a popular starting point for walks along this beautiful stretch of river. In summer the Manifold disappears underground north of the village to reappear below Ilam Hall. The village is also the place where the Rivers Manifold and Dove merge. The two rivers rise close together, on Axe Edge, and

for much of their course follow a parallel path, so it is fitting that they should also come together. Though Dovedale is regarded, and probably deservedly so, as the most scenic of the Peak District valleys, the Manifold Valley is very similar and while being marginally less beautiful it is often much less crowded.

WATERHOUSES
6 miles NW of Ashbourne off the A523

🏃 Hamps-Manifold Track

Between here and Hulme End, the Leek and Manifold Valley Light Railway, a picturesque narrow-gauge line, used to follow the valleys of the Manifold and the Hamps, criss-crossing the latter on little bridges. Sadly trains no longer run but its track bed has been made into the **Hamps-Manifold Track**, a marvellous walk which is ideal for small children and people in wheelchairs, since its surface is level and tarred throughout its eight miles. The Track can be reached from car parks at Hulme End, Waterhouses, Weags Bridge near Grindon, and Wetton.

WETTON
7 miles NW of Ashbourne off the B5053

🏛 Thor's Cave　🏃 Manifold Valley Trail

Wetton Mill has been sympathetically converted by the National Trust into a café, a very welcome sight for those walking the **Manifold Valley Trail**. There is also a car park here for the less energetic and a picnic area for those who would rather cater for themselves. Much of the hillside either side of the track also belongs to the National Trust and is a splendid place for walks.

Below the Mill can be found the ominous-sounding **Thor's Cave**, situated some 250 feet above the River Manifold. Though the cave is not deep, the entrance is huge, some 60 feet

1308. The market ceased in 1500 but the annual cattle sales continued right up until the beginning of the 20th century.

Its geographical location has helped to maintain the charm of this unspoilt village. There has been no invasion by the canal or railway builders (it lies at 900 feet above sea level) and it is still two miles from the nearest classified road. Around 150 years ago Alstonefield was at the centre of a huge parish which covered all the land between the two rivers. There has been a church here since at least AD892, but the earliest known parts of the present Church are the Norman doorway and chancel arch of 1100. There is also plenty of 17th century woodwork and a double-decker pulpit dated 1637. Izaak Walton's friend, Charles Cotton, and his family lived at nearby Beresford Hall, now unfortunately no more, but the family's elaborate greenish pew is still in the church, and the fishing temple built by Cotton survives in Beresford Dale.

The village also retains its ancient **Tithe Barn**, found behind the late-16th century rectory. The internal exposed wattle and daub wall and the spiral stone staircase may, however, have been part of an earlier building.

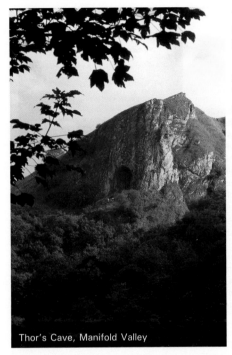

Thor's Cave, Manifold Valley

high, and the stiff climb up is well worth the effort for the spectacular views, all framed by the great natural stone arch. The acoustics too are interesting – conversations can easily be carried out with people far below. The openings at the bottom of the crag on which the cave sits are known as Radcliffe Stables and are said to have been used by a Jacobite as a hiding place after Bonnie Prince Charlie had retreated from Derby.

ALSTONEFIELD
7 miles NW of Ashbourne off the A515

🏠 Tithe Barn

This ancient village, situated between the Manifold and the Dove valleys, lies at the crossroads of several old packhorse routes and had its own market charter granted in

Chesterfield

🏠 Crooked Spire

This friendly, bustling town on the edge of the Peak District National Park grew up around its open-air market which was established over 800 years ago and claims to be England's largest. As the town lies at the crossroads of England, the hub of trade routes from all points of the compass, the town's claim seems easily justified. It was earning Royal revenue in 1165, as the Sheriff of Derbyshire recorded

FRANK HILL JEWELLER

5 West Bars, Chesterfield S40 1AQ
Tel: 01246 232155 Fax: 01246 278221
e-mail: Andrew@24ctjewllery.co.uk
website: www.24ctjewellery.co.uk

Thirty-five years of experience and expertise go into the design and manufacture of the highest quality jewellery at 24CT Ltd in association with **Frank Hill Jeweller**, with a level of service to match. The main specialities are wedding and engagement rings made in gold, white gold, platinum and titanium. All are made in the workshop on the premises from the highest quality metals hallmarked to British standards. Stones used include diamonds, emeralds, rubies, topaz, sapphire, aquamarine, amethyst and the increasingly popular modern tanzanite.

Clients can browse the website or visit the shop to see examples of what is offered, and can have their own pieces made to their specification. Andrew Thomson and his staff are happy to advise on design and the selection of metals and gemstones. They also offer a jewellery valuation service and a total repair service, including re-mounting stones, re-sizing rings, repairing chains and on-the-spot cleaning. They can also remodel an old piece or melt it down to make a totally new item.

TALLULAH

39 Chatsworth Road, Chesterfield S40 2AH
Tel: 01246 555132

'Something Beautiful for You and Your Home' is the motto of Joanne Rose, who owns and runs her delightful shop **Tallulah**. The shop is filled with lovely things on eyecatching display behind the quaint little shopfront.

The constantly changing stock includes chic home accessories, exquisite costume jewellery, fabulous handbags, handmade bath products from the Littlecote Soap Company, greetings cards for all occasions and beautiful gift wrap. For a gift to remember or just to spoil yourself, Tallulah is well worth a visit; opening hours are 10 to 4.30 Tuesday to Saturday.

in the Pipe Rolls and, in that year, the market earned the princely sum of £1 2s 7d for the Crown. The Pipe Roll of 1182 also mentions a fair in Chesterfield. Such fairs were large markets, usually lasting for several days and drawing traders and buyers from a much wider area. Chesterfield's formal charter, however, was not granted until 1204, but this charter made the town one of the first eight free boroughs in the country. Escaping the prospect of redevelopment in the 1970s, the markets are as popular as ever and are held every Monday, Friday and Saturday, with a flea market each Thursday and a farmers' market on the second Thursday of every month.

The town centre has been conserved for future generations by a far-sighted council, and many buildings have been saved, including the Victorian Market Hall built in 1857. The traditional cobbled paving was restored in the Market Place, and New Square was given a complete facelift. There are several Tudor buildings in the heart of Chesterfield, most notably the former Peacock Inn which is now home to a café. The Tourist Information Centre that was here is now in a new purpose-built centre in Rykneld Square, near the Crooked Spire church. Visitors to the town are drawn to this peculiarly graceful spire reaching high into the skyline; twisting and leaning, it is totally confusing to the eye. The **Crooked Spire** of St Mary and All Saints Church has dominated the skyline for so long that local folk have ceased to notice its unusual shape. Superstition surrounds it, and sadly the real story to its unusual appearance

OLIHOLPHO CLOTHING

255 Chatsworth Road, Chesterfield, Derbyshire S40 2BL
Tel: 01246 229900 Fax: 01246 229988
e-mail: garneed@aol.com
website: www.oliholpho.com

The husband-and-wife team of Carmel and Gary Needham own and run **Oliholpho Clothing**, which they named after their three daughters Olivia, Holly and Phoebe. It's an intimate, cosy and very friendly place, with two floors of display space, and the customers really appreciate how relaxed the atmosphere always is. The shop numbers Sandwich, Noa Noa, Numph and Part Two among the brands, and men's labels include Fly53, Solid, Pepi Jeans and Front shoes.

Accessories come from Johnny Loves Rosie, Hultquist (jewellery from Denmark) and shoes for men and ladies by J-Shoes. The owners are always looking out for new, interesting and innovative brands, which makes their shop very different from the High Street stores; they often go for Danish labels for their style and quality. Oliholpho is open from 10.30 to 5.30; closed Wednesday and Sunday.

has been lost over the years. The truth – or at least the best guess – could be the amount of green timber used to build the spire. Green timber is more easily shaped and becomes much stronger as it dries, finally setting like concrete. The builders would have expected the wood to move as it dried and allowed for it, but it's impossible to predict exactly how green timber will dry. It can split, defects can appear and develop – anything can happen. And, clearly, anything did! As well as this, there's no cross bracing in the eight sides of the spire, and the bottom timbers decayed, which is why it leans. Add to that 32 tons of lead that cover the wooden structure, 600 years of weather and, according to one 'expert', bell-ringing, and you get a crooked spire! However, some stories say it was the Devil who, pausing for a rest during one of his flights, clung to the spire for a moment or two. Incense from the Church drifted upwards and the Devil sneezed, causing the spire to twist out of shape.

This magnificent spire rises to 228 feet and leans 9 feet 4 inches from its true centre-point. It is eight-sided, but the herringbone pattern of the lead slates trick the eye into seeing 16 sides from the ground. The Crooked Spire is open most Bank Holidays and at advertised times; the church is open all year, Monday to Saturday 9am to 5pm (9am to 3pm, January and February), and Sundays at service times only.

Around Chesterfield

WHITTINGTON
3 miles NE of Chesterfield off the B6052/A61

🏛 Revolution House

During the 17th century, **Revolution House**

was part of an alehouse called the Cock and Pynot (*pynot* being the local dialect word for magpie). It was here that three local noblemen – the Earl of Devonshire, the Earl of Danby and John D'Arcy – met to begin planning their part in the events which eventually led to the overthrow of James II in favour of his daughter Mary and her husband, William of Orange. The Glorious Revolution took place later in the same year, November 1688, and it was in the year of its 250th anniversary that this modest house was turned into a museum.

Revolution House, a tiny cottage with thatched roof, flower border and charming garden gate which belies its rather incendiary name, is now open to the public from Easter to the end of September and features period furnishings and a changing programme of exhibitions on local themes. A video relates the story of the Revolution and the role which the house played in those fraught and dangerous days.

BARLBOROUGH
7 miles NE of Chesterfield off the A619

Lying close to the county borders with both Nottinghamshire and Yorkshire, this village still retains its manor house. Lying just north of the village centre, Barlborough Hall (private) was built in 1584 by Lord Justice Francis Rodes to plans drawn up by the designer of Hardwick Hall, Robert Smythson. Those who visit both houses will notice the strong resemblance. As well as building houses, Rodes was also one of the judges at the trial of Mary, Queen of Scots. The Hall is supposed to be haunted by a grey lady, said to be the ghost of a bride who received the news of her groom's death as she was on her way to the 12th century village church. Barlborough Hall should not be confused with Barlborough

Old Hall: this is an easy mistake to make as Barlborough Old Hall is actually the younger of the two! Built in 1618, as the date stone over the front door states, the Old Hall is of a large H-plan design and has mullioned windows.

CRESWELL
9 miles E of Chesterfield off the A616

🏛 Creswell Crags

Lying close to the Derbyshire-Nottinghamshire border, the limestone gorge known as **Creswell Crags** is well worth seeing. Formed thousands of years ago by the erosion of a river which cut through the limestone, this rock, which is porous and subject to erosion underground as well as on the surface, contributes by its very nature to the forming of natural chambers. The subterranean movement of water created a vast network of caves, which were subsequently exposed and used by Neanderthal man as shelters while out hunting. Tours can be taken from the visitor centre where there is also a display of

artefacts found in the area. Testimony to the artistry of the later inhabitants of these caves was the discovery of a bone carved with the head of a horse. The carving is about 13,000 years old and can now be seen in the British Museum. The largest cavern, Church Hole Cave, extends some 170 feet into the side of the gorge; it was here that hand tools and the only known Ice Age rock art in Britain were found.

BOLSOVER
7 miles E of Chesterfield off the A632

🏛 Castle

The approach to Bolsover from the north and east is dominated by the splendid, sandstone structure of **Bolsover Castle** (English Heritage), which sits high on a limestone ridge. A castle has stood here since the 12th century, though the present building is a fairytale 'folly' built for Sir Charles Cavendish during the early 1600s on the site of a ruined castle. By the mid-1700s much of the building had been reduced to the ruins seen today, though thankfully the splendid keep has withstood the test of time.

Pevsner remarked that not many large houses in England occupy such an impressive position as Bolsover Castle, as it stands on the brow of a hill overlooking the valley of the River Rother and Doe Lea. The first castle at Bolsover was built by William Peverel, illegitimate son of William the Conqueror, as part of his vast Derbyshire estates. Nothing remains of that Norman building. Visitors can explore the Little Castle, or Keep,

Bolsover Castle

which is decorated in an elaborate Jacobean style with wonderful fireplaces, panelling and wall paintings. The whole building later descended to the Dukes of Portland, and it remains a strangely impressive place, though even now it is threatened by its industrial surroundings and the legacy of centuries of coal-mining beneath its walls: subsidence.

AULT HUCKNALL
6 miles SE of Chesterfield off the A617

🦅 Hardwick Hall

The strange name of this village probably means 'Hucca's high nook of land', and this pleasant place, standing on a ridge close to the Nottinghamshire border, is home to the magnificent Tudor house, **Hardwick Hall** (National Trust). "More glass than wall", it is one of Derbyshire's Big Three stately homes alongside Chatsworth and Haddon, all three glorious monuments to the great landowning families who played so great a role in shaping the history of the county. The letters E S can be seen carved in stone on the outside of the house: E S, or Elizabeth of Shrewsbury, was perhaps better known as Bess of Hardwick. This larger-than-life figure had attachments with many places in Derbyshire, and the story of her life makes for fascinating reading.

She was born in the manor house at Hardwick in 1520. The house stood only a little distance from the present-day Hall and was then not much more than a farmhouse. The young Bess married her neighbour's son, Robert Barlow, when she was only 12. When her young husband, himself only 14, died a few months later she naturally inherited a great deal of property. Some 15 years later she married Sir William Cavendish and, when he died in 1557, she was bequeathed his entire fortune. By this time she was the richest

woman in England, save for one, Elizabeth, the Queen.

Bess began the building of Hardwick House in 1590, towards the end of her life and after her fourth lucrative marriage to George Talbot, 6th Earl of Shrewsbury. It stands as a monument to her wealth and good taste, and is justly famous for its magnificent needlework and tapestries, carved fireplaces and friezes, which are considered as among the finest in Britain.

Though Bess is the first person who springs to mind with regard to Hardwick Hall, it was the 6th Duke of Devonshire who was responsible for the Hall's antiquarian atmosphere. He inherited the property in 1811 and, as well as promoting the legend that Mary, Queen of Scots stayed here, he filled the house with furniture, paintings and tapestries from his other houses and from Chatsworth in particular.

PILSLEY
5 miles S of Chesterfield off the B6039

🌿 Herb Garden

The Herb Garden in Pilsley is one of the foremost gardens in the country. It consists of four display gardens, the largest of which is the Mixed Herb Garden, boasting an impressive established parterre. The remaining three gardens are the Physic, the Lavender and the Pot Pourri, each with its own special theme and housing many rare and unusual species. Areas of native flowers and wild spring bulbs can be enjoyed from March to September.

HOLYMOORSIDE
3 miles W of Chesterfield off the A632

Surrounded by attractive moorland and lying in the picturesque valley of the River Hipper,

JMJ POTTERY

140 Chatsworth Road, Brampton,
Chesterfield S40 2AR
Tel: 01246 555461
e-mail: orders@jmjpottery.com
website: www.jmjpottery.com

In historic Brampton, where there were once 12 potteries, **JMJ Pottery** is the domain of Janine Mannion Jones, who makes individual, colourful pieces that are both practical and attractive. She throws stoneware domestic pottery, from eggcups right up to large bread crocks and casseroles. She specialises in personalised pottery for weddings, birth plates and children's sets or for any occasion; she welcomes commissions, and customers can watch their pottery being thrown and choose the shape and glaze.

She also offers tuition in small groups, teaching everything from hand-building to throwing, glazing and firing their own pots. Janine is ecologically very aware. She minimises waste, recycling clay, water and paper. She buys pottery materials from as close as possible to Chesterfield. Pots are air-dried, she makes her own glazes from raw materials and only fires full kilns.

this scattered village has grown into a popular residential area for the nearby towns. The custom of well-dressing in the village was revived in 1979 after a gap of about 80 years. Two wells are dressed, a large one and a smaller one for children, on the Wednesday before the late summer Bank Holiday in August.

The dressers follow the tradition of Barlow, where only flowers and leaves are used and not wool, seed and shells, though they do not stick to biblical themes. In 1990 the well-dressing depicted a scene commemorating the 50th anniversary of the Battle of Britain, one of their most spectacular dressings to date, and won the dressers pictures in the national press.

CUTTHORPE
4 miles W of Chesterfield off the B6050

🏃 Linacre Reservoirs

Before the Second World War the well-dressings in this village, which take place on the third Friday in July, had no religious links. After the war the custom died out, but was revived again by three people from nearby Barlow in 1978. The three dressed wells are blessed during a service of thanksgiving for the pure water.

Near the village are the three **Linacre Reservoirs**, set in the attractive wooded Linacre Valley. Built between 1855 and 1904, until recently they supplied water to Chesterfield. Today the area is home to many species of fish, waterfowl, mammals and plant life, and is considered one of the most important ecological sites in the area. There are very pleasant walks, nature trails and fishing and a scenic picnic area.

BARLOW
3 miles NW of Chesterfield off the B6051

Barlow is mentioned in the Domesday Book, and was the home of Robert Barlow, the first of Bess of Hardwick's four husbands. Although situated outside the limestone area, Barlow has been dressing its main well for longer than most. It is not known for certain when the custom began in the village, though it *is* known that, like Tissington, the well here provided water throughout the drought of 1615; this may have marked the start of this colourful practice. The wells are dressed during the second week of August every year. West of the village, Barlow Woodseats are not as uncomfortable as they sound for this is the name of an irregular gabled 16th century house, also called Woodseats Hall (private), which has a cruck barn in its grounds. It was home to the Mower family, one of whom, Arthur Mower, was the agent to the Barlow family in the 16th century, and kept a truly remarkable diary from 1555 to 1610. All 52 volumes are now kept in the British Museum. He records the death of Bess of Hardwick in 1608, recalling her as "a great purchaser and getter together of much goods" and notes that she "builded Chattesworth, Hardwick and Owlcotes".

Alfreton

🏚 Alfreton Hall

This historic town dates back to Saxon times and, despite local legends to the contrary, Alfred the Great was not immortalised in the

naming of the place. This attractive former coal-mining town stands on a hill close to the Nottinghamshire border. Along the charming High Street can be found the George Hotel, a fine Georgian building that looks down the length of the High Street. There are also a number of other 18th century stone built houses, the most impressive of which is **Alfreton Hall**, the centrepiece of an attractive public park. In soft mellow stone, the Hall was built around 1730, with 19th century additions. The home until fairly recently of the Palmer Morewood family, owners of the local coal mines, it is now used as an Arts and Adult Education Centre. The park is quite extensive, boasting its own cricket ground and a horse-riding track around its perimeter. In King Street there is a house of confinement, or lock-up, which was built to house lawbreakers and catered mainly for the local drunkards. The close confines of the prison with its two cells, minute windows and thick outer walls must have been a very effective deterrent.

Around Alfreton

SOUTH WINGFIELD
2 miles NW of Alfreton off the A6

🏚 Wingfield Manor

Above the village, on the rise of a hill, stand the graceful ruins of the 15th century **Wingfield Manor**. Built by Ralph Lord Cromwell, the manor house was used as Mary, Queen of Scots' prison on two separate occasions in 1569 and 1584 when she was held under the care of the Earl of Shrewsbury. The local squire, Anthony Babington, attempted to rescue the Queen and lead her to safety but the plot failed and, instead, lead to them both being beheaded. One of the less well-known of Derbyshire's many manor houses and mansions, the history and architectural interest provided by the ruins make it one of the more fascinating homes in the area. A wander around the remains reveals the large banqueting hall with its unusual oriel window and a crypt which was probably used to store food and wine. Whatever its use, it is a particularly fine example and rivals a similar structure at Fountains Abbey.

CRICH

4 miles SW of Alfreton off the A6

🏠 Crich Stand   🏛 National Tramway Museum

This large village, with its hilltop church and market cross, is probably most famous as the home of the **National Tramway Museum**. Referring to itself intriguingly as 'the museum that's a mile long', it offers a wonderful opportunity to enjoy a tram ride along a Victorian Street scene. The trams are of course the main centre of interest and include one of the ex-London Transport Feltham trams, considered by many to be the most elegant ever built.

Back in the centre of the village is the tower of **Crich Stand**, a local landmark that looks rather like a lighthouse. In fact this is the Regimental Memorial for the Sherwood Foresters and, erected in 1923, stands almost 1,000 feet above sea level. From its viewing gallery, on a clear day, it is said that seven counties can be seen: a climb to the top certainly offers some fantastic views. This large, straggling village, which retains its medieval market cross, was also a flourishing knitting centre at one time; the telltale 18th century cottages with their long upper windows can still be seen. The part-Norman parish Church of St Michael has a built-in

Crich Tramway Village

Crich Tramway Village, Nr Matlock,
Derbyshire DE4 5DP
Tel: 01773 854321
e-mail: enquiries@tramway.co.uk
website: www.tramway.co.uk

Crich Tramway Village offers a family day out in the relaxing atmosphere of a bygone era. Explore the re-created period street with its genuine buildings and features, fascinating exhibitions and most importantly, its trams. Unlimited tram rides are free with your entry fee, giving you the opportunity to fully appreciate the Village and surrounding countryside.

Journey on one of the many beautifully restored vintage trams, as they rumble through the cobbled street past a traditional police telephone known as the 'TARDIS', the Red Lion Pub & Restaurant, exhibition hall, workshops, children's play and picnic area, before passing beneath the magnificent Bowes Lyon Bridge. Next it's past the bandstand, through the woods, and then on to Glory Mine taking in spectacular views of the Derwent Valley.

🎭 stories and anecdotes   🐦 famous people   🎨 art and craft   🎵 entertainment and sport   🚶 walks stone lectern which, though common in Derbyshire, is rare elsewhere in the country.

AMBERGATE
6 miles SW of Alfreton off the A6

🌱 Shining Cliff Woods

Where the River Amber joins the mighty Derwent, Ambergate is one of the main gateways to the Peak District for travellers going north on the A6. A marvellous bridge crosses

The Amber Valley

the Derwent. The village itself is surrounded by deciduous woodland, including the fine **Shining Cliff Woods**, an important refuge for wildlife. The railway, road and canal here are all squeezed into the tight river valley, and the railway station, standing 100 feet above the road, was one of the few triangular stations in Britain. Built in the late 19th century, the church of St Anne was a gift to the village from the Johnson family of the Ambergate Wire Works, now known as the business concern Richard Johnson and Nephew.

RIDDINGS
2 miles S of Alfreton off the A38/A610

Riddings, now a tranquil village, has twice been the scene of important discoveries. In the mid-1700s, 800 precious Roman coins were uncovered here. A century later, James Oakes, a colliery proprietor and ironmaster, discovered a mysterious liquid flowing on his property. He called in the assistance of his brother-in-law, Lyon Playfair, one of the most brilliant practical scientists of his day. Playfair

found the liquid to be petroleum – then an unknown product commercially, although it had been known (as naphtha, 'salt of the earth'), from Biblical times.

Playfair summoned the help of his friend James Young, who soon after he came to Riddings approached Playfair in dismay to show him that the oil was in a turbid condition. Playfair recognised at once the presence of paraffin, and instructed Young to extract enough paraffin to make two candles – the first paraffin-wax candles ever produced. With one candle in his left hand and the other in his right, Playfair illuminated a lecture he gave at the Royal Institution. From these small beginnings date the enormous petroleum industry and the rich trade in paraffin and its wide range of by-products.

Ripley

Once a typical small market town, Ripley expanded dramatically during the Industrial Revolution when great use was made of the iron, clay and coal deposits found nearby. The town's Butterley ironworks, founded in 1792 by a group of men which included renowned engineer Benjamin Outram, created the roof for London's St Pancras station. Outram's even more famous son, Sir James, enjoyed an illustrious career that saw him appointed Bayard of India, and earned him a resting place in Westminster Abbey.

Around Ripley

HEAGE
1 miles W of Ripley off the B6013

🏠 Windmill

This village is home to a famous tower **Windmill**, the only one in Derbyshire to retain all its six sails, fan tail and machinery. The Grade II listed building, situated to the west of the village, is built of local sandstone. Now more than 200 years old, the mill has been restored to full working order and is open to the public at weekends and Bank Holidays.

DENBY
2 miles S of Ripley off the A38/B6179

🏛 Visitor Centre

Denby Visitor Centre is one of the biggest visitor attractions in Derbyshire. The centerpiece is the famous pottery; it was established in 1809 and nearly 200 years later, classic ranges such as Imperial Blue and Regency Green are still best sellers. Other on-site attractions include a Factory

Shop, a Cookery Emporium offering cookery demonstrations and a stock of more than 3,000 kitchen gadgets, supplies and equipment.

HEANOR
3 miles SE of Ripley off the A608

🌷 Memorial Gardens   🎿 Shipley Country Park

The hub of this busy town centres on the market place, where the annual fair is held, as well as the twice-weekly market (Fridays and Saturdays). Away from the bustle of the market are the **Memorial Gardens**. This peaceful setting always promises a magnificent spread of floral arrangements, herbaceous borders and shrubberies.

To the south of Heanor is the **Shipley Country Park**, on the estate of the now demolished Shipley Hall. In addition to its magnificent lake, the Country Park boasts over 600 acres of beautiful countryside which

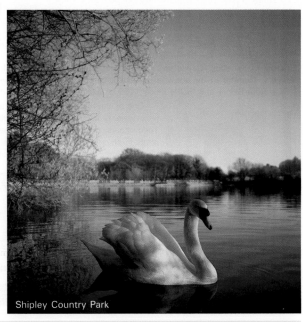

Shipley Country Park

🎬 stories and anecdotes   🐦 famous people   🎨 art and craft   ✒ entertainment and sport   🎿 walks should keep even the most enthusiastic walker busy. Well known as both an educational and holiday centre, there are facilities for horse riding, cycling and fishing. Restoration over the years has transformed former railways into wooded paths, reservoirs into peaceful lakes, and has re-established the once-flowering meadows and rolling hills which had been destroyed by colliery pits.

Belper

🏛 Mills   📷 Visitor Centre   ⚵ River Gardens

Famous for its cotton mills, the town is situated alongside the **River Derwent** on the floor of the valley. In 1776, Jedediah Strutt, the wheelwright son of a South Normanton farmer, set up one of the earliest water-

powered cotton mills here to harness the natural powers of the river to run his mills. With the river providing the power, and fuel coming from the nearby South Derbyshire coalfield, the valley has a good claim to be one of the cradles of the Industrial Revolution. Earlier, in 1771, Strutt had gone into profitable partnership with Richard Arkwright to establish the world's first water-powered cotton mill at Cromford. Great benefactors to Belper for 150 years, the Strutt family provided housing, work, education and even food from the model farms they established in the surrounding countryside.

The mills are still standing and, along with them, are some unique mill-workers' cottages. To discover more about the cotton industry, a visit to the **Derwent Valley**

FREARSONS

10 Bridge Street, Belper, Derbyshire DE56 1AX
Tel: 01773 823244   Fax: 01773 828030
e-mail: silvermanandson@yahoo.co.uk

Frearsons has been selling lovely gifts and things for the home since 1954, and in April 2007 it was bought by Steve Silverman, a talented and experienced maker and repairer of jewellery. The interior of the shop is cosy and inviting, and Steve has a warm welcome for all his browsers and buyers. The star of the show is the extensive collection of Royal Crown Derby, based a few miles from Belper and maker since 1750 of exclusive bone china gifts and collectables.

One of the most popular ranges is the wonderful selection of paperweights inspired by cats and dogs, birds, wild animals, Teddy bears, country life and 'Treasures of Childhood'. They are made in cheerful contemporary style with the appeal of bright Imari colours, hand-decorated so each piece is unique. This

collector's paradise also stocks Blue john jewellery from Derbyshire, crystal from Royal Scot, Royal Doulton and Tutbury, pewter tankards, wrist and pocket watches and pens by Parker, Sheaffer and Waterman.

🏛 historic building   📷 museum   🏛 historic site   ⚶ scenic attraction   🦋 flora and fauna

Visitor Centre is a must. It records the influence of the Strutt family on the town and of Samuel Slater, Strutt's apprentice who emigrated to America in 1789, built a mill there and went on to become "the Father of American manufacturers".

The oldest mill still surviving is the two-storey **North Mill** at Bridgefoot, near the magnificent crescent-shaped weir in the Derwent and the town's main bridge. Built in 1876, the mill has cast-iron columns and beams, and hollow tile floors which provided a warm-air central heating system. It is now the visitor centre. The massive, neighbouring redbrick **East Mill** was constructed in 1912, but now is largely empty. A Jubilee Tower in terracotta was erected on the mill site in 1897 to mark Queen Victoria's 60 years on the throne.

Train travellers through Belper are among those treated to a glimpse of George Stephenson's mile-long cutting, walled in gritstone throughout and spanned by no fewer than ten bridges. When completed in 1840 it was considered the engineering wonder of its day. In addition to all its industrial history the town goes back to well before the Industrial Revolution. Not only was it mentioned in the Domesday Book (as Beau Repaire - the beautiful retreat), but in 1964 the remains of a Roman kiln were found here.

The River Gardens were established in 1905 and today they are a pleasant place for a stroll among the beautifully tended gardens. Rowing boats can be hired for a trip along the Derwent. The Gardens are a favourite with the film industry, having been used in Ken Russell's *Women in Love*, as well as television's *Sounding Brass* and *In the Shadow of the Noose*.

Around Belper

DUFFIELD
2 miles S of Belper off the A6

🏛 Castle

This ancient parish is a charming place, with Georgian houses and cottages lining the banks of the River Ecclesbourne. For such a cosy place, it seems odd that the Parish Church is situated in isolation down by the river. Inside the Church there is an impressive monument dedicated to Anthony Bradshaw whose great-nephew went on to officiate over the court which called for the execution of Charles I. Also in the village is a large mound, all that remains of **Duffield Castle** (National Trust) which was ransacked and burnt to the ground in 1266.

Ilkeston

🏛 Museum

The third largest town in Derbyshire, Ilkeston received its royal charter for a market and fair in 1252; both have continued to the present day. The history of the town, however, goes back to the days when it was an Anglo-Saxon hilltop settlement known as Tilchestune. Once a mining and lace-making centre, its history is told in the **Erewash Museum**, housed in a fine Georgian house on the High Street. Other fine examples of elegant 18th century houses can be found in East Street while in Wharncliffe Road there are period houses with art nouveau features.

Ilkeston commands fine wide views from the hillside above the valley of the Erewash, which here bounds the county. The town's church-crowned hilltop is a landmark that can be seen from far afield.

Around Ilkeston

WEST HALLAM
2 miles W of Ilkeston off the A609

🏛 West Hallam Hall　🎋 The Bottle Kiln

West Hallam stands on a hilltop; its church, set between the great expanse of **West Hallam Hall** and the rectory, is approached via a lovely avenue of limes. The rector's garden has a glorious lime tree, and looks out over the valley to a great windmill with its arms still working as they have done since Georgian times.

One of the premier attractions in the area, **The Bottle Kiln** is a handsome and impressive brickbuilt former working pottery, now home to contemporary art and craft. Visitors can take a leisurely look at exhibitions

Dale Abbey Ruins

(changing throughout the year) of both British studio ceramics and contemporary painting in the European tradition. From figurative and descriptive to abstract, many styles and media are displayed here. In addition there is a selection of imaginative contemporary British jewellery and craftware on display in and around the old kiln. Two shops filled with jewellery, cards, gifts, objets-d'art, soft furnishings and housewares with an accent on style, design and originality can also be found at this superb site.

DALE ABBEY
3 miles SW of Ilkeston off the A6096

🏛 Windmill　🌲 Hermit's Wood

The village takes its name from the now ruined abbey that was founded here by Augustinian monks in the 13th century. Beginning life in a very humble manner, local legend has it that a Derbyshire baker came to the area in 1130, carved himself a niche in the sandstone and devoted himself to the way of the hermit. The owner of the land, Ralph FitzGeremunde, discovered the baker and was so impressed by the man's devotion that he bestowed on him the land and tithe rights to his mill in Borrowash. The sandstone cave and the romantic ruined 40-feet high window archway are popular attractions locally and a walk around the village is both an interesting and pleasurable experience. Nearby **Hermit's Wood** is an ancient area of woodland with beech, ash, oak and lime trees. It is wonderful at any time of year, but particularly in the spring when the woodland floor is covered with a mist of bluebells.

To the north of the village stands the **Cat and Fiddle Windmill**, built in the 1700s and a fine example of the oldest type of mill. The stone roundhouse is capped with a box-like

🏛 historic building　📷 museum　🏚 historic site　🝔 scenic attraction　🌿 flora and fauna wooden structure which houses the machinery and which is fitted onto an upright post round which it can rotate to catch the wind.

RISLEY
4 miles S of Ilkeston off the B5010

This small village has once again become a quiet backwater now that the main Derby to Nottingham road bypasses it to the south. Apart from ribbon building along the former main road, Risley consists of no more than a small group of old buildings, but they are unique and well worth a visit. In 1593, Michael Willoughby started to rebuild the village church. Although small, even by the standards of the day, it is charming and essentially Gothic in style. In the same year his wife founded a school and, although none of the original schoolhouses exist, those seen today date from the early 1700s and were constructed by a trust founded by the family. The central school building is a perfect example of the Queen Anne style and acted as both the school and schoolhouse, with the boarders sleeping in the garrets. The trustees still maintain this wonderful building, along with the Latin School of 1724, the English School of 1753 and another School House built in 1771.

BREASTON
5 miles S of Ilkeston off the A6005

🏛 Church

On the southern borders of the county, close to Nottinghamshire and Leicestershire, Breaston occupies the flat countryside near

PEAR TREE YARD CRAFT CENTRE

Town Street, Sandiacre,
Derbyshire NG10 5DU
Tel: 0115 949 7411
Fax: 0115 939 0504
e-mail: crafts@peartreeyard.co.uk
website: www.peartreeyard.co.uk

Pear Tree Yard Craft Centre is a family-run business in an old mill building.

It sells what is probably the largest and best selection of crafts and craft materials in the whole region, and shoppers who can't get to the shop (open 9am to 5pm Monday to Saturday) can order online through the excellent website.

Beads and braids, card making and scrapbooking, découpage, cards and envelopes, stickers, rub-ons and peel-offs, paper and paints, punches and stamps, jewellery and gift ideas, poly bags, cake decorations, all kinds of materials...........the list goes on, and if you don't see what you want in the shop there will always be someone there to help.

The Yard also includes a complementary therapy clinic providing a wide range of therapies.

📖 stories and anecdotes   🦜 famous people   🎨 art and craft   🎭 entertainment and sport   🚶 walks the point where the River Derwent joins the River Trent before continuing on its long journey to the North Sea. The mainly 13th century **Church of St Michael** boasts the 'Boy of Breaston' – a small, chubby-faced child immortalised in the 13th century by the mason of the nave arches. He has smiled down on worshippers and visitors for the past seven centuries. The story has it that this boy would come in and watch the masons at work while the church was being built. The master mason decided to make the child part of the church, so that he could always have a good view of it!

Coffins had to be carried to neighbouring **Church Wilne** for burial up until the early 1800s, as there was no burial ground at Breaston until that time. For this reason the footpath over the fields of Wilne continues to be known by villagers as the 'Coffin Walk'.

ELVASTON
8 miles SW of Ilkeston off the B5010

🏛 Castle

Elvaston is gathered around the edge of the **Elvaston Castle** estate, home of the Earls of Harrington. The magnificent Gothic castle seen today replaced a 17th century brick and gabled manor house; part of the original structure can be seen on the end of the south front. Designed by James Wyatt, the castle was finished in the early 1800s but, unfortunately, the 3rd Earl died in 1829 and had little time to enjoy his new home.

The grounds of Elvaston Castle were originally laid out and designed for the 4th

Earl by William Barron. Barron, who was born in Berwickshire in 1805, started work in 1830 on what at first appeared to be an impossible task. The 4th Earl wanted a garden 'second to none', but the land available, which had never been landscaped, was flat, water-logged and uninspiring with just two avenues of trees and a walled kitchen garden (but no greenhouses or hot houses). First draining the land, Barron then planted trees to offer shelter to more tender plants. From there the project grew. In order to stock the gardens, Barron began a programme of propagation of rarer tree species and, along with the tree-planting methods he developed specially to deal with Elvaston's problems, his fame spread. The gardens became a showcase of rare and interesting trees, many to be found nowhere else in Britain. Now owned by Derby County Council, the gardens, after years of neglect, have been completely restored and the delights of the formal gardens, with their fine topiary, the avenues and the kitchen garden can be enjoyed by all visitors to the grounds, which are now a Country Park.

No visit to Elvaston would be complete without a walk down to the Golden Gates. Erected in 1819 at the southern end of the formal gardens, the gates were brought from the Palace of Versailles by the 3rd Earl of Harrington. Little is known of the Gates' history, but they remain a fine monument and are the symbol of Elvaston.

Derby

🏛 Cathedral   🏛 Pickford House

🏛 Museums and Heritage Centre

Essentially a commercial and industrial city, Derby's position, historically and geographically, has ensured that is has

remained one of the most important and interesting cities in the area. Consequently there is much for the visitor to see, whether from an architectural or historical point of view. There are, however, two things almost everyone, whether they have been to the city before or not, associate with Derby: Rolls-Royce engines and Royal Crown Derby porcelain. When in 1906 Sir Henry Royce and the Hon C S Rolls joined forces and built the first Rolls-Royce (a Silver Ghost) at Derby, they built much more than just a motor car. Considered by many to be the best cars in the world, it is often said that the noisiest moving part in any Rolls-Royce is the dashboard clock! The home of **Royal Crown Derby**, any visit to the city would not be complete without a trip to the factory and its museum and shop. The guided tours offer an intriguing insight into the high level of skill required to create the delicate flower petals, hand-gild the plates and to hand-paint the Derby Dwarves.

The city's **Cathedral of All Saints** possesses a fine 16th century tower, the second highest perpendicular tower in England. The airy building was actually built in the 1720s by James Gibbs. Inside is a beautiful wrought-iron screen by Robert Bakewell and, among the splendid monuments, lies the tomb of Bess of Hardwick. Originally Derby's Parish Church, it was given cathedral status in 1927.

One of Derby's most interesting museums is **Pickford House**, situated on the city's finest Georgian street at number 41. It is a Grade I listed building, erected in 1770 by the architect Joseph Pickford as a combined family home and place of work. Pickford House differs from the majority of grand stately homes; unlike most it does not have a wealth of priceless furniture and works or art. Instead, visitors are able to gain an insight into everyday middle-class life during the 1830s.

Just a short walk from Pickford House is the **Industrial Museum**. What better place to house a museum devoted to the preservation of Derby's industrial heritage than the beautiful old **Silk Mill,** a building which stands on one of the most interesting sites in the country and which preceded Richard Arkwright's first cotton mill by over 50 years.

The **City Museum and Art Gallery** is also well worth visiting. Opened in 1879, it is the oldest of Derby's museums and the displays include natural history, archaeology and social history exhibits. One section of the museum is devoted to a Military Gallery and relates to Derby's local historical regiments. The walk-in First World War trench scene attempts to capture the experience of a night at the front. A ground floor gallery houses the city's superb collection of fine porcelain, manufactured in Derby from the mid-18th century. The **Derby Heritage Centre** has local history displays, tea room and souvenir shop housed in one of the city's oldest buildings. Another of the city's treats is the **Derbyshire Constabulary Memorabilia Museum**, which has a display of uniforms and weapons dating from the mid-1600s to the present day.

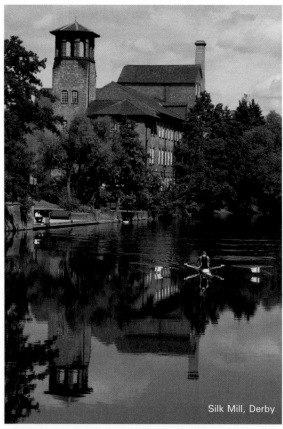

Silk Mill, Derby

Around Derby

KEDLESTON
4 miles NW of Derby off the A52

🏛 Kedleston Hall

Kedleston Hall has been the family seat of the Curzon family since the 12th century and, until it was taken over the by National Trust, it had the longest continuous male line in Derbyshire and one of the longest in the country. The present elegant mansion was built between 1759 and 1765 by Robert Adam and it remains one of the finest examples of his work. Since taking over the property, the National Trust have embarked on a major restoration programme. The three-mile Long Walk was created in 1776. Along with the

🏛 historic building   📷 museum   🏛 historic site   🍃 scenic attraction   🌿 flora and fauna house itself, there is the park with its lakes, boat house and fishing pavilion to explore.

SUDBURY
12 miles W of Derby off the A50

🏛 Sudbury Hall   🏛 Museum of Childhood

Sudbury is the estate village to **Sudbury Hall**, the late-17th century mansion and home of a branch of the Vernon family who lived at Haddon Hall. The house is intriguing, the garden restful. Gifted to the National Trust in 1967, the Hall is an unexpected mixture of architectural styles. A splendid example of a house of Charles II's time, the interior of Sudbury Hall contains elaborate plasterwork and murals throughout, wood carvings by Grinling Gibbons, and some fine examples of mythological paintings by Laguerre. Of particular interest is the **Museum of Childhood**, which is situated in the servants' wing and provides a fascinating insight into the lives of children down the ages. Fascinating displays range from a wealthy family's nursery and an Edwardian schoolroom to a 'chimney climb' and coal tunnel for the adventurous. The formal gardens and meadows lead to the tree-fringed lake. Wildlife abounds, including kestrels, grey herons, grass snakes, dragonflies, newts, frogs, toads, little and tawny owls and woodpeckers. Special events are held throughout the year.

Swadlincote

Here at the extreme edge of Derbyshire, well south of the River Trent, Swadlincote shares many characteristics with Staffordshire. Among the town's thriving industries, based on the clay and coal on which it stands, are large potteries founded in 1795 as well as brickworks.

Around Swadlincote

NETHERSEAL
6 miles S of Swadlincote off the A444

Netherseal is a picturesque village on the banks of the River Mease. 'Seal' means forested and Netherseal was recorded in the Domesday Book as a wooded area on the edge of Ashby Woulds. It was once a mining community with a two-shaft colliery and several related industries. The mining activity has long ceased and the centre of the village is now a conservation area with many listed buildings including some charming 17th century almshouses.

CALKE
5 miles NE of Swadlincote off the B587

🏛 Abbey

In 1985 the National Trust bought **Calke Abbey**, a large Baroque-style mansion built in 1701 on the site of an Augustinian priory founded in 1133. However, it was not until 1989 that the Trust was able to open the house to the public, for this was no ordinary house at all. Dubbed 'the house that time forgot' since the death of the owner, Sir Vauncy Harpur-Crewe in 1924 nothing had been altered in the mansion! In fact, the seclusion of the house and also the rather bizarre lifestyle of its inhabitants had left many rooms and objects untouched for over 100 years. There was even a spectacular 18th century Chinese silk state bed that had never been unpacked.

Today, the Trust has repaired the house and returned all 13,000 items to their original positions so that the Abbey now looks just as it did when it was bought in 1981. The attention to detail has been so great that none

CALKE ABBEY RACING STABLES

Heath Lane, Boundary,
South Derbyshire DE11 7AY
Tel/Fax: 01283 225294
e-mail: atackatack@calkeabbeyracing.co.uk
website: www.calkeabbeyracing2007.co.uk

Calke Abbey Racing Stables are ideally situated on the Derbyshire/Leicestershire border near Ashby-de-la-Zouche and just two miles from Junction 13 off the M42. The yard is licensed to train both flat and national hunt horses on their 6.5 furlong all weather gallop, which is also available for private hire. Also based at the stables is **A-TACK-A-TACK**, a comprehensively stocked, high-quality tack shop selling a wide range of horse and rider wear including

Charles Owen, Mark Todd, Legacy, Tagg, Dever, Georg Schumacher, Belstane, Falpro, Kakadu, Global Herbs, Grand Meadows feed supplements and many more.

of the rooms has been redecorated. Visitors can enjoy the silver display and trace the route of 18th century servants along the brewhouse tunnel to the house cellars. Calke Abbey stands in its own large park with gardens, a chapel and stables that are also open to the public. There are three walled gardens with their glasshouses, a restored orangery, vegetable garden, pheasant aviaries and the summer flower display within the unusual "auricular" theatre.

MELBOURNE

6 miles NE of Swadlincote off the B587

🏛 Church   🌱 Melbourne Hall

This small town, which lent its name to the rather better-known city in Australia, is a successful market garden centre. A famous son of Melbourne, who started his working life in one of the market gardens, was Thomas Cook, who was born here in 1808. He went on to pioneer personally conducted tours and established the famous worldwide travel company.

Full of Georgian charm, Melbourne has many fine buildings which include one of the noblest Norman churches in the country, the **Church of St Michael and St Mary**. This seems rather a grand church for this modest place and indeed, it is no ordinary parish church. In the 12th century, when the Bishopric of Carlisle was formed, there needed to be a place of safety for the clergy when Carlisle was being raided by the Scots. So this church was built at Melbourne and, while Carlisle was subjected to raids and violence, the Bishop

CHANTRY FARM SHOP

Kings Newton Lane, Kings Newton, Derbyshire DE73 8DD
Tel/Fax: 01332 865698
e-mail: sales@chantryfarm.com   website: www.chantryfarm.com

Chantry Farm Shop is a family-run business that has earned a reputation and a following that reaches far beyond this part of Derbyshire. Owners Helen and Philip Sread are passionate about their and are proud to offer discerning customers the best of both worlds – high-quality food and exceptional value for money.

Everything they sell is absolutely top-notch, from their own free-range poultry and quality meats (rare breeds as well as locally produced), the finest cottage industry products, prime fresh fruit and vegetables and delicious ice creams and puddings. Accolades come from the happy regular customers and from nationally known experts, notably the celebrity Rick Stein, who includes Chantry Farm Shop among his Food Heroes.

Opening hours are 8.30 to 5 Monday to Friday, 8 to 4 Saturday.

retired to Melbourne and continued to carry out his duties. The church was built between 1133 and 1229 and, in 1299, the then Bishop built a palace on land that is now home to Melbourne Hall.

The birthplace of the 19th century statesman Lord Melbourne, and also the home of Lady Caroline Lamb, **Melbourne Hall** is another fine building in this area of Derbyshire. A modest building, the Hall is surrounded by beautiful gardens, the most notable feature of which is a beautiful wrought-iron birdcage pergola built in the early 1700s by Robert Bakewell, a local blacksmith from Derby. The house is only open to the public in August, but the formal gardens are open throughout the summer season.

SWARKESTONE
9 miles NE of Swadlincote off the A5132

Bridge

It was at **Swarkestone Bridge** in 1745 that Bonnie Prince Charlie's hopes of seizing the English crown were finally dashed. To everyone's surprise, his advance guard had successfully penetrated so far south and victory seemed within his grasp. But when the Jacobite soldiers reached the bridge with its seven arches and three-quarter-mile long causeway crossing the River Trent they were confronted by a strong force of King George's troops. If Prince Charles's soldiers had managed to force their way across the river at this point, they would have faced no

Swarkestone Causeway

other natural barriers along the 120-mile march to London. As it transpired, the Scottish army retreated and fled north. Bonnie Prince Charlie himself managed to escape but the Jacobite Rebellion was all over bar the shouting.

Legend has it that the original bridge at Swarkestone was built by two daughters of the Harpur family in the early 13th century. The girls were celebrating their joint betrothals when their fiancés were summoned to a barons' meeting across the river. While they were away torrential rain fell, flooding the river, and the two young men drowned as they attempted to ford the raging torrent on their return. The girls built the bridge as a memorial to their lovers. Both girls later died impoverished and unmarried.

REPTON
5 miles N of Swadlincote off the B5008

🏛 Church 🏛 College

This village, by the tranquil waters of the River Trent, is steeped in history. The first recorded mention of Repton was in the 7th century when it was established as the capital of the Saxon kingdom of Mercia. A monastery, housing both monks and nuns, was founded here sometime after 653 but the building was sacked by the Danes in 874. A battleaxe, now on display in the school museum, was excavated a little distance from the church. It had apparently lain undisturbed for well over 1,000 years.

The parish **Church of St Wystan** is famous for its Anglo-Saxon chancel and crypt, but it also contains many of the major styles

THE NEWTON SOLNEY DELI

16a Main Street, Newton Solney, nr Burton-on-Trent,
Derbyshire DE15 0SJ
Tel: 01283 703328
e-mail: newtonsolney@aol.com   website: www.newtonsolneydeli.co.uk

Fiona Smith established the **Newton Solney Delicatessen** in November 2005 in the restored Post Office Building (it still also operates as the PO). She lost no time in putting her stamp on the place, bringing an excellent variety of fine food to South Derbyshire. Among the many goodies in the shop are bacon, sausages, hams and other cooked meats, Patchwork pâtés, up to 30 super cheeses, bread from the local bakery, Stokes dressings and mayonnaise, jams, honey, chutneys, olives, olive oil, Kimberleys handmade chocolates, farm eggs, Needwood ice creams and organic and Fairtrade coffee. Fiona also makes splendid cakes for weddings and other special celebrations.

of medieval architecture. When the chancel and part of the nave were enlarged in 1854, the original Anglo-Saxon columns were moved to the 14th century porch. The crypt is believed to be one of the oldest intact Anglo-Saxon buildings in England. The burial place of the Kings of Mercia, including St Wystan in 850, the crypt was rediscovered by chance in 1779 by a workman who was digging a hole for a grave in the chancel floor.

The ancient Cross, still at the central crossroads in the village, has been the focal point of life here for centuries and it has also stood at the heart of the Wednesday market. Right up until the late 1800s a Statutes Fair, for the hiring of farm labourers and domestics, was held here at Michaelmas.

Parts of an Augustinian priory, founded in 1170, are incorporated in the buildings of **Repton College**, itself founded in 1557. Sir John Port had specifically intended the college to be a grammar school for the local poor children of Etwall, Repton and Burnaston. These intentions have somewhat deviated over the passing years and now Repton stands as one of the foremost public schools in the country. Interestingly, two of its headmasters, Dr Temple and Dr Fisher, went on to become Archbishops of Canterbury. A third archbishop, Dr Ramsey, was a pupil at the school under Dr Fisher's guiding light. Film buffs will recognise the 14th century gatehouse and causeway, as they featured in both film versions of the popular story *Goodbye, Mr Chips*.

LOCATOR MAP

ADVERTISERS AND PLACES OF INTEREST

🏛 historic building   🏛 museum   🏛 historic site   ⚘ scenic attraction   ⚘ flora and fauna

6| Nottinghamshire

The county of Nottinghamshire, in the north Midlands, lies mainly on the low ground basin of the River Trent between the peaks of Derbyshire and South Yorkshire and the lowlands of Lincolnshire. It is a county of contrasts: it has plenty of industry but it has also retained much of its rural heritage as well as the remains of the famous Forest of Sherwood.

As any local lad will be happy to tell you, Nottingham used to be called 'Snotingham' after the unfortunately named Snot, chief of a 6th century Anglo-Saxon tribe. But there was a settlement here long before then. In Celtic times it was known as Tigguocobauc, 'the house of caves', an appropriate name since this ancient people lived in the caves that occur naturally in the soft local sandstone. When the Vikings arrived in England in 878, they recognised Nottingham's importance by making it one of the five boroughs of the 'Danelaw' - the area of Middle England they controlled. There was more significant development in Norman times when the famous castle that features so prominently in the Robin Hood legends was built.

The glory of the central part of the county is Southwell Minster, a uniquely graceful building which is perhaps the least well-known cathedral in the country. Southwell itself is small, with a population under 7,000, but it is a delightful town with many fine buildings and a picturesque old coaching inn where Charles I spent his last night of freedom. Surrounding this appealing little town is a maze of country lanes and ancient villages.

With an historic castle, magnificent parish church and a host of fine buildings, Newark is an immensely likeable place. In medieval times, the town thrived as a centre for the wool trade, benefiting from its position on the Great North Road and beside the River Trent. The Civil War brought great suffering but, apart from the castle, surprisingly little damage to the town's buildings. South of Newark lies the Vale of Belvoir, an unspoilt pastoral landscape dotted with the spires of village churches and overlooked by the mighty towers and turrets of Belvoir Castle, just across the border in Lincolnshire.

Sherwood Forest is known to old and young alike, all over the world, thanks to the tales of Robin Hood and the various stories, films, and TV series made about this legendary hero of the people. Sherwood, the shire wood of Nottinghamshire, was once part of a great mass of forest land which covered much of central England. Now officially designated as "Robin Hood Country", the tract of land running north from Nottingham is an attractive mix of woodland and rolling hills.

To the north of the forest is the area known as The Dukeries, which is scenically one of the most attractive parts of the county. Here, in the 18th century, no fewer than four different Dukes acquired huge estates: Rufford, Welbeck, Clumber, and Thoresby. All their great houses are now put to different uses but the glorious parks they created, especially at Clumber, make this a delightful area to visit.

The area around Mansfield was once the industrial heart of Nottinghamshire, its landscape dominated by pit-head wheels and chimneys, and the serried ranks of miners' terraced houses. This is "Pilgrim Fathers' Country" since it was here that the unorthodox worship of Richard Clyfton inspired such men as William Brewster of Scrooby, and William Bradford of Austerfield, later Governor of New England. The best introduction to their story is to follow the "Mayflower Trail", devised by Bassetlaw District Council, which follows a circular route starting from Worksop. Also in Worksop is the unusual National Trust property, Mr Straw's House, a time-capsule from the 1920s where nothing has altered in the subsequent 80 years. Retford and Blyth are both attractive old market towns: the former with some fine Georgian buildings, the latter boasting one of the most monumental Norman churches in the country.

Nottingham

A lively city of some 300,000 inhabitants, Nottingham offers a vast choice of shops, restaurants (more than 200 of them), cinemas, art galleries, two theatres, a world-class concert hall, and a host of other visitor attractions. The city also boasts a leading university, a major medical centre and a legendary football team, Nottingham Forest. The self-proclaimed 'Queen of the Midlands', Nottingham is known worldwide because of the legendary Robin Hood and his persecutor, the villainous Sheriff of Nottingham. Others associate the city with Boots the Chemist, Players cigarettes (whose packets carry a picture of Nottingham Castle), Raleigh cycles and motor-cycles, and with the ice skaters Torvill and Dean - their world-beating performances led directly to the siting in Nottingham of the National Ice Centre. Alan Sillitoe, the author of *Saturday Night and Sunday Morning*, was born in Nottingham in 1928 and for a while worked at the Raleigh bicycle factory. *Birthday* is a sequel to *Saturday Night*, and in his 2004 novel, *A Man of his Time*, Alan Sillitoe tells the story of a womanising Nottinghamshire blacksmith. JM Barrie and Graham Greene both had spells working on the *Nottingham Daily Journal.*

A good place to begin exploring the city is in the Old Market Square, known to locals as Slab Square and believed to be largest market square in the country. Although no market has been held here since the 1920s, the vast expanse of the square still lies at the centre of Nottingham life. At its eastern end stands the dignified Council House with its porticoed frontage and

a dome that is a replica of St Paul's in London. Part of the stately ground floor with its lofty ceilings and neo-classical architecture now houses some prestigious shops.

Until the Council House was built, the Market Square was the setting for the famous Nottingham **Goose Fair** which began in medieval times and gained its name from the large flocks of geese that were sold here around Michaelmas. Mentioned in a charter dated 1284, the Goose Fair still takes place in early October but has grown so much it is now held at Forest Fields on the edge of the city.

A short walk from the Market Square, in the appropriately named Maid Marian Way, **The Tales of Robin Hood** tells the story of the celebrated outlaw through a series of historically accurate displays depicting scenes such as Robin's imprisonment by the Sheriff of Nottingham to feasting in Sherwood Forest. After a tour by chair, ride visitors can then explore the history of the legend and also learn about the detective work undertaken in the 1930s in an attempt to authenticate the legend.

A further couple of minutes walk brings you to the entrance to **Nottingham Castle** (see panel opposite), which commands an imposing position on a rocky outcrop high above the city centre. However, those looking for the famous castle which features so frequently in the tales of Robin Hood will be sorely disappointed as the present buildings date from after the English Civil War and precious little remains of the original medieval fortification.

The original castle was built soon after the Battle of Hastings by William Peveril as part of William I's general fortification of many strategically important sites. Its elevated position, overlooking the city and the River Trent, made Nottingham Castle one of the foremost castles in Norman England and it

Nottingham Castle

Castle Place, Nottingham,
Nottinghamshire NG1 6EL
Tel: 01159 153700
website: www.nottinghamcity.gov.uk

Nottingham Castle is a magnificent 17th century ducal mansion built on the site of the original Medieval Castle, with spectacular views across the city. A vibrant museum and art gallery housing collections of silver, glass, armour and paintings, plus fifteen centuries of Nottingham history. The galleries also bring the best regional, national and international artist's work to the city. Nottingham Castle is 10 minutes walk from Nottingham City centre, with easy access from train and bus stations. Parking is close by.

The Castle is a great place for children, with interactive displays and an activity - led gallery bringing paintings to life, specifically for the under 5s plus a medieval - style playground in the grounds with covered picnic area.

Underneath the Castle are many manmade caves and tunnels, some of which date back to medieval times. Visitors can take a guided tour to see Mortimer's Hole, King David's dungeon and the old wine cellar. The tour is strenuous and includes steep steps. Many visitors choose to descend through hundreds of years of history, learning on the way gruesome tales about Roger Mortimer and King David of Scotland.

played host to many important visitors. Of a typical Norman motte and bailey design, the stone walls are thought to have been added in the early 12th century and it was further fortified by Henry II. Nottingham Castle's heyday came in the 14th and 15th centuries however, when not only was King David II of Scotland held prisoner here for a while around 1346 but, in the mid-1400s, Edward IV proclaimed himself king from Nottingham Castle. Later his brother, Richard III, rode out from here to the Battle of Bosworth field and his death.

For some reason, the Tudors shunned the castle which gradually fell into disrepair until Charles I came to Nottingham in 1642 and raised his standard, marking the beginning of the Civil War. Unfortunately, the king found little support for his cause in the city (only 30 citizens joined his troops) so he moved on to Shrewsbury, leaving Nottingham and its castle in the hands of the Parliamentarians. During the course of the war, the Royalists made several attempts to recapture the castle but Cromwell's supporters held out. After the fighting was over the castle building was rendered uninhabitable and was finally demolished in 1674 by the Duke of Newcastle who then built his own palace on the site.

Today, that palace is home to the **Castle Museum and Art Gallery**. Some remains of the original castle still stand, most notably the 13th century gatehouse, though much restored, and parts of the moat and outer bailey are visible. The museum, when it was opened by the Prince of Wales in 1878, was the first municipal art gallery in the country outside London. Today, the collection is particularly noted for its fine selection of Victorian paintings. The museum also has an outstanding collection of silverware and ceramics.

Alongside the Castle Museum is the **Sherwood Foresters Regimental Museum,** which continues the castle's connections with the military. The regiment was first raised in 1741 and, among the many displays, there is an area dedicated to the Nottingham flying ace of World War I, Captain Albert Ball, VC. He died in 1917, at the age of 20, having shot down 43 enemy aircraft. A statue erected to his memory stands in the castle grounds.

At the base of Castle Rock lies the famous **Trip to Jerusalem Inn** where crusaders are said to have stopped for a pint before setting off on their long journey to the Holy Land. Dating back to around 1189, it claims to be the oldest pub in England, a claim hotly contested by other hostelries inclding another Nottingham hostelry Ye Olde Salutation Inn. Set back into the sandstone rock, the building was once the brewhouse for the castle and from here travellers to the Holy Land bought their ale. In the pub's cellars is **Mortimer's Hole**, a cave hewn out of the sandstone rock which leads to the castle. It is through this passageway that some two dozen conspirators crept to capture Roger de Mortimer, the lover of Queen Isabella. When her husband, Edward II was murdered, Isabella had allowed Mortimer to effectively rule in place of her 18-year-old son, Edward III. De Mortimer's presumption was later punished by death. Edward III was in the castle at the time of Mortimer's capture and is believed to have

known about, and encouraged, the plot.

Also at the base of Castle Rock and housed in a terrace of four 17th century cottages, is the **Brewhouse Yard Museum**. Depicting the life of the people of the city up to the 1990s, the museum has accurately furnished rooms as well as a series of reconstructions that includes a Victorian kitchen and shop window displays of the 1920s.

Just around the corner, the **Museum of Costume and Textiles** in Castle Gate contains a fine collection of costumes from 1790 to the mid-20th century, all displayed in period rooms. There are also many other exhibits on show including tapestries; knitted, woven and printed textiles; and fashion accessories through the ages. The museum is housed in a terrace of brick houses that was constructed in 1788 by Cornelius Launder, a former High Sheriff. Castle Gate is an interesting street in itself and well worth a second look. The entrance to the museum has one of the finest examples of an 18th century doorcase and fanlight to be seen in the area.

Further down Castle Gate is **Newdigate House,** built in a refined fashion in 1680 and distinguished by a wrought iron screen and gates dating from the early 1700s. The house now forms part of the United Services Club but between 1705 and 1711 it was the home of Marshal Tallard, commander of the defeated French army at the Battle of Blenheim in 1704.

Nearby, in Castle Road, is a charming medieval building that is home to the **Lace Centre**. As well as holding lace-making demonstrations, the Centre stocks a vast selection of high quality lace available for purchase. A remarkably well-preserved example of a timber framed house of around 1450, the building was moved from its original site on Middle Pavement in 1968. Continuing the textiles theme, not far away and set in the heart of Nottingham's historic and recently revitalised Lace Market, is the Lace Market Centre, occupying a restored chapel in High Pavement. Here the story of Nottingham's famous industry is told, from the days when it was a cottage craft through to mechanisation and the days of the great textile factories. Visitors can see some of the giant machines that produced the delicate material and also various types of lace being made.

Across the road from the Museum, in the impressive Shire Hall, the **Galleries of Justice** provides an unusual and interesting insight into justice 19th century style. 'Condemned', a major crime and punishment experience, allows visitors to put themselves in the place of an accused in the harsh days around 1833. Real trials are re-enacted in the imposing Courtroom where the hapless criminal faced the possibility of capital punishment or transportation to the New World. Their discomfort is made very real by the restored period settings.

Also in High Pavement is Nottingham's largest parish church, St Mary's, which is also probably the city's oldest as it appears to have been founded in Saxon times. However, today's church dates from the 15th century though there are some 19th and early 20th century additions which include windows by a series of renowned stained glass makers. Also inside is a Bishop's Throne carved in 1890 when it was thought that the church would become the cathedral for the diocese of Southwell.

A ARNOLD & SONS

33 Abbey Road, West Bridgford, Nottinghamshire NG2 5NG
Tel: 01159 811057
website: a-arnoldandsons.co.uk

A Arnold & Sons is a long-established family business raising its own meat and selling it through two retail outlets. Their beef cattle and pigs are raised on the farm and fed a diet of home-produced rations from home-grown crops, guaranteed hormone- and antibiotic-free. As well as prime joints and cuts, the shops sell home-cured bacon and hams, chickens, game, burgers, sausages (plain pork, Lincolnshire, pork & leek, pork with tomato & basil) and for the Christmas season geese and white and bronze turkeys are available. They can supply meat for barbecues and other get-togethers. West Bridgford is located a short drive south of Nottingham.

The other shop also sells fruit, vegetables and general groceries and is at 41 Main Road, Long Bennington, by the A1 south of Newark. Tel: 01400 281398

Another short walk brings visitors to the **Caves of Nottingham**, a popular attraction which lies beneath the Broadmarsh Centre, one of the city's major shopping precincts. The city is built on sandstone and throughout Nottingham's history the rock has been tunnelled to provide first shelter and then hiding places. More than 400 man-made caves run beneath the city streets. Now, thanks to local voluntary groups, these caves have been saved for future generations. The most spectacular cave in the system, the Pillar Cave, was carved out back in 1250 and contains remnants of the country's only underground tannery. The caves were commonly used as pub cellars: the constant temperature being ideal for the storage of beer and wine. More recently, they served as air raid shelters during the blitz of World War II and one of the caves has been left as a memorial to those desperate times.

Alan Sillitoe, the author of *Saturday Night and Sunday Morning*, was born in Nottingham in 1928 and for a while worked at the Raleigh Bicycle Factory.

Around Nottingham

WOLLATON
2 miles W of Nottingham on the A609

🏛 Wollaton Hall   🏛 Museum

Built in creamy white Ancaster stone, **Wollaton Hall** is one of the most attractive and elaborate Elizabethan mansions in the Midlands. Set in a spacious park, the house was built in the 1580s to the designs of Robert Smythson, who also designed Hardwick Hall in Derbyshire. His client was Francis Willoughby whose family had made a fortune from the local coal mines. The Elizabethan passion for symmetry is extravagantly displayed on the magnificent front façade with its matching classical columns, busts of philosophers and mythological characters, and flamboyant gables.

The building is also home to the **Natural History Museum** which is based on the collection of Francis Willoughby, a noted naturalist of the mid-1600s, while some of the Hall's outbuildings have been transformed into the Nottingham Industrial Museum where the city's major industries are all represented. The park surrounding the Hall is one of the city's great amenities. The 525 acres are contained within a seven-mile long wall, providing security for the

Wollaton Park

🏛 historic building   🏛 museum   🏛 historic site   🔱 scenic attraction   🌱 flora and fauna herds of deer that roam here as they have for more than 400 years.

BULWELL

3 miles N of Nottingham on the B682

Originally the whole area surrounding the village was covered by forest and it is probable that the settlement took its name from a spring in the old woodland. However, a local legend tells the story of the naming of the village rather differently. Apparently, an enraged bull gored a rock here and released a stream of sparkling spring water.

BESTWOOD

6 miles N of Nottingham off the A60

🜲 Country Park

Bestwood was a favourite hunting ground of Charles II who often stayed here with Nell Gwynne. One local story tells of a wager the king struck with Nell, saying she could have all the land she could ride around before breakfast. Nell, not known for being an early riser, made an exception on this occasion. The next morning, she rose at dawn and rode around the countryside dropping handkerchiefs along the way. Arriving back before breakfast, Nell claimed her winnings and Charles kept his side of the bargain. Whether or not the story is true, the king certainly gave Nell substantial landholdings in the area.

Part of the old royal hunting park is now **Bestwood Country Park** whose 450 acres offer many differing landscapes. Here you'll also find the Bestwood Pumping Station, erected in the early 1870s. The Duke only gave his permission for it to be built after the architect solemnly promised that it would look nothing like a pumping station. With its 150ft tower, cooling pond disguised as an ornamental lake, and surrounded by beautifully maintained gardens, the station certainly lives up to the architect's promise.

SNEINTON

1 mile E of Nottingham on the A612

🏠 Windmill 🜲 William Booth Birthplace Museum

Sneinton's main claim to fame is as the birthplace, in 1829, of William Booth, the founder of the Salvation Army. The small terraced house where he and his family lived until 1831 is still standing in Notintone Place, fronted now by a statue of the great man. The family home has become the **William Booth Birthplace Museum**: entry to the house is by appointment only.

After his father's early death, Booth's mother was forced to move to Goosegate, Nottingham where she ran a shop selling toys and sewing materials and it was while living in this deprived area that Booth first became aware of the appalling conditions in

Green's Windmill, Sneinton

🎞 stories and anecdotes 🐦 famous people 🎨 art and craft 🌿 entertainment and sport 🜲 walks which the urban working classes lived. He was only 16 when he gave his first sermon in a house in Kid.

In 1849, Booth left Nottingham for London where he became a Methodist minister. But, finding the church structures too constraining, he established, in 1865, the Christian Missions which, in 1878, was renamed the Salvation Army. During the next 10 years, the movement spread to all corners of the world, including America, Australia and South Africa. The Army is still mobilised, with more than 1,000 local corps in the UK involved in both social and evangelistic work. Its missing persons bureau traces anything up to 5,000 people each year.

In Windmill Lane, Steinton, **Green's Windmill** is a Grade II listed working windmill that produces its own organic flour. It is the only inner city windmill in the UK and was once the home of the 19th century mathematician George Green.

HOLME PIERREPONT
3 miles E of Nottingham off the A52

🏛 Holme Pierrepont Hall

🏞 National Water Sports Centre

Although Holme has been in the hands of the Pierrepont family since 1284, the present **Holme Pierrepont Hall** dates from the early 1500s and is regarded as one of the best examples of a brick built house in the county. Opening times are restricted but the hall is well worth a visit. Some of the ground floor rooms have been restored to their original state and furnished in the style of the early 17th century, and the Upper Lodging still has superb ceiling timbers dating from the 1400s. There are two Victorian bedrooms with four-poster beds, one with its original William Morris fabrics. Refreshments are available in

the Long Gallery with its walnut furniture and family portraits gazing down from the walls. Outside, the Charles II Grand Staircase leads down to a formal Courtyard Garden with an elaborate parterre, created around 1875, and in the park Jacob sheep graze peacefully.

These days, Holme Pierrepont is more widely known as the home of the **National Water Sports Centre**. Built to Olympic standards, the Centre boasts a full size rowing course and a wild water slalom course, all man-made from the pasture and quarries which once dominated the area.

BEESTON
3 miles SW of Nottingham off the A52

🏛 Boots the Chemist

Lying on the southwest outskirts of Nottingham, Beeston is famous as the home of **Boots the Chemist**. Jesse Boot was born in 1850 and left school at the age of 13 to work in his mother's herbalist shop in the centre of Nottingham. She had started the business to supplement her husband's meagre income as a farm labourer. Following his death, when Jesse was only 10 years old, the shop became the mainstay of the family. Jesse quickly learnt the trade and in 1888 he set up the Boots Pure Drug Company.

In a business where quacks and charlatans abounded, Boot's emphasis on the purity of his drugs and medicines (and his competitive prices) attracted customers everywhere and by 1896 the company had a chain of over 60 shops. It was at his wife's suggestion that Jesse expanded the lines in the shops to include jewellery, stationery, books and art. In 1920 the business was sold to an American company only to be bought back by Jesse's son during the depression in 1933. A great benefactor to the city and surrounding area,

Jesse was knighted in 1903, created a baronet in 1917, and finally raised to the peerage as Lord Trent in 1929, two years before his death.

STAPLEFORD
4 miles SW of Nottingham off the A52

🏛 Hemlockstone

In Stapleford churchyard can be found the best preserved Saxon carving in the county in the form of a 10ft cross shaft. Dating from the late 11th century, the intricate carving depicts an eagle standing on a serpent - said to be the symbol of St Luke, the physician. The church, which dates mainly from the 13th and 14th centuries, has many war memorials to lost heroes. The village was once a thriving centre for framework knitting and terraced cottages built specifically for the workers can

Saxon Cross, Stapleford

still be seen in Nottingham Road.

One other feature of Stapleford worthy of a look is the **Hemlockstone,** a massive redstone boulder standing 30 feet high and weighing around 200 tons situated opposite Bramcote Park. Geologists believe the rock was probably deposited here by glacial action, while wind erosion has contributed to its brooding appearance. Its geological make up consists of sandstone, cemented by the mineral barite which is found in large quantities throughout the Stapleford and Bramcote Hills.

The village school was renamed the Arthur Mee Centre in memory of the writer who grew up in the town and was educated at the school. Born in 1875, Mee left school at 14 to work for the *Nottingham Evening Post* before moving to London and finding his niche writing for children. His works include the *Children's Bible*, the *Children's Encyclopaedia*, and the *Children's Shakespeare* but it is probably for *The King's England*, a series of guide books that ran to some 80 volumes, that Mee is best remembered.

CLIFTON
4 miles S of Nottingham on the A453

🚶 Clifton Grove

At first sight this village near the River Trent seems swamped by modern development but the character of the old village can be found in and around the green. The manor of Clifton was held by the family of that name from the 13th century up until 1953 when they gave up the hall to what is now Nottingham Trent University.

Along the banks of the River Trent is **Clifton Grove**, a wooded cliff above the riverbank, where visitors can stroll in the footsteps of Paul Morel and Clare Dawes, characters in DH Lawrence's *Sons and Lovers*. This stretch of the River Trent was also the setting for a tragic love story. In 1471, a young squire called Henry Bateman went to the Crusades with his master. When he returned, he discovered that his sweetheart Margaret had fallen for another man and married him. The heartbroken lover threw himself into the Trent from Clifton Grove. Some time later, Margaret herself took the same way out, presumably in remorse.

Ruddington

🏛 Museums

This historic village, whose name is derived from the Saxon word Rudda - meaning headman - was once the home of many hosiery workers and several of their cottages still remain. In 1829, a factory and frameworkers cottages were built around a courtyard in Chapel Street. Later, a school was built and this is now occupied by the **Ruddington Framework Knitters' Museum** which depicts community life through several reconstructed shops and an Edwardian schoolroom. Of the 25 hand frames seen here today, most are fully operational and there is an opportunity to buy samples made at the museum.

The industry reached its height in 1880, with the staggering number of 20,000 frames operating in Nottingham, Derbyshire and Lincolnshire. As well as the knitting frames on show, the museum also has other machinery of specific importance to the village and to the hosiery industry. Regular demonstrations are given using the working exhibits. Visitors can try out their own weaving skills on one of the collection of circular sock machines.

Not far away is the **Ruddington Village**

Museum, housed in the old village school building of 1852. Concentrating on the everyday life of the villagers, the museum has reconstructions of several shops and craftsmen's workshops including an Edwardian fish and chip shop. As well as having one of the school rooms restored to look as it once did, there is also a room devoted to a collection of farming implements.

Around Ruddington

GOTHAM
3 miles SW of Ruddington off the A453

The name is actually pronounced 'Goat'm' and the village should not be confused with the home of the caped crusader, Batman. However, the village is remembered as the home of the Wise Men. King John had decreed that he wished to build a hunting lodge here in the village. Naturally displeased at having to give up their land to the king's whims, the villagers devised a plan. They decided that the best way to dissuade the royal presence was to feign madness. When the king's messengers entered the village, the inhabitants reacted in such a peculiar way that the men returned to His Majesty with the suggestion that the mad men of Gotham should be left well alone. Such were the odd tales of their bizarre acts that Dr Andrew Borde published the *Merrie Tales of the Mad Men of Gotham* in the 16th century. There are many bizarre stories but one of the finest is kept alive in the name of the village pub - The Cuckoo Bush. A group of villagers, captivated by the song of a cuckoo, decided to capture the bird by encircling the bush in which it was sitting by a fence. Unfortunately, the men did not think to build a roof so the cuckoo simply flew away.

RATCLIFFE ON SOAR
6 miles SW of Ruddington off the A453

The tiny village of Ratcliffe on Soar has a pretty little church, with an eye-catching blackened spire, and a handsome manor farmhouse set picturesquely on the meadow banks of the River Soar. Although a massive power station looms over everything and the railway clatters by, this charming village is still definitely worth a visit.

EAST LEAKE
4 miles S of Ruddington off the A60

Like its neighbour, West Leake, the village name is derived from the Anglo-Saxon word Leche, meaning water meadow, and both villages lie on the banks of a tributary of the River Soar. The village church, which was mentioned in the Domesday Survey of 1086, was extensively restored in the 19th century but has retained its prize possession, a Vamp Horn or shawm. This extraordinary instrument is some eight feet long and only five others are known to exist. Invented in 1670 by Samuel Morland, the horn was used by the bass singer to lead the choir from the gallery.

STANTON ON THE WOLDS
4 miles SE of Ruddington off the A606

This rural village, which was until the 1960s home to seven dairy farms, has few really old buildings though the village dates back to Norman times. In the late 18th century, Stanton was hit by a freak storm in which giant hailstones rained down on the cottages and smashed their roofs. The ancient village Church of All Saints did, however, survive and can be found standing alone in a field,

reached by a footpath. Dating from the 11th century, the church, one of the smallest in south Nottinghamshire, is built mostly of boulders some of which, undoubtedly, were purloined from the nearby Fosse Way.

BUNNY
2 miles S of Ruddington on the A60

This pretty village has a wealth of lovely architecture and owes much of its charm to the eccentricities of its one-time squire, Sir Thomas Parkyns (1663-1741). A man obsessed with the sport of wrestling, Sir Thomas employed two full-time professionals to spar with him at Bunny Hall. He also organised an annual tournament in the village to promote local wrestling talent and this event continued for nearly 70 years after his death. In St Mary's Church, which was designed by Sir Thomas, his memorial graphically illustrates his commitment to the sport. It depicts the squire standing victorious over his defeated opponent on a wrestling mat, while Old Father Time stands by, perhaps as referee.

Another of Sir Thomas' hobbies was collecting stone coffins which he provided free to those of his tenants in need of one. During his long lifetime he rebuilt much of the village to his own designs, provided a school, gave his tenants free medical and legal advice and also found time to write a Latin Grammar and a book on wrestling, *Cornish Hugg Wrestling*.

KEYWORTH
3 miles E of Ruddington off the A606

In the heart of south Nottinghamshire's farming country this, until very recently, small village prides itself on having produced no fewer than 30 professional cricketers, one of whom went on to be capped for England.

THREADS

2c Main Street, Keyworth,
Nottinghamshire NG12 5AD
Tel: 0115 937 6010

Threads is located on the quaint village square of
Keyworth, in the heart of Nottinghamshire's farming
country. The village is known for the number of
professional cricketers it has produced, but anyone with
an interest in sewing and knitting will be bowled over by a
visit to this very special place. Owner Sheila Grudzinski
and her assistants have created a very friendly, relaxed
ambience in which customers shop for an amazing selection of
threads, yarns, wools, cottons, zips, needles, ribbons, buttons, bows
and patterns from across the world – everything, in short, for sewing
and knitting. And if it's not in stock, they'll do their very best to
order it as quickly as possible.

Threads also stocks a small boutique range of children's and
ladies' clothes and kits for beading and jewellery. Shop hours are
9am to 5.30pm Monday, Tuesday and Friday, 9am to 5pm
Wednesday, Thursday and Saturday. Once a fortnight, Sheila holds
classes in the village hall – informal but informative sessions which
she calls 'Knit, Stitch and Natter' evenings.

THE GEOLOGY SHOP

The British Geological Survey, Keyworth, Notts. NG12 5GG
Main tel: 01159 363100 Shop tel: 01159 363581
website: www.bgs.ac.uk Online Shop: www.geologyshop.com

The Geology Shop is part of the British Geological Survey, which
was founded in 1835 and is presently located in the village of
Keyworth. The Geology Shop deals with the oldest materials in
Britain - the rocks that shape and give character to the country's
varied landscapes. An incredibly wide range of objects can be
crafted from rocks and minerals, and in the Geology Shop you'll find
some stunning gift ideas - onyx, agate and soapstone ornaments,
bookends, candle-holders, paperweights, bowls and
vases.Jewellery, of course, makes brilliant use of precious stones,
so the display includes classic jewellery featuring amethyst, topaz,
opal, amber and jade, and there is designer jewellery from Hot
Diamonds, Silver Willow, Java and Goldmajor.

The shop also features fascinating fossils such as ammonites,
trilobites and prehistoric fish along with fabulous natural minerals and
crystals – amazing amethyst and citrine cathedrals and exotic natural
minerals for collectors as well as fun packs for kids. Geologists and
students will find a wide range of specialist geological maps, books
and reports, and the shop also stocks a comprehensive range of
Ordnance Survey maps, guides, compasses, pedometers, map measurers, map cases and much
more. The Geology Shop is open Monday to Friday (excluding national holidays) from 8.30am to
5pm and there is free on-site parking through the security barrier.

🏛 historic building   📷 museum   🏛 historic site   🏞 scenic attraction   🌱 flora and fauna

The village too has had its share of scandals and one local legend tells of a tenant farmer who was visited by the rector who had a complaint to discuss. The farmer was not very agreeable to the criticism and soundly horse-whipped the clergyman before sending him on his way. This whip is still in existence though the nature of the complaint the rector was making is unknown.

Southwell

Southwell is undoubtedly one of England's most beguiling towns, miraculously preserved from developers and with scarcely an ugly building to be seen. From whichever direction you approach, it is the twin towers of **Southwell Minster** that first catch the eye. With their pyramidal 'Rhenish Caps', these towers are unique in this country although they would look perfectly in place anywhere in the Rhineland.

James VI of Scotland was mightily impressed by Southwell when he passed through the town in 1603 en route to his coronation as James I: "By my blude," he is said to have exclaimed, "this kirk shall justle with York or Durham or any other kirk in Christendom."

Perhaps the least well-known of English cathedrals, Southwell's history goes back to 956 when Oskytel, Archbishop of York,

THE HEN HOUSE

1 Bull Yard, off King Street, Southwell,
Nottinghamshire NG25 0EH
Tel/Fax: 01636 812855
e-mail: info@henhouseinteriors.co.uk
website: www.henhouseinteriors.co.uk

Since 2001 Jo Hetherington has run **The Hen House** in premises just off King Street in the delightful minster town of Southwell. This is *the* place to come for an impressive range of interior design and decorative items to enrich a house or garden, or to find the perfect gift for any occasion. Bright, practical Danish design-led products include quilts, cushions, tea towels, aprons, bath mats and storage boxes, tins and jars of all sizes; there are lovely fabrics in linen and cotton by Vanessa Arbuthnott and Kate Forman; pottery from Gabriella Miller; handpainted children's mugs; basketware; stoneware; lovely scented French soaps; Teresa Green purses; antique and vintage chairs, stools and other pieces of furniture; and all kinds of antiques and collectables.

Jo and her well-trained staff are always ready with help and advice at the Hen House, which is open all day Monday to Saturday. Customers can also order online through the excellent website.
Opening hours: 10am to 5pm.

Southwell Minster

"Other churches may be older, a few may be larger, but none are more beautiful".

There is no space here to detail all the cathedral's other treasures but the striking eagle lectern in the choir has an interesting story attached to it. The lectern was originally installed at Newstead Abbey. However, during the widespread looting at the time of the Dissolution of the Monasteries, the monks threw the lectern into the lake, intending to retrieve it later. Later turned out to be 200 years later, in 1750 in fact. Half a century after that, the 5th Lord Byron presented the lectern to the Minster.

The Minster stands in a delightful precinct, surrounded by attractive buildings. To the south stand the ruins of the palace of the archbishops of York built in the 14th and 15th centuries. Parts of the old palace, closest to the minster's south doorway, have been incorporated into the present Bishop's Palace.

established a church here. The present building was erected in three phases. The nave, transept and western towers are the oldest parts, completed around 1150; the east end was built around 1240, and the superb Chapter House around 1290.

Octagonal in design, the Chapter House has been hailed as the pinnacle of the Decorated period of architecture - "among chapter houses as the rose among flowers". The architectural historian, Nikolaus Pevsner devoted a whole book, *The Leaves of Southwell*, to the incredible wealth of stone carvings of foliage decorating the arcades above the Canons' seats.

The word most often applied to the cathedral is "serene" and, as one visitor put it,

At the east end of the minster is **Vicar's Court,** a charming group of five Queen Anne houses built for the Vicars Choral around 1702. Just across the road from the Minster is a picturesque old coaching inn, the 16th century Saracen's Head. Charles I spent his last hours of freedom before his final surrender in this delightful half-timbered building. At that time, the inn was known as the King's Head: the name was changed after Charles was beheaded.

Just to the north of the Saracen's Head is Burgage Manor, a handsome Georgian pile where the young Lord Byron stayed with his mother between 1803 and 1807 while on holiday from Harrow and Cambridge. He joined the local theatrical group and it was his friends in the town who encouraged him to publish his first set of poems. Under the title *Hours of Idleness*, the book was published by Ridges of Newark and brought great acclaim to the young poet. **The Workhouse** in Upton Road is the only 19th century workhouse in existence offering visitors the opportunity to explore the building and its history, the segregated work yards, dayrooms, dormitories, master's quarters and cellars. Tel: 01636 817250.

Southwell can also be credited as the birthplace of the Bramley apple. The story goes that in the early 19th century, two ladies planted some apple pips in their cottage garden in the nearby village of Easthorpe. Nature took its course and one of the seedlings grew into a tree. By this time, Matthew Bramley owned the cottage and the quality of the tree's fruit began to excite public interest.

Mr Henry Merryweather, a local nurseryman, persuaded Bramley to let him take a cutting, which he consequently propagated with enormous success. Permission had been granted on the condition that the apples took Mr Bramley's name and not the two ladies'! The **Bramley Apple Exhibition** in Halam Road explains the full history and development of this famous fruit. While in the town, visitors should also look out for a Southwell Galette, a scrumptious pastry confection of hazelnuts, sultanas, and, of course, Bramley apples.

The disused railway line from Southwell to Mansfield, opened in 1871, is now an attractive footpath known as the **Farnsfield to Southwell Trail**. As well as the varied plant and wildlife that can be found along the 4½ mile walk, there is also plenty of industrial archaeological interest including the Farnsfield

Waterworks of 1910, a late 18th century cotton mill, and Greet Lily Mill, a corn mill on the banks of the River Greet.

Norwood Park is the only one of the four original parks around Southwell that remains today. The property of the Archbishops of York, the park remained in the possession of the Church until 1778. A house was built here in Cromwell's day but the present building dates from 1763. Open to visitors during the summer months, the house has a very lived-in feel. The surrounding parkland was laid out in the 18th century at the same time as the ice house and temple were built, and the lime avenue planted. Southwell has a racecourse that stages racing throughout the year, most of it flat racing on an all-weather surface.

Around Southwell

KIRKLINGTON
3 miles NW of Southwell on the A617

Kirklington's church is partly Norman and anyone venturing inside will see that the pulpit has some small holes in its side that have been plugged with more recent wood. The explanation for this odd feature is that in the early 1800s, Kirklington's sporting rector would use the pulpit as a portable screen when he went duck shooting. He would fire at the ducks through the holes in the pulpit's sides.

CAUNTON
7 miles NE of Southwell off the A616

The village Church of St Andrew was rebuilt by the Normans at the beginning of the 13th century but by the 1800s the building had fallen into such a state of disrepair that the altar, a wooden box, was only used as a resting place for the hat and gloves of visiting curates.

GONALSTON FARM SHOP

Southwell Road, Gonalston,
Nottinghamshire NG14 7DR
Tel: 0115 9665 666
e-mail: info@gonalstonfarmshop.co.uk
website: www.gonalstonfarmshop.co.uk

A warm welcome and a feast of culinary delights await visitors to **Gonalston Farm Shop**, which stands between Lowdham and Gonalston on the A612 Nottingham-Southwell road. Opened in 2003 by Georgina (George) and Ross Mason, it is recognised as one of the finest in its field in the county. The majority of the produce on sale is local, and pride of place goes to the extended meat counter with its impressive selection of cuts and joints.

The farm is coupled with Riverlands Farm in Gunthorpe village, and both specialise in producing high-quality cattle from their own pastures in the Trent Valley. The beef is hung for a minimum of 21 days to develop the full flavours. Almost all the meat is locally sourced, including lamb from nearby Shelford and pork from Arnold, thus fully traceable, with food miles kept to a minimum. Over 30 varieties of sausage are made on the premises, some of which have won the Great Taste Awards in London – the Oscars of the food industry. Other meat products include Parma hams, salami, pork and game pies, marmalade-glazed hams and Gold Award ox tongues. The new fresh fish counter sells wet fish, shellfish and smoked fish from Wednesday to Sunday.

The farm shop and delicatessen are filled with a wonderful array of fresh fruit and vegetables, 100 different cheese's, pickles and chutneys, herbs and spices, ice creams from Thaymar of Retford, hand-made cakes and pastries, beer, cider and wine, cards, gift wrap, gift vouchers and hampers made up to order for any occasion. Awards and accolades came quickly to Gonalston Farm Shop, winning the Best Newcomer Award from the National Farmers' Retail and Markets Association, and other recognition has assured that George and Ross, the fourth generation of the Mason family to be involved in livestock farming and butchery, are officially Food Heroes and not just farmers; another sign of their success is that the shop has almost doubled in size for 2007. The customer always comes first, and excellent relations are strengthened by loyalty cards, comments cards, newsletters and regular events and tastings. Summer opening hours are 9 to 7 Tuesday to Friday, 9 to 6 Saturday and 10 to 4 Sunday and Bank Holidays; Winter opening hours are 9 to 6 Tuesday to Thursday, 9 to 7 Friday, 9 to 6 Saturday and 10 to 4 Sunday. Look at the excellent website for events and e-sales.

HALL FARM HOUSE

Gonalston, nr Southwell, Nottinghamshire NG14 7JA
Tel: 0115 966 3112

Ronald and Rosemary Smith have lived here at their 17th century farmhouse for more than 50 years and since 1990 they have been providing comfortable, civilised Bed & Breakfast accommodation. The three guest rooms – a double, a twin and a family room – are tastefully decorated and furnished in keeping with the age of the building, and guests have the use of a games room and the lovely garden with an outdoor pool and tennis court. An Aga-cooked breakfast is served in the farmhouse kitchen. Ronald and Rosemary have created a particularly warm, friendly and informal ambience at Hall Farm, with a little help from their lovely briard, Sasha. The farm lies just off the A612 Nottingham- Newark road.

Restored in 1869, the church contains many monuments to the Hole family, Lords of the Manor here since Elizabethan times.

The best known member of the Hole family was Samuel Reynolds Hole who became known as the Rose King - a title bestowed on him by Tennyson. Before becoming Dean of Rochester, Hole lived at Caunton Manor as the squire and vicar and it was here that he began his extensive study of roses. By 1851, Samuel recorded that he possessed over 1,000 rose trees in more than 400 varieties, a collection which was to make him the most famous amateur rose grower of all.

UPTON

2 miles E of Southwell on the A612

🏛 National Exhibition of Time

Upton boasts a couple of very good pubs and its nine-pinnacled church is worthy of a visit too. A famous son of the village was James Tenant, the man who cut the world-renowned Koh-I-Noor diamond. But perhaps the most impressive building here is Upton Hall, a stylish Grecian villa with a central dome and elegant colonnade, built in the early 1800s. The hall is now the headquarters of the British Horological Institute and, inside,

visitors can see the **National Exhibition of Time** - a fascinating display of clocks, watches, and other horological pieces.

ROLLESTON

3 miles E of Southwell off the A617

🏛 Church

Holy Trinity Church is certainly one of the county's finest churches and is also the source of a great treasure: a portion of the original paper register covering the years 1584 to 1615. An interesting and historic document completed by the vicar of the time, Robert Leband, it gives the local gossip as well as the price of corn and notes of local events. A curiosity in the church is a fragment of a Saxon cross, built into the wall and scratched with the words 'Radulfus Me Fe' (Radulfus made me). It is one of very few surviving Saxon works in England to bear its author's signature.

EAST BRIDGFORD

7 miles S of Southwell off the A6097

The village is situated on a ridge overlooking a crossing of the River Trent and the edge of Sherwood Forest beyond. The village Church of St Peter is believed to stand on one of the earliest Christian sites in Nottinghamshire.

There was already a church here in the 9th century since it is known to have been plundered by the Danes when they came up the river to Nottingham.

SHELFORD
8 miles S of Southwell off the A6097

The name Shelford means the place of the shallow ford so, presumably, there was once a ford here across the River Trent which flows in a horseshoe bend around the village. Though now a quiet and tranquil place, in the winter of 1644, Shelford was the site of a particularly fierce battle. Royalist soldiers, taking shelter in the church tower, were smoked out by the Parliamentarian army who set fire to straw at the tower's base. During the same weekend, some 140 men were slaughtered by Cromwell's men at the manor house which was subsequently burnt to the ground.

The Royalist troops were commanded by Shelford's Lord of the Manor, Philip Stanhope, a member of the illustrious family who later became Earls of Chesterfield. There are some fine memorials to the Stanhopes in the village church, including one by Nollekens.

OXTON
4 miles SW of Southwell on the B6386

🏛 Oldox Camp

A charming village near the edge of Sherwood Forest and surrounded by parkland, Oxton has a goodly number of 17th and 18th century houses and cottages. The Sherbrooke family have been the lords of the manor here since the 16th century and Oxton still retains the feel of an estate village even though the hall was demolished in 1957. An oddity is to be found in a yard opposite the Green Dragon Inn. Here stands the tomb of Robert Sherbrooke who died in 1710. The unusual location is explained by the fact that Sherbrooke was a Quaker and this was the site of their meeting house.

The uncovering of **Oldox Camp**, one of the largest and best preserved Iron Age hill forts in Nottinghamshire, to the north of the village suggests that this was the original site of Oxton. Extending over some three acres, the fort is surrounded by a single ditch and bank, except at the entrance to the fort where the defences are doubled.

CALVERTON
6 miles SW of Southwell off the B6386

🌱 Patchings

The charming cottages in this industrial village date back to the early 19th century and were once the homes of framework knitters. Carefully restored by the Nottinghamshire Building Preservation Trust, the cottages originally formed three sides of a rectangle, though one side is now missing. Unusually, the large windows which provided the light for the knitters are found on the ground floor instead of the more usual upper storey.

It was a curate of Calverton, William Lee, who invented the stocking knitting frame in 1589. According to an old story, his invention was the result of an unsuccessful love affair. Whenever William visited the girl he wanted to marry she "always took care to be busily employed in knitting…He vowed to devote his further leisure to devising an invention that should effectually supersede her favourite employment of knitting". Lee succeeded in creating an immensely complicated machine that could produce top quality work between 10 and 15 times as quickly as the fastest hand knitters. To develop it further he sought the patronage of Elizabeth I but the queen refused to encourage something that would mean great job losses for her loyal subjects.

After being refused a patent by Elizabeth I, Lee travelled to France and gained the promise of support from Henry of Navarre. Unfortunately, Henry was assassinated before any promises were made good and it is believed that Lee died in Paris in 1610. Lee's brother, James, brought the frame back to London where the hosiery industry first developed before it settled in the Midlands later in the 17th century.

Also at Calverton is **Patchings,** formerly known as Painters' Paradise, a series of gardens that have been designed with the artist in mind. Here, amongst the rolling hills of north Nottinghamshire, is a perfect reconstruction of Claude Monet's garden at Giverney, complete with the elegant little bridge and the pool of water lilies that he painted so often. Attractive gazebo studios are dotted around the 50 acres of grounds, each designed to provide a picturesque view. An impressive building of Norwegian spruce – one of the largest wooden structures in England – offers further facilities for artists and visitors: studios, workshop and dark room as well as a licensed restaurant.

Newark-on-Trent

🏯 White Hart Inn   🏯 Town Hall   🏯 Castle

🏯 Church   🏯 Henrietta Maria's Lodgings

🏯 Governor's House   🏛 Folk Museum

🏛 Air Museum   🏚 Beacon Hill

John Wesley considered Newark one of the most elegant towns in England; more recently the Council for British Archaeology included it in their list of the best 50 towns in the country; and in 1968 Newark town centre was designated as one of the first Conservation Areas. Its medieval street plan remains intact, complete with a fine market square which is still busy every day of the week, except Tuesdays, with a market of one kind or another - plus a Farmers' Market once a month. Newark has become firmly established as one of the most important centers in Europe for the antiques trade, and together with Swinderby hosts the biggest European Antiques Fair every two months. The town also has long musical connections. The composer John Blow, who was born in the town in 1649, taught Henry Purcell and held major positions at Westminster Abbey and St Paul's Cathedral. Newark and Sherwood College's International School of Violin Making is now one of the world's top violin schools and attracts students from all over the world.

The square is lined with handsome houses and inns. The most remarkable of them is the 14th century former **White Hart Inn** (now a building society/estate agent), which has a magnificent frontage adorned with 24 plaster figures of angels and saints. Close by are the Saracen's Head where Sir Walter Scott often stayed, and the Clinton Arms, the preferred lodging of WE Gladstone during his 14 years as Newark's Member of Parliament.

Dominating one side of the square is the noble Georgian **Town Hall**, built in 1777 and recently fully restored. It now houses the town's civic plate and regalia, and an art gallery displaying works by Stanley Spencer, William Nicholson and notable local artists.

The grandest building of all is the **Church of St Mary Magdalene**, by common consent the finest parish church in the county. Its slender, elegant spire soars above the town and serves as a landmark for miles along the Trent Valley. The church dates back to the

🎦 stories and anecdotes   🐦 famous people   🎨 art and craft   🐚 entertainment and sport   👣 walks

River Trent

of their major arterial roads, Fosse Way, passes close by on its way to Lincoln. Saxons and Danes continued the settlement, the latter leaving a legacy of street names ending in 'gate', from *gata*, the Danish word for street.

When the Normans arrived, they replaced the wooden **Castle** with one of stone. The present building is mostly 12th century and for some 300 years it was owned by the powerful Bishops of Lincoln. Then in 1483, ownership of the castle was transferred to the Crown and leased out to a succession of noblemen.

early 12th century though all that survives of that structure is the crypt which now houses the treasury. Much of the building seen today dates from the 14th, 15th and 16th centuries and its exterior is a fascinating blend of carvings and tracery. The interior is spacious and airy, and the treasures on display include a huge brass commemorating Alan Fleming, a Newark merchant who died in 1373; a dazzling Comper reredos of 1937; a splendid east window depicting Mary Magdalene; a Victorian mosaic reproducing Van Eyck's *Adoration of the Lamb*; and fragments of a painted Dance of Death from around 1500.

Newark's recorded history goes back to Roman times when the legionaries established a base here to guard the first upstream crossing of the River Trent. One

The castle's most glorious days occurred during the Civil War. The people of Newark were fiercely loyal to Charles I and endured three separate sieges before finally surrendering to Cromwell's troops. Parliament ordered the 'slighting' of the castle, rendering it militarily useless, but left the demolition work to the townspeople. Understandably, they showed little enthusiasm for the task of demolishing the 8ft thick walls. As a result, the ruins are quite substantial, especially the mighty gateway that Pevsner called "the biggest and most elaborate of its period (1170-75) in England". It was here that King John, devastated by the loss of his treasure while crossing the Wash, came to die in 1216. The castle crypt and an intimidating beehive dungeon have also survived. Guided tours of the castle (and the town) are available and its history is colourfully interpreted at the Gilstrap Centre. This lies within the Castle Grounds which, with its gardens and Victorian bandstand, is a popular venue for special events as well as a pleasant spot for a picnic.

Newark Air Museum

Newark possesses several other reminders of the Civil War. As a defensive measure, two small forts were built to guard this strategic crossing over the River Trent. The King's Sconce, to the northeast, has since disappeared but its twin, the Queen's Sconce, still lies to the southeast. Named after Queen Henrietta Maria, who brought supplies into the town after the first siege in 1643, this square earthwork has a bastion in each corner and a hollow in the middle.

stories and anecdotes   famous people   art and craft   entertainment and sport   walks

In the town centre, on Kirk Gate, are **Henrietta Maria's Lodgings** where, according to tradition, the queen stayed in 1643. Travelling from Bridlington to the king's headquarters at Oxford, the queen was bringing with her men and arms from the continent. She had paid for them by selling off some of the Crown Jewels.

Nearby is the **Governor's House**, where the governors of Newark lived during the Civil War and where Charles I quarrelled with Prince Rupert after the prince had lost Bristol to Parliament. This wonderful timber framed building was restored in the late 19th century and during the work a medieval wall and some beam paintings were revealed along with graffiti dating from 1757. Occupying a former riverside warehouse, the **Millgate Folk Museum** concentrates on everyday life in the 19th and 20th centuries. The exhibits include an interesting array of shops and shop fronts, and there is also a reconstruction of an early 20th century terraced house. The Mezzanine Gallery within the museum hosts temporary exhibitions featuring the work of local artists, designers and photographers.

On the outskirts of the town, at **Beacon Hill**, one of the greatest victories over the Roundheads took place, in 1644, when Prince Rupert arrived to lift the second of Newark's sieges. Under Sir John Meldrum, the Parliamentarians lost more arms and equipment than during any other engagement of the Civil War.

Just east of the town, close to the A1, lies the **Newark Air Museum**, one of the largest privately managed collections in the country. Opened in the 1960s, the museum has more than 50 aircraft and cockpit sections on display. Visitors can see jet fighters, bombers, and helicopters which span the history of aviation as well as a great deal of aviation memorabilia, relics and uniforms on display in the Exhibition Hall.

Around Newark-on-Trent

CROMWELL
5 miles N of Newark off the A1

🏛 Museum of Dolls and Bygone Childhood

The large 17th century rectory in the village is now home to the **Vina Cooke Museum of Dolls and Bygone Childhood**. Appealing to adults and children alike, there are all manner of children's toys on display but perhaps the most fascinating are the handmade dolls depicting royalty, stars of stage and screen, and famous historical characters. Vina Cooke, a well-known doll artist, exhibits her own handmade dolls here.

SUTTON ON TRENT
7 miles N of Newark off the B1164

🏛 Mering Chapel

One of the largest Trentside villages, Sutton was once famous for basket-making, fishermen's baskets in particular. It has a fine church, first established in Saxon times and noted for its Mering Chapel. Dating from the early 1500s, the chapel was brought here from the village of Mering on the other side of the Trent. Mering has since vanished completely into the watery lowlands surrounding the Trent. The superb **Mering Chapel,** however, contains a distinguished memorial in Purbeck marble to Sir William Mering. The tomb is separated from the aisle by a very rare oak screen crafted around 1510. Sir William's family, like his village, is extinct.

🏛 historic building 🏛 museum 🏛 historic site 🐾 scenic attraction 🌿 flora and fauna

SOUTH CLIFTON
9 miles N of Newark off the A1133

This pleasant village along the banks of the River Trent still has the remains of an old wharf where the coal from Derbyshire and Yorkshire was unloaded before being distributed throughout the surrounding area. The river here is still much used though the local fishermen now have to contend with water-skiers travelling up and down. On the village green stands a young oak tree, planted in 1981, along with a plaque commemorating the achievements of a local farmer, Dusty Hare, who has lived in the parish all his life and scored the highest number (7,000) of points in Rugby Union Football and was honoured with an MBE in 1989.

NORTH CLIFTON
10 miles N of Newark off the A1133

♣ Japanese Garden

The village, like its neighbour South Clifton, also lies on the east side of the Trent, close to the border with Lincolnshire. The two villages are, however, quite separate, but they share the same church, dedicated to St George the Martyr, which lies between them and has an imposing 15th century tower.

An unusual attraction here is the **Pure Land Meditation Centre and Japanese Garden**, which offers a haven of peace for all ages who wish to come and experience the benefits of relaxation and meditation. Buddha Maitreya, a former Zen monk from Japan, offers tuition in meditation to individuals and groups, and has devoted 25 years to creating the delightful Japanese garden with its large central pond, bridges, and a small pagoda where visitors can relax and meditate amidst an abundance of

flourishing plants and trees. The garden is open every afternoon, except Mondays, between April and October.

THORNEY
11 miles N of Newark off the A57

In 1805, this once peaceful little village was the site of a dreadful murder. A local labourer, Thomas Temporell, also known locally as Tom Otter, was forced to marry a local girl whom, it was claimed, he had made pregnant. Tom was so upset by the accusations and the enforced marriage that, in a frenzy, he murdered his bride on their wedding night. The story goes that he then took her body and left it on the steps of a public house in Saxilby, Lincolnshire. Caught and tried, Tom was sentenced to death with the extra penalty of gibbeting (the practice of hanging the offender's body in chains at the scene of their crime).

Small though it is, Thorney possesses a huge and magnificent church, built in 1849 by the Nevile family of nearby Thorney Hall (now demolished). Constructed in the Norman style, the church contains a wealth of superb stone carvings, both inside and out. Among them are no fewer than 17 fearsome dragons' heads.

TUXFORD
12 miles NW of Newark off the A1

This pleasant little town used to have its own market and, because of its position on the Great North Road, prospered greatly during the days of stage coach travel. A devastating fire in 1702 destroyed most of the town but the rebuilding produced some attractive Georgian buildings. Among the buildings that did survive are the pleasing little Grammar School with its hipped roof and dormer windows, founded in 1669, and the medieval Church of St Nicholas. The church contains some interesting memorials to the White family and a striking font of 1673 standing beneath a magnificent hanging canopy.

KELHAM
3 miles W of Newark on the A617

Originally an estate village serving Kelham Hall, the village farms were among the first to grow sugar beet when it was introduced to England during World War I. A lane still leads from the village to the huge sugar beet factory a mile or so to the west. Kelham Hall, now council offices, is the third manor house to be built on the site. The first was the 'Kelum Hall' where Charles I was briefly imprisoned. That building was destroyed by fire in 1690. Another mansion was built for the Sutton family, Lords of the Manor of Kelham. That too went up in flames, in 1857. The present building was designed by George Gilbert Scott and opinions are sharply divided over the merits of its red-brick towers, pinnacles, gables and Gothic windows.

Like the Hall, Kelham's bridge over the Trent also suffered misfortune: during the frightful winter of 1881 ice packs floating down the river demolished the old wooden structure.

AVERHAM
4 miles W of Newark on the A617

⚖ Robin Hood Theatre

Pronounced locally as Airam, this pleasant town has a picturesque corner off the main road where the Norman church and Georgian rectory form an appealing little group on the edge of the Trent. In the rectory grounds stands the remarkable **Robin Hood Theatre**, established by a former Rector and built by a local carpenter. The Rev. Cyril Walker opened it in 1913 as a private theatre for opera lovers. It had a fully equipped stage and orchestra pit, and boasted the rare amenity of being lit by electricity. The late, great Sir Donald Wolfit, a local man born at nearby Balderton, gave his first performances here. The theatre went through a rocky period in the 1960s and closed for several years but it is now operating successfully again, offering a variety of shows and plays throughout the year.

EAST STOKE
4 miles SW of Newark on the A46

🏛 Battle of Stoke Fields

The village is the site of the last great conflict of the War of the Roses: the **Battle of Stoke Fields** that took place here on 16th June 1487. The battle saw the army of Henry VII defeat the Yorkists and the pretender Lambert Simnel in a bloody conflict that lasted for three hours and left a toll of 7,000 deaths. The defeated army fled across the meadows to the river which is known locally to this day as the Red Gutter. Many of those who died in battle lie in Deadman's Field nearby, and local farmers have occasionally uncovered swords and other relics from the battle when ploughing their fields.

ELSTON
7 miles SW of Newark off the A46

🏛 Chapel

This rural village was once well-known for the local trade of skep-making, or basket-making, using specially grown willows, but the craft has all but died out. A curious building on the outskirts of the village is the deserted **Elston Chapel**, a quaint little building with a Norman doorway and many other Norman and medieval features. Its origins have been shrouded in mystery but recent research has suggested that the building was the chapel to the hospital of St Leonard that once existed in this locality.

SIBTHORPE
5 miles S of Newark off the A46

🏛 Dovecote

All that remains above ground of a priests' college, founded here in the 14th century, isthe parish church and a **Dovecote** (NT). Standing in the middle of a field and some 60 feet high, this circular stone building has a conical tiled roof and provided nesting places for more than 1,200 birds.

SCREVETON
7 miles S of Newark off the A46

🏛 Church

Sibthorpe Dovecote

The ancient village, whose name means 'farm belonging to the sheriff', has a delightful, small 13th century church which lies in a secluded position some way from the village. Reached by a footpath, the **Church of St Wilfrid** is home to a fine alabaster tomb of Richard Whalley, who is depicted with his three wives and 25 children at his feet.

CAR COLSTON
8 miles S of Newark off the A46

Now a conservation area, this village is fortunate in that it has remained unspoiled by modern development. Of particular interest here are the village's two greens which both date from the reign of Elizabeth I. At that time individual strips of land were cultivated by the villagers and the typical ridge and furrow appearance can still be made out. In 1598, the parish was enclosed, the land being turned into the fenced fields that became the norm, but the land in the middle of the village was left open

so that the villagers could graze their cattle. The Large Green, at 16.5 acres, is the largest in the county and, at the other end of the village lies Little Green (a mere 5.5 acres).

There are several interesting houses in the village but **Old Hall Farm**, which dates from 1812, is probably the one that receives most attention. The interest is generated, not so much by the building itself but because it was the home of Robert Thoroton, who in 1677 published his *Antiquities of Nottinghamshire*. The first major history of the county, the work was updated in the late 18th century by John Throsby and remains today one of the prime sources for local historians.

SCARRINGTON
8 miles S of Newark-on-Trent off the A52

The main attraction of this small village is not a grand house or a splendid village church but a remarkable man-made edifice. A pile of around 50,000 horseshoes towers 17 feet high and was built by the former

---

🎭 stories and anecdotes   🦜 famous people   🎨 art and craft   🎬 entertainment and sport   🚶 walks blacksmith, Mr Flinders. Over the years, souvenir hunters have taken the odd shoe here and there, with the result that the monument is bending over very slightly at the top.

However, the obelisk which Mr Flinders began in 1945 stands rock solid though all he used to bond the shoes was his skill and a great deal of luck! At one time it was coveted by an American visitor who wished to buy it and transport it to the United States.

ALVERTON
7 miles S of Newark-on-Trent off the A52

A small hamlet of just a handful of houses, Alverton's tiny population is occasionally augmented by two resident ghosts. The first has been seen in the old Church of England schoolhouse, which is now a private residence, and is believed to be the ghost of a teacher who was murdered at the school.

Alverton's second ghost, an elderly lady dressed in Victorian clothes, has been sighted at one of the hamlet's larger houses. The lady is believed to be Mary Brown, a sewing maid to Queen Victoria, who gave up her job after the death of her sister-in-law. Mary moved back to her brother's house to act as housekeeper to him and his four children and, by all accounts, she proved to be a formidable woman. She ruled the house with a rod of iron. In later years, when noises were heard on the upper floors, it was said that "Aunt Polly was on the warpath again"!

Bingham

The unofficial 'capital' of the Vale of Belvoir, Bingham is an ancient medieval

---

THE CURTAIN POLE

30-31 Market Place, Bingham, Nottingham Ng13 8AN
Tel: 01949 838734 Fax: 01949 875875
e-mail: accounts@curtainpole.com
website: www.thecurtainpole.com

Directors Nikki and Lorne Foster and their friendly, qualified staff offer a complete bespoke interior design service at the **Curtain Pole**. In relaxed, welcoming surroundings they offer anything from a single room scheme to a complete design and project management for the whole premises.

Among the specific offerings are wallpapers and paints; bespoke curtains, blinds, shutters and awnings; upholstery and re-upholstery; bespoke quality furniture; handcrafted and modular kitchens, bedrooms and bathrooms; lighting and design accessories; carpets, stone and ceramic floor and wall tiles and timber flooring. In addition to consultations for the needs of each client, the Curtain Pole also sells individual items for the home and offers alteration and restoration services.

🏛 historic building   🏚 museum   🏛 historic site   🍃 scenic attraction   🌱 flora and fauna market town that grew up around the church. After passing through a period of depression in the 20th century, the town is once again thriving. The area around the market square has been smartened up and the octagonal Butter Cross with its Victorian tiles and inscriptions provides an attractive focus here. Most of the buildings around the market place are also Victorian but All Saints' Church is medieval, dating from the 13th century though, again, there are many Victorian additions and decorations.

Bingham was the third Nottinghamshire town to provide an Archbishop of Canterbury. George Abbot's tenure of office was almost as unremarkable as that of Thomas Secker of Sibthorpe except for one unfortunate accident in 1621. Abbot was out shooting deer with a crossbow when he missed and killed a gamekeeper instead.

Around Bingham

COTGRAVE
4 miles SW of Bingham off the A46

🏛 Mill Hill

The discovery of an Anglo-Saxon burial ground on **Mill Hill**, Cotgrave's highest point, confirms that there has been a settlement here for many centuries. The excavation team uncovered the skeletons of nearly 100 people including some 13 children and the remains have been dated to around the mid to late 6th century.

Close to the burial ground stood the village's old post mill, itself the site of an unsolved mystery. One of the millers disappeared without trace after having been accused of pilfering corn. Rumours in the 19th century suggested that a body had been

discovered in the mill foundations and, despite believing that this could be the remains of the missing miller, the villagers kept quiet and the rumour was never investigated. During an excavation of the post mill site in the 1970s the skeleton of a male was uncovered which showed injuries that suggested that the unfortunate man was killed by a blow to the head. Whether or not this was all that remained of the missing miller has never been established.

Cotgrave is probably most well known as the home of Cotgrave Colliery which opened in 1964 and was a showplace mine for a number of years. The promise of work here for the next 100 years brought many miners from other coalfields to the village and also generated a huge expansion and building programme. Unfortunately, major geological faults made it impossible to mine the huge reserves and the colliery is now closed.

Kinoulton
6 miles S of Bingham off the A46

🏛 Church

The village, on the edge of the wolds, stands on high ground and from this vantage point there are views over the Vale of Belvoir to Belvoir Castle. Today, Kinoulton is a large commuter village but it has a long and interesting past. In the 12th century, there was a castle here, its commanding position being ideal since it was also close to the Fosse Way. Archbishop Cranmer had a palace nearby and, to the west of the village, lies the spring which brought the village to prominence in Georgian times as a spa with curative properties. Later, the arrival of the Grantham Canal ushered in a period of mild prosperity. (The canal still passes through the village and provides some pleasant walking.)

HORTORS NURSERIES & FARM SHOP

Hickling Lane, Kinoulton, Nottinghamshire NG12 3ED
Tel: 01949 81312

Friendly, well-informed staff, with Jill Hortor at the helm, add to the pleasure of a visit to **Hortors Nurseries & Farm Shop**, which is located midway between Kinoulton and Hickling. Hanging baskets are a speciality, and there's always a good stock of herbaceous and bedding plants whilst bouquets and arrangements can be made to order.

The farm shop on the same site sells an abundance of locally produced fruit and vegetables, home-grown and local summer salad leaves, cordials and juices from Belvoir Fruit Farms, dairy products from the Manor Farm Dairy at Thrussington, honey, jams, preserves and Colston Bassett cheese.

There's plenty of good walking in the vicinity, and the picturesque Grantham Canal runs through the village close to the nursery.

Standing beside the canal, Kinoulton's **Church of St Luke** was a gift of the squire, the Earl of Gainsborough, in the 1760s. The earl felt the old church was too near what was then a major thoroughfare, the Fosse Way. The slate headstones in the old churchyard have some fine inscriptions but not all of the stones have survived. Some were 'borrowed' by the local baker to line his oven, a piece of recycling that was exposed when a customer noticed that his loaf was imprinted with the words "in loving memory".

HICKLING

7 miles S of Bingham off the A606

Lying on the western edge of the Vale of Belvoir, this agricultural village was the site of a busy basin on the Grantham Canal. Building work on the basin finished in 1797 and the canal, which carried coal, building materials, and agricultural goods, was in constant use until the 1930s when it began to fall into disrepair. Recently cleared, Hickling Basin is once again attracting people, this time visitors who come to see the resident flocks of wildfowl.

COLSTON BASSETT

4 miles S of Bingham off the A46

🏚 The Cross

For centuries this small village was the property of the Bassett family and later the Hackers and the Goldings. Between them they planted the many trees that shade the winding lanes, built a noble manor house, landscaped the gracious park, and in 1892 added a striking if rather over-elaborate church. The cumulative effect is to make Colston Bassett one of the most picturesque villages in the Vale of Belvoir.

At one time the village was large enough to sustain its own weekly market and the partly medieval Market Cross can still be seen. Since 1933, the **Cross** has been owned by the National Trust - the first property it acquired in Nottinghamshire. The Cross stands near the old post office, itself a picture postcard building that used to feature in GPO advertisements during the 1960s.

On the outskirts of the village stand the forlorn ruins of the former village church which has been abandoned since 1892.

CROPWELL BISHOP
3 miles S of Bingham off the A46

🏛 Church

Much of the furniture from Colston Bassett's old church was moved to Cropwell Bishop and installed in **St Giles' Church**. St Giles is the oldest building in this sizeable village and dates back to around 1215.

The village lies close to the old Roman road, the Fosse Way, now the A46. The coaching inns of Cropwell Bishop are said to have given shelter to highwayman Dick Turpin while he was plundering the coaches using the busy thoroughfare.

In modern times, the village has prospered from gypsum works. Two of the works' bottle kilns still stand alongside the Grantham Canal.

LANGAR
3 miles SE of Bingham off the A52

🏛 Church   🌼 Wild Flower Farm Visitor Centre

"Really, the English do not deserve great men," declared George Bernard Shaw. "They allowed Butler to die practically unknown." He was referring to Samuel Butler, author of *The Way of All Flesh*, who was born in the elegant Georgian rectory at Langar on December 4th, 1834. A trenchant satirist, Butler mocked the pomposity and exposed the hypocrisy of the Victorian middle classes. No wonder they didn't much care for him. Langar itself appears in his major work as Battersby-on-the-Hill and the portraits of its residents are far from flattering. The year 2002, the centenary of Butler's death, provided an opportunity to commemorate one of the village's most famous residents in some way but no-one bothered. '*One* of the village's most famous residents', because this small rural village in the heart of the Vale was also the home of Admiral Richard, Earl Howe (1726-99), "Black Dick of Lanagar". Richard achieved national fame on the Glorious 1st of June, 1794, at the Battle of Ushant where his victory included the capture of seven French ships of the line. The Admiral himself merits only a modest plaque in **St Andrew's Church**, but other generations of the Howe family; their predecessors, the Scropes, as well as the Chaworths from nearby Wiverton Hall, are all celebrated by an extraordinary gathering of monuments. The most splendid is a four-poster free-standing alabaster monument to Thomas, Lord Scrope, who died in 1609, and his wife: according to Pevsner "the figures are good enough to be in Westminster Abbey".

To the south of Langar, the former airfield is surrounded by an unsightly industrial estate which nevertheless contains the **Wild Flower Farm Visitors Centre**, part of a commercial nursery, where visitors are able

🎭 stories and anecdotes   🌱 famous people   🎨 art and craft   ✒ entertainment and sport   🚶 walks

LANGAR HALL

Langar, Nottinghamshire NG13 9HG
Tel: 01949 860559 Fax: 01949 861045
e-mail: info@langarhall.co.uk
website: www.langarhall.co.uk

"Once in a blue moon it is still possible to come across a country house that makes one want to jump for joy." These are the words of someone who definitely knows his hotels, and anyone who visits **Langar Hall** will agree with his praise. Langar Hall is a house of immense charm in the beautiful Vale of Belvoir, built in 1837 on the site of a great historic house, the home of Admiral Lord Howe. It stands quietly secluded overlooking lovely gardens, with sheep grazing among the trees, a croquet lawn, and beyond it a network of medieval fish ponds stocked with carp. It is the family home of Imogen Shirving, who combines the highest standards of good hotel keeping with the hospitality of an informal country house.

The en suite accommodation comprises eight double/twin rooms, a four-potser room and a suite; most enjoy lovely views, and all are quiet, very comfortable and well equipped for both business and leisure stays. Among the day rooms are the Study, for reading or small meetings; the White Sitting Room for afternoon tea and pre-dinner drinks; the Indian Room for private parties and conferences; and two meeting rooms for up to 45.

The food at Langar Hall is as distinguished as the accommodation. In the elegant pillared hall, fresh seasonal produce, including home-reared lamb, locally-raised pork, beef and poultry, fish from Brixham,

game in winter and home-grown vegetables and herbs, is the basis of the menus. English country cooking with a twist, with the emphasis on freshness and flavour provides memorable signature dishes such as twice-baked cheese soufflé, pan-fried scallops with squid ink risotto and a trio of Langar lamb. The enjoyment level stays high right to the end with scrumptious desserts like gooseberry and crème fraiche tart or hot chocolate fondant with caramelised banana and chocolate sauce. In the Garden Room, snacks and light dishes are served from 11am to 7pm Monday to Friday, and afternoon tea from 4 pm Monday to Thursday.

🏠 historic building 🏛 museum 🏚 historic site ⚘ scenic attraction ❦ flora and fauna

THE WILD FLOWER FARM

Lapwing Meadows, Coachgap Lane, Langar, Nottinghamshire NG13 9HP
Tel: 01949 860592 Fax: 01949 869047
e-mail: sales@naturescape.co.uk
website: www.naturescape.co.uk

Lovers of gardens and gardening, nature and the countryside will be in their element at the **Wild Flower Farm**, a family business producing wildflower plants and seeds, native trees and shrubs. Liz and Brian Scarborough, their son Mark are acknowledged experts in their field, and they and

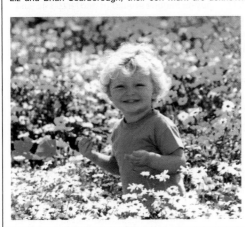

their staff are always willing to give help and advice. The 250 + varieties of plants and seeds, many of them rarely found elsewhere, include wild flowers, wild climbers, wild roses, cottage garden plants, herbs and pond and marsh plants.

The farm has 40 acres of crops, a mile of hedgerows, woodland walks, a wildlife cottage garden, a dragonfly pond, a wetland meadow, a picnic site, a children's play area, a tea room and a pine cabin selling plants and gifts. Visitors can enjoy walks around the farm and spot the abundant wildlife, including birds and butterflies, hares and voles. The Wild Life Farm is open from 11 to 5.30 between April and September.

to explore the wild flower meadows and see a wide variety of species in their natural habitat.

GRANBY

4 miles SE of Bingham off the A52

This small, once self-sufficient village is still proud that its name was adopted by the Dukes of Rutland, of nearby Belvoir Castle, as the courtesy title of their eldest son. It was John, son of the 3rd Duke, who brought most lustre to the name as Commander in Chief of the British forces in Germany in the mid-1700s. The Marquis was immensely popular with his troops, many of whom followed an old tradition on leaving the Army and became publicans. Which explains why so many hostelries up and down the country are named

The Marquis of Granby – including naturally the inn at Granby itself.

WHATTON

3 miles E of Bingham off the A52

The Norman St John's Church was restored in the 1860s under the direction of Thomas Butler, rector of Langar, and the stained glass windows, including some crafted by William Morris to the designs of Burne-Jones, were added later that century. The font, which is dated 1662, replaced one that had been damaged during the Commonwealth. This church was used by Thomas Cranmer and his family until he left the area to take up his studies at Cambridge. A memorial to his father, Thomas Cranmer senior, who died in 1502, can be found inside.

🎭 stories and anecdotes   🦜 famous people   🎨 art and craft   🎟 entertainment and sport   🥾 walks

ASLOCKTON
2 miles E of Bingham off the A52

This village is now separated from its neighbour, Whatton, by the main Nottingham to Grantham railway line, though the footpaths linking the two can still be walked today. This was the village in which Thomas Cranmer was born and spent his early years. Born in 1489, he attended the parish church at Whatton and also a local grammar school, possibly at Southwell, before leaving at the age of 14 to continue his education at Cambridge. It was in 1533 that Henry VIII proposed this obscure theologian and academic as Archbishop of Canterbury, an appointment which had to be approved by the Pope – the last time Rome had any say over who should be Primate of All England.

One of Cranmer's first duties on gaining his appointment was to pronounce the marriage between Henry VIII and Catherine of Aragon null and void. During the course of his 23 years in office, Cranmer also pronounced invalid Henry's marriage to Anne Boleyn and granted him a divorce from Anne of Cleves. Loyal to his monarch throughout, Cranmer aided Henry in effecting the independence of the Church in England from Rome. He was also responsible for drafting much of the *Common Prayer Book* that was used right up until the 1970s when it was replaced by a modern language version. Following the death of Henry VIII, Cranmer was convicted of treason under Mary I and burnt at the stake in 1556.

Though not built until the late 19th century, Aslockton Church is appropriately dedicated to Thomas while the village school also bears the name of its most famous resident. Cranmer's Mound, to the east of the church, is a high Norman motte some 15 feet high which is clearly visible from the footpath to Orston. Further along this same footpath can be seen the site of the manor house where Cranmer was born.

Sherwood Forest

It seems likely that it was William the Conqueror who designated Sherwood as a Royal Forest, an administrative term for the private hunting ground of the king. The land was not only thickly wooded but also included areas of rough heathland as well as arable land, meadow land, small towns, and villages. The Norman kings were passionate about their hunting and, to guard their royal forests, there were a set of rigidly upheld laws, to conserve the game (known as the venison) and vegetation (known as the vert). No one, even those with a private estate within the royal forest, was allowed to kill or hunt protected animals, graze domestic animals in the forest, fell trees or make clearings within the boundaries without the express permission of the king or one of his chief foresters. It is little wonder then, with such strict rules imposed upon them, that the people turned to the likes of Robin Hood and others who defied the laws and lived off the king.

Edwinstowe

🌿 Major Oak   🐾 Vicar Water Country Park

📷 Sherwood Forest Visitor Centre   🏛 Church

🍃 Sherwood Forest Fun Park   🌿 Farm Park

Lying at the heart of Sherwood Forest, the life of the village is still dominated by the forest, as it has been since the 7th century. Edwin, King of Northumbria, who gave the village its name, died in the Battle of Hatfield in 632. The village developed around the church built on the spot where he was slain. In 1912 a cross was erected by the

Duke of Portland to mark the king's grave. From then on until the time of the Domesday Survey, Edwinstowe remained small. Following the Norman Conquest, the village found itself within the boundaries of the royal hunting forest of Sherwood and it became subject to the stringent laws of the verderers. Dating from the 12th century, the **Church of St Mary** was the first stone building in Edwinstowe and according to legend it was here that the marriage took place between Robin Hood and Maid Marian. Buried in the graveyard is Dr Cobham Brewer whose *Dictionary of Phrase & Fable*, first published in 1870 and still in print, is possibly the most readable reference book ever compiled.

A little way up the road leading northwards out of Edwinstowe is the **Sherwood Forest Visitor Centre** (see panel below). Sherwood, the 'Shire Wood', was once a great woodland mass stretching from Nottingham to Worksop. Although only relatively small pockets of the original forest remain today, it is still possible to become lost among the trees. Whether or not Robin and his Merry Men ever did frolic in the greenshawe is, however, debatable. Arguments still rage as to which particular historical figure gave rise to the legend of the famous outlaw. Records

Sherwood Forest Country Park & Visitor Centre

Edwinstowe, Nottinghamshire
Tel: 01623 823202
e-mail: sherwood.forest@nottscc.gov.uk
website: www.nottinghamshire.gov.uk/countryparks

The magnificent former Royal Hunting Forest of Sherwood – the legendary home of Nottinghamshire's world-famous outlaw, Robin Hood - once covered 100,000 acres. Today, Sherwood Forest Country Park & Visitor Centre, the largest remnant of the original forest, is just 450 acres but is home to over 900 veteran oak trees which are over 500 years old. Waymarked pathways lead from the Visitor Centre through the forest to Sherwood's most famous tree, the mighty Major Oak, which is known world-wide as Robin Hood's tree.

This great tree, weighing an estimated 23 tons and with a waistline of 33 feet has grown here for something between 800 and one thousand years, although its exact age can only be estimated. Its large canopy - that part of the tree made up of leaves and branches - has a spread of 92 feet, showing that the tree has grown with little or no competition from other large oaks.

Tales of Robin Hood have been told for over 700 years and the fascination with Sherwood's legendary hero continues into the 21st Century.

The Visitor Centre, next to the car park at the entrance to the country park, is the starting point for any visit to Sherwood Forest. Here, the *Robyn Hode's Sherwood Forest* exhibition shows visitors what life in Sherwood Forest would have been like in medieval times while, in the video studio you can find out more about this famous forest.

stories and anecdotes   famous people   art and craft   entertainment and sport   walks

Major Oak, Sherwood Forest

outlaw's exploits can be found on a piece of parchment which dates from the mid-15th century but it was not until William Caxton set up his printing press in London in 1477 that cheaper books could be produced. From then on, the story of Robin Hood, his merry band of men, Guy of Gisborne, and the evil Sheriff of Nottingham has inspired countless books and at least a dozen major films. Among others, the medieval outlaw has been portrayed by Douglas Fairbanks, Kevin Costner and Sean Connery.

from the 12th century suggest a number of possible candidates, including the Earl of Huntingdon.

During the 15th century, several references to the outlaw can be found in the writings of two Scottish historians. In 1521 a third Scotsman, John Major, wrote "

> *About the time of King Richard I, according to*
> *my estimate, the famous English robbers*
> *Robert Hood and Little John were lurking in*
> *their woods, preying on the goods of the wealthy.*"

However, none of the historians gave any clues as to the sources of their writings. By the 16th century, there were two conflicting stories emerging as to the birthplace of Robin, one suggesting Kirklees while the other suggested Locksley.

Tracing the stories of Robin Hood is a difficult task as the tales, which have been told for over 600 years, were spoken rather than written since few local people could read and write. One of the earliest known stories of the

Undeterred by the vague foundations upon which the legend is built, visitors still flock to see the great hollow tree which the outlaws purportedly used as a meeting place and as a cache for their supplies. The **Major Oak** is located about 10 minutes walk along the main track in the heart of the forest and presents a rather forlorn appearance. Its 33ft girth and branches 260 feet in circumference are now supported by massive wooden crutches and iron corsets. There is no denying that the tree is at least 500 years old, and some sources claim its age to be nearer 1,000 years. Despite its decayed appearance the tree is still alive thanks to careful preservation. Recent tests have established that some parts of the tree have successfully taken to grafting and there are hopes that at some stage a whole colony of minor oaks may be produced.

The visitor centre also houses a display of characters from the Robin Hood stories, with appropriate scenes of merry making. This

THE CAFÉ IN SHERWOOD FOREST

Forest Corner, Edwinstowe, Nottinghamshire NG21 9RN
Tel: 01623 824033   Fax: 07092 178236
e-mail: café@stop4t.co.uk
website: www.stop4t.co.uk

The café in Sherwood Forest is situated within the Sherwood Forest Art and Craft Centre. A former coach house and stables, believed to have been built by Lord Manvers in the 1850s. The café is open all day for a fine selection of light snacks and more substantial meals. Homemade scones and Cornish clotted cream teas a speciality. Jams, chutneys, biscuits and pickled produce also available. There is seating capacity for 24 inside the café, 30 in the courtyard and a further 24 seats in the atrium. The café is open 10am to 5pm in the summer season and 10am to 4pm in the winter months (closed Mondays).

theme has also been successfully translated to the city of Nottingham in the Tales of Robin Hood exhibition.

Another impressive attraction in Edwinstowe is the **Sherwood Forest Fun Park**, which can be found to the north of the A6075 Mansfield to Ollerton road. This family-run funfair contains a variety of popular fairground rides including dodgems, a ghost train, and a giant Astroglide. The park is open daily from 10 o'clock to dusk between mid-March and mid-October, and admission is free, pay as you go on the rides.

Not far from Edwinstowe, off the A6075, is the **Sherwood Forest Farm Park,** a naturalist and animal lover's delight, beautifully laid out, with picturesque water gardens and three wildfowl lakes. Enjoying a peaceful setting in a secluded valley on the edge of Sherwood Forest, the Farm Park boasts no fewer than 30 of Britain's rarest breeds of farm animals and other endangered and protected species. A peaceful spot to relax can be found by visitors even on the busiest of days. The pets' corner with its goats and the exotic bird garden are just two of the delights, and among the many other attractions are the family of kune kune pigs,

the water buffalo Raquel and Curly, Little John the Shire Horse, Dizzy Lizzie the Suffolk Punch, a group of wallabies, a tree house, tractor and trailer rides and the summer maize maze. A miniature steam railway meanders through the grounds.

A couple of miles south-east of Edwinstowe is **Vicar Water Country Park.** Open daily throughout the year, from dawn to dusk, the Park covers 80 hectares of attractive countryside, complete with a large lake, and provides excellent walking, fishing, cycling and horse-riding. Footpaths and bridleways link the Park to the Sherwood Pines Forest Park; the Timberland Trail; the Maun Valley Way and the Robin Hood Way. The Visitor Centre has ample information about the area and also a café.

Around Edwinstowe

CUCKNEY
5 miles NW of Edwinstowe on the A60

Five main roads converge on this sizeable village which in medieval times was a marshy island. A large mound in the churchyard is all that is left of Thomas de Cuckney's 12th century castle. Because the nearby church was built on the marshes it was necessary in the 1950s to shore it up by building a concrete platform underneath. In the course of this work the remains of hundreds of skeletons were uncovered. At first it was thought the bones were the grisly relics of some 12th century battle. More recent research has revealed that the remains are much older. They have now been linked to the 7th century Battle of Heathfield between Edwin of Northumbria and Penda of Mercia.

An estate village to the country seat of the Dukes of Portland, Welbeck Abbey, Cuckney is made up of farm workers cottages. Along with Clumber House, Thoresby Hall and Rufford Abbey, **Welbeck Abbey** makes up the four large estates in this area of Nottinghamshire, all owned by Dukes. Naturally, the area became known as The

Dukeries. It was the 5th Duke of Portland who began, in 1854, an extensive building programme that turned Welbeck into what is seen today. The most impressive of his additions was the riding school, the second largest in the world, complete with a peat floor and gas jet lighting. The building is now leased to the Ministry of Defence and is used as an Army training college, though the abbey and the grounds have been maintained in perfect condition.

CLUMBER PARK
4 miles N of Edwinstowe off the A614

🏛 Chapel of St Mary the Virgin   ⚘ Clumber Park

Clumber Park was created in 1707 when the 3rd Duke of Newcastle was granted permission by Queen Anne to enclose part of the Forest of Sherwood as a hunting ground. The building of Clumber House began in 1760, though it was much altered in the early 19th century. After a devastating fire in 1879, the house was rebuilt in an Italianate style but, due to the vast expense of its upkeep, Clumber House was demolished in 1938. All that remains today are the foundations.

However, any sense of disappointment is quickly dispelled by the charm of the buildings that remain in this lovely setting. The estate houses with their high pitched gables and massive chimneys are most picturesque. The redbrick stables are

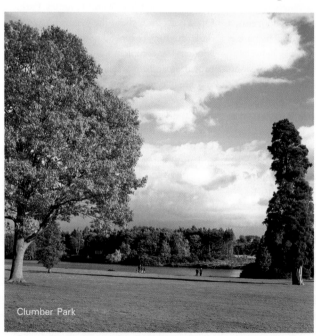

Clumber Park

particularly fine as they are surmounted by a clock tower crowned by a domed cupola. The inset clock in the tower dates back to 1763 and the stables now house the café and visitor centre.

By far the most striking building on the estate, however, is the **Chapel of St Mary the Virgin,** built by GF Bodley in the 1880s. It was commissioned by the 7th Duke of Newcastle to commemorate his coming of age. A fervent Anglo-Catholic, he spent the then-colossal sum of £30,000 on its construction. The church has many elaborate features including some wonderful stone and woodwork and stained glass by Kempe.

The 4,000-acre Clumber Park is owned by the National Trust and attracts more than a million visitors each year. The man-made lake is particularly lovely and is crossed by a fine classical bridge. Five different roads enter the park and each entrance is marked by an impressive gateway. Most imposing of them all is the Apleyhead Gate, off the A614, which leads into the glorious Duke's Drive. Stretching for a distance of two miles, the drive is the longest double avenue of limes in Europe and contains some 1,300 trees.

PERLETHORPE
4 miles NE of Edwinstowe off the A614

🖈 Thoresby Gallery

Situated in the valley of the River Meden, Perlethorpe lies within the estate of Thoresby Hall, at the eastern end of Thoresby Lake. The first hall was built in the late 17th century for the Earl of Kingston but this was destroyed in 1745 and replaced by a Palladian-style mansion. The hall seen today is a Victorian mansion built by Anthony Salvin in 1864 for the Pierrepont family and is surrounded by the largest park in the county.

The Hall itself is now a hotel.

The village church, which was completed in 1876, was built by Salvin at the same time as he was working on the hall. At the beginning of the 20th century Countess Manvers of the great hall took a keen interest in the welfare of the village children and was always informed of any who did not attend Sunday school. She would then visit them and scold those who had failed in their duty. But if a child had been absent because of sickness, she would ensure that hot soup was delivered until the child was well again. The **Thoresby Gallery** in Thoresby Park is an imaginative conversion with three well-lit exhibition areas. There is a permanent exhibition of the works of Marie-Louise Pierrepont, Countess Manvers. Free admission.

OLD OLLERTON
2 miles E of Edwinstowe off the A614/A6075

🖭 Water Mill

Not to be confused with the more workaday town of New Ollerton, Old Ollerton is a delightfully preserved cluster of old houses, a charming Georgian coaching inn covered in creeper, and a church set beside the River Maun. Straddling the river is **Ollerton Water Mill**, more than 300 years old. Visitors are welcome to wander around the ancient building with its huge water wheel, browse in the Exhibition Area, watch a short video illustrating the age-old milling process, or sample the refreshments in the tea room. The name of the village was originally Alreton, or Allerton, meaning farm among the alders, and the alders still grow here along the banks of the River Maun. The village lay on the road from London to York (though now it is bypassed) and also on the roads from Newark to Worksop and Lincoln to Mansfield. As a consequence, Ollerton developed as a meeting

THORESBY PARK COURTYARD

Thoresby Park, nr Ollerton, Newark,
Nottinghamshire NG22 9EP
Tel: 01623 822365   Fax: 01623 822315
e-mail: info@thoresby.com
website: www.thoresby.com

For retail therapy with a difference, the **Courtyard** in the heart of Thoresby Park is *the* place to go. An eclectic mix of stylish outlets sell a variety of arts and crafts, homeware, clothes and gifts, and the site also has an art gallery and a café. **Barton Dawes** (Tel: 01623 822533) is filled with a huge selection of stylish items for the home, with everything from tableware and ceramics to French mirrors and chandeliers, and a wide range of gifts for every occasion. **Craft Corner** (Tel: 01623 824002) offers a wide choice, materials for jewellery making, fabric, crafts, card-making and paper crafts. Handcrafted items are available to buy and daily workshops help customers learn new crafts and techniques.

Hazel Walker (Tel: 01623 825111) sells a superb selection of clothes and accessories for style-conscious ladies, from swimsuits, beachwear and casual wear to formal evening outfits. For lovers of Teddy Bears, **7th Heaven** is just that, a paradise for collectors of bespoke teddies and for anyone who just wants a more modest teddy to love; Teddy Bear workshops; Teddy Bear Hospital; also unusual gollies, dolls house furniture, soft furnishings and home accessories. Tel: 01623 823565. **Thoresby Gallery** (Tel: 01623 822009) shows an exciting range of pictures, prints and innovative and affordable art, all for immediate purchase and collection. The Gallery houses a permanent collection of works by Marie-Louise Pierrepont.

place for Sherwood Forest officials and the inns became staging posts during the coaching era.

WELLOW

2 miles SE of Ollerton on the A616

🏛 Maypole   🏛 Church

This pretty conservation village is located on the site of an early settlement and was once fortified by an earthwork and, on the western side, by Gorge Dyke. The remains of the earthwork can still be seen and villagers have retained the right to graze their cattle on enclosed land. On the village green stands the tallest permanent **Maypole** in England – 60 feet high, colourfully striped like a barber's pole, and with a cockerel perched on the top. Because earlier wooden poles rotted away,

were stolen or got knocked down, this one is made of steel and firmly fixed in place. It was erected to commemorate Elizabeth II's Silver Jubilee in 1976 and forms the focus for the May Day festivities held on the Spring Bank Holiday Monday. The jollities include dancing around the Maypole and the crowning of a May Queen.

Other notable features of this surprising village include a Ducking Stool; part of the old stocks; and a 17th century case clock in the 12th century parish **Church of St Swithin**. The clock face was made locally to commemorate the coronation of Elizabeth II in 1953. Each year on 19th September, the three church bells, which are between 300 and 400 years old, are rung in memory of a certain Lady Walden. Some 200 years ago she was

Wellow Maypole

paying a visit to Wellow and became lost in a local wood. Following the sound of the church bells, Lady Walden eventually found her way to the village and, such was her relief, that she left money for the bells to be rung each year on that day.

LAXTON
4 miles E of Ollerton off the A6075

🏠 Dovecote Inn   🏛 Castle Mound

Laxton is unique since it is one of a handful of places in the country that have managed to retain their open field farming system. Devised in the Middle Ages, this system was generally abandoned in the 18th and 19th centuries when the enclosure of agricultural land took place. The fields have been strip farmed here for about 1,200 years and the system ensured that farmers had an equal share of both good and poor land. A farmer could hold as many as 100 strips, representing about 30 acres. In the 1600s the strips were, on average, about half an acre in size but, with the advent of more efficient means of ploughing, this increased to three-quarters of an acre. The familiar three year crop rotation also ensured productive use of the land.

Another unique feature of this fascinating village is the magnificent **Dovecote Inn**, which is owned (but not run) by the Queen. Here, a form of manorial government that has survived from medieval times still continues. Each winter, villagers gather at the inn each winter to appoint a jury which is then responsible for inspecting the fallow fields in the next cycle. The jurors tour the fields left fallow for the past year then adjourn for lunch back at the Dovecote. During the afternoon they then discuss any offences committed by farmers. A week later comes the Court meeting. The 18th century was a great time of rebuilding in Laxton and many of the houses display the patterned brickwork that was typical of this period. The still visible stonework around the bottom of some buildings suggests that the foundations were of much older timber framed constructions.

Just north of the village, along a lane close to the church, is another fascinating aspect of Laxton's medieval history. This is the Norman motte, or **Castle Mound**, which lies almost hidden beneath the trees. At the beginning of the 12th century, the stewardship of Sherwood Forest moved to Laxton and the village became the administrative centre for the forest. As a consequence, the motte and bailey castle was one of the biggest in this part of the country. Although no ruined keep or crumbling walls exist today, the castle earthworks are still the largest and best preserved in the county.

Egmanton and Laxton

Distance: *6.0 miles (9.6 kilometres)*

Typical time: *180 mins*

Height gain: *50 metres*

Map: *Explorer 271*

Walk: *www.walkingworld.com ID:1440*

Contributor: *David Berry*

ACCESS INFORMATION:

Egmanton lies between the A6075 (Ollerton to Tuxford road) and the A616 (Newark – Ollerton). It is only a short distance off the A1; northbound, leave at Tuxford, southbound at Markham Moor. There are bus services to Egmanton village from Tuxford, Newark, Ollerton and Retford.

DESCRIPTION:

This walk is set in the undulating Nottinghamshire countryside ten miles to the north-west of Newark. The old coalmining area of Ollerton is five miles to the west but does not impinge on the scenery of this walk. Egmanton is a typical, small, red-brick village of this area with church and pub. Laxton is a little bigger, again with church and pub. It is England's last open field farming village with an ancient strip field system. There is a visitors' centre explaining this feudal scheme and on the walk, a couple of explanatory placards are passed. The majority of the walk is on farm tracks and field footpaths, but the last mile is along a quiet country road with little traffic.

FEATURES:

Pub, Toilets, Museum, Church, Wildlife, Great Views

WALK DIRECTIONS:

1 | From 'The Old Plough Inn' walk in an easterly direction. Shortly, take the right fork, Weston Road. Proceed along this road for 150 metres.

2 | Turn right up Wood Lane, which is between some expensive-looking new properties and a council-looking row of houses. The road becomes a stone track and climbs up, heading for the right-hand corner of Egmanton Wood. Ignore a turning left into the woods. Continue to the corner and stay on the track as it follows the edge of the wood.

3 | When the track ends, continue more or less straight ahead on a path across a field. In the middle of the field, there is a small tree on this path. In the distance, in line with the path, is a pylon. Walk to the hedge and turn left for 18m. Go through a gap in the hedge. Turn left and follow the edge of the field to your left.

4 | Turn right when you get to the footpath, which is identified by having an electricity pole and two large trees on it.

5 | Continue along the path to the far side of the field, which will lead you to a gateway (with no gate). Through the gateway, turn sharp right along a farm track. Over the brow of the hill you will see Laxton church tower.

6 | Having walked one third of a mile along this track, you will see a footpath off to the left. Follow this and you will now be heading slightly to the left of the church

tower. The path enters a playing-field. Keep left and walk the edge of the field. At the pavilion, continue on your heading to pass through the hedge. Turn immediately right for 30m.

7 | Turn left through the hedge and under a wooden bar at a footpath that once more heads towards the church. Go diagonally across the field to a footpath sign in the corner. Keep to the left edge of the next field to a stile. The next short footpath takes you down to a village road. Turn right and head for Laxton village centre. On the right you will pass one of the several placards explaining the open field system. Ahead is The Dovecote Inn. Beside it there is a visitors' centre explaining the field system – and toilets. You might at this stage take in the centre and explore some of the fields. You might also choose to patronise the pub.

8 | When all this is complete, the walk continues along the road to the left, signposted 'Boughton and Ollerton'. Ignore a footpath by Cross Hill Farm and a bridleway sign by the information placard opposite the church. Pass the post office and a B&B at Lilac Farm.

9 | Take the right fork – 'No Through Road'. In 400m there is a public footpath sign to right, just before a bungalow. Follow a well-defined footpath across the crop field to the left hedge, which the path then follows to the corner of the field.

10 | At the corner of the field, take the stile and go through the gateway beyond. Walk down this narrow field to a stile on the left. Cross the stile and you will see, down to the left, a footbridge. Make for that by following the hedge to your right and then turning left on reaching a ditch. Cross the footbridge and the stile immediately beyond it.

11 | Continue straight ahead, along a well-defined path through the crop, keeping the hedge of the field to your right. As you reach higher ground, notice that you are heading towards a communications tower in the middle distance. To your right you can see your destination, Egmanton.

It might seem that you are in the middle of nowhere, but beyond Egmanton you can see the A1 traffic and to the left and right, cooling towers. So, 'civilisation' is not that far away! The path is now diverging away from the hedge, but you are still heading towards the communications tower.

12 | The well-defined path ends at the corner of another field projecting into this one. Climb the mound at that corner and turn right along a track. A short way along that track there is a gateway (no gate) with a yellow arrow, the direction of which seems to indicate walking across the crop. It seems that previous walkers have not done this but have followed the track made by the wheels of a tractor. This runs parallel to the hedge, displaced into the field some 30m. As the hedge bends to the left and then curves right, so does the tractor-wheel track. As the track starts dropping down the hill, look for the line where previous walkers have turned left through the crop, which is the proper line of the footpath, towards a fingerpost in the far hedge. At the fingerpost over the stile, turn right and follow the fence, keeping it on your right.

13 | In the right-hand corner there is a wooden barrier, with a footpath sign. Go over the stile. Navigation is now simple – just follow a straight line keeping the hedge / ditch on your left. Look for quite an incredible amount of badger activity. Their paths for their nightly runs are long-established. It is almost a mile along this footpath. Reassurance that all is well is when you cross over a substantial private road up to a farm. You know you have reached the last field when you notice some strange mounds to your right. On the OS map they are labelled as an antiquity – 'Fish Ponds'.

14 | At the corner of this field, the footpath ends and there is a rather dilapidated gate. Go through it onto a short track.

15 | The track leads to the road to Egmanton. Turn right.

16 | Entering Egmanton – the end is in sight!

EGMANTON

5 miles E of Ollerton off the A1

🏛 Shrine of Our Lady of Egmanton

Reached by quiet winding lanes, Egmanton is little visited these days but during the Middle Ages a local woman claimed to have had a vision of the Virgin Mary. The **Shrine of Our Lady of Egmanton** became a major place of pilgrimage right up until the Reformation.

The cult was revived in 1896 by the 7th Duke of Newcastle who commissioned Sir Ninian Comper to completely restore and redecorate the church. The result is an exuberant recreation of a medieval church with all its colour and graven images. The exterior is really quite modest but the interior is resplendent and inspiring, with the light from many tapers and candles helping to create a mesmerising atmosphere.

RUFFORD

2 miles S of Ollerton off the A614

🏛 Abbey   🐦 Country Park   ✒ Craft Centre

Rufford Abbey was founded in 1148 by Gilbert de Gant as a daughter house to Rievaulx Abbey. During the Dissolution it suffered the fate of many religious houses and came into the hands of the 6th Earl of Shrewsbury, fourth husband of the redoubtable Bess of Hardwick. The Earl pulled down most of the abbey and built a grand Elizabethan mansion. All that remains of the abbey is a vaulted crypt, said to be haunted by the ghost of a giant monk with a skull-like face. According to the parish register for Edwinstowe, a man died of fright after catching sight of this unholy visitor!

The abbey's stable block now houses an impressive craft centre and a ceramics centre, and the restored 18th century Orangery features a changing display of outdoor sculptures and large-scale ceramics. In the vaulted stone undercroft, 'Rufford the Cistercian Abbey' traces the varying functions of the Cistercian order in England from the 12th century through to the Dissolution of the Monasteries in the reign of Henry VIII.

The grounds of the abbey, now the **Rufford Country Park and Craft Centre**, are well worth a visit. In addition to the variously themed formal gardens near the house, there are also some hides where birdwatchers can overlook a portion of the lake which has been designated a bird sanctuary. In the grounds too stands an 18th century corn mill, now home to a display of Nottinghamshire history, and two icehouses dating from the mid-1800s. As well as the majestic Lime Avenue, there is also the

Rufford Abbey

Broad Ride, at the southern end of which are several animal graves. Most were pets belonging to the family at the house but one grave is that of the racehorse Cremorne, the 1872 Derby winner. Events throughout the year include the Earth & Fire Ceramic Fair in June. Tel: 01623 822944.

BILSTHORPE
4 miles S of Ollerton off the A614

The hall where, during the Civil War, Charles I is reputed to have hidden in a cupboard still exists but is now incorporated into a farm that stands opposite the village church.

Bilsthorpe remained a quiet farming community, as it had been for many centuries, right up until 1922 when a coal mine was sunk in the village by Stanton Ironworks. An explosion at the mine with a subsequent loss of life brought the vicar and the mine manager into a dispute over compensation. The manager, unwilling to pay out, built a wooden church away from the main part of the village and near the temporary accommodation provided for the mine workers.

FARNSFIELD
7 miles S of Ollerton off the A614

🐾 Farm Centre   🦋 Wonderland

Close to the crossroads of the A614/A617 near Farnsfield are two popular family attractions. **White Post Modern Farm Centre** is a working farm with more than 4,000 animals, among them llamas, deer, owls, piglets, chicks and even mice. **Wonderland Pleasure Park & Garden Centre** has a

---

THE WHITE POST FARM CENTRE

Mansfield Road (A614), Farnsfield, nr Newark, Nottinghamshire NG22 8HL
Tel: 01623 882977 Fax: 01623 883499
e-mail: marketing@whitepostfarmcentre.co.uk
website: www.whitwpostfarmcentre.co.uk

A great day out for the whole family is guaranteed at the **White Post Farm Centre**, which has been attracting crowds and awards ever since it first opened its doors in 1988. The three young owners who took over in 2004, all with children of their own, provide visitors with an experience that is both exciting and educational. Twenty-five acres of picturesque farmland include pleasant walks through paddocks of farm animals both native and exotic, from sheep, cows, pigs, goats and ducks to llamas and wallabies. The Reptile House is home to an amazing collection of creatures large and small, including stick insects, crickets, locusts and leaf-cutter ants, boa constrictors and a Burmese python, tarantulas, turtles and terrapins, frogs, snails, axolotls, angel fish and clown fish. The site contains

tea rooms and a burger barn, indoor and outdoor play areas (the go-kart track is a must for the kids!), and a recently opened farm shop adds a new dimension with a wide range of fresh local produce.

The Centre stands on the A614 ten miles north of Nottingham in the heart of Robin Hood country.

---

wealth of attractions for visitors of all ages: a large tropical house with exotic butterflies and birds, fish and insects, including a colony of leafcutter ants; a large indoor soft play area with a giant pirate ship and a Jungle Room; adventure play areas including a 54ft trawler in a giant sandpit; one of the largest hedges in the country; trails and woodland; a pet shed; a water fun fountain, a miniature railway; a garden centre and much more.

In Farnsfield village itself traces of a Roman camp can be found and the ghost of a Roman soldier is reputed to haunt one of village's pubs. More recently, the village was the birthplace of the explorer, Augustus Charles Gregory. After emigrating to Australia, Gregory became the first person to explore the country's interior. The Royal Geographical Society commissioned an expedition led by him in 1855, a journey during which 5,000 miles of the country was mapped. Gregory's respect for the native culture earned him the unofficial title of 'Protector of the Aborigines'.

RAINWORTH
7 miles SW of Ollerton off the A617

🕊 Rainworth Water

Pronounced 'Renoth' locally, this is a mining village and its development is solely due to the now closed pits. There are, however, two very different places of interest within the village. **Rainworth Water**, a series of lakes and streams, which attracts walkers, naturalists, and fishermen, is also the site of a bird sanctuary founded by the naturalist Joseph Whitaker.

Rainworth's other claim to fame is its fish and chip shop which found itself on the front pages of the national newspapers in the early 1980s as the place where the Black Panther

was caught. A local shopkeeper had noticed a man loitering in the area and had contacted the police who kept a watch for the suspicious man on the main street of the village. Suddenly realising that he was being followed, the suspect began shooting at the police, injuring one, but the customers in the chip shop, seeing what was going on, apprehended the man. Though at the time the police did not know the identity of the gunman he later turned out to be the notorious Black Panther who was later convicted of murder.

RAVENSHEAD
9 miles SW of Ollerton on the A60

🏛 Pumping Station   🎨 Rural Craft Centre

Although the name Ravenshead appears in the Domesday Book, the village of Ravenshead is relatively new and dates from 1966 when the three hamlets of Fishpool, Larch Farm, and Kighill merged. Situated by the side of the main road is the Bessie Shepherd Stone which marks the spot where, in 1817, Bessie was murdered as she walked from Mansfield to Papplewick.

Longdale Lane Rural Craft Centre was established in the 1970s and it is the oldest such centre in the country. It's a re-creation of a 19th century village, complete with flagstones and Victorian street lamps. Behind the decorative, period shop fronts a whole host of professional artists can be seen making both traditional and modern objects. **Papplewick Pumping Station** is Britain's finest Victorian water pumping station, recently restored as a spectacular example of Victorian craftsmanship. Original features include an ornate engine house, an ornamental cooling pond and a boiler house with six Lancashire boilers. Tel: 0115 963 2938.

Mansfield

🏛 Bentinck Monument   🏛 Museum

The second largest town in the county, Mansfield stands at the heart of what were once the great North Nottinghamshire coalfields. That industry has now vanished but Mansfield still has the atmosphere of an industrial town although its economy is now based on a broader spread of varying businesses.

The most distinctive structure in Mansfield is undoubtedly the great railway viaduct that sweeps through and above the town, carried by 15 huge arches of rough-hewn stone. Built in 1875, it is one of the largest viaducts to be found in an English town and gives some dignity to a community which suffered badly from thoughtless development in the 1960s.

The old market place still hosts markets on Mondays, Thursdays, Fridays and Saturdays with colourful stalls gathered around the impressive Gothic **Bentinck Monument**. This was erected in 1848 in memory of Lord George Bentinck, the younger son of the Duke of Portland. Bentinck was a long serving Member of Parliament for the town and a great friend of Disraeli. The memorial was raised by public subscription but unfortunately funds ran out before the finishing touch, a statue of Bentinck himself, could be placed in the central space.

Standing just to the northwest of the market place, **Mansfield Museum** concentrates its collections largely on local interest and includes a model of a Roman villa that once stood at nearby Mansfield Woodhouse. The collection spans the centuries from that early occupation right up to more recent times, with pictures and artefacts relating to the industry of the town

and surrounding villages. The adjoining art gallery also carries a local theme and features works by artists of the area including the water-colourist AS Buxton, who is well known for his paintings of Mansfield.

Around Mansfield

MANSFIELD WOODHOUSE
2 miles N of Mansfield on the A60

🏛 Church

Originally a settlement within Sherwood Forest, Mansfield Woodhouse is now virtually a suburb of Mansfield but the core of the village remains remarkably intact and several interesting buildings have survived.

Opposite The Cross, in the heart of the town, stands one of these fine houses, the Georgian Burnaby House. Still retaining many of its original, elegant features the house was obviously built for a prosperous family and, during the mid-1800s, it was occupied by the Duke of Portland's land agent. On the other side of the road stands a stump which is all that remains of the Market Cross, erected here after a great fire in 1304. The village stocks also stood close by and they were once used to detain George Fox, the Quaker Movement founder, after he had preached the gospel to the villagers.

At the bottom of the street stands the oldest building in Mansfield Woodhouse, **St Edmund's Church**. Most of the original church was lost, along with the parish records, when fire swept through the village in the early 14th century. The present church was built on the same site though it underwent some severe restoration in the 19th century. Standing not far from the church is a manor house known as Woodhouse Castle because of the battlements which were added to the building in the early 1800s. Dating from the 1600s, this was the home of the Digby family and, in particular, of General Sir John Digby, Sheriff of Nottingham, who distinguished himself during the Civil War.

Another building of note is the essentially 18th century Wolfhunt House found just off the High Street. The unusual name is derived from a local tale which suggests that the land on which the house is built once belonged to a man who was employed to frighten away the wolves in Sherwood Forest by blowing a hunting horn.

SKEGBY
2 miles W of Mansfield off the A6075

Skegby's church had to be rebuilt in the 1870s because of mining subsidence but some interesting features were salvaged from the old church: some monuments to the Lindley family; a fine east window; and two delightful effigies from the early 1300s showing a Sherwood Forester and his wife. She is dressed in a wimple and long gown; he carries a hunting horn.

The village is lucky in having a particularly fine example of a 14th century cruck cottage though this was not discovered until restoration work was taking place on the building in the 1950s. The village's pinfold, the place where stray animals were held until their owner claimed them, has also been restored and can be found on the Mansfield road.

TEVERSAL
3 miles W of Mansfield off the B6014

A rural oasis in the heart of this former mining district, Teversal stands on a hill looking across to the lovely Elizabethan Hardwick Hall which is actually just over the

border in Derbyshire. Teversal village is the fictional home of Lady Chatterley and the woodlands of the Hardwick Hall estate were the meeting place for her and gamekeeper Mellors in DH Lawrence's *Lady Chatterley's Lover*.

The village also boasts, according to Pevsner, "one of the most rewarding village churches in the county". It has a Norman door, 12th century arcades and a 15th century tower but eclipsing all these are the wonderful 17th century fittings, all marvellously intact. A wealth of colourful hatchments, ornate monuments to the Molyneux and Carnavon families, Lords of the Manor, and original box pews all add to the interest. The Carnavons own family pew has embroidered cushions and is set apart from the lowlier seating by four spiral columns which give it the appearance of a four-poster bed.

SUTTON IN ASHFIELD
2 miles SW of Mansfield on the A38

This once small village expanded over the years as a result of local coal mining and modern development has not been kind. However, a few of the original 17th and 18th century cottages can be seen near the Church of St Mary Magdalene. The church contains some Norman work on the west wall, 13th century arcades and a 14th century spire. A tombstone lying beside the path leading to the porch commemorates a certain Ann Burton who achieved the remarkable feat of dying on the 30th February 1836.

ANNESLEY WOODHOUSE
5 miles SW of Mansfield on the A608

All that remains of old Annesley is the roofless ruin of what DH Lawrence described as a "mouldering church standing high on a bank by the roadside…black and melancholy above the shrinking head of the traveller". Another great writer also knew the village well. Annesley Hall was the home of Mary Chaworth, a lady for whom Lord Byron formed an early affection. The poet and the beautiful heiress would often walk up to the breezy summit of Diadem Hill, 578ft high and visible for miles around. The liaison was a little odd since Mary had inherited her great fortune from William Chaworth: William had been killed in a duel by Byron's great uncle, the 5th Lord Byron. Perhaps because of this unfortunate event, Mary did not succumb to the poet's charms. Instead she married John Musters, the sporting squire of Colwick Hall near Nottingham. She died there in 1832 as the result of an attack on the Hall by Reform Bill rioters.

NEWSTEAD
5 miles S of Mansfield off the A608

🏛 Abbey

A magnificent 13th century ruin attached to a Victorian reworking of a Tudor mansion provides one of the county's most historic houses. **Newstead Abbey** was founded by Henry II around 1170 as part of his atonement for the murder of Thomas à Becket, and sold at the Dissolution of the Monasteries to Sir John Byron who destroyed much of the Abbey and converted other buildings into a mansion. The Newstead estate remained in the Byron family for almost 300 years, its last owner being the celebrated poet George, Lord Byron.

He inherited the property from his great uncle, the 5th Lord Byron, better known as 'Devil Byron'. As mentioned earlier, the 5th Lord had killed an old family friend in a duel and although he was only convicted of manslaughter, he was obliged to pay huge punitive costs. Ostracised by London society, he retreated to Newstead in malevolent mood. To pay his debts he virtually denuded the estate of its great plantations of oaks. And just to spite his son and expected heir he ordered the slaughter of the deer herd that had grazed the parkland for generations. As it happened, his son died before him and the estate passed to that "brat from Aberdeen", as he referred to his impoverished great nephew who was living there in poverty with his mother.

When the poet arrived at Newstead in 1798, he found that the only room in this huge mansion without a leaking roof was the scullery. The estate was burdened with debts, and so was Byron. He managed to let the estate out for some years but when

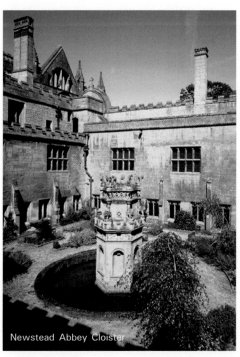
Newstead Abbey Cloister

he finally took up residence in 1808 he was still hard put to make the house even reasonably habitable. In 1817 he gave up the struggle, sold the estate to an old Harrow schoolmate, Col. Thomas Wildman, for £94,000, removed himself to Italy and never saw Newstead again.

Col. Wildman spared no expense in refurbishing and extending the dilapidated house, an undertaking that took 12 years to complete. The house and grounds that visitors see today is essentially the creation of Thomas Wildman, but the presiding spirit of the house is undeniably that of the wayward poet.

Over the years, many Byron manuscripts, letters, books, pictures and personal relics have found their way back to the Abbey, and both the house and grounds are beautifully maintained by the present owners, the City of Nottingham, to whom the estate was bequeathed in 1931. The house is open every afternoon from April to September, and the grounds all year round. These include a secret garden; a beautifully carved fountain decorated with fantastic animals; the famous and elaborate memorial to Byron's dog Boatswain, and a large lake where the 5th lord used to re-enact naval battles.

Byron died from a fever while travelling in Greece supporting the patriot's war of independence against the Turks. His body was returned to England but his scandalous reputation for womanising made a proposed burial in Westminster Abbey unthinkable. Instead, he was interred at Hucknall, a couple of miles south of Newstead Abbey (see below).

LINBY
6 miles S of Mansfield on the B6011

"One of the prettiest villages on the north side of Nottingham," was Pevsner's rather cautious praise of this small village where a stream runs along the main street with broad grass verges, and enough stone built houses to face down the unfortunate sprawl of 1930s red brick houses near the church.

The village is situated on the banks of the River Leen which, during the late 18th century, was a busy, bustling place with six cotton mills being powered by the water. The mills were strictly functional but George Robinson, their owner, did not want to be out done by his near neighbours at Newstead Abbey so he added battlements and other ornate features and thus gave Castle Mill its name. Young apprentices were brought in from as far away as London to work in Castle Mill. Housed in small lodges near the mill, the children worked long hours weaving cotton cloth in terrible conditions with minimal food and clothing provided. Brought to work in the mills from a young age (some were no more than ten years old) many died early. In Linby churchyard the graves of 42 apprentice children bear witness to Robinson's callous pursuit of profit.

When the 5th Lord Byron dammed the River Leen upstream from Linby, in order to create a lake on his estate, he also played havoc with the water supply to the mills. With a reduction in power, Robinson had to find another reliable power source and in 1786 his sons were the first to apply steam power to a cotton mill when they installed a Boulton and Watt engine.

HUCKNALL
7 miles S of Mansfield off the A611

🕊 Church

Hucknall attracts a constant stream of visitors to **St Mary Magdalen Church,** not so much for its 14th century font or for the

27 attractive stained glass windows by Kempe, but to gaze at a simple marble slab set in the floor of the chancel. It bears the inscription: *BYRON, Born January 22nd, 1788, Died April 19th, 1824.*

The inscription is surmounted by a laurel wreath, in classical times the only award to winners in the original Olympic Games. The memorial was presented to the church in 1881 by the King of the Hellenes in appreciation of Byron's support for the Greeks against their imperial masters, the Turks.

Byron died in Greece where his body was embalmed and transported to England. For several days the body was exhibited at an inn in Nottingham before being buried in the Byron family crypt at Hucknall. Many years later, in 1938, the vicar of Hucknall entered the now closed crypt to challenge a tradition that the poet's body had been removed. He found the lid of the coffin loose and its lead lining cut open. "Very reverently, I raised the lid, and before my eyes lay the embalmed body of Byron in as perfect condition as when it was placed in the coffin 114 years ago...The serene, almost happy expression on his face made a profound impression on me. The feet and ankles were uncovered, and I was able to establish the fact that his lameness had been that of his right foot." Another occupant of the family vault is Ada, Countess of Lovelace, Byron's only daughter. Ada was a friend and associate of Charles Babbage, inventor of the forerunner of the computer.

Hucknall boasts another famous son. Eric Coates, the son of a local doctor, was born here on 27th August 1886. He displayed musical talent at an early age, (he demanded and got his first violin at the age of six), and became the most celebrated viola player of his generation. But Coates became even more famous as a composer of light music – his *Sleepy Lagoon* is immediately recognisable to millions as the signature music of BBC Radio's long-running programme *Desert Island Discs.*

SELSTON
9 miles SW of Mansfield on the B600

Mentioned in the Domesday Book as a place with a church and three acres of meadows, like many other village communities in this western area of Nottinghamshire, Selston was at that time very much a farming community. But beneath the fertile agricultural land lay coal and leases for coal mining were granted as early as 1206. For centuries the coal mining operation remained small scale but by the 1850s Selston had taken on many of the aspects of a modern colliery village. The last coal pit in Selston closed in 1956 but almost half a century later the village still has a lacklustre air to it.

From the churchyard of the partly-Norman Church of St Helen there are some splendid views across the neighbouring Derbyshire hills. The graveyard is the last resting place of Dan Boswell, king of the gypsies. For many years newborn gypsy babies were brought to Boswell's gravestone to be baptised and many gypsies made special journeys to the church to pay their respects.

Eastwood

🏛 Heritage Centre

⚒ DH Lawrence Birthplace Museum

"I have always hated it," wrote DH Lawrence of the mining town where he was born in 1885. Reviling the "ugliness of my native village", he wished it could be pulled down "to the last brick". Local people reciprocated his dislike: "He were nowt but a big soft gel," said one of his contemporaries many years later when the gawky lad whose mum insisted he should never go down the pit had become a writer and painter of internatonal repute.

The Lawrence family home, a two up, two down, terrace house at 8a Victoria Street is now the **DH Lawrence Birthplace Museum.** It has been furnished in a late 19th century style with which the Lawrence family would have been familiar. There are also some household items on display which belonged to the family and anyone visiting the museum will see that the house's front window is larger than others in the same street. This is where Mrs Lawrence displayed children's clothes and other linen items which she made and sold to supplement the fluctuating wages brought home by her miner husband.

In 1887, the Lawrence family moved to a larger, end of terrace house in Eastwood which today is known as the Sons and Lovers Cottage since it featured as the Morels' house, The Bottoms, in Lawrence's novel. This house too is open to the public, though by

appointment only, and is also laid out with furnishings and artefacts which are appropriate to the time. Lawrence's father was a miner at the nearby Brinsley Pit and though the family moved house in Eastwood several times, the Lawrences remained short of money. Young Lawrence attended the local school and was the first Eastwood boy to gain a scholarship to Nottingham High School where he was a pupil until 1901. Lawrence started his working life as a clerk before undertaking a teacher training course and moving to teach in a school in Croydon. The offices where as a boy D H Lawrence would pick up his father's wages are now the **Durban House Heritage Centre**, which houses a range of exhibitions and the Rainbow Gallery.

Though Lawrence had already begun writing, his major novels were not written until after 1912, the year he eloped with his former professor's wife and left England. Drawing heavily on the influences of his upbringing in Eastwood, *Sons and Lovers,* first published in 1913, not only describes the countryside around Eastwood but also portrays many local personalities. The unflattering descriptions of, among others, Lawrence senior, caused a great deal of local resentment, a resentment that astonishingly persists to this day in the village. Lawrence and his wife, Frieda Weekley, returned to England during World War I but they were unable to settle and at one point were detained as suspected German spies. They were

DH Lawrence Birthpace Museum

soon on their travels once again.

In the early 1920s, Lawrence published *Women in Love* and, a few years later, was diagnosed with tuberculosis, the disease from which he died in 1930. It was while he was in Florence, trying unsuccessfully to find a cure for his crippling condition, that Lawrence wrote his most famous novel, *Lady Chatterley's Lover*. First published in 1928, the full text of the controversial story was not printed until 1960 and, even then, it was the subject of a court case that is almost as famous as the book.

A place of pilgrimage for devotees of Lawrence, Eastwood also attracts those with an interest in railway history. It was at the Sun Inn in the Market Place that a group of "Iron Masters and Coal Owners" gathered on 16th August, 1832 to discuss the construction of a railway that would eventually become the mighty Midland Railway. A plaque on the wall of the inn commemorates the seminal meeting.

The railway was formed to compete with the Erewash Canal, completed in 1779 and effectively put out of business by the 1870s. Almost a century later, following years of neglect, the canal was cleared and made suitable for use by pleasure craft. The towpath was resurfaced and now provides a pleasant and interesting walk.

Around Eastwood

AWSWORTH
1 mile S of Eastwood on the A6096

In order to lay the tracks for the Great Northern Railway line from Derby to Nottingham, a viaduct was needed to carry the railway over the Erewash Canal, the River Erewash and the Nottingham Canal which all lie close to Awsworth. The resulting construction, built in 1876-7, is still an impressive sight though the line is now disused. One of only two viaducts in England to be made of wrought iron lattice girders, the Bennerley Viaduct has 16 spans, which are set on pillars 56 feet high.

KIMBERLEY
1 mile S of Eastwood off the A610

Kimberley – the name means a clearing in the forest – was first mentioned in the Domesday Book, and for many centuries it remained a small rural farming hamlet. The village church

---

LOU LOU'S

4 James Street, Kimberley, Nottingham,
Nottinghamshire NG16 2LP
Tel: 0115 854 4784
website: www.loulous.org.uk

Quality comes first at **Lou Lou's**, a delightful café and bistro in one of Kimberley's cobbled streets. All products are carefully selected to guarantee the finest in food service. Everything on the menu is homemade and at lunchtime includes soup, sandwiches, baguettes, lasagne and specials of the day and can be eaten in the charming conservatory or enclosed rear garden. Lou Lou's offers speciality drinks and the world famous Italian Musetti coffee. The café is open from 9am to 4pm, Monday to Saturday and a bistro menu is served on Friday and Saturday evenings (booking essential). Lou Lou's also specialises in outside catering and is the perfect venue for private functions.

🎭 stories and anecdotes 🐦 famous people 🎨 art and craft 🎭 entertainment and sport 🚶 walks fell into ruin down the centuries, but with the arrival of industries such as brewing, mining and silk making and the growth of the population a new church, Holy Trinity, was built in 1847. A well-known landmark is the War Memorial, which commemorates the villagers who fell in the two World Wars. It is thought to be the only domed war memorial in the country. Most villages in Britain have their little eccentricities, and in Kimberley they stage 'pram' races on a day in July in support of local charities.

COSSALL
3 miles S of Eastwood off the A6096

Now a conservation area, this village draped across a low hill boasts some attractive buildings, notably the picturesque 17th century Willoughby almshouses and a farmhouse which includes part of the original home of the Willoughby family. They were a branch of the Willoughbys of Wollaton, a dynasty that was founded by a wealthy 13th century wool merchant from Nottingham named Ralph Bugge. This rather unfortunate name (which means hobgoblin) was understandably changed by his descendants to the more acceptable Willoughby; a name taken from the village of Willoughby-on-the-Wolds, on the border with Leicestershire, where Ralph owned a fair acreage of land.

Cossall was another of DH Lawrence's haunts and it featured in his novel *The Rainbow* as the village of 'Cossethay', home of the Brangwen family. The fictional character, William Brangwen, is said to have been based on Alfred Burrows, to whose daughter, Louise, Lawrence was engaged for some time. She duly appears as Ursula Brangwen. The Burrows family lived in a cottage, now marked by a plaque, near the charming village church

which contains a fine marble tomb of the Willoughbys.

Retford

🏛 Bassetlaw Museum

🏛 Percy Laws Memorial Gallery   🏯 Cannon Square

Retford is actually two communities, East and West Retford, set either side of the River Idle. West Retford is the elder settlement; its twin grew up during the 1100s as a place where tolls could be collected from travellers making the river crossing. Retford has been a market town since 1246 and markets are still held here every Thursday and Saturday.

Retford received a major economic boost in 1766 when the Great North Road was diverted through the town. That was when the Market Square was re-developed and some of the elegant Georgian buildings here, and in Grove Street, still survive from that time. The grand and rather chateau-like Town Hall, however, dates from 1868 and replaced the Georgian hall. Outside the Town Hall can be found the Broad Stone, which is probably the base of an old parish boundary cross. Tradition has it that during the times of the plague in Retford, in the mid-16th and mid-17th centuries, coins were placed in a pool of vinegar in the hollow in the top of the stone to prevent the disease from spreading while trading was taking place at the market.

In the northwestern corner of the square is an archway that leads down to the River Idle. Bearing the inscription "JP Esquire 1841", the archway once led to the gardens of John Parker who lived in a nearby house, now business premises. A close inspection of the garden wall will reveal that it has a hollow curve. This was in order to funnel hot air along the wall to warm the fruit trees grown in its shelter.

Cannon Square is home to one of Retford's more unusual attractions: a Russian cannon. Dating from 1855 and weighing over two tons, the cannon was captured by British soldiers at Sebastopol and brought to Retford at the end of the Crimean War. The townsfolk paid for its transportation and, in 1859, after arguments raged about its siting, the cannon was finally placed in the square and named the Earl of Aberdeen after the incumbent Prime Minister. During World War II the cannon was threatened with being melted down to help the war effort and was only saved after a Retford gentleman bought it and hid it until the war was over.

One of Retford's most infamous visitors was the highwayman Dick Turpin, and several historic inns still stand as a reminder of the romantic days of stage coach travel. Another man who stood and delivered here, though in a more respectable fashion, was John Wesley, who conducted many open air meetings in East Retford.

While in Retford, it is well worth visiting the **Bassetlaw Museum** in Amcott House, Grove Street. This imposing late 18th century town house was once the home of the Whartons, the woollen drapers; Sir Wharton Amcotts, MP for the Borough of East Retford; and the Peglers, local industrialists. It was extensively restored and opened as a museum for the District of Bassetlaw in 1986. The house is noted for its finely executed internal plasterwork and elegant wrought iron staircase which the restoration has returned to their full Georgian splendour. The museum has a distinct local emphasis, with displays of local archaeology, civic, social and industrial history, and fine and applied art. Occupying

the former service wing of the house, the **Percy Laws Memorial Gallery** has a permanent display of historic Retford civic plate and also hosts short term exhibitions.

Around Retford

MATTERSEY
6 miles N of Retford off the B6045

🏛 Priory

From the eastern end of the village, a rubbly lane leads down to the sparse ruins of the romantically sited **Mattersey Priory,** founded in 1185 for the Gilbertine Order, the only monastic order to be established by an Englishman, Roger de Mattersey. When the Priory was founded, it had only six canons. Though the number of priests fluctuated over the years, Mattersey was never a wealthy institution: at the time of the Dissolution of the Monasteries only five canons had to be turned out onto the streets. The original priory buildings at Mattersey were destroyed by fire in 1279 so the remains seen today are of the 14th century dormitory, refectory and the walls of the Chapel of St Helen. The site is rarely visited by tourists but, with the River Idle flowing nearby, it is a peaceful and picturesque hidden place, well worth seeking out.

GRINGLEY ON THE HILL
7 miles NE of Retford on the A631

Gringley commands some astonishingly wide views over Yorkshire, Lincolnshire, and Nottinghamshire. The best vantage point is Beacon Hill (235ft), on the east side of the village. As the name suggests, Beacon Hill was used as the site for beacon fires designed to warn of impending invasion.

🎭 stories and anecdotes   🕊 famous people   🎨 art and craft   ✏ entertainment and sport   🚶 walks

GOACHER'S

Green Acres, Wood Lane, North Wheatley,
Retford, Nottinghamshire DN22 9BG
Tel: 01427 880341   Fax: 01427 884309
e-mail: Judith@goforgoachers.fsnet.co.uk
website: www.goforgoachers.co.uk

Generations of the Goacher family have farmed here since the 1850s, and their 165 acres provide much of the top-quality produce sold in the farm shop. **Goacher's** sells an unrivalled selection of fruit and vegetables, including up to 12 varieties of apples, eight kinds of plums, three sorts of pears, dessert cherries (the only ones in the North), strawberries, raspberries, Tayberries, redcurrants, blackcurrants, asparagus, pumpkins and a whole lot more. Among other goods for sale are homemade pies and cakes, turkeys reared on the farm, free-range eggs, fresh and frozen fruit and vegetables, honey from their orchards, homemade jams and chutneys, fruit vinegars, milk, cream and ice cream made locally using fruit from the farm.

Pick Your Own is an important part of the business, and the farm has a picnic area with a children's play area and pets galore. Goacher's is open from 9am (10am on Sunday, closed Wednesdays November to April). They also attend many farmers' markets in Nottinghamshire and Lincolnshire.

The village Church of St Peter and St Paul dates from the 12th century and one of the church bells is, rather unusually, dated to the time of the Commonwealth. During that period, bells and other decorative items were considered frivolous and were generally dispensed with but, as the parish records show, the people of Gringley did not subscribe to such kill-joy ideas: they also celebrated Christmas in defiance of Puritan edicts forbidding the festival.

NORTH LEVERTON
5 miles E of Retford off the A620

🏛 Windmill   🐾 Adventureland

The correct name for this attractive village is 'North Leverton with Habblesthorpe', a mouthful which has been hailed in the *Guinness Book of Records* as the longest multiple place name in England.

The 12th century village Church of St Martin is reached via a bridge over a stream and, with its 18th century Dutch gables, looks rather like an import from Holland. So, too, does the splendid **North Leverton Windmill**, the only one in Nottinghamshire still grinding corn. When the mill was built in 1813, it was known as the 'North Leverton Subscription Mill' in acknowledgement of the farmers from four surrounding parishes who subscribed to the cost. Three storeys high, the elegant structure has four sails, one of which was struck by lightning in 1958. Thanks to the efforts of local people, assisted by financial support from the County Council, the mill is now fully operational and visitors can follow the whole milling process in action. If they wish, they can also purchase some of the freshly ground flour.

About three miles south of the village, **Sundown Kiddies Adventureland** is a unique theme park designed especially for the under tens. There's a pet shop where the animals join in and sing a musical chorus; a Witches' Kitchen where the kids are in charge of the gruesome cuisine; rides; an adventure play area; café and much more.

BABWORTH
1 mile W of Retford on the A620

Babworth has a fine Georgian Hall, a church with Pilgrim Father associations and a spacious park laid out by Humphrey Repton – but virtually no village. Its inhabitants were moved to the village of Ranby, two miles to the west, when the park was 'improved'. The old Great North Road used to pass through Babworth and it was here, in 1503, that Margaret Tudor was entertained by the Alderman of Retford at a cost of £12.11s (£12.55p). She was on her way to marry James IV of Scotland.

Inside the porch of the small Church of All Saints, with its battlements and pinnacles, a plaque records that the Pilgrim Fathers William Brewster and William Bradford worshipped here before sailing on the *Mayflower*.

Worksop

🏛 Priory Gatehouse   🏛 Mr Straw's House

⛴ Chesterfield Canal

Despite the unattractive modern houses lining the roads leading into Worksop, there are some fine Georgian buildings to be found in Bridge Street. One of the major attractions of Worksop is the **Priory Gatehouse**, which is best approached from Potter Street where the full glory of the 14th century building can be seen. Its great niches house large and beautifully carved statues and the immense entrance is rather reminiscent of a cave opening. Originally the portal to a large Augustinian monastery, the gatehouse together with the Church of St Mary and St Cuthbert, is all that remains. There is also a

Mr Straw's House

7 Blyth Grove, Worksop, Nottinghamshire S81 0JG
Tel: 01909 482380
e-mail: mrstrawshouse@nationaltrust.org.uk
website: www.nationaltrust.org.uk

This modest semi-detached Edwardian house was the family home of well-to-do grocers William and Florence Straw from 1923. It is remarkable because the Straws' two sons preserved it almost unaltered till it came to the National Trust in 1990. The interior with its 1920s wallpaper, heavy Victorian furniture and household objects provides a rare glimpse into interwar middle-class life. There are displays of family costume, letters and photos and a typical suburban garden.

🎞 stories and anecdotes   🐦 famous people   🎨 art and craft   ✏ entertainment and sport   🥾 walks

wayside shrine, which makes it a unique ecclesiastical attraction. Today, the upper floor of the gatehouse houses an art gallery and exhibitions are put on here regularly.

The first canal to be built in Nottinghamshire was the **Chesterfield Canal**, which runs from Chesterfield in Derbyshire to the River Trent. Some 46 miles long, work on the canal was begun in 1771 and it took six years to complete under the supervision of John Varley, the deputy of the great canal engineer, James Brindley. In the mid-1800s, the canal was taken over by the Sheffield and Lincoln Junction Railway, which in 1863 decided to cease maintaining the waterway and allowed it to run down. The collapse of one of the canal's two tunnels, at Norwood in 1908, hastened its decline by effectively cutting off Chesterfield from the rest of the waterway.

During the canal's heyday, in the early 1800s, it was indeed a busy waterway and many buildings lined its route, particularly through Worksop. Pickford's Depository, spanning the canal in the centre of the town, was typical of this time. The trap doors in the stone archway over the canal were used for the loading and unloading of the 'cuckoos', as the narrowboats on the Chesterfield Canal were called.

A recent acquisition by the National Trust, **Mr Straw's House** (see panel on page 289) at 7 Blyth Grove, is quite unique and well worth visiting. The house, together with an endowment of one million pounds, was left to the Trust by William Straw in his will. The Trust's surveyors were surprised to find upon inspection of the Edwardian semi-detached house that they were actually stepping back in time. Inside, everything had remained untouched since the death in 1932 of William Straw senior, a grocer and seed merchant in

Worksop. His wife, who died seven years later, neither altered nor added anything. Nor did her two sons, William and Walter, who lived a bachelor existence at the house. Walter, who took on the family business, died in 1976; his brother William in 1990.

In all those years, virtually nothing had changed in the house. The parents' bedroom had been closed up and everything left as it was. A 1932 calendar was still hanging on the wall; William Senior's hats were still perched in the hall; his pipes and tobacco pouch lay ready by the fireside.

The Mayflower Trail starts at Scrooby church and guides visitors around the local sites connected with the Pilgrim Fathers, including William Brewster's Manor House at Scrooby and Gainsborough Old Hall, just across the Trent in Lincolnshire.

Around Worksop

CARLTON-IN-LINDRICK
3 miles N of Worksop on the A616

🏛 Old Mill Museum

This village's name has a delightful meaning – the "freedmen's enclosure in the lime wood". In fact it is not one, but two villages, North Carlton and South Carlton, the latter of which is the more ancient. Believed to have been a Saxon settlement, South Carlton, or Carlton Barron as it was also called, is home to the village church. With its massive Saxon tower, the church is quite awe-inspiring as it soars above the village. In Church Lane is the **Old Mill Museum**, housed in a converted 18th century water mill. On display are some unusual linen pictures, used by the Victorians as educational material, as well as farming implements and mill machinery.

BLYTH

5 miles NE of Worksop on the A634

🏛 Church

A village on the old Great North Road, Blyth is distinguished by a fine church and, until the 1970s, also boasted a stately home, Blyth Hall. The latter was demolished and the site is now covered by executive homes. But the magnificent **Church of St Mary and St Martin** still stands, its great tower surmounted by eight lofty pinnacles soaring high above the village.

The original church was built around 1100 and much of that Norman building has survived in all its sturdy strength. Pevsner thought that there was "nothing like Blyth to get a feeling for early Norman grimness." Opinions differ on that, since the now bare and rough-hewn walls were originally brightly painted. However, most agree that the medieval Gothic additions to the church were eminently successful. The most treasured possession here is a 15th century wall painting of the Last Judgment, one of the largest and most complete medieval murals in England. Restored in 1987, the mural has been described as 'unsophisticated', 'probably done by a travelling artist', but it is still mightily impressive.

There are many other buildings of note in the village, including a handsome stable block and the former rectory, surmounted by a cupola. Among the redbrick Georgian houses there are also a number of coaching inns providing a reminder that Blyth was once an important staging post on the Great North Road.

Just to the southwest of the village lies Hodsock Priory (private) and its beautiful Gardens surrounded by parkland and meadows. Although this would seem to be the perfect setting for a medieval monastery, no priory ever stood here. The present house was built in 1829 in the Tudor style to complement the marvellous 16th century gatehouse. The gatehouse is approached across an ancient rectangular moat and, within this area, the gardens have been laid out. The southern arm of the moat was made into a small lake around 1880. The Snowdrop Garden and Snowdrop Woodland Walk are open to visitors for four weeks from early February.

Between Blyth and the nearby village of Styrrup, to the north, lies the Tournament Field. Dating back to the Middle Ages, the field was one of only five in the country to be granted a royal licence by Richard I.

CRESWELL

3 miles SW of Worksop on the A616

🏛 Creswell Crags

Creswell village is actually in Derbyshire but its most famous feature lies just inside the Nottinghamshire border. **Creswell Crags** form a dramatic limestone gorge pitted with deep, dark and mysterious caves. Here the bones of prehistoric bison, bears, wolves, woolly rhinos and lions twice the size of their modern descendants have been found. Around 45000BC, humans took over the caves. One of them was a gifted artist, as a bone fragment engraved with a fine carving of a horse bears witness. The Visitors' Centre contains some fascinating archaeological finds and there are some pleasant walks past the lakes to the crags.

LOCATOR MAP

ADVERTISERS AND PLACES OF INTEREST

🏠 historic building   🏛 museum   🏛 historic site   🌳 scenic attraction   🌿 flora and fauna

7| Lincolnshire

Known to the Romans as Lindum Colonia, Lincoln stood at the junction of two major Imperial thoroughfares, Fosse Way and Ermine Street. By the time of the Domesday Book, it had grown into a settlement of around 1,000 households. William the Conqueror won few friends here by peremptorily ordering 166 of these houses to be destroyed to make way for an imposing castle. Around the same time, he authorised the building of a cathedral and made Lincoln the ecclesiastical centre of a vast bishopric that extended from the Humber to the Thames.

The city reached its peak of prosperity during the Middle Ages but when Henry VIII visited in 1541 the town fathers were reduced to begging relief from taxation or "they would be compelled in short time to forsake the city, to its utter desolation". Henry rejected their plea. When Daniel Defoe passed through Lincoln in the 1770s he found "an ancient, ragged, decayed and still decaying city". Half a century later, another traveller dismissed the historic city as *"an overgrown village"*.

Happily, improvements in roads and canals, and the arrival of the railway in the 1840s, returned the city to prosperity and Lincoln became a major centre for heavy engineering, -

steam engines, agricultural machinery, excavators, motor cars and other heavy duty items. But you only have to climb the hill to the old town to enter the serenity of the cathedral close, a tranquil enclave lying in the shadow of the noblest and most majestic of all English cathedrals.

The south bank of the River Humber is indeed Lincolnshire's most industrial area but that is only part of the story. Rural north Lincolnshire is as peaceful and unspoilt as anywhere in the county, with scenery that ranges from the northern tip of the Wolds in the east, to the level plains of the Isle of Axholme in the west. The area also includes the largest town in the county, Grimsby (pop. 92,000), once one of the busiest fishing ports in the world and now an important centre of the food processing industry. A few miles up-river, and even more imposing, is the colossal Humber Bridge, the largest single span suspension bridge in Europe.

The Lincolnshire Wolds, a sweeping chalk

Lincolnshire Wolds

downland stretching up the middle of the county, includes some of the most beautiful and largely undiscovered countryside in England. This is great walking and cycling country, but there are a few hills, too – Nab Hill and Tetford Hill both rise to over 400 feet. Picturesque villages and small towns such as Aby, Bag Enderby, Normanby-on-the-Wold, Somersby, Spilsby and Walesby are well worth exploring, as are the larger towns – Market Rasen on the western edge, Horncastle in the south and Louth in the east.

Stretching from Wainfleet and Skegness in the south to Cleethorpes and the mouth of the Humber to the north, the Lindsey Coastal Plain runs for about 40 miles, north to south, and extends between five and 10 miles wide, east to west. The Plain offers a good range of

animal sanctuaries and nature reserves. The area's other main attraction, the splendid sandy beaches running virtually the whole length of the coast, didn't come into their own until the railways arrived in the mid-1800s. The coastal villages of Skegness, Mablethorpe and Cleethorpes have grown steadily to become popular resorts for East Midlanders, each one offering a wide range of family entertainment.

The Elizabethan writer Michael Drayton must have deterred many of his contemporaries from visiting southeast Lincolnshire by his vivid word picture of the "foggy fens". It was, he wrote, "a land of foul, woosy marsh…with a vast queachy soil and hosts of wallowing waves". It can't have been quite that bad - the Romans farmed extensively here, for example. Since Drayton's day, various drainage schemes, from the 16th century onwards, have reclaimed many thousands of waterlogged acres. Spalding is known around the world for its annual Tulip and Spring Flower Festival when a procession of floats, adorned with millions of tulip heads, progresses through the town.

The Great North Road, now the A1, brought Grantham and Stamford a constant stream of travellers and trade, a traffic whose legacy includes some fine old coaching inns. One visitor during the early 1800s regarded this as "the only gentrified region" of Lincolnshire. Belton House, Belvoir Castle, Grimsthorpe Castle and the breathtaking Elizabethan splendour of Burghley House are four of the grandest stately homes in England.

Five-Sailed Windmill, Alford

Lincoln

🏛 Cathedral 🏛 Bishops Old Palace 🏛 Jews House
🏛 Castle 🏛 The Stonebow 🏛 Ellis Mill
🏛 Museum of Lincolnshire Life ⚘ Usher Gallery
🏛 Lincolnshire Road Transport Museum

Bishop's Old Palace

Apart from Durham, **Lincoln Cathedral** is the only one in England to occupy a magnificent hilltop location, its towers soaring high above the Lincolnshire lowlands and visible for miles around. William the Conqueror ordered the first cathedral to be built here but that was almost entirely destroyed by an earthquake on April 15th 1185. The rebuilding that followed, under the energetic direction of Bishop Hugh of Avalon, resulted in the creation of one the country's most inspiring churches. Among its many superb features are the magnificent open nave, stained-glass windows incorporating the 14th century Bishop's Eye and Dean's Eye, and the glorious Angel Choir, whose carvings include the Lincoln Imp, the unofficial symbol of the city.

The imposing ruins of the **Bishops Old Palace** (English Heritage) in the shadow of the Cathedral, reveal the sumptuous lifestyle of the wealthy medieval bishops whose authority stretched from the Humber to the Thames. Visitors can wander through splendid apartments, banqueting halls and offices, explore the dramatic undercroft, gaze at the views from inside the Roman city walls, relax in the peaceful Contemporary Heritage Garden and see one of Europe's most northerly vineyards.

A good way to explore the city is to follow the Lincoln Heritage Trail which takes in the city's "Magnificent Seven" tourist attractions. The cathedral, naturally, takes pride of place

but close by is **Lincoln Castle** which dates from 1068. Visitors can climb to the ramparts, which include Observatory Tower, to savour some fine views of the city. Interesting features abound, notably the keep, known as Lucy Tower, Cobb Hall, where the public gallows were located, and the Victorian prison whose chapel has separate pews like upright coffins. The building also houses an original version of Magna Carta.

There are some fine Norman buildings on a lesser scale in Steep Hill and the Strait. **Jews House**, which dates from about 1170, is thought to be the oldest domestic building in England to survive intact. Its neighbour is Jews Court, a reminder of the time when there was a thriving Jewish community in Lincoln. Medieval splendour lives on in the

🎬 stories and anecdotes 🪶 famous people ⚘ art and craft ✏ entertainment and sport 🚶 walks

Jews House, Lincoln

lunatic asylum and set in eight acres of beautiful grounds and gardens, is an elegant porticoed building whose attractions include a tropical conservatory with a display dedicated to the botanist Sir Joseph Banks, an aquarium, a specialist shopping mall and a fully licensed pub and restaurant.

Lincolnshire's largest social history museum is the **Museum of Lincolnshire Life** which occupies an extensive barracks built for the Royal North Lincoln Militia in 1857. It is now a listed building and houses a fascinating series of displays depicting the many aspects of Lincolnshire life. The Domestic Gallery turns the clock back to the beginning of the 20th century, showing what life was like in a middle-class home; settings include a nursery, bedroom, kitchen, parlour and wash house. The Transport Gallery shows the skills of the wheelwright and coachbuilder in such items as a carrier's cart and a horse-drawn charabier (hearse). It also contains a fully restored 1925 Bullnose Morris and a Lincoln Elk motorcycle. In the Agricultural and Industrial Gallery notable exhibits include a First World War tank built by William Foster of Lincoln; a 20-ton steam ploughing engine; a steam traction engine and a number of tractors. Commercial Row features a builder's yard, a printing press, a village post office and several shops. All the above represent just part of the scope of this marvellous museum, where visitors can also pause for refreshment and perhaps a slice of the local speciality plumbread in the Hungry Yellowbelly café. (That peculiar name is applied to anyone born in Lincolnshire!)

black and white half-timbered houses on High Bridge and in the old city Gateways, while the residences in the Cathedral Close and Castle Square are models of Georgian elegance.

The most impressive survival of the old town walls is **The Stonebow** which spans the High Street pedestrianised shopping mall. The three-storey building houses the city's Guildhall, its civic insignia, royal charters and other historic artefacts. The Mote Bell on the roof, dated 1371, is still rung to summon the City Fathers to council meetings.

The Collection is a new museum, standing next to the region's premier art gallery, the Usher. The archaeology collection contains over 2,000,000 artefacts from the Iron Age, Roman, Saxon, Viking and Medieval eras. **The Usher Gallery** was built in 1927 with funds bequeathed by a Lincoln jeweller, James Ward Usher. It is a major centre for the arts, with collections of porcelain, glass, clocks and coins, and a display of memorabilia connected with the Lincolnshire-born Poet Laureate, Alfred Lord Tennyson. The gallery also houses an important collection of works by Peter de Wint and paintings by Turner, Lowry, Piper, Sickert and Ruskin Spear.

The Lawn, originally built in 1820 as a

Ellis Mill is the last survivor of a line of windmills that once ran along the Lincoln Edge, a limestone ridge stretching some 70 miles from Winteringham by the Humber to Stamford on the county's southern border. This tower mill dates back to 1798 and is in full working order. For those interested in Lincoln's commercial past, the Lincoln Engineering Society has produced a leaflet detailing an Industrial Heritage Trail that guides visitors to a score of the city's manufacturing companies, past and present.

Lincoln stages several major annual events, including a flower festival in the Cathedral and the Lincolnshire Show at the Showground just north of the city. The Lincoln Waterfront Festival is a family-oriented street arts festival based around the Brayford Waterfront in the bustling city centre. Each year a free programme combines exciting and innovative acts with well-established favourites such as the World Champion Jet Skiers, street theatre performers and a firework finale.

Around Lincoln

Just southeast of the city are the popular open spaces of Hartsholme Country Park and Swanholme Lakes Local Nature Reserve, 200 acres of woodland, lakes and meadows to explore. A little way further south is Whisby Nature Park, set on either side of the Lincoln-Newark railway line and home to great crested grebes, teal and tufted duck. Also on the

Doddington Hall & Gardens

Estate Office, Doddington Hall & Gardens, Doddington, Lincoln. LN6 4RU
Tel: Estate Office 01522 694308
e-mail: info@doddingtonhall.com
website: www.doddingtonhall.com

Doddington Hall is a stunning Elizabethan family home set in six acres of romantic wild and walled formal gardens, with a continuous pageant of colour form earliest spring until autumn. It has never been sold since it was built in 1595 by Robert Smythson and is still a lived-in and much-loved family home, alive with history and interest.

As well as the fascinating house history, its contents and its beautiful gardens, it has children's activities, summer concerts and a Christmas shop. Freshly made meals using locally-sourced produce, and home made teas and cakes are served in the fabulous new café. There are award-winning facilities for the disabled and the Hall makes an ideal venue for a wedding or corporate event.

Opening Times: Gardens Only: Every Sunday, 18ᵗʰ Feb to end of April,
also Easter Monday, 1-5pm.

House and Gardens: Every Wednesday and Sunday and Bank Holiday Mondays, 1-5pm, May to end of September. Gardens open 12 midday-5pm.

Guided party tours of both House and Gardens welcome
at other times by prior arrangement.

🎬 stories and anecdotes   🦜 famous people   🎨 art and craft   🌿 entertainment and sport   🚶 walks southern outskirts of the city is the **Lincolnshire Road Transport Museum** where 40 vintage cars, commercial vehicles and buses span more than 70 years of road transport history. Also on display is a wide variety of old road signs, ticket machines and early bus timetables.

DODDINGTON
5 miles W of Lincoln off the B1190

🏛 Doddington Hall

About five miles west of Lincoln, **Doddington Hall** is a very grand Elizabethan mansion completed in 1600 by the architect Robert Smythson, and standing now exactly as then, with wonderful formal gardens, a gatehouse and a family church. The interior contains a fascinating collection of pictures, textiles, porcelain and furniture that reflect four centuries of unbroken family occupation.

BARDNEY
10 miles E of Lincoln on the B1190/B1202

🏛 Abbey

The dominating feature of this little town beside the River Witham is the British Sugar Corporation's towering beet processing factory. In medieval times, a more elegant structure distinguished the town, and was just as important to its prosperity. **Bardney Abbey** was famous then because it housed the holy remains of St Oswald, an 8th century King of Northumbria. Pilgrims flocked here in their thousands. The original Saxon abbey was demolished by Viking raiders in 870 and its Norman successor fared little better at the Dissolution of the Monasteries. Only the ground plan is now distinguishable. Some fragments from the abbey were incorporated into Bardney's Church of St Lawrence which is otherwise mostly 15th century. Features of

interest here include a tomb slab of Abbot Richard Horncastle, who died in 1508, and two unusual Charity Boards dated 1603 and 1639. These list benefactors of the parish, complete with colour portraits of these generous souls.

Connoisseurs of unusual churches will be well rewarded by a short detour to **Southrey**, a remote hamlet set beside the River Witham. Built of timber by the parishioners themselves in 1898, St John the Divine is painted brilliant white outside and sky blue within. Resembling some Mission station in the Australian outback, this quaint little church stands on a plinth incorporating gravestones from Bardney Abbey.

BASSINGHAM
7 miles SW of Lincoln off the A46

🏛 Auburn

A pleasant little village with houses mostly of local warm red brick; an Elizabethan manor house (private) and, on one of the many little greens, an oak seat carved in the shape of a bull. This striking feature is part of an admirable enterprise masterminded by North Kesteven Arts to enhance both the natural and built-up areas of the District with all kinds of sculpture and art work. These imaginative pieces, many of them serving as public benches, range from the Dorrington Demons, based on a local legend, to the Scopwick Woman whose seat, in the lap of her skirt, has become a kind of letterbox with local people leaving tokens, messages or gifts for others to pick up. A booklet titled *In View*, which gives full details of these fascinating works, is available from TICs.

A couple of miles north of Bassingham, **Aubourn** is a charming Elizabethan and Jacobean manor house set in attractive

BRILLS FARM B&B AND THE CATS WHISKERS

Brills Hill, Norton Disney, Lincolnshire LN6 9JN
Tel: 01636 892311 Fax: 01636 892326
e-mail: admin@brillsfarm-bedandbreakfast.co.uk
website: www.brillsfarm-bedandbreakfast.co.uk

Brills Farm B&B offers superb comfort and
sophistication in beautiful surroundings on top of
one of the few hills in Lincolnshire. The farmhouse
is early Georgian, and the White family, Sophie and
Charlie, have sympathetically restored and
renovated it, preserving the structure and many
original features. Each of the three letting bedrooms,
all doubles, has its own individual style and
character, and days at the farm start with a super
breakfast that includes home-produced bacon and
eggs. The hosts can also arrange a picnic lunch,
afternoon tea and a splendid 4-course evening meal.
Brills Farm, which is located off the A46 between
Lincoln and Newark, is a mixed farm with crops,
pigs and horses – and two lakes. Parts are a
designated Site of Scientific Interest and a haven for
wildlife, including deer, badgers and foxes. Sophie

also runs the **Cats Whiskers**, a bespoke catering service covering Lincolnshire, Derbyshire,
Nottinghamshire and Leicestershire. Quality and true flavours are to the fore in everything they
do, from small intimate dinner parties to wedding receptions and hog roasts.

---

gardens and notable for a finely carved oak
staircase. Nearby, the tower of Aubourn's
Victorian church stands alone, all that was left
after the church was demolished in 1973 and
parishioners reverted to worshipping in the
chancel of the old church amidst the clutter
of memorials to the Meres and Nevile
families.

GAINSBOROUGH

15 miles NW of Lincoln on the A156

🏠 Old Hall 🏠 All Saints Church

Britain's most inland port, Gainsborough is
located at the highest navigable point on the
River Trent for seagoing vessels. During the
17th and 18th centuries particularly, the town
prospered greatly and although many of the
lofty warehouses lining the river bank have

been demolished, enough remain to give some
idea of its flourishing past.

The town's most famous building is the
enchanting **Gainsborough Old Hall,** one of
the most striking architectural gems in the
county. The Hall was built in the 1470s by Sir
Thomas Burgh, a Yorkist supporter in the
Wars of the Roses. Sir Thomas later
entertained Richard III in the Great Hall with
its vast arched roof. The kitchens also remain
virtually unchanged since those days. A
century or so later, around 1597, a London
merchant, William Hickman, extended the
building in Elizabethan style. The Hall is
generally considered one of the best
preserved medieval manor houses in the
country. Today, it is run jointly by Lincolnshire
County Council and English Heritage, and is

Gainsborough Old Hall

open most days throughout the year.

Gainsborough also boasts an outstanding church. Beautifully set in its own grounds in the centre of the town, **All Saints** is a magnificent example of a Georgian classical "city" church. The interior, with its massive columns, box pews and gallery, is richly decorated in gold and turquoise. It is open during daylight hours, tours are available and there's even a cafeteria and gift shop.

Another notable building is Marshall's Britannia Works in Beaumont Street, a proud reminder of Gainsborough's once thriving engineering industry. Built around 1850, the quarter-of-a-mile long frontage bears an impressive figure of Britannia herself.

Gainsborough is believed to have provided material for George Eliot's *The Mill on the Floss*.

THE BLACK SWAN GUEST HOUSE

21 High Street, Marton, nr Gainsborough,
Lincolnshire DN21 5AH
Tel/Fax: 01427 718878
e-mail: info@blackswanguesthouse.co.uk
website: www.blackswanguesthouse.co.uk

Superb service is one of the hallmarks of the **Black Swan Guest House**, which was a coaching inn in the 18th century. The buildings were totally refurbished in the 1990s using many of the original materials, and the house and stable block now provide very comfortable guest accommodation. All the rooms have showers en suite, TV and tea/coffee-making facilities, and the large Premier Room boasts a four-poster bed.

There are six rooms in the main house and four large rooms in the stable block, which can also be used as family rooms. Breakfasts, using locally sourced foods, freshly cooked to order are served in the comfortable dining room. A range of drinks is available in the cosy lounge in the evening. There is room for 10 cars in the private off-road car park. Resident proprietors Judy and John Patrick offer a warm welcome to all their guests at the Black Swan, which stands on the A156 at the junction with the A1500.

ACCENT ON HOME DESIGN

3a Southolme, Gainsborough,
Lincolnshire DN21 2EQ
Tel: 01427 679494

Sherree Barker, with 25 years experience in the business, owns and runs **Accent on Home Design** on a corner site in historic Gainsborough. The large windows give glimpses of the array of stylish furnishings, fabrics, homeware and gifts on display within. The ever-changing stock runs from cards, ceramics and gifts for the home to cushions, fabrics, blinds and wallpapers from the leading manufacturers. Sherree is on hand to offer help and advice along with a design, making up and installation service for all your window dressing needs.

The now-demolished Ashcroft Mill on the River Trent was the model for Tulliver's mill and the eagre, or tidal bore, that precipitates the tragic climax of the novel is clearly based on the surge that happens at Gainsborough. This usually takes place about 50 minutes after high tide at Grimsby and the bore can be anything between eight feet and 13 feet high.

Scunthorpe

🏛 Appleton Frodingham Railway Preservation Society

🏛 North Lincs Museum

Up until the 1850s the main activity around Scunthorpe was the maintaining of rabbit warrens - the local breed with their silvery coats being much in demand with furriers. Then a local landowner, Rowland Winn, discovered that the poor local soil lightly covered vast deposits of ironstone. Scunthorpe's rapid rise to becoming a major steel town was under way. Today, the Corus plant produces more than four million tonnes of liquid steel, from a 690-hectare site which contains 90 miles of railways.

On selected summer weekends, the **Appleby Frodingham Railway Preservation Society** runs two-hour rail

tours around the plant. Pulled by a restored steam locomotive, the fully guided tour takes in all aspects of iron and steel making and includes a glimpse of red hot steel being rolled in the mills.

More of Scunthorpe's industrial and social heritage is on display at the **North Lincolnshire Museum,** with exhibits that include an ironmonger's cottage. The town has also created a Heritage Trail which takes visitors through three of the parks created by Victorian benefactors - Scunthorpe is proud of its parks and gardens.

Around Scunthorpe

NORMANBY
4 miles N of Scunthorpe off the B1430

🏰 Normanby Hall 🏛 Farming Museum

Normanby Hall was built in 1825 for the Sheffield family and extended in 1906. The interior is decorated in Regency style, and displays include eight rooms that reflect the changes made down the years, as well as two costume galleries. The 300-acre Park has plenty to see and enjoy, including a deer park, duck ponds, an ice house in the middle of the

🎭 stories and anecdotes 🦢 famous people 🎨 art and craft ✍ entertainment and sport 🚶 walks miniature railway circuit, a Victorian laundry, a Victorian walled garden and a new children's play area. The **Normanby Hall Farming Museum** majors on rural life in the age of the heavy horse and, among the exhibits illuminating the workings of a 19th century country estate, are traditional agricultural equipment and transport and country crafts. Near the park gates, some picturesque estate cottages bear witness to the Sheffield family's reputation as good landlords. Rents were low and job security was good, so perhaps the only drawback was that the Sheffield family restricted the number of public houses they would allow on their lands.

A mile or so northwest of the Hall, St Andrew's Church in the agreeable village of Burton-on-Stather contains an impressive range of memorials to the Sheffield family, the oldest of which dates back to the 1300s.

ALKBOROUGH

11 miles N of Scunthorpe off the A1077

🔶 Julian's Bower

A scenic walk leads from Burton-upon-Stather to Alkborough, where the medieval maze known as **Julian's Bower** is a perplexing talking point. Not a maze made of hedges, but a pattern cut in the turf, it occupies a beautiful location on a clifftop overlooking the River Trent. The design of the maze is reproduced

Julian's Bower, Alkborough

in the porch of the 11th century village church, and again in a window high above the altar.

BARTON-UPON-HUMBER

10 miles NE of Scunthorpe off the A15

🏠 Baysgarth House   🔶 Water's Edge Country Park

🔶 Far Ings   🔶 Barton Clay Pits

Today, Barton is dominated by the colossal south tower of the Humber Bridge, connecting Lincolnshire with East Yorkshire. This has been a major crossing point for more than 1,000 years. The Domesday Book recorded a ferry here and the community was then the largest town in North Lincolnshire. In the 1770s, Daniel Defoe gave a vivid description of his passage across the Humber "in an open boat in which we had about 15 horses, and ten or 12 cows, mingled with about 17 or 18 passengers, we were about four hours tossing about on the Humber before we could get into the harbour at Hull". (The river at this point is about two-and-a-half miles wide.)

The heart of the town still has some pleasant streets - Fleetgate, Bargate, Beck Hill and Priestgate, all distinguished by mainly Georgian and early Victorian buildings. **Baysgarth House**, now a museum, is an 18th century mansion with a collection of 18th and 19th century English and Oriental pottery, a section on country crafts and an industrial museum in the stable block. The surrounding park has a picnic area, play area and various recreational facilities. Once an area of severe industrial contamination, **Water's Edge Country Park** is now home to an impressive number of species – bird, mammal, plant and insect – and its easy paths and tranquil surroundings make it a great place to unwind. Opened in April 2006, it is an environmentally friendly visitor centre with displays on the wildlife of the Park, a coffee shop, and interactive cameras in nesting boxes (the first in the country).

Just to the north of Barton, on the banks of the Humber, is an observation area for viewing the mighty Humber Bridge. Opened in 1981, this is Europe's longest single-span suspension bridge with an overall length of 2,428 yards. This means that for more than a third of a mile only four concrete pillars, two on each bank, are preserving you from a watery death. From these huge pylons, 510 feet high, gossamer cables of thin-wired steel support a gently curving roadway. Both sets of pylons rise vertically, but because of the curvature of the earth they actually lean away from each other by several inches. The bridge is particularly striking when the vast structure is very occasionally floodlit at night.

Around the bridge are important nature reserves. **Barton Clay Pits** cover a five-mile area along the river bank and offer a haven for wildlife and recreation for sporty humans. **Far Ings,** with hides and waymarked trails, is home to more than 230 species of wild flowers, 50 nesting bird species and hundreds of different sorts of moths.

BRIGG
7 miles E of Scunthorpe on the A10

🖉 Brigg Fair

King John was not universally liked but one of his more popular deeds was the granting of a charter (in 1205) which permitted this modest little town to hold an annual festivity on the 5th day of August. **Brigg Fair**, along with

---

THE WHITE HORSE

5 Wrawby Street, Brigg,
North Lincolnshire DN20 8JJ
Tel: 01562 652242

Julian and Sarah Newell run three outstanding establishments in Wrawby Street in the market town of Brigg. **The White Horse** at No 5 is a popular, welcoming pub serving traditional ales, excellent wines and top-quality meals that attract discerning diners from throughout the region. An across-the-board menu, supplemented by daily specials, is served lunchtime and evening, and all day on Sunday, when prime roasts are the centrepiece.

At No 17, **Newells of Brigg** (Tel: 01652 654411) is a high-class delicatessen selling a wide range of cheeses, olives, pâtés, cooked meats, salads, made-to-order sandwiches, chutneys, preserves, milk, cream and wine. Julian first made his name in Brigg as a first-class butcher, and still owns **Waters & Son, Butcher** at No 18 (Tel: 01652 653111).

Waters sells a fine selection of meat and poultry, seasonal game and some more exotic choices such as crocodile, kangaroo, bison and ostrich. The shop has a strong local following and supplies many local establishments, naturally including Julian's pub and deli. Newells and Waters are open from 8am to 5pm Monday to Saturday.

🖪 stories and anecdotes   🐦 famous people   🎨 art and craft   🖉 entertainment and sport   🐾 walks

Widdecombe and Scarborough, joined the trio of 'Best Known Fairs in England', its celebrity enhanced by a traditional song (twice recorded by Percy Grainger), and the haunting tone poem, *Brigg Fair*, composed by Frederick Delius in 1907.

King John's son, Henry III, also showed favour to the town. He granted the loyal burghers of Brigg the right to hold a weekly market on Thursdays, a right they still exercise to the full. Each week, the market place is crammed with around 100 stalls. A farmers' market is also held on the 4th Saturday of each month, attracting producers of quality local produce and crowds of shoppers. A pedestrianised town centre, combined with ample parking nearby, has made Brigg's markets some of the busiest in North Lincolnshire.

Many visitors to Brigg, including the architecture guru Nikolaus Pevsner, have commented that some of the town's most interesting buildings are its pubs. Pevsner picked out for special mention the Lord Nelson, with its broad Regency bow window, the Dying Gladiator, remarkable for the *"gory realism"* of its pub sign, and the Black Bull which boasts "a vigorous Edwardian pub front".

HAXEY
8 miles SW of Scunthorpe on the A161

🎭 Haxey Hood Game

Haxey is the site of a nature reserve, but is best known for the **Haxey Hood Game,** launched around 2.30 on the afternoon of Twelfth Night in front of the parish church. Three hundred men divided into four teams compete to push a leather 'hood' into the pub of their team's choice. The game apparently started in the 12th or 13th century when Lady

de Mowbray lost her hood and a number of village men scrambled to retrieve it. The strongest man caught the hood but was too shy to hand it back, and was labelled a fool by the lady, while the man who eventually handed it over was declared a lord. The lady suggested that the scene should be re-enacted each year, and gave a plot of land for the purpose. The 'sway' of men struggle across the fields working the hood towards the appropriate pubs and always staying within the sway - no open running. When the sway reaches the winning pub, the landlord touches the hood to declare the game over, and free drinks paid for by a collection end the day in time-honoured style. Rather an elaborate build-up to a drinking session, but just one of the quaint traditions that make English country life so colourful.

EPWORTH
12 miles SW of Scunthorpe on the A161

🏛 Old Rectory   🏛 St Andrew's Church

This small town, the southern 'capital' of the Isle of Axholme, is a hallowed place for Methodists from all over the world. From 1696 until his death in 1735 the Revd Samuel Wesley was Rector here. John Wesley was born at the **Old Rectory** on June 17th, 1703; his brother Charles on December 18th, 1707. Two years later, inflamed by one of the Rector's outspoken sermons, local people set fire to the Rectory. The house was rebuilt incorporating ribs and keels from ships broken up in the nearby River Trent. The house still stands today, a charming Queen Anne building. Several of its rooms have been refurnished in period style and some of the brothers' possessions are on display. There are also collections of portraits and prints.

St Andrew's Church, where Samuel Wesley was minister, is a short walk from the town centre. His table tomb stands near the southeast door and it was from this vantage point that John would address his followers after he had been refused access to the church. Inside, the 12th century font in which both John and Charles were baptised, can still be seen.

The best way to follow the footsteps of the Wesleys is to join the Wesley Trail which has information boards placed at various locations connected with the family. A pamphlet giving full details of the Trial is available from various outlets in the town.

SANDTOFT
10 miles W of Scunthorpe off the A161 or Exit 2 of M180

🏛 Trolleybus Museum

On a wartime airfield on the Isle of Axholme, the **Trolleybus Museum at Sandtoft** is home to Britain's largest single collection of trolleybuses and motorbuses. Started in 1969 by a small and enthusiastic group of volunteers, the collection includes vehicles dating from 1927 to 1985, including magnificent six-wheeled double-decker trolleybuses and a fascinating one-and-a-half decker from Aachen in Germany.

Skegness

🏛 Church Farm Museum 🦭 Seal Sanctuary

🦭 Gibraltar Point National Nature Reserve

🎨 The Jolly Fisherman

In the early 1800s, when the Tennyson family used to visit Skegness with the future Poet Laureate, Alfred, in tow, it was still a tiny fishing village but already famous for its miles of firm sandy beaches and its 'oh-so-bracing' sea air. As late as 1871, the resident population of Skegness was only 239 but two years later the railway arrived and three years after that the local landowner, the Earl of Scarborough, built a new town to the north of the railway station.

A huge pier, 1,843ft long, was erected. This survived for almost 100 years before a gale on the night of January 11th, 1978 left it sadly truncated. Other amenities provided by the Earl of Scarborough for visitors included the Lumley Hotel, St Matthew's Church and a grand promenade. The Jubilee Clock Tower on the seafront was added in 1899 and, in 1908, the town fathers amazed even themselves by a stroke of advertising genius – their adoption of the Jolly Fisherman as the town's mascot.

The Jolly Fisherman has an interesting story behind him. In 1908 the Great Northern Railway purchased an oil painting of the plump and prancing fisherman for £12. After adding the famous slogan 'Skegness is so Bracing', they used the painting as a poster to advertise trips from London to Skegness (fare 3/-, 15p). Almost a century later the same Jolly Fisherman is still busy promoting Skegness as a holiday resort. There are two statues of him in town, one at the railway station, another in Compass Gardens and, during the summer months, he can also be seen strolling around the town.

Naturally, the town is well-provided with funfairs – Bottons, Fantasy Island, and Butlin's, the latter two of which are actually in the contiguous town of Ingoldmells. It was in 1936 that Billy Butlin opened his very first holiday camp with the slogan 'A Week's

Gibraltar Point Nature Reserve

Distance: *1.9 miles (3.0 kilometres)*

Typical time: *80 mins*

Height gain: *0 metres*

Map: *Explorer 274*

Walk: *www.walkingworld.com ID:1833*

Contributor: *Sam Roebuck*

ACCESS INFORMATION:

The walk starts at the South Car Park, by the Visitor Centre of Gibraltar Point, though it is easy enough to pick up the walk from the North Car Park. Gibraltar Point itself is only accessible by car (or a good cycle track) via Skegness town centre, but is very well signposted and the South Car Park and Visitor Centre are at the very end of the access road.

ADDITIONAL INFORMATION:

The map does not represent the main paths too well, but don't despair - it is all but impossible to get lost. There are many bird hides accessible from this route and it is well worth exploring at least one - don't forget your binoculars.

DESCRIPTION:

This is a gentle walk around one of England's best-known nature reserves, around the dunes of Gibraltar Point. Enjoy the peace and tranquillity, disturbed only by birdsong and the gentle rolling of the waves on the miles of quiet beach. An ideal walk for a summer's evening.

FEATURES:

Sea, Toilets, Wildlife, Birds, Gift Shop, Good for Kids, Mostly Flat, Nature Trail, Ancient Monument Description:

WALK DIRECTIONS:

1 | Look for the notice-board in the corner of the car park and go through the gate on its right. Turn immediately right over a footbridge.

2 | In 400m, by a notice-board and immediately before the wooden walkway continues over the dunes, turn right, keeping the dunes on your left.

3 | In 200m, at the bird observatory, turn left to ascend the steps that run to the right of the building.

4 | The path emerges on the edge of the beach, onto a sandy track which runs northwards with the dunes on the left. Follow this track for half a kilometre. There are many opportunities during this stretch to divert from the path towards the sea to explore the quiet, sandy beach.

5 | The dunes on the left give out as the track bends to the left, leaving you in front of a World War II pill-box. Walk up to the pill-box and turn left. Within 100m, pick up a vague,

sandy track and quickly another track that turns right into the dunes.

6 | At a high and distinctive dune, as the path bends left, climb the steps that ascend the dune, to the viewpoint. Continue over the dune and down the far side.

7 | At the junction of paths, fork right and follow this path for another 400m.

8 | As you reach the bird hide on your right, turn left and follow this path back to the car park.

Holiday for a Week's Wage' – about £2.50 in those days. The price included accommodation, meals and entertainment and the holidays were understandably popular with workers – a new law had just guaranteed them a statutory week's leave with pay. Just three years later, World War II erupted and the holiday market imploded. But Billy Butlin still prospered. The government bought his camps to use as army barracks, appointed him Director-General of Hostels and, at the end of the war, sold the camps back to him at a knock-down price. The camp is still operating, now named the Butlin's Family Entertainment Resort, and day visit tickets are available.

Alongside the obvious attractions of the beach and all the traditional seaside entertainment, Skegness and Ingoldmells have other places of special interest. **Church Farm Museum,** a former farmhouse, is home to a collection of old farm implements and machinery, re-created village workshops, a paddock of Lincoln Longwool sheep and a fine example of a Lincolnshire "mud and stud" thatched cottage brought here from the nearby village of Withern. Craft demonstrations can be viewed on most Sunday afternoons and a programme of special events - sheep shearing, steam

threshing and so on, continues throughout the season.

Natureland Seal Sanctuary (see panel on page 308) on North Parade provides interest and fun for all the family with its seals and baby seal rescue centre; aquarium; tropical house with crocodiles, snakes and tarantulas; a pets corner and Floral Palace; a large greenhouse teeming with plant, insect and bird life, including butterflies and flamingoes.

Serious birdwatchers should head south along the coast to **Gibraltar Point National Nature Reserve,** a field station among the salt marshes and dunes with hides, waymarked routes and guided tours.

Around Skegness

WAINFLEET
5 miles SW of Skegness on the A52

🏛 Magdalen College School

Formerly a thriving port, Wainfleet now finds itself several miles from the sea. Narrow roads lead off the market place with its medieval stone cross, making this a place you really have to explore on foot. The most striking building in the town is the former **Magdalen College School,** built in dark red brick in 1484 for William of Wayneflete, Bishop of Winchester and Lord Chancellor to Henry VI. William first founded Magdalen College, Oxford and later established the college school in the town of his birth. It continued as a school until 1933 but now houses the public library, a small museum, a tea room and a walled tea garden.

This attractive little town has a Friday market, held in the unspoilt Market Place with its Buttercross and Clock Tower, and among the variety of family-run shops there is one which

Skegness Natureland Seal Sanctuary

North Parade, Skegness, Lincolnshire PE25 1DB
Tel: 01754 764345
website: www.skegnessnatureland.co.uk

Natureland is situated at the northern end of Skegness seafront and has a specialised collection of animals including seals, penguins, tropical butterflies (April to October), tropical birds, sea life exhibit, aquarium, reptiles, pets corner and many more. It has become known world wide for it's rescue of orphaned baby seal pups that become stranded on beaches around the Wash and has been successful in rearing and returning to their natural environment a large number of these beautiful creatures. When they first arrive, the pups need very careful nursing and treatment that is carried out in the Seal Hospital by the dedicated staff.

Feeding time is a great favourite with both children and adults. The seals like to show off their talents to the visitors and an informative talk is given on Seals, Penguins and Seal Rescue work, whilst they are being fed. The Sea Life Exhibit is a large 25ft long tank containing 5,000 gallons of seawater and is home to British sharks, rays, lobsters, crabs and many other species of marine life.

In the Floral Palace you can walk through a plant lovers paradise with tropical butterflies flying freely through the luscious vegetation around you (April to October). In another section free flight tropical birds are the main attraction, whilst Cacti from around the world can be seen in the third section.

Another children's' favourite is the Pets Corner where goats, calves (in the summer), rabbits, geese and chickens can all be hand fed with food available from the Gift Shop. Large displays of tropical marine and freshwater fish and smaller displays of local marine invertebrates make the Aquarium a fascinating and educational experience not to be missed. Snakes, scorpions, crocodiles and tarantula spiders plus other reptiles and insects inhabit the Tropical House. These are all made to feel at home by the jungle sound effects.

🏛 historic building   🏛 museum   🏛 historic site   ⚜ scenic attraction   🌿 flora and fauna offers an unusual culinary treat: - traditional fish and chips cooked on a coal range.

A curious feature lies about a mile south of the town, on the western side of the A52. Rows and rows of small, rounded mounds are all that remain of an important industry that flourished here from the Iron Age to the 1600s - the extraction of salt from sea water. Throughout these long centuries, salt was an expensive, but absolutely vital, commodity, both as a preservative and a condiment. During the Roman occupation of Britain, part of an Imperial soldier's remuneration was a pouch of salt, his *salarium* or salary. When the mounds at Wainfleet were excavated in the 1950s they were found to contain *salterns* - low hearths surrounded by brick in which fires were lit to evaporate pans of sea water and leave behind the precious salt.

BURGH LE MARSH
4 miles W of Skegness on the A158

🏃 Peddars Way   🏛 Gunby Hall

Pronounced 'Borough', this small town was once the terminus of a Roman road from Lincoln. Although Burgh is now several miles inland, it was from here, centuries ago, that travellers boarded a ferry to cross The Wash and join the **Peddars Way** in Norfolk.

About three miles northwest of Burgh, **Gunby Hall** (National Trust) is reputed to be the setting Tennyson had in mind when he wrote of:

"an English home – gray twilight pour'd
On dewy pastures, dewy trees
Softer than sleep – all things in order stored,
A haunt of ancient peace".

Built in 1700 and extended in the 1870s, Gunby Hall is a delightful William & Mary house of plum-coloured brick surrounded by sweeping lawns and flower gardens. The Hall has long been associated with the Massingberd family whose portraits, including several by Reynolds, are on display along with some very fine English furniture. The walled garden is particularly charming and beyond it the Church of St Peter contains some life-size brasses of early Massingberds.

WILLOUGHBY
11 miles NW of Skegness on the B1196

🐦 Captain John Smith

Willoughby is best known as the birthplace of **Captain John Smith**, founder of what is now the State of Virginia in the USA. A farmer's son, Smith was born in the village in 1580 and educated in nearby Louth. He left England as a young man and, after a spell as a mercenary in Europe, set sail with other optimistic colonists for Chesapeake Bay in 1607. A forceful character, Smith was elected Governor of the new settlement but his diplomatic skills proved unequal to the task of pacifying the local Native Americans. They took him captive and were intent on killing him until one of the chieftain's daughters, Pocahontas, interceded and saved his life. Pocahontas later married one of Smith's fellow colonists, John Rolfe, and returned with him to England. Beautiful and intelligent, the dark-skinned Pocahontas was welcomed as an exotic celebrity. King James I graciously allowed her to be presented at his Court but within a few months the lovely Indian princess died "of a fever". Four hundred years later, the romantic tale continues to furnish the material for songs, stories, plays and musicals.

Willoughby village celebrates its most famous son with a fine memorial window in the church (a gift from American citizens), and in the Willoughby Arms pub where a portrait painted on an outside wall and, inside, accounts of his adventures may be seen.

Horncastle

🏛 Church

"Few towns of Horncastle's size can have so many Regency bow-windows", noted Nikolaus Pevsner. These attractive features, and the houses that went with them, were a direct result of the town's increased prosperity and the building boom that followed the opening of the Horncastle Navigation Canal in 1802. The town also has an unusual number of hostelries; many of them were built to accommodate visitors to the annual Horse Fair, which started some time in the 1200s and continued until 1948. Its modern successor is

the Summer Fayre, a popular event that takes place each June.

St Mary's Church has some interesting features, including a brass of Lionel Dymoke, dated 1519. The Dymokes were the hereditary King's Champions who, at the coronation feast of medieval monarchs, challenged anyone who disputed the validity of the king's succession to mortal combat. Above an arch in the Lady Chapel hang 13 scythe blades. These agricultural tools were the only arms available to the local people who took part in the Pilgrimage of Grace of 1536. This was a mostly northern protest against Henry VIII's policy of closing down every monastery in the country. Their rebellion failed. The king graciously pardoned those who had taken part and the rebels returned peacefully to their

SECRETS @ SARAH PEARS INTERIORS

15 Bull Ring, Horncastle,
Lincolnshire LN9 5HU
Tel/Fax: 01507 525212
e-mail: info@sarahpearsinteriors.co.uk
website: www.sarahpearsinteriors.co.uk

The mother and daughter team of Ann Bishop and Sarah Pears and run **Secrets @ Sarah Pears Interiors** in the Bull Ring in the heart of Horncastle. The shop specialises in interior design and stocks all the leading designers of fabrics, wallpaper and paints. Farrow & Ball, Designer Guild, Jane Churchill and GP & J Baker are among the leading brands, and the range of home accessories, jewellery, glassware, fragrances and other lifestyle products and gifts includes leaders in their fields like East of India, Garden Trading, Nougat Body to Home and new parent gifts from the Flower Stork.

For anyone looking for something special for the home or a gift idea with a difference, this is the place to go, a splendid one-stop that's open from 9.30 to 4 (closed Wednesday and Sunday).

BAUMBER PARK

Baumber, nr Horncastle, Lincolnshire LN9 5NE
Tel: 01507 578235 Mobile: 07977 722776 Fax: 01507 578417
e-mail: baumberpark@amserve.com
website: www.baumberpark.com

A spacious and elegant farmhouse of character, **Baumber Park** was originally built around 1680 and much enlarged in the 1800s. It is surrounded by parkland in which cows and calves graze all summer and there's also a small flock of pedigree Lincoln Longwool sheep which lamb in April. Other traditional farm animals at home here are horses, cats and dogs and chickens to lay eggs for breakfast. Your hosts at Baumber Park are Clare Harrison, who looks after her bed & breakfast guests, and husband Michael who runs the adjoining farm.

Clare is also an accomplished horticulturalist who propogates and sells some plants from the well-stocked garden. The accommodation comprises three guest bedrooms – two are spacious with bay windows giving excellent views over the garden and farmland. The third bedroom is a double with a lovely big new en suite bathroom and with views onto the farm. All rooms have antique furniture, portable TV, radio and hospitality tray. Downstairs is a large guest lounge with open log fire, piano and TV, and a dining room with a big mahogany table and a collection of Lincolnshire books. Guests also have the use of a grass tennis court. Tourist Board gradings are no longer sought as there are additional things on offer such as character, space, tradition, extensive gardens, home-produced fare and especially a warm welcome.

---

homes. Once the crisis had been defused, Henry ordered the summary execution of the most prominent leaders and supporters of the uprising.

Around Horncastle

SOMERSBY

7 miles NE of Horncastle off the A158

🦜 Bag Enderby

For pilgrims on the Tennyson trail, a visit to Somersby is essential. The poet's father, Dr George Clayton Tennyson, was Rector of the village and the adjoining parish of Bag Enderby. Alfred was born here in 1809 and for most of the first 30 years of his life

Somersby Rectory was his home. Many of his poems reflect his delight in the surrounding scenery of the Wolds, Fens and coast. When the family left Somersby in 1837, following the death of Dr Tennyson, Alfred wrote:

We leave the well-beloved place
Where first we gazed upon the sky;
The roofs, that heard our earliest cry,
Will shelter one of stranger race.

The Rectory, now Somersby House (private), still stands, complete with the many additions Dr Tennyson made to accommodate his family of 10 children. He is buried in the graveyard of the small church where he had been minister for more than 20 years and which now contains a fine bust of his famous son. Also in the graveyard, where a simple

---

🎞 stories and anecdotes 🦜 famous people 🎨 art and craft 🥾 entertainment and sport 🥾 walks

Medieval Cross, Somersby

tombstone marks the Doctor's burial place, stands a remarkably well-preserved medieval cross.

The nearby village of **Bag Enderby** is associated with another celebrated figure, John Wesley. He preached here on the village green beneath a noble elm tree. The hollow trunk still stands. The church also has a special treasure: a beautifully carved 15th century font "worth crossing Lincolnshire to see". The carvings include a tender Pietà, a hart licking the leaves of a tree growing from its back, and a seated figure playing what appears to be a lute.

SPILSBY
10 miles E of Horncastle on the A16

🏛 Church   🌱 Northcote Heavy Horses Centre

A pleasant little market town with a

population of about 2,000, Spilsby sits near the southern edge of the Wolds. Market day is Monday, (with an open air auction as part of the fun), and there's an annual May Day Carnival with dancing round the may pole in the market square. The **Church of St James** has many interesting features, most notably the incredible array of tombs and memorials of the Willoughby family from the 1300s to the early 1600s. Perhaps the most striking of them, a 1580s memorial to the Duchess of Suffolk and Richard Bertie, fills the whole of the original chancel arch. Another monument honours Spilsby's most famous son, the navigator and explorer Captain Sir John Franklin, who lost his life while in charge of the expedition that discovered the North West Passage. A handsome bronze of the great man stands in the square facing the market hall of 1764.

About two miles east of Spilsby, on the B1195, the **Northcote Heavy Horses Centre** offers a unique "hands-on" experience with these gentle giants. Visitors have the options of participating in morning or all day sessions during which they have close contact with the horses, including grooming them if they wish. The afternoon programme is for those who simply want to walk around on their own, explore the museum/vehicle workshop, watch the video display of the Centre's activities, enjoy a half-hour horse dray ride through country lanes, or settle down for tea and scones in the Hen's Nest Tea Room.

OLD BOLINGBROKE
8 miles SE of Horncastle off the A155 or B1195

🏛 Bolingbroke Castle

Old Bolingbroke is the site of **Bolingbroke**

Castle, now in the care of English Heritage. Originally built in the reign of William I it later became the property of John of Gaunt whose son, afterwards Henry IV, was born at the castle in 1367. During the Civil War, Bolingbroke Castle was besieged by Parliamentary forces in 1643, fell into disuse soon after and very little now remains.

EAST KIRKBY

8 miles SE of Horncastle on the A155

🏛 Heritage Centre

The airfield beside the A155 is the setting for the **Lincolnshire Aviation Heritage Centre,** based in the old control tower. Displays include an Avro Lancaster bomber, a Shackleton, cockpits from Canberras, military vehicles and a wartime blast shelter.

Louth

🏛 Church of St James   🏛 Museum   ⚘ Art Trail

One of the county's most appealing towns, Louth is set beside the River Lud on the eastern edge of the Wolds in an Area of Outstanding Natural Beauty. Louth can make the unusual boast that it stands in both the eastern and western hemispheres since the Greenwich Meridian line passes through the centre of the town.

There was a settlement here long before the Romans arrived. By the time of the *Domesday Book* in 1086, Louth was recorded as a prosperous market town. It still is. There's a cattle market on Thursdays; a general market on Wednesdays (with an open air auction), Fridays and Saturdays; and a

OLD MALTINGS ANTIQUES CENTRE

38 Aswell Street, Louth, Lincolnshire LN11 9HP
Tel: 01507 600366

Norman and Margaret Coffey, both Lincolnshire-born, owned a jewellery shop in Grimsby before coming here, first to manage and then to own the **Old Maltings Antiques Centre**. In the two-storey converted Victorian maltings up to 30 dealers sell a wide range of furniture (mainly Victorian and Edwardian), bric-a-brac and collectables at all prices, including silver, glass and ceramics.

Norman and Margaret have an antique jewellery shop at the entrance to the Centre, and they also provide a pine-door stripping service and a house-clearing service. The stock changes all the time, so every visit will offer excellent browsing and lots of new things to buy. Opening hours are 10am to 4.30pm Monday to Friday, 10am to 5pm Saturday; closed Sundays and Bank Holidays.

Farmers' Market on the last Wednesday of each month.

The town is a pleasure to wander around, its narrow winding streets and alleys crammed with attractive architecture and bearing intriguing names such as Pawnshop Passage. Westgate in particular is distinguished by its Georgian houses and a 16th century inn. A plaque in nearby Westgate Place marks the house where Tennyson lodged with his grandmother while attending the King Edward VI School. Founded in the 1200s, the school is still operating and among its other famous old boys are Sir John Franklin and Captain John Smith of Pocahontas fame. Broadbank, which now houses the **Louth Museum,** is an attractive little building with some interesting artifacts including some amazing locally-woven carpets that were displayed at the 1867 Paris Exhibition. And Tennyson fans will surely want to visit the shop in the market square that published *Poems by Two Brothers* and is still selling books.

But the town's pre-eminent architectural glory is the vast **Church of St James,** which boasts the tallest spire of any parish church in England. Nearly 300 feet high and built in gleaming Ancaster stone, this masterly example of the mason's art was constructed between 1501 and 1515. The interior is noted for its glorious starburst tower vault,

beautifully restored Georgian pine roof, a wonderful collection of Decorated sedilia, and a fascinating array of old chests. On summer afternoons, visitors can climb to the base of the spire for a panoramic view that stretches from the Wolds to the North Sea.

An interesting recent addition to the town's attractions is the **Louth Art Trail** linking commissioned works of art, each of which will have some significant connection with the town's history. Already in place are sculptures outside St James's Church, Louth Library and around the Louth Navigation Canal and the River Lud. Both waterways have made important contributions to the town's prosperity although the Lud has also brought disaster. In 1920 a flash flood destroyed hundreds of homes and killed 23 people. A plaque on the side of the town watermill shows how high the river rose during that disastrous inundation. Another Art Trail commission is based on the theme of the Greenwich Meridian, and there's a further sculpture located in Hubbards Hills, a picturesque public park lying in a 125ft-deep glacial valley to the west of the town.

Lincolnshire Wolds

🏢 historic building   🏛 museum   🏛 historic site   🗨 scenic attraction   🌿 flora and fauna

LINCOLNSHIRE

Lincolnshire Wolds Railway

Around Louth

LUDBOROUGH
6 miles N of Louth on the A16

🏛 Lincolnshire Wolds Railway

The only standard gauge steam railway in the county, the **Lincolnshire Wolds Railway** is a noble volunteer enterprise with the ambitious aim of extending its present half-mile track to a full 10 miles. The line is part of the original Great Northern Railway which opened in 1848 and closed in 1980. The old Ludborough station has been restored, visitors can watch ongoing restoration in the engine shed and, on steaming days, travel along the line. The former ticket office now houses a collection of railway memorabilia; there's a gift shop and a buffet car serving homemade light refreshments. Entrance to the site is free.

MABLETHORPE
13 miles E of Louth on the A52 &A1104

🐾 Animal Gardens   🐾 Seal Sanctuary   🏛 Museum

Mablethorpe is the northernmost and most "senior" of the three Lincolnshire holiday resorts that almost form a chain along this stretch of fragile coast which has frequently been threatened by the waves, and whose contours have changed visibly over the years. Much of the original village of Mablethorpe has disappeared into the sea, including the medieval Church of St Peter. In the great North Sea flood of January 31st, 1953, seven Mablethorpe residents were drowned.

Long popular with day trippers and holidaymakers, Mablethorpe offers all that could be asked of a traditional seaside town, and a little more. One of the most popular attractions is the **Seal Sanctuary** at North End. This complex houses creatures of all kinds, with special wildcat and barn owl features, and includes a seal and seabird hospital, as well as a nature centre with many fascinating displays. The lynx caves are particularly interesting, displaying three-dimensional scenes of Mablethorpe as it was 9,000 and 20,000 years ago, along with prehistoric tools and fossils.

A unique collection is on view at **Ye Olde Curiosity Museum** where Graham and Sue Allen have amassed an astonishing collection of more than 18,000 curios. One of the oddest is an 1890 'fat remover', which looks like a rolling pin with suction pads and was used in massage parlours. The Museum also houses the most complete collection of Pendelfin in the world.

ABY
10 miles SE of Louth on minor roads

🐾 Claythorpe Watermill & Wildfowl Gardens

Claythorpe Watermill & Wildfowl Gardens

🎭 stories and anecdotes   🗣 famous people   🎨 art and craft   ✐ entertainment and sport   🚶 walks are a major draw for visitors of all ages to this small village at the tip of the Lincolnshire Wolds. A beautiful 18th century watermill provides the central feature, surrounded by attractive woodlands inhabited by hundreds of waterfowl and other animals. There are peacocks and pheasants, cockerels, wallabies, goats and even a miniature Shetland pony. Built in 1721, the mill is no longer working but it provides a handsome setting for a restaurant, gift shop and Country Fayre shop. Open daily between March and October, the gardens also have a Bygone Exhibit Area.

ALFORD
12 miles SE of Louth on the A1114

🏛 Manor House   🏛 Windmill

🏛 Church of St Wilfrid   🎡 Alford Festival

Often described as Lincolnshire's Craft Centre, Alford is a flourishing little town with markets that were first established in 1238 still taking place on Tuesdays and Fridays. These are supplemented by a regular Craft Market every Friday throughout the summer.

Small though it is, Alford boasts some outstanding buildings. **Alford Manor House**, built around 1660, claims the distinction of being the largest thatched manor house in England. It's an attractive building with brick

Five-Sailed Windmill, Alford

gabling and a beautifully maintained thatched roof. It serves now as a folk museum where visitors are invited to step back into the past and take a look at local life through time-warp shops, an old-fashioned veterinary surgery and a Victorian schoolroom. Reaching even further back into the past, the History Room contains a collection of interesting Roman finds and also displays from the salt works

---

THE OLIVE TREE DELICATESSEN

23 Market Place, Alford, Lincolnshire LN13 9EB
Tel/Fax: -1507 463892
e-mail: wilburn159@aol.com website: www.simplyorganics.co.uk

On the Market Place in a conservation area of Alford, the **Olive Tree Delicatessen** sells a mouthwatering selection of top-quality food. Owners Darren and Maxine Wilburn seek out the very best produce from the very best suppliers, from Lincolnshire, the UK or overseas. Lincolnshire Poacher, Yellow Belly and Cotehill Blue head a wonderful selection of English and Continental cheeses; there are a dozen salamis, olives from Italy, Spain and Greece, ice cream from Joe Delucci in Turin, sugar-free and gluten-free goods, and a busy takeaway service offering excellent coffee and tea, soup, sandwiches and jacket potatoes.

🏛 historic building   🖼 museum   🏛 historic site   🌄 scenic attraction   🌿 flora and fauna that once prospered in this part of the county. Another exhibit explores the still-flourishing connections between Alford and the USA.

An even more tangible link with the past is provided by **The Five Sailed Windmill** on the eastern side of the town. It was built by a local millwright, Sam Oxley, in about 1837. Standing a majestic six floors high, it has five sails and four sets of grinding stones. This sturdy old mill came perilously close to total destruction in 1955. Thanks to the efforts of local enthusiasts it is now back in full commercial operation, complete with a vintage oven producing bakery items with the full flavour that only the old-fashioned methods seem able to produce. Other attractions here include a wholefood shop, tea room and garden.

Alford's handsome medieval **Church of St Wilfrid** dates from the 14th century and

among its treasures are a curiously carved Jacobean pulpit, the marble tomb of the former Manor House residents, (the Christopher family), and an amazing collection of tapestry kneelers. With so many parish churches nowadays locked for most of the time, it's good to know that St Wilfrid's is open daily from 9am to 4pm. In August, St Wilfrid's hosts a Flower Festival, part of the **Alford Festival**, which began in 1974 and over the years has attracted a growing variety of craftspeople, joined nowadays by dancers, singers, poets and actors.

DONINGTON-ON-BAIN
10 miles SW of Louth via A153/A157

🐦 Red Hill Nature Reserve   🚶 Viking Way

Country roads lead westward into wonderful walking country at Donington-on-Bain, a peaceful Wolds village on the **Viking Way**.

Watermill, Donington-on-Bain

📖 stories and anecdotes   🐦 famous people   🎨 art and craft   🎭 entertainment and sport   🚶 walks

This well-trodden route, which was established in 1976 by Lincolnshire County Council, runs 147 miles from the Humber Bridge to Oakham in Rutland and is waymarked by Viking helmet symbols. While in Donington, have a look at the grand old water mill and the 13th century church. There is a story that it was usual at weddings for old ladies to throw hassocks at the bride as she walked up the aisle. This boisterous custom was ended in 1780 by the rector after he was hit by a badly aimed hassock!

To the east of Donington and south of Goulceby is the celebrated **Red Hill Nature Reserve.** The hill itself is an outcrop bearing a vein of spectacular red chalk that is rich in fossil finds. The small reserve is home to several species of butterflies and moths, the meadow pipit, common lizard and grass snake. From the clifftop there are some wonderful views across the Wolds. The hill also provides the setting for a Good Friday procession when the vicar of Asterby and three parishioners carrying crosses climb the steep lane. The three crosses are erected above a chalk pit and a short service takes place with music provided by the Horncastle Brass band.

Grimsby

🏛 Dock Tower   🏛 Fishing Heritage Centre

🏛 The Time Trap   🌿 People's Park

🏃 Freshney Park Way

According to tradition it was a Dane called Grim who founded Grimsby. He had been ordered to drown the young Prince Havelock after the boy's father had been killed in battle. Grim could not bring himself to murder the child so he set sail for England. After a tempestuous crossing of the North Sea, Grim

and the boy arrived at the Humber estuary where he used the timbers of their boat to build a house on the shore. They lived by selling fish and salt, thus establishing the foundations of an industry for which Grimsby would become known the world over.

But until 1848, Grimsby didn't even rank among Lincolnshire's ten largest towns. That was the year the railway arrived, making it possible for fish to be swiftly transported to major centres of population inland. Only four years later, the town's most famous landmark, the elegant, Italianate **Dock Tower,** was built, soaring more than 300 feet above the busy docks. The Tower now enjoys Grade I listed building status, ranking it alongside such national treasures as Buckingham Palace and Chatsworth House. The tower's original function was purely utilitarian, the storage of 33,000 gallons of water to operate the hydraulic system that worked the lock gates. But shortly after it was built in 1852 it was discovered that water in a pressurised tube worked just as well so the tower became redundant. On open days, visitors can undertake the gruelling climb up the inside of the tower to enjoy the breathtaking views from the top.

The Tower stands beside Alexandra Dock, which enjoyed its heyday during the 1950s when Grimsby was the world's largest fishing port. The story of those boom days is told in vivid detail in the **Fishing Heritage Centre** in Alexandra Dock, where visitors are challenged to navigate the icy waters of the Arctic, experience freezing winds, black ice, and lashing rain as the trawler decks, literally, heave and moan beneath your feet. As well as recreating the deep-sea fishing industry in its heyday, the Centre also explores the social setting of that period, with reconstructions of the twisting back streets and alleys of 1950s Grimsby. Pre-booked parties can visit **The Time Trap**, housed deep in old prison cells of the Town Hall, which recreates the seamier side of life on dry land and has proved a very popular annexe to the Heritage Centre. Visitors pass through dark, twisting corridors, explore mysterious nooks and crannies, discovering en route some unexpected facets of the town. The Town Hall itself, built in 1863, is a dignified building whose frontage has a series of busts depicting Queen Victoria, Prince Albert, local man John Whitgift, later Archbishop of Canterbury, Edward III (who granted the land around here to the Freemen of Grimsby), the Earl of Yarborough, (local landowner and High Steward of the borough at that time), and the historian Gervase Holles who was Mayor of Grimsby in 1640.

Many Victorian buildings were destroyed during World War II but a surviving legacy from that era is the **People's Park** where the facilities include a heart-shaped lake, children's play area, bowling greens, croquet lawn, ornamental gardens and plenty of open space. The Floral Hall is vibrant with colour all year round and houses both tropical and temperate species, and a large variety of house and garden plants, shrubs and conifers are on sale. Away from the centre, by the banks of the River Freshney, is **Freshney Park Way,** 300 acres of open space that attracts walkers, cyclists, anglers and birdwatchers as well as picnickers.

A final note for football fans. Be prepared for the question: Why does Grimsby Town Football Club play all its games away? Answer: Because the Mariners' ground is actually in Cleethorpes, a resort which has spread northwards to meet up with Grimsby itself.

Around Grimsby

IMMINGHAM
7 miles NW of Grimsby off the A180

🏛 Pilgrim Father Monument   🏛 Museum

A small village until the early 1900s, Immingham's breakthrough came when a new port on the south bank of the Humber was proposed. Grimsby naturally thought that the honour should be hers but consultants favoured Immingham because the deep water channel of the river runs close to the shore here. The new Docks were opened by King George V in 1912 and rapidly grew in importance, especially when the Great Central Railway switched its passenger liner service from Grimsby. The Docks expanded yet further when the Humber was dredged in the late 1960s to accommodate the new generation of giant tankers and a huge refinery now stands to the west of the town. Not promising country for tourists but the heart of the old village has survived with St Andrew's Church at its centre.

The **Immingham Museum** traces the links between the Docks and the railways and there's also an exhibit about the group of Puritans who, in 1607, set sail from Immingham to the New England. A memorial to this event, the **Pilgrim Father Monument**, was erected by the Anglo-American Society in 1925. It originally stood near the point of embarkation but is now located near the church. Most of the 20ft-high column is made from local granite but near the top is a block of hewn from Plymouth Rock in New England where these religious refugees first landed.

CLEETHORPES
1 mile S of Grimsby on the A180

🏛 Ross Castle   🏛 Cleethorpes Coast Light Railway

🏛 Humber Estuary Discovery Centre

One of Cleethorpes' claims to fame is that it stands on zero longitude, i.e. on the Greenwich Meridian line. A signpost on the coastal path marks the Meridian line and points the way to London, the North Pole and other prominent places, an essential snap for the family album.

Just south of Grimsby and almost merged with it, Cleethorpes developed from a little village into a holiday resort when the railway line was built in the 1860s. The Manchester, Sheffield & Lincolnshire Railway Company developed much of the town and also built the splendid promenade, a mile long and 65ft wide, below the cliff. Above the promenade they built the sham ruin known as **Ross Castle**, named after the railway's general secretary, Edward Ross. Swathed in ivy, the folly marked the highest point of the cliffs which the promenade now protects from erosion.

The railway company also funded the construction of a pier. This was opened on August Bank Holiday Monday 1873, when nearly 3,000 people paid the then princely sum of sixpence (2½p) for admission. The toll was reduced the next day to a much more reasonable penny (½p), and it is recorded that in the first five weeks 37,000 people visited. The pier, like many others, was breached during the Second World War as a defence measure to discourage enemy landings, and it was never restored to its full length. The pier now measures 355ft compared to its original 1,200ft but the Edwardian pavilion of 1906 is still in place and is currently the largest nightclub in the area.

The town also boasts the last surviving seaside steam railway, the **Cleethorpes Coast Light Railway.** This narrow-gauge steam railway runs along the foreshore and lakeside every day from Easter to September, and on weekends throughout the year. A recent addition to the town's attractions is the **Cleethorpes Humber Estuary Discovery Centre.** Here visitors can become time travellers, discover extinct creatures and submerged forests, and work off their aggression by participating in a Viking raid. The Lincolnshire clockmaker, John Harrison, who solved the problem of finding longitude, is celebrated in one of the many exhibits and the complex also offers refreshments in the Boaters Tea Room.

NORTH SOMERCOTES
12 miles SE of Grimsby off the A1031

🌿 Donna Nook Nature Reserve

Olney's Shrove Tuesday pancake races may be better known but those at North Somercotes are equally popular. Contestants run the length of this straggling village tossing their pancakes as they go. There are separate contests for adults and children.

To the east of the village is the **Donna Nook Nature Reserve** which stretches six miles south along the coast to Saltfleet. In summer it's a favoured nesting site for many species of birds, among them dunnock, little grebe and meadow pipits. Large colonies of Brent geese, dunlin and other waders are attracted to the mudflats while common and grey seals pup on the sandflats. As well as marram grass and sea buckthorn, the dunes also provide a support for the much rarer pyramidal orchids.

🏛 historic building   🏛 museum   🏛 historic site   🌊 scenic attraction   🌿 flora and fauna

Roman Walls, Caister

CAISTOR
10 miles SW of Grimsby on the A46

🏛 Church   🏛 Pelham's Pillar

Caistor's market place stands on the plain, looking across corn fields to the distant towers of Lincoln Cathedral; but its narrow streets wind their way up the western slopes of the Wolds. Caistor's name makes it clear that this agreeable little market town did indeed start life as a small Roman camp. Just a few hard-to-find fragments of the once massive walls remain. However, it's known that the camp measured just 300 yards by 100 yards and that the present **Church of St Peter & St Paul** stands at the exact centre of the Roman enclosure. The church, whose oldest part is the Anglo-Saxon tower, contains a curiosity kept in a glass case. This is the famous Gad Whip, which until 1847 was "cracked over the head of the vicar on Palm Sunday by a man from Broughton in payment for certain parcels of land". Another version of the tradition claims that the whip, which had a purse containing two shillings tied to it,

was simply waved over the head of the clergyman while the latter read the second lesson. Either way, Victorian opinion regarded the performance as not consistent with ecclesiastical decorum and it was suppressed.

A mile or so north of the town, **Pelham's Pillar** commemorates the planting of the surrounding woods by Charles Pelham, Earl of Yarborough. Between 1787 and 1828, the earl had planted 12,552,700 trees – at least that is what the inscription claims. The lofty tower cost a staggering £2,395 to build and when it was completed in 1849 no less a personage than Prince Albert came to view it. The tower is locked but if you want to climb up inside, a key can be obtained within reasonable hours from the Keeper's Cottage, Pillar Lodge.

The 147-mile long Viking Way passes through Caistor and about five miles south of the town climbs to **Normanby-on-the-Wold**, the highest village in Lincolnshire. The path continues through **Walesby**, where All Saints Church is known as the Ramblers' Church because of its stained glass window depicting Christ with ramblers and cyclists, and on to the delightful village of **Tealby**.

MARKET RASEN
18 miles SW of Grimsby off the A46

🏇 Racecourse

This pleasing little market town stands between the great plain that spreads north of Lincoln and the sheltering Wolds to the east.

SPRING

3 Market Place Walk, Market Rasen, Lincolnshire LN8 3HJ
Tel: 01673 849366   Fax: 01673 885324

Spring is a cosy, friendly shop in the centre of town selling a wide range of designer womens' wear and accessories. Linda Smithson and Sally Cordell have created a very welcoming

ambience for browsing and buying, and every customer passing through the door can be assured of helpful individual attention.

Among the many prominent names usually in stock are clothing by Seebago, Joules, Saint James, Blue Willis, Noli and James Lakeland; Quba Sails for ladies all at sea; Repeat cashmere; trousers by Gardent and Michele to fit and flatter all sizes; Royal Mer French knitwear; Gabour, Quayside and

Wolky shoes; Prickly Pear handbags; and Coeur de Lion jewellery. Quality, variety, value for money and personal service make every visit to Spring a real pleasure.

SUNNYSIDE UP FARM SHOP

Poplar Farm, Tealby Road, Market Rasen, Lincolnshire
LN8 3UL
Tel: 01673 844736   Fax: 01673 849227
e-mail: hammonds@poplar-farm.fsnet.co.uk
website: www.sunnyside-up.co.uk

Lincolnshire-born Hazel and Julian Hammond have farmed here for 15 years and in November 2005 they opened their farm shop. In custom-built premises on the B1203 between Market Rasen and Tealby, they sell cuts and joints from their rare-breed Lincoln Red beef and Berkshire and Gloucestershire Old Spot pigs. All their meat is butchered on the premises and hung for a minimum of three weeks. Lamb comes from a neighbouring farm, and poultry includes free-range chickens, ducks and guinea fowl.

The emphasis throughout is on local produce, including award-winning Cotehill Blue, Yellow Belly and Lincolnshire Poacher cheese, milk and other dairy products, fish from Grimsby on Fridays, prize-winning sausages, fruit and vegetables, cakes, biscuits and chocolate – even Lincoln Red beer from Tom Woods Highwood Brewery. Also in stock are organic flour, jams, preserves, pickles and produce from a local Grammar School Enterprise Project.

EAST FARMHOUSE

Mill Lane, Middle Rasen, nr Market Rasen,
Lincolnshire LN3 5AQ
Tel: 01673 842283   Mobile: 07836331424
Fax: 01673 849041
e-mail: emmalouise.grant@btconnect.com

Nestling at the foot of the Lincolnshire Wolds, **East Farmhouse** is a listed mid-18th century property surrounded by open fields and delightful views. Bed & Breakfast guests at Jim and Gill Grant's farm enjoy home comforts in two spacious double bedrooms – one en suite, the other with private facilities. Each has a TV, radio and tea/coffee tray, and guests have the use of an oak-beamed sitting/breakfast room with an open log fire. Gill is a keen cook, and her breakfast, featuring home-laid eggs and local produce, makes the perfect start to the day.

A self-catering cottage sleeping four guests is available nearby, and both the farmhouse and the cottage are ideal bases for exploring the Wolds and the historic city of Lincoln. Jim and Gill have lived and farmed here for over 30 years; both have a keen interest in conservation, and the farm has won two conservation awards for environmental stewardship. Guests can enjoy farm walks, where abundant wildlife is usually to be seen, and the extensive gardens are a special delight in the summer, with a large duck pond, a grass tennis court and a summer house. The accommodation (non-smoking) is open all year except Christmas and New Year.

Now happily bypassed, the town still has a market on Tuesdays and throughout the year there are regular meetings at the **Market Rasen Racecourse.**

Taking its name from the little River Rase, Market Rasen was once described by Charles Dickens as being "the sleepiest town in England". Much of the central part is a conservation area.

Boston

🏠 Boston Stump   🏠 Guildhall   🏠 Windmill

An important inland port on the River Witham, Boston's fortunes reached their peak during the Middle Ages when the town was second only to London in the amount of taxes it paid. Today, it's a prosperous market town of around 37,000 inhabitants and the administrative centre for the region. The market, more than 450 years old now and the largest open air market in Lincolnshire, takes place every Wednesday and Saturday.

The town's most famous landmark is St Botolph's Church, much better known as the **Boston Stump.** 'Stump' is a real misnomer since the tower soars 272ft into the sky and is visible for 30 miles or more from land and sea. Building of the tower began around 1425 and was not completed for 100 years. The body of the church is older still - it dates back to 1309 and is built mainly in the graceful Decorated style of architecture. St Botolph's is the largest parish church in England (20,070 square feet in all) and its spacious interior is wonderfully light and airy. The church is noted for its abundance of often bizarre medieval carvings in wood and stone - a bear playing an organ, a man lassooing a lion, a fox in a bishop's cope taking a jug of

CHERRY HOLT STUDIO

Dowdyke Road, Sutterton, nr Boston,
Lincolnshire PE20 2 LB
Tel: 01205 460558

Cherry Holt Studio is a delightful modern gallery built in 2003, owned and run by Joyce Colam with her daughters Lindis and Caroline.

Lindis is a talented artist specialising in oils and pastels, and her work can be seen hanging with paintings by up to 30 other artists, most of them local, with regular exhibitions showcasing individual or groups of artists.

Lindis and other artists hold art and pottery classes, while Caroline is in charge of a bespoke framing service that includes framing all kinds of mementoes as well as paintings and prints.

Browsers are always very welcome, and the studio has a charming little tea room serving home baking, sandwiches, light lunches, salads and cream teas. When the sun shines, it's a particular delight to take refreshment by the little pond in the garden.

Also included at Cherry Holt is a well-stocked art store.

ARTS CORITANI

Granary Lane, High Street, Swineshead, Lincolnshire PE20 3LH
Tel/Fax: 01205 820014
e-mail: artscoritani@btopenworld.com
website: www.artscoritani.com

An old granary in the village of Swineshead, sited at the junction of the A17 and the A52 has been renovated and converted to provide 2,000 square feet of display space for showing contemporary art.

Arts Coritani opened its doors in August 2002 and the honour of the first exhibition fell to Lincolnshire's best known and respected living artist, Andrzej Kuhn: 90% of his work sold on the opening day. The Gallery is available for hire to selected artists and the owners welcome contact by progressive artists and collectors. The East Coast Artists Group of about 12 professional artists is associated with the Gallery; their work is available for exchange exhibitions in galleries in other parts of the world.

Arts Coritani is developing an interest in all aspects of computer arts and New Media, and the site has an IT room and an acre of park for outdoor events and displays.

🏛 historic building   🏛 museum   🏛 historic site   🝏 scenic attraction   🌱 flora and fauna water from a baboon.

One of Boston's most striking secular buildings is the 15th century **Guildhall**, which for 300 years served as the Town Hall; it has recently re-opened after major refurbishment. Another impressive building is the **Maud Foster Windmill** (1819), the tallest working windmill in Britain and unusual in having five sails, or "sweeps". Visitors can climb to the top of the mill, see the machinery and millstones in action, and enjoy some fine views from the outside balcony. There's a tea room and a Mill Shop that sells the mill's own stone-ground organic flour as well as local books and souvenirs.

If you enjoy seeking out architectural curiosities, then there's a splendid one in a quiet back street of the town. The frontage of the **Freemason's Hall** represents a miniature Egyptian temple, complete with columns crowned by papyrus fronds. Half a century earlier, following Napoleon's Egyptian campaign there had been a spate of such monumental buildings, but Boston's temple, built in the 1860s, presents a very late flowering of the style.

Around Boston

FISHTOFT
3 miles SE of Boston off the A52

This village has just one claim to fame. It was from an obscure creek near the village that the Pilgrim Fathers made their first attempt to escape England's oppressive religious laws. A simple monument is inscribed with the words:

Near this place in September 1607 those
later known as the Pilgrim Fathers
set sail on their first attempt to
find religious freedom across the seas.

DONINGTON
10 miles SW of Boston on the A52

A small market town, Donington boasts some elegant Georgian buildings, among them the former Grammar School, and a huge church which was bountifully re-endowed in the 14th century when Donington was flourishing as the centre of trade in flax and hemp. Like Deeping St James the church has its own rather elegant *hude*, or movable hut. If inclement weather coincided with a burial, the hut would be moved to the graveside. Standing inside the shelter (complete with its own coat hook) the parson could smugly observe the mourners being drenched. Inside the church there are a number of memorials to the Flinders family. Their most famous son, Matthew, was born at Donington in 1774 and later became celebrated for his exploration of the Australian coastline. Returning from Australia to England via the Indian Ocean in a decrepit ship, Flinders put in at Mauritius for repairs. At that time, Mauritius was governed by the French who had watched British expansion in Australasia with alarm. They arrested Flinders as a spy and it was seven long years before they allowed him to continue his journey back to England and his home town of Donington.

Spalding

🏛 Gordon Boswell Romany Museum	
🐦 Flower Parade	🐦 Springfields Festival Gardens
🏛 Ayscoughfee Hall Museum & Gardens	

This small market town is known around the world for its annual **Flower Parade** which attracts half a million visitors each year. Established in 1959, the Festival is held in

---

🎬 stories and anecdotes   🦜 famous people   🎨 art and craft   ✒ entertainment and sport   🚶 walks early May when marching bands lead a succession of colourful floats, each adorned with thousands of tulip heads and spring flowers, through the town. The floats are then displayed at **Springfields Festival Gardens** whose 30 landscaped acres include marvellous show gardens, a carp lake, a shopping outlet, a play barn and Fenscape, a unique experience where you can discover how the landscape was created and what life is like for those living on the Fens.

The two weeks around the Flower Parade coincide with the South Holland Arts Festival featuring open air concerts, workshops, exhibitions and a host of other activities and performances. The festival is based on the South Holland Centre, a stylish venue which is active throughout the year and also has a café-bar on the first floor overlooking the Market Place.

Spalding itself is an interesting place to stroll around, with Georgian terraces lining the River Welland and with many of the buildings revealing Dutch architectural influences. Before the days of mass car ownership, most visitors to the Tulip Festival arrived by excursion trains and a great mesh of sidings stretch to the north of the town. To cross them, the longest iron footbridge in Lincolnshire was built. Two, actually, because another equally impressive construction stands south of the station, spanning the main line and a now defunct branch line.

The jewel in Spalding's crown is undoubtedly **Ayscoughfee Hall Museum and Gardens,** a well-preserved medieval mansion standing in attractive gardens by the river and with some venerable yew tree walks. Pronounced "Asscuffy", the Hall was built around 1429 for Sir Richard Aldwyn. It later became the home of Maurice Johnson (1688-

1755), a member of the Royal Society and a leading figure in the intellectual life of his day. In 1710, he founded the Gentlemen's Society of Spalding, which still flourishes from its headquarters and small museum in Broad Street. Part of the Gentlemen's extensive collection of stuffed birds, dating back to 1800, is on display in Ayscoughfee Hall, which also has a prominent exhibit honouring the explorer and oceanographer Capt. Matthew Flinders who has been mentioned earlier under his birthplace in Donington. Other galleries record Spalding's social and economic history.

Located in the lovely grounds of Ayscoughfee Hall is Spalding's War Memorial which stands at one end of an ornamental pool which in winters past would freeze over. Blocks of ice were hewn from it and stored in the icehouse which still survives, tucked away in a corner of the garden walls.

Connoisseurs of odd buildings should make their way down a lane off Cowbit Road to a red brick building that belongs to no recognisable school of architecture. Known as the Tower House, it was built in Victorian times but no one has any idea who built it, why or exactly when. It's a bizarre medley of medieval towers and crenellations, a random obelisk, Georgian-style windows and other bits and pieces. One writer described it as being ' like a giant Lego construction'. It is now a private house, but the exterior can be enjoyed from the lane.

A couple of miles south of Spalding, the **Gordon Boswell Romany Museum** has a colourful collection of Romany Vardos (caravans), carts and harnesses along with an extensive display of Romany photographs and sketches covering the last 150 years. A slide show and conducted tour are available and

---

🏛 historic building   🏛 museum   🏛 historic site   🌿 scenic attraction   🌾 flora and fauna there's also a fortune telling tent. Gordon Boswell and his wife Margaret also arrange Romany Days Out in a horse-drawn vardo, a trip which includes a meal cooked over a traditional Romany stick fire. The museum is open from March to October but closed on Mondays (except Bank Holidays) and Tuesdays.

Around Spalding

PINCHBECK
2 miles N of Spalding on the B1356

📷 Pinchbeck Engine & Land Drainage Museum

📷 Spalding Bulb Museum   🌱 Tropical Forest

For an interesting insight into how the South Holland Fen has been transformed by man, a visit to the **Pinchbeck Engine and Land Drainage Museum** is strongly recommended. The star exhibit here is the Pinchbeck Engine, a sturdy monster which was built way back in 1833. Each year for almost 120 years, up until 1952, the 20hp engine lifted an average of three million tons of water from the soggy fens at a rate of 7,500 gallons per minute.

In 1988 the Drainage Board and South Holland Council restored this superb piece of machinery and it now operates regularly, and is the centrepiece of the museum, which is open daily from April to October.

Also in Pinchbeck is the **Spalding Bulb Museum** which follows the growth of the bulb-growing industry down the years with the aid of tableaux and artefacts, as well as audio-visual and seasonal working demonstrations. A third attraction is **Spalding Tropical Forest**, actually a water garden centre but promising "a tropical paradise full of plants, waterfalls, fountains and streams".

SURFLEET
4 miles N of Spalding off the A16

The River Glen provides an attractive feature in this popular village with its yachts on the water and holiday homes on the banks. Surfleet church has a tower that leans at an alarming angle, more than six feet out of true, the result of subsidence in the boggy ground. The north door is pockmarked with musket shot, a permanent reminder of an unwelcome visit from Cromwell's soldiers during the Civil War.

WESTON
3 miles NE of Spalding on the A151

🏛 Church   🏛 Mounton Mill

This small village surrounded by tulip fields boasts a fine church, **St Mary's,** which is notable for having one of the most complete Early Gothic interiors in the country. The superb arcades have been compared to those in Lincoln Cathedral and there's a wealth of carving known as Lincolnshire stiff-leaf. The 13th century font is carved with huge flowers decorating each panel of the bowl and the Victorian pulpit has openwork panels somewhat Islamic in style. An eye-catching feature in the rather dimly-lit interior, is the display of colourful kneelers placed on the shelves of the pews.

Just to the southeast of Weston is **Moulton Mill**, the largest survivng windmill in the country. Open to the public after many years use as a grain store, it offers a unique experience. A visitor centre, gift shop and The Granary tea room will complete your visit.

HOLBEACH
10 miles E of Spalding on the A151/B1168

Located deep in the heart of the Fens, Holbeach stands at the centre of one of the largest parishes in the country. It extends some 15 miles from end to end and covers 21,000 acres.

Holbeach is a pleasing little town with a market on both Thursday and Saturday and also boasts an impressive church with a lofty spire visible for miles across the flat fields. The curious entrance porch, with its two round towers, is believed to have been "borrowed" from the now vanished Moulton Castle, a few miles to the west.

When William Cobbett passed through Holbeach on his *Rural Rides* in the 1840s he was delighted with the "neat little town, a most beautiful church, fruit trees in abundance and the land dark in colour and as fine in substance as flour". Surprisingly little has changed since William visited.

GEDNEY
13 miles E of Spalding off the A17

🏛 Church

Of all the fine churches in this corner of the county, **St Mary's** at Gedney is perhaps the most spectacular. It is supernaturally light inside, an effect produced by its magnificent clerestory in which the medieval masons reduced the stonework to near-invisibility. The 24 three-light windows drench the interior with light, brilliantly illuminating the carvings and bosses of the roof, and the interesting collection of monuments. The best known of these is a brass in the south aisle which depicts a lady who died around 1400 with a puppy crouching in the folds of her gown.

LONG SUTTON
15 miles E of Spalding on B1359

🦋 Butterfly & Wildlife Park　🎿 Peter Scott Walk

🎿 King John's Lost Jewels Trail

Long Sutton is a very appropriate name for this straggling village. St Mary's Church has an unusual two-storeyed porch, the upper floor of which was once used as a school, and a rare, lead-covered spire 160 feet high.

The surrounding area borders The Wash and is a favourite place with walkers and naturalists, especially bird-watchers. One of the most popular routes is the **Peter Scott Walk** – during the 1930s the celebrated naturalist lived in one of the two lighthouses on the River Nene nearby. Another route, **King John's Lost Jewels Trail**, covers 23 miles of quiet country roads and is suitable for cyclists and motorists. It starts at Long Sutton market place and passes Sutton Bridge where the unfortunate king is believed to have lost all his treasure in the marsh. Sutton Bridge itself is notable for the swing bridge over the River Nene. Built in 1897 for the Midland and Great Northern Railway, it is one of very few examples still surviving of a working swing bridge.

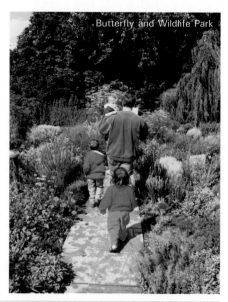
Butterfly and Wildlife Park

🏛 historic building　📷 museum　🏚 historic site　🌿 scenic attraction　🦋 flora and fauna

OTHELLO BAKERY

31 High Street, Long Sutton,
Lincolnshire PE12 9DB
Tel/Fax: 01406 363228
e-mail: rg218@aol.co.uk

Owner Richard Green learned the baker's art in London and opened **Othello Bakery** in 2000 in the main street of Long Sutton. There has been a bakery on this corner site for more than 80 years, but the locals will confirm that it's never been better. Bread and cakes are baked fresh daily and offer an impressive choice of traditional goodies: square tin loaves, bloomers, wholemeal, malt and soda bread, scones, flapjacks, Eccles cakes, Bakewell tarts, Viennese pastries, apple puffs, cream cakes, celebration cakes for special occasions. All these can be bought to take away or enjoy in the pine-furnished tea room, along with rolls and sandwiches with a variety of fillings, light or full English breakfasts and hot snacks including jacket potatoes, sausage rolls, pies and pasties.

Friendly staff and a congenial band of regulars create a very warm and welcoming ambience at Othello Bakery, which is open from 8am to 3.30pm; closed Sunday.

The Butterfly and Wildlife Park has one of the country's largest walk through tropical butterfly and bird houses. With its wallaby enclosure, reptiles, birds of prey flying displays and a host of other amenities, it makes the perfect family day out.

CROWLAND

10 miles S of Spalding on the A1073

🏛 Abbey   🏛 Trinity Bridge

It was in AD699 that a young Mercian nobleman named Guthlac became disillusioned with the world and took to a small boat. He rowed off into the Fens until he came to a remote muddy island, (which is what the name Crowland means). Here he built himself a hut and a small chapel. Guthlac's reputation as a wise and holy man

attracted a host of visitors in search of spiritual guidance. He died in 714 and shortly afterwards his kinsman, King Ethelbald of Mercia, founded the monastery that became known as **Crowland Abbey.**

The abbey buildings have suffered an unusually troubled history. Nothing but some oak foundations remains of the first abbey - the rest was destroyed by Danish invaders. The monastery was rebuilt in Saxon style in about 950 when the community began to live according to the rule of St Benedict. That abbey was also destroyed, on this occasion by a great fire in 1091. An earthquake in 1117 interrupted the rebuilding. Some 50 years later, the third abbey was completed, in the Norman style. Parts of this splendid building can still be seen, notably in the dog-tooth west

---

📖 stories and anecdotes   🐦 famous people   🎨 art and craft   🎭 entertainment and sport   🚶 walks

arch of the central tower. Another fire caused massive damage in 1143 and the restoration that followed provides most of the substantial ruins that remain. They present an impressive sight as they loom forbiddingly over this small Fenland village. Happily, the abbey's former north aisle survived and now serves as the parish church.

Trinity Bridge, Crowland

Crowland is also noted for its extraordinary 'Bridge without a River', also known locally as the 'Three Ways to Nowhere Bridge'. When it was built in the 1300s, **Trinity Bridge** provided a dry crossing over the confluence of three small streams. Hence its unique triangular shape. But the streams dried up and the bridge now serves no purpose apart from being extremely decorative. At one end, there's a large seated figure, possibly of Christ and almost certainly pilfered from the West Front of the abbey where a surprising number of these 15th century statues are still in place.

Stamford

🏠 St Leonard's Priory   🏠 Burghley House

🏛 Museum   🏛 Steam Brewery Museum

Proclaimed as "the finest stone town in England", Stamford was declared the country's first Conservation Area in 1967. Later, "England's most attractive town" (John Betjeman's words), became familiar to millions of TV viewers when its wonderfully unspoilt Georgian streets and squares provided an authentic backdrop for the BBC's dramatisation of George Eliot's *Middlemarch*. Stamford is a thriving little town with a wide

variety of small shops (including a goodly number of antiques shops), and a bustling street market on Fridays.

A dubious local legend asserts that Stamford was founded in the 8th century BC by the Trojan king of Britain, Bladud, and continued as a seat of learning until the 14th century AD when it was supplanted by the upstart universities of Oxford and Cambridge. Whatever its past, what gives the present town its enchanting character is the handsome Georgian architecture, evidenced everywhere in private houses and elegant public buildings such as the Town Hall, the Assembly Rooms, the theatre and the well-known George Hotel whose gallows sign spans the main street.

Stamford's most ancient ecclesiastical building is **St Leonard's Priory**, founded by the Benedictines in the 11th century and a fine example of Norman architecture with an ornate west front and north side arcade.

Secular buildings of note include Browne's Hospital in Broad Street which was founded in 1494 by the same Browne brothers mentioned above. It now houses the **Museum of Almshouse Life** - the ground floor presenting aspects of almshouse life, the upper hosting various exhibitions.

The town is well provided with museums. The **Stamford Museum** includes an exhibit celebrating one of the town's most famous visitors. Daniel Lambert earned a precarious living by exhibiting himself as the world's heaviest man. As an additional source of income he would challenge people to race along a course of his choosing. Daniel would then set off along the corridors of the inn, filling them wall to wall and preventing any challenger from passing. For most of his adult life he weighed well over 50 stones. When he died in the Waggon & Horses Inn at Stamford in 1809 the wall of his bedroom had to be demolished in order to remove his body.

Railway buffs will want to pay a visit to the Stamford East Railway Station. The station was built in 1855-6 for the branch line of the Great North Railway. Because the land was owned by the Marquess of Exeter, of nearby Burghley House, the architect William Hurst was obliged to build in the classical style using the local honey-coloured stone. The result is surely one of the most elegant small stations in the country.

A rather more specialised museum is the **Stamford Steam Brewery Museum** which has a collection of original 19th century brewing equipment. The museum is housed in the malt house and brewery, which was established by William Burn in 1825 and continued brewing right up until 1974. It is now open to the public by prior arrangement.

Two more of Stamford's famous residents should be mentioned. Buried in the town cemetery is Sir Malcolm Sargent, the 'pin-up' conductor of the Henry Wood Promenade Concerts in the 1960s and '70s. The cross on his grave is inscribed with the Promenaders' Prayer. And in St Martin's Church is the splendid tomb of William Cecil, 1st Lord Burghley, who was Elizabeth I's Chief Secretary of State from her accession until his death in 1598. Cecil's magnificent residence, Burghley House, lies a mile south of the town.

"The largest and grandest house of the Elizabethan Age", **Burghley House** presents a dazzling spectacle with its domed towers, walls of cream coloured stone, and acres of windows. Clear glass was still ruinously expensive in the 1560s so Elizabethan grandees like Cecil flaunted their wealth by having windows that stretched almost from floor to ceiling. Burghley House also displays the Elizabethan obsession with

Burghley House

🎭 stories and anecdotes   🦜 famous people   🎨 art and craft   🎬 entertainment and sport   🚶 walks symmetry - every tower, dome, pilaster and pinnacle has a corresponding partner.

Contemporaries called Burghley a 'prodigy house', a title shared at that time with only one other stately home in England – Longleat in Wiltshire. Both houses were indeed prodigious in size and in cost. At Burghley, Cecil commissioned the most celebrated interior decorator of the age, Antonio Verrio, to create rooms of unparalleled splendour. In his 'Heaven Room', Verrio excelled even himself, populating the lofty walls and ceiling with a dynamic gallery of mythological figures. The State rooms house the earliest inventoried collection of Japanese ceramics in the West, rare examples of European porcelain and wood carvings by Grinling Gibbons. Four magnificent state beds stand majestically against fine examples of Continental furniture and important tapestries and textiles.

In the 18th century, Cecil's descendants commissioned the ubiquitous Capability Brown to landscape the 160 acres of parkland surrounding the house. These enchanting grounds are open to visitors and are also home to a large herd of fallow deer which was first established in Cecil's time. Brown also designed the elegant Orangery which is now a licensed restaurant overlooking rose beds and gardens.

Twelve acres of scrub woodland have been reclaimed and planted with specimen trees and shrubs and now provide a sylvan setting for the Sculpture Garden, featuring a number of dramatic artworks by contemporary sculptors.

Throughout the summer season, Burghley hosts a series of events of which the best known, the Burghley Horse Trials, takes place at the end of August.

Around Stamford

THE DEEPINGS
8 miles E of Stamford off the A16

🏛 Priory Church

There are four Deepings in all and they lie alongside the River Welland which here forms the county boundary with Cambridgeshire. The largest is Market Deeping which was once an important stop on the London to Lincoln coaching route. The triangular town centre has some imposing Georgian buildings, a large antique and craft centre, and a church dating back to 1240.

Today, Deeping St James merges imperceptibly with its larger neighbour. The old village sits on the banks of the Welland which at this point is controlled by two locks. The **Priory Church of St James** is an impressively large structure and was originally built as a satellite cell of Thorney Abbey. Among its possessions is a *hude* - a small shelter rather like a sentry box which was designed to keep the Vicar dry when conducting burial services in the rain. Another interesting curiosity is the small square building in the centre of the village. It was originally the Market Cross but was converted into a lock-up in 1819 to contain village drunks and other troublemakers. Three semi-circular stone seats with chains can still be seen through bars in the doors. Incongruously, the rather elegant little building is topped by a graceless modern street lamp.

BOURNE
10 miles N of Stamford on the A6121

🏛 Heritage Centre   🌿 Bowthorpe Oak

🌳 Bourne Wood

A small, attractive town, Bourne has a fine

church, an impressive Town Hall of 1821 with an unusual staircase entry, delightful Memorial Gardens, and a variety of family shops, craft and antiques emporia, as well as modern shopping precincts. A colourful market takes place every Thursday and Saturday.

It was the springs of clear water that enticed the Romans to settle here. Today, the springs flow into St Peter's Pool from which a small stream known as the Bourne Eau runs into the town and Memorial Gardens. Here, willow trees border the crystal clear water, home to fish, wildfowl and small roosting houses. En route, the Bourne Eau passes Baldocks Mill which functioned between 1800 and the 1920s, and now houses the **Bourne Heritage Centre.**

Notable sons of Bourne include Raymond Mays, who founded the BRM motor company in 1949, and Charles Frederick Worth, the couturier and founder of the House of Worth. A mile west of the town, beside the A151, stands **Bourne Wood,** 400 acres of long-established woodland with an abundant and varied plant and animal life. Once part of the great Forest of Brunswald, it's a great place for walking or cycling, and has some interesting modern sculpture in wood and stone. The waters around Bourne and the Deepings are credited with curative properties and the Blind Well, on the edge of the wood,

is reputed to be particularly efficacious in healing eye complaints.

About four miles south of Bourne, near the village of Witham on the Hill, stands the **Bowthorpe Oak**, which is believed to be the largest in terms of its girth than any other tree in Britain. When last measured, the oak was just over 39 feet around. The tree is hollow and it's claimed that on one occasion 39 people stood inside it.

GRIMSTHORPE
5 miles NW of Bourne on the A151

🏰 Castle

Grimsthorpe Castle is definitely two-faced. Seen from the north, it's a stately 18th century demi-palace. Viewed from the south, it's a homely Tudor dwelling. The Tudor part of the house was built at incredible speed in order to provide a convenient lodging place in Lincolnshire for Henry VIII on his way north to meet James V of Scotland in York. The royal visit to Grimsthorpe Castle duly took place in 1541 but the honour of the royal presence was tarnished by the adultery that allegedly took place here between Henry's fourth wife, Katherine Howard, and an attractive young courtier, Thomas Culpepper. In Tudor times, royal misbehaviour of this nature constituted an act of high treason. The errant Queen and her ardent courtier paid a

Grimsthorpe Castle

📖 stories and anecdotes   🦜 famous people   🎨 art and craft   🎭 entertainment and sport   🚶 walks fatal price for their nights of passion at Grimsthorpe Castle. Both were condemned to the executioner's axe.

The imposing Georgian part of Grimsthorpe Castle was built in the early 1700s. The 16th Baron Grimsthorpe had just been elevated by George I to the topmost rank of the peerage as Duke of Ancaster. It was only natural that the new Duke should wish to improve his rather modest ancestral home. He commissioned Sir John Vanbrugh, the celebrated architect of Blenheim Palace and Castle Howard, to completely redesign the building. As it happened, only the north front and the courtyard were completed to Vanbrugh's designs, which is why the castle presents two such different faces.

There's no such confusion about the grounds of Grimsthorpe Castle. These could only be 18th century and were landscaped by who else than Capability Brown. His fee was £105, about £100,000 in our money. In return for this substantial consideration, Brown miraculously transformed the flat fields of south Lincolnshire into an Arcadian landscape of gently rolling hills, complete with an artificial lake and a sham bridge.

Seventeen generations of the Willoughby family have been Lords of the Manor of Grimsthorpe since they first arrived here in 1516. During that time they have borne a bewildering variety of other titles. All have held the Barony but at different times have also been Earls of Lindsey, Dukes of Ancaster and, later, Earls of Ancaster. The Willoughby genealogy is further complicated by the fact that the Barony is one of the very few peerages in Britain that can descend

🏛 historic building 🏛 museum 🏚 historic site ⌘ scenic attraction 🌿 flora and fauna

through the female line. A marriage in 1533 between the 49-year-old Duke of Suffolk and the 14-year-old Margaret Willoughby added yet another title, Duchess of Suffolk, to the Barony's pedigree.

Grantham

🏠 The Conduit	🏠 St Wulfram's House
🏠 Grantham House	🏠 Methodist Church
🏛 Museum	🎨 Arts Centre

A lively market town set beside the River Witham. Turn a blind eye to the charmless environs that surround the town from whichever direction you approach. Make your way to its centre which boasts a pleasing core of old buildings. These cluster around the town's famous church, **St Wulfram's,** whose soaring spire, 282 feet high, has been described as "the finest steeple in England". When completed in 1300 it was the loftiest in England and is still the sixth highest. St Wulfram's interior is not quite so inspirational, dominated as it is by uncharacteristically drab Victorian stained glass, but the rare 16th century chained library of 150 volumes is occasionally open to the public and well worth seeing.

Just across from the church, **Grantham House** in Castlegate is a charming National Trust property, parts of which date back to around 1380. Additions were made in the 16th and 18th centuries. The house stands in 25 acres of garden and grounds sloping down to the

River Witham and, although the house itself open by appointment only, there is a right of way through the meadows on the opposite bank of the river. Also in Castlegate, look out for the only living pub sign in the country. In a lime tree outside the Beehive Inn is a genuine bee hive whose bees produce some 30lbs of honey each year. This unique advertisement for the pub has been in place since at least 1830.

After St Wulfram's Church, Grantham's most venerable building is that of the Angel and Royal Hotel in High Street. The attractive 15th century façade still bears the weather-beaten sculptured heads of Edward III and Queen Philippa over its central archway. King John held his court here and it was in one of the inn's rooms that Richard III signed the death warrant of the 2nd Duke of Buckingham in 1483.

A hundred yards or so from the inn stands an unusual Grantham landmark. The **Conduit** is a miniature tower built by the Corporation in 1597 as the receiving point for the fresh water supply that flowed from springs in the

The Conduit, Grantham

nearby village of Barrowby. At the southern end of the High Street stands a monument to Sir Isaac Newton who was born nearby and educated at the town's King's School. It's an impressive memorial, cast in bronze from a Russian cannon captured during the Crimean War. Behind the statue is the ornate Victorian Guildhall (1869), which now houses the Guildhall Arts Centre. Originally, the building incorporated the town's prison cells but these now serve as a box office for the Arts Centre.

Next to the Conduit, the **Grantham Museum** provides a fascinating in-depth look at local history - social, agricultural, industrial, and has special exhibits devoted to Sir Isaac Newton, and to Lady Thatcher, the town's most famous daughter. When elevated to the peerage she adopted the title Baroness Thatcher of Kesteven - the local authority area in which Grantham is located. She still retains close links with the town and once declared, "From this town I learned so much and am proud to be one of its citizens".

There is another connection with the former Prime Minister in **Finkin Street Methodist Church**, just off the High Street. Inside this imposing building with its pillared entrance and spacious balcony is a lectern dedicated to Alderman Alfred Roberts, a Methodist preacher, grocer, and father of Margaret Thatcher who worshipped here as a child.

The Thatcher family lived over Alderman Roberts' grocery shop in Broad Street. For a while this became The Premier Restaurant but is currently a chiropractic centre. Margaret Thatcher was Britain's first woman Prime Minister, but Grantham can also boast another distinguished lady who was the first in her profession. Just after World War I,

Edith Smith was sworn in as the country's first woman police officer. Edith was reputed to be a no-nonsense lady who made the lives of the town's malefactors a misery.

Before leaving the town, do try to track down the local delicacy, Grantham Gingerbread. It was created in 1740 by a local baker who mistakenly added the wrong ingredient to his gingerbread mix. The unusual result was a white crumbly biscuit, completely unlike the regular dark brown gingerbread. Traditionally, the sweetmeat was baked in walnut-size balls and, until the 1990s, was always available at Catlin's Bakery and Restaurant whose baker possessed the secret recipe. Sadly, Catlin's Bakery is now closed and Grantham Gingerbread is no longer easy to find.

Around Grantham

BELTON
3 miles N of Grantham on the A607/A153

🏚 Belton House

"An English country-house at its proudest and most serene", **Belton House** stands in 1,000 acres of parkland surrounded by a boundary wall five miles long. Built in 1685 of honey-coloured Ancaster stone and in the then fashionable Anglo-Dutch style, Belton was the home of the Brownlow family for just under 300 years before being given to the National Trust in 1983. The Trust also acquired the important collections of pictures, porcelain, books and furniture accumulated by 12 generations of Brownlows. With its Dutch and Italian gardens, orangery, deer park, woodland adventure playground and indoor activity room, Belton provides a satisfying day out for the whole family.

BELTON GARDEN CENTRE

Lincoln Road, Belton, Grantham,
Lincolnshire NG32 2LN
Tel: 01476 563700 Fax: 01476 591946
e-mail: info@beltongardencentre.co.uk
website: www.beltongardencentre.co.uk

Once the kitchen garden to the neighbouring National Trust property, **Belton Garden Centre** is a thriving family-run business.

High Victorian walls surround the centre, providing shelter for the wide range of attractively presented plants that flourish here. The Centre also sells a wide range of pots, stoneware, water features, water garden products, quality garden furniture and other garden accessories.

The shop area is filled with gift ideas, including beautiful silk flowers and glass by Sia, natural candy and traditional toys. The Interiors Store is stocked with bespoke furniture, home accessories, lighting and gifts for all occasions, and in the Belton Design Studio Alison Hutchinson, a gold medal winning garden designer, offers bespoke garden designs, construction and planting for domestic or commercial properties.

Visitors can take a break from browsing and buying with a light snack or hearty meal in the coffee shop, and a children's play area will keep the little ones happy – and in sight.

Anyone interested in follies should make a short detour from Belton to the village of Londonthorpe. The original purpose of the "heavily rusticated stone arch with a horse on the top" has long since been forgotten but it now serves as a bus shelter.

OSBOURNBY
8 miles E of Grantham on the A15

Set in rolling hill country, 'Ozemby' is an attractive village with a pleasing mix of architectural styles from the 16th to the 19th centuries. The large church, unusually for Lincolnshire, has a tower rather than a spire and is also notable for its fine collection of medieval bench ends. Hanging on the wall of the nave are paintings of Moses and Aaron of which Pevsner enquires:

"Are they the worst paintings in the county? Anyway, one cannot help liking them".

ROPSLEY
6 miles E of Grantham off the A52

Described in Elizabethan times as *"a considerable village remarkably situated as it were in a bason with hills all around"*, Ropsley was famous then as the birthplace of Richard Fox (1448-1528), a trusted advisor of Henry VII. Fox was appointed to a succession of bishoprics, two of which, Exeter and Wells, he never visited. But he did spend the last 12 years of his life in Winchester as its bishop. Fox founded Corpus Christi College at Oxford, and also established the King's School in Grantham where Sir Isaac Newton was later educated.

📖 stories and anecdotes   🐦 famous people   🎨 art and craft   ✒ entertainment and sport   🚶 walks

THE HOUBLON INN

Oasby, nr Grantham, Lincolnshire NG32 3NB
Tel: 01529 455215
website: houblon-inn.co.uk

The Houblon Inn is a fine old stone building in a village off the A52 northeast of Grantham. When Hazel and Eddie came here in August 2001 they found the old inn somewhat neglected, and since then they have devoted care and energy into restoring the splendid original features and developing it into one of the finest hostelries in the region. Everards Tiger Brew is the house ale, with up to four changing guests, and there's a good selection of other beers and lagers. Hazel and Eddie have always had a keen interest in real food, and the blackboard menus at the Houblon makes excellent use of the best seasonal ingredients and herbs from the garden.

The dishes are never too complicated but always full of interest, and this exceptional food is accompanied by a well-chosen wine list that includes many by the glass. Overnight accommodation is available in four delightful en suite bedrooms in a converted barn across the courtyard. A gravel garden at the rear features comfortable wooden chairs and tables, old-fashioned garden benches and herb-fringed flower beds. The inn takes its name from the local dignitary Sir John Houblon, the first governor of the Bank of England (see him on the back of the current £50 note).

The house in which Fox was born still stands on Ropsley High Street.

FOLKINGHAM

8 miles E of Grantham on the A15

Once a market town and an important coaching stop, Folkingham was also the venue until 1828 of the Kesteven Quarter Sessions, which were held in the former Greyhound Inn facing the Market Square. Convicted prisoners were confined in the nearby House of Correction of which only the forbidding gatehouse-cum-governor's house survives. This surprisingly roomy edifice is now available to rent as a holiday 'cottage' through the Landmark Trust. Also recalling the penal provisions of the past are Folkingham's village stocks which are preserved in St Andrew's Church.

WOOLSTHORPE BY COLSTERWORTH

7 miles S of Grantham off the A1 at Colsterworth

🏠 Woolsthorpe Manor

Voted 'Man of the Last Millennium', Isaac Newton was born in 1642 in the modest Jacobean farmhouse, **Woolsthorpe Manor,** which has scarcely changed since he lived here. It was at Woolsthorpe that the Father of Modern Science later made some of his greatest inventions and discoveries. The Manor is now owned by the National Trust which has furnished the rooms to reflect life of the period and has converted a 17th century barn into a Science Discovery Centre, which helps explain the achievements of one of the country's most famous men. Almost as

🏠 historic building   🏛 museum   🏯 historic site   ✧ scenic attraction   🌱 flora and fauna famous is the legendary apple tree which helped clear Newton's thinking about the laws of gravity: the apple tree in the garden here is said to have been grafted from the original tree beneath which Newton was sitting when the apple fell on to his head. Newton's interests were wide and varied: from 1696 he was involved in reforming the nation's corrupt coinage system and from 1699 until his death in 1727 he held the post of Master of the Mint.

A rather strange memento of the young Newton is preserved in the church at nearby Colsterworth. It's a sundial crafted by Newton when he was nine years old. It seems odd to place a sundial *inside* a church and even odder to install it upside down.

BELVOIR
8 miles SW of Grantham off A607

🏛 Castle

In Victorian times, the Dukes of Rutland could stand on the battlements of **Belvoir Castle** comfortable in the knowledge that, in whichever direction they looked along the pastoral Vale of Belvoir, everything in sight formed part of their estate, some 30,000 acres in all, (plus large holdings in other parts of the country). William the Conqueror granted this spectacular site to his standard-bearer at the Battle of Hastings, Robert de Todeni and, more than 900 years later, his descendants, now the Dukes of Rutland, still live here. Perched on the hilltop, the present castle looks convincingly medieval with its great tower, turrets and castellations, but it was in fact built in the early 1800s and is the fourth to occupy the site. The opulent interior contains some excellent paintings, including works by Gainsborough, Reynolds and Poussin, and the familiar portrait of Henry

VIII by Holbein. In the 130ft long Regent's Gallery are some remarkable Gobelin tapestries, while other magnificent rooms display elegant Regency furniture, a dazzling ceiling copied from the Church of Santa Maria Maggiore in Rome, a dramatic array of 18th century weaponry and a monumental silver collection which includes a wine cooler weighing more than 112lbs. The castle also houses the Museum of the Queen's Royal Lancers. The grounds provide a marvellous setting for special events, among which the medieval jousting tournaments are undoubtedly the most colourful. (Incidentally, Belvoir Castle lies just across the county boundary, in Leicestershire, but has always been regarded as a Lincolnshire attraction.)

Sleaford

🏛 Cogglesford Mill 🏛 Church ✏ The Hub

The history of this busy market town stretches back to the Iron Age. In Roman times there was a massive mint here (730 coins were discovered in one dig), and when a railway was being constructed in Victorian times, a vast Anglo-Roman cemetery was uncovered. Later, the Normans built a sizeable castle of which only a small portion of a wall remains, but much of their other major contribution to the town, the **Church of St Denys**, still survives. Its tower, 144 feet high and dating from around 1200, stands separate from the main body of the church, and is among the oldest stone-built towers in England. The interior is notable for the superb 14th century tracery in the north window, two magnificent monuments to the local Carre family, some stained glass by William Morris, and a striking rood loft restored by Ninian Comper in 1918.

🎦 stories and anecdotes 🦜 famous people ✏ art and craft 🎭 entertainment and sport 🚶 walks

Cranwell Aviation Heritage Centre

Heath Farm, North Rauceby, Sleaford, Lincolnshire
Tel: 01529 488490
e-mail: tic@n-kesteven.gov.uk
website: www.heartoflincs.com

The Royal Air Force College at Cranwell in Lincolnshire is probably the most famous landmark in R.A.F history. The Cranwell Aviation Heritage Centre portrays the history of this renowned Royal Air Force officer training establishment, from its early days as a Royal Naval Air Service balloon base to present day.

The attraction features photographs, exhibits and archive film. It also has a computerised flight simulator, outside courtyard area with Jet Provost aircraft, Vampire nose pod, an exhibition hall with interpretation panels, artefacts, and exhibits and video theatre, and an information and retail area which sells souvenirs and memorabilia.

For opening times, more information on the centre, or details of special events contact Sleaford Tourist Information Centre on 01529 414294

Collectors of old inn signs will be interested in the Bull and Dog pub in Southgate. Set in the wall above its ground floor is a stone bearing the date 1689 and depicting a bull being baited by dogs. The scene is thought to be unique in the country and the stone itself the oldest surviving pub sign in England. **The Hub** centre for contemporary craft is based in a restored seed warehouse by the Banks of the River Slea. Regularly changing exhibitions are held in the two galleries, as well as special events and craft courses, and the retail area, the rooftop viewing area and the riverside café complete the visitor experience. On the eastern edge of the town, **Cogglesford Mill** has been restored to working order and is open to the public. Probably built around 1750, the Mill contains an exhibition detailing its history.

Other features of interest in Sleaford include the 15th century Vicarage near the church, the landmark Handley Monument, a memorial erected to the town's MP in 1846

and reminiscent of an Eleanor Cross, and the Old Playhouse, purpose-built as a theatre in 1824 and now home to the local theatre company.

Around Sleaford

NAVENBY
10 miles NW of Sleaford on the A607

🏠 Mrs Smith's Cottage

One of the county's most unexpected attractions is **Mrs Smith's Cottage**, just off the High Street of this village where Hilda Mary Craven was born on October 28th, 1892. After spending her childhood in Navenby, Hilda moved out of the county but returned in the 1920s to live in a tiny cottage in East Road. At the age of 64 she married, becoming Mrs Smith, but her husband Joseph died less than four years later. Hilda stayed on in the cottage, resisting any change she thought unnecessary, until she was 103.

🏛 historic building   🏠 museum   🏛 historic site   🏞 scenic attraction   🌱 flora and fauna

During her 80 years of living here, she created a spellbinding time warp. The original ladder access to the first floor is still in place; Hilda's rocking chair and shawl still remain in her favourite place by the range; the original outside privy and washhouse can still be viewed. Opening times are restricted: for more details call 01529 414294.

NORTH RAUCEBY
5 miles W of Sleaford off the A17

🏛 Cranwell Aviation Heritage Centre

Generations of RAF personnel have trained at the Royal Air Force College, Cranwell. When it opened on February 5th, 1920, it was the first Military Air Academy in the world and it later chalked up another first when a jet plane designed by Frank Whittle, a Cranwell

graduate, took off from the runway here in 1941. In the nearby village of North Rauceby the **Cranwell Aviation Heritage Centre** (see panel opposite) tells the Cranwell story and that of the other numerous RAF bases in the region, with the help of photographs, exhibits and film. The museum is open Wednesday, Thursday and Sunday from 10.30am to 4.30pm during the season.

HECKINGTON
5 miles E of Sleaford off the A17

🏭 Windmill   🏭 Church

There's plenty of variety and interest here, in particular the tall Church of St Andrew, the Victorian almshouses and the magnificent eight-sailed **Heckington Windmill** by the railway station. When built in 1830 the mill's

G SIMPSON BUTCHERS LTD

11 Cameron Street, Heckington, nr Sleaford, Lincolnshire NG34 9RW
Tel: 01529 460403

The annual village show (one of the largest in the country), the Church of St Andrew and the famous windmill all attract visitors to Heckington but, for anyone who demands the very best in locally reared meat, **G Simpson Butchers Ltd** should be at the top of the list.

As well as the recently refurbished shop, Gary Simpson with his experienced members of staff supply pubs and restaurants as well as the local community.

Their beef, pork, lamb and poultry is consistently of the highest quality, as are the bacon and sausages, the pies and pasties and the locally-made pickles and chutneys.

Always in demand are specialities such as homemade Lincolnshire sausages, stuffed chine, haslets, stir frys and much more.

🎞 stories and anecdotes   🐦 famous people   🎨 art and craft   🎭 entertainment and sport   🚶 walks

sails numbered a modest five, but after storms damaged the mill in 1890, eight sails were removed from another mill nearby and installed here. The only surviving eight-sailed mill in Britain rises to five floors and was in use up until 1942. It is now owned by Lincolnshire County Council and can be visited on weekend afternoons, Thursday and Friday afternoons in the season, and at other times by appointment.

Heckington's other major attraction is its early-14th century **Church of St Andrew**, which is famous for the wealth of stone carvings on its tower. Inside, there's an outstanding Easter Sepulchre on which medieval master masons depicted the events of Christ's Crucifixion and Resurrection. The same masons were also responsible for the nearby sedilia (stone seats), beautifully carved with scenes from village life and figures of saints.

DORRINGTON
5 miles N of Sleaford on the B1188

🏛 North Ings Farm Museum

Run entirely by volunteers, **North Ings Farm Museum** is a fascinating place where vintage

tractors, stationary engines, a narrow-gauge railway and a small foundry are among the attractions. The museum is open Sundays during the summer and steam train rides are operational on the first Sunday of each month.

SCOPWICK
8 miles N of Sleaford on the B1188/B1191

Stone cottages line the main street of this small village and a stream splashes alongside the road. In 1838, the Revd George Oliver noted in his booklet, *Scopwickiana,* that the stream invariably overflowed in wet weather making progress along the street possible only by means of stepping stones. This inconvenience continued until fairly recent times. The Revd. Oliver also recorded that the village's only ale house was kept in good order by a formidable landlady who permitted her customers no more than a couple of pints before sending them home to their wives.

Just south of Scopwick is RAF Digby, which was the first Lincolnshire airfield to be attacked by the Luftwaffe in World War II. In the RAF Digby Operations Room Museum the wartime setting has been recreated,

THE STABLES STUDIO & THE OLD BREWHOUSE

94 High Street, Martin, Lincolnshire LN4 3QT
Tel: 01526 378528
e-mail: stablesstudio@homecall.co.uk
website: www.stablesstudio.co.uk

The Stables Studio is located in a quiet situation within the rural village of Martin, three miles west of Woodhall Spa and only 20 minutes from Lincoln's historic city centre. Also close to RAF heritage sites and many golf courses including the National Golf Centre. The new owners offer characterful en suite accommodation in the 18th century Old Brewhouse or in the renovated stable block, staying in self-contained units such as Pigswill or The Tack Room. Guests start the day with an excellent breakfast featuring prime local produce. This establishment enjoys a 4 star rating from the English Tourist Board.

🏛 historic building   🏛 museum   🏛 historic site   🔱 scenic attraction   🌾 flora and fauna complete with plotting table, maps and personnel, and the airfield's story is told with the help of many exhibits, photographs and documents. Guided tours take place on summer Sundays: further details on 01529 414294 (Sleaford TIC).

METHERINGHAM
9 miles N of Sleaford on B1188

🏠 Airfield Visitor Centre

Just outside this large, straggling village is the Metheringham **Airfield Visitor Centre**, one of many Lincolnshire airfields established by the RAF during World War II. A leaflet available from local TICs gives details of the North Kesteven Airfield Trail which includes Metheringham. Here, the Centre's exhibits, photographs and documents tell the story of the airfield and of 106 Squadron, Bomber Command, whose base it was.

Woodhall Spa

🏠 Cottage Museum   📖 Kinema in the Woods

Woodhall Spa is something of an anomaly – a chunk of the Home Counties transplanted to the heart of Lincolnshire. Surrounded by pine and birch woods, spacious Victorian and Edwardian villas are set back from tree-lined avenues and it's said that not a single house in the town is older than the 1830s. Woodhall became a spa town by accident when a shaft sunk in search of coal found not coal but mineral-rich water. In 1838 a pump room and baths were built, to be joined later by hydro hotels. Here, real or imagined invalids soaked themselves in 'hypertonic saline waters' heated to 40ºC (103º F). The arrival of the railway in 1855 accelerated Woodhall's popularity, but by the early 1900s the spa had fallen out of favour and the associated buildings disappeared one by one. But this beautifully maintained village has retained its decorous spa atmosphere, pleasantly relaxed and peaceful, and also boasting a championship golf course.

One interesting survivor of the good old days is a former tennis pavilion, now the **Kinema in the Woods**. When it was converted to a cinema during World War II, it inevitably became known as the Flicks in the Sticks. It's one of very few back projection cinemas in the country and the entertainment on offer includes performances on an original Compton Organ. The **Cottage Museum** on Iddsleigh Road, also the Tourist Information Centre, tells the story of the establishment of the town as a spa resort.

Woodhall Spa had close connections with 617 Squadron, the Dambusters, during World War II. The Petwood Hotel was used as the officers' mess. Memorabilia of those days are displayed in the hotel's Squadron Bar, and in Royal Square a memorial to those intrepid airmen takes the form of a 20ft long model of a breached dam.

There are several sites of interest outside the town. To the north stand the ruins of a 15th century hunting lodge called the Tower on the Moor, built for Ralph, Lord Cromwell of Tattershall Castle. And, standing all alone on Thimbleby Moor in the hamlet of Reeds Beck, is a 36ft high memorial to the Duke of Wellington, erected in 1844 and topped by a bust of the Iron Duke. The column celebrates the successful cultivation of Waterloo Woods, an oak forest planted just after the battle in 1815.

At Kirkstead, off the B1191, stands a towering piece of brickwork, the only visible remains of a 12th century Cistercian Abbey.

Close by is the fine 13th century Church of St Leonard, "a gem of Early Gothic…with an interior like a cathedral aisle", according to Simon Jenkins. Originally built as a "chapel outside the gates" for visitors to the abbey, St Leonard's was closed in 1877, but restored in 1914 by the Society for the Protection of Ancient Buildings. Miraculously, its beautifully carved chancel screen has survived intact. Dating back to the 13th century, it is believed to be the second oldest such screen in England.

Around Woodhall Spa

CONINGSBY
4 miles S of Woodhall Spa on the A153

🏛 RAF Coningsby

The centre of this large village, which started life as a Danish settlement, is dominated by the church tower of St Michael, notable for its enormous single-handed clock; at over 16ft in diameter, this 17th century clock claims to be the largest working example of its kind. South of the village is **RAF Coningsby**, which operates every type of current RAF fast jet. The mission of the base is 'to deliver the future, develop the present and commemorate the past of the RAF's combat air power'. It is also the home of the Battle of Britain Memorial Flight, created in 1957 in memory of the gallant airmen who flew in that crucial battle. The Flight operates a Lancaster, five Spitfires, two Hurricanes, two Chipmunks and a Dakota. These historic World War II aircraft are not just museum pieces - they are all still flying and can be seen at a variety of air shows during the summer months. Over 7,000 Lancasters were built

in the 1940s and Coningsby's veteran took to the air to celebrate the Memorial Flight's 50th anniversary in April 2007 after a full restoration in Coventry. It is one of only two surviving Lancasters – the other is in Canada. Visiting these wonderful machines on their 'home territory' provides an added dimension, and knowledgeable guides provide informative tours. The Centre is open throughout the year, Monday to Friday, and at weekends for special events. More details on 01526 344041.

TATTERSHALL
4 miles S of Woodhall Spa on the A153

🏛 Castle   🏛 Holy Trinity Church

Tattershall lies on the opposite bank of the

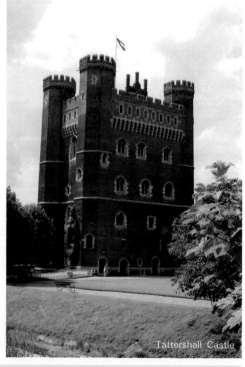
Tattershall Castle

River Bain from Coningsby and is known all over the world for the astonishing keep of **Tattershall Castle.** Its six storeys rise 110ft, a huge rectangular slab built in local red brick. In the 1400s it must have appeared even more formidable than it does now. Construction began around 1445 on the orders of the Lord Chancellor, Ralph Cromwell, and it was clearly designed more as a statement of his power and wealth rather than for defence. Military fashion had moved on from such huge Keeps and in any case the peaceful heart of 15th century Lincolnshire had no need for fortifications on this scale. Originally, the Keep was surrounded by a large complex of other buildings but these have almost entirely disappeared and the tower stands menacingly alone. Despite its magnificence, Tattershall had fallen into near ruin by the early 1900s. There was a very real possibility that it would be dismantled brick by

brick, transported to the United States and re-erected there. Happily, the tower was rescued by Lord Curzon who bequeathed it to the National Trust on his death in 1925.

In the shadow of the castle is Tattershall Country Park, set in 365 acres of woods, parks and lakes and offering all sorts of sporting facilities.

As well as this superb castle, Tattershall boasts one of the county's finest churches. **Holy Trinity** was also commissioned by Ralph Lord Cromwell. That was in 1440: the church was finally completed in 1480, long after Ralph's death. Constructed of Ancaster stone, this "glasshouse church" is dazzlingly light and airy inside, but because of its scale and the absence of all but a few adornments, more imposing than likeable. Among the items of note is a striking brass of Ralph himself, but sadly his image is headless.

LOCATOR MAP

ADVERTISERS AND PLACES OF INTEREST

 historic building   📖 museum   🏛 historic site   🌣 scenic attraction   🌿 flora and fauna

8 Leicestershire & Rutland

Leicestershire's most attractive features are shy and quiet and have to be sought out but they amply reward the explorer. The county is divided into two almost equal parts by the River Soar, which flows northward into the Trent. It separates the east and west by a broad valley, flowing like a silver ribbon through historic Leicester in the very heart of the county. This capital town was thriving in Roman days and is one of the oldest towns in England. It has managed to retain outstanding monuments of almost every age of English history. Red Leicester cheese was made in the southern part of the county in the 1700s, but now the only genuine product is made at Melton Mowbray, which also makes Stilton and, of course, the superlative pork pies. And every schoolchild knows the name of Bosworth Field, one of the momentous battles which changed the course of English history.

Just 20 miles across and covering a mere 150 square miles, Rutland delights in its status as England's smallest county. Its 37,800 inhabitants were incensed when the Local Government changes of 1974 stripped the county of its identity and merged it with neighbouring Leicestershire. It took more than 20 years of ceaseless campaigning before bureaucracy relented and Rutland was re-instated as a county in its own right once again. Rutland has villages of thatch and ironstone, clustered around their churches, and the countryside is rich in pasture where once deer were hunted. Its central feature is Rutland Water, its 3,100 acres making it one of the largest man-made lakes in northern Europe. Started in 1971 to supply water to the East Midlands towns, it was created by damming the valley near Empingham.

Rutland Water

Leicester

🏛 Church of St Mary de Castro   🏛 Guildhall

🏛 Newarke Houses Museum   ⚔ Castle Gardens

🏛 Jewry Wall & Museum   🏛 National Space Centre

🏛 New Walk Museum & Art Gallery

🏛 Wygston's House   🏛 Guru Nanak Gurdwara

Designated Britain's first Environment City in recognition of its commitment to green issues and the environment, Leicester has numerous parks and open spaces, is one of the country's top 10 shopping destinations, has a buzzing nightlife and also boasts a rich architectural heritage with no fewer than 350 listed buildings.

When the Romans built a town here in the 1st century AD they called it Ratae Corielauvorum, and when they left 300 years later it survived in some form. It was the seat of a Christian bishop in the 7th century, and in the 9th century was conquered and settled by the Vikings along with Lincoln, Nottingham, Derby and Stamford. The city flourished in the Middle Ages when the cloth and wool trades became important, and the coming of the canals and the railways brought further prosperity. The development of road transport changed the face of the city, and modern Leicester is a thriving industrial and commercial city with superb shopping and recreational facilities and a mixture of cultures and communities as rich and diverse as any in the land.

At the heart of Leicester's heritage is Castle Park, the old town, an area of gardens, churches, museums and other fine buildings. Here are concentrated many of the city's main visitor attractions. **Castle Gardens** was just an area of marshland by the River Soar until it was drained and opened as gardens to the public in 1926. In the gardens is a statue of Richard III who, on a sunny August day in 1485, rode out from the Blue Boar Inn to his death at the Battle of Bosworth Field. After the battle, his body was hung from the parapet of Bow Bridge before being buried at Greyfriars Church. After the Dissolution, his body was disinterred and thrown into the river, later to be recovered and buried near the bridge. Cardinal Wolsey died in Leicester while on his way to London to face a treason charge. He

Leicester Guildhall

died after falling from his mule and was buried in the Lady Chapel of Leicester Abbey. The Abbey is now in ruins, and a simple memorial can be found in Abbey Park.

Castle Motte is a man-made mound built around 1070 by Leicester's first Norman lord; like the gardens, it is open to the public during daylight hours; interpretation boards explain its history. Adjacent to the gardens is the **Church of St Mary de Castro**, founded in 1107 and still in use. The chancel, stained glass, carvings and tombstones are all well worth taking time to examine. Geoffrey Chaucer was married here and Henry VI was knighted in the church in 1426. Next to the church is the Great Hall of Leicester Castle. The Hall was built in the 12th century by Robert le Bossu and used by successive Earls of Leicester as their administrative headquarters; it is open to the public on special event days. Also in the same space is **Newarke Houses Museum**, a museum of social and domestic history contained in two 16th century houses. Displays include clocks, toys, furniture, a 1940s village grocer's shop and a reconstructed Victorian street scene. Leicester's diverse cultural heritage is represented by the Jain Centre, the only one of its kind in the Western world, housed in a converted 19th century Congregational chapel surmounted by a wondrously ornate facade; and the **Guru Nanak Gurdwara**, a Sikh temple and museum. Across the road from the Jain Centre is the **Jewry Wall and Museum.** The Wall is not only the oldest surviving Roman civil building in Britain but its wall is also the highest in the country and was part of the public baths, whose foundations are still visible. The museum chronicles the history and archaeology of the city and the county from Roman times to 1485. The adjacent St

Nicholas Church dates back to Anglo-Saxon times and, despite later alterations, Saxon work and re-used Roman bricks can be seen in the walls and tower. The Church of St Martin, which was in existence before 1086, was extended in the 14th and 15th centuries, restored in the 19th century and hallowed as the Cathedral of Leicester in 1927. Stained glass and carvings are impressive, and the memorial to Richard III is a highlight.

One of the very finest buildings in Leicester is the **Guildhall**, built around 1390 for the Guild of Corpus Christi and used as the Town Hall from the late 15th century to 1876. Concerts and theatrical performances are held regularly in the Great Hall. Across the road from the Cathedral is **Wygston's House**, a part timber-framed building, one of the oldest in the city, which now houses displays of fashion, textiles and crafts from around the world, along with a reconstruction of a 1920s draper's shop. This museum section also has an activity area where children are encouraged to dress up in replica historical costumes.

Leicester City Museums also include The **New Walk Museum and Art Gallery**, with displays including natural history, geology, ancient Egyptian mummies, a dinosaur skeleton more than 175 million years old, and a fine German Expressionist collection; Belgrave Hall and Gardens, a Queen Anne house whose rooms reflect Edwardian elegance and Victorian cosiness; the Abbey Pumping Station, an 1891 station with massive beam engines and several exhibitions; and the Gas Museum on Aylestone Road.

The city's most recent major attraction is the **National Space Centre,** opened in 2001 as part of the new millennium celebrations and the UK's largest attraction dedicated to space. This multi-million pound project offers real rockets and satellites, interactive challenges and the most advanced space theatre in the world, transporting the audience on an awe-inspiring journey through the universe and beyond.

In Western Park, EcoHouse is an environment-friendly show home featuring energy efficiency, sustainable living and an organic garden.

Around Leicester

KIRBY MUXLOE
2 miles W of Leicester off the B5380

🏛 Castle

Kirby Muxloe Castle is a picturesque ruined fortified manor house dating from 1480. Built

of brick rather than the more usual stone, it was started by William, Lord Hastings, but not completed by him – he was executed by Richard III. Only the great gatehouse and one of the four angle towers remain intact.

DESFORD
4 miles W of Leicester off the A47

🐦 Tropical Birdland

Tropical Birdland, which opened its doors to the public in 1987, is a breeding centre for rare and endangered species: birds of the rainforest, 85 species, walk-through aviaries, chick room, woodland walk, koi ponds, picnic gardens, bird shop, free parking – all this adds up to one of the county's most popular attractions. Open Easter to end October.

REAL FLAVOURS DELICATESSEN

Unit 2, Enterprise House, Main Street, Kirby Muxloe, Leicestershire LE9 2AF
Tel: 0116 239 4802
e-mail: alan_hill@ntlworld.com
website: www.realflavoursdeli.com

May 2007 saw the re-opening of **Real Flavours Delicatessen** after a top-to-toe refurbishment programme carried out by owner Alan Hill.

The spotless premises display an impressive array of top-quality deli produce, much of it organic. Customers are regaled with superb charcuterie, home-cooked gammon, quiches, pies and pâtés, salad items, olives, olive and other oils and vinegars.

Bread is delivered fresh daily from a local bakery, and among the wide variety of cheeses is the local speciality Sparkenhoe Red Leicester. Food for specialised diets can be supplied with a little notice. Kirby Muxloe lies a short distance west of Leicester.

TOOLEY PARK FARM SHOP

Peckleton Common Road, Peckleton, Leicestershire LE9 7RF
Tel: 01455 822876 Fax: 01455 824677
e-mail: peteandsuedraycott@btinternet.com

Dorothy Draycott, her son Peter and daughter-in-law Sue represent the third generation of farmers at **Tooley Park Farm**, which enjoys a lovely rural setting west of Leicester, easily reached from the A47 or A447. The shop is filled with top-quality produce, including prime beef reared on the farm on a diet of naturally grown food and hung for a minimum of two weeks to allow the full flavours to develop. Also on display are locally reared pork, lamb and poultry. A new shop extension is due to open later in the year, offering a variety of home-made pies and pastries, along with frozen vegetables and fruit.

The area around the farm has plenty to attract the visitor, including the Tropical Birdland at Desford, Bosworth Battlefield and Mallory Park motor racing circuit, but for those who appreciate fine food naturally produced Tooley Park Farm Shop should definitely be top of the list of places to visit. Opening hours are 10 to 5.30 Monday and Thursday, 10 to 6.30 Friday, 10 to 4 Saturday and 10 to 2 Sunday.

NEWTOWN LINFORD
5 miles NW of Leicester off the A50

🏠 Bradgate House 🚶 Bradgate Country Park

A picturesque village of thatched dwellings and timbered style buildings, Newtown Linford lies alongside the River Lin, which flows through the village and into **Bradgate Country Park**. This is the largest and most popular park in the county with well over a million visitors every year exploring its 850 acres. The park was created from Charnwood Forest 700 years ago as a hunting and deer park, and the scene is probably little changed since, a mixture of heath, bracken, grassy

Bradgate Country Park

slopes, rocky outcrops and woodland – and the deer are still there. Man-made features of the park include a well-known folly called Old John Tower. Built in 1784 by the 5th Earl of Stamford in memory of a former member of his household, it stands nearly 700 feet above sea level and affords fine views.

Also here are the ruins of **Bradgate House**, built of brick at the beginning of the 16th century. This was the home of the Grey family and it was here that Lady Jane Grey was born in 1537. Her father was the scheming and ambitious Duke of Suffolk who forced her, at the age of 16, to marry the son of the Duke of Northumberland, Regent to Edward VI. With his own eye on power, Northumberland prevailed on the dying

Edward to name Jane as heir to the throne. On hearing the news, Jane fell fainting to the ground. Public opinion recognised Mary Tudor as the rightful heir and within days both Jane's father and father-in-law had deserted her. Jane spent nine days as reluctant queen and a further seven months as a prisoner in the Tower of London – before a swift death on the executioner's block on 12th February 1554. Today the lovely rose-red ruins of Bradgate House where Jane passed much of her brief life look too benign and inviting ever to have been involved in such a murderous tale of 16th century politics. The story is that the foresters at Bradgate cut off the heads of the oaks in the park as a mark of respect to Lady Jane; pollard oaks can still be seen here.

PARK VIEW RIDING SCHOOL

Anstey Lane, Thurcaston,
Leicestershire LE7 7JB
Tel: 0116 236 4858   Fax: 0116 236 8050
e-mail: bev@parkviewridingschool.co.uk
website: www.parkviewridingschool.co.uk

The owners of **Park View Riding School** have built up an enviable reputation over 25 years for making sure that every visit is an occasion to remember. The setting is a great asset, and management and tuition are in the safe, fully qualified hands of Bev Rossi, Lance McDonald and their friendly team. The 80 acres of beautiful countryside include private access to parkland and bridleways for safe and enjoyable riding, exploring the forests of Charnwood, Bradgate Park and Swithland Woods, perhaps stopping for a spot of refreshment on the way.

An indoor school and large outdoor floodlit area ensure continuous riding, and on-site amenities include stables and grazing for up to 60 horses and ponies, a livery and grazing service and a coffee shop. The school has 15 horses and 25 ponies to choose from for the daily lessons and hacks and for the popular week-long riding holidays for 9 to 16-year-olds of all abilities in carefully chosen groups.

ANSTEY
3 miles NW of Leicester off the A46

Packhorse Bridge

The 16th century **Packhorse Bridge** that
crosses Rothley Brook at Anstey is a
particularly fine specimen: 5ft wide to give
space for the horse's bulging panniers, 54ft
long and supported by five low arches. In the
late 18th century when the bridge was the
only way to get to Leicester, some four miles
distant, it would have been crossed many
times by Ned Ludd, who was born in Anstey
in 1811. He was apprenticed to a local weaver
and one night broke two stocking frames.
Groups of workers took this as a sign to rebel
against the unemployment and hardship the
new equipment was causing, and set about
destroying other machines in the new textile
milles. They gained the name of Luddites, a
term now used to describe anyone opposed to
modern technology. The government's
response to the damage was to swoop on six
of the leaders and hang them all at
Nottingham.

REARSBY
5 miles NE of Leicester on the A607

According to meticulous accounts that have
survived, the lovely old bridge in Rearsby was
built by six men in just nine days during the
summer of 1714. The village constable's
accounts showed the total cost as £11 2s 2d
(£11.11p) – with the largest expense £2 12s
6d being for 21 quarters of lime, the smallest
a payment of 5d (2p) "to George Skillington
for Nailes". The bridge was paid for by a levy
of ratepayers of 8d in the pound but,
according to constable Richard Harrison, he
ended up '£1 11s 0 ½ d out of Pockett'. A
small consolation must have the inscription on
the sixth arch of his initials, RH, alongside the
date 1714.

OADBY
3 miles SE of Leicester off the A6/A47

Stoughton Farm Park   **Botanical Gardens**

James Hawker   **Brocks Hill Country Park**

Effectively a suburb of Leicester, Oadby
nevertheless has three venues of interest to
those who care for the environment. There's a
treat for horticulturalists in the form of the
University of Leicester's **Botanical Gardens**
which include an arboretum, herbaceous
borders, water garden and glass houses that
shelter tropical and temperate plants, alpines
and succulents.

In Gartree Road is the entrance to
Farmworld at **Stoughton Farm Park**,

stories and anecdotes   famous people   art and craft   entertainment and sport   walks

Britain's biggest and brightest working farm park. A great family day out is provided by shire horses, cart rides, rare farm animals, lakeside and woodland walks, a working dairy farm, toy tractor park, chicken hatchery, milking parlour, children's farmyard and playgrounds. There's also a café and pub.

In Washbrook Lane, **Brocks Hill Country Park & Environment Centre** is a remarkable building, completely self-sufficient and needing no electricity, gas or water supplies – not even a sewer. It was built to demonstrate wind and solar power, photovoltaics, rainwater re-cycling and sewage composting. The centre stands in 67 acres of newly planted Country Park with woodland, meadowland, community orchard and arboretum. There's an Exhibition Area, café and classroom facilities.

In Oadby graveyard is the tombstone of **James Hawker**, one of the most engaging rogues of all time. In his entertaining autobiography, *James Hawker's Journal*, he reveals that he found his vocation when he was 18 years old and poached his first bird. That was in 1844 and from then until his death in 1921 he honoured his declaration that "I will poach 'till I die". He was only caught once and on that charge, he indignantly claims, he was innocent – "They knew me and seized the occasion to punish my earlier misdemeanours". In later life James combined a respectable daytime career as a parish councillor and member of the school board with a nocturnal pastime of depleting his aristocratic neighbour's lands of their edible game. For 60 years his grave remained unmarked until EMMA Theatre Company, which had performed a play about his life, erected a simple monument bearing as epitaph his defiant, and true, claim:

"I will poach 'till I die".

WISTOW
6 miles SE of Leicester off the A6

Only two churches in the country are dedicated to St Wistan, a Christian prince of Mercia who was murdered by his wicked uncle Brifardus near this tiny hamlet in 849AD. Wistow's Church of St Wistan was largely remodelled in 1746 so its interior has mainly Georgian fittings including box pews and ironwork communion rails. There are striking memorials to members of the Halford family of nearby Wistow Hall (private) where they lived continuously from 1603 to 1896. Their most distinguished visitor, albeit in some distress, was Charles I who stopped here briefly to change horses on his flight from the Battle of Naseby. In their haste, the king and his party left their battle horses with their saddles and other gear still in place. Charles even left his sword behind; many years later it was given to George IV by Sir Henry Halford, physician to George III, George IV and William IV. The saddles and other equipment are now held by the New Walk Museum in Leicester. A popular family attraction is the Wistow Maze, comprising eight acres of maize and sunflowers, with a quiz trail amid the three miles of paths designed by the famous maze expert Adrian Fisher. It stands opposite Wistow Rural Centre.

KIBWORTH HARCOURT
8 miles SE of Leicester on the A6

The earliest type of windmill used in the county was the post mill, where the whole wooden body complete with the machinery was positioned on a post and could be turned so that the sails faced the wind. The only surviving one – dating from the early 18th century – is here.

🏛 historic building   🏛 museum   🏛 historic site   💧 scenic attraction   🌱 flora and fauna

QUILTERS PARADISE

Unit 1, Churchill Way, Fleckney,
Leicestershire LE8 8UD
Tel: 0116 240 3191
e-mail: micksharpe@quiltersparadise.co.uk
website: www.quiltersparadise.co.uk

For anyone interested in quilts and quilting, **Quilters Paradise** fully lives up to its name. It has firmly established itself as the leading quilting and patchwork shop in the county, with all the fabrics and other materials, along with all the advice that the quilter should ever need. The business, which is owned and run by Walter and June Sharpe, is located in Fleckney village, 8 miles south of Leicester and close to Market Harborough, Wistow Park and Foxton Locks.

Always in stock is an impressive selection of quilts and quilting kits, cushions and cushion covers, cottons, silks, patchwork, and all kinds of fabrics and materials including the Makower range. Friendly staff are on hand with advice, and among the services offered by Quilters Paradise are custom design, quilting classes and printing photographs on cotton, linen or silk. Customers are free to browse, to sit and sew or just relax with a cup of tea or coffee in this most welcoming of places, which is open between 11 and 4 Wednesday to Saturday.

Market Harborough

🏛 Church of St Dionysius   🏛 Old Grammar School

🏛 Museum

Halfway between Leicester and Northampton at a crossing point of the River Welland, Market Harborough was created as a planned market town in the mid-12th century. The booths that filled its market place were gradually replaced by permanent buildings, and many of these, along with the courts that led off the High Street, still stand. In 1645 Charles I made Market Harborough his headquarters and held a council of war here before the Battle of Naseby. The development of turnpike roads - the motorways of their day – led to prosperity and the establishment of coaching inns in the town, many of them still in business. The canals and the railways transformed communications and manufacturing industry became established, the most notable company being RW & H Symington, creators of the Liberty Bodice.

The town trail takes in the major buildings, including the 14th century parish **Church of St Dionysius** with its superb limestone broach. The church has no graveyard because it was, until the early 1900s, a daughter church of St Mary in Arden with the status of a chapel. The **Old Grammar School** is a timber-framed building with an open ground floor; built in 1614 to serve the weekly butter market and "to keepe the market people drye in time of fowle weather", it later became a school, a role which it sustained until 1892. The factory of the Symington Company,

📖 stories and anecdotes   🕊 famous people   🎨 art and craft   🎵 entertainment and sport   🚶 walks

LAVENDER BLUE

15 Church Street, Market Harborough,
Leicestershire LE16 7AA
Tel: 01858 419090
e-mail: frenchgray@btconnect.com website: www.french-grey.co.uk

Kate and Dean Lascelles work closely with *Country Living* suppliers to stock   **Lavender Blue** and regularly exhibit at *Country Living* fairs. Their lovely shop in Church Street is filled with good things for the home or gift ideas, from pottery and china, glassware and enamelware to candles, soaps and soft furnishings. Customers who can't visit the shop can browse the website which features a small, but ever changing selection of their stock. Lavender Blue also stocks an interesting range of metal folding furniture, 'for outside, inside and everywhere inbetween'.

Old Grammar School, Market Harborough

by road to Leicester he conceived the idea of an outing using the then newly opened railway. He organised the excursion from Leicester to Loughborough on July 7th 1841; the fare of a shilling (5p) included afternoon tea. Cook later moved to Leicester, where he is buried at Welford Road cemetery.

which grew from a cottage industry of staymakers to a considerable economic force in the town, now houses the Council offices, the library, the information centre and the **Harborough Museum,** which incorporates the Symington Collection of Corsetry.

Among the town's distinguished past residents are William Bragg, whose nephew and son shared the Nobel Prize for Physics in 1915; Jack Gardner, who was British Empire and European Heavyweight boxing champion between 1950 and 1952; and Thomas Cook, who spent 10 years of his life here and was married in the town. While travelling one day

Around Market Harborough

HALLATON

6 miles NE of Market Harborough
off the B664

🐦 Hare-Pie contests 🏛 Village Museum

On the village green of this picturesque village in the rich grazing lands of the Welland Valley stands an unusual conical Buttercross. Every Easter Monday the cross is the setting for the crowning ceremony of the **Hare-Pie**

🏛 historic building 🏛 museum 🏛 historic site 🐦 scenic attraction 🌿 flora and fauna

Scrambling & Bottle-Kicking contest. The captain of the winning team is lifted to the top of the conical monument and there he broaches a bottle of ale. The contest is a free-for-all struggle between the neighbouring villages of Hallaton and Medbourne to get two out of three bottles of ale across the village boundary by whatever means possible. (The 'bottles' are actually small oak casks.) As many as 400 players may be milling around in the scrum and the battle has been known to continue for eight or nine hours). The day's events begin with a procession to Hare Pie Bank where pieces of a huge hare pie are thrown to the crowd. The antiquarian Charles Bilson believed the custom was a relic of a time when the hare was worshipped as a divine animal, but he has no explanation for the origins of the bottle-kicking contest. A display of this curious event is on show in the **Hallaton Village Museum**, along with relics from the motte and bailey castle and some unusual agricultural items. The museum is open Saturday, Sunday and Bank Holiday afternoons in summer.

FOXTON

2 miles NW of Market Harborough off the A6

🏛 Locks & Canal Museum

The most famous site on the county's canals is the **Flight of Ten Locks** on the Grand Union Canal, one of the great engineer Thomas Telford's most impressive constructions. Alongside the 10 locks are the remains of a remarkable inclined plane. This was built to by-pass the locks by moving boats in steel tanks to a different level. In the **Canal Museum** is a working model of the inclined plane. There are several other buildings and bridges of interest (including a swing-bridge) in this pretty village.

LUTTERWORTH

12 miles W of Market Harborough on the A4304

🏛 Stanford Hall B Museum

John Wycliffe was made Rector here under the tutelage of John of Gaunt as a reward for his diplomatic services. His instigation of an English translation of the Bible into English caused huge dissent. He died in 1384 and was buried in the church here, but when he was excommunicated in 1428 his body was exhumed and burned and his ashes scattered in the River Swift. Most of his Bibles were destroyed by the Church and the Latin versions continued to be used until William Tynedale produced an English Bible during the reign of Henry VIII. Close to the church, **Lutterworth Museum and Historical Society** contains a wealth of local history from Roman times to World War II.

About three miles southeast of Lutterworth and set in meadows beside the River Avon, **Stanford Hall** has been the home of the Cave family since 1430. The present house – pleasantly-proportioned, dignified and serene – was built by the celebrated architect William Smith of Warwick in the 1690s. A superb staircase was added around 1730, one of very few structural alterations to the house in its 300-year history. One other was the Ballroom which contains paintings that once belonged to Bonnie Prince Charlie's younger brother, Henry Stuart. They include the last major portrait of the middle-aged Bonnie Prince Charlie, two of James III – the Old Pretender – and a particularly fine portrait of Charles II by Sir Peter Lely. The Cave family became Barons and it was the 6th Baron, Adrian, whose fascination with motor-cars is perpetuated in Stanford's collection of cycle-cars and motor cycles. Adrian was also closely

WISHBONE

23 Church Street, Lutterworth,
Leicestershire LE17 4AE
Tel: 01455 554550
e-mail: ctiivas@btinternet.com

Opposite the Frank Whittle Memorial in the centre of Lutterworth, **Wishbone** is a gem of a boutique-style shop that's well worth seeking out for its array of speciality gifts for all occasions.

The staff are friendly and well-informed, and the whole place has a wonderfully welcoming feel that makes every visit a sheer delight. Browsers are certain to find just the right gift for a birthday, an anniversary, a wedding, a children's party, or something for a personal treat or a keepsake.

There are greetings cards by Second Nature and Woodmasters, silver and costume jewellery, candles and lamps, photo frames and much, much more, and with the stock changing all the time every visit will reveal something new and exciting to buy.

associated with the pioneer aviator, Percy Pilcher who, in 1895, had accomplished the first controlled flight in Britain. Pilcher made several experimental flights in Stanford Park but a flight in his glider, *The Hawk*, on September 30th 1899 ended in disaster when a bamboo strut in the tail fractured, the machine turned on its back and crashed. In the stable Block at Standord there's a fascinating full-size replica of *The Hawk* 'with its innumerable wires like the ribs of an umbrella'.

Lutterworth has another, more successful connection with aviation: it was the home of Sir Frank Whittle, inventor of the jet engine.

Hinckley

🏛 Museum

Few of the old timbered houses still stand in the town of Hinckley, whose Fair is

mentioned in Shakespeare's *Henry IV*. Now a thriving industrial and market town, Hinckley was already an established community in Saxon times. When the Domesday Book was compiled, Hinckley had 60 families – four times as many as in contemporary Birmingham. The turning point in its fortunes came in 1640 when William Illife set up the first stocking frame in Hinckley and so initiated the hosiery and knitwear industry that has made the town known internationally. A surviving example of 17th century cottages once used for framework knitting still stand in Lower Bond Street and are home to **Hinckley & District Museum**. The Museum illustrates the history of town and district, and includes among its hosiery exhibits a stocking frame of 1740.

It was in 1727 that gossip across the county told of a tombstone in Hinckley churchyard that drips blood. Richard Smith, a young man of 20, was killed in Market Place by an army recruitment sergeant he had offended by some trifling joke. The tombstone, though moved from its original location when St Mary's Church was enlarged in the 19th century, is reputed to 'sweat blood' at midnight on the anniversary of his murder.

Ghostly visitations have been reported at several places around the town, including The Union Inn in the Borough, The Barley Sheaf in Lower Bond Street and the Concordia Theatre in Stockwell Head. The

Stocking Factory, Hinkley

theatre, housed in the former Britannia Hosiery Works, hosts a wide variety of dramatic and musical entertainment.

THE ART STUDIO, TEN-TWO GALLERY & ART CAFÉ

102 Castle Street, Hinckley, Leicestershire LE10 1DD
Tel: 01455 636339
e-mail: roseandlinda@ten2gallery.co.uk   website: www.ten2gallery.co.uk

The owners of **The Art Studio, Ten-Two Gallery and Art Café** aim to provide a stimulating selection of fine artwork and a valuable service to the local art community. Quality is the keynote throughout the range of products, whether it's a card, art materials, giftware, pictures and prints, bespoke picture framing or a cup of coffee and a slice of homemade cake. The beautiful Ten-Two contemporary gallery sells originals, open and limited edition prints, glassware, ceramics, sculpture and jewellery. The Art Studio is stocked with an impressive range of art materials and provides a superb picture framing service; it also offers a programme of creative classes and workshops.

This is the perfect place to find a special present or something for the home or office, and there are plenty of catalogues to browse through over a cup of coffee or tea in the Art Café – the menu includes sandwiches, paninis, jacket potatoes and home-made cakes and slices. The owners and staff also have the expertise and resources to search for customers' favourite pieces of art. The handsome Oak Room is available for hire, and they have an extensive programme of classes and workshops. See website for details. Opening hours are 9 to 5 Monday to Saturday.

BIGGIE BEST

7 Windsor Street, Burbage, Leicestershire LE10 2EE
Tel: 01455 615068   Fax: 01509 674346
e-mail: info@biggiebestleicester.co.uk   website: www.biggiebestleicester.co.uk

Biggie Best started up in Cape Town in the early 1980s and is now a household name. Biggie Best fabrics have the natural earthy appearance of 100% cotton. The inspiration for the designs have been mostly classical and traditional and have been influenced by English style. Designs, therefore are not linked to the latest fashion: instead they are subtle and timeless with a nostalgic, yet up-to-date feel which can transform the essentially basic and functional into something very special.

Also in stock are soft furnishings, mirrors, jewellery, bears, clocks etc. Biggie Best is open Tuesday to Saturday 10am to 5pm and for those who can't make it to the shop the excellent website illustrates the wide range of fabrics.

FOSSE EQUESTRIAN

Fossefield Farm, Broughton Road, Stoney Stanton,
Leicestershire LE9 4JA
Tel: 01455 284587
e-mail: sales@fosseequestrian.co.uk
website: www.fosseequestrian.co.uk

Owner Lorna Wickham heads a family business selling an impressive range of equestrian products for horse and rider. They have their own horses and many years' experience in all aspects of matters equestrian. Their aim is to deliver top brands at a great price, with exceptional service to match. Their stock is expanding all the time, and all the big names in the business are represented in the well-laid-out displays.

The range includes saddles and saddlery accessories, grooming kits, training reins, horse-riding equipment and equestrian supplies, jodhpurs, breeches, hats, crops, bridles, rugs, stable equipment, horse care products and grooming kits. Among the top names featured are John Whitaker, Ariat, Georg Schumacher, Equinox, Harry Hall, Masts, legacy, Caldene, Cottage Craft, Dever, Toggi, Champion, Charles & Owen and Mark Todd. In a rural location between Hinckley and Leicester, Fosse Equestrian is open from 9 to 3 Monday to Wednesday, 10 to 5 Thursday, and 9.30 to 5.30 Friday and Saturday. Customers can also shop online or by mail order.

Around Hinckley

BURBAGE

1 mile E of Hinckley on the B4668

🌱 Burbage Woods

The village was originally called Burbach, a name that came from the burr thistles that grew in profusion in the fields. The 9th Earl of Kent was an early incumbent, being rector here for 50 years at the Church of St Catherine, whose spire is a landmark for miles around. **Burbage Woods** are nationally important because of the spectacular ground flora, and Burbage Common is one the largest areas of natural grassland in the locality. For the visitor there's a network of footpaths, bird observation hide, picnic tables and a visitor centre.

MARKET BOSWORTH

5 miles N of Hinckley off the A447

🚂 Battlefield Railway   🚣 Leisure & Water Park

🌳 Country Park

This market town is most famous as the battle site for the turning point in the Wars of the Roses – Richard III (Duke of York "White Rose" county) was routed here by Red Rose forces (Henry Bolingbroke, later Henry IV, of Lancaster) and killed in 1485. This was the battle immortalised in Shakespeare's play *Richard III*, where the desperate king is heard to cry, *"My kingdom for a horse"*. Richard's defeat led to the accession of the Tudor dynasty, Shakespeare's patrons and perhaps,

therefore, the impetus behind his less-than-complimentary portrayal of Richard which is disputed by historians to this day. **Bosworth Battlefield** is the historic site of the battleture King Henry VII. The Visitor Centre gives a detailed insight into medieval times with the aid of models, replicas and a film theatre, and also on site are a picnic area, a country park and a battle trail, a self-guided trail of 1¾ miles which takes the visitor round the field of battle, passing the command posts of Richard and Henry. Huge flags are frequently flown from these sites, adding colour and poignancy to the scene. Visitors can see the well where Richard drank during the battle, and pause at the memorial stone on the spot where Richard died. A fascinating addition to the site is a display of weapons from the Tudor period, found on the *Mary Rose,* one of Henry VIII's warships, which sank in Portsmouth Harbour in 1545. Call 01455 290429 for details of visits, events, etc.

The Battlefield is on the route of the **Ashley Canal**, whose towpath offers delightful walks through beautiful countryside. Opened in 1804, this lock-free

Bosworth Battlefield

Market Bosworth Country Park

Distance: *4.0 miles (6.4 kilometres)*

Typical time: *120 mins*

Height gain: *10 metres*

Map: *Explorer 232, Landranger 140*

Walk: *www.walkingworld.com* *ID:1505*

Contributor: *Roy Davenport*

ACCESS INFORMATION:

Served by buses from Leicester, Hinckley and Coalville. Car parking is in the Country Park situated on the B585 between Market Bosworth and the A447 Hinckley to Ashby Road.

ADDITIONAL INFORMATION:

Refreshments are available at several different places in Market Bosworth and also at the Royal Arms and Hercules public houses in Sutton Cheney and sometimes at the Arms Houses. Toilets are available in the Country Park and in the town. Gift shops and craft shops can be found in Market Bosworth. Almost flat throughout an easy walk. Good views across the Leicestershire borders into Warwickshire.

DESCRIPTION:

Market Bosworth is a small & pretty town in Leicestershire. This walk commences in the Bosworth Country Park a large area of parkland with a lake, and a variety of ducks, swans, moorhens and an abundance of wild birds.

The Park also contains an Arboretum with many of the trees marked to show their individual species. The Park is an ideal place for picnics and playing games with the children.

This walk leaves the Park via fields and makes it way to Sutton Cheney a small Leicestershire village. This village it close to the Bosworth Battlefield (see walk 1973) and contains the lovely little Battlefield church. Here King Richard III and his men passed by on the way to the battlefield and King Richard himself heard mass on the morning of the battle. In the church will be found battle emblems and a commemorative plaque.

Here to you will see the picturesque "Alms Houses" as you make your way up the church path.You will then return via more fields and an avenue of trees to pass through the arboretum and back to the lake in the park.

Depending on the height of crops you may see 3 memorials. One is a giant stone pillar bearing the figure of Hercules, which may have been put up originally by the fourth or fifth Baronet of Bosworth Park and could be 200 years old. Also two memorial stones over a pit where 3 horses are buried. The sandstone plaques are now almost unreadable. The larger one refers to "Trumps", charger of Capt. Norton Legge A.R.C. The smaller one reads "In memory of "Scots Grey" 10 seasons without a fall. Born 1876 died 1892. A trusty steed a faithful friend makes good the journey to the end". Sadly no public path actually allows access to the memorials.

FEATURES:

Lake/Loch, Pub, Toilets, Play Area, Church, Wildlife, Birds, Flowers, Great Views, Butterflies, Cafe, Gift Shop, Food Shop, Good for Kids, Mostly Flat, Public Transport, Restaurant, Tea Shop, Woodland, Ancient Monument

Market Bosworth

Bosworth Park

Cadeby

Spring Wood

Sutton Cheney

0 200 400 600 800metres 1
KILOMETRES
0 200 400 600yards ½ MILES

WALK DIRECTIONS:

1 | Walk across to the lake called, Bow Pool, and facing the lake turn left. Ignore the first footpath right along side the boathouse and find the next footpath to the right on the edge of the wood sign posted 'Woodland Walk'. Follow this path until you reach a 'T' junction with another footpath with a wooden fence on the far side. Turn left and exit the wood. Turn immediate right and passing a bench continue in almost a straight line through the plantation passing three more benches on the way and exit via the kissing gate.

2 | Ignoring the two wooden gates to your left go forward to the stile in the hedgerow. From the stile make your way forward keeping the hedgerow on your left. Continue along the

edge of a small wood, after that again continue forward with the hedge on your left until you reach the next stile. The way marker shows two footpaths one straight ahead and one angling to the right.

3 | The stile after this has a sign stating NO DOGS so dog walkers follow the divert route and rejoin main route at Waymark 7.

3 | **Divert Route** - Follow right hand marker, going close to corner of wood and forward to stile in hedgerow, then head for gap in the hedgerow ahead.

4 | On reaching the gap ignore the path ahead and turn left to the hedgerow. Follow this with the hedges on your left.

5 | At the first corner turn right and crossing the gap and keeping to the right of the hedge follow it to the end. At the end of this hedge you are at main walk point number 7. Turn right and follow the main route.

3 | **Main route -** Cross stile and continue forward with hedge on your left then through tree line and over the ditch. Bear slightly left and head up towards the farmhouse. The path passes between the farm on your left and hedgerow on your right and along farm drive. Just after end of the farm garden and before metal gate cross the stile on your right.

6 | Head towards the large house and on reaching the hedge turn right to follow the hedge round. At the far end of the garden, and end of the conifer trees go slightly right to the waymarker at the left hand end of the hedgerow on the right. Divert route walkers rejoin main route at this point.

7|The path now goes slightly left to a waymarker at the end of a hedgerow on the left. Go forward over the track and head towards the left hand telegraph pole of the two that can be seen ahead of you. As your reach a path junction in the middle of the field opposite 'The Royal Arms', it's worth looking right to note the waymarker at the end of a hedgerow in front of an old tree. This is a walk point for the return journey. Turn left at this junction and go to the stile in front of the pub car park

8|Cross the stile and go through the car park (or the bar!) to reach the road and turn right. Make your way through Sutton Cheney village to the church, passing The Square and The Old Bakery on the right and The Hercules pub on the left. (Pub so called because it stands in a direct line with Hercules Monument and Bosworth Park Hall).

9|Enter the churchyard on the right and as you pass through the second gate observe The Old Alms Houses on the right. When you exit the church door turn right and leave the yard via the small gate next to a cottage. After the gate turn sharp right to pass between the cottages. Pass between 'Church Cottage' and the very pretty 'Bumblebee Cottage'. Continue forward past the gates at the entrance to the Alms Houses and down the grass lane ahead of you.

10|At the next cottage (The opposite end of The Square passed earlier) go diagonally left across the corner of the field to the hedge corner between the two telegraph poles. Follow the hedge right to the next field. You will now see the paths ahead of you that you came along earlier and the 'Royal Arms' over on the right. Ignore the direct path ahead and angle slightly left to reach the waymark at the end of the hedge you noted on your outward journey. Follow the hedgerow down to the right in the direction of 'The Leicester Round' markers (Black circle of arrows) to the bottom of the field.

11|Go diagonally left across the corner of the field and head in the direction of the house that can be seen on the edge of the wood in the distance. At the bottom of the slope (divert walkers came to this point earlier on their outward journey) continue forward keeping the hedge on your left. At the end of the hedge go left and right over the stream (interesting old weir here) and with the wood on your right go up towards the house. Cross over the drive and continue forward to the stile.

12|Cross the stile and then turn left for about 50 yards and face right. Looking across to the right corner of the left wood on the brow of the slight hill you may see 'Hercules'. Return to the stile and turn left to walk down the avenue of trees passing a pool on the left. As you approach the corner of the wood look to your right and again you may spot 'Hercules' on his pedestal.

13|Continuing forward at the end of the wood look through the hedgerow on your right to see the Horse Memorials in the field. Continue forward. As you approach the end of the avenue you may see GIANT HOGWEED - DO NOT TOUCH - IT CAN STING AND SOME PEOPLE ARE HIGHLY ALLERGIC TO IT. Pass through the gate into the Arboretum. After going through the gate ignore waymarkers ahead and turn left to follow the main pathway. Follow down to the bottom crossing the stream over the third bridge. Continue back up on the opposite side of the stream. At the junction of the paths continue forward keeping the Wooden Toadstool on your left, over the bridge and back to Bow Pool.

canal connects Hinckley, Bosworth Battlefield, Market Bosworth, Battlefield Railway, Measham Museum and Moira Furnace.

Market Bosworth Country Park is one of many beautiful open spaces in the area. Another is **Bosworth Water Trust's Leisure and Water Park** on the B585 west of town. This is a 50-acre leisure park with 20 acres of lakes for dinghy sailing, boardsailing and fishing. Railway nostalgia awaits at Shackerstone, three miles northwest of Market Bosworth, where the **Battlefield Railway** offers a steam-hauled nine-mile round trip from Shackerstone to Shenton through the delightful scenery of southwest Leicestershire. At Shackerstone is an impressive museum of railway memorabilia, locomotives and rolling stock. On summer weekends there's a steam and diesel service; this also runs on Wednesdays in July and August. Call 01827 880754 for timetable details.

TWYCROSS
7 miles NW of Hinckley off the A444

🐾 Zoo

Five miles northwest of Market Bosworth, on the A444 Burton-Nuneaton road, **Twycross Zoo** is an ideal family attraction, home to a wide variety of animals including gorillas, chimps, orang-utans, gibbons, marmosets, elephants, lions, giraffes, flamingos and penguins. Open daily throughout the year.

On a side road parallel to the A444 three miles north of Market Bosworth lies a village with the wonderful name of **Barton-in-the-Beans**. The county was apparently once known as 'bean-belly' Leicestershire, on account of the large reliance on the bean crops that formed part of the staple diet in

needy times. The beans were said to have been sweeter and more tender than anywhere else in the country.

Coalville

🏛 Snibston Discovery Park

Originally called Long Lane, the town sprang up on a bleak common when Whitwick Colliery was opened in 1824. The big name in the early days was George Stephenson, who not only established the railway here (in 1832) but also built the churches.

At Ashby Road, Coalville, **Snibston Discovery Park** (see panel on page 366) is built on the 100-acre site of the former Snibston Colliery. Visitors can explore a unique mixture of nature, history, science and technology: topics covered include the industrial heritage of Leicestershire, and former miners conduct a lively surface tour of the colliery. There are rides on board a diesel locomotive on the restored colliery line and the Extraordinary Gallery allows visitors to lift a Mini Cooper, beat a robot or make fire. You can test your strength against a pulley system in the Engineering Gallery or relax in the Grange Nature Reserve and Victorian arboretum. The Fashion Gallery houses over 1,000 items from the 1750s to the present day, the largest such collection outside London. Tel 01530 278444 for opening times.

Around Coalville

OAKS IN CHARNWOOD
2 miles NE of Coalville off the B587

🏠 Mount St Bernard Abbey

In a beautiful elevated position in Charnwood Forest, **Mount St Bernard Abbey** was the first

Snibston Discovery Park

Ashby Road, Coalville, Leicestershire LE67 3LN
Tel: 01530 278444
e-mail: snibston@leics.gov.uk

One of the largest and most dynamic museums in the Midlands, Snibston is Leicestershire's all-weather science and industry museum, where visitors can get their 'hands-on' loads of fun in the popular Science Alive! Gallery, or explore the County's rich heritage in the Transport, Extractives, Engineering and Textiles and Fashion Galleries, with its amazing selection of historic and contemporary costumes.

Try and lift a Mini Cooper in the hands on gallery Extra Ordinary, which shows how technology has affected our every day life. Join real life miners on a tour of the colliery and experience what it was like to work underground. Take a ride on the diesel locomotive and get creative with the holiday activities. Other attractions outdoor science and water playgrounds, sculptures and Nature Reserve, where you can enjoy the sunshine or let off steam in our adventure play area. Opening: Daily: 10am – 5pm

Please see website for further details. Some activities incur an additional charge.

Catholic abbey to be founded in England after the Reformation. It is a Cistercian Monastery of white monks founded in 1835 as a continuation of Garendon Abbey (1133-1538).

SWANNINGTON
1 mile NW of Coalville on the A511

One of the first railway lines in Britain to use steam engines was the Leicester & Swannington Railway, which was opened in 1833 to bring coal to the city. The incline at Swannington is now part of one of the many heritage trails in the county. Traces of some of the many shallow 'bell pits' once common in this mining area can be seen in scrubland near the windmill on Swannington Common. Three floors of the restored Swannington Mill are open to the public on Sunday afternoons between April and September.

IBSTOCK
3 miles S of Coalville off the A447

🌿 Country Park   🏚 Donington Le Heath Manor House

Sense Valley Forest Park, at Heather near Ibstock, is a 150-acre site that has been transformed from an opencast mine into a woodland and wildlife haven. The site includes several large lakes and areas of conservation grassland, and the number of species of birds recorded grows each year.

Also a little way south of Coalville is **Donington Le Heath Manor House**, an attractive stone manor that is one of the few of its period (1280) to remain intact. It is now a museum.

Ashby-de-la-Zouch

🏠 Castle 🏠 St Helen's Church 🏛 Museum

🌲 National Forest

A historic market town whose name comes from the Saxon Aesc (ash) and Byr (habitation); the ending de la Zouch was added in 1160 when a Norman nobleman Alain de Parrhoet la Zouch became lord of the manor by marriage. In the 15th century Edward IV granted Ashby Manor to his favourite counsellor, Lord Hastings, who converted the manor house into a castle and rebuilt the nearby St Helen's Church. During the Civil War **Ashby Castle** was besieged for over a year by the Parliamentarian Army until the Royalists surrendered in 1646. After the war the castle was partly destroyed to prevent its further use as a centre of resistance and almost wholly forgotten until the publication of Sir Walter Scott's *Ivanhoe* in 1820. He used the castle as the setting for the archery competition which Robin Hood won by splitting the shaft of his opponent's arrow in the bull's eye. The most striking feature of the imposing ruins is the 80-ft Hastings Tower of 1464, which visitors can still climb to enjoy the view. The earliest parts predate the conversion and include parts of the hall, buttery and pantry of the 12th century manor house.

Hard by the castle ruins stands **St Helen's Church**, built by Lord Hastings in the 1400s on the site of an 11th century church. Restored and enlarged in 1880, it contains

---

BANGLES & TAT

Unit 3, Pass Courtyard, Ashby-de-la-Zouch, Leicestershire LE65 1AG
Tel: 01530 560930 Fax: 01283 760630
website: www.banglesandtat.co.uk

Hilary and Celia run **Bangles & Tat**, a friendly shop selling a wide range of beads and jewellery-making equipment. The beads include glass, wooden, semi-precious and freshwater pearls, and the stock offers everything needed to make jewellery, including cords and wires, buttons, sequins, felting wool, and ribbons in organza and velvet. The handmade jewellery on display, including some splendid tiaras, can be bought or reproduced to order in a variety of sizes and styles.

Visitors to this splendid little place can learn to make their own jewellery and other decorative pieces in the small, informal workshops that are held during shop hours (up to four participants) or in the evenings (up to 10 per course). Subjects include wire & bead jewellery, fabric collage, wet and dry felting, peg loom weaving, silk paper making and papier maché. Shop hours are 9.30am to 5pm Monday to Saturday.

🎬 stories and anecdotes   🍴 famous people   🎨 art and craft   🎭 entertainment and sport   🚶 walks

ASHBY AQUATICS & WATER LILY TABLES

163 Nottingham Road, Ashby-de-la-Zouch, Leicestershire
Tel: 01530 560834 Fax: 01530 416314
e-mail: enquiries@ashbyaquatics.co.uk
website: www.ashbyaquatics.co.uk

Ashby Aquatics is a friendly family-run enterprise in the National Forest, specialising in aquatic plants, exotic fish and associated supplies and accessories. The main building stands next to a lake close to a roundabout on the A511 and a short drive from the main A42. The stock includes an impressive variety of plants for the water's edge and floating plants, and knowledgeable staff are always ready with help and advice on lake planting and related topics.

In the summer they hold special kids days when youngsters can spend a few hours having fun while learning about pond life, aquatics, plants and even birdlife. In the Tropical Room there are tanks of Koi carp and other exotic fish, and Ashby also sells coldwater fish, fish tanks, pumps and heaters, fish food and tank plants. The owners have recently opened Water Lily Tables, a delightful lakeside café where visitors can enjoy a cup of tea or coffee and a snack throughout the centre's opening hours, which are 9 to 6 Monday to Saturday and 10 to 4 on Sunday.

much of interest, including some exceptionally fine stained glass depicting the life of Christ. There are several monuments to the Hastings family and an unusual relic in the shape of a finger pillory used to punish parishioners misbehaving in church. **Ashby de la Zouch Museum** contains a permanent display of Ashby history, the highlight being a model of the castle during the Civil War siege.

Ashby was for a while in the 19th century promoted as a spa town; the Ivanhoe baths were designed in 1822 by Robert Chaplin in Grecian style and had a 150ft colonnaded front with 32 Doric columns. Nearby Georgian terraces, also by Chaplin, stand as testimony to the seriousness of the spa

project, but a period of decline set in and the baths closed in the 1880s; the buildings were demolished in 1962. Yet another Chaplin building, the grand railway station, ceased to function as a station when the Leicester-Burton line was axed in the 1960s but was restored in the 1980s for use as offices. In the Ashby Tourist Information Centre (Tel: 01530 411767) visitors can pick up a copy of the National Forest & Beyond Visitor Guide. The **National Forest** is Britain's boldest environmental project to create a new forest for the nation covering 200 square miles and spanning parts of Leicestershire, Staffordshire and Derbyshire. Since its inception, more than seven million trees have been planted.

🏛 historic building   🏛 museum   🏛 historic site   🜄 scenic attraction   �, flora and fauna

Around Ashby de la Zouch

MEASHAM
5 miles S of Ashby off the A42

🏛 Museum

Measham was a place of brick-making and coal-mining, with the Ashby Canal flowing past and the River Mease nearby. It was in his warehouse near the canal at Measham that Joseph Wilkes produced his double-size bricks, known as *gobs* or *jumbies*, to try to avoid the brick tax of 1784. Those bricks can still be seen in some of the buildings in the village. In the High Street, opposite St Lawrence's Church, **Measham Museum** is a small village museum with an interesting collection of artefacts, documents and illustrations preserved by a former village doctor and his father. They provide a unique personal history of a community over a period of almost 100 years. Look out for the collection of colourful Measham Teapots which were once very popular on canal boats. Many prehistoric artefacts have been found preserved in peat in the area, including stone hammerheads, solid wooden wheels and flint wedges bound in hazel.

MOIRA
2 miles SW of Ashby on the B586

🏛 Moira Furnace   🎨 Conkers

Conkers, an award-winning attraction in the centre of the National Forest (see under Ashby-de-la-Zouch), is located off the B5003 Ashby-Overseal road. It has 120 acres of themed trails, demonstrations, two licensed lakeside restaurants, shop, garden and plants centre, amphitheatre and a number of craft workshops, as well as the Discovery &

Waterside Centres with over 100 interactive exhibits. The site adjoins Sarah's Wood, a 25-acre farmland site transformed into a woodland and wildlife haven, with trails and paths suitable for wheelchairs and a children's play area.

Near Donisthope, two miles south of Ashby, Willesley Wood was one of the first National Forest planting sites and is now an attractive 100-acre area of mature woodland, a lake and meadows. One of the walks leads to Saltersford Valley, which features woodland sculptures, a lake and a picnic area.

The industrial heritage of the region is remembered in the **Moira Furnace**, an impressive, perfectly preserved blast furnace built in 1804 by the Earl of Moira. The site includes lime kilns, a casting shed and engine house, and a range of craft workshops, woodland walks, nature and industrial trails, country park and children's playground.

STAUNTON HAROLD
4 miles N of Ashby off the B587

🎨 The Ferrers Centre   🏛 Calke Abbey   🚶 Reservoir

Another craft centre here, with 16 craft workshops within a magnificent Georgian courtyard. Crafts at **The Ferrers Centre** include contemporary furniture, ceramics, copper-smithing and forge, picture framing and sign studio, designer clothing and textiles, automata, stained glass, china restoration, stone carving and silver jewellery. Gift shop, gallery and tea room on site. Staunton Harold Hall and Holy Trinity Church are surrounded by the beautiful parkland and lakes of the Staunton Estate. The Palladian-style hall is not open to the public, but the church is open for afternoon visits April to September daily except Thursday and Friday. In the care of the National Trust, the church is one of the few to have been built during the Commonwealth period in 1653 and retains the original pews, cushions and hangings, together with fine panelling and a painted ceiling.

Staunton Harold Reservoir, covering over 200 acres, has two nature reserves, fishing, sailing and a visitor centre with exhibitions and 3-D models. Footpaths and nature walks provide a link with the nearby 750-acre Calke Abbey park at Ticknall, near Melbourne. The National Trust's **Calke Abbey** is a baroque mansion built in 1701-3 which has remained virtually unchanged since the death of the last baronet, Sir Vauncey Harpur-Crewe, in 1924.

Loughborough

🏛 Carillon   🏛 Museums   🏛 Great Central Railway

🏛 John Taylor Bellfoundry Museum

In Loughborough's Market Place is a statue of a seated man admiring his sock. Titled *The Sock,* this whimsical piece by sculptor Shona Kinlock celebrates the town's premier industry in times past, beginning with wool, then woollen stockings and progressing to knitwear and hosiery machinery and engineering.

Another major industry since mid-Victorian times is represented by the lofty **Carillon** in Queen's Park which was opened in 1923 as an imaginative War Memorial to the dead of the First World War. The 151ft carillon tower, the first to be built in Britain, contains a unique carillon of 47 bells, covering four chromatic octaves, under the care of the borough carilloner. Carillon recitals are given on Thursday and Sunday afternoons during the summer months. Visitors who climb the 138 steps to the viewing gallery are rewarded with magnificent views of the Charnwood scenery. The **Museum of Armed Forces** in Queen's

Park has displays relating to the Great War and is open seven days a week.

Loughborough's connection with bells began in 1858 when the bell foundry of John Taylor moved here from Oxford. It is still producing and restoring bells for customers all over the world. Situated alongside the working factory, the **John Taylor Bellfoundry Museum** covers all aspects of bell-founding from early times and shows the craft techniques of moulding, casting, tuning and fitting up of bells. The foundry made Great Paul, which hangs in St Paul's Cathedral. It is the biggest bell in Britain, weighing 17 tons and standing nine feet high. Call 01509 233414 for opening times and details of tours.

The **Charnwood Museum** displays the natural and local history of Charnwood, the district around Loughborough that includes the majestic Charnwood Forest.

For many visitors to Loughborough, the

Bellfoundry, Loughborough

SPENCERS TRADITIONALS

Spencers Bakery, rear of 154 Loughborough Road, Hathern, Loughborough,
Leicestershire LE12 5JB
Tel/Fax: 01509 842375

'Acorns were good till bread was found' Juvenal

'Gentle bakers, make good bread! For good bread doth comfort, confirm and doth establish
the heart' Andrew Boorde, 1542

'Bread, dear brothers, is the staff of life' Jonathan Swift

From Biblical times, man has praised the qualities of bread, which has since time immemorial
been a staple of his diet. The smell of freshly baked bread is hard to resist, and for more than
150 years that smell has been luring customers to Hathern. Ian Spencer is the third generation
of bakers running **Spencers Traditionals**, where bread is baked the way it used to be, with a

natural proving process and none of the nasty
additives that make so much mass-produced
bread unpleasant and indigestible. A look
through the back door will not only seduce
you with its aroma but will also tell you that
the kneading process is an excellent way of
de-stressing and exercising the arm muscles.
Customers can buy the fresh-baked bread
from here between 8am and 3pm (till 1pm on
Saturdays).

Also at 51 Brook Street, Shepshed,
Loughborough, Leicestershire LE12 9RF
Tel: 01509 650958

most irresistible attraction is the **Great Central Railway**, Britain's only main line steam railway. Its headquarters are at Loughborough Central Station, where there is a museum, a working signal box and a collection of historic steam locomotives. The station, with its ornate canopy over the island platform, is worth a visit in its own right, and is in regular demand from film companies. It was used a few years ago for the filming of *Shadowlands* – other stars who have been filmed here include Nicole Kidman, Anthony Hopkins and Kate Winslet. The line runs eight miles from Loughborough to Leicester, crossing the Swithland Reservoir viaduct, and the service operates every weekend and Bank Holiday throughout the year, and weekdays from June to September. Call 01509 for details of timetables and special events. In the Phantom & Firkin,

Loughborough's only brew pub, visitors can see how traditional cask ales are made. Call 01509 262051 for details of free brewery tours.

Loughborough Market is one of the finest street markets in the country. Full of tradition and atmosphere, it is held in the market place and adjacent streets every Thursday and Saturday. November sees the annual Loughborough Fair, with stalls, shows, rides and other attractions.

Around Loughborough

CASTLE DONINGTON
7 miles NW of Loughborough off the A6

Donington GP Collection

Originally just Donington – the 'Castle' was added when the Norman castle was built to defend the River Trent crossing. It was demolished by King John to punish the owner for supporting Magna Carta and was rebuilt in 1278.

The **Donington Grand Prix Collection**, in Donington Park, is the world's largest collection of single-seater racing cars. The five halls contain over 130 exhibits of motor racing.

WYMESWOLD

5 miles NE of Loughborough on the A6006

A large conservation village whose Georgian houses give it the air of an 18th century market town – more than 30 of them are Grade II listed. The 14th century parish church was restored by Pugin in 1844.

MOUNTSORREL

5 miles SE of Loughborough off the A6

🏠 Stonehurst Family Farm & Motor Museum

Peaceful since the A6 bypass was opened, Mountsorrel lies on the west bank of the Soar. Its elegant Butter Market, or Dome, lends distinction to an otherwise unremarkable little town. The Dome was built in 1793 by the eccentric Lord of the Manor, Sir John Danvers, and the town was surprised that he didn't have it painted red – almost everything else in Mountsorrel that could be painted was covered in brilliant red, a colour for which Sir John had an insatiable appetite. His clothes were predominantly red, set off by discreet touches of black: "being a broad-set man his appearance was like that of the Knave of Spades".

WYMESWOLD COUNTRY FURNITURE LTD

17 Far Street, Wymeswold,
Leicestershire LE12 6TZ
Tel/Fax: 01509 880309
website: www.wymeswoldcountryfurniture.co.uk

This is a real treasure trove! It is housed on two floors in converted Georgian stables and is full of beautiful things. The business was founded in 1983 and has become one of the most respected and successful dealers in genuine old pine furniture. Here there are extensive stocks of furniture for all rooms of the house - beds, chests of drawers, wardrobes, boxes, desks, cupboards, tables, chairs, dressers, plate racks, old shop counters and much more.

However, there is more than just furniture - the shop is packed with home accessories, both old and new, and there is a room devoted to selling limited editions by successful artists, hand-coloured etchings, as well as original artwork.

The business is owned and run by Bill and Jenny McBean. Bill takes care of the restoration work and picture framing, while Jenny concentrates on buying all the wonderful gifts and accessories which include

Deliveries are made in our original 1936 Bedford Van

An original 7', 6 drawer, 2 cupboard sideboard c1840

mirrors, ceramics, glassware, candle and electric lighting, cushions, jewellery, cards and the artwork. "I like to try to find different things which are not readily available on the High Street," says Jenny - and she certainly does. It really is well worth a visit.

🏠 historic building   🏛 museum   🏚 historic site   🌊 scenic attraction   🌱 flora and fauna

A great attraction in the village for the whole family is **Stonehurst Family Farm & Motor Museum**. Highlights range from baby rabbits and guinea pigs in Cuddle Corner to all the familiar farm animals, free tractor rides, a working smithy and an impressive collection of vintage cars, motorcycles and other vehicles including Leicestrshire's first motor bus. Restaurant, tea shop, farm shop are all open daily all year.

OLD WOODHOUSE
3 miles S of Loughborough on minor roads

🏛 Beaumanor Hall

The most impressive stained glass window in Leicestershire is to be found not in any of the county's churches but at **Beaumanor Hall**, the seat of the Herrick family from 1595 to the 1930s. The present Tudor-style mansion was built in 1848 and it was then that the extraordinary window, 15ft high and 25ft wide, was installed by William Perry Herrick. All his life William was obsessed with his family pedigree so each of the 21 panels in the great window features the brilliantly coloured coat-of-arms of one of his ancestors. It's a breathtaking riot of heraldry. Sadly, for a man who took such pride in his ancestry, William died without a direct heir to succeed him. Beaumanor Hall is now a Leicestershire County Council training centre but the window may be viewed by prior arrangement by calling 01509 890119.

WOODHOUSE EAVES
3 miles S of Loughborough on minor roads

🌿 Long Close Gardens 🌳 Beacon Hill Country Park

The oldest house in this attractive village is Long Close, which is thought to have once been a royal hunting lodge. Secluded behind a high wall, the five acres of **Long Close**

Gardens have become known as the Secret Garden. They've also been described as "a Cornish Garden in Leicestershire" because of the rare and interesting plants that flourish here. The gardens are open from March to July and group visits can be arranged at other times by appointment.

Woodhouse Eaves takes its name from being on the edges, or eaves, of Charnwood Forest. The views are superb, especially from the summit of **Beacon Hill Country Park**, one of the highest points in Leicestershire at 818ft.

SHEPSHED
4 miles W of Loughborough on the A512

The hosiery industry was once the principal activity here with some 900 stocking frames clattering away at the peak of the town's prosperity. Shepshed still offers factory outlet shopping for knitwear and clothing as well as traditional and farmers' markets. Around the medieval marketplace are some thatched cottages once used by framework knitters in the 1800s.

Melton Mowbray

🏛 St Mary's Church 🏛 Ye Olde Pork Pie Shoppe

The very name of this bustling market town makes the mouth water, being home to the pork pie, one of the most traditional of English delicacies. The Melton Hunt Cake, a rich fruit cake spiced with Jamaican rum, is another local speciality, and Stilton, 'king of English cheeses', is also made here. The cheese has the longest history, dating back possibly as far as the 14th century and first made in the village of Little Dalby. It is only manufactured in Leicestershire, Nottinghamshire and Derbyshire. Of the six

Parish Church, Melton Mowbray

St Mary's Church, considered the largest and stateliest parish church in the whole county, dates from 1170. It has a particularly imposing tower and impressive stained glass windows.

Around Melton Mowbray

GRIMSTON
3 miles W of Melton off the A6006

Perhaps because of its unappealing name, Grimston tends to be overlooked by guide books. It is in fact one of the county's most appealing villages. At its centre is a lovely green where a set of ancient stocks stands beneath a chestnut tree. Overlooking the green are two venerable hostelries and the Church of St John the Evangelist. Here the curious custom of "bidding by candle" continued until the early 1900s.

A small stump of candle was lit and buyers would then make their bids for the item being auctioned. Whoever made the last bid before the candle guttered acquired the lot at that price.

EASTWELL
5 miles N of Melton off the A607

🏚 Crossroads Farm Museum

Just outside the village, **Crossroads Farm Museum,** in a 17th century barn, is a treasure trove of farming equipment and memorabilia from Victorian times to the present day.

STATHERN
7 miles N of Melton off the A607

A peaceful village nestling in the Vale of Belvoir, Stathern has a medieval church with a beautifully carved 13th century doorway, an

producers, four are in the Vale of Belvoir and one in Melton itself. The noble cheese became nationally popular in the 1740s when Frances Pawlett of Wymondham came to an arrangement with the landlord of The Bell Inn at Stilton to market the cheese. The inn was a coaching stop on the Great North Road and travellers who sampled the noble cheese soon spread its fame. Later, Melton Mowbray became the market centre for Stilton and from 1883 to 1914 three specialist fairs were held each year – 12,672 cheeses were sold at the first! A 16lb Stilton takes 17 gallons of milk to produce and a minimum of two months to mature. The town is also known for its Red Leicester cheese.

Hand-raised pork pies have been made here since 1831 and since 1851 in the oldest surviving bakery, **Ye Olde Pork Pie Shoppe**, where visitors can watch the traditional hand-raising techniques and taste the pies.

Markets have long been a feature of life in Melton Mowbray, and the Domesday Book of 1086 records the town's market as the only one in Leicestershire. Large street markets are held on Tuesdays and Saturdays in the Market Place, and butter and corn crosses still stand at two of the town's former market points. The town also has regular livestock auctions and a farmer's market

---

🏛 historic building   🏚 museum   🏛 historic site   🝔 scenic attraction   🌱 flora and fauna

CROSSROADS FARM SHOP & MUSEUM

Scalford Road, Eastwell, Melton Mowbray,
Leicestershire LE14 4EF
Tel: 01949 860242

Third-generation farmers Alan and Jane Hewson attract lovers of top-quality home-produced food from many miles around. The range of British beef, pork and lamb is truly impressive, either in cuts and joints or in home-cured hams, bacon, preservative-free sausages and haslet. Among the biggest sellers are the gold award-winning meat pies: steak, steak & kidney, chicken & mushroom, pork apple & cider and many more. Fresh homemade cakes are made daily in their bakery on the farm. Also to be found are free-range eggs, preserves, soft drinks and an extensive range of Fair Trade foods. The farm is going back to its dairying roots with on-site milking and bottling, handmade and hand-patted jersey butter, cream and old-recipe farmhouse cheeses.

Another development is a group of local residents growing organic fruit and vegetables in greenhouses on the farm. Customers can enjoy superb cream teas in the 17th century barn or out on the lawn, and wander round the little museum above the shop with a fascinating collection of old farm implements. Eastwell lies off the A617 a short distance north of Melton Mowbray.

arcaded 14th century font, and some fine modern glass. A one-time resident here was Colonel Hacker who acted as "master of ceremonies" at the execution of Charles I. After the Restoration he, too, was dispatched by the executioner's axe.

WALTHAM ON THE WOLDS
5 miles NE of Melton on the A607

Straddling the A607, high up on the Leicestershire Wolds, Waltham is an attractive village with an excellent hostelry and a tall-spired medieval church. Roman pavements and Saxon stone coffins have been discovered here, testifying to the antiquity of the settlement. The country lane that leads from Waltham to Harby is unusually wide because, it is believed, it was an ancient drovers' road leading to Nottingham.

BELVOIR CASTLE
12 miles N of Melton off the A607

🏰 Castle   🏛 Queen's Royal Lancers Museum

The Leicestershire home of the Duke of Rutland is an imposing mock-medieval

Vale of Belvoir

🎪 stories and anecdotes   🐦 famous people   🎨 art and craft   🎭 entertainment and sport   🚶 walks

RUTLAND STUDIO & BESPOKE KITCHENS

7 Market Street, Bottesford, Leicestershire NG13 0BW
Tel: 01949 843330/842513

The **Rutland Studio** is situated in the village of Bottesford, in the beautiful Vale of Belvoir and 10 minutes from Belvoir Castle. At the shop, which is found on Market Street right opposite the old buttercross, you will find an eclectic mix of antique and good quality reproduction furniture. The antiques are sourced usually from France, Italy and also here in England. Margaret, the proprietor, says even she never knows what she will find on her many quests to find quality, decorative items. The shop offers a bespoke furniture service where customers can order any size or design required. Customers can choose from an extensive range of furniture from the catalogue and have the piece custom finished as Margaret also specialises in hand painted furniture. In

addition you will also find an exclusive range of children's furniture and headboards, antique and modern chandeliers together with a range of decorative items and gift ware.

The shop opened in 1999 and in 2002 Margarets partner, Andrew Goodson, launched **Rutland Studio Kitchens**. Andrew is happy to arrange a visit for a no obligation survey and quotation. This side of the business has grown rapidly with many satisfied clients. Andrew is able to offer customers a very hands on approach and takes great care to supervise his designs through to completion. The shop opens Wednesday - Saturday, 10.30am - 4.30pm and Sundays by appointment.

As Margaret says "Step Inside - Be Inspired".

STAPLEFORD PARK COUNTRY HOUSE HOTEL & SPORTING ESTATE

Stapleford, Leicestershire LE14 2EF
Tel: 01572 787000 Fax: 01572 787001
e-mail: reservations@stapleford.co.uk
website: www.staplefordpark.com

The approach to the house through the 500-acre **Stapleford Park** offers the first glimpse of Georgian grandeur, confirmed when guests pass under the stone arch and into the welcome, warmth and grace of a bygone era. Most of the building is late 17th century, and the long history of hospitality is maintained by impeccable (but always approachable) hosts and staff. Oak floors, panelled walls, heavy drapes, fresh flowers, fine carvings and sumptuous armchairs and sofas set the scene in the day rooms, and the bedrooms are equally striking. The 55 rooms have 55 designers, and the easy chairs, soft settees, beautiful beds and sumptuously appointed bathrooms put hem in a class of their own. Most enjoy glorious views of the grounds designed by Capability Brown. Dining here is also a memorable experience, the finest and freshest seasonal

ingredients used to create superb dishes complemented by a superb cellar. The private dining areas make a wonderful venue for a special celebration, and modern technology is available for meetings, conferences and seminars. Stapleford also excels in its sporting and leisure facilities, which range from golf and tennis to riding, shooting, falconry, archery, croquet, boules and off-road driving. The Lifestyle Club in the old stable block has a well-equipped gym, and the spa features a swimming pools, sauna, steam room, Jacuzzi and a range of body treatments.

building in an equally imposing setting overlooking the pastoral Vale of Belvoir. The present **Belvoir Castle** was completed in the early 19th century after previous buildings had been destroyed during the Wars of the Roses, the Civil War and in the major fire of 1816. In the stunning interior are notable collections of furniture and porcelain, silks and tapestries, sculptures and paintings. There are works by Van Dyck, Reynolds, Hogarth and, most familiar of all, Holbein's imposing portrait of Henry VIII. Also within the castle is the **Queen's Royal Lancers Museum**. The grounds are as splendid as the castle and are used for medieval jousting tournaments on certain days in the summer.

WYMONDHAM
6 miles E of Melton off the B676

🌾 Windmill and Craft Centre

A must for visitors here is the six-sailed **Windmill** dating from 1814 and currently being restored. It is one of only four of its kind in the country and most of its massive machinery is still intact. The mill's former outbuildings have been converted into a **Craft Centre** with workshops for wrought iron work, candle-making, pine furniture, hand-made kitchens, playhouses and architectural antiques. There's a tearoom serving light lunches and home-baked cakes, a free bouncy castle and play area. Bed & breakfast accommodation is also available.

BURROUGH-ON-THE-HILL
5 miles S of Melton off the B6047

Burrough Hill is an Iron Age fort rising to almost 700ft overlooking the Wreake Valley. There are grand views from its flat summit which in Victorian times was used for horse racing.

TILTON ON THE HILL
7 miles S of Melton on the B6047

🕊 Owston Woods

The highest habitation in the county, some 700 feet above sea level, Tilton has a charming little church with some striking Norman gargoyles and stone carvings of human heads and animals, and some impressive monuments to members of the Digby family. About three miles east of the village, there's pleasant walking in the Forestry Commission's **Owston Woods** – look out for the 800-year-old lime tree which is still in remarkably good shape.

Rutland

🌱 Rutland Water

The motto of the county is, appropriately, 'multum in parvo' ('much in little'). It has two delightful market towns, Oakham and Uppingham, and 52 small, unspoilt villages of thatch and ironstone cottages clustered round their churches. The county's central feature is **Rutland Water** which extends over 3,300 acres and is the largest man-made reservoir in Europe. Started in 1971 to supply water to East Midlands towns, it was created by damming the valley near Empingham. There's good walking and cycling around its 26-mile shoreline, some great bird-watching (including wild ospreys), excellent trout and pike fishing, a wide variety of watersports and a rock climbing wall. St Matthews Church on the edge of the reservoir houses a museum.

The county boasts two leading public schools, Oakham and Uppingham; one of the most striking and best-preserved Norman churches in the country, at Tickencote; a grand 12th century Great Hall and the home of the original 'Tom Thumb', both in Oakham.

📖 stories and anecdotes   🐦 famous people   🌾 art and craft   🎭 entertainment and sport   🕊 walks

GOLDMARK GALLERY

Uppingham, Rutland LE15 9SQ
Tel: 01572 821424
e-mail: info@goldmarkart.com
website: www.goldmarkart.com

Mike Goldmark has been a 'shopkeeper' (his description!) in Uppingham for more than 30 years and in that time he has masterminded the growth and great success of his **Goldmark Gallery**. He ran a bookshop on the site before converting it into a gallery that has become known in all parts of the world. The Gallery specialises in original prints and also sells paintings, drawings, sculptures, etchings, lithographs and woodcuts. Mike's boundless enthusiasm has seen a non-stop growth of the business, with the result that there are now more than 20,000 items in stock.

The artists featured on the two floors of display space, the superbly produced catalogues (works of art in themselves) and the websites include many of the most familiar names in the world of art: Henri Matisse, Henry Moore, Eric Gill, Elisabeth Frink, John Piper, Marc Chagall, Graham Sutherland, Pablo Picasso, Terry Frost, Howard Hodgkin and long-time gallery artists George Large, Robert Dawson and Rigby Graham. More than 30 websites are devoted to individual artists, with over 2,000 images and more added daily (access these sites via the gallery's website). The Gallery shows some of the finest in UK studio ceramics, with a sumptuous catalogue for each exhibition. On the publishing side, a series of illustrated books has been launched, adding to the occasional art biography; a number of art films have also been produced, the latest with the collaboration of Charles Mapleston, who has made art films for more than 30 years for TV.

Other services include expert advice on framing, and Mike has recently opened a print work-shop with master printer Ian Wilkinson and wife and assistant Jan. Sales by mail order started in a small way in 2000 and now accounts for over half the business, with customers all over the world. The gallery ships daily in its own-brand made-to-measure boxes, ensuring quick and safe delivery. The staff have a long tradition of sitting down together for lunch, visitors are always welcome to join them for a bite and a chat, but they have one request – 'please don't all come at once'. The gallery is open Monday to Saturday 9.30am to 5.30pm, also Sunday afternoons and Bank Holidays.

Curiously for such a pastoral, peaceful county, it was Rutland men who were prime movers in two of the most dangerous conspiracies in England's history. In a room over the porch of Stoke Dry church, the Gunpowder Plot was hatched with the local lord of the manor, Sir Everard Digby, as one of the ringleaders. Some 75 years later, Titus Oates and his fellow conspirators hatched the anti-Catholic 'Popish Plot' at his home in Oakham.

Uppingham

🏫 School

This picturesque stone-built town is the major community in the south part of the county. It has a long, handsome high street and a fine market place where traders have hawked their wares every Friday since 1280. The town is known for its bookshops and art galleries, but whereas other places are dominated by castles or cathedrals, in Uppingham it's the impressive **Uppingham School** that gives the town its special character. The school was founded in 1584 by Robert Johnson, Archdeacon of Leicester, who also founded Rutland's other celebrated public school at Oakham. For more than 250 years,

Uppingham was just one of many such small grammar schools, giving rigorous instruction in classical languages to a couple of dozen sons of the local gentry. Then, in 1853, the Rev Edward Thring was appointed headmaster. During his 43-year tenure the sleepy little school was transformed.

The Old School Building still stands in the churchyard, with trilingual inscriptions around the walls in Latin, Greek and Hebrew – *Train up a child in the way he should go* is one of them. In its place rose a magnificent complex of neo-gothic buildings: not just the traditional classrooms and a (splendid) chapel, but also a laboratory, workshops, museum, gymnasium and the most extensive school playing fields in the country.

Dr Thring wrote extensively on educational matters, championed education for girls and founded the Headmasters Conference. When he retired in 1897 he could look back with pride on the creation of one of the country's most successful public schools, both academically and financially. The old school, the 18th century studies, the Victorian chapel and schoolrooms, and the 20th century great hall, all Grade I or Grade II listed, can be visited on a guided tour on Saturday afternoons in summer.

HOME FARM

Main Street, Ayston, Uppingham, Rutland LE15 9AE
Tel/Fax: 01572 823345
e-mail: sue@homefarmayston.co.uk
website: www.homefarmayston.co.uk

Home Farm is a traditional farmhouse B&B in the heart of Rutland, on a working farm producing high-quality beef cattle and a variety of arable crops. Just one mile from Uppingham, it has two letting bedrooms sleeping up to 5 guests, airy, roomy and relaxing, with TV, tea/coffee making facilities and hairdryer. Guests can choose the full English breakfast or a Continental-style alternative, and packed lunches are available by prior arrangements.

📰 stories and anecdotes   🦜 famous people   🎨 art and craft   🎵 entertainment and sport   🚶 walks

Around Uppingham

STOKE DRY
3 miles S of Uppingham on the A6003

There are some striking monuments in the church at Stoke Dry to the Digby family, particularly an engraved alabaster slab to Jaquetta Digby who died in 1496. One of her descendants, Sir Everard Digby, was to bring great shame on the family. He was born in the village in 1578 but when the Protestant James I ascended the throne, Sir Everard and his Catholic friends became involved in the conspiracy now known as the Gunpowder Plot. It was in the priest's room over the porch of St Andrew's Church that the conspirators met. After his conviction in 1609 Sir Everard endured the gruesome ordeal of death by hanging, drawing and quartering. The porch where the plotters met has another macabre story attached to it – it's said that one vicar locked a witch in the room and left her to die by starvation.

Stoke Dry overlooks Eyebrook Reservoir, a 300-acre trout fishery in an idyllic location in the Welland Valley, by the border with Leicestershire and Northamptonshire. Good bank and boat fishing from April to October.

LYDDINGTON
3 miles SE of Uppingham off the A6003

🏛 Bede House

A quiet village where English Heritage oversees the **Bede House,** one of the finest examples of Tudor domestic architecture in the country. This house of prayer was once part of a retreat for the Bishops of Lincoln and was later converted to a hospital (bede house) for 12 poor men, two women and a warden. It remained in use right up until 1930. The fine 16th century rooms can be visited daily from April to October. The small gardens contain a notable herb garden with over 60 herbs, both culinary and medicinal, and just outside the grounds lie the fish ponds that used to supply the bishop's kitchen.

WING
2 miles NE of Uppingham off the A6003

🌿 Maze

The little village of Wing is best known for a Maze in which it's impossible to get lost. The medieval **Turf Maze** is made of foot-high turf banks and measures 40 feet across. Its design is identical to the mosaic patterns in the floors of Chartres Cathedral and other French cathedrals. An old tradition asserts that penitents were required to crawl around the maze on their knees, stopping at various points to say prayers. Once a fairly common sight, only eight such turf mazes are known to still exist in

Turf Maze, Wing

England. They were already falling into disfavour by Shakespeare's time. In *A Midsummer Night's Dream* he wrote:

And the quaint mazes in the wanton green
For lack of tread, are indistinguishable.

Oakham

🏛 Castle   🏛 All Saints Church   🏛 Museum

🏛 Flore's House   🏛 School   🎞 Burley-on-the-Hill

Oakham is one of England's most appealing county towns, a friendly place with many old hostelries, a regular twice weekly market, a wide variety of family-owned shops, a fine church and a major public school.

Just off the Market Place with its charming market cross and stocks is **Oakham Castle**, a romantic, evocative fortified manor house built between 1180 and 1190, with the earliest surviving example of an aisled stone hall in the country. A unique feature is a collection of over 200 horseshoes hanging all around the walls of the hall. For centuries, any peer of the realm passing through the town has been required to present a horseshoe to the castle. When this custom began isn't clear although one plausible story says that it began in the days of William the Conqueror when his farrier lived here. (The farrier's descendants, the Ferrers family, later built the Great Hall). This unusual tax is still being imposed – amongst the hundreds of horseshoes of every size, some ornately gilded, others rusty, is one presented by Queen Elizabeth II.

All Saints Church is the spiritual centre of town, a fine parish church with a 14th century tower. On the capitals in the nave are striking carvings of traditional subjects, including dragons, the Green Man, Adam and Eve, and Reynard the Fox.

Rutland County Museum, housed in a splendid 18th century riding school in Catmose Street, has displays of farm equipment, machinery and wagons, domestic collections and local archaeology. The riding school belonged to the Rutland Fencibles, a volunteer cavalry regiment raised in 1794 and now remembered in a gallery in the museum.

Flore's House is one of the oldest buildings in the town. It dates from the late 1300s and was built by William Flore and his son Roger, who was a wealthy merchant and four times Speaker of the House of Commons.

Notable natives of Oakham include the infamous conspirator Titus Oates who was born here in 1649 and lived in Mill Street. A minor cleric, he played the leading role in fabricating the 'Popish Plot' of 1678. Oates claimed to have uncovered a secret Jesuit plot to assassinate Charles II and return the Catholic Church to power. Many innocent Catholics were killed as a result of this alarm, but Oates, when the truth was discovered, did not escape lightly. He was sentenced to yearly whippings and was not freed until 1688; he died in obscurity in 1705.

Another Oakham man involved in Titus Oates' conspiracy was the famed midget Jeffery Hudson, 'the smallest man from the smallest county in England'. He lived in a thatched cottage which still stands on Melton Road opposite the White Lion pub. By the age of nine Jeffery stood a mere 18 inches high and he never grew to more than 3ft 6. His father, who was above average height, worked on the Duke of Buckingham's estate at nearby **Burley on the Hill,** a couple of miles north-east of Oakham. The duchess took a fancy to the minuscule lad, dressed him in costly silk and satin, and kept him by

SWANS ANTIQUES & INTERIORS

No 17 Mill Street, Oakham,
Rutland LE15 6EA
Tel: 01572 724364   Fax: 01572 755094
e-mail: info@swansofoakham.co.uk
website: www.swansofoakham.co.uk
website: swanslinen.co.uk

Swans of Oakham is located in the centre of Oakham's prestigious shopping area, Mill Street. Swans offers you a unique and impressive range of original antique and quality reproduction furniture with the accent on the more unusual, decorative (but always practical) pieces. Among the most striking is one of the country's largest collections of original French beds in all sizes and styles, including the hard to find 5ft wide kingsize and wider. The large showroom, spread over two floors, is filled with complementary furniture, such as bedside and dressing tables, armoires, pairs of bedroom chairs and many other lovely pieces. You will find around a dozen French beds fully made up on display with fine quality bedding, throws and quilts, with approximately a further 50 beds standing.

Swans also makes bespoke beds, especially four-posters in solid oak and cherry, often using original 19th century front posts and basing the whole design of a bed around them. The two workshops also produce a range of handmade furniture, made to your specification which includes kitchen dressers, centre islands, bookcases, TV cabinets and their impressive kitchen/dining tables. Swans offers a comprehensive furnishing service that enables clients to furnish their properties - whether a compact apartment, or a grand country house, all with good quality, unusual antiques along with some quality handmade pieces made to fit.

The business is owned by Peter and Linda, who both travel widely to source the very best and more unique pieces, and the shop along with the impressive website, is managed by their son Tom. With the addition of their constantly updated website, for seven years furniture has been supplied to clients all over the world, including regular customers based in the USA, Malaysia and New Zealand. Swans has certainly contributed to Mill Street becoming well known as "The Knightsbridge of Rutland", as there are a superb selection of shops and eateries, fabrics, ladies and gents fashions, galleries, oriental rugs, a herbal dispensary and fantastic fishing tackle shop to help out with all you may need for a day at the nearby Rutland Water!

Opening hours are:- Monday to Saturday 9am to 5.30pm and Sundays are by welcome appointment. Just call 01572 724364 if you can't make it between these times and one of the family will be happy to meet you.

To see almost everything currently in the shop, go to www.swansofoakham.co.uk - there is also www.swansbedlinen.co.uk now open so you can see over 400 items, from bedding, to nightwear, to bathroom accessories.

her as a kind of mascot. When Charles I and his Queen Henrietta Maria were guests at Burley, a huge cold pie was placed on the table before them and when the pie was cut open out popped Jeffery. The Queen was so delighted with the midget that she took him back to the royal court, where he became a popular figure, was knighted and had his portrait painted by Van Dyck. But Jeffery was an extremely quarrelsome character and on one occasion challenged Lord Crofts to a duel in which the latter was killed. Jeffery was banished for a time but while travelling back to England was captured by Turkish pirates and sold as a slave. Ransomed by the Duke of Buckingham, he returned to Oakham and the house in the High Street. With his usual impetuosity he became

involved in Titus Oates' Popish Plot and was imprisoned.

Oakham School was founded in 1584 by Archdeacon Robert Johnson, who also founded Uppingham School. As at Uppingham, the original single room school building still stands, its walls inscribed with Hebrew, Latin and Greek quotations. Both schools expanded greatly in the 19th century but while the school buildings at Uppingham dominate the little town, at Oakham they are spread across the town centre, partly hidden away off the attractive market place where the ancient Butter Cross still provides shelter for the town stocks. Now co-educational, Oakham School has around 1,000 pupils.

On the outskirts of town, the road to Uppingham crosses Swooning Bridge, where

---

THE CHOCOLATE BAR

49a High Street, Oakham, Rutland LE15 6AJ
Tel: 01572 724554
e-mail: enquiries@echocolatebar.co.uk
website: www.echocolatebar.co.uk

Looking for a special gift for Christmas, Easter, Mothers Day, Fathers Day, Valentines Day, a Wedding, a Birthday,......or any other occasion? Look no further than the **Chocolate Bar**, which offers a wide range of the finest Belgian chocolates available in Rutland. There is also a selection of gluten-free, sugar-free and dairy-free chocs, along with orgainic and Fairtrade chocolate. The Chocolate Bar was opened in 2001 by two chocoholic friends Sharon and Lesley, who transformed a small café and unexceptional chocolate shop into this thriving business. In addition to the mouthwatering display of individual chocolates, they have novelty chocolate gifts

  and personally gift-boxed chocolates.

In the Café, a treat not to be missed is the Chocolate Bar Special – the finest hot chocolate laden with whipped cream, a smattering of marshmallows adorned with a flake and crowned with a dusting of cocoa powder. The menu also offers savoury snacks and something more substantial as well as lots of lovely cakes. Customers can order their chocolates by phone or on the website for delivery anywhere in the UK.

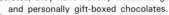

🎬 stories and anecdotes   🦜 famous people   🎨 art and craft   🎭 entertainment and sport   🚶 walks

Rutland Railway Museum

Ashwell Road, Cottesmore, Oakham,
Rutland LE15 7BX
Tel: 0572 813203

Located in the pleasant countryside of the ancient county of Rutland, four miles from Oakham, the Museum is dedicated to telling the story of railways in industry, especially local ironstone quarrying. It goes back to the days before mass road transport when most freight was carried by rail and factories, works and quarries had their own railway systems.

The Museum's open air steam centre hosts a large collection of steam and diesel locomotives, wagons, vans and coaches, together with other related items and artefacts. Train rides and demonstrations are a regular feature of steam days – part of the ongoing development and restoration of the Museum site by volunteer members.

🏛 historic building   🏛 museum   🏛 historic site   🏞 scenic attraction   🌱 flora and fauna

CROMWELL HOUSE

76 High Street, Oakham, Rutland LE15 6AS
Tel: 01572 724364
website: www.cromwellhouseselfcatering.co.uk

The team behind Swans Antiques also own **Cromwell House**, a handsome Regency townhouse in the centre of Oakham. Two newly converted and fully serviced luxury apartments are available for private or corporate lets, combining the standards of a top-class hotel with the space, comfort and amenities of a home environment. Each of the apartments occupies an entire floor and consists of a double bedroom (king size bed, hairdryer, personal safe), large lounge, kitchen/diner and bathroom (full-size bath with shower over bath, toilet, basin, heated mirror and towel rail). The lounge is provided with books, tapes, CDs, a hi-fi system and multi-channel TV with video and DVD.

THE OLIVE BRANCH

Clipsham
Tel: 01780 410335 website: www.rutlandinnco.co.uk

The management at Cromwell House have a family link with the **Olive Branch** at nearby Clipsham. Combining the best aspects of country pub and high-class restaurant, it offers visitors an excellent choice of food and drink, from bar snacks and locally brewed cask ales to classic pub food and daily changing menus of fine country cooking complemented by a superb wine selection.

condemned felons going on their last journey from the town gaol first saw, on top of a small rise called Mount Pleasant, the gallows from which they were about to hang.

Around Oakham

TEIGH

5 miles N of Oakham on a minor road

Teigh (pronounced 'tea') is one of the 31 'Thankful Villages', those communities where all the men and women who served in World War I survived. A brass inscription in the church gives thanks for the safe return of the 11 men and two women from the village who came back.

The Old Rectory, which stands next to the Strawberry Hill-style Gothic church, has a delightful partly-walled garden that was first laid out in the 1950s.

COTTESMORE

5 miles NE of Oakham on the B668

Railway Museum

The **Rutland Railway Museum** (see panel opposite) is the big attraction here. The working steam/diesel museum is based on local quarry and industrial railways. The open-air steam centre is home to a large collection of steam and diesel locomotives, wagons, vans and coaches, together with many related items and artefacts. Call 01572 813203 for details of steam days and gala days. A little further along the B668 is the village of Greetham on the Viking Way, one of the three long-distance walks that converge on Oakham.

stories and anecdotes   famous people   art and craft   entertainment and sport   walks

Hambleton Peninsula

Distance: *3.7 miles (6.0 kilometres)*

Typical time: *90 mins*

Height gain: *0 metres*

Map: *Explorer 15 Rutland Water*

Walk: *www.walkingworld.com ID:29*

Contributor: *Nicholas Rudd-Jones*

Turning off A606About 8 miles form A1/ StamfordPark the car at the pub (if you intend to use it later) or in the road just outside.

Rutland Water is a created lake, supplying water to the east Midlands. It is basically a huge success story, attracting lots of active visitors.

A very pleasant walk around the edge of the Hambleton Peninsula, which looks out in all directions over Rutland Water, a man-made success. Rutland Water has many leisure pursuits, notably sailing and cycling. It's a very good place to come with the family.

The walk itself is simple, suitable for all ages with lots to distract youngsters. The Finch Arms at the end of the walk is an excellent place for (posh) snacks and refreshment, and welcomes children. It can be very muddy; cyclists can be numerous on Bank Holidays.

Lake/Loch, Pub, Wildlife, Birds, Flowers, Great Views

1 | Cross a cattle-grid at the end of the road, and strike out along a stony track which runs east along the side of the lake. Very shortly you should turn left, pass through another cattle-grid and continue on eastwards. The walk is very straightforward, flat and passing through interesting woods. There is always a lovely view of the lake to your right. Up on the hill on your right, you will soon see a splendid Victorian hunting lodge – Hambleton Hall, now a famous restaurant. After about 2kms the track takes a sharp left inland and then shortly afterwards, just before hitting the road, takes a sharp right.

2 | Go north from this point along the stone track (not down the road). The path soon reaches the other side of the promontory and swings back westwards. Stay on undulating path for about 3kms, until you reach the road.

3 | When you reach the road, turn left – a short walk takes you back to the pub and the car.

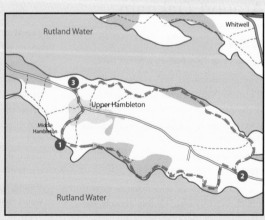

CLIPSHAM
10 miles NE of Oakham off the B668

🌱 Yew Tree Avenue

Just to the east of this small village is one of the most extraordinary sights in the county, **Yew Tree Avenue**. In the 1870s Amos Alexander, head forester to the Clipsham Hall Estate, began clipping the yew trees around his lodge into chimerical shapes – a fantastic parade of animals, chess pieces and abstract forms. The Squire of Clipsham admired them greatly and gave Amos a free hand with the 150 yew trees lining the approach to the hall. Along the 700 yard avenue appeared a dream-like succession of figures, some commemorating local or national events, others recording family events.

Amos died in the early 1900s and the trees were left untended until in 1955 the Forestry Commission assumed responsibility for the avenue and renewed the topiary tradition. Each of the trees is between 15 and 20ft high, and each is shaped individually. An elephant looks across to a ballerina; a Spitfire takes off towards a battleship, Diddy-men cavort near a windmill – there's even a Big Mac hamburger in there somewhere!

EXTON
5 miles NE of Oakham off the A606

🏛 Church 🌱 Barnsdale Gardens

A charming village in one of the largest ironstone extraction areas in the country with a church set in delightful parkland. The **Church of St Peter & St Paul** is remarkable for its wealth of fine monuments, a sumptuous series commemorating members of the Noel and Harington families interred here from the early 1500s to the late 1700s.

This imposing collection is dominated by a colossal memorial to Baptist Noel, 3rd Viscount Campden, who died in 1683. Sculpted in black and white marble by Grinling Gibbons, it stands 22ft high and 14ft wide, almost filling one wall of the north transept. A lengthy inscription extols Viscount Campden's many fine qualities which had "justly rendered him the admiration of his contemporaries and the imitation of postery".

Barnsdale Gardens, in The Avenue, were made familiar to millions by the late Geoff Hamilton, who designed the gardens, on TV's *Gardeners' World*. They are now run by his son and daughter-in-law and embrace many themes, including cottage, allotment and kitchen gardens, woodland, parterre and town and country paradises. Open all year.

EGLETON
1 mile E of Oakham on a minor road

🌱 Birdwatching Centre

Egleton is home to **Anglian Water's Birdwatching Centre**, located on two storeys on the west shore. It has an osprey platform with CCTV.

EDITH WESTON
5 miles E of Oakham off the A6003

🏛 Normanton Church

This village takes its name from Edith, wife and then widow of King Edward the Confessor (1042-66), who gave her this part of the county as a gift. A peaceful spot in the heart of really lovely countryside on the south shore of Rutland Water. Near the village, off the A606 and A6121, stands Rutland's best-known landmark. **Normanton Church**, on the very edge of Rutland Water, was formerly part of the Normanton Estate and now houses a display dedicated to the construction of the reservoir by Anglian Water and a history of the area. Open April to September. The estate was the property of the big local landowner Sir Gilbert Heathcote, sometime Lord Mayor of London, who pulled down the village of Normanton to enlarge his park and moved the villagers to nearby Empingham.

EMPINGHAM
5 miles E of Oakham on the A606

🏛 Dovecote   🌱 Butterfly Farm & Aquatic Centre

This pleasant little town is dominated by the tower and spire of St Peter's Church, whose interior features include fragments of ancient glass. In a field just outside the village stands a well-preserved **Dovecote** containing 700 nests. It could have been in this very field that one of the bloodiest slaughters of the Wars of the Roses took place, on 12th March 1470 – in all, some 10,000 men were killed. This gory clash of arms became known as the Battle of Losecoat Field because the defeated Lancastrians shed their uniforms as they fled in the hope of avoiding recognition, capture and certain death.

At Sykes Lane, North Shore, just west of Empingham, is the Rutland Water **Butterfly Farm & Aquatic Centre**. A great place to spend a few hours, with 5,000 square feet of walk-through jungle that is home to free-flying butterflies and tropical birds. Other creatures at the centre include koi carp, terrapins, iguanas, tarantulas, tropical creepy-crawlies and monitor lizards. Open daily April to October.

TICKENCOTE
8 miles NE of Oakham off the A1

🏛 Church

Apart from Canterbury Cathedral there is nothing in England to compare with the astonishing Norman sexpartite vaulting over the chancel of the parish **Church of St Peter** in the tiny village of Tickencote. Equally breathtaking is the chancel arch, a mighty six-layered portal leading to a miniscule nave beyond. Built around 1140, each of the overlapping six arches is carved with a different design – foliage, chevrons, double zig-zags, beak-head ornament or just plain round mouldings. In addition to these masterpieces of Norman architecture, St Peter's also contains a remarkably fine 13th century font and an unusual wooden life-size effigy of a 14th century knight.

LITTLE CASTERTON
9 miles E of Oakham via the A606/A1

🏛 Tolethorpe Hall

Tolethorpe Hall, just off the A1 and close to the Lincolnshire border, is best known as the home of the Stamford Shakespeare

Tickencote Church

Company, which each summer performs three different plays on an open-air stage in an idyllic woodland setting facing a 600-seat covered auditorium. The old manor house has another claim to fame as the birthplace in 1550 of Robert Browne, one of the earliest 'congregationalists'. His radical views led to his arrest and it was only through the intervention of his kinsman Lord Burghley that he was released. Browne's religious views mellowed with the passing of the years – his fiery temper did not. At the age of 80 Browne was consigned to Northampton for an assault on a constable and it was there that he died in 1633.

PICKWORTH
9 miles NE of Oakham off the A1

Pickworth's most famous resident was John Clare, surely one of the saddest figures in the pantheon of English poets. Born in 1793 in a village near Peterborough, Clare came to Pickworth as a young man, finding work on a nearby farm. Over the course of a year he managed to save £1 from his meagre wages

and used it to publish a prospectus of his poems. The poems were eventually published, in 1820, but did not sell. Poverty, poor health and incipient madness stalked him throughout his life. His happiest years may well have been spent at Pickworth for it was here that he met 18-year-old Patty Turner whom he immortalised in one of his most charming poems:

And I would go to Patty's cot,
And Patty came to me,
Each knew the other's every thought
Under the hawthorn tree.
And I'll be true for Patty's sake
And she'll be true for mine,
And I this little ballad make
To be her Valentine.

They married soon afterwards and eventually had seven children. But Clare was working beyond his strength and gradually his habitual melancholy deteriorated into madness. He spent the last 27 years of his life in asylums. His youngest son went to see him once; Patty could never bring herself to visit.

LOCATOR MAP

ADVERTISERS AND PLACES OF INTEREST

🏠 historic building   🏛 museum   🏛 historic site   🏞 scenic attraction   🌱 flora and fauna

9 | Northamptonshire

Although it is a relatively small county, Northamptonshire has a lot to offer but, as it is crossed by some of the country's major routes, it is also one that is often bypassed. The county town, Northampton, along with other local towns, is famed for its shoe industry although Northamptonshire remains, essentially, a farming county littered with ancient market towns and rural villages. However, it is its long history that is most interesting – the decisive battle of Naseby was fought on its soil and it was at the now ruined Fotheringay Castle that Mary Queen of Scots was executed.

Northamptonshire is shaped like a laurel leaf, with the River Nene a distinctive feature. Wherever one journeys across the county one is never far from its banks and the reflection of the trees in high summer on its shimmering waters can be quite breathtaking. The alluvial soils and gravel terraces of the Nene Valley have been continuously farmed since Neolithic times and there are remains of many Anglo-Saxon settlements.

A county of great landowners, Northamptonshire also has many royal connections. The original Rockingham Castle was built by William the Conqueror; Richard III was born at Fotheringhay Castle, Mary Queen of Scots was beheaded there; Charles I spent several months in captivity at Holdenby Hall, at that time the largest house in England; and in more recent times, Althorp entered the national consciousness as the childhood home of Diana, Princess of Wales, and as her final resting place.

Another royal death is commemorated by the two elaborate Eleanor Crosses erected by a grieving King Edward I to mark the places where the coffin bearing his wife Eleanor to London from Nottinghamshire rested overnight. One is at Geddington, near Kettering; the second on the outskirts of Northampton; only two others of the original 12 crosses survive.

The county boasts two extraordinary Elizabethan buildings – the Triangular Lodge at Rushton, and Lyveden New Bield near Brigstock, both of them expressing a deeply religious symbolism. The roll-call of outstanding churches in the county includes All Saints at Brixworth, one of the finest Anglo-Saxon churches in England and the only one still in use; the tiny church at Slapton with its glorious medieval wall paintings; and the Church of the Holy Sepulchre in Northampton – the largest and best-preserved Norman round church in the country.

Land-locked though it is, Northamptonshire has an abundance of canals, rivers and lakes. The River Nene is navigable right from the Wash into the heart of Northampton and links up with the Grand Union Canal. The Canal Museum in the popular canalside village of Stoke Bruerne provides an insight into 200 years of history and traditions on the county's waterways.

Sporting enthusiasts will find plenty to interest them, including National Hunt racing at Towcester, football (Northampton Town, Rushden & Diamonds), motor racing at Silverstone which has hosted the Formula 1 Grand Prix for the past 10 years, drag racing at Santa Pod.....and the world conker championships at Ashton near Oundle!

Northampton

🏛 Church of the Holy Sepulchre   🏛 Guildhall

🏛 Briar Hill   🏛 Eleanor Cross

🏛 Central Museum & Art Gallery

🏛 Abington Museum   🍃 Nene White Water Centre

Much of its face is modern, but the capital of
the county has a wealth of history for the
visitor to discover. At least 6,000 years ago a
camp was set up at **Briar Hill**, and more recent
traces of early settlements in the area date from
between 700BC and 50AD. The Domesday
Book of 1086 shows Northampton as a town
of 300 houses, comparable in size to Derby or
Nottingham. Richard I granted the town its
first charter in 1189 and, by the
13th century, Northampton had
become a major market town, and
its market square, dating from that
period, is reputed to be the second
largest in the country.

For centuries Northampton has
been associated with the
shoemaking trade. Tradition has it
that in 1213 a pair of boots was
made here for King John, and the
first large order came in 1642
when 4,000 pairs of shoes and
600 pairs of boots were made for
the army. The industry grew
rapidly throughout the county and
by the end of the 1800s, 40% of
the population was involved in
the shoe trade. People like Philip
Manfield and William Barrett
were just two of the major players
who started their businesses in
Northampton and grew them into
extensive chains. William Barrett
gave his name to the maternity

hospital, and Manfield gave his to another of
the town's hospitals. St Crispin, the patron
saint of shoemakers, is portrayed in several
churches, and Northampton Town Football
Club are known as the Cobblers. The **Central
Museum and Art Gallery** has the world's
largest collection of footwear, showing shoe
fashions down the centuries and the machines
that made the shoes. There is also an
outstanding collection of British and Oriental
ceramics, leathercraft from around the world
and some fine paintings including Italian
works of the 15th to 18th centuries and
British art. The **Abington Museum**, set in a
15th century manor house in Abington Park,
has a number of interesting exhibits, including

Church of the Holy Sepulchre

a room with 16th century oak panelling, exhibits detailing the county's military history, a 19th century fashion gallery, and a display titled "Northampton Life – from the cradle to the grave".

Northampton has two outstanding churches: All Saints, designed by Henry Bell in the Wren style, with ornate plasterwork by Edward Goudge and two organs by JS Walker; and the wonderful **Church of the Holy Sepulchre,** one of only four remaining round churches in the kingdom. Founded by Simon de Senlis, 1st Earl of Northampton, to commemorate his safe return from the Crusades in 1100, it is often known as the "Soldiers Church" and carries battle scars from the Wars of the Roses. It is the oldest standing building in Northampton and is almost identical to the original in Jerusalem.

The most prestigious building in town is certainly the **Guildhall,** a gem of Victorian architecture built in 1864 by Edward Godwin and later extended by Matthew Holding and Arnold Jeffrey. Grand tours of the building take in the old prison cells, the Mayor's parlour, the Great Hall, the Godwin Room and the Council Chamber. The Royal Theatre is another Victorian gem, built in 1884 in opulent Italianate style and home to one of the oldest repertory companies in England. The Welsh House, one of the few buildings to survive the disastrous fire of 1675, dates from 1595 and recalls the time when Welsh drovers would bring their cattle to the market. Another striking building is No. 78 Derngate, designed by the Scottish architect Charles Rennie Mackintosh.

In 1290 the funeral procession of Queen Eleanor, wife of Edward I, stopped for the night at Delapre Abbey. In the south of town, at **Hardingstone** on the London Road A508,

stands one of the three surviving **Eleanor Crosses** of the 12 originally erected to mark each night of the progress of the mournful cortege to London. See under Geddington for more about the Eleanor Crosses.

Northampton boasts more than 150 parks and open spaces, most notably **Abington Park** with lakes, aviaries and the museum mentioned above. Northampton's racecourse is the setting for the International Hot Air Balloon Festival, a summer highlight that attracts visitors from far and wide. Other outdoor attractions include Delapre Park, where the Cluniac Abbey was built in 1145; and Hunsbury Hill Country Park, where the Iron Age hill fort can still be seen – this park is also home to the Northamptonshire Ironstone Railway Trust's museum and railway. Northampton's sports and leisure facilities are abundant: two of the best are Billing Aquadrome with extensive fishing and moorings and, opened in 1999, the **Nene White Water Centre** with facilities for canoeing, rafting, rowing and orienteering.

Around Northampton

EARLS BARTON
5 miles NE of Northampton off the A45

⛪ Church of All Saints

A great treasure here is the village **Church of All Saints**, with one of the most impressive Anglo-Saxon towers in the whole country, its surface adorned with purely decorative masonry strips. The tower is 10th century, the south doorway is 12th, the aisles are 13th, the tower arch 14th, the south porch 19th but they all co-exist in great architectural harmony. Beyond the remarkably well-preserved Norman doorway the most amazing sight is

JEYES OF EARL BARTON

26-28 The Square, Earls Barton,
Northamptonshire NN6 0NA
Tel: 01604 810289 Fax: 01604 810289
e-mail: info@dollylodge.com
website: www.dollylodge.com

You'll be amazed what you will find behind the chemist door at **Jeyes on The Square** in Earls Barton. David and Georgina Jeyes established their traditional local pharmacy over 25 years ago. Family roots go back to Philadelphus Jeyes in The Drapery, Northampton and the well-known Jeyes Fluid, invented by John Jeyes in 1810 but still used worldwide today. Together they have built a treasure trove of varied shops all under one roof. **The Keepsake Gift Shop** in the old Nat West Bank, **The Dolly Lodge**, a unique and fascinating dolls house shop, with **The Dolly Lodge Den** for children. The Dolls and Teddy Kingdom is special too.

Enjoy refreshments in the friendly **Apothocoffee Shop** with the **Walled Garden** open on warm, summer days. There are even books for the whole family and local interest books too. **Earls Barton's Museum of Village Life** with free entry is a fascinating insight into Victorian life, and a display of **Jeyes Pharmacy Memorabilia**.

The family cannot stand still - so new for Easter 2007 is a conservatory for **Potty About Flowers** - special gifts for flower lovers - everyone has a favourite flower and here you will find a gift to match. Friends can catch up in comfort in **The Blossom Tea Lounge**. No wonder everyone calls Jeyes an Aladdin's Cave. Pay a visit soon, you will receive a warm welcome. Open: Monday - Saturday, 8.30am - 5.30pm. Free parking.

the 15th century chancel screen, ablaze with hundreds of dazzling butterflies on the wing; next to it is a wonderful, heavily carved Jacobean pulpit in black oak.

CASTLE ASHBY
6 miles E of Northampton off the A428

🏛 Castle   ✐ Craft Centre

Two major attractions for the visitor here. **Castle Ashby** is a fine Elizabethan mansion, home of the Marquess of Northampton, standing in Capability Brown parkland with Victorian gardens and a lake. The building of Castle Ashby was started in 1574 on the site of a 13th century castle that had been demolished. The original plan of the building was in the shape of an 'E' in honour of Queen Elizabeth I, and is typical of many

Elizabethan houses. About 60 years later the courtyard was enclosed by a screen designed by Inigo Jones. One of the features of Castle Ashby is the lettering around the house and terraces. The inscriptions, which are in Latin, read when translated *"The Lord guard your coming in"* and *"The Lord guard your going out"*. Inside there is some wonderful restoration furniture and paintings of the English and Renaissance schools.

On a much smaller scale the old **Manor House** makes a delightful picture by the church; it has a dungeon and there is a 13th century window with exquisite tracery set in the oldest part of the house near a blocked Norman arch. The poet, Cowper, loved to wander amongst the trees, some of which are said to have been planted by the Countess

THE BUTTERY CAFÉ & VANILLA JADE

The Rural Shopping Yard, Castle Ashby,
Northamptonshire NN7 1LF
Tel: 01604 696728 (Buttery)
01604 696515 (Vanilla Jade)

Brick buildings set around a farm courtyard have been converted into two delightful enterprises, the **Buttery Café** and **Vanilla Jade**.

Kate Brown's coffee shop provides a very pleasant, relaxed setting for enjoying a cup of excellent coffee with a snack. Savoury choices include soup, panini, made-to-order plain and toasted sandwiches and jacket potatoes, while among the home-made cakes are coffee & walnut, banana, carrot, tea loaf, slices, flapjacks and brownies. Traditional cream teas feature freshly baked scones with fresh cream and strawberry jam. The coffee shop has seats for 38 inside and 20 more under sunshades in the yard.

In the same location, Kate also owns Vanilla Jade, a lovely little boutique filled with clothes, gift ideas and things for the home and garden. Among the goods on display, all personally chosen by Kate, are ladies' light, informal clothes, handbags, jewellery, kitchenware, mugs, soft toys, candles, fragrances, greetings cards and garden accessories – a great place to find a treat or a gift that's just that little bit different. The café and the shop are both open Tuesday to Sunday and Bank Holiday Mondays.

Judith herself. The tree that attracts the most visitors is called Cowper's Oak, the branches of which spread twice as far across as the tree is high. There is a tradition that it will never die because Cowper stood beneath it one day during a heavy thunderstorm and was inspired to write his famous hymn: *"God moves in Mysterious Ways"*.

Castle Ashby Craft Centre & Rural Shopping Yard is set in an old farmyard and comprises a farm shop and delicatessen, craft shops, pottery, goldsmith's studio, art gallery and tea room.

HORTON

6 miles SE of Northampton on the B526

🌱 The Menagerie

A mile south of the village a gate leads off the road and across fields to **The Menagerie**, a fascinating garden surrounding the great house (pulled down in 1936) where Lord Halifax once had a private zoo. A lime avenue, water gardens, a rose garden and thatched arbours are among the delights of a garden that is still being developed. A distinguished son of Horton was Ralph Lane, the first Governor of Virginia.

SALCEY FOREST

8 miles S of Northampton off the B526

Reached from the A508 at Roade or the B526 between Horton and Stoke Goldington, the 1,250-acre Salcey Forest has been owned and managed by the Forestry Commission since the 1920s. Part of the chain of ancient Royal Hunting Forests that stretched from Stamford

THE SARACENS HEAD

Main Street, Little Brington,
Northamptonshire NN7 4HS
Tel: 01604 770640
e-mail: info@thesaracensatbrington.co.uk

The Saracens Head is a friendly inn on the main street of Little Brington, which lies in pleasant countryside between Northampton and Daventry. The Evans family – Duncan, Sarah and their son Tom – have a warm welcome for visitors of all ages, whether they've come for a quick drink, a meal or an overnight or longer stay. The interior has bags of old-world appeal, with exposed beams and brickwork, flagstones, sturdy darkwood furniture, old advertising boards – even an authentic red telephone box. There are seats for 70 inside, and 80 more outside, providing a year-round choice for enjoying a glass or two of the well-kept real ales.

Food is an important part of the inn's business and regularly attracts diners from all over the region. The talented team in the kitchen prepare an impressive selection of dishes from a repertoire that takes its inspiration from around the world. Thai mussels delicately fragranced with coconut cream will get the meal off to a delicious start, followed perhaps by sea bass with chilli, ginger, garlic and lime; braised lamb shanks; or richly-sauced beef with Guinness with a puff-pastry topping. There's always a good choice for vegetarians, and desserts such as home-made bread & butter pudding or honey-glazed mango with Greek yoghurt are very hard to resist. Lunch snacks include sandwiches (white or brown baguette or tortilla wrap) with interesting fillings like chicken, boursin & spinach or hot gammon with red onion chutney. Good food deserves good wine, and there's a well-chosen selection on offer at this outstanding inn.

Guest accommodation comprises three well-appointed en suite double rooms and a twin-bedded room. This is first-class walking country, and one marked walk of about four miles crosses arable and grazing fields in the vicinity of Althorp House. There are also several bridal paths in the vicinity, and the inn has a paddock where guests can keep their horses.

🏛 historic building   🏛 museum   🏛 historic site   ♤ scenic attraction   ☘ flora and fauna to Oxford, it produces quality timber while providing a home for a wide variety of animal and plant life, and recreational facilities for the public. There are three circular trails at Salcey, named after the three woodpeckers found there: the Lesser Spotted Trail of a leisurely hour; the Great Spotted Trail of about two miles; and, for the more energetic, the Green Woodpecker Trail of about 2½ hours. The forest is open to visitors all year round.

CHAPEL BRAMPTON
4 miles NW of Northampton off the A508

🏛 Northampton & Lamport Railway

Steam train buffs will want to pay a visit to the **Northampton & Lamport Railway**, which is home to an interesting collection of railway-related vehicles. Visitors can enjoy a journey hauled by vintage locomotives; there are heritage displays and special events throughout the year. Trains run regularly on Sundays and Bank Holiday Mondays, March to November, from Pitsford and Brampton Station. More details on 01604 820327.

ALTHORP
5 miles NW of Northampton off the A428

The home of the Spencer family since 1508, Althorp remains exactly that – a classic family-owned English stately home that the Spencers have stamped with their style ever since John Spencer, a large-scale sheep farmer, acquired the estate. The present house was begun in 1573, and behind the stark tiling of the exterior is a wealth of fine paintings, sculpture,

porcelain and furniture. Known widely by connoisseurs for generations, Althorp is now known across the whole world since the tragic death of Diana, Princess of Wales, in 1997. She lies in peace in the beautiful, tranquil setting of the Round Oval, an ornamental lake, surrounded by her family's ancestral heritage. For many centuries the Spencers were buried at nearby Great Brington, where the church has memorials to 20 generations (see walk on page 398).

HOLDENBY
7 miles NW of Northampton off the A428

🏛 Holdenby Hall

The Royal connections go back more than 400 years at **Holdenby Hall**, which was built by Elizabeth I's Lord Chancellor and favourite, Sir Christopher Hatton, for the purpose of entertaining the Queen. At the time, it was the largest Elizabethan house in England and, for the diarist John Evelyn, "one of the most pleasing sights that ever I saw". It was visited but once by Elizabeth; it later became the palace and eventually the prison of Charles I, who was kept under guard here for five months after his defeat in the Civil War. The house, which appeared as Limmeridge House

Holdenby Hall

Great and Little Brington

Distance: *4.3 miles (6.9 kilometres)*

Typical time: *120 mins*

Height gain: *55 metres*

Map: *Explorer 223, Landranger 152*

Walk: *www.walkingworld.com ID:2025*

Contributor: *Peter Chrighton*

ACCESS INFORMATION:

There is a car park at the Saracens Head pub in Little Brington. If visiting Althorp House, there is a car park at the front entrance to the grounds that is on the route of the walk (start at Waymark 5).

From M1 J16, take the A45 towards Northampton. Turn left at the roundabout. Follow the road to the end and turn left at the next roundabout. Take the second right into Little Brington after 4.5km. Turn left into Main Street and park in the Saracens Head car park.

DESCRIPTION:

The walk starts and finishes at The Saracens Head pub in Little Brington and is across arable and grazing fields in the vicinity of Althorp House, the resting-place of Princess Diana. It is an easy walk and could be combined with a visit to the house (tickets required). The church in Great Brington is often open. The walk is over rolling agricultural land, giving good views of the countryside and also has views of Althorp House.

FEATURES:

Pub, Church, Stately Home, Wildlife, Birds, Butterflies, Gift Shop, Mostly Flat, Woodland, Ancient Monument

WALK DIRECTIONS:

1 | From the Saracens Head turn east along Main Street to follow the road for 100m. Continue straight ahead at the end of the road onto a track alongside a house and pass through the gate. At the next gate aim straight ahead, ignoring the footpath to the right. This takes you onto Carriage Drive, which although not a public right of way, the Althorp Estate permits walking along to the next footpath. Follow the drive for 900m.

2 | Turn left onto the footpath through the gap in the hedge. Cross the stile and walk straight ahead, aiming for the right-hand end of the houses.

3 | Go through the gate and along the drive for 100m. At the footpath sign to Harlestone turn right and walk along the driveway down the side of the house.

4 | Where the footpath splits in two (no signposts), keep following the path straight ahead, ignoring the path to the left. Enter the wood and follow the path around to the left.

5 | At the road turn left and follow it for 400m, with views of Althorp House. Turn left and walk up the avenue of trees to Great Brington church, another path that Althorp Estate permits one to use although not a public right of way.

6 | At the end of the avenue of trees, turn right to reach the car park for Great Brington church.

right, aiming for the left-hand end of the trees, to a gate. Go through the gate. Head diagonally across the field, slightly to the right of the clump of trees. At the corner of the field go through the small gate and turn left onto the road. Follow the road for 500m.

11|At the first footpath on the left, cross the stile and follow the right-hand edge of the field up to the edge of the woods. Go through the gate and follow the edge of the woods. As the edge of the wood turns to the left, head diagonally across the field, to the right of the telegraph pole in the distance. Following the marker-post, head uphill with the next section of woodland on the right. Cross the stile and take the footpath straight ahead, following the line of the telegraph poles.

12|At the hedge field boundary, walk straight ahead with the hedge on your right. Follow the footpath straight ahead across three fields. At this point you join the Macmillan Way. Head across the field, aiming for the footpath to the right of the metal shed.

13|Go through the gate to the right of the metal shed and walk straight ahead along the right-hand edge of the narrow field. Turn left to reach the car park.

7|From the car park, head east along the road for 100m. At the footpath sign, turn right and cross through the field. Continue straight ahead at the avenue of trees. Climb over the stile and continue ahead along the right-hand side of the field.

8|Go through the gate and follow the left-hand edge of the field, continuing through the next gate. Continue through the kissing-gate on the pathway between the houses.

9|At the road turn left and follow it for 100m. Turn right at the next road and follow to its end (a further 100m).

10|At the end of the road, continue straight ahead into the field. Then head slightly to the in the BBC's *The Woman in White*, stands in magnificent grounds, which contain a falconry centre, a smaller scale reconstruction of Hatton's original garden, a fully working armoury and a 17th century farmstead that evokes the sights and smells of life in days gone by. There's a museum, a children's farm and a lakeside train ride together with tea in the Victorian Kitchen.

EAST HADDON
7 miles NW of Northampton off the A428

🌿 Haddonstone Showgardens

A village of thatched cottages, a village pump protected by a neat thatched cone, a 14th century church and an 18th century hall. It is best known for **Haddonstone Showgardens**, which has walled gardens on different levels and a huge stock of garden ornaments of every kind.

GUILSBOROUGH
9 miles NW of Northampton off the A5199

🌿 Coton Manor Garden

A handsome, dignified village where Wordsworth came to stay in the vicarage and, it is said, brought with him the yellow Cumberland poppy that is often seen here. The church has lovely windows by William Morris and Burne-Jones, and Guilsborough Grange has a wildlife park and areas for walking and picnicking. A short distance south of the village, in the tiny community of Coton, **Coton Manor Garden** is a traditional garden originally laid out in 1925 and embracing several delightful smaller gardens. Beyond the garden are a wildflower meadow and a magical five-acre bluebell wood. The nursery

propagates over 1,000 varieties of plant, and in the stable yard are a restaurant and tea room.

KINGSTHORPE
2 miles N of Northampton on the A508

Once a small riverside village, Kingsthorpe is now effectively a suburb of Northampton but its ancient church still looks across meadows to the River Nene. Inside, there are some massive Norman arches with varied ornamental carving.

PITSFORD
4 miles N of Northampton off the A508

Off the A508 just north of the village, Pitsford Water is an 800-acre reservoir with trout fishing and boats for hire, sailing, a picnic area, nature reserve and information

Pitsford

centre. The reservoir is also accessible from the village of Holcot.

COTTESBROOKE
9 miles N of Northampton off the A5199

🏠 Cottesbrooke Hall

In secluded countryside near the site of the Battle of Naseby, **Cottesbrooke Hall** is one of the finest of all the grand houses in the county. The magnificent Queen Anne house, reputedly the model for Jane Austen's *Mansfield Park*, was begun in 1702 and is home to an impressive collection of pictures, porcelain and furniture. The grounds are quite superb, featuring the Statue Walk (statues from the Temple of Ancient Virtue, at Stowe), the Dilemma Garden with old roses and rare trees, the Dutch Garden, the Pine Court and many other charming gardens and courtyards. The hall and gardens are open to visitors on certain days in the summer.

Daventry

🏛 Museum ⛰ Borough Hill ⚔ Country Park

Old and new blend intriguingly in this historic market town whose streets are shared by dignified Georgian houses and modern shops. A colourful market is held along the High Street every Tuesday and Friday, and in the Market Place stands the Moot Hall, built in 1769 of ironstone. Originally a private house, it became the moot hall, or town hall, in 1806 after the former town hall was demolished. It is now home to the Tourist Information Centre and to **Daventry Museum**, which illustrates the social history of the town and its environs. It also shows regularly changing arts and crafts exhibitions and contains archaeological finds from **Borough Hill** and some of the equipment used by the BBC

when it had a transmitter station on the hill. The oval hill, which rises to 650 feet above sea level, is more than two miles round and covers an area of 150 acres. It was the third largest Iron Age hill fort in Britain and in more recent times was topped by the huge radio masts that transmitted the World Service of the BBC. This was the site of the world's first radar station, masterminded by Sir Robert Watson-Watt, a descendant of steam pioneer James Watt.

Daventry was once an important stop on the coaching routes, and it is said that King Charles I spent several days at the Wheatsheaf Inn before the Battle of Naseby, where he lost the battle and his kingdom. Shakespeare mentions the town in *King Henry IV (Part 1)*, when Falstaff tells Bardolph the tale of a shirt stolen from a "red-nose innkeeper". During the coaching era the chief industry of Daventry was whip-making.

Daventry Country Park is a beautiful 133-acre site centred on the old Daventry Reservoir. Coarse fishing, a picnic area, adventure playground, nature trails, nature reserve and visitor centre are among the amenities. Open daily all year.

Around Daventry

ASHBY ST LEDGERS
3 miles N of Daventry on the A361

📖 Gunpowder Plot

From 1375 to 1605 the manor house at Ashby was the home of the Catesby family, and it was in a room above the gatehouse that Guy Fawkes is said to have met Robert Catesby to hatch the **Gunpowder Plot**. On the 5th of November, 1605, Catesby rode the 80 miles from London in seven hours with the news

---

📖 stories and anecdotes   🐦 famous people   🎨 art and craft   🖋 entertainment and sport   🚶 walks

ABRAXAS COOKSHOP

The Heart of the Shires Shopping Village, Top Floor,
Barn Arcade,
A5 - 2 miles North of Weedon,
Northamptonshire NN7 4LB
Tel: 01327 341080 Fax: 01327 341740
e-mail: info@abraxascookshop.com
website: www.abraxascookshop.com

When Sarah George and Helen Sparrow met for coffee at The Heart of The Shires Shopping Village in 1996 and looked at an empty unit, they had little idea of what was to be the result. Eleven years later, and winners of no less than eight awards for Excellence in Housewares, including *Cook & Housewares* Retailer of The Year 2005, the flagship store has expanded into three local towns, Rugby, Banbury and Northampton.

Abraxas Cookshop, situated on the top floor of the Barn Arcade at The Heart of The Shires Shopping Village, is one of the finest of its kind and has been described as "an inspired shopping experience". The family-run and owned business with the emphasis on quality goods and personal customer service together with the warm and convivial atmosphere created by the highly trained friendly staff. makes this a magical journey not to be missed.

Abraxas Cookshop is an 'Aladdin's cave' of cookware for use by the everyday cook to the professional chef. The layout of the shop is in different sections for easy exploration by the customer. Begin at the Aga section carrying a varied selection of Aga cookware, bakeware and accessories then browse the many saucepan ranges on offer, brands include Mauviel French copper, Swift Supreme, Meyer-Prestige, Hahn, Fissler and Stellar. Moving on past butchers blocks and kitchen work stations, salt & pepper mills, pestle & mortars, chopping boards, steamers and frying pans customers arrive at the electrical section housing KitchenAid, Magimix, Cuisinart and Dualit food mixers, blenders, coffee machines and toasters in an array of eye-catching colours and finishes. Customers can then peruse the Nigella Lawson designer range and the complete range of Le Creuset cast-iron cookware together with textiles and accessories. Spend some time in our specialist bakeware section where everything from roasting pans, speciality cake tins and silicone bakeware is available. Abraxas Cookshop also stocks a large range of knives; brands include Global, Sabatier, Wusthof, Henckels, I.O.Shen, Porsche and Victorinox. Tools, gadgets, textiles and jam making equipment are all housed in a large central area.

Extend this unique experience by visiting other shops on the site owned by the sisters, namely Abraxas China & Glass (stocking the entire Emma Bridgewater range), Dressage Outdoor Clothing and Ladies Fashions, The Garden Room and The Pickle Room, all on site at The Heart of The Shires Shopping Village.

For more information visit the website – www.abraxascookshop.com

🏛 historic building   🖼 museum   🏚 historic site   🐟 scenic attraction   🌱 flora and fauna

IN THE CELLAR UPSTAIRS

The Heart of the Shires Shopping Village,
A5 (Watling Street), 2 miles N of Weedon,
Northamptonshire NN7 4LB
Tel: 01327 342263
e-mail: merc300sl@hotmail.co.uk

The Heart of the Shires Shopping Village is a beautiful courtyard of model farm buildings dating from 1867 and comprising an exquisite array of shops and tearooms. One of the most interesting for browsers and buyers is **In the Cellar Upstairs**. It is owned and run by Kimberley Egan-Humphries, who moved here from nearby Weedon, where she cleared the stock from her cellar and sold it upstairs – hence the name of the new enterprise.

The items on display change constantly, ranging from antique furniture in pine, mahogany, oak and other woods, paintings and prints, mirrors, oriental rugs, clocks, vintage luggage, china, porcelain, glassware, lamps and jewellery. With the rapid turnover of stock, every visit to the Cellar Upstairs is a delight and revelation. Open 10 to 5 Tuesday to Saturday, 11 to 5 Sunday and Bank Holidays.

that the plot had failed. He fled to Holbeach in Staffordshire, where he was shot dead after refusing to surrender. The Church of St Mary & St Leodegarious has much to interest the visitor, including Jacobean box pews, an elaborately carved rood screen, a Norman font, a number of Catesby brasses and, most notably, some medieval wall paintings depicting the Passion of Christ.

FLORE
3 miles E of Daventry on the A45

🐿 Adams Cottage

Called *Flora* in the Domesday Book, the village has a wide green that slopes gently down to the River Nene. **Adams Cottage** was the home of the ancestors of John Adams (1797-1801), President of the United States, whose

son was also President. In the 13th century church are several memorial windows, one of them dedicated to Bruce Capell, an artillery officer who was awarded the Military Cross at the age of 22 for courage and devotion to his wounded men. A simple wooden cross from Flanders hangs on the wall, and his window depicts the farewell between David and Jonathan.

UPPER STOWE
5 miles SE of Daventry off the A5

A short drive up the A5 from Towcester brings the visitor to the village of Upper Stowe and the Old Dairy Farm Centre. The community of Stowe Nine Churches is very oddly named, particularly as there is only one church, late Anglo-Saxon. The story is that the builders tried eight times to build the church but each time the Devil took away the stones. At the ninth attempt they succeeded – hence the name.

CANONS ASHBY
7 miles S of Daventry off the A361

🏛 Canons Ashby House

This pretty village contains the Church of St Mary, once part of the Black Canons' Monastery church and much reduced in size at the time of the Dissolution of the Monasteries. **Canons Ashby House**, built from part of the ecclesiastical building after the Dissolution, is one of the finest of Northamptonshire's great houses. Home of the Dryden family since the 1550s and now in the care of the National Trust, it contains some marvellous Elizabethan wall paintings and sumptuous Jacobean plasterwork. The grounds are equally delightful, with yews, cedars and mulberry trees, terraces and parkland. Open afternoons, April to October, except Thursdays and Fridays.

CHARWELTON
4 miles SW of Daventry on the A361

The chief claim to fame of Charwelton is that it is the spot where the River Cherwell rises, in the cellar of Cherwell House. The river forms the county boundary as it travels south into Oxfordshire before joining the Thames. In the village is a lovely old packhorse bridge.

BYFIELD
5 miles SW of Daventry on the A361

⚲ Boddington Reservoir

The tall tower of the rich-stone 14th century church is one of the major local landmarks. A major leisure attraction just west of the village is **Boddington Reservoir**, a balancing reservoir for the Oxford Canal. A good place to start a walk, or to fish, sail or windsurf on the reservoir itself.

Towcester

📍 Racecourse   📍 Leisure Centre

A busy little place, Towcester is popular with seekers of antiques – there are at least half a dozen different establishments selling antiques.

In Roman times the town was called Lactodorum and it stood on the major highway Watling Street (now the A5). The Romans improved the road and built a fort to guard their troop movements. During the Civil War it was the only Royalist stronghold in the area and in the following centuries it was an important stop on the coaching route between London and Holyhead. By the end of the 18th century there were 20 coaching inns in the town, servicing up to 40 coaches every day. Charles Dickens stayed at the Saracen's Head, then called the Pomfret Hotel, and immortalised it in *The Pickwick Papers*. The parish church of St Lawrence, built on the site of a substantial Roman building, is one of the loveliest in the county, with features from several centuries: the crypt, reached by a doorway from the sanctuary, is 13th century, the arcades 13th and 14th. On the arch of the south chapel is a carved jester's head probably from the 14th century, while the massive tower and the font are from the 1400s. Close to the church is the Chantry House, formerly a school, founded by Archdeacon Sponne in 1447.

Towcester Racecourse is set in the beautiful parkland estate of Easton Neston, the family home of Lord Hesketh. The course, which has its entrance on the A5, came into being in 1876, when the Empress of Austria was staying at Easton Neston and

🏛 historic building   🏛 museum   🏛 historic site   ⚲ scenic attraction   🌿 flora and fauna

PRESENT THINKING

9 Museum Court, Towcester, Northamptonshire NN12 6BX
Tel: 01327 359300
e-mail: jane@present-thinking.co.uk   website: www.present-thinking.co.uk

In a courtyard in the centre of Towcester, **Present Thinking** is an inspired name for one of the most interesting gift and lifestyle shops in the region. Hands-on owner Jane Astle brings her considerable design skills and instinctive sense of style to a collection of gift ideas sourced in large part from individual craftspeople.

There are gifts for all ages and pockets, from handmade silver jewellery from Thailand, to mugs and tea sets, unique photo frames, books, fragrances, silk scarves and handbags and a selection of cards for all occasions. Jane chose Towcester because it is a vibrant, successful market town with a sense of style and confidence that reflects her own values and philosophy.

attended an Easter steeplechase held in her honour. The course now stages about 16 National Hunt meetings a year, including a couple in the evening.

At Springfields, off the A43 south roundabout, **Towcester Leisure Centre** has a five-lane swimming pool, floodlit tennis court, gymnasium, sports hall and art exhibitions.

Around Towcester

GREENS NORTON
1 mile NW of Towcester off the A5

🚶 Knightley Way

A village at the southern end of the 12-mile **Knightley Way**, one of several mapped walking routes in the county. At this point the

Grafton Way takes over, continuing to Cosgrove in the very south of Northamptonshire. The church at Greens Norton is well worth a visit, with its Saxon stonework, Norman font and commemorative brasses of the Green family.

BLISWORTH
3 miles NE of Towcester off the A43

🏛 Blisworth Tunnel

The building of the Grand Union and Oxford Canals brought trade and prosperity to the area and now provides miles of quiet, picturesque walks or boat trips. On the Grand Union Canal, the **Blisworth Tunnel** between Blisworth and Stoke Bruerne, opened in 1805, is the longest in England, at nearly two miles. The pretty village of Blisworth is a mass of

🎭 stories and anecdotes   🦚 famous people   🎨 art and craft   🎵 entertainment and sport   🚶 walks

YOUNGS NURSERIES

33 Northampton Road, Blisworth,
Northamptonshire NN7 3DW
Tel: 01604 858574
e-mail: youngs_nurseries@hotmail.co.uk
website: www.youngs_nurseries.co.uk

On the old A43 (now an unclassified road) between Blisworth and Stoke Bruerne, **Youngs Nurseries** sell a wide selection of plants for house and garden, shrubs and trees, and hanging baskets for all seasons. Many of the plants, including fuchsias and geraniums, are grown on site. There's also an excellent range of accessories, from composts and plant nutriments to pots and planters, fountains, sundials and birdbaths. David and Carolyn Young have built up the business from nothing on a site where their parents had a property and sold produce from a wooden shed.

The nurseries expanded with greenhouses and a brick-built shop selling garden accessories, and the original shop is now the floristry department. David and Carolyn and their friendly, capable staff are always on hand with help and advice for visitors to the nurseries. The Young family, whose name continues in the nurseries, are well known in the area through David and Carolyn's parents and their grandfather, who had a village shop and was an expert tea-blender.

roses in summer, in the cottage gardens, in the Tudor and Jacobean houses and around the 13th century church. The most significant treasure in the church is a high screen of the 15th century complete with doors. Also of interest is a tablet near the altar that tells of the wife of a sergeant-at-arms to Queen Elizabeth I. The tablet records that she lived a maid for 18 years, was a wife for 20 years and a widow for 61, dying in her 99th year.

STOKE BRUERNE

3 miles NE of Towcester off the A508

🏛 Stoke Park   🏛 Canal Museum

A picturesque canalside village at the southern end of the famous Blisworth Tunnel. The canal provides the major attractions, with waterside walks, boat trips to the tunnel and a

visit to the fascinating **Canal Museum**. Housed in a converted corn mill, the museum displays 200 years of canal history and life on the narrow boats (many of which are still in use for pleasure trips). The exhibits include working engines, old photographs, waterway wildlife and the tools used by canal workers and boatmen. The museum, which is open throughout the year, has a tea room and a souvenir shop. The canal has a series of locks at this point, and visitors can stop in the car park at the lower lock on the A508 and walk into the village along the towpath, passing seven locks en route. There are shops, pubs and restaurants at this popular place, which is the perfect location for a family day out and an ideal starting point for a canal holiday.

A private drive on the Stoke Bruerne to

Shutlanger road leads to **Stoke Park**, a great house standing in a 400-acre estate. Attributed to Inigo Jones, the house was built in Palladian style (the first in this country) around 1630 for Sir Francis Crane, head of the Mortlake Tapestry Works. The main house burnt down in 1886, and only the pavilions and a colonnade remain.

SILVERSTONE
4 miles SW of Towcester on the A43

🏛 Church 🏎 British Grand Prix

The home of British motor racing, located off the A43 in the village. The **British Grand Prix** is the highlight of the year, but the circuit hosts a large number of other events, including rounds of the *Auto Trader* touring car championship and the International Historic Car Festival. Members of the public can test their skills in a single-seater racer, a Lotus Elise, a rally car or a 4x4 off-road vehicle.

Tucked away on country roads northwest of Silverstone are two of the many interesting churches for which Northamptonshire is famous. The **Church of St Mary** at **Wappenham** has a sculpture by Giles Gilbert Scott from the renowned family of architects, who had local connections; two fonts; a clock from the 17th century; and brass memorials to the Lovett family.

SLAPTON
4 miles SW of Towcester off the A43 or A45

🏛 Church 🪶 Weedon Lois

Slapton is little more than a hamlet but its tiny **St Botolph's Church,** set on the hillside above the River Tove, contains some of the finest medieval wall paintings in the county. Hidden under limewash for three centuries, the paintings were discovered in the mid-

1800s and magnificently restored. Covering almost all of the interior walls, they colourfully depict Bible stories and scenes from the life and works of various saints. Slight variations in style suggest they belong to two separate periods, one in the late 1200s, the other in the mid-1300s.

The village of **Weedon Lois,** a mile or so to the west of Slapton, is the final resting place of Edith Sitwell (1887-1964). She often visited her brother Sacheverell at his home at nearby Weston. Her grave is marked with a restrained memorial by Henry Moore with a bronze of two intertwined hands depicting Youth and Age. It is inscribed with the last lines of her poem, *The Wind of Early Spring.*

BRACKLEY
10 miles SW of Towcester off the A43 or A422

🏛 School

A town of Saxon origins with houses clustered round a tangle of streets. A castle was built here in the early part of the 12th century, which some accounts claim as the meeting place for the rebel barons who drew up the first version of Magna Carta in 1215. King John did not approve of their proposals, and it took almost a year before he relented and signed. Wool brought prosperity in the Middle Ages, allowing the rebuilding of the Church of St Peter with a fine early English west tower and south aisle. A free hospital and chapel which had been built by Robert le Bossu for the benefit of the poor was sold to Magdalen College, Oxford, in 1484 and halfway through the following century a school was opened on the site. The buildings have been much altered down the years, but the school exists to this day, now known as **Magdalen College Comprehensive School**. A notable landmark on the High Street is the baroque town hall, with its handsome clock

🎬 stories and anecdotes 🪶 famous people 🎨 art and craft 🎭 entertainment and sport 🚶 walks tower, built in 1706 at the instigation of the Duke of Bridgwater. During the 19th century, Brackley was served by two railway companies, the London & North Western and the Great Central, with stations at either end of town. Alas, the lines were axed in the 1960s.

AYNHO
16 miles SW of Towcester on the B4100

🏛 Aynho Park

A peaceful, picturesque limestone village of leafy lanes and lovely old cottages. The former manor house, **Aynho Park**, is a very grand 17th century country house in the care of the Country Houses Association. It was originally the property of the Cartwright family who, it is said, claimed the rents from their tenants in the form of apricots; some apricot trees can still be seen trained into fan shapes and growing on the walls of cottages. The house was burnt down by Royalist troops during the Civil war but was rebuilt by the Cartwrights, who at the same time rebuilt the village church with the same proportions as the house, so the church too has the appearance of a country villa. Later changes were made to the house by Archer and Soane. Public rooms and the grounds are open to the public on Wednesday and Thursday afternoons from May to September. The Wharf at Aynho on the Oxford Canal has holiday boats for hire and a canalside shop.

KING'S SUTTON
15 miles SW of Towcester off the A4260

🏛 Church

Located at the southernmost tip of the county, King's Sutton boasts one of Northamptonshire's finest church towers. The 15th century spire of **Church of St Peter and St Paul** soars almost 200ft towards the heavens and in a county famous for its elegant spires, King's Sutton is unmatched in its beauty. The interior, heavily restored by George Gilbert Scott in 1866, is less inspiring but is worth visiting to see the macabre memorial to Thomas Langton Freke who died in 1769. It represents Christ rising above His own skeleton which is depicted with gruesome realism and has a rib cage moulded in iron.

A famous son of the village was William Lisle Bowles, born in 1762. The poems written by this vicar's son so delighted Samuel Taylor Coleridge that he changed from studying theology to writing poetry himself.

SULGRAVE
10 miles W of Towcester off the B4525

🏛 Sulgrave Manor

The best-known attraction here is **Sulgrave Manor**, a Tudor manor house built by the ancestors of George Washington, first President of the United States of America. Lawrence Washington, sometime Mayor of Northampton, bought the manor from Henry VIII in 1539. In 1656, Lawrence Washington's great-great-grandson Colonel John Washington left England to take up land in Virginia, which later became Mount Vernon. This man was the great-grandfather of George. The Washington family arms, which are said to have inspired the stars and stripes design of the American flag, are prominent above the front door, and the house is a treasure trove of George Washington memorabilia, including documents, a velvet coat and even a lock of his hair. The house is open daily (except Monday) from April to October, and at weekends in March, November and December. A lottery grant has allowed the construction of a series of buildings in the grounds which are part of major educational programmes covering all aspects of Tudor history. The lovely gardens include yew hedges, topiary, herbaceous borders and a formal rose garden planted in 1999. There's a gift shop and a buttery serving light refreshments.

Kettering

🏛 Manor House Museum 　 🎨 Alfred East Gallery

An important town standing above the River Ise, Kettering gained fame as a producer of both clothing and shoes. It was in Kettering that the missionary William Carey and the preacher Andrew Fuller founded the Baptist Missionary Society in 1792, giving a new impetus to the cause of foreign missions all over the world. The parish church of St Peter and St Paul, with its elegant crocketed spire, is one of the finest in the country and a landmark for miles around. Much of the old town has been swallowed up in modern development, but there are still a few old houses in the narrow lanes, and the Heritage Quarter around the church gives a fascinating, hands-on insight into the town's past.

The **Manor House Museum**, housed in an 18th century manor house, has impressive collections of social and industrial history, archaeology and geology. Individual items range from a macabre mummified cat to an example of the Robinson car built in Kettering in 1907.

In the adjacent **Alfred East Gallery** a constantly changing programme of

THE VICTORIA FURNITURE COMPANY

27 Victoria Street, Kettering,
Northamptonshire NN16 0BU
Tel: 01536 516203
e-mail: victoriapine@btconnect.com
website: www.victoriapine.com

In all respects, the **Victoria Furniture Company** lives up to its motto 'beautifully crafted furniture to fit any space or budget'.

15,000 square feet on two floors of showroom space in Victoria Street, close to the town centre, provides a generous amount of room for displaying an impressive range of occasional and dining room furniture, a good selection of genuine antique furniture, bespoke and fitted bedrooms, hand-crafted kitchens showroom stock and bespoke office furniture and granite and hardwood worktops.

Many varieties of wood are used, and choices include modern and traditional, reproduction antique, distressed, reclaimed, plain and painted tables, chairs, chests, cupboards, dressers, wardrobes, beds, cabinets and bookcases. Among the many other services available are:

- Planning & Design Services
- Antique furniture
- Free estimates, house visits by appointment
- In-house Fitter
- Paint Stripping
- Wood Turning
- Furniture Restoration
- Architectural Salvage
- Hand wax and laquer finishing

Victoria Furniture's highly qualified team pride themselves on the quality of service supplied. Their large following of regular customers all providing Victoria Furniture with solid recommendations, as the number one in tailor-made furniture locally. They also specialise in tailor made furniture from reclaimed timbers.

Shop hours of the Victoria Furniture Company, (A Member of the Guild of Master Craftsmen) are, 9am to 5.30pm, Sunday 10am to 4pm. There's also a superb website where a large selection of the stock can be viewed.

exhibitions of paintings, crafts, sculpture, photography and children's work ensures that there will be something new to see on every visit. Among the items on permanent display are works by Alfred East RA and Thomas Cooper Gotch. In between visits to the museum and gallery (both wheelchair-accessible) the Heritage Gardens are a pleasant place for a stroll or a picnic. The Tourist Information Centre is at the same location.

On the A6, on the outskirts of town, **Wicksteed Park** is a 148-acre site of leisure and pleasure, with 40 rides and attractions, including roller coaster, pirate ship, train ride, Mississippi river boat and pitch & putt. There are several catering outlets, shops, a pottery, a photographic studio and two playground areas. Open daily Easter-September, weekends to November.

Around Kettering

GEDDINGTON
3 miles NE of Kettering off the A43

🏛 Eleanor Cross   🏛 Boughton House

This attractive village, like many in the county, has known royal visitors: monarchs from the time of William the Conqueror used a summer palace as a base for hunting in the Royal Forest of Rockingham. In the centre of the village is an ornately carved stone cross almost 40 feet high. This is the best preserved of the three surviving **Eleanor Crosses** that marked the funeral procession of Queen Eleanor, who had died at Harby in Nottinghamshire in 1290. Her devoted husband, King Edward I, accompanied the body south to London, and he ordered the crosses to be erected to mark the places where the coffin rested. William Rishanger, a monk at St Albans, records the event: "The King gave orders that in every place where her bier had rested, a cross of the finest workmanship should be erected in her memory, so that passers-by might pray for her soul". Other crosses were raised at Lincoln (where the Queen's heart was buried), Grantham, Stamford, Hardingstone in Northampton (this still exists), Stony Stratford, Dunstable, St Albans, Waltham (this still exists), Cheapside and Charing Cross.

Off the A43, on a minor road between Geddington and Grafton Underwood (where there is a monument to the crews of B17 bombers), stands one of the very finest houses in the country. The origins of **Boughton House**, the Northamptonshire home of the Duke of Buccleuch, go back 500 years to a small monastic building. Extended over the years, it was transformed into "a vision of Louis XIV's Versailles". In addition to the wonderful architecture, Boughton is

Boughton House

noted for its French and English furniture, its paintings (El Greco, Murillo, 40 Van Dycks) and its collection of armoury and weaponry. The grounds, which include parkland, lakes, picnic areas and woodland play areas, are open May to September, the house in August only.

Large tracts of the ancient woodland of the region have survived, and in the fields by Boughton House are the remains of more recent planting. The 2nd Duke of Montagu, nicknamed John the Planter, had the notion of planting an avenue of trees all the way from the house to his London home. The plan hit immediate trouble when his neighbour, the Duke of Bedford, refused to let the trees cross his estate; instead, the Planter set down many avenues on his own estate, amounting to the 70 miles of the distance to London. Dutch Elm disease destroyed much of his planting, but the old trees are being replaced with limes and beeches.

TWYWELL
4 miles E of Kettering off the A14

Twywell (the name means 'double spring') has a history that includes the Romans, the Saxons and the Normans, but the strongest, and most surprising connection is with Africa. Two African boys, Susi and Chuma, faithful servants and companions of David Livingstone, were with him when he died and carried his body hundreds of miles to the sea before accompanying it to Westminster Abbey. They had saved all Livingstone's papers and stayed at Twywell as guests of the explorer's friend Horace Waller while

DAIRY FARM

Cranford St Andrew, nr Kettering,
Northamptonshire NN14 4AQ
Tel: 01536 330273

At the centre of a 350-acre mixed farm, **Dairy Farm** is a thatched Jacobean manor house opposite Cranford Hall, with outstanding views over open countryside. It's a place of great character, and the three guest bedrooms are tastefully appointed; one of the double rooms boasts a four-poster bed. Breakfast is based on farm and local produce, and with a little notice resident owner Audrey Clarke will also prepare a splendid evening meal.

In the garden are an imposing medieval stone dovecote and a charming summer house, and the 12th century village church is just beyond the garden wall. The area around the farm is perfect for pleasant country walks, and though peaceful and serene, Dairy Farm is within easy reach of the local amenities. And with the A14 close by it is ideally suited for touring and sightseeing. Open all year except Christmas.

🏠 historic building   🏛 museum   �🏛 historic site   ᕓ scenic attraction   🌱 flora and fauna

Livingstone's Journals were being prepared. In the church are three stones from Calvary in the window by the altar. They were sent by the rector's friend, General Gordon, who wrote a letter saying that he hoped to visit the Pope on his way back from Palestine. That letter is preserved in the church.

WOODFORD
6 miles E of Kettering off the A14

A bizarre story here. A human heart was found in one of the columns of the Norman church during restoration work in the 19th century. It is thought to belong to one of the Traillys, who died while fighting in the Crusades; his heart was brought back by his followers so that he could rest with the other Traillys, who were the local lords of the manor at the time. Also of note in the church are over 100 carved oak figures, some medieval brasses and a tablet commemorating

John Cole, bookseller, schoolmaster and writer on antiquities. He lived from 1792 to 1848, dying in great poverty. Woodford was the home of a certain Josiah Eaton, a man of small stature (5'2") but great stamina. A prodigious walker, he set out in 1815 on a marathon walk around Blackheath, completing a mile every hour for six weeks, without ever stopping. At the end of this amazing feat of endurance he had covered 1,100 miles.

THRAPSTON
5 miles E of Kettering on the A605

The Medieval Bridge at Thrapston crosses the River Nene on one of its loveliest stretches. The town is surrounded by fine pastureland, created when the flood waters and rich mud subsided after the two Ice Ages. The main attraction in the church is a stone tablet carved with stars and stripes. It is thought by some that this motif was the inspiration for the American flag, being the coat of arms of Sir John Washington, who died in 1624. The church and nearby Montagu House, home of Sir John, are places of pilgrimage for many American tourists.

RAUNDS
7 miles SE of Kettering on the B663

A small town in the Nene Valley with a lofty (183ft) church spire. It was at the heart of the Northamptonshire shoemaking trade, specialising in army boots, and was also known for the manufacture of dolls. In May 1905 Raunds hit the headlines when 200 men marched to London to protest at the poor

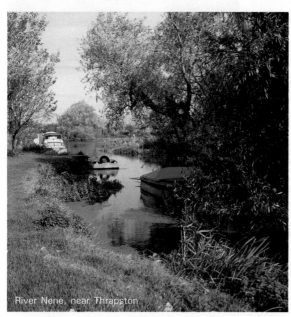
River Nene, near Thrapston

rates of pay for bootmakers. They were delighted to find on their arrival that a crowd of 10,000 supporters was waiting for them. After 10 days, the strikers won concessions and returned victorious.

IRTHLINGBOROUGH
7 miles SE of Kettering on the B571/A6

A small town noted for its leather and iron industries. It boasts two fine bridges across the Nene, one built in the 14th century, the other in the 20th. The medieval bridge has 10 ribbed arches, and the arms of an ancient monastery carved into one if its stones, suggesting perhaps that it was built by monks, perhaps from Peterborough. The modern one, running parallel to the old, is an impressive sight, its great arches stretching for half a mile over the low-lying land by the river. Irthlingborough is home to Rushden & Diamond Football Club, whose stadium is located in the magnificent Diamond Centre. Also in the centre is the Doc Shop, selling Dr Martens boots.

HIGHAM FERRERS
10 miles SE of Kettering off the A45

🏛 Chichele College

Just off the Market Place in this delightful old town a narrow lane leads to a unique group of ecclesiastical buildings. These include the 13th century spired Church of St Mary the Virgin, a chantry and bede house, and a 13th century market cross. Also here is **Chichele College**, a college for secular canons founded in 1422, named in honour of a local worthy called Henry Chichele. Born here in 1362, he progressed from baker's boy to Archbishop of Canterbury, a position he filled for 30 years until his death in 1443.

Market Cross, Higham Ferrers

PYTCHLEY
2 mile S of Kettering off the A509

🐎 Pytchley Hunt

The location of the old headquarters of the **Pytchley Hunt**. One of the most famous Masters of the Hunt (1827-1834) was Squire Osbaldeston, a man of boundless energy and stamina, who once successfully wagered 1,000 guineas that he could ride 200 miles in 10 hours, changing horses as necessary. He used 32 horses and completed the 200 miles with more than an hour to spare. No one took up his offer of a vast sum of money if they could achieve the same feat with the same horses. The good squire was a crack shot, a talented underarm bowler and a fine boxer. He was evidently less accomplished at backing horses than riding them, for he ended his days in London in obscurity and comparative poverty.

WELLINGBOROUGH
8 miles S of Kettering off the A509 or A45

🏛 Church of St Mary   🏯 Croyland Abbey

🌿 Summer Leys Nature Reserve

This important market and industrial town, known for its iron mills, flour mills and tanneries, sits near the point where the River Ise joins the River Nene. The spire of the medieval All Hallows Church rises among trees in the centre of town, and the other church, whose great tower can be seen on the further bank of the Nene, is the **Church of St Mary**. It was built in the first decades of the 20th century and is regarded as Sir Ninian Comper's masterpiece. He declared St Mary's his favourite church and wished to be buried here with his wife but Comper's fame demanded interment in Westminster Abbey. Funded by two Anglo-Catholic spinster sisters, St Mary's has been described as "a sort of fantastical King's College, Cambridge", a sumptuous medley of extravagant Gothic features complete with gilded columns and golden angels. Not to be missed!

Wellingborough was granted its market charter in 1201 and markets are still held four days a week. In and around the market square are several interesting old buildings, including the gabled Hind Hotel. One of its rooms is called the Cromwell Room because it was being constructed while the Battle of Naseby was in progress.

Another fine building is **Croyland Abbey**, now a Heritage Centre with a wealth of local history, and near it is a splendidly restored old tithe barn originally used for storing the manorial tithes. Stone-walled and thatch-roofed, it is 70 feet long and 22 feet wide. It

dates from the 1400s and has two great doorways at either side, one of them 13 feet in height. An attraction in the centre of town is the Millennium Rose Garden at **Swanspool Gardens**. The Embankment at Wellingborough is a great place for a family outing, where a thriving population of swans lives next to the outdoor paddling pool that dates from the 1930s. South of the town, **Summer Leys Nature Reserve** is a year-round haven for large numbers of birds. Each May, thousands of people visit the town for the International Waendel Weekend of walking, cycling and swimming.

IRCHESTER
2 miles SE of Wellingborough off the A45

🚶 Country Park

Originally a Roman settlement, a fortified town whose walls were eight feet thick. A Saxon cemetery was also discovered here, and Norman England is represented by the plinths in the church. The six-arched bridge that crosses the River Nene is 14th century and bears the crossed keys of Peterborough Abbey and the wheel of St Catherine. On the B570 is **Irchester Country Park**, 200 acres of woodland walks, wayfaring course, nature trail, picnic meadows and ranger service in a former ironstone quarry.

PODINGTON
4 miles SE of Wellingborough off the A509

The noisiest place for miles around, this is the location of the Santa Pod Raceway, where the fastest motorsport on earth takes place on selected days between March and November. The Top Fuel Dragsters can accelerate from 0 to 100mph in under a second, so put in your ear plugs and don't blink!

🎬 stories and anecdotes   🦜 famous people   🎨 art and craft   ✒ entertainment and sport   🚶 walks

THE COUNTRY HOUSE HOTEL

63 Loddington Road, Great Cransley, Northamptonshire NN14 1PY
Tel: 01536 791600 Fax: 01536 791369
e-mail: jenny@the-country-house-hotel.co.uk website: www.the-country-house-hotel.co.uk

'Continental Charm in the Heart of England'. That's the promise of **The Country House Hotel**, where resident owners jenny and Steve Adams offer comfortable, stylish accommodation at

affordable prices. The seven spotless bedrooms, all decorated and furnished to a very high standard, are equipped with telephone, TV, wireless broadband, trouser press, hairdryer and beverage tray, providing a peaceful, civilised retreat for business or leisure guests.

Traditional English and Continental cuisine produces an interesting supper menu, and picnic hampers can be ordered; a room service menu is also available. The hotel has a comfortable lounge bar and conservatory, and sports guests will find golf, tennis and swimming facilities a short drive away.

THE TOLLEMACHE ARMS

49 High Street, Harrington, Northamptonshire NN6 9NU
Tel: 01536 710649 e-mail: enquiries@tollemacheharrington.com
website: www.tollemacheharrington.com

A notable landmark on the main street of Harrington, the **Tollemache Arms** has been dispensing fine food and drink since Henry VIII was on the throne. This fine country inn is open seven days a week, with food and drink available from midday onwards. Excellent menus make top-class use of local produce in dishes that range from traditional pub lunches with cask-conditioned ales to a fine dining experience complemented by well-chosen wines. Families are made welcome, and the inn has a large garden offering stunning country views.

CHURCH FARM LODGE

Tel: 01536 713320 e-mail: info@churchfarmlodge.com
website: www.churchfarmlodge.com

Across the road from the Tollemache Arms, **Church Farm Lodge** offers top-class accommodation a short drive from Market Harborough, Kettering and Northampton, and with easy access to many local attractions. A great place to stay whether for pleasure or on business, the lodge comprises 14 luxurious en suite rooms stylishly converted from barns and farm buildings. All rooms have TV with Freeview and wireless broadband as well as tea/coffee-making facilities, and they retain many features of the original buldings.

 historic building   museum   historic site   scenic attraction flora and fauna

LAMPORT

8 miles SW of Kettering off the A508

🏛 Lamport Hall

Lamport Hall is a fine 16th century house enlarged in the 17th century by John Webb. Home to the Isham family from 1560 to 1976, it features an outstanding collection of furniture, books, paintings and china. It has gardens and parkland, including the first Alpine garden and the first garden gnomes in England, plus a shop and tea room and a farm museum.

NASEBY

10 miles W of Kettering off the A5199

🏛 Battle of Naseby

Two monuments and interpretation panels mark the site of the **Battle of Naseby**, where, in 1645, Oliver Cromwell's Parliamentarian forces defeated King Charles I and determined the outcome of the Civil War, thereby giving the English people the right to rule their own country. Cromwell and Fairfax with 14,000 Roundheads faced the Royalist forces, who advanced outnumbered two to one. The first attack came at 10 o'clock on the morning of June 14th and, after heavy fighting, Fairfax won a decisive victory, capturing all the King's baggage and a fortune in gold and silver. The King surrendered in Newark some months later and the Civil War was at an end. Naseby Battle and Farm Museum, in the village, contains a model layout of the battle, relics from the fight and a collection of bygone agricultural machinery.

Many of the defeated Royalists who fled after the battle were surrounded and killed at the village of Marston Trussell on the Leicestershire border. Their remains lie in the churchyard.

KELMARSH

6 miles W of Kettering on the A508

🏛 Kelmarsh Hall

Near Junction 2 of the A14, just outside the village of Kelmarsh, **Kelmarsh Hall** (see panel on page 418) is an early 18th century house designed in Palladian style by an outstanding pupil of Sir Christopher Wren, James Gibbs (who is perhaps best known as the architect of the Church of St Martin in the Fields, London). One of only two surviving houses outside London by Gibbs in this style, it stands in 3,000 acres of farmland, with a lake, beautiful topiary and rose gardens and woodland walks. The Great Hall is the focal point of the house, with many of Gibbs' original features. One of the most attractive rooms is the Chinese Room, where the hand-painted wallpaper, from Kimberley Hall in Norfolk, dates from the 1840s. The church opposite the main entrance to the Hall contains fine marble from Rome, some William Morris furnishings and the vaults of the families who have lived at the Hall – the Hanburys, the Naylors and the Lancasters.

RUSHTON

4 miles NW of Kettering off the A6

🏛 Rushton Triangular Lodge   🏛 Rushton Hall

One mile west of the village, on an unclassified road, stands **Rushton Triangular Lodge**, described as "the purest folly in the country". It was built by Sir Thomas Tresham in 1597 and symbolises the Holy Trinity, with three walls, each with three windows, three gables and three storeys, topped with a three-sided chimney. Thomas Tresham, known as Thomas the Builder, was brought up a Protestant but courageously returned to the Roman Catholic faith of his ancestors. At

Kelmarsh Hall

Kelmarsh, Northampton,
Northamptonshire NN6 9LT
Tel: 01604 686543

Built in 1732 to a James Gibbs design, Kelmarsh Hall is surrounded by its parkland and beautiful gardens. Much of the interior was decorated in the 1920s and 30s by Nancy Lancaster of Colfax & Fowler in the manner that has become known as the English country house look.

Geoffrey Jellicoe and Norah Lindsay helped to create the remarkable RHS Partner gardens which include a stunning triangular walled garden. From Snowdrop Sunday through to the Autumn splendour of the cutting garden, visitors will not be disappointed.

From Easter 2007 Kelmarsh Hall will be the home to the Croome Collection. Croome Court in Worcestershire was home to the Earls of Coventry until 1948. Thanks to the foresight of the Croome Trustees and family much of the furniture and chattels together with their original bills of sale were retained. This fine collection of furniture, paintings and porcelain will be available for group visits.

Opening Times: 2pm-5pm

House & Gardens: Easter until the end of September, Bank Holiday Sundays & Mondays, plus Thursdays 3rd May-27th September

Gardens: Easter until the end of September, Bank Holiday Sundays & Mondays, plus Tuesdays, Wednesdays, Thursdays & Sundays

Rushton Hall, the Tresham family home since the 14th century, he was caught harbouring the renowned Jesuit Edmund Campion and was sentenced to seven years' imprisonment. Responsible for several intriguing buildings, he died soon after proclaiming the first Stuart king and just before his son Francis was arrested as a protagonist in the Gunpowder Plot.

Neighbouring **Rushton Hall**, also dating back 400 years, is described as a "dazzling example of Tudor and Stuart splendour". Built by Sir John Tresham, enlarged by Sir Thomas and completed by the Cockayne family, it now houses a Royal Institute for the Blind school, but is open to the public by appointment and for special events. Tel: 01536 710506

DESBOROUGH

5 miles NW of Kettering on the A6

Desborough has the appearance of being a relatively modern town, but its history can be traced back to the Bronze Age. The oldest standing building is the Church of St Giles, built around AD1225, and other buildings of architectural interest include the 18th century Church House and the late 17th century Old Manor House coloured with the rich reds of Northamptonshire ironstone.

CORBY
6 miles N of Kettering off the A43

🍃 Top Lodge

A modern industrial town, but one with a history. Taking its name from a Scandinavian chieftain during the Danish occupation, it grew in significance in the mid-10th century, when King Edgar set up the Corby Hundred, with a local Moot Court governing the affairs of other villages in the area. True industry arrived at Corby in the later years of Queen Victoria's reign, with the building of the Kettering-Manton railway. Many of the bricks used in the building of the viaduct at Harringworth were made at Corby brickworks, which closed at the beginning of the 20th century. But Corby was still essentially a small village until the 1930s, when Stewarts & Lloyds built a huge steel-making plant based on the area's known reserves of iron ore. That industry virtually stopped in 1980, but Corby remains a go-ahead modern town, with many cultural and leisure opportunities for young and old alike. It also treasures its heritage, both historic and geographic. 170 acres of woodland have been preserved intact at the very heart of the town,

and there is much to interest the visitor in the surrounding villages that make up Corby Borough: Cottingham, East Carlton, Middleton, Rockingham, Stanion and Weldon. At **Top Lodge** visitor centre, two miles south of the roundabout at Duddington, The Barn enables visitors to watch live televised pictures of a family of red kites on their nest and offers the chance of seeing theses wonderful birds soaring above the barn and nearby woodland.

EAST CARLTON
1 mile W of Corby on the A427

🌲 Countryside Park

East Carlton Countryside Park comprises 100 acres of parkland with nature trails and a steel-making heritage centre with craft workshops, a forge and a cafeteria.

ROCKINGHAM
2 miles N of Corby on the A6003

🏰 Rockingham Castle

"450 Years a Royal Castle, 450 years a family home". Nine hundred years of history are contained within the walls of **Rockingham Castle**, built by William the Conqueror on the slopes of Rockingham Hill, overlooking the Welland Valley and the thatched and slate-roofed cottages of the village. The grand rooms are superbly furnished, and the armour in the Tudor Great Hall recalls the Civil War, when the castle was captured by the Roundheads. Owned and lived in since 1530 by the Watson family, the castle was put to atmospheric use by the BBC in the series *By*

Rockingham Castle

the Sword Divided, in which it was known as Arnescote Castle. Charles Dickens wrote much of *Bleak House* at Rockingham.

HARRINGWORTH
4 miles N of Corby off the B672

🏛 Viaduct

An impressive sight here is the great **Viaduct** carrying the railway from Kettering to Oakham a mile across the Welland Valley. Completed in 1879, it has 82 spans, each 40 feet wide. In the village are a notable village cross and the Church of St John the Baptist (12th to 14th centuries).

DEENE
4 miles NE of Corby off the A43

🏛 Deene Park   🏛 Kirby Hall

Surrounded by beautiful gardens and grounds filled with old-fashioned roses and rare trees and shrub stands **Deene Park**. Originally a

Deene Park

medieval manor, it was acquired in 1514 by Sir Robert Brudenell and has been occupied by the family ever since. One of the family's most distinguished members was James, 7th Earl of Cadogan, who led the Charge of the Light Brigade at the Battle of Balaclava. The Earl survived the slaughter but was killed four years later when he fell from the horse that had carried him safely at Balaklava. The horse's head is on display at Deene. Transformed from medieval manor to Tudor and Georgian mansion, Deene Park contains many fine examples of period furniture and some beautiful paintings. The oldest visible part is an arch of about 1300 in the east of the house; the Great Hall was completed in the late 1500s and has a magnificent sweet chestnut hammer-beam roof. The house is open on Bank Holiday Sunday and Monday afternoons from Easter to the end of August and all Sunday afternoons in June, July and August.

Also near Deene, in the parish of Gretton, is **Kirby Hall** (English Heritage), one of the loveliest Elizabethan ruins in England. Now only partly roofed, the hall dates from 1570 and was given by Elizabeth I to her Lord Chancellor and favourite courtier Sir Christopher Hatton. Alterations attributed to Inigo Jones were made in the 17th century.

The fine gardens with their peacock population are being restored. A version of Jane Austen's *Mansfield Park* was filmed here in 1998.

WELDON
2 miles E of Corby on the A427

This sizeable village is best known for the honey-coloured building stone quarried here. The stone was used to build nearby Rockingham Castle and Great St Mary's Church in distant Cambridge. An interesting

🏛 historic building   📷 museum   🏛 historic site   ⚜ scenic attraction   🌱 flora and fauna house on the village green, is the windowless Round House, once used as a lock-up.

BRIGSTOCK
5 miles SE of Corby on the A6116

On the banks of a tributary of the River Nene called Harpers Brook, the Saxon village of Brigstock has many delightful old cottages, a 16th century manor house, and a church with an unusual circular extension to its tower. The village was once deep in Rockingham Forest, and the church bells were rung three times a day to guide travellers. By the little tree-covered village green a quaint Elizabethan cross topped by a ball weather vane stands on four steps.

EASTON-ON-THE-HILL
12 miles NE of Corby on the A43

🏠 Priest's House

An attraction here at the far northern tip of the county is the **Priest's House**, a pre-Reformation priest's lodge which is of specialist architectural interest and is in the care of the National Trust. In the village church is a tablet commemorating one Lancelot Skynner, a rector's son, who died in 1799 when the ship *La Lutine*, laden with gold, sank off Holland. The ship's bell was recovered and now hangs in the London headquarters of Lloyd's who had insured the cargo.

Oundle

🏠 School   🎨 International Festival

Oundle is a beguiling little town with some fine stone buildings dating from the 17th and 18th centuries, ancient hostelries and a variety of specialist shops. The town is probably best known for its **Public School**, founded by Sir

William Laxton in 1556. An inscription to his memory is written above the 17th century doorway in Greek, Latin and Hebrew. The medieval church, with its magnificent tower and 200-feet spire, is an impressive sight, and other notable buildings include three sets of almshouses. The museum, in the old courthouse, paints a picture of local life and the farming heritage down the years.

In mid-July, the town hosts the **Oundle International Festival** – 10 days devoted to a vibrant mix of classical music, theatre, jazz and film. The festivities include a hugely popular open-air jazz and firework spectacular.

Around Oundle

LYVEDEN NEW BIELD
4 miles SW of Oundle via the A427

🏠 Lyveden New Bield Lodge

Another of Sir Thomas Tresham's creations, **Lyveden New Bield** is a cross-shaped Elizabethan garden lodge erected to symbolise the Passion. Begun around 1595 as a garden lodge for his main residence, the Old Bield, it remains virtually unaltered since work on it stopped with the death of Sir Thomas in 1605. An intriguing and haunting roofless shell, it features some interesting exterior frieze work and stands in beautiful open countryside, with the remains of late-Elizabethan water gardens adjoining the site. The new orchard contains many old varieties of apples, pears and plums.

ASHTON
1 mile E of Oundle off the A605

The National Dragonfly Museum, once located in Ashton, is now located at Wicken

Fen in Cambridgeshire. The village remains the home of the World Conker Championships, which take place in October each year.

FOTHERINGHAY
4 miles NE of Oundle off the A605

🏠 Lyveden New Bield Lodge Castle

🏠 Lyveden New Bield Lodge

🏠 Church of St Mary & All Saints

🏛 Prebendal Manor Medieval Centre

The first **Fotheringhay Castle** was built around 1100 by the son-in-law of William the Conqueror; the second in the 14th century by Edmund of Langley, a son of Edward III. Richard III was born here; Henry VIII gave the castle to Catherine of Aragon and it later became the prison and place of execution of Mary, Queen of Scots, who was brought here in bands of steel and beheaded in the Banqueting Hall in 1587. Sir Christopher Hatton, a favourite of Elizabeth I, was one of the judges who sentenced Mary to death. Following her death, it is said that her jewellery was stolen and hidden in the woodlands around Corby. If so, it lies there still. The castle was pulled down in 1627 and

Prebendal Manor House

Nassington, Peterborough, Northamptonshire PE8 6QG
Tel: 01780 782575
e-mail: info@prebendal.co.uk
website: www.prebendal-manor.co.uk

The Grade I listed Prebendal Manor House is the earliest surviving dwelling in Northamptonshire. It forms the focus of a group of stone buildings, which includes a 16th century dovecote, a large 18th century tithe barn and a 15th century lodgings building. The present stone house dating from the early 13th century stands on a historic site, which includes two medieval fishponds and archaeological and historical evidence of one of King Cnut's royal timber halls. The Prebendal Manor and church stand on a promontory over looking the village and river Nene.

   Alan Titchmarsh described the gardens at Prebendal Manor as a "stunning example of a recreated medieval garden". (Royal Gardeners Pub., BBC, 2003) The gardens were established to represent both practical and decorative features that could be found in a high status garden between the 13th and 15th centuries. The plants have been selected from several plant lists. These include the earliest English gardening book by 'Jon Gardener' and a 15th century 'Leech Book', that contains the sort of medical recipes that Nicholas Colnet, who was physician to Henry 5th during the Agincourt campaign in 1415. He was given the Prebendal Manor in 1417, probably in return for his services. The gardens are at their best from late May until mid July. The ephemeral beauty of gardens was noted by many medieval poets:

   'Now shrinketh rose and lilye-flour, That whilen ber that swete savour. In somer, that swete tide.'

🏠 historic building   🏛 museum   🏯 historic site   🌀 scenic attraction   🌿 flora and fauna

Fotheringhay Castle

The neighbouring village of **Woodnewton** has retained much of its historic character, and the many houses of limestone, thatch and Collyweston slate in Main Street have led to its designation as a Conservation area. In the graveyard of St Mary's Church is the grave of Nicolai Polakovs, better known as Coco the Clown, who retired to Woodnewton in 1973 and died there shortly afterward. A short drive to the north, at **Nassington**, stands the **Prebendal Manor Medieval Centre** (see panel opposite). At its heart is the manor, a 13th century Grade I listed building that for many centuries was home to Prebendaries, officials of the Church. The Centre provides an insight into the lives of these powerful men, including Simon of Sudbury, who later became Archbishop of Canterbury and was beheaded in the Tower during the Peasants Revolt of 1381.

200 years later a gold ring was found with a lovers' knot entwined around the initials M and D - Mary and Darnley? Perhaps the ring fell from the Queen's finger as she was executed. The evocative site of the castles by the River Nene is rich in atmosphere, and visitors to Fotheringhay should not leave the village without seeing the **Church of St Mary and All Saints**, a 15th century former collegiate church in a prominent position overlooking the Nene Valley. Notable features include an unusual octagonal lantern tower.

LOCATOR MAP

ADVERTISERS AND PLACES OF INTEREST

🏛 historic building   🏛 museum   🏛 historic site   🏛 scenic attraction   🌿 flora and fauna

10 | Warwickshire & West Midlands

A rich vein of medieval and Tudor history runs through Warwickshire and the romantic ruins of Kenilworth Castle, the grandeur of Warwick Castle and the elegance of Royal Leamington Spa set the tone for this most delightful of counties. However, it is Stratford-upon-Avon that is the focal point for most visitors and, known throughout the world as the birthplace of William Shakespeare, the old part of the town is completely dominated by this exceptional man who died nearly 400 years ago. Along with the various timber-framed houses that are linked with the Bard, Stratford is also the home of the Royal Shakespeare Company, which holds a regular programme of performances of his plays each year.

Another town that has found fame through one of its young citizens is Rugby, as it was a pupil who, in the early 19th century, broke the rules of football during a match and, in so doing, founded the game that bears the name of the town. Close by is the ancient village of Dunchurch that is often dubbed the 'Gunpowder Plot Village' as it was here, in 1605, that the conspirators waited to hear if they had succeeded in blowing up the Houses of Parliament.

The West Midlands and the extreme north of the county of Warwickshire is dominated by the major cities of Birmingham and Coventry. It often gets overlooked by visitors but repays a closer look. It is an area rich in natural beauty, with a wealth of beautiful gardens, some excellent museums and historic buildings, and a long and distinguished industrial and cultural heritage.

Stratford-upon-Avon

Warwick

🏛 Castle   🏛 Church of St Mary

🏛 Museums   🌿 Racecourse

Over the past ten centuries **Warwick Castle** has witnessed some of the most turbulent times in English history. From the era of William the Conqueror to the grand reign of Queen Victoria, the Castle has left us a fascinating legacy to enjoy today. Dominating the town, it is surely everyone's ideal of a medieval building, one of the country's most splendid castles and certainly one of the most visited. It still serves as a home as well as retaining the greater part of its original masonry. Standing by the River Avon, Warwick is in a good defensive position and became part of Crown lands as recorded in

the Domesday Book in 1086.

A tour of this palatial mansion takes you from the grim austerity of the original dungeons with their gruesome torture chambers to the gloomy but sumptuous opulence of rooms later adapted for comfortable living. The castle's magnificent State Rooms, once used to entertain the highest members of the nobility, house some superb art treasures including works by Holbein, Rubens and Velasquez. As the castle is owned by Madame Tussaud's, striking waxworks play their part in the displays. In the castle's Ghost Tower, visitors can learn of the dark and sinister secrets surrounding the fatal stabbing of Sir Fulke Greville who is said to haunt the premises to this day. In the Great Hall visitors come face to face with Oliver

THE WARWICK ARMS HOTEL

17 High Street, Warwick, Warwickshire CV34 4AT
Tel: 01926 492759   Fax: 01926 410587
e-mail: reception@warwickarmshotel.com
website: www.warwickarmshotel.com

■   ■   ■
WARWICK ARMS HOTEL
EST. 1717

The building dates back almost 300 years, but guests at **The Warwick Arms Hotel** will find every up-to-date comfort and convenience as well as many handsome original features. The Hotel offers 34 en suite bedrooms, many with both bath and shower, and all pleasantly restored and modernised. Guests will feel instantly at home in the relaxing day rooms, which include three spacious lounge and bar areas.

The Warwick Arms is not just a great place to stay, very close to the castle and the shops, but an excellent choice for a meal. Chef Ben Patterson's modern English cooking provides plenty of mouthwatering choices, from salmon fishcakes and salt & pepper calamari to braised half-shoulder of lamb, corn-fed breast of chicken, Aberdeen Angus ribeye steak and vegetable Thai green curry. There's a bar menu for lighter appetites, and the 'grazing boards' – cheese, charcuterie, fish or antipasti – are perfect for snacking or sharing. The fine food is complemented by well-priced wines on a globe-trotting list, and three real ales are always on tap.

🏛 historic building   🏛 museum   🏛 historic site   🌣 scenic attraction   🌿 flora and fauna

Cromwell's death mask. And the armoury houses one of the best private collections in the country.

The castle exterior is best viewed from **Castle Bridge**, where the 14th century walls can be seen reflected in the waters of the River Avon. There is a walk along the ramparts, and much to explore within 60 acres of grounds, including a re-created Victorian formal rose garden, the Peacock Gardens and an expanse of open parkland designed by Capability Brown. Events throughout the year

Warwick Castle

PRESENT DAYS

14 Swan Street, Warwick, Warwickshire CV34 4BJ
Tel: 01926 494927 Fax: 01926 403229
e-mail: info@presentdays.co.uk web: www.presentdays.co.uk

Womens' fashion, arts and crafts, jewellery and gifts fill the shelves and display cases behind the smart black-and-white frontage of **Present Days** in the old part of town. Pottery from Bell of Charlbury and Bridgwater, Neals Yard remedies, fragrances and scented candles and Burts Bees products make perfect gifts or pampering treats. Among other ranges are children's books, educational and soft toys, including Jelly Cat and Moulin Roty toys from France, Pilgrim jewellery from Denmark, gift wrap and gift boxes, greetings cards, paper napkins and stationery.

Upstairs is a range of womens' fashions in an attractive choice of colours and styles. The Avoca and Adini labels are strongly represented, and there's an exclusive range of Irish knitwear. Gill and David Way, who have many years' experience in the retail trade, are rightly proud of their delightful shop, where every visit brings a new choice of gift ideas and treats.

[f] stories and anecdotes   🐦 famous people   ✒ art and craft   🎭 entertainment and sport   🚶 walks

include **Medieval Tournaments**, open-air firework concerts and special entertainment days.

A strong link with the castle is found in the **Collegiate Church of St Mary** in Old Square, a splendid medieval church on the town's highest point. Of pre-Conquest origin, the church contains the magnificent fan-vaulted Beauchamp Chapel, built to house the monuments of Richard Beauchamp, Earl of Warwick, and his family. The chapel contains an outstanding collection of Warwickshire tombs, a chapter house and a Norman crypt (complete with a tumbrel, part of a medieval ducking stool). In summer visitors can ascend the tower to enjoy the excellent views. The politician and scholar Enoch Powell is buried in his Brigadier's uniform in the churchyard of St Mary, the Church of his old regiment, the Royal Warwickshire. (An earlier service for Enoch Powell was held at St Margaret's Church, Westminster, and included part of hos own translation of the Gospel of St Matthew.)

The centre of Warwick was rebuilt after a fire in 1694, and though many older buildings survived, the centre is dominated by elegant Queen Anne buildings. A walk around High Street and Northgate Street takes in some of the finest buildings, including **Court House** and **Landor House**. Court House on Jury Street houses the Tourist Information Centre and the **Warwickshire Yeomanry Museum**, with displays of uniforms, arms, swords, sabres and selected silver.

Some of the town's oldest structures can be

LA MAISON

13 Swan Street, Warwick CV34 4BJ
Tel: 01926 497711 Fax: 01926 497710
e-mail: info@lamaisonwarwick.co.uk
website: www.lamaisonwarwick.co.uk

The two floors of display space at **La Maison** are filled with a splendid collection of inspirational furniture, accessories, homeware and gifts. Owner Charlotte Yarnold has always considered quality and design as of the utmost importance, and the unique handmade furniture includes some of the most stylish contemporary and traditional pieces to be found outside London. The large range of accessories and original gift ideas include fabrics and soft furnishings, cushions, mirrors, lamps and lighting, vases, candles, clocks and picnic hampers.

Among the many famous brands are John Sankey and Henderson Russell furniture and fabrics, Vincent Sheppard traditional Lloyd Loom furniture, Artcopi and Felix Monge furniture, Lampe Berger perfumed lamps, Flambeau lamps featuring distressed finishes in gold and silver, Middle Kingdom porcelain, Millefiore toiletries, and Japanese dolls from Kokeshi and Momiji. La Maison also stocks a wide range of cards and gift wrapping, and a wedding and wish list service is available. Shop hours are 9.30am to 5.30pm Monday to Friday, 9.30am to 5pm Saturday.

🏚 historic building   🏛 museum   🏚 historic site   🦆 scenic attraction   🌱 flora and fauna

RUMPS THE BUTCHERS

49 Brook Street, Warwick, Warwickshire CV34 4BL
Tel: 01926 419166
website: www.rumpsthebutchers.com

It it's top-quality meat you're looking for, **Rumps the Butchers** is definitely the place for you. Most of the outstanding range of meat on display is sourced from the region, including beef from the Cotswolds, traditionally dry aged on the bone, lamb from Cheltenham, grass-bedded pork from Witney, chickens from Balsall Common and turkeys from Bishops Tachbrook. Superb sausages are made on the premises, bacon is dry-cured plain or smoked in house. Cheeses come from Earlsden and Broadway. A mail order service is available throughout the UK.

found around Mill Street, an attractive place for a stroll, with several antiques shops along the way. The **Mill Garden** at the end of Mill Street is home to a delightful series of plantings in a breathtaking setting on the Avon beside the castle. Here visitors will find a herb garden, raised beds, small trees, shrubs and cottage plants including some unusual varieties.

Warwickshire Museum in Market Place occupies an imposing 17th century market hall housing collections that illustrate the geology, wildlife and history of the county. Notable exhibits include giant fossils, live bees, ancient jewellery and the historic Sheldon Tapestry map of Warwickshire. Changing programmes in the ground floor galleries offer exciting exhibitions of acclaimed local and national artists' work.

One of the most important buildings in Warwick is St John's House, dating from 1666 and considered a very good example of the period. Today the building houses a museum where visitors can find out how people lived

Mill Street Bridge, Warwick

in the past. Upstairs is the **Museum of the Royal Warwickshire Regiment**.

Two of Warwick's medieval town gateways survive, complete with chapels. Of these, Westgate Chapel forms part of **Lord Leycester's Hospital**, a spectacularly tottering and beautiful collection of 15th century half-timbered buildings enclosing a pretty galleried courtyard. Inside, the main interest is provided by the **Queen's Own Hussars Regimental Museum**. This 600-year-old medieval treasure has a unique chantry Chapel dating back to 1123, a magnificent Great Hall and Guildhall together with other timber-framed buildings, first established by the Earl of Leicester as an old soldiers' home in 1571. The historic Master's Garden, featuring a Norman arch and 2,000 year-old vase from the Nile, is a spectacular summer attraction.

In the heart of Warwick, just 400 yards from the castle, the Lord Leycester Hotel occupies Grade II listed buildings steeped in history: in 1694 they halted the Great Fire of Warwick; in the 1700s they housed the Three Tuns Inn; and by the 19th century they were elegant townhouses.

Warwick Racecourse in Hampton Street offers flat and National Hunt racing throughout the year. This picturesque racecourse makes a good day out for all the family, with a

programme of some 25 meetings throughout the year. The central grandstand incorporates the first stand built in 1809, among the oldest surviving in the country. On the city side of the racecourse stand the recently restored Hill Close Gardens.

Around Warwick

KENILWORTH
4 miles N of Warwick on the A452

🏛 Castle   🏛 Abbey

Although the town was here before the Domesday Book was compiled, Kenilworth's name is invariably linked with its castle. Today the remains of this castle stand as England's finest and most extensive castle

---

LET'S CREATE

Unit 6, Millar Court, Station Road, Kenilworth, Warwickshire CV8 1JD
Tel: 01926 863701
e-mail: kareneveritt@letscreate.co.uk
website: www.lets-create.co.uk

Karen Everitt has been immersed for more than 20 years in the world of arts and crafts, and she invites others to share her passion and enthusiasm in her shop **Let's Create**. The main specialities are cardmaking, scrapbooking and beaded jewellery, but there's much, much more to intrigue and interest the visitor. Kits and ready-made products are available, but the way to make the most of what Karen has to offer is to participate in the many activities that fill the year.

Workshops, courses and demonstrations cover a wide range of creative activity, from making belts, handbags, plastic embellishments and Christmas cards to decoupage, parchment craft, and using inks and powders in distress techniques to create an aged look in an object of choice. Let's Create can also organise and host parties on the Kenilworth premises, and runs a membership scheme that lets members make the most of all that Karen and her staff have to offer. The shop is open from 9.30am to 5pm Monday to Saturday (half-day Wednesday).

🏛 historic building   🏛 museum   🏛 historic site   🏞 scenic attraction   🌿 flora and fauna ruins, dramatically ensconced at the western edge of the town.

Kenilworth Castle's red sandstone towers, keep and wall glow with an impressive richness in the sun, particularly at sunrise and sunset. Here you can learn about the great building's links with Henry V (who retired to Kenilworth after the Battle of Agincourt), King John, Edward II and John of Gaunt. The tales of this great fortress, immortalised (if enhanced) in Sir Walter Scott's novel *Kenilworth* written in 1821, are many and varied. The marvellous Norman keep, the oldest part of the ruins, was built between 1150 and 1175. John of Gaunt's Great Hall once rivalled London's Westminster Hall in palatial grandeur. After Simon de Montfort's death at the Battle of Evesham in 1265, Kenilworth was held by his son. At that time the castle was surrounded by the Kenilworth Great Pool, a lake covering about 120 acres.

An audio tour guides you on a revealing journey around the Castle, recounting stories of Kenilworth's turbulent past. There are fine views from the top of Saintlowe Tower, and lovely grounds for exploring and picnicking, as well as beautifully reconstructed Tudor gardens. Special events throughout the year include a festival of Tudor Music, Saxon and Viking exhibitions, medieval pageantry, various re-enactments, plays and operas in the grounds and much more. Excavation work has recently unearthed the foundations of the original Elizabethan gardens built in the 1570s by Robert Dudley for a visit by Queen Elizabeth I. The gatehouse he built has been fully restored and is open to the public for the first time in decades. It was here that Dudley, Earl of Leicester, courted the Queen. It is said that she kept his last letter in a casket until the day she died. A copy of the latter is on display in

the new Elizabeth and Dudley exhibition. The remains of **Kenilworth Abbey** can be seen in the churchyard of the Norman parish church of St Nicholas in the High Street. Much of interest was discovered during excavations and there are many relics on display in the church, including a 'pig' of lead. It is said that this formed part of the roof at the time of the Dissolution but was then melted down and stamped by the Commissioners of Henry VIII.

ASHOW
4 miles NE of Warwick off the A46

Avon Cottage in Ashow, at the far end of this attractive village adjacent to the church is a charming cottage garden surrounding a picturesque 18th century Grade II listed building. It stretches for one-and-a-half acres with extensive River Avon frontage. Diverse and interesting plantings make for year-round interest. There is also an attractive orchard area with free-range domestic hens and waterfowl.

HATTON
2 miles NW of Warwick off the A41

🌱 Hatton Country World

Hatton Country World is a uniquely charming blend of family fun and country

Hatton Country World

📖 stories and anecdotes   🐦 famous people   🖌 art and craft   🚲 entertainment and sport   🚶 walks

THE COOK SHOP

112 Regent Street, Royal Leamington Spa,
Warwickshire CV32 4NR
Tel: 01926 888588
website: www.cookshop.co.uk

Owner Toni McLennan has almost 30 years' experience in selling cookware, and since 1995 she has put that experience to excellent use in running the **Cook Shop** at Caterers Hire & Sales in Royal Leamington Spa's fashionable Regent Street. Knives are a speciality, sold singly and in sets, along with knife holders and knife sharpeners. All the leading brands from England, France, Germany and Japan are kept in stock, and visitors to the shop's website can browse through the whole range. Knives are just one of the huge range of items in stock, and with just about everything to do with the preparation, cooking and serving of food, this really is a paradise for cooks.

On display are collections of everything from saucepans and casseroles to sieves, scales, baking trays, processors, coffee-making machines, plates and dishes, aprons and oven gloves. Literally hundreds of brands are represented on the shelves, including Global, Wusthof, Sabatier, La Cafetière, Le Creuset, Kitchen Devils, Gaggia, Krups, Magimix, Salter, Lock & Lock, Hahn, Kaiser, Dualit, Alan Silverwood, Bialetti, Cornsih Blue, Mermaid, Typhoo......the list is almost endless. No one with an interest in cooking should miss a visit to this wonderful shop when in Royal Leamington Spa.

*W*ith over forty years experience in the family, from sorting Diamonds in Antwerp, Sapphires and Rubies in Thailand, to choosing jewellery and watch ranges in Switzerland, Colin and Sandy Scamp have a wealth of knowledge and experience. Peter Stephan don't just sell jewellery they are real jewellers! Because they are an independent company they can draw on many varied sources for their ranges of Jewellery, Watches, Gifts and Silver. Apart from their own ranges they prefer to initially select pieces from UK manufacturers, but also source their ranges from across Europe and the Far East to ensure they offer a different look, just for you!

At Peter Stephan we specialise in Platinum Engagement, Wedding and Eternity rings. Whilst we can produce most of our rings in either 18ct White or Yellow gold we strongly recommend the special qualities of Platinum.

If you do not find anything suitable from our extensive stock ranges we can source or have a unique piece of jewellery specially designed and manufactured for you. Having worked at the jewellery repair bench and being involved for many years in jewellery manufacturing Colin can advise how to transform an idea into what will be the ideal style just for you!

From modern design to smart classic Peter Stephan is the place to go

Peter Stephan

P.S... UNIQUE JEWELLERY

98 Warwick Street, Royal Leamington Spa, CV32 4QG
Tel: +44 (0)1926 431400 Fax: +44 (0)1926 431500
e-mail: info@peterstephan.co.uk website: www.peterstephan.co.uk

🏛 historic building   🏛 museum   🏛 historic site   ♺ scenic attraction   🌿 flora and fauna shopping. On this 100-acre farm, visitors will find the largest collection of rare breed farm animals in Britain and the largest craft village in England with some 35 workshops employing over 100 people. Known by many old boaters as the 'Stairway to Heaven', the Hatton Lock flight has 21 locks and lifts the Grand Union Canal 144 feet out of Warwick in two-and-a-half miles.

BARFORD

3 miles S of Warwick on the A429

The name of Joseph Arch may not be known to many nowadays, but in his time he was one of the leading figures in the world of farming. Born in a tiny house in 1826 (the house still stands), he was a scare-crower, ploughboy, stable lad and champion hedge-cutter before his radical views led him to found the Warwickshire Agricultural Labourers Union, and later the National Union. He became the first truly working-class Member of Parliament (for North West Norfolk) and was a friend of the Prince of Wales, but he never forgot his roots and he died, at the grand old age of 93, in the little house where he was born. A much grander building is the Regency Barford House, notable for its giant Ionic columns. The Church of St Peter was mainly rebuilt in 1884 by RC Hussey.

SHERBOURNE

3 miles S of Warwick on the A46

🌱 Sherbourne Park

Set in lovely countryside with views over fields to the River Avon, **Sherbourne Park** is one of the very finest gardens in the county. Highlights of the gardens, which were designed by Lady Smith-Ryland in the 1950s, include a paved terrace covered by clematis, wisteria and a magnolia; an 'orchard' of sorbus trees; a box-edged, rose-filled parterre and the White Garden surrounded by yew hedges. The redbrick house of the Park is early Georgian, and the view is dominated by the parish church, built in 1863 by Sir George Gilbert Scott. Open on certain afternoons and by appointment. Tel: 01926 624255

Royal Leamington Spa

🏛 Pump Rooms   🏛 Museum & Art Gallery

This attractive town boasts a handsome mixture of smart shops and Regency buildings, and The Parade is undoubtedly one of the finest streets in Warwickshire. At the beginning of the 19th century very few people knew of the existence of Leamington, but by 1838 all this had changed. By this time the

DRIFTWOOD

39 Park Street, Leamington Spa,
Warwickshire CV32 4QH
Tel: 01926 450351

Kate Thacker has been in womens' retail fashion for more than 20 years, and since 2000 she has run **Driftwood** in this smart town-centre street. She is the main stockist in the region for Jackpot womens' clothes from Denmark. Other brands featured prominently include Great Plains, well known for the quality of its smart casual garments, Rose Black scarves and Balagan jewellery. Friendly, knowledgeable staff are a major plus at Driftwood, which also offers an alteration service on garments purchased from the store.

famous waters were cascading expensively over the many 'patients' and the increasingly fashionable spa was given the title 'Royal' by permission of the new Queen, Victoria. **The Pump Rooms** were opened in 1814 by Henry Jephson, a local doctor who was largely responsible for promoting the Spa's medicinal properties. This elegant spa resort was soon popularised by the rich, who came to take the waters in the 18th and 19th centuries. A converted swimming pool and Turkish Bath houses the **Art Gallery & Museum**, which contains paintings by British and European artists, a 'Cabinet of Curiosities' with activities and trails for children, the story of Leamington and its people, a Hammam – part of the Victorian Turkish Baths, and changing exhibitions and regular events. Immediately opposite the Spa itself are Jephson's Gardens containing a Corinthian temple which houses a statue of him. Acclaimed as one of the country's finest ornamental gardens, it has many unusual trees and plants and a glass house with a range of habitats from desert to tropical.

UFTON FIELDS NATURE RESERVE
5 miles E of Leamington Spa off the A425

This haven is open every Sunday from 11am till 4pm. It boasts an all-weather footpath and a wealth of butterflies, dragonflies and wild flowers, as well as a bird hide.

HARBURY
5 miles SE of Leamington Spa off the B4452

The history of this area goes back many years – dinosaur fossils have been found in

the local quarries and the Fosse Way, a major Roman road, passes close by. Just outside the village lies Chesterton Windmill, an unusual mill built in 1632.

Stratford-upon-Avon

- 🏛 Hall's Croft   🏛 Holy Trinity Church
- 🪶 Nash's House   🌱 Butterfly Farm
- 🪶 Shakespeare's Birthplace
- 🏛 Harvard House & Museum of British Pewter
- 🖋 Royal Shakespeare Company & Theatre

After London, many visitors to England put Stratford-upon-Avon next on the itinerary, and all because of one man. William Shakespeare was born here in 1564, found fame in London and then retired here, dying in 1616. Needless to say, the places connected with his life and work have become Meccas for anyone interested in the cultural history, not just of these islands, but of the entire world.

Each of the houses associated with the Bard has its own fascinating story to tell, and staff at the houses are happy to guide visitors on a journey encompassing what life might have been like in Stratford-upon-Avon during

Shakespeare's Birthplace

🏛 historic building   🏛 museum   🏛 historic site   🪶 scenic attraction   🌱 flora and fauna

Shakespeare's day. The half-timbered house that is **Shakespeare's Birthplace** has been returned to the way it would have looked in his day. Household inventories, books and pictures have been assembled, and a room thought to have been his father John's workshop was been re-created with the help of the Worshipful Company of Glovers. The garden is planted with flowers and herbs mentioned in the plays. An adjoining exhibition charts Shakespeare's life and features many rare local artefacts and an edition of the collected plays published in 1623.

Further along, on Chapel Street, stands **Nash's House**. This half-timbered building was inherited by Shakespeare's granddaughter, Elizabeth Hall, from her first husband,

Thomas Nash. It now contains an exceptional collection of Elizabethan furniture and tapestries, as well as displays, upstairs, on the history of Stratford. The spectacular Elizabethan-style knot garden is an added attraction. Next door, in New Place, Shakespeare bought a house where he spent his retirement years, from 1611 to 1616. Today all that can be seen are the gardens and foundations of where the house once stood. An exhibit in Nash's House explains why this, Shakespeare's final home in Stratford, was destroyed in the 18th century. Opposite New Place is the Guild Chapel, and beyond this is the Grammar School, where it is believed that Shakespeare was educated.

Hall's Croft in Old Town is one of the best examples of a half-timbered gabled house in

AUTOGRAPH INK MEMORABILIA

8 Old Red Lion Court, Bridge Street, Stratford-upon-Avon, Warwickshire CV37 6AB
Tel: 01789 267766
e-mail: slaes@autographink.co.uk
website: www.autographink.co.uk

Saturday the 11th of March 2006 saw the grand opening of **Autograph Ink Memorabilia**, a shop and showroom stocked with hundreds of genuinely signed autographed photographs and memorabilia. They can be sold unframed or delicately set in a hand-crafted wooden frame. Certain items can be prepared for dedication to a special friend, and another service enables customers' pictures to be reproduced on high-quality linen stretched on a solid wooden frame.

The two floors are packed from ground to ceiling with pictures of the famous, including sporting celebs, stars of stage and screen, and singers from Ol' Blue Eyes to Madonna. The shop began as a hobby for owner Tony King, and meetings with Stratford-born photographer Stuart Stanley and Canadian caricature artist Marshall Caplin spawned the idea for the shop. Their work dominates the space, but there's plenty more besides the photographs and drawings, including film scripts, posters, books, signed football shirts and boxing gloves – even divorce papers and wills, all one-off originals, and all with authentic signatures.

This is a great place for browsing and, as the owner says, retail therapy is rarely this fascinating. Shoppers can also order online.

Stratford. It was named after Dr John Hall, who married Shakespeare's daughter Susanna in 1607. This impressive house contains outstanding 16th and 17th century furniture and paintings. There is also a reconstruction of Dr Hall's 'consulting room', accompanied by an exhibition detailing medical practices during Shakespeare's time. Outside, the beautiful walled garden features a large herb bed; visitors can take tea near the 200-year-old mulberry tree or have lunch in the restaurant here.

Hall's Croft is near **Holy Trinity Church**, an inspiration for many poets and artists because of its beautiful setting beside the River Avon. It is here that Shakespeare is buried. Dating partly from the 13th century, it is approached down an attractive avenue of limes. The north door has a sanctuary knocker, used in the past to ensure any fugitive who reached it 37 days' grace. Shakespeare's wife, Anne Hathaway, and their daughter Susanna and her husband John Hall are also buried here.

Shakespeare is not the only illustrious name to have associations with the town. **Harvard House** in the High Street, dating from 1596, was the childhood home of Katherine Rogers. Her son, John Harvard, went to the American Colonies in the early 1600s and founded the university named after him in 1636. In 1909 Harvard House was restored and presented to

---

THE NUTCRACKER CHRISTMAS SHOP

44-45 Harley Street, Stratford-upon-Avon,
Warwickshire CV37 6QW
Tel: 01789 268987
e-mail: info@thenutcrackerchristmasshop.co.uk

Nobody knows more about Christmas decorations than Robert Newman, who owns the **Nutcracker Christmas Shop** in Stratford and several other outlets throughout the UK. In a fine old black-and-white half-timbered building in a pedestrianised shopping street, every day is Christmas Day, with more than 2,000 items to adorn the home or to hang on the festive tree. There are toys and angels, dolls and a veritable army of Santas, sourced from all over Europe and North America, and themed on all parts of the United Kingdom. And the Nativity displays are among the loveliest you'll ever see.

WOODSTOCK GUEST HOUSE

30 Grove Road, Stratford-upon-Avon,
Warwickshire CV37 6PB
Tel: 01789 299881
e-mail: jackie@woodstock-house.co.uk
website: www.woodstock-house.co.uk

Visitors to Stratford-upon-Avon have a wealth of history and culture to discover, and **Woodstock Guest House** provides the ideal place for exploring its heritage. Denis and Jackie have created an excellent base for a quiet, civilised stay, and the five comfortable en suite guest bedrooms include a family room; one room is situated on the ground floor. A good English or Continental breakfast starts the day, and Woodstock offers all-day secure parking for residents.

Harvard University. It boasts the most ornately carved timbered frontage in the town. Cared for by the Shakespeare Birthplace Trust, it houses the **Museum of British Pewter** based on the nationally important Neish Collection.

There are many fascinating old buildings in Stratford. The old market site in Rother Street has a history dating from 1196, when a weekly market was granted by King John. In the square is an ornate fountain-cum-clock tower, a gift from GW Childs of Philadelphia in the jubilee year of Queen Victoria. It was unveiled by the actor Sir Henry Irving, who in 1895 became the first Knight of the Stage.

Stratford has become a Mecca for theatre-lovers, who flock to enjoy an evening at one of the town's three theatres. The first

commemoration of Shakespeare's passing was organised by the actor David Garrick (of Garrick Theatre and the Garrick Club fame), 150 years after the Bard's death. People have been celebrating this illustrious poet and playwright's life and times ever since. The **Royal Shakespeare Company** has an unrivalled reputation both in the UK and worldwide, and wherever the RSC perform, the audience are certain of witnessing performances of the highest standard. The **Royal Shakespeare Theatre** opened in 1879 with a performance of *Much Ado About Nothing* starring Ellen Terry and Beerbohm Tree. The season was limited to one week as part of a summer festival. It was so successful that, under the direction of FR Benson, it grew to spring and summer seasons, touring

BROADLANDS GUEST HOUSE

23 Evesham Place, Stratford-upon-Avon, Warwickshire CV37 6HT
Tel: 01789 299181 Fax: 01789 551382
e-mail: philandjohn@broadlandsguesthouse.co.uk
website: www.broadlandsguesthouse.co.uk

The guest always comes first at **Broadlands Guest House**, where resident proprietors Phil Gray and John Worboys are the most welcoming and attentive of hosts. The bay-windowed house in a quiet road was completely refurbished a couple of years ago, and the six guest bedrooms offer a peaceful, civilised and very comfortable base for a break in historic Stratford. The three doubles, one twin and two singles, each with its own individual charm, all have en suite facilities, TV, hairdryer, good toiletries, bottle water and hairdryer, and some of the bathrooms feature attractive tiles fitted by the owners.

Excellent freshly cooked breakfasts start the day, and guests can browse through a supply of magazines spread out on a chaise longue on the stairs. The house has a pretty little front garden, and private car parking is available. Situated in the Old Town conservation area, Broadlands is well placed for visiting Shakespeare's birthplace, the theatres, the River Avon and the town's many other attractions. Children over 12 are welcome, but not dogs.

🏠 historic building 🏛 museum 🏛 historic site 🌂 scenic attraction 🌱 flora and fauna

NAQUIBA

Shop 5, 7-9 Union Street, Stratford-upon-Avon, Warwickshire CV37 6QT
Tel: 01789 205252
e-mail: info@naquiba.com website: www.naquiba.com

Naquiba is a funky, feel-good boutique selling a unique range of clothing, jewellery, accessories and gifts making this essential shopping for bright-minded individuals. Chief attractions among the wide-ranging displays include exquisite handmade jewellery, ethnic and boho clothing, Dr Martens boots and shoes (traditional and in funky colours), beautifully detailed handbags in vintage and gothic styles, cosmetics and body glitter. Naquiba, which also has a body piercing studio, prides itself on excellent customer service, and the staff are always ready with help and advice. Open 9.30am-5.30pm Monday to Friday, 9.30am-6pm Saturday, 11am-5pm Sunday.

the nation in between. In 1925, because of the excellence of the performances and direction, the company was granted a Royal Charter. Sadly, a year later the theatre was destroyed by fire. At the time, playwright George Bernard Shaw sent a one-word telegram: Congratulations! Apparently the building was a bit of an eyesore, but there are few such buildings in today's Stratford. The company, undeterred, continued by giving performances in cinemas while a worldwide fundraising campaign was launched to build a new theatre, which was opened on 23rd April 1932, the 368th anniversary of the Bard's birth.

Quite apart from the industry that has grown around Shakespeare and his life and times, Stratford boasts a number of other world-class attractions. Stratford's **Butterfly Farm** provides a specially designed and constructed habitat for Europe's largest collection of butterflies. There is also an area devoted to Insect City and, for the brave of heart, Arachnoland where the world's largest spider, rain forest scorpion colonies and other 'spinners' can be seen in perfect safety.

The Royal Shakespeare Theatre Summer House on Avonbank Gardens

is home to the Stratford Brass Rubbing Centre, which contains a large collection of exact replicas of brasses of knights and ladies, scholars, merchants and priests of the past.

Around Stratford-upon-Avon

SHOTTERY
1 mile W of Stratford off the A422

🐾 Anne Hathaway's Cottage

This was the birthplace of Anne Hathaway, Shakespeare's wife. Here visitors will find the Elizabethan farmhouse now known as **Anne Hathaway's Cottage**, and can retrace the steps which the courting couple, who married

Anne Hathaway's Cottage

🏛 stories and anecdotes   🐾 famous people   🎨 art and craft   ✒ entertainment and sport   🚶 walks

STRATFORD GARDEN CENTRE

Campden Road, Clifford Chambers, nr Stratford-upon-Avon,
Warwickshire CV37 8LW
Tel: 01789 205745
e-mail: mail@stratfordgardencentre.co.uk
website: www.stratfordgardencentre.co.uk

On the B4632 south of Stratford-upon-Avon, **Stratford Garden Centre** is Warwickshire's premier centre for horticulture, with a mix of flowers, plants, trees, gifts and fine foods that represent the best the county has to offer. The range of indoor and outdoor plants, mainly grown locally, changes with the seasons, and there's always a wide selection of plant aids and garden accessories. The Centre also sells a range of stylish outdoor furniture, along with gas and charcoal barbecues and patio heaters. Smaller items run from seasonal decorations, gifts, gift wrap and cards to glassware, pottery, books, candles and fragrances.

Tasty light lunches, freshly made teas, coffees and juices are served in the bright, modern 80-seat café, and the deli section tempts with a fine array of meats, cheese, bread and cakes. The centre has many franchised retail outlets, including Arctic Spas hot tubs, Maidenhead Aquatics, Playopolis, Prior Products, Craft Central, Slippery Hill Baby Clothing and Cotton Traders clothes. Opening hours are 9am to 6pm (Sunday 10.30am-4.30pm).

🏚 historic building   📷 museum   🏛 historic site   🭪 scenic attraction   🌱 flora and fauna

WARWICKSHIRE & WEST MIDLANDS

in 1582, might have taken. The epitome of the traditional thatched cottage, this delightful spot was home to Hathaways since the 15th century, up until some 70 years ago when the Shakespeare Birthplace Trust decided it was time to open up the home to the public. The Hathaway bed, settle and other pieces of furniture owned by the family remain, and there is a traditional English cottage garden and orchard – plants and herbs grown by the Shakespeare Trusts' gardeners can be purchased. Other attractions of this handsome village are the Shakespeare Tree Garden, the tranquil Shottery Brook, a

STRATFORD ANTIQUES & INTERIORS

Dodwell Trading Estate, Evesham Road, Dodwell, nr Stratford-upon-Avon,
Warwickshire CV37 9SY
Tel: 01789 297729 Fax: 01789 297710
website: www.stratfordantiques.org.uk

Stratford Antiques & Interiors is one of the largest of its kind in the Midlands, with over 10,000 square feet of display space and more than 20 dealers under one roof. The stock includes antiques, reproduction and contemporary pieces and an abundance of interior design goods, all of the best quality and all with a touch of the inspirational. Visitors can browse through well-laid out themed displays of antique furniture, reproduction pieces, antique and reclaimed pine, oak and pine furniture made to order, Knowle settees, painted French furniture, fitted kitchens, soft furnishings, beds and bedding and lovely silk flowers.

   This outstanding out-of-town shopping experience is located a mile-and-a-half out of Stratford on the B439 road to Bidford-on-Avon. Opening hours are 10am to 5pm seven days a week.
Access is easy and there's plenty of parking space, and shoppers can take a break in the Copper Kettle Tea Rooms.

TALTON MILL FARM SHOP & DELI

Oxford Road (A3400), Alderminster,
nr Stratford-upon-Avon, Warwickshire CV37 8UG
Tel: 01789 459140
website: www.talton-mill.co.uk

Talton Mill has been selling top-quality food for 25 years, including home-reared meat and poultry, local game and seasonal vegetables. Mark and Liz Holberton also offer a range of superb cooked products prepared in the farmhouse kitchen, including terrific pies (chicken, leek & mushroom, fisherman's, steak & ale), quiches, paella and scrumptious fruit crumbles. The River Stour flows through the 20-acre farm, which stands on the A3400 opposite the entrance to the Ettington Park Hotel.

sculpture garden and an Elizabethan-style yew maze planted in 2001. A growing willow cabin inspired by *Twelfth Night* allows visitors to hear reading of the Sonnets by well-known actors.

WILMCOTE

3 miles NW of Stratford off the A34

🏠 Palmers Farm   🏵 Mary Arden's House

Another notable house connected with the poet is that of his mother, situated here in the village of Wilmcote, slightly off the well-beaten tourist track. **Palmers Farm** is a striking Tudor farmhouse, now home to the Shakespeare Countryside Museum of farming and rural life. **Mary Arden's House** is next to the farmhouse. Note in particular the bread oven doors, which are made of bog oak, which never burns, and are seen only very rarely now in England. Special events and demonstrations of traditional sheep shearing, weaving and spinning, crook making and other country crafts are held throughout the year, as well as celebrations and entertainments based on accounts from Shakespeare's plays, in particular *A Winter's Tale*. Best of all, however, is the dovecote of the house. Robert Arden, who was lord of the manor, was in this capacity the only villager allowed to have one. It has over 600 pigeon holes and, at nesting time, would house about 3,000 birds.

Wilmcote is also one of the few small villages left which retains its Victorian Gothic railway station.

CHARLECOTE

3 miles E of Stratford off the B4086

🏛 Charlecote Park   🏛 Mill

The National Trust's **Charlecote Park** (see panel below) is a magnificent stately home occupying extensive grounds overlooking the River Avon. Home of the Lucy family since 1247, the present house was built in the mid-1500s. Thomas Lucy was knighted here by Robert Dudley, Earl of Leicester, deputising for Elizabeth I, who spent two nights here in 1572. The house was comprehensively modernised during the 1700s, but when George Hamilton Lucy inherited it in 1823 he took the decision to 'turn the clock back' and create interiors according to rich Victorian 'Romantic' ideals of the Elizabethan era. The

Charlecote Park

Warwick, Warwickshire CV35 9ER
Tel: 01789 470277
e-mail: charlecote.park@nationaltrust.org.ue

The home of the Lucy family for over 700 years, the mellow brickwork and great chimneys of Charlecote seem to sum up the very essence of Tudor England. There are strong associations with both Queen Elizabeth and Shakespeare who knew the house well – he is alleged to have been caught poaching the estate deer. The Rich early Victorian interior contains many important objects from Beckford's Fonthill Abbey and, outside, the balustraded formal garden opens onto a fine deer park landscaped by 'Capability' Brown. Visitors can see a video film of life at Charlecote Park in the Victorian period.

🏛 historic building   🏠 museum   🏛 historic site   ⚶ scenic attraction   🌱 flora and fauna house, apart from the family wing which is still used by descendants of these early Lucys, has not been changed since. The lavish furnishings of the house include important pieces from William Beckford's Fonthill Abbey sale in 1823. A treasure trove of historic works of sculpture and painting, no visitor can fail to be impressed by the house's sheer magnitude, grace and beauty. The park was landscaped by Capability Brown and reflects his use of natural and man-made features complementing each other. The park supports herds of red and fallow deer (in about 1583 the young William Shakespeare is alleged to have been caught poaching Sir Thomas' deer; years later he is said to have taken his revenge by using Sir Thomas as his inspiration for the fussy Justice Shallow in *The Merry Wives of Windsor*), as well as a flock of Jacobs sheep first introduced here in 1756.

Charlecote Mill is situated on the site of an earlier mill mentioned in the Domesday Book, at which time it was valued at six shillings, eight pence (33p). In 1978 this 18th century building was restored with the help of volunteers from Birmingham, and the west waterwheel was repaired at the expense of the BBC for their film of George Eliot's novel, *The Mill on the Floss.*

MORETON MORRELL
7 miles E of Stratford off the B4455

🏛 Church

In the **Church of the Holy Cross** (Norman with 14th and 15th century rebuilding) is an effigy of Richard Murden, High Sheriff of Warwickshire in 1635. The village has an American connection. Richard Randolph had seven children baptised in the church, and

his third son, William, went to Virginia in 1672. William was an ancestor of Thomas Jefferson, the third President of the USA and the man chiefly responsible for the drafting of the Declaration of Independence. In the same family were John Marshall, America's first Chief Justice, and General Robert E Lee, whose surrender to General Grant in 1865 brought the American Civil War to an end.

WELLESBOURNE
4 miles E of Stratford off the A429

🏛 Wartime Museum   🏭 Watermill

Wellesbourne Wartime Museum is located on the site of a wartime airfield. On display are tools, ration books and an exhibit in the style of a contemporary battle operations control room. **The Wellesbourne Watermill** is a genuine brick-built working flour mill dating back to 1834. This restored mill on the River Dene, a tributary of the River Avon, is one of the few in the country which visitors can see working as it did when new. A video presentation prepares visitors for the mill itself, providing an insight into this heritage site. Demonstrations of the art and skill of milling stoneground flour are enacted and

Wellesbourne Watermill

THE COUNTRY PURSUIT

1 Banbury Street, Kineton,
Warwickshire CV35 0JS
Tel: 01926 641230
website: www.countrypursuit.co.uk

Popular owner Sue Wixey has built up a strong following among the local sporting community at her shop **The Country Pursuit**. She stocks everything for the horseman, from saddles, bridles and other tack to boot, jodhpurs, shirts and ties, and caters equally well for the fishing and shooting fraternity. Associated gift ideas range from limited edition sporting prints to books on country sports, to greetings cards, Border Fine Art and Thelwell.

explained by the miller, and visitors are encouraged to take part. Apart from the working demonstrations, there are guided walks alongside the river and two ponds, tree trails, and coracle boats along the river. There is also a display of antique farm implements, a craft shop, and a tea room in the wonderful 18th century timber-framed barn where teas and lunches are served.

Compton Verney
6 miles E of Stratford off the B4086

🏛 Manor House

Before crossing the Fosse Way, the Roman road that runs from Exeter to Lincoln passes **Compton Verney Manor House**. For many years closed to the public, this magnificent manor has been renovated and is now open to visitors. An exquisite collection of works of art has been assembled, including British portraiture, European Old Masters and modern works, along with a unique collection of British Folk Art. Workshops, evening talks, lectures and special events bring to life the processes and inspiration behind some of these great works. The manor house stands in 40 acres of parkland landscaped by Capability Brown and rich in flora and fauna, with a lake, arbour, stirring stone obelisk, Victorian

watercress bed, Cedar of Lebanon, and Adam Bridge. The handsome avenue of Wellingtonias lines what was once the entrance to the estate.

KINETON
8 miles E of Stratford on the B4086

🏛 Battle of Edgehill

This pleasant old market town is a peaceful retreat with an old courthouse and several 17th and 18th century houses. To the south-east of the town is the site of the **Battle of Edgehill,** fought here in October 1642. For the Royalists this was the first and one of the most devastating clashes of the Civil War. A year after the battle, Charles I was again in Kineton to meet his wife, Henrietta Maria, who had spent the previous night in Shakespeare's house as the guest of the poet's daughter Susanna.

GAYDON
8 miles E of Stratford off the B4100

📷 Heritage Motor Centre

The **Heritage Motor Centre** in Gaydon hosts a most impressive collection of historic British cars, and also offers a variety of outdoor activities for the whole family. This fascinating Centre tells the story of the British motor industry from 1896 to the present day.

🏛 historic building   📷 museum   🏛 historic site   🐸 scenic attraction   🌿 flora and fauna

It boasts about 200 exclusively British vehicles from the world-famous makes of Rover, Austin, Morris, Wolseley, Riley, Standard, Triumph, MG and Austin Healey. Open 10am to 5pm daily. The 65-acre site also features a 4 x 4 off-road demonstration circuit.

FENNY COMPTON
11 miles E of Stratford off the A423

🏕 Country Park

This charming village close to **Burton Dassett Hills Country Park** and just half a mile from the Oxford Canal provides endless opportunities for scenic walks along the edge of the Cotswold Scarp. Burton Dassett Park itself is distinguished by rugged open hilltops topped by a 14th-century beacon with marvellous views in all directions.

FARNBOROUGH
11 miles SE of Stratford off the B4086

🏛 Farnborough Hall

The National Trust's **Farnborough Hall** is a lovely honey-coloured stone house built in the mid-1700s and the home of the Holbech family for over 300 years. The interior features some superb plasterwork, and the delightful grounds include a terrace walk, 18th century temples and an obelisk.

WARMINGTON
10 miles SE of Stratford on the B4100

🌿 National Herb Centre

The **National Herb Centre** enjoys a great location on the northern edge of the Cotswolds on the B4100 close to the Warwickshire-Oxfordshire border. A centre for research and development work for the UK herb industry, the site has been developed with an eye towards providing visitors with a fascinating range of activities and sights. The

Plant Centre has one of the widest selections of plants, trees and shrubs with herbal uses in the country. The Herb Shop stocks a range of herbs, health foods and gifts, many produced on site.

OXHILL
8 miles SE of Stratford off the A422

A charming village of brown and redbrick cottages on a tributary of the Stour. The Church of St Laurence is mainly Norman with a unique 12th century font lavishly sculpted and depicting Adam and Eve at the Tree of Life and an impressive Norman doorway decorated with strange faces peering through foliage.

UPTON HOUSE
11 miles SE of Stratford off the A422

🏛 Upton House

Here on the border with Oxfordshire, **Upton House** is a late 17th century National Trust property built of the mellow local stone. The house was remodelled in 1927-9 for the second Viscount Bearsted to house his growing art collection and also to modernise the premises. The collections in the house are the chief attractions, featuring paintings by English and Continental Old Masters including El Greco, Brueghel, Bosch, Hogarth and Stubbs. Brussels tapestries, Sèvres porcelain, Chelsea figures and 18th century furnishings are also on display. In the fine gardens, in summer, there can be seen the typically English scene of white-clad cricketers; in winter, the Warwickshire Hunt holds its meet here.

UPPER TYSOE
8 miles SE of Stratford off the A422

🏕 Windmill Hill 🏕 Compton Wynyates Park

From Upper Tysoe there is a lovely walk south

over **Windmill Hill** (which actually has a windmill on it), taking you to the church on the edge of **Compton Wynyates Park**, with views of the attractive Tudor manor below – a refreshing bit of brick building in this Cotswold-edge stone country.

HONINGTON
8 miles SE of Stratford off the A3400

🏛 Honington Hall

Honington Hall encapsulates the architectural and decorative styles popular in the late 17th and 18th centuries. Opening times are limited but the Hall is well worth a visit, presenting many delightful examples of Regency tastes and refinements.

SHIPSTON-ON-STOUR
9 miles SE of Stratford off the A3400

For centuries, Shipston-on-Stour was an important agricultural centre, in the heart of a rural district known as 'Feldon'. From the 1200s tradesmen and craftsmen helped shape the town, that remains to this day a centre for fascinating shops, galleries and antiques shops.

The hills that surround the town are perfect for gentle strolls and cycling. This small town has quite a busy shopping centre, but is rewarding to stroll through, with a nice church and many handsome old stone buildings.

THE BAKERY SANDWICH SHOP & COFFEE BAR

14 Sheep Street, Shipston-on-Stour, Warwickshire CV36 4AF
Tel: 01608 661563

The Peacock family can be proud in their claim that **The Bakery Sandwich Shop** offers 'much, much more than your daily bread'. Their well-loved establishment does indeed sell excellent freshly baked bread, in loaves or for the made-to-order sandwiches, but they also sell scrumptious cakes and cater for lunchtime appetites with a menu of savouries that includes hearty soups. To accompany the food, in the coffee bar or to take away, is a selection of freshly ground Italian coffee. Friendly, efficient service is another plus at the Bakery, which is open from 7.30am to 3.30pm Monday to Friday, 8.30am to 2pm Saturday.

TALLET BARN B&B

Yerdley Farm, Vicarage Lane, Long Compton,
Shipston-on-Stour, Warwickshire CV36 5LH
Tel: 01608 684248
e-mail: talletbarn@btinternet.com
website: www.countryaccom.co.uk/yerdley-farm

Yerdley Farm and the **Tallet Barn** annexe enjoy a quiet position in the village of Long Compton on the A3400. Tallet Barn is a medieval expression for a building that combines animal shelter, feed loft and outside steps. Many original features remain in a fine conversion that provides two comfortable non-smoking rooms for Bed & Breakfast guests. One is a double/family room on the ground floor, the other a twin-bedded room on the first floor; both have TV, radio and hot drinks tray. Farmland offers access to circular walks and glorious scenery.

🏛 historic building   🏛 museum   🏛 historic site   🏞 scenic attraction   🌿 flora and fauna

LONG COMPTON
12 miles SE of Stratford off the A3400

🌳 Whichford Wood

🏛 Rollright Stones

Just a short distance from the Oxfordshire border, this handsome village lies close to the local beauty spot known as **Whichford Wood**. It is a pleasant Cotswold village of thatched stone houses and some antiques shops. A mile or so to the south of Long Compton, straddling the Oxfordshire border, are the **Rollright Stones**, made up of the King Stone on one side of the lane, with the other two stone groupings – known as the King's Men and the Whispering Knights – on the other. Legend has it that this well-preserved stone circle is a king and his men, tricked by a sorceress into falling under her spell, and then petrified.

Solihull

🏛 National Motorcycle Museum

Solihull began life as a sparsely populated village in a relatively under-populated part of the country. It did not begin to grow in size and importance until the 1930s. Its motto – *Urbs in Rure* (town in country) – is well deserved. Its cottages and houses have since medieval times always blended well with the greenery that covers a large swathe of the surrounding region. Today, Solihull's 17th and 18th century houses clearly demonstrate the good planning that has always been a hallmark of the town's social and architectural design. The chief glory of Solihull's Church of St Alphege is some fine glass by Kempe. At nearby Bickenhill, the **National Motorcycle Museum** is a tribute

WARWICKSHIRE & WEST MIDLANDS

Rollright Stones, Long Compton

🎭 stories and anecdotes 🕊 famous people 🎨 art and craft 🎭 entertainment and sport 🚶 walks

EARLSWOOD LAKES

Earlswood Lakes Craft Centre, Wood Lane, Earlswood, Solihull, West Midlands B94 5JH
website: www.earlswoodlakescraftcentre.co.uk

Earlswood Lakes were built around the 1820s to supply water to the Startford-upon-Avon Canal. They are now home to an abundance of wildlife but still retain traces of an industrial heritage. On the northern edge of the Lakes is a craft centre housing a number of enterprises, including shops and a tea room. Trading hours are 10am to 5pm Tuesday to Sunday

ELSPETH & MARY

Tel: 01564 702999

Country crafts and gifts for all ages make up the ever-changing stock at **Elspeth & Mary**. On display are costume accessories, such as new clothing, vintage linen, bags, aprons, kitchenware and other items ranging from tea cosies to fascinators. Enjoy a trip down memory lane in Humbugs Olde World Icecream and Sweet Shop.

HAMISH BOWIE

Tel: 0800 056 6608/07980 959 662
website: www.hamishbowie.com

Hamish Bowie is a top jewellery designer specialising in wedding, engagement and eternity rings, handmade in gold, platinum, palladium, titanium and other precious metals. Some are set with fine diamonds and gemstones, and all are tailored to suit an individual's finger. Hamish also sells necklaces, earrings and holds a stock of clocks and watches – repair and restoration undertaken.

DILLY CRYSTAL

Tel: 01564 700382
website: www.reikibythelakes.co.uk

Dilly Crystal stocks a variety of lifestyle items and remedies, including crystals, gemstones, dowsing pendulums, books, candles, oils, incense and angels. Dilly offers reiki – 'human, equine, canine and feline' – and other therapies including hypnotherapy and personal development.

EARLSWOOD TEA BARN

Tel: 01564 702570

In the old egg-grading barn by the cowshed in the courtyard, Hamish Bowie's wife Jill runs **Earlswood Tea Barn** with Dilly. They offer a warm, comfortable and friendly ambience for enjoying a menu of breakfasts, light lunches, snacks and afternoon teas.

🏛 historic building   🏛 museum   🏛 historic site   🜀 scenic attraction   🌱 flora and fauna

to, and a priceless record of, the once-great British motorcycle industry.

Around Solihull

KNOWLE
1 mile SE of Solihull off the A4141

🏛 Grimshaw Hall   🏛 Chester House

The Elizabethan **Grimshaw Hall** in Knowle is a fine example of a carefully restored building of great historic significance (but is not open to the public). Nearby **Chester House** was built in the mid-1300s; it has been successfully refurbished and is today used as a library, thus offering a practical service to today's population.

LAPWORTH
5 miles S of Solihull off the A3400

🏛 Baddesley Clinton   🏛 Packwood House

Here, where the Grand Union and Stratford Canals meet, handsome Lapworth boasts some characterful old buildings. At Chadwick End, a mile west of the A4141, **Baddesley Clinton** is a romantic, medieval moated manor house which has changed little since 1633. Set against the backdrop of the Forest of Arden, this National Trust-owned property has had strong Catholic connections throughout its history. There is a tiny chapel in the house, and secret priests' holes, used to hide holy fathers during the fiercely anti-Catholic times during the reign of Charles I. The grounds feature a lovely walled garden and herbaceous borders, natural areas and lakeside walks. Lunches and teas are available. Nearby **Packwood House**, also in the care of the National Trust, is a Jacobean country mansion with a beautiful interior filled with rare furniture, tapestries, stained glass and

ornaments. The recently restored Carolean garden features an unusual topiary – a series of yew trees created to represent The Sermon on the Mount. 2007 sees the 80th anniversary of a visit by Queen Mary, and a small exhibition tells the story of the Royal visit.

HENLEY-IN-ARDEN
7 miles S of Solihull off the A3400

🏛 Beaudesert Castle   🏛 Church

Possibly the finest old market town in Warwickshire, its mile-long High Street brimming with examples of almost every kind of English architecture from the 15th century onwards, including many old timber-framed houses built with Arden oak. Little remains today of the Forest of Arden, the setting adopted by William Shakespeare for his *As You Like It*, as its stocks were diminished in the 1700s by the navy's demand for timber, but nothing could diminish the beauty of Henley itself.

The town emerged initially under the protection of Thurston de Montfort, Lord of the Manor in 1140. **Beaudesert Castle**, home to the de Montfort family, lies behind the churches of St John and St Nicholas, where remains of the castle mound can still be seen. Famous visitors of the past to this delightful town have included Dr Johnson, his friend James Boswell, and the poet Shenstone.

The 15th century **Church of St John the Baptist** has a tower which dominates the High Street where it narrows near the ancient Guildhall. The roof of the Guildhall is supported by oak beams which were growing at the time of the Norman invasion, and a wooden candelabra hangs from the ceiling. At one end of the hall is a huge dresser displaying a set of pewter plates dating back to 1677. The charter granted to the town has a

Ullenhall and Henley-in-Arden

Distance: *4.5 miles (7.2 kilometres)*

Typical time: *120 mins*

Height gain: *69 metres*

Map: *Explorer 220*

Walk: *www.walkingworld.com ID:2920*

Contributor: *Richard and Kathy Wood*

ACCESS INFORMATION:

Take the A4189 from Henley in Arden. Take a right turn, along Ullenhall Lane sign posted to Ullenhall. When you arrive in the village of Ullenhall, before reaching the pub turn left up Church Hill. Park along the roadside before the church.

DESCRIPTION:

This beautiful circular walk begins in the picturesque Warwickshire village of Ullenhall. It starts from the church slowly crossing fields and lanes towards Hallend which follows the Arden Way. Before crossing Henley in Arden Golf & Country Club there are a couple of benches, ideal for that well earned rest and bite to eat. The walk then follows the perimeter of the Golf course for a while before returning to Ullenhall across farmland.

FEATURES:

Pub, Church, Wildlife, Birds, Flowers, Great Views, Mostly Flat Description:

WALK DIRECTIONS:

1 | After leaving the attractive Ullenhall church, walk down Church Hill to the main Ullenhall road in the village. Cross the main road and head up Watery Lane. Walk to the right of the white railings and then go through the gate. Turn right to follow the footpath behind the house.

2 | Cross the road and go straight through the gate. Continue straight on over the hill and down the other side to the gateway by the road junction. Continue straight on along Chapel lane for 200 metres.

3 | At the road junction turn right up towards a small church. Go through the church yard to the left of the church and through the gate. Go down the hill following the hedge eventually leading to a road. Turn right onto the road.

4 | Follow the road until you meet the entrance to Hall end farm. Go through the gate to the farm. On passing through the gate to the farm turn

left into the field. Go straight across the field towards a small group of trees at the top of the hill. Go down the other side to a stile by a lane. Turn right onto lane.

5 | Continue along the lane passing a couple of cottages on a left hand bend. Immediately after this bend turn right by a barn to follow the Arden Way. Keeping on the Arden Way the path crosses the Golf course before running between the Tennis courts and a couple of houses, finally emerging at the Golf Club House.

6 | Turn left at the Club house to go across the car park. Do not go over the Railway bridge, follow the footpath to the right of the bridge, also signed up for the first golf tee. Follow the footpath along side the railway line and edge of the golf course. Cross over the stile by the railway bridge and down the steps to the road.

7 | Turning right on the road and head up towards a gate. Go through the gate and follow the edge of the golf course until arriving at a stile.

8 | Cross the stile and go straight across the field to arrive at a small wooden bridge. After crossing the bridge cross the fields keeping the farm house on your left. Carry on up the hill crossing three further stiles. Keeping the hedge to your left, carry on up the hill to another stile. Cross the next field to a gateway on the lane. Turn right onto the lane.

9 | Immediately turn left down Perry Mill Lane. Follow the lane down until you reach the junction of Watery Lane.

10 | Turn left and continue down Watery lane until you meet the main road. Cross the road then go up Church Hill back to your starting point by Ullenhall church.

royal seal embossed in green wax, kept in its own glass case in the Guildhall.

The town's Court Leet still meets yearly with the lord of the manor at its head, as it has for centuries. Members of this distinguished grouping have included the High Bailiff, Low Bailiff, Ale-taster, Butter-weigher, Mace bearer, Town Crier, Town Constable, Two Affearers and Two Brook Lockers. Just outside Henley lies **Beaudesert**, a village even older than its near neighbour Henley, with a good few timber-framed cottages and the beautifully restored Norman church of St Nicholas.

WOOTTON WAWEN
9 miles S of Solihull off the A3400

🏠 Church   🏠 Wootton Hall   🗿 Saxon Sanctuary

Handy for walks on nearby **Stratford Canal**, Wootton Wawen also contains some fine timber-framed buildings and Warwickshire's oldest church – **St Peter's,** an impressive structure that still has its Saxon tower, now more than 1,000 years old. The main building is actually three churches in one; there are three completely separate chapels tacked on to each other with a refreshing disregard for architectural design which does not in any way detract from the church's charm. One of these chapels, the barn-roofed Lady Chapel, is now **The Saxon Sanctuary**, a colourful exhibition that traces the history of 'Wagen's' woodland village in the Forest of Arden. It reveals how this small village conceals a Roman road, two monasteries, an ancient fort, mysterious underground passages, a river that changes with fashion, a disappearing pond and an aqueduct!

St Peter's stands within a picturesque churchyard which has won the Diocesan 'Best Kept' award several times. Next to the church stands **Wotton Hall**, dating from 1637. Maria

YEW TREE FARM SPECIALITY SHOPS

Stratford Road, Wootton Wawen, nr Henley-in-Arden, Warwickshire B95 6BY

On the A3400 close to J16 of the M40, **Yew Tree Farm** houses a delightful variety of crafts and speciality shops, open Tuesday to Sunday. In this pleasant country setting, summer visitors can stroll down to the waterfall meadow and pick flowers from the field.

HURO JEWELLERY

The Milling Shed   Tel: 01564 794391
e-mail: hurojewellery@hotmail.com website: www.hurojewellery.co.uk

Huro Jewellery is a small family business with an enviable reputation for quality and reliability. They specialise in the design and fabrication of unique pieces of jewellery at prices to suit all tastes and ages. Expert craftsmen work in all precious metals and, in addition to stock pieces, they will make new and exciting pieces to customers' individual requirements. Huro Jewellery also offers a comprehensive repair, alteration and cleaning service, and for 2007 they have started beginners' classes in jewellery making.

KNOT JUST WOOD BESPOKE KITCHENS

The Tool Shed   Tel: 01564 794785
website: www.knotjustwood.co.uk

Bespoke handmade kitchens and furniture are the speciality of **Knot Just Wood**, whose aim is to provide classic, timeless designs combined with traditional craftsmanship. They have the experience and expertise to provide a tailor-made solution for even the most awkward and difficult spaces, with designs and costings to suit all tastes and requirements. Knot Just Wood also stocks a range of kitchenware and unusual gifts for the home.

DELLA AND JAMES LINGERIE & SWIMWEAR

The Old Bull Pen   Tel: 01564 794255
e-mail: allisongile@dellaandjames.co.uk website: www.dellaandjames.co.uk

Della and James is a gem of a lingerie shop, a haven where clients can shop at leisure, be professionally fitted and order their favourites in different styles and colours. Many of the products stocked by owner Allison Gile are rarely found in this country, and the size of the shop and a close relationship with the customers enables her to respond quickly to their needs. Among the brands in stock are Rosy, Chantelle, Lejaby, Passionata and Panache, plus Nick and Nora sleepwear.

LE GRENIER ANTIQUES

Tel: 01564 795401
e-mail: info@legrenierantiques.co.uk website: www.legrenierantiques.co.uk

Le Grenier is a specialist supplier of antique and country French furniture. The retail space is filled with a dazzling array of fine pieces; the owners' passion for fine wood and a strong connection with the South of France are essential elements of the business, and among the speciality items on display are beds, tables, cabinets, armoires and commodes. The selection of English antique furniture is equally impressive, and the whole of the current range, French and English, can be viewed on Le Grenier's superb website.

Fitzherbert, wife of George IV, spent her childhood here and is thought now to return in ghostly form as the 'Grey Lady' who has been seen wandering about the Hall.

ALCESTER

15 miles S of Solihull off the A435

🏛 Roman Heritage Centre   🏛 Ragley Hall

Alcester is an ancient Roman market town built on the Icknield Street Encampment. **Roman Alcester Heritage Centre** explores everyday life in and around Roman Alcester. The museum houses an interactive exhibition of discoveries from the town and surrounding area. Local excavations have made Alcester one of the most understood small Roman towns in the country. There are many interesting properties in the medieval streets of Alcester, including the Church of St Nicholas with its 14th century tower and the early 17th century town hall. Alcester is popular for good local walks along the confluence of the Rivers Alne and Arrow. The town has been regional winner of a Britain in Bloom award. Alcester has many interesting buildings, including the 13th century Church of St Nicholas. One of its treasures is a painted alabaster effigy of Lord of the Manor Sir Fulke Greville, his wife and his 15 children (two of the children died in infancy and are represented by swaddling).

The adjacent village of Arrow is interesting to stroll around (despite some development) - as is the pretty stream that divides Arrow and Alcester. Though fruit farming around here is much rarer than it used to be, there are still to be found delicious fresh dessert plums for sale in the late summer and early autumn.

VOYAGE HOME

12 High Street, Alcester,
Warwickshire B49 5AD
Tel: 01789 765126
e-mail: info@voyagehome.co.uk
website: www.voyagehome.co.uk

The gift and interiors shop **Voyage Home** first opened its doors in Walton in 2001, and soon attracted the attention of celebrities and the style sections of newspapers and magazines. The second branch opened here in Alcester in September 2006 and is destined to be a magnet for locals and visitors alike. The shop is run by the mother and daughter duo Marie Kennedy and Natasha Minchella who have dedicated themselves to seeking out an exquisite range of stylish gifts and interior accessories.

    The shop has a fascinating range from vintage chairs and furniture, often reupholstered in funky modern fabrics, to chic smaller accessories, including the popular Bombay Duck and lisbeth Dahl ranges. There are stylish gifts for men, and children are well catered for with products including exclusive driftwood furniture or old-fashioned gifts such as a message in a bottle kits or pocket sundial. The move to Alcester is like a homecoming, with grandparents and great grandparents born and bred in the town, and Marie and Natasha ensure a warm and relaxed atmosphere in the shop.

🎬 stories and anecdotes   🐿 famous people   🎨 art and craft   🖊 entertainment and sport   🚶 walks

Nearby **Ragley Hall** is a genuine 17th century treasure. The Warwickshire home of the Marquess and Marchioness of Hertford, it is a perfectly symmetrical Palladian house set in 400 acres of parkland and gardens landscaped by Capability Brown. One of England's great Palladian country houses, it was inherited by the eighth Marquess in 1940 when he was only nine. During the Second World War the house was used as a hospital, and thereafter became almost completely derelict. In 1956 the Marquess married, and he and his wife set about making the Hall their home. All the main rooms have been redecorated in colours similar to the original ones that would have been used, and the process of restoring and improving continues. This magnificent stately home boasts James Gibb's elegant Baroque plasterwork in the Great Hall, as well as Graham Rust's stunning 20th century mural, *The Temptation.* A tour takes in Ragley Hall's fabulous collection of treasures from a bygone age, featuring paintings (including some modern art), china, furniture and a goodly assortment of Victorian and Edwardian dolls and toys. The Stables house an impressive carriage collection.

The main formal garden, to the west of the Hall, descends in a series of wide terraces, now entirely occupied by roses. The rest of the garden, covering 24 acres, consists of shrubs and trees interspersed with spacious lawns providing vistas across the 400-acre park. The lake, created in 1625, is now used for fishing, sailing, swimming

and water skiing; there is also a lakeside picnic area. The cricket pitch is in regular use. A country trail of about two miles wends its way through the park and the woods, to end at a very popular adventure playground. The Hall also boasts licensed terrace tea rooms. Special events such as craft fairs, gardeners' weekends, dog trials and outdoor concerts are held throughout the year.

COUGHTON
3 miles N of Alcester off the A435

🏛 Coughton Court   🏛 Dovecote

The parish church of this very pretty village was built by Sir Robert Throckmorton between 1486 and 1518. It has six bells which were restored in 1976 but are still carried in their original wooden frame. Inside there are some interesting oddments: a faceless clock, fish weather vanes and a dole cupboard from which wheaten loaves were distributed to the needy.

The crowning glory of the village is one of the great Tudor houses, **Coughton Court**, home of the Throckmorton family since 1409. The family were very prominent in Tudor times and were instigators of Catholic

Coughton Court

emancipation, playing a part in the Gunpowder Plot – the wives of some of the Gunpowder Plotters awaited the outcome of the Plot in the imposing central gatehouse. This, and the half-timbered courtyard, are particularly noteworthy, while inside there are important collections of paintings, furniture, porcelain and other family items from Tudor times to the present day. Treasured possessions include the chemise of Mary, Queen of Scots and the Throckmorton Coat; the former was worn by Queen Mary at her execution in 1587. The Coat was the subject of a 1,000 guinea wager in 1811. The priest's hole found in the house was constructed by one of the most famous builders of hiding places, Nicholas Owen.

This National Trust property has extensive gardens and grounds, a lake, a riverside walk and two churches to add to the interest. The fountain pool in the courtyard leads out to formal paths of lime trees. Spring heralds a magnificent display of over 100,000 daffodils and other spring blooms. The grounds also boast a walk planted with willows and native shrubs and trees beside the River Arrow, a new bog garden, a formal orchard and a walled garden project opened in 1996 and maturing into a splendid example of garden 'rooms' set with their own particular plant themes. One herbaceous border is planted with cool blues and yellows, the other with hot reds and orange. Also on site there is the Tudor Restaurant serving coffee, lunches and teas, an attractive gift shop and a plant centre.

A little way east of Coughton, at **Kinwarton** just south of the B4089, there stands another National Trust property in the shape of **Kinwarton Dovecote**. This circular 14th century dovecote still houses doves and retains its 'potence', a pivoted ladder by which

access is possible to the nesting boxes. Visitors can home in every day from April to October.

LONG MARSTON
6 miles SE of Alcester off the B4632

🚶 The Greenway

Charles I stayed at a house in Long Marston after his flight from the Battle of Worcester. The village's 14th century church has a half-timbered turret and porch. From Long Marston there's access to **The Greenway**, a converted railway line ideal for cycling or walking. This open public greensward boasts two-and-a-half miles of surfaced paths amid beautiful scenery, with picnic areas and a tranquil atmosphere of rural calm.

ILMINGTON
9 miles SE of Alcester off the B4632

🏠 Ilmington Manor   🚶 Ilmington Downs

🏛 Meon Hill

Along the northeastern Cotswolds, at the foot of the Wilmington Downs, you'll come to the village of Ilmington. This eye-catching place has several lovely old houses. Its part-Norman church, which features oak furnishings by Robert Thompson of Yorkshire, is approached through a Norman arch. This is truly a hidden place and one of the most picturesque one could hope to find. Lying in the valley between the Campden and Foxcote hills, it is surrounded by green fields and Cotswold countryside. Here there are fine old stone cottages with roses round the doors, and gardens full of colour. The village's name means 'the elm grown hill'. It was made famous on Christmas Day 1934, when the first radio broadcast by George V was introduced by Walton Handy, the village shepherd, and relayed to the world from **Ilmington Manor**,

Ilmington

the fine Elizabethan house once owned by the de Montfort family. The remains of a tramway, once the main form of transport to the village, can still be seen.

The nearby **Ilmington Downs** are, at 850 feet, the highest point in the county, commanding fine views of the surrounding country. Across the B4632 you will pass **Meon Hill**, where an Iron Age fort stood dominating the valley.

Birmingham

🏛 Sarehole Mill   🏛 Soho House

🖼 Museum & Art Gallery   🌿 Botanical Gardens

🌿 Nature Centre   ℘ Barber Institute

Birmingham rewards a visit many times over with its wealth of museums, marvellous public spaces, historic buildings and myriad other sights, sounds and attractions. It is a city with a rich and varied industrial history taking in everything from the first steam engine to button, buckles, clocks and chocolate.

Peter de Bermingham obtained rights of trading in a Market Charter granted in 1166 by King Henry II. By the mid-16th century there were some 1,500 people living in 200 homes, as well as one main street and a number of side-streets, markets for grain and livestock, and mills for tanning. Already the smiths were selling their knives and all manner of tools throughout England. This growth was helped along by the demands of the Parliamentarians, who during the Civil War needed a virtually endless supply of swords, pikes and armour. So it was that Birmingham emerged with a strong reputation as a metal centre.

By the 1750s the population had swelled to over 20,000 and, by the time of the Industrial Revolution, Birmingham had become the industrial, commercial and cultural capital of the Midlands. This was due in large part to the industriousness of the native 'Brummies'. Today this tradition continues, enhanced by the influx of peoples of differing nationalities and cultures, each adding their own unique gifts and talents to the mix.

The Birmingham Symphony Orchestra, recognised as one of the finest in the world, performs a regular season in the classical Roman-inspired Town Hall, built by Joseph Hansom, of hansom cab fame.

There are no fewer than 6,000 acres of parkland and open space in Birmingham. Cannon Hill Park in Edgbaston is one particular highlight. It has 80 acres of flower and ornamental gardens. Also in Edgbaston, on Westbourne Road, the **Botanical Gardens** (see panel below) comprise 15 acres and boast a Tropical House with lily pond, banana and cocoa trees, the Palm House, Orangery, National Bonsai Collection, Cactus House and the gardens themselves, filled with rhododendrons, azaleas and a good collection of trees. **Birmingham Nature Centre**, not far away on Pershore Road, has British and European wildlife – including wallaby, fallow deer, otters and reptiles – in indoor and outdoor enclosures resembling as closely as possible the creatures' native habitats.

The focus for shopping is the area bounded by New Street and Corporation Street; away from these areas there are some very attractive Victorian arcades which house the smaller speciality shops, including jewellers: Birmingham is traditionally a centre of jewellery, indeed there is an 18th century church in St Paul's Square known simply as The Jewellers Church. The Jewellery Quarter Discovery Centre is a good place to start if you'd like to learn more about times past and present in the Birmingham jewellery trade. It is located on Vyse Street, centred round the

The Birmingham Botanical Gardens And Glasshouses

Westbourne Road, Edgbaston,
Birmingham, B15 3TR
Tel: 0121 454 1860
e-mail: admin@birminghambotanicalgardens.org.uk
website: www.birminghambotanicalgardens.org.uk

The lush rainforest vegetation in the Tropical House includes many economic plants. Palms, tree ferns, orchids and insectivorous plants are displayed in the Subtropical House. The Mediterranean House features a wide variety of citrus plants, a pelargonium collection and seasonal displays of conservatory plants. A desert scene, with its giant agaves and opuntias, fills the Arid House.

Outside there is colourful bedding on the Terrace and a tour of the Gardens includes rhododendrons and azaleas, herbaceous borders, an impressive Rock Garden and a collection of over 200 trees. There are Herb and Cottage Gardens, a Water Garden, Alpine Yard, Historic Gardens, Organic Garden and the National Bonsai Collection. Ferns, grasses and sensory plants all have their own areas.

A magnificent Lawn Aviary stands at the far side of the main lawn, in front of which is a formal sunken Rose Garden. From a deep red centre the roses shade to pale pink and cream. A collection of shrub roses continues the rose theme behind the aviaries. A Sculpture Trail takes you to every corner of the Garden. The Children's Adventure Playground and Children's Discovery Garden provide excitement for our younger visitors who are also enthralled by our bird collection. The Gallery has different exhibitions each month. The 'Shop at the Gardens' stocks a wide range of gifts and plants.

Refreshments are available in the Pavilion. Bands play every Sunday afternoon throughout the summer. Open daily from 9 am. (10 am. Sunday) until dusk (7 pm. Latest).

preserved workshops of Smith & Pepper, still much as they were at the end of the 19th century.

The Museum and Art Gallery in Chamberlain Square represents the 17th, 18th and 19th centuries, including the world's finest collection of works by the Pre-Raphaelites. The contemporary art of sculpture is also well represented. Costume, silver, textiles and ceramics as well as works of ethnography from around the world, among which is a large and rare copper Buddha from Sultangani.

The Barber Institute at Birmingham University houses an excellent collection of paintings and sculptures. There is a wealth of Impressionist pieces, as well as the work of European masters.

Soho House is a handsome Georgian building which has been carefully restored to its original elegance. Former home of the pioneering industrialist Matthew Boulton, James Watt's business partner and founder of the Soho Mint, who lived here from 1766 to 1809, it contains some of his original furnishings. Displays relate the story of the man and his times, and offer a chance to see some of the fruits of Boulton's nearby factory – buttons and buckles, ormolu clocks and vases, silver and Sheffield plate tableware – where he and Watt developed the steam engine.

There are some 2,000 listed buildings in Birmingham, dating from the Elizabethan, Jacobean, Georgian and Victorian periods. The 1879 neo-Renaissance Council House is an impressive testament to the city's success and achievements. The Curzon Street Goods Station is a colonnaded building dating from 1838. Built by Philip Hardwick, its Ionic portico celebrates the wonder of the then-new railway industry.

Sarehole Mill in Cole Bank Road in Hall Green is Birmingham's only working water mill. The former childhood haunt of JRR Tolkien (author of *The Hobbit* and *Lord of the Rings*), it was used as a flour mill and also to roll and smooth metal needed during the Industrial Revolution. The present buildings are mainly Georgian, having been rebuilt in the 1760s, and were in commercial use right up to 1919. The mill then fell into disrepair, though it was later carefully restored to working order. Another nearby attraction well worth a visit is Castle Bromwich Hall Gardens, on Chester Road, about four miles east of the city centre. This boasts a collection of plants grown here in the 18th century, including historic herbs and vegetable species, shrubs and border plants, in a classic formal layout popular in the 1700s. Guided tours available.

Around Birmingham

ASTON
2 miles N of Birmingham off the A34

🏛 Aston Hall

Aston Hall was one of the last great Jacobean country houses to be built in England. Like Hatfield House and Blickling Hall, it has a highly intricate plan and a dramatic skyline of turrets, gables and chimneys. It is also administered by Birmingham Museum and Art Gallery, who have done much to make it a memorable place to visit. The house was built between 1618 and 1635 by Sir Thomas Holte, and remained the seat of the Holte family until it was sold off in 1817. King Charles I came to Aston Hall in 1642, at the beginning of the Civil War, and it was later besieged and sacked by Parliamentarian soldiers.

KINGSBURY

7 miles NE of Birmingham off the A4097

🎣 Water Park 🐤 Children's Farm

Kingsbury Water Park boasts over 600 acres of country park, with loads to see and do, including birdwatching, picnic sites, nature trails, fishing and a good information centre. There is also a cosy café and special unit housing the park's shop and exhibition hall. Also with the park, **Broomey Croft Children's Farm** makes for an enjoyable and educational day out for all the family, with a wealth of animals housed in renovated early 19th century farm buildings.

YARDLEY

2 miles E of Birmingham off the A45/A4040

🏛 Blakesley Hall

Blakesley Hall is Birmingham's finest Elizabethan building. Built in 1590, it is an extremely attractive timber-framed farmhouse which has been carefully restored. Its rich, decorative framing and jettied first and second floors reflect the wealth of its Elizabethan owner and builder, Richard Smallbroke, one of the leading merchants of the time. A diminutive and rare Long Gallery survives, while in Smallbroke's bedroom the original wall paintings were uncovered in 1950. Some of the 12 rooms are furnished to look as they did in 1684, when an inventory of the house's contents was drawn up.

Old Yardley village is one of Birmingham's outstanding conservation areas. Within walking distance of Blakesley Hall, it is truly remarkable for its medieval church and **Trust School**. Of particular note are the pretty Georgian cottages.

Blakesley Hall

WHITACRE GARDEN CENTRE

Tamworth Road, Nether Whitacre, Coleshill,
Warwickshire B46 2DP
Tel: 01675 481306
e-mail: mail@whitacregardencentre.co.uk
website: www.whitacregardencentre.co.uk

Whitacre Garden Centre is an independently-run enterprise in the heart of the North Warwickshire countryside, easily reached from the M6 (J4) or the M42 (J9). A wide range of indoor and outdoor plants is always available, along with garden tools and accessories, pots and ornaments, fencing, arches and pergolas. Also on site are a gift shop with a floristry, a wild bird care centre, a children's play area and the stylish modern Café Camellia. Friendly staff are always ready with help and advice. Opening hours are 9am to 5.30pm (Sun 10.30am to 4.30pm, Thursdays till 8pm April to December).

BOURNVILLE
4 miles S of Birmingham off the A4040

📷 Cadbury World

This planned village built by the Cadbury family, which moved its factory from the city centre in 1879, is a testament to good labour relations. **Cadbury World** is located in the heart of the famous Bournville factory. Here visitors can follow the story of chocolate, from tropical rain forests to 16th century Spain and on to Georgian London and, finally, Victorian Birmingham. Of course, a highlight of any tour here is the chance to sample the modern day product!

Coventry

🏛 Cathedral   🏛 St Mary's Guildhall

📷 Phoenix Initiative   📷 Priory Visitor Centre

📷 Toy Museum   ⚓ Canal Basin   🦢 Lady Godiva

📷 Herbert Art Gallery & Museum

📷 Transport Museum

Although on the fringe of the West Midlands conurbation, Coventry is surrounded by some of the finest scenery and places of historic interest in the country. It claims among many of its famous sons and daughters the novelist George Eliot, who attended school in Warwick Row and lived with her father on Foleshill Road between 1841 and 1849, and the poet Philip Larkin, son of Coventry's city treasurer and born in the city in 1922.

The famous three medieval spires of Coventry - Christchurch, Holy Trinity and St Michael's - are still prominent on the city skyline. During the terrible bombing inflicted on the city during the Second World War, St Michael's, a former parish church elevated to Coventry's cathedral in 1918, suffered direct

hits. Its spire and outer walls are all that remain, evoking both the horror and the spirit of reconciliation that arose from those times. Standing in the ruins of this 14th century church can be a strange and moving experience. The altar is made of broken stones gathered from the destruction on the night of 14th November 1940. It is surmounted by a cross of charred roof beams and a cross of medieval nails, behind which are inscribed the words, 'Father Forgive.'

The new **Cathedral**, designed by Basil Spence, stands at right angles to the old, and together they symbolise sacrifice and resurrection. The cathedral's worldwide ministry of peace and reconciliation has been echoed by the city fathers in Coventry, who in the years since the Second World War have aquired 26 twin towns and cities around the world, many of the links forged from a shared experience of war. Though unashamedly modern, the vast and striking interior of Spence's cathedral conveys a powerful sense of the past. It is also an unrivalled gallery of post-war British art, with Jacob Epstein, Elizabeth Frink, John Piper and Graham Sutherland among those artists represented. In a national poll conducted by English Heritage and Channel Four in 1999, it was voted Britain's most popular 20th century building.

Coventry has ancient links with the myth of St George the dragon-slayer, but its most famous legend is, of course, **Lady Godiva**, who rode the streets naked to protest against taxation on the 11th century town-dwellers. A bronze statue in Broadgate stands to her memory. It was Godiva's husband Leofric who started commerce and industry in Coventry as early as 1043, when he chose the small Saxon township as the site for a Benedictine priory. He gave the monks land on which to raise sheep, laying the basis for the wool trade which by 1400 had turned Coventry into the 4th biggest and most powerful city in England. Leofric and Godiva's church, dating from the 1040s, was later turned by the Benedictines into the Cathedral Church of St Mary, and was fated to become the only English cathedral to be destroyed on the orders of Henry VIII.

The site of the city's lost first cathedral has in recent years become the focus of the **Phoenix Initiative**, a Millennium project that has blended archaeology and the restoration of historic buildings with the creation of new public spaces and cutting edge architecture.

Medieval Coventry

Among the new buildings is the **Priory Visitor Centre,** which tells the story of the great lost cathedral and displays artefacts from archaeological excavations. Beneath another new building nearby are the Priory Undercrofts, standing archaeology that allows visitors to make conducted tours of cellars where monks once lived. The Phoenix is the first piece in a £1 billion regeneration jigsaw that, over the next decade, will transform Coventry's somewhat angular and splintered city into a much more attractive and welcoming place, built on heritage and striking new buildings.

Despite its roller-coaster history, modern Coventry still has many ancient treasures: Bond's Hospital in Hill Street is a beautiful timber-framed almshouse, founded in the 16th century and restored by the Victorians. It forms one side of a courtyard, open to the public, that also includes the 16th century Bablake School and the 14th century Church of St John the Baptist, used as a prison for Royalist soldiers during the Civil War and almost certainly the origin of the expression Sent to Coventry. Ford's Hospital in Greyfriar's Lane is another half-timbered Tudor almshouse, founded in 1509 by Coventry merchant William Ford as a home for elderly women and still in use as that today.

Nearby, in New Union Street, is the gatehouse to Cheylesmore Manor, once owned by the Black Prince and the only unfortified royal palace in England. This attractive half-timbered building is Coventry's Register Office, the oldest building in the country to be used for such a purpose. Not far away stands Whitefriars, a Carmelite friary established in the 1340s. It is not open to the public at present, but in its picturesque gatehouse is the privately run Coventry Toy Museum, which houses a collection dating from the 18th century. Coventry's main civic museum, the **Herbert Art Gallery and Museum**, houses a permanent exhibition of the city's history. The complex is now in the throes of a multi-million development that will give it a state-of-the-art History Centre and new gallery space in a landmark building very close to the cathedral.

A few yards away stands the jewel in Coventry's medieval crown, **St Mary's Guildhall**, where Kings and Queens have been entertained and the city's mayors appointed to their office since the middle of the 14th century. Its tower once imprisoned Mary, Queen of Scots, and it has a restored 600-year-old crypt. One of England's finest guildhalls, St Mary's Hall also features a superb Arras tapestry made for its north wall in 1500 and a window above that portrays nine English kings, including a rare representation of the legendary King Arthur. The building is a treasure house of oak carving, suits of armour and stained glass and has associations with many famous people, including George Eliot and Oliver Cromwell.

At Holy Trinity, just along the street, experts have recently restored and uncovered the *Coventry Doom*, a 15th century Judgement Day wall painting that is regarded as one of the finest works of medieval art to have survived in this country.

Coventry's history since the Middle Ages had been a roller coaster ride of boom and slump, with staple industries like silk-weaving and watch-making falling victim to foreign competition in the 19th century. It was cycle manufacture and then automotive engineering

that laid the foundations for the city's 20th century prosperity and growth. Back in 1885, the first modern bicycle was invented and manufactured in Coventry. A decade later Daimler opened a factory in a disused Coventry cotton mill – and the British motor industry was in business.

The **Coventry Transport Museum** (see panel opposite) in Hales Street examines the enormous contribution made by the city to the transport industry, spanning more than a century, from the first cycles to the latest in automotive technology. Its collection of more than 400 British-made cars, motorcycles and bicycles, is the largest in the world and features, among many other treasures, Thrust SSC, the current holder of the World Land Speed record. The Museum is open every day and admission is free.

The engineering boom made Coventry a magnet for skilled engineers from all over Britain, among them the father of Coventry-born Frank Whittle, inventor of the jet engine. But there is a surviving relic too from an earlier period of the city's industrial history.

On the edge of the city centre, a few minutes walk from the main shopping areas, is **Coventry Canal Basin**, the only canal terminus in the country to be located in the centre of a city. Its warehouses, some dating from the 18th century, are now home to artists' studios and specialist craft workshops, and the basin has been the focus in recent years of a new development of offices, apartments and shops. The five-mile canal towpath to the boundary of the city features around 40 works of art – the longest art trail in the country.

For an industrial city, Coventry also boasts many 'green' credentials, with acres of protected ancient woodland, outstanding parkland and public spaces.

Museum of British Road Transport Coventry

Hales Street, Coventry CV1 1PN
Tel: 02476832425
e-mail: museum@mbrt.co.uk
website: www.mbrt.co.uk

Coventry is the home of British road transport, and the Museum offers the largest display of British cars, cycles and motorcycles anywhere in the world. Step back in time to pioneering cycles and motorcars and the beginning of mass production. Experience the recreated Coventry Blitz and share in the City's spirit of optimism as it rebuilt after the war. Find out about Coventry's *Boomtime* in the 50s, 60s and 70s and reflect on past and future designs in the *Icons* Gallery. Includes the land speed record cars 'Thrust 2' and 'ThrustSSC', the Coventry Blitz Experience, and the world famous Tiatsa model collection.

Lady Herbert's Garden, recently restored as part of the Phoenix Initiative, lies between the last two surviving medieval city gates. Incorporating part of the old city wall, it forms a link between a new public square, Millennium Place, and the new Garden of International Friendship.

Greyfriars Green close to the city's railway station, is a conservation area with attractive gardens and two terraces of fine buildings. The War Memorial Park in Kenilworth Road is Coventry's premier park, with tree-lined walkways, giant children's water feature and Cenotaph.

Coombe Country Park, close to the city's eastern boundary, comprises almost 400 acres of historic Capability Brown landscapes surrounding a luxury hotel in what was the medieval Cistercian abbey of Coombe.

And what of the expression 'sending to Coventry'? There are many possible explanations, the most likely being that a garrison was once based here that was so unpopular with the locals that they shunned the soldiers. Another, less likely, theory is that the name of Coventry derived from the covin-tree, an oak that stood in front of the castle. It was used as the gallows!

Around Coventry

BAGINTON
5 miles S of Coventry off the A444

 Midland Air Museum

The **Midland Air Museum** at Coventry Airport in Baginton houses a unique collection of aircraft, engines and exhibits telling the story of the jet engine. In this hands-on museum visitors can sit in the cockpit of a Vulcan Bomber or Meteor, and with over 35 aircraft on display there is something to interest everyone. This very relaxed and informal museum features local aviation history, with a 'Wings Over Coventry' gallery and a wealth of Coventry-produced aircraft and other exhibits, dominated by the giant Armstrong Whitworth Argosy freighter of 1959.

STONELEIGH
6 miles S of Coventry off the A444

🏛 Abbey

This attractive village has a sandstone Norman church, several timber-framed houses and, nearby, the headquarters of the Royal Agricultural Society of England, and the Showground famed for its annual Royal Show. The history of **Stoneleigh Abbey** began in 1154 when Henry II granted the lands to a community of Cistercian monks, who built their abbey on the site. Visitors can view the superb interior only on guided tours (Tel: 01926 858535) but are welcome to stroll through the grounds, which were landscaped by Humphry Repton in 1809. They contain many beautiful trees, including a 1,000-year-old oak.

BUBBENHALL
7 miles SE of Coventry off the A445

🦌 Country Park

Between Bubbenhall and Ryton-on-Dunsmore, off the A445, **Ryton Pools Country Park** is a 100-acre country park with an exciting range of facilities, including a Visitors Centre, picnic areas, bird hide, numerous footpaths, model railway, fishing site and two adventure playgrounds.

Rugby

🏛 School   📷 Webb Ellis Museum
🌿 Cock Robin Wood   🦌 The Pathway of Fame
🦌 Great Central Walk

The only town of any great size in north-eastern Warwickshire, Rugby has a Market Place surrounded by handsome buildings and

the striking Church of St Andrew, built by the Rokeby family after their castle had been destroyed by Henry II. The old tower dates from the 1400s. With its fireplace and three foot-thick walls, it looks more like a fortress and was, indeed, a place of refuge.

Rugby is probably most famous for its **School**, founded in 1567. Originally situated near the Clock Tower in the town, it moved to its present site in 1750. There are many fine buildings, splendid examples of their period, the highlight being the school chapel, designed by William Butterfield. These buildings house treasures such as stained glass believed to be the work of Albrecht Durer, the 15th century German artist and engraver.

There are few places in the world where you can gaze with any certainty over the birthplace of a sport that gives pleasure to millions. The game of Rugby originated here at the school when William Webb Ellis broke the rules during a football match in 1823 by picking up and running with the ball. The **Webb Ellis Rugby Football Museum** is open from 9am to 5pm Monday to Saturday, and the **Rugby Pathway of Fame** begins at the Visitor Centre and follows a series of bronze plaques, each dedicated to a famous player or a historic moment in the development of the game. Rugby Town Trail is a two-hour walk that brings to life the town's history from its Saxon beginnings to the present day. The walk begins and ends at the **Clock Tower** in Market Place. This edifice was intended to commemorate the Golden Jubilee of Queen Victoria in 1887, yet it was not completed until 1889 because over-indulgent citizens had dipped too deep into the Tower funds to feast and drink at the Jubilee. The Trail takes in many of the town's main tourist attractions, including the house where Rupert Brooke was born, and his statue in

Regent Place. Caldecott Park, in the centre of town, has beautiful floral displays, trees and a herb garden. Picnicking areas and a play area are two more of the highlights of this lovely park, and there are also facilities for bowls, putting, tennis and boules.

Rugby is bounded by two of the greatest Roman roads, Fosse Way and Watling Street, which meet just northwest of Rugby, at High Cross, one of the landmarks of the area.

The town is as far inland as it is possible to get in the British Isles, yet Rugby is an excellent centre for all kinds of water sports and aquatic activities. The Oxford Canal winds its way through the borough, and the Rivers Avon, Leam and Swift provide good angling, pleasant walks and places to picnic.

Cock Robin Wood is a nature reserve on Dunchurch Road, near the junction with Ashlawn Road. Here the visitor will find extensive areas of oak, ash, rowan, cherry and field maples, as well as grassy areas and a central pond, a haven for insects, frogs and butterflies.

The **Great Central Walk** is a four-mile ramble through Rugby. Along the way visitors will encounter an abundance of wildlife, plants and shrubs, as well as conservation areas and picnic sites.

Around Rugby

ASHBY ST LEDGERS
4 miles SE of Rugby off the A361

The Gunpowder Plot conspirators took refuge here in the manor house owned by Robert Catesby. Though not open to visitors,

---

CLIFTON CRUISERS CANAL HOLIDAYS

Vicarage Hill, Clifton-on-Dunsmore, nr Rugby,
Warwickshire CV23 0DG
Tel: 01788 543570 Fax: 01788 579799
e-mail: info@cliftoncruisers.com
website: www.cliftoncruisers.com

Clifton Cruisers is a family-run business based at Clifton Wharf on the North Oxford Canal, from where the Garfield family offer canal holidays with a choice of day trips, short breaks, weeks, romantic weekends, Christmas trips and longer bookings of up to two months. The boats are individually designed for comfort, with a very varied choice of layout and accommodation to satisfy the requirements of most family and other holiday groups. All have centre ropes for easy mooring, radiator central heating, fridge/freezer, gas hob, oven and grill, microwave, toaster, cutlery and crockery, bed linen as required, TV and DVD player, radio/CD player or radio/tape player, hairdryer and 240 and 12V sockets.

All the boats come ready to go, with no hidden extras for diesel, gas or car parking. Clifton Cruisers will give full handover instructions to the British Marine federation standard and are also happy to provide a 'driving lesson' and full lock instruction. Along with canal etiquette and advice on routes and key times. The base on the North Oxford Canal is convenient for the Warwickshire Ring, the Ashby and Grand Union Canals and the Grand Union Leicester Arm. Warwickshire boasts some really beautiful countryside, and the major tourist attractions such as Stratford-upon-Avon, Warwick Castle and Coventry Cathedral are within easy reach.

Napton Windmill

Distance: *4.5 miles (7.2 kilometres)*
Typical time: *150 mins*
Height gain: *60 metres*
Map: *Explorer 222*
Walk: *www.walkingworld.com ID:350*
Contributor: *Ron and Jenny Glynn*

ACCESS INFORMATION:

By car: parking at village green.

ADDITIONAL INFORMATION:

Stout footwear is needed for this walk.

DESCRIPTION:

From the peaceful village green, surrounded with attractive houses and cottages, the route climbs the High Street, then drops to pasture-land below the village. It leads to the Oxford Canal on its descent from the summit via the locks. Following the towpath past the Folly Pub, famous for its pies, the canal then follows the twisting, winding route round the contours of the land, eventually leaving it to start the ascent back to the village.

The walk passes the huge crater where once clay was quarried to make bricks. The climb to a height of 500ft provides distant views across the wide vista of seven counties. The windmill at the top is a fine feature of Napton and the Church of St Lawrence nearby also occupies a lofty position. It is but a short distance down to the village green.

WALK DIRECTIONS:

1 | With the Crown Pub on left, walk uphill along High Street into Hackwell Street and on.

2 | Turn right opposite Vicarage Road sign, by side of The Granary, down steps to take a stile. Follow line of two telegraph poles and on, to cross a stile and down a bank.

3 | Turn right along narrow lane to come out onto road and follow round to Dog lane.

4 | Turn left just before school, into bridleway. Ignore footpath on left and continue straight ahead to go through middle metal gate and continue then out into another field in same direction. At third gateway turn left to another gate. Go through and turn right. Pass a pond and go through a walkers' gate over stream.

5 | At the next gate turn right, with hedge and fence on right. Go through gate at end of field and out onto road. Continue at junction along Chapel Green and past "Pondarosa" on left.

6 | Turn left at "Eureka" along private drive and into gate, right along back of garage and tight to hedge on right to cross a stile. Walk diagonally left and head for dip in westerly direction. Look for concrete footbridge downhill. Cross and head diagonally left (aim for collapsed pylon) and once past, look for the gate that leads out onto the road. Turn right and walk over canal bridge.

7 | Turn left down onto towpath by a lock, then left under the bridge. Notice the windmill on the hill as you walk down to the bottom lock. Pass the Folly Pub on left and walk on. Enjoy now the tranquillity of still waters, wild life, domestic animals and far distant views, along the winding Oxford Canal in this glorious setting.

8 | At Bridge 112 turn left and walk over it to pass buildings on left.

9 | Turn left over stile and walk on over uneven land, keeping close to fence overlooking old disused quarry. Walk uphill where roam Jacob sheep and donkeys. Follow line of fencing round to left, past huge rock boulders, then uphill with hedge on left. Pause for breath (several times) on the steep ascent, and look across the panoramic views across 7 counties.

10 | The line of the hedge bends to the right, to take a narrow path along to a stile that leads out onto the driveway of Napton Windmill. Turn left and continue.

11 | Take left fork, to pass Leys Farm and then the parish church of St Lawrence.

12 | Turn right a few yards on, into enclosed downhill path. Come out on road opposite the Granary and retrace steps to start point.

J.R.C.S. FALCONRY

Tel: 01788 890096   mob: 077736 524512
e-mail: jan@jrcsfalconry.co.uk
website: www.jrcsfalconry.co.uk

'Exciting', Entertaining' and 'Educating' are apt descriptions of the courses offered at **J.R.C.S. Falconry.** Owner Jan Prymaka, a falconer with many years' experience, started his professional career with the Bird of Prey display team at Wobrun Abbey and his work has covered all aspects of rearing, training, working with and caring for a wide range of birds of prey.

Set up in 2001, J.R.C.S. Falconry is based not far from Rugby near the Warwickshire/Northamptonshire border close to some beautiful flying countryside and easily reached from the motorway network.

The main courses, lasting 5 or 10 days, cover such topics as the law relating to birds of prey; their food, nutrition and health; tools and equipment; housing and husbandry; and training and caring for the birds. These course end with a written and practical exam, and one-day experience and hawking days are also available.

Jan's private collection of birds includes vultures and buzzards, the beautiful barn owl, the hunting hawk, the feisty falcon, the canny kestrel and the glamorous golden eagle. Applicants can book courses by telephone, by e-mail or online.

Ashby St Ledgers Manor House

the manor house is close to the road and worth seeing, as it is very evocative of the times. This charming village also rewards a stroll, with some cottages designed by Lutyens. Parts of the handsome village church date back to the early 1500s.

NAPTON ON THE HILL
9 miles S of Rugby off the A425

This attractive village on a rounded hill above a curve in the Oxford Canal - one of the prettiest in this part of the world, with pleasant towpath walks. There are views of seven counties from the hilltop.

DUNCHURCH
1 mile S of Rugby off the A426

🐦 Guy Fawkes

'The gunpowder plot village': on November 5th, 1605, the Gunpowder Plot conspirators met at the Red Lion Inn, Dunchurch, to await the news of **Guy Fawkes'** attempt to blow up the English Houses of Parliament. The Red Lion still exists today, as a private residence known as **Guy Fawkes House**. This attractive village with its rows of thatched cottages has a 14th century church built by the monks of Pipewell Abbey, with one of the oldest parish registers in England.

Such was the considerable trade in looking after travellers who stopped over in Dunchurch during the great coaching days (up to 40 coaches a day stopped here), it is said that every property in the centre of the village was at some time an inn or ale house. For centuries Dunchurch has been a popular stopover point for travellers on the main Holyhead-London road. A coaching stop to take on fresh horses, Dunchurch was also the staging post for pupils, masters, parents and visitors travelling to Rugby School. Many famous and important people have stayed in the village over the centuries, including Princess Victoria, Longfellow, the Duke of Wellington and William Webb Ellis of Rugby Football fame. Today, the village is in a designated conservation area with a lovely village green complete with village stocks and maypole, charming 16th, 17th and 18th century buildings, many of which retain the traditional Warwickshire thatched roofs. In

1996 the village won the prestigious Best Kept Large Village in Warwickshire award.

The Old Smithy which stands on the Rugby Road, is believed to have been the inspiration for Henry Wadsworth Longfellow's poem *Under the Spreading Chestnut Tree*.

DRAYCOTE
4 miles SW of Rugby off the A426

🐾 Draycote Water   🎣 Country Park

Draycote Water is a centre of watersports, fishing, sailing, birdwatching and attractive walks around the reservoir. Fly fishing permits are available from the Fishing Lodge. **Draycote Country Park**, next to Draycote Water, boasts 21 acres for walks, kite flying, picnicking by the lake, and magnificent hilltop views over Draycote Water, one of the largest reservoirs in the region.

LONG ITCHINGTON
8 miles SW of Rugby off the A423

🏛 Church of the Holy Trinity

The picturesque village of Long Itchington straddles the lovely Grand Union Canal. The Anglo-Saxon 'Farm by the River Itchen' boasted a population greater than that of Coventry at the time of the Domesday Book.

Dunchurch Village Stocks

The village **Church of the Holy Trinity** dates in part from 1190. The tower has only the remains of its original spire, which collapsed when struck by lightning during a Sunday morning service in 1762. The carvings in the chancel bear a closer look: one depicts a monkey with her young, another the head and shoulders of what is believed to be a jester.

🏛 historic building   📷 museum   🏛 historic site   ⌘ scenic attraction   🌱 flora and fauna

THE FRAGRANT ROOM

37 Coventry Street, Southam, Warwickshire CV47 0EP
Tel: 01926 811933

In 1642 Southam, on the River Itchen, saw the first skirmishes of the English Civil War. Things have been much more relaxed since those far-off days, and there is no more pleasant and inviting place to visit than **The Fragrant Room**. Owner Jan Watts personally sources a wide range of fragrant things for the home, including pots pourris and candles in all shapes and sizes and fragrance oils. Also among the stock are costume and silver jewellery, New World CDs for relaxation, lovely silk scarves by Lucy Harper, greetings cards (some handmade), wrapping paper and Tisserand Lavender products.

SOUTHAM

9 miles SW of Rugby off the A426

Southam is an attractive town along the River Itchen. It is first mentioned in a charter of King Ethelred in 998, but there was probably an Anglo-Saxon village here before this, and Roman coins found within the parish hint at an earlier community. It repays a visit for the lovely rural scenery surrounding the town, and the wealth of good walking in the area. The Battle of Southam in 1642 was the first skirmish of the Civil War, and it was here in Southam that Charles I spent the night before the battle of Edge Hill. In the main street is the surprisingly named Old Mint Inn, a 14th century stone building taking its name from an occurrence following the Battle of Edge Hill. Charles I commanded his local noblemen to bring him their silver treasure, which was then melted down and minted into coins with which he paid his army.

WOLSTON

5 miles W of Rugby off the A428

The Church of St Margaret is Norman in origin, but was substantially rebuilt after the steeple collapsed into the chancel in 1759. A stone in the churchyard poses the simple question: *'Tell me which is best, the toilsome journey*

or the traveller's rest?' Near the 1837 railway bridge are the earthworks of Brandon Castle, which was destroyed not very long after it was built in the 13th century.

RYTON-ON-DUNSMORE

6 miles W of Rugby off the A45

🌱 Henry Doubleday Research Association

🌱 Ryton Pools Country Park   🌱 Pagets Pool

This village is home to the **Henry Doubleday Research Association** at Ryton Gardens. This organic farming and gardening organisation leads the way in research and advances in horticulture. The grounds are landscaped with thousands of plants and trees, all organically grown. Also on site are a herb garden, rose garden, garden for the blind, shrub borders and free-roaming animals. **Ryton Pools Country Park** is a 100-acre country park opened in 1996. The 10-acre Ryton Pool is home to great crested grebes, swans, moorhens and Canada geese. There is also an attractive meadow area for strolling or picnicking, a Visitor Centre, shop and exhibition area. **Pagets Pool** near the north-eastern end of the park is one of the most important sites in Warwickshire for dragonflies, with 17 species including the common blue, emperor dragonfly and black-tailed skimmer. Other highlights include

WARWICKSHIRE & WEST MIDLANDS

guided walks and a model railway run by Coventry Model Engineering Society.

BRANDON
6 miles W of Rugby off the A428

🌱 Nature Reserve

Brandon Marsh Nature Centre is 200 acres of lakes, marshes, woodland and grassland, providing a home and haven for many species of wildlife. There are bird hides, an informative Visitor Centre and a nature trail, as well as guided walks, pond-dipping and changing exhibitions.

STRETTON UNDER FOSSE
5 miles NW of Rugby off the B4112

🏛 Prison Museum

For a slightly unusual day out, **H M Prison Services Museum** at Newbold Revel, Stretton under Fosse has displays on the history of imprisonment from medieval times to the present. Visits are strictly by appointment; contact the Curator on 01788 834168.

NEWBOLD-ON-AVON
1 mile N of Rugby off the B4112

🌳 Quarry Park

Newbold Quarry Park affords visitors the opportunity for a country walk just north of Rugby town, with hilly woodland and extensive waterside walks. This bit of countryside is a haven for birds and wildlife.

NUNEATON
8 miles N of Coventry on the A444

🏛 Museum & Art Gallery

Originally a Saxon town known at Etone, Nuneaton is mentioned in the Domesday Book of 1086. The 'Nun' was added when a wealthy Benedictine priory was founded here in 1290.

The Priory ruins left standing are adjacent to the church of St Nicholas, a Victorian edifice occupying a Norman site which has a beautiful carved ceiling dating back to 1485.

The town has a history as a centre for coal-mining, which began in Nuneaton as early as the 14th century. Other industries for which the town has been famous include brick and tile manufacture and ribbon-making on hand looms. As the textile and hatting industries boomed, the town began to prosper. Today's Nuneaton is a centre of precision engineering, printing, car components and other important trades.

Nuneaton Museum and Art Gallery, located in Riversley Park, features displays of archaeological interest ranging from prehistoric to medieval times, and items from the local earthenware industry. There is also a permanent exhibition of the town's most illustrious daughter, the novelist and thinker George Eliot. Born to a prosperous land agent at Arbury Hall in 1819, Eliot (whose real name was Mary Ann Evans) was an intellectual giant and free thinker. She left Warwickshire for London in adulthood, and met George Henry Lewes, a writer and actor who was to become her lifelong companion. Lewes, married with three children, left his family so that he and Eliot, very bravely for the time, could set up house together. Eliot's novels return again and again to the scenes and social conventions of her youth, and are among the greatest works of English literature – in particular her masterpiece, *Middlemarch*.

MONKS KIRBY
9 miles SE of Nuneaton off the A427

🏛 Denmark Field

The Saxons were the first people to build a church in this ancient settlement, probably a wooden structure originally, being replaced by a stone building later. The Danes arrived about 864 AD as part of their conquest of this part of the country. The field at the rear of the church is still known as the **Denmark Field**.

After the Norman Conquest, a Benedictine Priory was established and a church rebuilt on the old site. Most of the present building dates from the 14th century. The tall spire, built above the tower in the 15th century, could be seen by travellers for many miles around until it was blown down by a great storm on Christmas night in 1701. From its earliest days Monks Kirby grew in size and importance, eventually taking on the full status of a market town. Pilgrims and merchants were accommodated in the Priory's guest house, which probably stood on the site of the current Denbigh Arms public house. This rural, quiet village, dominated by the ancient church, also boasts many pretty cottages along its main streets.

BEDWORTH
3 miles S of Nuneaton off the B4029

🌱 Miners' Welfare Park

This small town was once part of the North Warwickshire coalfield established at the end of the 1600s. Local people were largely responsible for the building of the Coventry Canal, running from Coventry to Fradley near Lichfield and completed in 1790, 22 years after work on it began. It was constructed to connect the fast-growing town with the great new trade route, the Grand Trunk – and to provide Coventry with cheap coal from the Bedworth coal field.

French Protestant families fleeing persecution sought refuge here, bringing with them their skill in silk and ribbon weaving.

The parish church, completed in 1890, is a good example of Gothic Revival. Its grounds include a scented garden. The open air market and main shopping precinct share the town's central All Saints Square with the splendid Chamberlaine almshouses, founded by a 17th century rector of Bedworth, the Rev. Nicholas Chamberlaine. Close by, the Old Meeting church dates from 1726 and is one of the earliest nonconformist chapels in the region. Bedworth's award-winning **Miners' Welfare Park** contains some of the finest spring and summer bedding layouts in the region, as well as areas devoted to tennis, bowls, pitch and putt, roller skating and cricket.

ARBURY HALL
3 miles SW of Nuneaton off the B4102

A visit to **Arbury Hall** (see panel on page 472) fits another piece in the jigsaw of George Eliot's life and times. She was born on the estate, where her father was land agent; in *Mr Gifgil's Love Story* she portrays Arbury as Cheverel Manor, and gives detailed descriptions of many of the rooms in the house, including the Salon and the Dining Room – comparing the latter, unsurprisingly given its grandeur, to a cathedral. The Hall's grounds include a delightful 10-acre garden with a real air of tranquillity.

ANSLEY
5 miles W of Nuneaton off the B4112

Ansley is best known for adjacent Hoar Park, which dates back to the 1430s. The existing house and buildings date from 1730, and now form the centrepiece of the 143-acre Park, which contains a handsome **Craft Village**. The Park, as well as being a craft, antiques and garden centre, is still a working farm.

Arbury Hall and Gardens

Nuneaton, Warwickshire CV10 7PT
Tel: 02476382804
e-mail: brenda.newell@arburyhall.net

Arbury Hall, standing in the midst of rolling lawns, surrounded by many acres of beautiful parkland, seven miles from the centre of England has been the home of the Newdegate family since the 16th century. This lovely Elizabethan mansion house with its 12th century monastic origins was Gothicised by Sir Roger Newdegate during the second half of the 18th century and with its soaring fan vaults, plunging pendants and filigree tracery, stands as the most breathtaking and complete example of early Gothick Revival architecture.

Arbury contains important collections of paintings, furniture, glass and china collected through the centuries by successive generations of the Newdegate family.

George Eliot, born on the estate in 1819 where her father was the agent, features Arbury in several of her novels, especially "Scenes of Clerical Life" where in "Mr Gilfil's Love Story" she portrays Arbury as Cheverel Manor and gives detailed descriptions of many of the rooms in the house including The Saloon and The Dining Room. The Gardens, wooded walks and lakes, provide the visitors with a superb example of the informal style of late 18th century English landscape gardening.

Daffodils and Bluebells in Springtime, the Azalea and Rhododendron Walks in May, the splendid Wisteria wall in June followed by a profusion of Roses all through the Summer, and wildfowl on the lakes offer tranquil surroundings in which to relax.

MANCETTER

5 miles NW of Nuneaton off the A5

🏛 Church of St Peter

This former Roman camp is situated on a rocky outcrop overlooking the valley of the River Anker. This camp was once one of a line of forts built by the Romans as they advanced northwards. The village is chiefly associated with the Mancetter Martyrs, Robert Glover and Joyce Lewis, both of whom were burnt at the stake for their religious beliefs. The martyrs are commemorated on wooden tablets in the fine **Church of St Peter**, which dates back to the early 1200s. The glory of this church is its rich glass in the east window of the chancel, most of which is 14th century in origin and thought to have been created by

John Thornton, builder of the great east window of York Minster. Between the manor and the church are two noteworthy rows of almshouses dating from 1728 to 1822.

ATHERSTONE

5 miles W of Nuneaton off the A5

🏛 St Mary's Church

Atherstone is a small market town situated on the Roman Watling Street at the eastern edge of the Warwickshire Forest of Arden, off the A5 between Nuneaton and Tamworth. Set against the wooded hills of the Merevale Estate, the picturesque town centre dates from medieval times and is unspoiled by modern development. Atherstone's history predates medieval times to the Anglo-Saxons;

at the time of the Norman Conquest it belonged to the Countess of Mercia, Lady Godiva. The Domesday Book of 1086 records 14 residents: 11 villagers, two smallholders and one slave. Its importance as a trading centre grew and grew over the ensuing years, so that by 1724 Daniel Defoe could describe it as 'a town famous for a great cheese fair on the 8th September'.

Atherstone's **St Mary's Church** was founded in 1365 as a chapel-of-ease, becoming a parish church in 1835, when Atherstone separated from Mancetter to become a parish in its own right. The tower was rebuilt in 1782 in 'modern Gothic' style. To the rear of the building, the 12th century Baddesley Porch, brought from Baddesley Ensor church when the latter was demolished in 1842, boasts lovely decorative detail.

GRENDON
3 miles NW of Atherstone off the A5

Grendon once boasted its own mint, owned by Sir George Chetwynd of Grendon Hall. It was this same Sir George who fell in love with the actress Lillie Langtry, and who fought Lord Lonsdale in a fist fight to win her favour. He led an extravagant life, spending a lot of time at race meetings and entertaining the Prince of Wales, with the result that his beloved Lillie began a liaison with the Prince, and Sir George lost so much money that Grendon Hall had to be sold off; it was pulled down in 1933.

NEWTON REGIS
6 miles NW of Atherstone off the B5493

One of the most unspoilt villages in Warwickshire, Newton Regis has been voted Best Kept Small Village on numerous occasions. Near the Staffordshire border and between the M42 and B5453, this lovely village is built around an attractive duck pond which was once a quarry pit. The village's name is thought to derive from its former royal ownership, having once been the property of King Henry II. It has in its day also been known as King's Newton and Newton-in-the-Thistles – the latter perhaps referring to the abundance of thistles or specially grown teasels which were used in the carding of flax fibre. Linen looms were worked in the house, which is now the Queens Head Inn.

ALVECOTE
6 miles NW of Atherstone off the M42

🏛 Priory 🏕 Priory Picnic Area

Alvecote Priory, just on the border with Staffordshire, was founded by William Burnett in 1159, who built it as a penance after having (mistakenly) believed that his wife had been unfaithful during his pilgrimage to the Holy Land. This small Benedictine Priory was founded as a cell to the Great Malvern Priory in Worcestershire. As with many others it was dissolved in 1536, when the buildings were converted into a house, which was pulled down in about 1700 when another house was constructed using some of the old materials. The 14th century remains include a fine moulded doorway and dovecote.

Alvecote Priory Picnic Area boasts canalside picnic spots and a nearby nature reserve. There is also an interesting circular walk that takes in lakes, wildlife, many unusual plants, the old North Warwicks Colliery tip, and handsome canal bridges.

TOURIST INFORMATION CENTRES

Derbyshire

ASHBOURNE
13 Market Place, Ashbourne, Derbyshire DE6 1EU
Tel: 01335 343666
Fax: 01335 300638
e-mail: ashbourneinfo@derbyshiredales.gov.uk

BAKEWELL
Old Market Hall, Bridge Street, Bakewell ,
Derbyshire DE4 1DS
Tel: 01629 816 558
Fax: 01629 814 782
e-mail: bakewell@peakdistrict.gov.uk

BUXTON
The Crescent, Buxton, Derbyshire SK17 6BQ
Tel: 01298 25106
Fax: 01298 73153
e-mail: tourism@highpeak.gov.uk

CHESTERFIELD
Rykneld Square, Chesterfield, Derbyshire S40 1SB
Tel: 01246 345 777 or 01246 345 778
Fax: 01246 345 770
e-mail: tourism@chesterfield.gov.uk

DERBY
Assembly Rooms, Market Place, Derby,
Derbyshire DE1 3AH
Tel: 01332 255802
Fax: 01332 256137
e-mail: tourism@derby.gov.uk
website: www.visitderby.co.uk

GLOSSOP
The Heritage Centre, Bank House, Henry Street, Glossop,
Derbyshire SK13 8BW
Tel: 01457 855 920
Fax: 01427 855 920
e-mail: info@glossoptouristcentre.co.uk
website: www.glossoptouristcentre.co.uk

MATLOCK
Crown Square, Matlock, Derbyshire DE3 3AT
Tel: 01629 583388
Fax: 01629 584131
e-mail: matlockinfo@derbyshiredales.gov.uk

MATLOCK BATH
The Pavillion, Matlock, Derbyshire DE4 3NR
Tel: 01629 55082
Fax: 01629 56304
e-mail: matlockbathinfo@derbyshiredales.gov.uk

RIPLEY
Town Hall, Market Place, Ripley, Derbyshire DE5 3BT
Tel: 01773 841 488 or 01773 841 486
Fax: 01773 841 487
e-mail: touristinformation@ambervalley.gov.uk

Herefordshire

BROMYARD
The Bromyard Centre, Cruxwell Street, Bromyard,
Herefordshire HR7 4EB
Tel: 01432 260 280 or 01432 261 845
Fax: 01432 260 282
e-mail: tic-bromyard@herefordshire.gov.uk
website: www.visitherefordshire.co.uk

HEREFORD
1 King Street, Hereford, Herefordshire, HR4 9BW
Tel: 01432 268 430 or 01432 260 701
Fax: 01432 342 662
e-mail: tic-hereford@herefordshire.gov.uk
website: www.visitherefordshire.co.uk

HEREFORDSHIRE TOURISM
Tourist Board, P.O. 4, Plough Lane, Hereford,
Herefordshire HR4 0XH
Tel: 01432 260621
Fax: 01432 383031
e-mail: tourism@herefordshire.gov.uk
website: www.visitherefordshire.co.uk

KINGTON
2 Mill Street, Kington, Herefordshire HR5 3BQ
Tel: 01544 230 778
e-mail: contact@kingtontourist.fsnet.co.uk
website: www.kingtontourist.info

LEDBURY
3 The Homend, Ledbury, Herefordshire HR8 1BN
Tel: 01531 636 147 or 01432 261 899
Fax: 01531 634 313
e-mail: tic-ledbury@herefordshire.gov.uk
website: www.visitherefordshire.co.uk

LEOMINSTER
1 Corn Square, Leominster, Herefordshire HR6 8LR
Tel: 01568 616460
Fax: 01568 615546
e-mail: tic-leominster@herefordshire.gov.uk
website: www.visitherefordshire.co.uk

QUEENSWOOD
Queenswood Country Park, Dinmore Hill, Leominster,
Herefordshire HR6 0PY
Tel: 01568 797 842
e-mail: queenswoodtic@herefordshire.gov.uk
website: www.visitherefordshire.co.uk

ROSS-ON-WYE
Swan House, Edde Cross Street, Ross-On-Wye,
Herefordshire HR9 7BZ
Tel: 01989 562768
Fax: 01989 565057
e-mail: tic-ross@herefordshire.gov.uk
website: www.visitherefordshire.co.uk

Leicestershire

ASHBY-DE-LA-ZOUCH
North Street, Ashby-de-la-Zouch,
Leicestershire LE65 IHU
Tel: 01530 411 767 or 01530 454 601
Fax: 01530 560 660
e-mail: ashby.tic@nwleices.gov.uk

HINCKLEY
Hinckley Library, Lancaster Road, Hinckley,
Leicestershire LE10 0AT
Tel: 01455 635 106
Fax: 01455 251 385
e-mail: hinckleytic@leics.gov.uk

LEICESTER
7/9 Every Street, Town Hall Square, Leicester,
Leicestershire LE1 6AG
Tel: 09062 941 113 (calls charged)
Fax: 01162 221 534
e-mail: info@goleicestershire.com

LOUGHBOROUGH
Loughborough Town Hall, Market Place, Loughborough,
Leicestershire LE11 3EB
Tel: 01509 218113
Fax: 01509 240617
e-mail: tic@charnwoodbc.gov.uk

MARKET HARBOROUGH
Council Offices, Adam and Eve Street, Market Harborough,
Leicestershire LE16 7AG
Tel: 01858 828 282

MELTON MOWBRAY
7 King Street, Melton Mowbray,
Leicestershire LE13 1XA
Tel: 01664 480 992
Fax: 01664 480 992
e-mail: tic@melton.gov.uk

RUTLAND WATER
Sykes Lane, nr Oakham, Empingham, Rutland,
Leicestershire LE15 8PX
Tel: 01572 653026
or Accommodation bookings: 01572 653026
Fax: 01572 653027
e-mail: tic@anglianwater.co.uk

Lincolnshire

ALFORD
7-8 West Street, Alford, Lincolnshire LN13 9HT
Tel: 01507 462 143
Fax: 01507 462 143
e-mail: alfordinfo@e-lindsey.gov.uk
website: www.poachercountry.co.uk

BOSTON
Market Place, Boston, Lincolnshire PE21 6NN
Tel: 01205 356656
Fax: 01205 356656
e-mail: ticboston@boston.gov.uk
website: www.boston.gov.uk

BRIGG
The Buttercross, Market Place, Brigg,
Lincolnshire DN20 8ER
Tel: 01652 657 053 or 01724 297 353
Fax: 01652 657 053
e-mail: brigg.tic@northlincs.gov.uk
website: www.northlincs.gov.uk/tourism

CLEETHORPES
42-43 Alexandra Road, Cleethorpes,
Lincolnshire DN35 8LE
Tel: 01472 323 111 or 01472 323 222
Fax: 01472 323 112
e-mail: cleetic@nelc.gov.uk
website: www.nelincs.gov.uk

GAINSBOROUGH
Tourism Development Unit, 26 Spital Terrace,
Gainsborough, Lincolnshire DN21 2HG
Tel: 01427 676666 Ext: 636
Fax: 01427 811553
e-mail: tourism.info@west-lindsey.gov.uk
website: www.west-lindsey.gov.uk

GRANTHAM
The Guildhall Centre, St Peter's Hill, Grantham,
Lincolnshire NG31 8PZ
Tel: 01476 406 166
Fax: 01476 406 166
e-mail: granthamtic@southkesteven.gov.uk
website: www.southwestlincs.com

HORNCASTLE
14 Bull Ring, Horncastle, Lincolnshire LN9 5HU
Tel: 01507 526636
Fax: 01507 526636
e-mail: horncastleinfo@e-lindsey.gov.uk
website: www.poachercountry.co.uk

LINCOLN (CASTLE HILL)
9 Castle Hill, Lincoln, Lincolnshire LN1 3AA
Tel: 01522 873213 or 01522 873256
Fax: 01522 541452
e-mail: tourism@lincoln.gov.uk
website: www.lincoln.gov.uk

LINCOLN (CORNHILL)
21 Cornhill, Lincoln, Lincolnshire LN5 7HB
Tel: 01522 873 256 or 01522 873 213
Fax: 01522 541 447
e-mail: tourism@lincoln.gov.uk
website: www.lincoln.gov.uk

LOUTH
The New Market Hall, off Cornmarket, Louth,
Lincolnshire LN11 9PY
Tel: 01507 609289
Fax: 01507 609289
e-mail: louthinfo@e-lindsey.gov.uk

MABLETHORPE
Unit 5, Louth Hotel, High Street, Mablethorpe,
Lincolnshire LN12 2AF
Tel: 01507 474939
Fax: 01507 474938
e-mail: mablethorpeinfo@e-lindsey.gov.uk
website: www.funcoast.co.uk

SCUNTHORPE

Scunthorpe Central Library, Carlton Street, Scunthorpe,
Lincolnshire DN15 6TX
Tel: 01724 297354
Fax: 01724 859737
e-mail: brigg.tic@northlincs.gov.uk
website: www.northlincs.gov.uk

SKEGNESS

The Kiosk, Tower Gardens, Grand Parade, Skegness,
Lincolnshire PE25 2UG
Tel: 01754 899887
Fax: 01754 767856
e-mail: skegnessinfo@e-lindsey.gov.uk
website: www.funcoast.co.uk

SLEAFORD

Advice Centre, Money's Yard, Carre Street, Sleaford,
Lincolnshire NG34 7TW
Tel: 01529 414294
Fax: 01529 414294
e-mail: tic@n-kesteven.gov.uk
website: www.heartoflincs.com

SPALDING

South Holland Centre, Market Place, Spalding,
Lincolnshire PE11 1SS
Tel: 01775 725 468
Fax: 01775 762 715
e-mail: tic@sholland.gov.uk

STAMFORD

Stamford Arts Centre, 27 St Mary's Street, Stamford,
Lincolnshire PE9 2DL
Tel: 01780 755 611
Fax: 01780 755 611
e-mail: stamfordtic@skdc.com
website: www.southwestlincs.com

WOODHALL SPA

Cottage Museum, Iddesleigh Road, Woodhall Spa,
Lincolnshire LN10 6SH
Tel: 01526 353775
Fax: 01526 353775
e-mail: woodhallspainfo@e-lindsey.gov.uk
website: www.poachercountry.co.uk

Northamptonshire

BRACKLEY

2 Bridge Street, Brackley, Northamptonshire NN13 7EP
Tel: 01280 700 111 or 01280 704 453
Fax: 01280 700 157
e-mail: tic@southnorthants.gov.uk
website: www.southnorthants.gov.uk

CORBY

Willows Art Complex, George Street, Corby,
Northamptonshire NN17 1QB
Tel: 01536 407 507
e-mail: tourist.information@corby.gov.uk
website: www.corby.gov.uk

KETTERING

The Coach House, Sheep Street, Kettering,
Northamptonshire NN16 0AN
Tel: 01536 410 210 or 01536 534 212
Fax: 01536 534 370
e-mail: tic@kettering.gov.uk
website: www.kettering.gov.uk

NORTHAMPTON

The Guildhall, St Giles Square, Northampton,
Northamptonshire NN1 1DE
Tel: 01604 838 800 or 01604 838 801
Fax: 01604 604 180
e-mail: northampton.tic@explorenorthamptonshire.co.uk
website: www.northampton.gov.uk

OUNDLE

14 West Street, Oundle, Northamptonshire PE8 4EF
Tel: 01832 274 333 or 01832 273 326
Fax: 01832 274 333
e-mail: oundletic@east-northamptonshire.gov.uk
website: www.east-northamptonshire.gov.uk

RUSHDEN

Newton Road, Rushden, Northamptonshire NN10 0PT
Tel: 01832 742 189

TOURIST INFORMATION CENTRES

Nottinghamshire

NEWARK
The Gilstrap Centre, Castlegate, Newark,
Nottinghamshire NG24 1BG
Tel: 01636 655765
Fax: 01636 655767
e-mail: gilstrap@nsdc.info

NOTTINGHAM
1-4 Smithy Row, Nottingham,
Nottinghamshire NG1 2BY
Tel: 08447 75678 or 01159 155 330
Fax: 0115 915 5323
e-mail: tourist.information@nottinghamcity.gov.uk

OLLERTON
Sherwood Heath, Ollerton Roundabout, nr Newark,
Ollerton, Nottinghamshire NG22 9DR
Tel: 01623 824 545
Fax: 01623 822 930
e-mail: sherwoodheath@nsdc.info

RETFORD
40 Grove Street, Retford, Nottinghamshire DN22 6LD
Tel: 01777 860 780
Fax: 01777 860 780
e-mail: retford.tourist@bassetlaw.gov.uk

WORKSOP
Worksop Library, Memorial Avenue, Worksop,
Nottinghamshire S80 2BP
Tel: 01909 501 148
Fax: 01909 501 148
e-mail: worksop.tourist@bassetlaw.gov.uk

Rutland

RUTLAND WATER
Sykes Lane, nr Oakham, Empingham,
Rutland LE15 8PX
Tel: 01572 653026
or Accommodation bookings: 01572 653026
Fax: 01572 653027
e-mail: tic@anglianwater.co.uk

Shropshire

BRIDGNORTH
The Library, Listley Street, Bridgnorth,
Shropshire WV16 4AW
Tel: 01746 763257
Fax: 01746 766625
e-mail: bridgnorth.tourism@shropshire-cc.gov.uk

CHURCH STRETTON
Church Street, Church Stretton, Shropshire SY6 6DQ
Tel: 01694 723 133
Fax: 01694 723 045
e-mail: churchstretton.scf@shropshire-cc.gov.uk

ELLESMERE INFO LINK
4 Ploughman's Corner, Wharf Road, Ellesmere,
Shropshire SY12 0EJ
Tel: 01691 624488
Fax: 01691 624477
e-mail: ellesmereinfo@northshropshiredc.gov.uk

ELLESMERE
The Mere's Visit or Centre, Mereside, Ellesmere,
Shropshire SY12 0PA
Tel: 01691 622 981
Fax: 01691 622 981
e-mail: ellesmere.tourism@shropshire-cc.gov.uk

IRONBRIDGE
Ironbridge Gorge Museum Trust, Telford, Coalbrookdale,
Shropshire TF8 7DQ
Tel: 01952 884 391
Fax: 01952 884 391
e-mail: tic@ironbridge.org.uk

LUDLOW
Castle Street, Ludlow, Shropshire SY8 1AS
Tel: 01584 875053
Fax: 01584 877931
e-mail: ludlow.tourism@shropshire-cc.gov.uk

MARKET DRAYTON
49 Cheshire Street, Market Drayton,
Shropshire TF9 1PH
Tel: 01630 653 114
Fax: 01630 652 226
e-mail: marketdrayton.scf@shropshire-cc.gov.uk

MUCH WENLOCK
The Museum, High Street, Much Wenlock,
Shropshire TF13 6HR
Tel: 01952 727 679 or 01746 763 257
Fax: 01952 727 679
e-mail: muchwenlock.tourism@shropshire-cc.gov.uk

OSWESTRY (HERITAGE CENTRE)
The Heritage Centre, 2 Church Terrace, Oswestry,
Shropshire SY11 2TE
Tel: 01691 662753
Fax: 01691 657811
e-mail: ot@oswestry-welshborders.org.uk

OSWESTRY (MILE END)
Mile End Services, Oswestry, Shropshire SY11 4JA
Tel: 01691 662 488 or 01691 657 876
Fax: 01691 662 883
e-mail: tic@oswestry-bc.gov.uk

SHREWSBURY
The Music Hall, The Square, Shrewsbury,
Shropshire SY1 1LH
Tel: 01743 281 200
Fax: 01743 281 213
e-mail: visitorinfo@shrewsbury.gov.uk

TELFORD
The Telford Centre, Management Suite, Telford,
Shropshire TF3 4BX
Tel: 01952 238 008 or 01952 238 009
Fax: 01952 291 723
e-mail: tourist-info@telfordshopping.co.uk

WHITCHURCH
12 St Mary's Street, Whitchurch, Shropshire SY13 1QY
Tel: 01948 664 577 or 01948 665 432
Fax: 01948 665 432
e-mail: whitchurch.heritage@ukonline.co.uk

Staffordshire

BURTON UPON TRENT
Coors Visit or Centre, Horninglow Street,
Burton upon Trent, Staffordshire DE14 1NG
Tel: 01283 508 111 or 01283 508 112
Fax: 01283 517 268
e-mail: tic@eaststaffsbc.gov.uk
website: www.eaststaffsbc.gov.uk

CANNOCK
The Valley Heritage Centre, Valley Road, Hednesford,
Cannock, Staffordshire WS12 5TD
Tel: 01543 877666
Fax: 01543 462317
e-mail: museum@cannockchasedc.gov.uk
website: www.museumofcannockchase.co.uk

LEEK
1 Market Place, Leek, Staffordshire, ST13 5HH
Tel: 01538 483 741
Fax: 01538 483 743
e-mail: tourism.services@staffsmoorlands.gov.uk
website: www.staffsmoorlands.gov.uk

LICHFIELD
Lichfield Garrick, Castle Dyke, Lichfield,
Staffordshire WS13 6HR
Tel: 01543 412121 or 01543 412112
Fax: 01543 412 120
e-mail: info@visitlichfield.com
website: www.visitlichfield.com

TOURIST INFORMATION CENTRES

NEWCASTLE-UNDER-LYME
Newcastle Library, Ironmarket, Newcastle-under-Lyme,
Staffordshire ST5 1AT
Tel: 01782 297 313
Fax: 01782 297 323
e-mail: tic.newcastle@staffordshire.gov.uk
website: www.newcastle-staffs.gov.u

STAFFORD
Market Street, Stafford, Staffordshire ST16 2LQ
Tel: 01785 619619 or 01785 619136
Fax: 01785 619134
e-mail: tic@staffordbc.gov.uk
website: www.staffordbc.gov.uk

STAFFORDSHIRE TOURISM
Development Services, Riverway, Stafford,
Staffordshire ST16 3TJ
Tel: 01785 277 397
Fax: 01785 215 286
e-mail: tourism@staffordshire.gov.uk
website: www.staffordshiretourism.com

STOKE-ON-TRENT
Victoria Hall, Bagnall Street, Hanley, Stoke-on-Trent,
Staffordshire ST1 3AD
Tel: 01782 236 000 or 01782 236 005
Fax: 01782 236 005
e-mail: stoke.tic@stoke.gov.uk
website: www.stoke.gov.uk/tourism

TAMWORTH
29 Market Street, Tamworth, Staffordshire B79 7LR
Tel: 01827 709 581 or 01827 709 618
Fax: 01827 709 582
e-mail: tic@tamworth.gov.uk

Warwickshire

KENILWORTH
Kenilworth Library, 11 Smalley Place, Kenilworth,
Warwickshire CV8 1QJ
Tel: 01926 748 900
Fax: 01926 748 901
e-mail: kenilworthlibrary@warwickshire.gov.uk

LEAMINGTON SPA
The Royal Pump Rooms, The Parade, Leamington Spa,
Warwickshire CV32 4AB
Tel: 01926 742762
Fax: 01926 742766
e-mail: leamington@shakespeare-country.co.uk

NUNEATON
Nuneaton Library, Church Street, Nuneaton,
Warwickshire CV11 4DR
Tel: 02476 347 006 or 024 7638 4027
Fax: 024 76 350 125
e-mail: nuneatonlibrary@warwickshire.gov.uk

RUGBY
Visit or Centre, Rugby Art Gallery Museum & Library,
Little Elborow Street, Rugby, Warwickshire CV21 3BZ
Tel: 01788 533 217
Fax: 01788 533 212
e-mail: visitor.centre@rugby.gov.uk

STRATFORD-UPON-AVON
Bridgefoot, Stratford-upon-Avon,
Warwickshire CV37 6GW
Tel: 0870 160 7930
Fax: 01789 295 262
e-mail: stratfordtic@shakespeare-country.co.uk

WARWICK
The Court House, Jury Street, Warwick,
Warwickshire CV34 4EW
Tel: 01926 492 212
Fax: 01926 494 837
e-mail: touristinfo@warwick-uk.co.uk
website: www.warwick-uk.co.uk

West Midlands

BIRMINGHAM
Tourism Centre and Ticket Shop, The Rotunda,
150 New Street, Birmingham, West Midlands B2 4PA
Tel: 0870 225 0127 (information)
or 0121 202 5000 (tickets)
Fax: 0121 616 1038
e-mail: callcentre@marketingbirmingham.com
website: www.beinbirmingham.com

BIRMINGHAM (WECOME CENTRE)
Wecome Centre, New Street (at junction with Corporation St),
Birmingham, West Midlands B1
Tel: 0870 225 0127

COVENTRY
4 Priory Row, Coventry, West Midlands CV1 5EX
Tel: 024 7622 7264
Fax: 024 7622 7255
e-mail: tic@cvone.co.uk

MERRY HILL
Merry Hill Centre, Brierley Hill,
West Midlands DY5 1SR
Tel: 01384 487 900
Fax: 01384 487 910

SOLIHULL
Central Library, Homer Road, Solihull,
West Midlands B91 3RG
Tel: 0121 704 6130 or 0121 704 6962
Fax: 0121 704 8224
e-mail: ckelly@solihill.gov.uk

WALSALL
Tourist and Travel Information Centre, Walsall Bus Station,
St Pauls Street, Walsall, West Midlands WS1 1NR
Tel: 01922 625 540 or 01922 776 010
Fax: 01922 776 012
e-mail: walsalltt&i@travelwm.co.uk

WOLVERHAMPTON
18 Queen Square, Wolverhampton,
West Midlands WV1 1TQ
Tel: 01902 556 110 or 01902 556 112
Fax: 01902 556 111
e-mail: wolverhampton.tic@dial.pipex.com

Worcestershire

BEWDLEY
Load Street, Bewdley, Worcestershire DY12 2AE
Tel: 01299 404740
Fax: 01299 404740
e-mail: bewdleytic@btconnect.com

BROADWAY
1 Cotswold Court, Broadway, Worcestershire WR12 7AA
Tel: 01386 852937

BROMSGROVE
Bromsgrove Museum, 26 Birmingham Road, Bromsgrove,
Worcestershire B61 0DD
Tel: 01527 831809
Fax: 01527 577983

DROITWICH SPA
St Richard's House, Victoria Square, Droitwich Spa,
Worcestershire WR9 8DS
Tel: 01905 774312
Fax: 01905 794226
e-mail: heritage@droitwichspa.gov.uk

EVESHAM
The Almonry, Abbey Gate, Evesham,
Worcestershire WR11 4BG
Tel: 01386 446 944
Fax: 01386 442 348
e-mail: tic@almonry.ndo.co.uk

TOURIST INFORMATION CENTRES

MALVERN
21 Church Street, Malvern, Worcestershire WR14 2AA
Tel: 01684 892 289 or 01684 862 345
Fax: 01684 892 872
e-mail: malvern.tic@malvernhills.gov.uk

PERSHORE
Tourism Association, Town Hall, 34 High Street, Pershore,
Worcestershire WR10 1DS
Tel: 01386 556 591
e-mail: tourism@pershore-tc.gov.uk
website: www.visitpershore.co.uk

REDDITCH
Palace Theatre, Alcester Street, Redditch,
Worcestershire B98 8AE
Tel: 01527 60806
Fax: 01527 60806
e-mail: info.centre@redditchbc.gov.uk

TENBURY WELLS
21 Teme Street, Tenbury Wells,
Worcestershire
Tel: 01584 810136
website: uk.geocities.com/TenburyTIC

UPTON UPON SEVERN
4 High Street, Upton Upon Severn,
Worcestershire WR8 0HB
Tel: 01684 594200
Fax: 01684 594185
e-mail: upton.tic@malvernhills.gov.uk

WORCESTER
The Guildhall, High Street, Worcester,
Worcestershire WR1 2EY
Tel: 01905 726 311 or 01905 722 480
Fax: 01905 722 481
e-mail: touristinfo@cityofworcester.gov.uk

INDEX OF ADVERTISERS

INDEX OF ADVERTISERS

INDEX OF ADVERTISERS

SPECIALIST FOOD SHOPS

Looking for more walks?

The walks in this book have been gleaned from Britain's largest online walking guide, to be found at *www.walkingworld.com*.

The site contains 300 walks across eastern England, so there is plenty more choice in this region alone. If you are heading further afield there are walks of every length and type across England, Scotland and Wales – ideal if you are taking a short break as you can plan your walks in advance.

Want more detail for the walks in this book? Next to every walk in this book you will see a Walk ID. You can enter this ID number on Walkingworld's 'Find a Walk' page and you will be taken straight to the details of that walk.

- **Over 1850 walks across Britain**
- **Print routes out as you need them**
- **No bulky guidebook to carry**

Walkingworld routes contain much more detailed instructions and mapping than can be given in a printed book. The walk descriptions have photographs at every major decision point to help you to navigate and each comes with an Ordnance Survey 1:50,000 scale map. Once you have found a walk you like, simply print it out on standard A4 paper and you are ready to go!

- **Convenient A4 sized maps**
- **Print copies for everyone in your party**
- **Find walks for holidays and short breaks**

A modest annual subscription gives you access to over 1850 walks, all in Walkingworld's easy to follow format. The database of walks is growing all the time and as a subscriber you gain access to new routes as soon as they are published.

Visit the Walkingworld website at *www.walkingworld.com*

ORDER FORM

To order any of our publications just fill in the payment details below and complete the order form. For orders of less than 4 copies please add £1 per book for postage and packing. Orders over 4 copies are P & P free.

Please Complete Either:

I enclose a cheque for £ [＿＿＿＿＿＿＿]   made payable to Travel Publishing Ltd

Or:

CARD NO: [＿＿＿＿＿＿＿]   EXPIRY DATE: [＿＿＿＿]

SIGNATURE: [＿＿＿＿＿＿＿]

NAME: [＿＿＿＿＿＿＿]

ADDRESS: [＿＿＿＿＿＿＿]

TEL NO: [＿＿＿＿＿＿＿]

Please either send, telephone, fax or e-mail your order to:

Travel Publishing Ltd, 7a Apollo House, Calleva Park, Aldermaston, Berkshire RG7 8TN
Tel: 0118 981 7777   Fax: 0118 940 8428 e-mail: info@travelpublishing.co.uk

	PRICE	QUANTITY		PRICE	QUANTITY
HIDDEN PLACES REGIONAL TITLES			**COUNTRY PUBS AND INNS TITLES**		
Cornwall	£8.99	....	Cornwall	£5.99	....
Devon	£8.99	....	Devon	£7.99	....
Dorset, Hants & Isle of Wight	£8.99	....	Sussex	£5.99	....
East Anglia	£8.99	....	Wales	£8.99	....
Lake District & Cumbria	£8.99	....	Yorkshire	£7.99	....
Northumberland & Durham	£8.99	....	**COUNTRY LIVING RURAL GUIDES**		
Peak District and Derbyshire	£8.99	....	East Anglia	£10.99	....
Yorkshire	£8.99	....	Heart of England	£10.99	....
HIDDEN PLACES NATIONAL TITLES			Ireland	£11.99	....
England	£11.99	....	North East of England	£10.99	....
Ireland	£11.99	....	North West of England	£10.99	....
Scotland	£11.99	....	Scotland	£11.99	....
Wales	£11.99	....	South of England	£10.99	....
HIDDEN INNS TITLES			South East of England	£10.99	....
East Anglia	£7.99	....	Wales	£11.99	....
Heart of England	£7.99	....	West Country	£10.99	....
South	£7.99	....	**OTHER TITLES**		
South East	£7.99	....	Off The Motorway	£11.99	....
West Country	£7.99	....			

TOTAL QUANTITY [＿＿＿＿]

TOTAL VALUE [＿＿＿＿]

READER REACTION FORM

The **Travel Publishing** *research team would like to receive readers' comments on any visitor attractions or places reviewed in the book and also recommendations for suitable entries to be included in the next edition. This will help ensure that the* **Country Living series of Rural Guides** *continues to provide its readers with useful information on the more interesting, unusual or unique features of each attraction or place ensuring that their visit to the local area is an enjoyable and stimulating experience. To provide your comments or recommendations would you please complete the forms below and overleaf as indicated and send to:*

The Research Department, Travel Publishing Ltd, 7a Apollo House, Calleva Park, Aldermaston, Reading, RG7 8TN

YOUR NAME:

YOUR ADDRESS:

YOUR TEL NO:

Please tick as appropriate: COMMENTS ☐   RECOMMENDATION ☐

ESTABLISHMENT:

ADDRESS:

TEL NO:

CONTACT NAME:

PLEASE COMPLETE FORM OVERLEAF

READER REACTION FORM

COMMENT OR REASON FOR RECOMMENDATION:

....

....

....

....

....

....

....

....

....

....

....

....

READER REACTION FORM

The **Travel Publishing** *research team would like to receive readers' comments on any visitor attractions or places reviewed in the book and also recommendations for suitable entries to be included in the next edition. This will help ensure that the* **Country Living series of Rural Guides** *continues to provide its readers with useful information on the more interesting, unusual or unique features of each attraction or place ensuring that their visit to the local area is an enjoyable and stimulating experience. To provide your comments or recommendations would you please complete the forms below and overleaf as indicated and send to:*

The Research Department, Travel Publishing Ltd, 7a Apollo House, Calleva Park, Aldermaston, Reading, RG7 8TN

YOUR NAME:

YOUR ADDRESS:

YOUR TEL NO:

Please tick as appropriate: COMMENTS   RECOMMENDATION

ESTABLISHMENT:

ADDRESS:

TEL NO:

CONTACT NAME:

PLEASE COMPLETE FORM OVERLEAF

READER REACTION FORM

COMMENT OR REASON FOR RECOMMENDATION:

....

....

....

....

....

....

....

....

....

....

....

READER REACTION FORM

The **Travel Publishing** *research team would like to receive readers' comments on any visitor attractions or places reviewed in the book and also recommendations for suitable entries to be included in the next edition. This will help ensure that the* **Country Living series of Rural Guides** *continues to provide its readers with useful information on the more interesting, unusual or unique features of each attraction or place ensuring that their visit to the local area is an enjoyable and stimulating experience. To provide your comments or recommendations would you please complete the forms below and overleaf as indicated and send to:*

The Research Department, Travel Publishing Ltd, 7a Apollo House, Calleva Park, Aldermaston, Reading, RG7 8TN

YOUR NAME:

YOUR ADDRESS:

YOUR TEL NO:

Please tick as appropriate: COMMENTS ☐ RECOMMENDATION ☐

ESTABLISHMENT:

ADDRESS:

TEL NO:

CONTACT NAME:

PLEASE COMPLETE FORM OVERLEAF

READER REACTION FORM

COMMENT OR REASON FOR RECOMMENDATION:

....

....

....

....

....

....

....

....

....

....

....

....

READER REACTION FORM

The **Travel Publishing** *research team would like to receive readers' comments on any visitor attractions or places reviewed in the book and also recommendations for suitable entries to be included in the next edition. This will help ensure that the* **Country Living series of Rural Guides** *continues to provide its readers with useful information on the more interesting, unusual or unique features of each attraction or place ensuring that their visit to the local area is an enjoyable and stimulating experience. To provide your comments or recommendations would you please complete the forms below and overleaf as indicated and send to:*

The Research Department, Travel Publishing Ltd, 7a Apollo House, Calleva Park, Aldermaston, Reading, RG7 8TN

YOUR NAME:

YOUR ADDRESS:

YOUR TEL NO:

Please tick as appropriate: COMMENTS ☐   RECOMMENDATION ☐

ESTABLISHMENT:

ADDRESS:

TEL NO:

CONTACT NAME:

PLEASE COMPLETE FORM OVERLEAF

READER REACTION FORM

COMMENT OR REASON FOR RECOMMENDATION:

....

....

....

....

....

....

....

....

....

....

....

READER REACTION FORM

The **Travel Publishing** *research team would like to receive readers' comments on any visitor attractions or places reviewed in the book and also recommendations for suitable entries to be included in the next edition. This will help ensure that the* **Country Living series of Rural Guides** *continues to provide its readers with useful information on the more interesting, unusual or unique features of each attraction or place ensuring that their visit to the local area is an enjoyable and stimulating experience. To provide your comments or recommendations would you please complete the forms below and overleaf as indicated and send to:*

The Research Department, Travel Publishing Ltd, 7a Apollo House, Calleva Park, Aldermaston, Reading, RG7 8TN

YOUR NAME:

YOUR ADDRESS:

YOUR TEL NO:

Please tick as appropriate: COMMENTS ☐   RECOMMENDATION ☐

ESTABLISHMENT:

ADDRESS:

TEL NO:

CONTACT NAME:

PLEASE COMPLETE FORM OVERLEAF

READER REACTION FORM

COMMENT OR REASON FOR RECOMMENDATION:

....

....

....

....

....

....

....

....

....

....

....

TOWNS, VILLAGES AND PLACES OF INTEREST

TOWNS, VILLAGES AND PLACES OF INTEREST

TOWNS, VILLAGES AND PLACES OF INTEREST

TOWNS, VILLAGES AND PLACES OF INTEREST

TOWNS, VILLAGES AND PLACES OF INTEREST

TOWNS, VILLAGES AND PLACES OF INTEREST

TOWNS, VILLAGES AND PLACES OF INTEREST

TOWNS, VILLAGES AND PLACES OF INTEREST

TOWNS, VILLAGES AND PLACES OF INTEREST

TOWNS, VILLAGES AND PLACES OF INTEREST

TOWNS, VILLAGES AND PLACES OF INTEREST

TOWNS, VILLAGES AND PLACES OF INTEREST